Manual of Insight

Manual of Insight

Venerable Mahāsi Sayadaw

Translated and Edited by the
Vipassanā Mettā Foundation
Translation Committee

Forewords by Joseph Goldstein and Daniel Goleman

Wisdom

Wisdom Publications
199 Elm Street
Somerville, MA 02144 USA
wisdomexperience.org

Library of Congress Cataloging-in-Publication Data
Names: Sobhana, Mahā caññ' Cha rā to' 'A rhaṅ', 1904–1982, author.
Title: Manual of insight / Mahasi Sayadaw ; translated and edited by the Vipassanā Mettā Foundation Translation Committee.
Other titles: Wịpaṭhạna shụ nī kyān. English
Description: Somerville, MA : Wisdom Publications, 2016. | Includes bibliographical references and index. | Translated from Burmese and Pali.
Identifiers: LCCN 2015041172 (print) | LCCN 2016008923 (ebook) | ISBN 9781614292777 (hardback) | ISBN 1614292779 (hardcover) | ISBN 9781614292913 (Ebook) | ISBN 9781614292913 (ebook) | ISBN 1614292914 (ebook)
Subjects: LCSH: Vipaśyanā (Buddhism) | BISAC: RELIGION / Buddhism / Rituals

ISBN 978-1-61429-277-7 ebook ISBN 978-1-61429-291-3

21
5 4 3

Design by Gopa & Ted 2. Set in Diacritical Garamond 13.92/11.9.

Wisdom Publications' books are printed on acid-free paper and meet the guidelines for permanence and durability of the Production Guidelines for Book Longevity of the Council on Library Resources.

Printed in the United States of America.

Vipassanā Mettā Foundation Translation Committee

Project Advisor
Sayadaw U Paṇḍita (Paṇḍitārāma Shwe Taung Gon Sasana Yeiktha, Yangon, Myanmar)

Managing Editor
Steve Armstrong

Translators
Hla Myint
Ariya Baumann

Abhidhamma and Pāḷi Research Consultants
Sayadaw U Janaka (Chanmyay Yeiktha, Yangon, Myanmar)
Sayadaw U Indaka (Chanmyay Myaing Meditation Center, Yangon, Myanmar)
Sayadaw U Sāgara (Chanmyay Myaing Study Monastery, Hmawbi, Myanmar)
Hla Myint (Myanmar and USA)
Akiñcano (Marc Weber) (Germany)

Pāḷi Quote Citations, Glossaries
Ven. Vīrañāṇī

Abhidhamma Charts
Steve Armstrong

Editors
Ven. Vīrañāṇī
Steve Armstrong
Ariya Baumann
Deborah Ratner Helzer
Kamala Masters

Funding provided by Vipassanā Mettā Foundation

All proceeds from the sale of this book will be used to freely distribute copies to Buddhist monastics, libraries, and meditation centers, and to support opportunities to practice the method outlined in the book.

For further information and to report errors, please visit: www.mahasimanualofinsight.org

Namo tassa bhagavato arahato sammāsambuddhassa![1]
Without equal is the Omniscient Buddha of nine attributes![2]
Without equal is the Dhamma of six attributes![3]
Without equal is the Saṅgha of nine attributes![4]

When we reflect in this way, the mind becomes particularly clear and delighted. At that moment we observe the mental states of reflection, clarity, and delight as well as the physical phenomena that depend on these mental states as they arise. May virtuous people who practice as instructed in this book attain path, fruition, and nibbāna in this very life. Thus have I composed this manual on the practice of insight meditation.

Publisher's Acknowledgment

The publisher gratefully acknowledges the generous contribution of the Hershey Family Foundation toward the publication of this book.

Contents

Foreword by Joseph Goldstein xvii

Foreword by Daniel Goleman xix

Managing Editor's Preface xxi

Introduction 1

1. PURIFICATION OF CONDUCT 7

The Purification of Conduct for Monks 7

Observing the Monastic Precepts 7 • Pursuing a Pure Livelihood 8 • Wisely Using Requisites 8 • Carefully Restraining the Senses 13 • Practicing Restraint Prior to the Practice of Meditation 16 • Restraint that Comes from Meditation 20 • Restraint as a Prerequisite for Meditation 22

The Purification of Conduct for the Laity 22

Comparisons to Monastic Morality 23 • The Five Spiritual Obstacles 24 • The Enlightenment of Immoral Laypeople 26 • How Different Types of People Are Suited to Different Trainings 31

Purifying Conduct with Meditation 37

Morality by Means of Abandonment 37 • Morality by Means of Abstinence 38 • Morality by Means of Mental Volition 39 • Morality by Means of Restraint 39 • Morality by Means of Nontransgression 39 • Morality as Remote and Immediate Conditions for Concentration and Knowledges 40 • The Power of Meditation to Purify Morality for Monastics 41 • Nota Bene: The Practice of Morality Is Essential 43

2. PURIFICATION OF MIND 45

Mental Purification 45
Three Types of Mental Purification 45 ◆ Two Vehicles for Going
to Enlightenment 46 ◆ Methods for Taking the Two Vehicles to
Enlightenment 49 ◆ Insight with Momentary Concentration 52 ◆
Methods for Developing Insight 56

Mental Purification for Those Who Take the Vehicle
of Insight to Enlightenment 57
Liberations and Hindrances 57 ◆ Helpful Contemplations
to Dispel Hindrances 75 ◆ Obstacles to Concentration and the
Methods to Overcome Them 78 ◆ States of One-Pointedness 89

3. ABSOLUTE AND CONVENTIONAL REALITIES 93

What Is Reality? 93
Ultimate Reality 93 ◆ Conceptual Illusions 94 ◆ Hearsay
and Such 97 ◆ Description vs. Experience 98 ◆ The Correct
Definition of Ultimate Reality 101 ◆ Transience 102

The Two Meanings of Activity 105
The Meaning that Ordinary People Know 105 ◆ The Meaning
that Insight Meditators Know 106

Two Kinds of Insight 108
Appropriate Objects for Meditation 108 ◆
The Present Moment 118 ◆ Inferential Insight: Knowledge
by Comprehension 124

Lessons to Learn from Those Who Take the Vehicle
of Tranquility to Enlightenment 126
Observation of the In- and Out-Breath 129 ◆ To What Extent
Must Insight Be Purified? 131 ◆ Venerable Sāriputta's Method 133 ◆
Venerable Moggallāna's Method 137 ◆ A Note of Caution 138

4. THE DEVELOPMENT OF MINDFULNESS 143

Checking Meditation against the Pāḷi Texts 143
Five Kinds of Phenomena 143

Contemplation of the Body 148

The Case of Seeing 148 • The Case of Hearing 169 • The Case of Smell 170 • The Case of Taste 171 • The Case of Touch 172 • Mindfulness of Breathing 174 • The Four Primary Material Elements 176 • How to Observe Thought 178 • How to Note General Activities 182 • Clear Comprehension 185 • Accurate Awareness 195

Contemplation of Feeling 195

Pleasant Feeling 195 • Unpleasant Feeling 197 • Neither-Unpleasant-nor-Pleasant Feeling 197 • Worldly Pleasure 199 • Unworldly Pleasure 200 • Worldly Displeasure 200 • Unworldly Displeasure 201 • Worldly Neither Displeasure nor Pleasure 204 • Unworldly Neither Displeasure nor Pleasure 204 • Realizing Feelings 205

Contemplation of Mind 206

Mental States 206 • Realizing Mind 208

Contemplation of Mental Objects 208

The Five Hindrances 208 • Wise Attention 210 • Unwise Attention 211 • The Five Aggregates 213 • The Six Senses 217 • The Ten Fetters 220 • The Seven Factors of Enlightenment 222 • Balancing Spiritual Faculties 224 • The Seven Types of Suffering 227 • The Four Noble Truths 229

Mindfulness of the Four Noble Truths 232

Truths in the Round of Existence and Truths Beyond It 232 • How Suffering Is Realized 234 • How the Origin of Suffering Is Realized 237 • How Cessation and Path Are Realized 239 • Cultivating Mundane Understanding 240 • Cultivating Supramundane Understanding 242 • How to Develop the Noble Eightfold Path 246 • The Moment of Path Knowledge 254 • Other Objects of Meditation 255

The Benefits of Mindfulness 257

The Only Way 257 • The Buddha's Acknowledgment 258 • Suitable Contemplations 260

5. PRACTICAL INSTRUCTIONS 263

Preparations for Practice 263

The Basic Practice 264

The Primary Object 264 • Distracting Thoughts 266 • Physical Discomfort 267 • Odd Experiences 268 • Getting a Drink 269 • Going to Bed 271 • Getting Up 272 • Eating a Meal 272 • Increasing the Number of Objects 273 • General Objects 274 • Mental States 274 • Diligence 275

Insight 275

Mind and Body 275 • Cause and Effect 277 • Effects of Concentration 279 • Seeing the Three Characteristics 280 • Distractions from the Path 283 • Disappearance 284 • Disillusionment 286 • Looking for Relief 288 • Equanimity 289

The Experience of Nibbāna 292

Entering Fruition 295 • Clarifying the Insight Knowledges 296 • Practicing for Higher Paths and Fruitions 298 • A Note on Pāramī 300

A Word of Advice 301

6. STAGES OF INSIGHT KNOWLEDGE 303

Insight Knowledge that Discerns Mental and Physical Phenomena: Purification of View 303

Awareness of Phenomena 303 • Discerning Mental and Physical Phenomena 304 • Seeing Things as They Really Are 306

Insight Knowledge that Discerns Conditionality: Purification by Overcoming Doubt 308

The First Way of Seeing Conditionality 309 • The Second Way of Seeing Conditionality 313 • The Third and Fourth Ways of Seeing Conditionality 314 • The Fifth Way of Seeing Conditionality 315 • The Lesser Stream Enterer 323

Insight Knowledge by Comprehension 325

Comprehension of Impermanence 327 • Comprehension of

Suffering 329 • Comprehension of Not-Self 330 • Contemplation of Mental Phenomena 334 • Other Types of Contemplation 335 • Strengthening the Mental Faculties 336 • Seven Ways to Contemplate Physical Phenomena 337 • Seven Ways to Contemplate the Mind 351 • Practical Advice 353

Insight Knowledge of Arising and Passing Away 356

Eliminating Attachment 357 • Continuity of Processes vs. Momentary Phenomena 358 • The Characteristics of Arising and Passing Away 362 • Observing True Arising and Passing Away 364 • The Ten Corruptions of Insight 367 • Purification by Knowledge and Vision of What Is Path and Not Path 378 • Purification by Knowledge and Vision of the Way 378

Insight Knowledge of Dissolution 379

Insight and Counter-Insight 380 • Inferential Knowledge 383 • Mature Knowledge 383

The Three Aspects of Disillusionment: Insight Knowledges of Fear, of Danger, and of Disenchantment 384

Insight Knowledge of Fear 384 • Insight Knowledge of Danger 385 • Insight Knowledge of Disenchantment 387

Insight Knowledge that Desires Deliverance 389

Insight Knowledge of Reobservation 390

The Ten Aspects of Insight into Impermanence 391 • The Twenty-Five Aspects of Insight into Unsatisfactoriness 392 • The Five Aspects of Insight into Not-Self 395 • Mature Reobservation 396

Insight Knowledge of Equanimity toward Phenomena 396

How Phenomena Are Observed from Two Aspects 398 • How Phenomena Are Observed from Four Aspects 398 • How Phenomena Are Observed from Six Aspects 400 • How Phenomena Are Observed from Eight Aspects 401 • How Phenomena Are Observed from Ten Aspects 402 • How Phenomena Are Observed from Twelve Aspects 402 • The Three Stages of Equanimity 403 • Peak Insight Knowledge of Equanimity toward Phenomena 405

Knowledge that Leads to Emergence 406

Adaptation 408 • Knowledge of Change-of-Lineage 411 • Path Knowledge and Fruition Knowledge 411 • A Word of Caution 418

Reviewing Knowledge 419

Five Subjects to Consider 419 • Abandonment of Defilements 420 • Confirming Stream Entry 430 • The Great Reviewing Knowledges (Mahāpaccavekkhaṇañāṇa) 441

Attainment of Fruition 445

Three Types of Insight 446 • The Benefit of Attaining Fruition 447 • Entering the Attainment of Fruition 447 • The Experience of the Attainment of Fruition 449 • Emerging from the Attainment of Fruition 451 • Unstable Attainment 452 • Varying Degrees of Mastery 453

Nibbāna 454

Definitions of Nibbāna 454 • Two Types of Nibbāna 458 • Experiencing Nibbāna 462

7. The Eighteen Great Insight Knowledges 467

The Seven Main Contemplations 468

Contemplation of Impermanence 468 • Contemplation of Unsatisfactoriness 489 • Contemplation of Not-Self 492 • Contemplation of Disenchantment 501 • Contemplation of Dispassion 502 • Contemplation of Cessation 504 • Contemplation of Relinquishment 507

The Remaining Contemplations 512

Contemplation of Destruction 512 • Contemplation of Fall 514 • Contemplation of Change 515 • Contemplation of the Signless 518 • Contemplation of the Desireless 520 • Contemplation of Emptiness 520 • Insight into Phenomena that Is Higher Wisdom 521 • Knowledge and Vision of Things as They Really Are 522 • Contemplation of Danger 523 • Contemplation of Reflection 524 • Contemplation of Turning Away 526

Mahāsi Sayadaw's Closing Words 528

List of Abbreviations 529

Notes 531

Pāḷi-English Glossary 591

English-Pāḷi Glossary 635

Bibliography 679

Index 681

About Vipassanā Mettā Foundation 709

Tables on the Removable Insert

Appendix 1: The Progress of Insight

Appendix 2: Mental Factors Present in Each Consciousness

Appendix 2a: Mental Factors Present in Each Consciousness (Continued)

Appendix 3: Stream of Consciousness

Appendix 4: Uprooting Defilements

Appendix 5: Materiality

Appendix 6: Planes of Existence

Appendix 7: Mental Process Functions

Foreword by Joseph Goldstein

The Venerable Mahāsi Sayadaw, one of the foremost Burmese monks of the twentieth century, played a critical role in disseminating the liberation teachings of early Buddhism. He was a rare example of someone who combined the most extensive and thorough knowledge of the Pali texts with the wisdom that comes from the deepest realizations of meditation. The range of both his theoretical and practical understanding was acknowledged when he was asked to be the chief questioner at the Sixth Buddhist Council, held in Yangon in 1954.

In his teaching role, Mahāsi Sayadaw was largely responsible for the widespread practice of *vipassanā*, or insight meditation. In Burma he established hundreds of meditation centers around the country where ordinary lay practitioners, as well as monastics, could come and receive instruction and guidance in Satipaṭṭhāna meditation, the practice of the Four Foundations of Mindfulness, which the Buddha declared to be the direct path to liberation. In these centers and those in other Asian countries, hundreds of thousands of people were introduced to this meditation practice. Through his disciples these teachings were later brought to India, the birthplace of the Buddha, and then to the West.

The widespread introduction of mindfulness now taking place in America and other Western countries has its roots largely in the teachings of Mahāsi Sayadaw, and his great ability to convey the practical means of awakening. Although mindfulness in its secular applications has tremendous benefits, it's helpful to remember that the original teachings of the Buddha are about liberation—that is, freeing the mind from those mental states that cause suffering to oneself and others.

In this extraordinary work, *Manual of Insight*, Mahāsi Sayadaw explains in depth and great detail the entire path of practice, beginning with the Purification of Conduct and ending with the realization of Nibbana, the highest freedom. It integrates some of the most abstruse elements of theoretical knowledge with the most direct and accessible practical teachings. *Manual of Insight* is a text to study slowly, it is a reference work to deepen our understandings, and it is ultimately a guide for our own path of awakening.

Foreword by Daniel Goleman

In *Manual of Insight*, the Burmese meditation master Mahāsi Sayadaw offers a gift from an ancient wisdom tradition that speaks to the urgent needs of the modern world. Many of the teachers who brought *vipassanā*, or insight meditation, to the West studied with Mahāsi Sayadaw or his students. And now that mindfulness meditation, a modified form of insight vipassanā, has become so popular, the time is auspicious for this deep explanation of the full path that mindfulness begins.

My own connection with these teachings was through studying with students of Mahāsi Sayadaw, mainly Sayadaw U Paṇḍita, with whom my wife Tara Bennett-Goleman and I spent remarkably fruitful time on retreat. Sayadaw U Paṇḍita has taken pride in following to the letter the path set out in the *Manual of Insight*. In contemporary vernacular, Sayadaw U Paṇḍita uses the term "SQ," spiritual intelligence, to refer to the deep insights and practical tools contained in *Manual of Insight*, the method he has taught to thousands of students in Burma—including Aung San Suu Kyi—and around the world.

From my perspective, SQ describes the spiritual level of emotional intelligence. The keystone in emotional intelligence is self-awareness, and vipassanā gives us that ability in the most profound way. With this lens on our mind and body we can re-experience the comings and goings in our own phenomenology in a fine-grained way that breaks down the illusory sense of self that cognitive science tells us we synthesize from disparate internal inputs, weaving together these random parts into an ongoing personal narrative. That narrative, we can see with vipassanā, hides more essential truths about our true nature.

Then there is self-regulation, the many ways in which we routinely apply that self-awareness to manage our lives. With vipassanā comes *sīla*, the voluntary self-discipline essential to balancing and focusing our mind freed from the routine distractions and attachments of our daily lives. With this self-discipline we can create an oasis in our life where the deep introspection of vipassanā allows us to experience deeper truths about our very being.

The third part of emotional intelligence, empathy, comes in three varieties: cognitive understanding, where we see how others think; emotional attunement, where we sense how they feel; and empathic concern, where we care about their wellbeing and stand ready to help if need be. This last quality of empathy creates a caring community, a quality that modern society sorely lacks. The practice of mettā and karunā, aspects of vipassanā where we cultivated compassion and lovingkindness, speak to this need.

And finally we put these capacities together in having fruitful relationships. In the evolution of being that this path of insight aims for, the end-result shows up in a transformation of being. As people approach the goal of that path, their personal qualities become a spiritual equivalent of the heights of emotional intelligence: equanimity in all circumstances, an absence of negatives like jealousy and anger, an abundance of lovingkindness and compassion, and being awake in the present moment.

While for centuries a materialist mentality could dismiss such claims as religious superstition or cultural myth, neuroscience has begun to tell us a very different story. As recent findings with highly advanced meditation practitioners are showing, the structural and functional changes in their brain are consistent with the ancient formulations of the enduring traits that intensive practice can bring.

Fresh news from the brain lab urges us to look more seriously at these maps of the mind and how to upgrade our very being. The timing of this translation appears fortuitous.

Managing Editor's Preface

As with all conditioned things, the publication of this book is the result of innumerable causes and conditions, some that are known and many that will go unrecognized. The proliferation of new applications of mindfulness within secular society for an increasing variety of purposes and the attendant increasing demand for well-qualified guidance in the development of mindfulness and liberating insight have been major factors spurring this book into being. A reading audience that, through study of Dhamma and the practice of meditation, has become ripe enough to appreciate the great clarity of instruction has finally appeared and is rapidly growing. There are now many Dhamma students who will be able to recognize the comprehensive and authoritative Buddhist knowledge, the clear understanding of the vast range of meditative experiences one can encounter on the path, and the refined grasp of insight knowledge and the subtlety of liberation that this book contains. The time has come to share this profound work, *Manual of Insight*, with the English reading world.

The Author

Mahāsi Sayadaw, the author of *Manual of Insight*, is recognized as one of the most accomplished Buddhist scholars and meditation masters of the twentieth century. Within his native Burma he was respected as an exceptional scholar who wrote over seventy books in the Burmese and Pāḷi languages. He was also honored by the worldwide Buddhist community at the Sixth Council of the Saṅgha, held in Burma in 1956, where he was asked to assume the role of questioner, a position that was held by Mahā Kassapa at the First Council of the Saṅgha three months after the passing of the Buddha. During the Sixth Council Mahāsi Sayadaw was also responsible for overseeing creation of an authoritative edition of the Pāḷi

Canon, along with its commentaries and subcommentaries. This edition of the Canon, called the *Chaṭṭha Saṅgāyana Tipiṭaka*, is still widely used and held in high regard throughout the Theravāda Buddhist world.

In addition to his prolific scholastic achievements, Mahāsi Sayadaw also developed a clear, simple, and easy to understand (if not easy to master) method for practicing mindfulness-based insight meditation based on his personal practice of meditation rooted in his studies. Having taught the method to his relatives, he found that they were quite successfully able to purify the progress of their insight. With this confirmation, in 1949 he accepted the invitation to teach his method to lay people as well as monastics and to guide students in the development of liberating insight at a newly created meditation center in Rangoon, the Mahāsi Sasana Yeiktha Meditation Center. Hundreds of thousands of Burmese and foreign students have since successfully practiced there. Since Mahāsi Sayadaw passed away in 1982, Sayadaw U Paṇḍita and other renowned Burmese meditation masters have preserved the Mahāsi Sayadaw tradition of teaching, making it available to thousands of Burmese, Western, and non-Burmese Asian Dhamma students.

Mahāsi Sayadaw's meditation method and retreat format are characterized by clarity and simplicity of instruction, suited even for those who do not have extensive academic knowledge of the Buddha's teachings—that is, instructions suited for lay people and householders as well as for monastics; intensive periods of retreat for a limited duration, rather than life-long monastic commitment; a clear method of tracking the progress of meditators—that is, a method of tracking the progress of insight; and the opportunity for foreign students to attend teachings and retreats and to practice and attain proficiency in mindfulness. These unique features of the Mahāsi Sayadaw method have led to his recognition as one of the "elders" or "grandfathers" of what has become the Western mindfulness movement and insight meditation tradition. A number of key figures in the contemporary spread of Buddhist meditation throughout the world belong to the Mahāsi Sayadaw lineage: the first generation of Western vipassanā teachers, Joseph Goldstein, Sharon Salzberg, and Jack Kornfield, are students of Mahāsi Sayadaw's disciple Anagarika Munindra and his student Dipa Ma.

These and subsequent generations of Western vipassanā teachers who follow the Mahāsi method using an intensive retreat format have established leading centers for training in vipassanā meditation, such as the

Insight Meditation Society (MA), Spirit Rock Meditation Center (CA), Tatagatha Meditation Center (CA), Gaia House (England), Meditation Centre Beatenberg (Switzerland), and numerous offshoot centers such as Cambridge Insight Meditation Center (MA), Common Ground Meditation Center (MN), Seattle Insight Meditation Society, Vipassanā Hawaii (Honolulu), Vipassanā Mettā Foundation (Maui), and many other groups. Mahāsi Sayadaw's teachings have thus had an undeniable and significant impact on the transmission of the Buddha's Theravāda teachings to the West, grounding them solidly in the practice of mindfulness.

The Book

In 2000 I learned that Mahāsi Sayadaw's comprehensive and authoritative *Manual of Insight* had never been translated into English. As a senior teacher leading mindfulness and insight retreats, I recognized the growing need for the type of guidance that the manual provides. So I set out to put together a team of scholar-practitioners, both lay and ordained, that could carry out the monumental work of making this book available to English-reading Dhamma students. The team of Western and Burmese Dhamma students who participated in the translation and editing of this work are all either currently ordained monks and nuns or have been in the past. Every member of the team has extensively practiced mindfulness and the development of insight within the Mahāsi Sayadaw tradition and remains engaged in spreading these teachings, through instruction and practice, around the world. The project was advised by Sayadaw U Paṇḍita and funded by the Vipassanā Mettā Foundation.

Mahāsi Sayadaw wrote *Manual of Insight* in Seikkhun, west of Mandalay, over a seven-month period in 1945, during which time the nearby city of Shwebo, only eight miles away, was under almost daily bombardment. The work he produced is a comprehensive and authoritative treatise that expounds the doctrinal and practical aspects of mindfulness (*satipaṭṭhāna*) and the development of insight knowledge (*vipassanā*) up to and including the attainment of the Buddha's ideal of enlightenment (*nibbāna*). Originally published in two volumes in Burmese, *Manual of Insight* comprises seven chapters that introduce the theory and practice of the Buddha's Noble Eightfold Path, which begins with the practice and development of mindfulness, continues through the unfolding of insight knowledge, and culminates in the realization of enlightenment.

The first chapter, "Purification of Conduct," offers an overview of how to establish an ethical foundation for one's practice through purification of speech and behavior (*sīla*), the second of the three foundations of the Dhamma and the first of three types of training undertaken on the Noble Eightfold Path. While there is a brief overview of ethical purity for monastics, particular attention is paid to ethical practice for lay practitioners, supplemented with orthodox and sometimes fundamental teachings from the Buddhist tradition.

The second chapter, "Purification of Mind," offers a detailed description of how to use mindfulness to develop concentration, stability or collectedness of mind (*samādhi*), the second of the three types of training employed on the Noble Eightfold Path and the first part of the third foundation of the Dhamma, development of mind (*bhāvana*). The establishment of continuous mindfulness temporarily purifies the mind of defilements (*kilesas*), which leads to tranquility or seclusion of the mind from distraction. Mahāsi Sayadaw's description of the development of concentration includes an important clarification of the difference between what is known as "fixed" or "tranquility" concentration and "insight" or "momentary" concentration. The clarity with which the venerable Sayadaw makes this distinction proves instructive of and essential to effective insight practice.

The third chapter, "Absolute and Conventional Realities," provides the foundation for insight practice by clearly articulating what are called the two views of reality: the relative, ordinary, consensual, or conceptual understanding of experience, and the experiential, empirical, or personal understanding of experience. Understanding the distinction between these two is essential to the skillful practice of insight and, ultimately, to realizing the Four Noble Truths, that is, to attaining enlightenment. While mindfulness can be practiced, and often is, without clearly distinguishing the difference between these two views or understandings, liberating insight (*nibbāna*) is not possible without it. The significance of material such as is laid out in this chapter is often glossed over in secular applications of mindfulness.

The fourth chapter, "The Development of Mindfulness," offers comprehensive instructions for developing mindfulness based on the Buddha's teachings on the four foundations of mindfulness, as outlined in the very well-known and highly regarded *Discourse on Mindfulness* (*Satipaṭṭhāna Sutta*).

The fifth chapter, "Practical Instructions," provides instruction in both the practices preliminary to undertaking insight meditation and in the actual practice of developing insight knowledge, ranging from the initial practices to advanced levels of practice. The remainder of the chapter is a narrative of meditative experiences from the initial days of practice up to and including the attainment of the first stage of enlightenment known as "stream-entry." It is in this chapter that Mahāsi Sayadaw lays out in plain language what a meditator is likely to experience through their practice and how they can come to understand those experiences as falling along a spectrum of unfolding insights known as the progress of insight. This clear articulation of the path of practice and of unfolding insight knowledges sets Mahāsi Sayadaw's teaching apart from those of other modern Buddhist teachers. The venerable Sayadaw's "Practical Instructions" provide a map of uncommon clarity that will confidently guide and encourage anyone willing to make the effort. An earlier translation of this chapter alone was published in Sri Lanka in 1965 under the title *The Progress of Insight*. Here in this volume, it is published for the first time in English in the full context of Mahāsi Sayadaw's comprehensive presentation on the subject.

The sixth chapter, "Stages of Insight Knowledge," presents a comprehensive template for evaluating one's practice and one's development of insight knowledge. Here Mahāsi Sayadaw explains in detail the various dazzling effects that come with the development of concentration as well as the ten corruptions of insight, sometimes called pseudo-nibbāna. The signs of attainment of each level of the progress of insight knowledge are identified, up to and including the experience of enlightenment. This material has not previously been widely available outside of Burma.

The seventh and final chapter, "The Eighteen Great Insight Knowledges," articulates the seven major and eleven minor insights to be realized through development of the path of practice. The contents of this chapter offer a very refined look at how insight purifies one's understanding, thereby uprooting the defilements that lay dormant within the mindstream. The clarity and subtlety of the shifts in understanding that must unfold for effective practice is unparalleled in Western Dhamma writings and teachings.

Taking into consideration the fact that the audience for which Mahāsi Sayadaw wrote *Manual of Insight* differs considerably from the contemporary English readership in terms of their likely knowledge of basic Abhidhamma, the Buddhist science of mind and matter, we have chosen to include robust appendices to provide readers some basic materials to help them navigate the more technical portions of this work. Abhidhamma contains the most exquisitely detailed description one can find anywhere of the mind, its processes, functions, and development through the practice of meditation. The various Abhidhamma categories of phenomena mentioned in the book have been compiled into a set of charts that conveniently display the relation between each of them and give an idea of how such subtle moments of consciousness unfold in sequence over time. This material has been provided as a supplement to Mahāsi Sayadaw's text and did not appear in the Burmese edition.

At the urging of Venerable Sayadaw U Paṇḍita, the senior Burmese advisor to the translation project, we have included in the numerous footnotes to the book the Pāḷi source text for the many citations of canonical texts Mahāsi Sayadaw makes. This has been done so that current and future scholars may directly and easily consult the Pāḷi and confirm for themselves the authenticity of the source material that Mahāsi Sayadaw used. Mahāsi Sayadaw deliberately and fully identified the traditional sources for everything he wrote about practice, mindfulness, and the unfolding of insight, referring to the discourses of the Buddha contained in the Pāḷi Canon or other Pāḷi language sources, such as commentaries, sub-commentaries, and so on. The translation team undertook the daunting task of locating and providing 599 Pāḷi quotations in Romanized script so that the reader could easily consult them if desired in this very volume. Those quotations from extra-canonical sources, for which we were unable to locate the English, have been translated from Mahāsi Sayadaw's own Burmese translations.

We also thought it useful to include an extensive dual glossary of technical terms—Pāḷi to English and English to Pāḷi—for those who may wish to consult the source language terminology that lies behind our translation.

Taken as a whole, the material in this manual provides a comprehensive, well-documented presentation of the practice of the Buddha's Noble Eightfold Path that verifiably leads one to the goal of liberation according to the Theravāda tradition.

The Team of Translators and Editors

Every member of the translation committee has undertaken decades of practicing the method outlined in this book. All have, at one time or another, taken up robes and lived as monks or nuns in Burma practicing the teachings in this book, some for more than twenty years. In this, we are grateful for the wise oversight and guidance of Sayadaws U Paṇḍita, U Janaka, U Indaka, U Lakkhaṇa, U Jaṭṭila, and Belin Sayadaw. Without their instruction and guidance in our own practice we would not have been able to prepare this book. In addition to these masters, many other nuns and monks in Burma assisted with the location of the many citations that Mahāsi Sayadaw includes to authenticate these teachings as the Buddha's.

The first draft of the translation was completed by Hla Myint, formerly ordained as Ven. Vaṇṇita, who holds a Monastic PhD (Abhivaṃsa) in Pāḷi Language and Buddhist Studies from Mahā-gandayone, one of the most prestigious Pāḷi Institutes in Burma. He currently writes, translates, and teaches Dhamma at Tathagata Meditation Center (TMC), San Jose, CA, and since 2000, has been teaching Buddha-Dhamma at the Buddhist Study Program of Antioch College.

Revision, review, and editing of the first draft of the translation was undertaken by Ariya Baumann, formerly ordained as Ven. Ariyañāṇī, a Swiss-born former Buddhist nun who lived and practiced in Burma for twenty years, is conversant in Burmese language and familiar with Pāḷi. She currently leads retreats in Burma, Europe, Australia, and the US.

As the managing editor, I myself oversaw the project from its conception to its publication, working closely with the translators and editors, and performing additional edits on the manuscript at each stage of the process. During my years of ordination as Ven. Buddharakkhita, I practiced primarily under the guidance of Sayadaw U Paṇḍita. Subsequently, as a cofounding director and guiding teacher of the Vipassanā Mettā Foundation, I have been leading mindfulness, insight, and *abhidhamma* retreats worldwide since 1990. I created the charts of abhidhamma data that are included in this book while studying abhidhamma with Sayadaw U Sāgara in Australia.

Ven. Virañāṇī, an American nun who has resided in Burma since 2005, assisted with the edit of the text, located the Pāḷi text of cited passages in Romanized editions of the texts, found available English translations of such for reference purposes, and compiled the extensive dual language glossaries provided at the back of the book. Ven. Virañāṇī has studied Pāḷi language and extensively practiced insight meditation in Burma and the US. She currently leads retreats in Burma, Europe, New Zealand, and Australia.

Kamala Masters, formerly ordained as Ven. Vipulañāṇī, has intensively practiced vipassanā and mettā meditations with Sayadaw U Paṇḍita since

1985, both as a nun and layperson. She has also practiced with Anagarika Munindra, who trained under the guidance of Mahāsi Sayadaw and passed on his method of practice. Kamala is a cofounding director and guiding teacher of the Vipassanā Mettā Foundation and has been leading mindfulness, insight, and lovingkindness retreats worldwide since 1993.

Deborah Ratner Helzer, formerly ordained as Ven. Gotamī, intensively practiced insight meditation under the guidance of Sayadaw U Paṇḍita. She has been teaching Dhamma and leading insight meditation retreats in the US since 2005.

The following Burmese monks have provided valuable research assistance for the translation of Pāḷi text and explanation of technical details of abhidhamma: Sayadaw U Janaka from Chanmyay Yeiktha, Yangon, Burma; Sayadaw U Indaka from Chanmyay Myaing Meditation Center, Yangon, Burma; Sayadaw U Sāgara from Chanmyay Myaing Study Monastery, Hmawbi, Burma and Akiñcano (Marc Weber), former monk from Germany.

The Time and Place of Publication

The first generations of Western vipassanā teachers chose not to reveal much of what they knew of this material in part due to the tendency of Western Dhamma students to strive with an "unwholesome" ambition to attain something, which can be more of a hindrance than a benefit. The refined guidance that Mahāsi Sayadaw provides in this book will lead practitioners to systemically and gradually purify their minds of attachment, aversion, and delusion, and to realize the successive stages of enlightenment, culminating in nibbāna.

However, numerous different methods and forms of meditation practice have now appeared to compete for the attention of sincere Dhamma students. The Mahāsi Sayadaw method, in particular the clarity of the progress of insight, has attracted and continues to attract and retain many students. It is the emerging consensus among the senior Western vipassanā teachers that given the growth and stability of sincere Dhamma communities in the West, the material in this book will now more than ever serve as a useful point of orthodox reference for all who take up the tradition.

This *Manual of Insight* offers a detailed description of the theory and practice of mindfulness that leads to insight knowledge and the realization of *nibbāna* that is unavailable in contemporary English-language

Dhamma writings. The inclusion of copious, accurately cited sources in the Pāḷi Canon and detailed supplementary abhidhamma materials within this book sets it clearly apart from the majority of Western or non-Burmese books on the subject. When the time came to seek a publisher for this important and monumental work, Wisdom Publications was our first choice. Wisdom enthusiastically recognized the value that the material in *Manual of Insight* would have for all Dhamma practitioners, regardless of tradition. We are grateful for the guidance of the editors at Wisdom who have helped us to strike a happy balance between a very faithful translation of Mahāsi Sayadaw's writing in his own voice and smooth readability in English.

I take personal responsibility for any errors that may appear in this book. It is important to us that all readers be informed of any errors that are found in the book. Should you find any, please report them to us at www.mahasimanualofinsight.org, where we will have a page of corrections for reference.

May the merit accrued by virtue of any and all actions taken to bring this book to publication support the development of the aspiration for liberation and accomplishment of the end of suffering for all beings.

Steve Armstrong

Introduction

According to the Buddha's teaching, the practice of insight meditation (*vipassanā*) enables one to realize the ultimate nature of mind and body, to see their common characteristics of impermanence (*anicca*), suffering (*dukkha*), and not-self (*anattā*), and to realize the Four Noble Truths.

To reject the practice of insight meditation is to reject the teaching of the Buddha, to undermine others' faith and confidence in the practice, and to abandon the prospect of attaining the path and fruition. The following verse from the *Dhammapada* shows how big an offense this is:

> The unwise who rely on evil views
> To malign the teachings of the noble arahants
> Who live the Dharma
> Produce fruit that destroy themselves,
> Like the *kathaka* reed that dies upon bearing fruit.[5]

The following reflections can arouse enthusiasm for the practice of insight meditation. Access to the Dhamma is a precious opportunity. We are very fortunate to be alive at this point in history when we have access to the teachings of the Buddha. It is a tremendous opportunity for all of us. We have the chance to profit by realizing the path, fruition, and nibbāna that are the most valuable Dhammas. But this opportunity will pass. Unfortunately this great opportunity does not last forever. The span of our lives ends before long. Even if our lifespans are not yet over, we can die at any time. And even while we are still alive, we may lose the ability to practice if we become weak or sick due to old age, if conditions are too dangerous, or if other problems or difficulties arise.

We should not waste our time. How should we make best use of this great opportunity after having read this book? Should we be satisfied just with academic learning or teaching? Should we continue to devote all of our time and energy to the pursuit of never-ending sense pleasures? Is it not better to practice so that we will not find ourselves helpless on our deathbeds, without any reliable spiritual achievement to support us? The Buddha reminded us constantly that we have to practice effectively beforehand as long as there is time.

> Today the effort must be made;
> Tomorrow Death may come, who knows?
> No bargain with mortality
> Can keep him and his hordes away.[6]

Regret is useless. If we do not practice although we have the opportunity, we will feel regret when we are sick, old and weak, lying on our deathbed, or being reborn in the lower realms. Before it is too late, keep in mind the Buddha's admonition:

> Meditate, bhikkhus, do not delay or else you will regret it later.
> This is our instruction to you.[7]

Do you have personal experience? Are you able to appreciate the attributes of the Dhamma from personal experience? Do you know its attributes for yourself? Do you know that it has been well explained by the Buddha? That it can be empirically experienced? That it gives immediate results? That it invites one to come and see, to realize the truth for oneself?[8]

How to Read This Book

Please keep in mind the following considerations as you read this book: Don't read carelessly. It is very important to read the whole book thoroughly and carefully, from the beginning to the end, in order to appreciate the author's meaning and examples taken from the Pāḷi texts, their commentaries, and subcommentaries.

Don't feel disheartened if you come across Pāḷi references that you don't understand. They are mentioned here primarily for serious scholars of Pāḷi. If you wish to understand, you may ask such scholars and obtain the meaning. Some of the Pāḷi found in the book is not translated. Again, it is included primarily for the benefit of serious scholars of Pāḷi. English translations of Pāḷi references from the Discourse on the Foundations of Mindfulness (*Satipaṭṭhāna Sutta*) are widely available.

In some places in the book, everyday language is used, rather than formal language. The Buddha himself used Māgadhī, the everyday language of his time, when he gave Dhamma talks, rather than classic Sanskrit. This should not be considered odd or a sign of the relative insignificance of the material. Those with little or no knowledge of the Pāḷi scriptures should concentrate on chapters 4 and 5. Even reading and studying only chapter 5 will enable you to practice insight meditation in a straightforward way, and you will be able to realize path knowledge, fruition knowledge, and nibbāna.

Finally, don't feel disheartened if you have not yet attained a satisfactory level in your meditation practice. Go to a teacher and practice systematically under his or her guidance for seven days, fifteen days, or one month according to the instructions given in this book. Your experience will be satisfactory and you will realize special insights. You will also realize for yourself that the Dhamma is endowed with the aforementioned attributes.

Manual of Insight

Purification of Conduct 1

The Purification of Conduct for Monks

According to the *Visuddhimagga*,[9] purification of conduct (*sīlavisuddhi*) refers to the four kinds of morality (*sīla*) that are completely purified.

> Moral purity is indeed completely cleansed
> through observing the monastic rules
> beginning with the fourfold morality.[10]

Purification of conduct refers to the purification of four kinds of morality that I will fully explain in this section: the morality of observing the monastic precepts (*pāṭimokkhasaṃvara*), the morality of pursuing a pure livelihood (*ajīvapārisuddhi*), the morality of wisely using requisites (*paccayasannissita*), and carefully restraining the senses (*indriyasaṃvara*).

There are two categories of morality, one for monks and one for laypeople. Since the morality of monks is quite extensive, I will explain it only in summary. As a monk, one should fully purify the four types of morality.

Observing the monastic precepts

Observing the monastic precepts that were established by the Buddha to restrain one's actions of body and speech from transgression is called "the morality of observing the monastic precepts." This kind of morality protects one from numerous kinds of danger and suffering. The guideline given to fully purify this morality is:

> . . . seeing danger in the slightest faults, observing the commitments he has taken on . . .[11]

A monk should take great care not to break any one of his precepts. He should consider even minor offenses to be dangerous, since they can interfere with his prospect of attaining the path and fruition and lead him to a rebirth in the lower realms.

If a monk happens to break a precept, he should correct it as soon as possible, just as a child would immediately drop a red-hot charcoal that he had accidentally picked up. A monk expiates his offense by observing the probation (*parivatta*) and penance (*mānatta*) of ostracism, or by relinquishing any money or materials according to the procedure given in scripture. Once an offense is restored in accord with the rules for monks (*vinaya*),[12] the monk should determine not to commit such an offense again. In this way he fully purifies observation of the monastic precepts.

Pursuing a pure livelihood

Seeking or receiving the four requisites[13] in accord with the rules for monks is called "the morality of pursuing a pure livelihood." The most important aspect of this kind of morality is making the effort to obtain the four requisites in ways that are in accord with the rules for monks. There are many ways of obtaining requisites that are not in accord with the rules for monks. A comprehensive list of these can be found in the *Visuddhimagga*.

If a monk obtains any of the four requisites by violating the rules for monks, the offenses are called "offenses meriting expulsion" (*pārājika*),[14] "offenses requiring a convening of the saṅgha" (*saṅghādisesa*), "serious infractions" (*thullaccaya*), or "improper conduct" (*dukkata*), depending on what kind of action he has committed. Improper conduct is the most common offense. The use of requisites that one has improperly acquired is also improper conduct. The observation of monastic precepts is also broken when one commits these offenses. This can damage the monk's prospects of celestial rebirth, path knowledge, and fruition knowledge. When these offenses are restored by way of the aforementioned procedures, the observation of monastic precepts can again be purified and one escapes from these dangers. So a monk must thoroughly purify this type of morality, too.

Wisely using requisites

The morality of wisely using requisites refers to keeping in mind the purpose for using the four requisites. To keep this morality purely, every time a monk uses any of the four requisites, he should consider its proper purpose. For example, when a monk wears or changes his robe, he should consider that the purpose of the robe is simply to protect him from the elements, not to make his body beautiful or attractive. When he eats he should consider the purpose of the food, one morsel after another. If he cannot do so at the moment of eating, he can do it some time before the next dawn. If he fails to do so until the dawn breaks, it implies that he uses the requisites "on loan" (*iṇaparibhoga*) as explained by the commentaries.

The term "use of requisites on loan" does not mean that a monk is accountable to repay his supporters for their donation in a future rebirth. It is given this name because the way that the monk utilizes the requisites resembles the way that someone procures something on loan. This is explained as follows: By donating requisites to a monk of pure morality, lay supporters fulfill one of the factors of perfect donation (*dakkhiṇāvisuddhi*). Thus they receive the greatest benefits possible from their generosity. If a monk fails to consider the proper purpose in using the requisites, his keeping in mind the purpose for using the four requisites is not pure, and the donors cannot enjoy the full benefits of their donations. For this reason, donors are then compared to someone who has sold something on loan or on credit. They have not received the full value for their donation. The recipient monk is similarly compared to someone who purchases on loan or on credit without giving the full value.

The *Mahāṭīkā*[15] says: "*Iṇaparibhoga* means 'use of something on loan.' A donation is compared to the use of something on loan since the recipient of it is not qualified for the factor of perfect donation."[16] But the *Mahāṭīkā* also says, "Just as a debtor cannot go where he wishes, so also the monk who uses things on loan cannot go out of the world."[17] So what is the point of this passage then? The point is that if a monk uses requisites without considering the purpose for doing so, his attachment to them is not cut. That attachment will lead him to the lower world after his demise. The story of a monk named Tissa illustrates this:

> A bhikkhu by the name of Tissa died with feelings of attachment to his brand new robe and was reborn as a louse on that very robe. When the robe was about to be shared among the other bhikkhus according to the rules for bhikkhus regarding a dead bhikkhu's possessions, the louse cried and accused the bhikkhus of robbing him of the robe. Through his psychic power, the

> Buddha heard the louse crying and asked the bhikkhus to postpone sharing the robe lest the louse should be reborn in a hell realm.[18] A week later the louse died and was reborn in the Tusitā celestial realm. Only then did the Buddha allow the robe to be shared among the bhikkhus as explained in the commentary of the *Dhammapada*.

This is a frightening thing! In view of his rebirth in the Tusitā celestial realm right after his louse's death, it is clear that if he had not been attached to his robe, he would have been reborn in that celestial realm immediately after his monk's death. Moreover if the Buddha had not postponed the sharing of his robe, he might even have been reborn in hell. Attachment is a serious misdeed and a frightening thing! The Buddha delivered the following verse regarding this event:

> As rust corrupts
> The very iron that formed it,
> So transgressions lead
> Their doer to states of woe.[19]

Some people assume that due to the use of materials on loan, a monk cannot attain path and fruition, as he is accountable to repay his loan. However, such an assumption is not in accord with the texts at all.

Some say that the use of materials on loan is a more serious offense than both enjoying the status of a monk on false pretenses and the four offenses meriting expulsion. This is so because when someone has become a layperson or a novice after committing an offense meriting expulsion or the offense of enjoying the status of a monk on false pretenses, that person can attain path and fruition.

For the Pāḷi reference, there is this passage from the Aṅguttara Nikāya commentary:

> After listening to this discourse,[20] sixty bhikkhus who had committed grave offenses were seized by spiritual urgency (*saṃvega*) and relinquished their bhikkhuhood. They then lived as novices (*sāmaṇera*), fulfilling the ten novice precepts. Later, cultivating good mental attitudes, some of them became stream enterers (*sotāpannā*),[21] some once returners (*sakadāgāmī*),[22]

> some nonreturners (*anāgāmī*),[23] and some were reborn in the celestial realms. Thus even bhikkhus who commit offenses meriting expulsion could be rewarded.[24]

The commentary explains that the Buddha had seen those sixty monks committing offenses meriting expulsion. So he made his journey with the purpose of delivering this discourse to them on the way. It is clear from this explanation that they had led their lives as monks on false pretenses for some time after committing grave offense. Even so, their grave offense and offense of enjoying the status of a monk on false pretenses did not destroy their prospects for path knowledge and fruition knowledge.

So how is it possible that using the requisites on loan, a minor offense, could destroy the prospects for enlightenment of a monk regardless of his otherwise good observation of monastic precepts? That is not reasonable, at all.

The monastic code and wisely using requisites

The instruction to consider the purpose for using the four requisites is not from the rules for monks but from the discourses. So a failure to consider the purpose for using the four requisites does not mean that a monk violates any monastic rule laid down by the Buddha. So it cannot cause any damage to the monk's prospect of path knowledge and fruition knowledge. Thus we should not say that use of requisites on loan is even as serious as the offense of improper conduct, which is the least serious offense of the monastic rules, aside from improper conversation (*dubbhāsita*).

One may ask here, "The commentary says that taking medicine without considering the purpose for doing so constitutes a breach of the monastic rules. So is it not reasonable to assume that not keeping the purpose for using the requisites in mind is also a breach of the monastic rules?" But this reasoning is not correct. A monk is allowed to take medicine only for medicinal purposes. If he takes that same medicine for a nutritional purpose, then it is an improper act according to the following monastic rule:

> If a bhikkhu eats for nutritional purpose the food allowed after noon (*yāmakālika*), the food allowed for a week (*sattāhakālika*), and the food allowed for life (*yāvajīvika*), it is an improper act every time he swallows it.[25]

So it is clear that this offense is due to the violation of the monastic precept, but it is not a violation of keeping in mind the purpose for using the medicine. For this reason, the subcommentary says that it is possible to purify a failure to keep in mind the purpose for using the four requisites by considering the purpose of the requisites used during the day some time before the next dawn.

Venerable Tipiṭaka Cūḷānāga Thera[26] was a highly respected senior monk. He was senior even to Venerable Buddhaghosa, the author of the commentaries. He was well versed in the Tipiṭaka, the three baskets of the Buddhist scriptures,[27] and was highly respected by the authors of the commentaries. So his views should be taken seriously. The notion that failing to consider the purpose for the four requisites is a breach of the monastic rules is contradictory to Venerable Tipiṭaka Cūḷānāga Thera's view. According to him, only the observation of the monastic precepts is morality. The other three classes of morality are not described as morality in any Pāḷi texts. Contrary to some other teachers, he explained that restraining the senses is simply restraint of the six senses, pursuing a pure livelihood is simply obtaining the four requisites in a fair and honest manner, and wisely using requisites is simply reflecting on the purpose of using the four requisites obtained fairly.[28]

Only observing the monastic precepts constitutes authentic morality. If a monk breaks this morality, he can be compared to a man whose head has been cut off. It is useless for him to consider lesser injuries to his limbs (the other three classes of morality). If a monk keeps this morality robust, he is compared to a man with a healthy head, who can therefore protect his life and limbs.

So according to this senior monk, as long as a monk's observation of the monastic rules is in good condition the other three moralities can be restored, however damaged they may be. Of course there is no doubt that a perfectly restored and purified morality helps a monk to realize path and fruition. According to other teachers, path and fruition cannot be attained when one uses requisites on loan, and a one-time failure to keep in mind the purpose for using requisites cannot be purified. These opinions contradict the above-mentioned Theravāda doctrine.

The method for reflecting on the purpose of the requisites is explained in the definition of moderation in eating (*bhojanemattaññū*) found in the Abhidhamma and in the Buddha's discourses, such as the *Sabbāsava Sutta*[29] and the *Āsava Sutta*.[30] However it is never directly referred to as "keeping in mind the purpose for using the four requisites." Instead it is called "moderation in eating," or "abandoning taints by using" (*paṭisevanāpahātabbāsavā*). For this reason Venerable Tipiṭaka Cūḷanāga Thera said that it is not described as morality in any Pāḷi texts.

Meditation and consideration

Reflecting on the purpose for using the requisites is, in an ultimate sense, wise reflection or reviewing (*paccavekkhaṇa*), and it more properly belongs to the field of training in wisdom (*paññāsikkhā*) than to the field of training in morality (*sīlasikkhā*). Reflecting on the purpose for using the requisites is not intended as a way to legitimize requisites according to the monastic rules, as are the practices of resolve (*adhiṭṭhāna*) and assignment (*vikappanā*), nor should such reflection simply be recited as a mantra. Reflection is instead meant to protect a monk from the mental defilements associated with the four requisites. So a monk should use the four requisites with proper consideration of their purpose.

Furthermore, an insight meditator automatically fulfills the practice of keeping in mind the purpose for using the four requisites, as demonstrated by the following passage:

> If a bhikkhu contemplates the requisites in terms of elements or loathsomeness when he obtains or uses them, then there is no offense for using or keeping overdue or extra robes and so on.[31]

This will be explained in detail later in the section on a layperson's morality. Thus, keeping in mind the purpose for using the four requisites can be completely purified in two ways: either by means of considering the purpose for using the requisites or through meditation on any object.

Carefully restraining the senses

Restraining the senses means to carefully restrain the senses in order to prevent the arising of defilements when one of the six types of sense objects enters one of the six sense doors and arouses one of the six sense consciousnesses. I will only give a detailed explanation of how to restrain oneself in order to have this kind of pure morality with regard to the eye-sense door. One can understand the other sense doors in a similar manner.

> On seeing a form with the eye, he does not grasp at its signs and features . . .[32]

When seeing a form with the eye, a monk should not recognize a person by his or her male or female form or by physical gestures and facial expressions. As the commentary says, "Let seeing be just seeing." The subcommentary explains that one should not allow one's mind to wander beyond the mere fact of seeing by paying attention to how beautiful or ugly a person is, and so forth.

The mental defilements of craving and so on often result from paying close attention to the face and limbs of the opposite sex. So one should not take an active interest in the body parts of a person of the opposite sex: the face, eyes, eyebrows, nose, lips, breasts, chest, arms, legs, and so on. Similarly one should not take an active interest in his or her gestures: the way he or she smiles, laughs, talks, pouts, casts a side glance, and so on. As the commentaries say, "He only apprehends what is really there."[33]

According to this quote one should pay attention only to what really exists in the person who is seen. What really exists in that person is hair of the head, hair of the body, nails, teeth, skin, flesh, sinews or tendons, bones, and so on. Alternately one should observe the four primary material elements and the secondary derived material elements in the person.[34] I will now explain how restraint arises in accordance with the commentary.

When a visible form stimulates the eye-door, a sequence of mind moments occur as follows: one attends to the object (*āvajjana*), eye-consciousness (*cakkhuviññāṇa*) sees the object, receives the object (*sampaṭicchana*), investigates the object (*santīraṇa*), determines the object (*votthapana*), and fully perceives the object or moves toward it (*javana*). Restraint may arise at the moment of full perception by means of morality (*sīla*), mindfulness (*sati*), knowledge (*ñāṇa*), forbearance (*khanti*), or effort (*vīriya*). If any one of these forms of restraint arises, the morality of restraining the senses is fulfilled. Alternately, self-indulgence may arise due to immorality, mindlessness, ignorance, impatience, or idleness.[35]

Restraint by means of morality

Restraint by means of morality is called *sīlasaṃvara* in Pāḷi. According to the commentaries, it refers to the observation of monastic precepts. A violation of this kind of restraint is called "self-indulgence through immoral conduct" (*dussīlya-asaṃvara*). Breaking the monastic precepts either verbally or bodily is a breach of the monastic code. With regard to self-indulgence via immorality, the subcommentaries[36] say that a transgression does not happen at the five sense doors with the arising of a transgressive defilement (*vītikkamakilesa*)[37] alone; the transgression only happens at the mind door. Transgressions via the remaining four self-indulgent behaviors arise at all six sense doors.

Restraint by means of mindfulness

Restraint by means of mindfulness is called *satisaṃvara* in Pāḷi. Restraint by means of mindfulness refers to restraint of the senses: restraint of the eye (*cakkhusaṃvara*), and so on. This is true restraint of the senses. In an ultimate sense, it is mindfulness that restrains the six sense doors in order to prevent the arising of defilements. On the other hand, forgetting to be mindful will lead to self-indulgence (*muṭṭhasacca-asaṃvara*) that manifests as covetousness (*abhijjhā*) and aversion, as described by the following Pāḷi passage:

> . . . greed and sorrow, evil unskilled states, would overwhelm him if he dwelt leaving this eye-faculty unguarded . . .[38]

Restraint by means of wisdom

Restraint by means of wisdom is called *ñāṇasaṃvara* in Pāḷi. According to such texts as the *Cūḷaniddesa* and the *Suttanipāta* commentary, restraint by means of wisdom occurs with the attainment of the path knowledges:

> The wisdom [of path knowledge] that restrains the current [of unwholesomeness such as craving, wrong view, defilements, misbehavior, ignorance, and so on.] is called "restraint by means of wisdom."[39]

According to the *Visuddhimagga*, restraint by means of wisdom also arises with keeping in mind the purpose for using the four requisites: "Restraint by means of [wisdom] is this . . . and use of requisites is here combined with this."[40]

Insight knowledge should also be included in restraint by means of wisdom. The practice of insight meditation that can abandon the defilements lying dormant in sense objects (*ārammaṇānusaya*) by means of partial removal (*tadaṅgappahana*) is even better than restraining defilements by means of reflection. The *Niddesa* states:

> Perceiving and seeing that all conditioned things are impermanent, one restrains the current of defilements through wisdom.[41]

Thus path knowledge, keeping in mind the purpose for using the four requisites, and insight knowledge are all considered part of restraint by means of wisdom. Nonrestraint is the opposite of these three kinds of wisdom, namely delusion (*moha*).

Restraint by means of forbearance

Restraint by means of forbearance is called *khantisaṃvara* in Pāḷi. This refers to exercising patience in dealing with cold, heat, severe pain, insults, very harsh words, and so on. It is, in an ultimate sense, nonaversion or nonhatred (*adosa*). Its opposite is self indulgence due to impatience (*akkhanti-asaṃvara*).

Restraint by means of effort

Restraint by means of effort is called *vīriyasaṃvara* in Pāḷi. "Effort" refers to exerting energy in order to abandon thoughts of sensual pleasure and so on. In an ultimate sense, it is the effort that is the right kind of striving (*sammapaddhanavīriya*), made according to the following Pāḷi passage:

> Here a bhikkhu awakens zeal for the non-arising of unarisen evil unwholesome states, and he makes effort, arouses energy, exerts his mind, and strives.[42]

According to the *Visuddhimagga*, the morality of pursuing a pure livelihood is included as part of restraint by means of effort. The opposite of restraint by means of effort is self-indulgence through idleness or laziness (*kosajja-asaṃvara*).

Practicing restraint prior to the practice of meditation

Of these five kinds of restraint, two cannot be included in the preliminary practice of restraint of the senses. Restraint by means of morality falls within the domain of the morality of observing monastic precepts. Restraint by means of wisdom, however, depends on having first developed insight and path knowledges. So it cannot be observed before taking up meditation.

In order to purify morality by means of carefully restraining the senses prior to the practice of meditation, one must cultivate three types of restraint: restraint by means of mindfulness, restraint by means of forbearance, and restraint by means of effort. The way in which to apply these restraints to purify this kind of morality is explained in the commentary called *Aṭṭhasālinī*:

> One can arouse wholesomeness by means of self-control, by means of transforming one's thoughts, by means of keeping busy doing good, and by means of steering one's mind towards wholesomeness.[43]

Exerting self-control

One should exert self-control: think, talk, and act only in wholesome ways; let only wholesomeness come in through one's six sense doors; take extra care to arouse only wholesomeness; bear patiently with whatever may happen; and make great effort not to entertain unwholesome thoughts. With this kind of self-control, one rarely thinks of anything unwholesome. When that happens, one does not allow unwholesomeness to be aroused within; one tries to think in a wholesome way.

For example, if a generous person obtains something precious and valuable, his first thought is to offer it to someone else rather than to use it for his own pleasure. In a similar way, self-control allows one to patiently bear anything unpleasant without reacting in an unwholesome way. This is a brief explanation of how to purify one's morality by means of restraining the senses by exerting self-control.

Transforming thoughts

If unwholesome thoughts arise, they should be transformed into wholesome thoughts. For example, if defiled thoughts arise when seeing a woman, they might be transformed in the following ways:

- Regard her as your own sister or mother, depending on her age, and reflect on her suffering, thereby arousing genuine thoughts of sympathy or kindness.
- Contemplate the disgusting substances in her body—tears, saliva, mucus, phlegm, feces, urine, and so on—by means of the perception of loathsomeness.

- Abandon defiled thoughts concerning the woman and substitute wholesome thoughts for them by discussing or teaching the Dhamma, reading books or scriptures, chanting, doing volunteer work, and so on.

There are many other ways to transform one's thoughts mentioned in the commentary on the *Satipaṭṭhāna Sutta*. This is just a brief explanation.

Keeping busy doing good

One should keep oneself occupied all the time with wholesome deeds such as: learning, teaching, memorizing, reading, scrutinizing, and chanting the Buddhist scriptures; discharging the daily duties of a monk; discussing the Dhamma, only speaking about the Dhamma; giving or listening to Dhamma talks; and practicing asceticism (*dhutaṅga*). When one does so, mental defilements do not have much opportunity to arise, and most of the time wholesome mental states will arise at the six sense doors instead. This is a brief explanation of how to uninterruptedly arouse wholesomeness.

Steering one's mind toward wholesomeness

One should encourage right attitude (*yoniso manasikāra*) by steering one's mind toward wholesomeness whenever one encounters sense objects. For example, if one is insulted without reason, one should bear in mind any of the following thoughts:

- "He insults me because he is not aware of the truth."
- "Frivolous people often insult others without good reason. That is the way they are."
- "When the truth comes to light, he or she will feel regret."
- "I might have insulted someone in a past life. So now I am suffering the same in return."
- "Insult is part of everyone's life; it is one of the worldly vicissitudes.[44] If even the Buddha himself was insulted, why not a person like me? The vicissitudes of life usually affect the minds of ordinary people. Only the noble can forebear the vicissitudes of life. I will follow their example."
- "The Buddha said that we must be patient even with a person who hacks us into pieces. If we become angry, we would not truly be his

disciples. Being insulted is much less painful than being hacked up. Why shouldn't I be able to follow this teaching of the Buddha?"

- "The one who insults me is, in an ultimate sense, made up of mental phenomena led by anger and physical phenomena generated by that angry mental state. There is no person insulting me but only the five aggregates[45] of mental (*nāma*) and physical (*rūpa*) phenomena that have already vanished at the moment of insult. They no longer exist. Now there is nothing to be angry with. If I remain angry, that would involve being angry with the subsequent phenomena, which would be similar to a person who hates the parents but takes revenge on their children or grandchildren after the parents have passed away."
- "The five aggregates of mental and physical phenomena were only there while I was being insulted, and they have also already vanished. So if I remain angry with the subsequently arisen mental and physical phenomena, it would be like trying to take revenge when the children, grandchildren, or great-grandchildren are there, but the parents are no longer living."

There are many other ways of thinking, too, that will encourage a right attitude. Whichever way one steers one's mind toward wholesomeness is honored as a right attitude. This is a brief explanation of how purification by means of right attitude comes about.

Attaining the three kinds of restraint

By employing the means described above, only wholesome mental states arise at the six sense doors, and one therefore attains morality by means of restraining the senses. Practicing in this way whenever there is contact with the six sense objects, wholesome awareness prevails, and one therefore attains restraint by means of mindfulness. If unwholesome thoughts should arise from time to time, one should make up one's mind not to think them again. One also fulfills restraint of the senses in this way. Moreover, when one encounters unpleasant sense objects, one is able to be patient with them, which is restraint by means of forbearance. When one makes a great effort to prevent the arising of mental defilements, such as thoughts of sensual pleasure, or makes a great effort to ensure that unwholesome thoughts disappear, this is restraint by means of effort.

In addition, one can restore one's morality by means of restraint of the senses in the same way as one restores one's morality by confessing one's offense to a fellow monk and promising not to commit it again.

Restraint that comes from meditation

The means of fulfilling morality by means of restraining the senses as mentioned above may sound easy, but in practice it is not. The mind is very disobedient unless it is tamed through meditation. It often goes to sense objects against one's wish or determination. This is how the mind is unless it is tamed by means of meditation. Some people have the notion that morality by means of restraining the senses can be attained without or before practicing meditation. They assume that one should meditate only after having attained all four types of morality.

However we should consider the instruction emphasized by the commentaries and subcommentaries that the mind should just be with the seeing and so on, and let absolutely no defilements arise at the six sense doors. Who can do that every time sense objects strike any of the six sense doors and produce the six sense consciousnesses? No one can do that, not even a very mature insight meditator! The defilements to be overcome by means of restraining the senses are not the ones that result in verbal or physical transgressions that can be overcome by means of morality. They are the obsessive and dormant defilements that can only be rooted out by means of concentration (*samādhi*) and wisdom (*paññā*).

Restraint of the senses is not really morality in the same sense as the morality of observing the monastic precepts. The mindfulness, wisdom, forbearance, and effort that characterize restraint of the senses actually belong to the training of concentration and wisdom, not to the training of morality. That is why restraint by means of wisdom refers to path knowledge as shown in the *Cūḷaniddesa* and in the commentary to the *Suttanipāta*. This evidence proves that restraint of the senses cannot be fully purified without or before meditation. The mind tamed by means of meditation becomes gentle and obedient. It follows one's wishes, and one can direct it to any object one wants. That is the way it is.

Therefore, restraint of the senses can only be fully purified by means of meditation. The more one's meditation matures, the purer one's restraint of the senses becomes. When one's meditation is fully mature, this kind of morality will be fully purified as explained in the commentaries and subcommentaries. To illustrate this point, the *Visuddhimagga* encourages us to follow the example of a senior monk called Mahātissa.

> *Mahātissa*
> Venerable Mahātissa was a senior bhikkhu who had been practicing the contemplation of the impurity of the body (*asubhabhāvanā*) for years. One day, he saw a woman smiling alluringly at him somewhere in the forest. Far from yielding to temptation, the sight of her teeth caused the perception of impurity (*asubhasaññā*) to arise in him, which led him to attain the first *jhāna*. He then proceeded to practice insight meditation based on that very jhāna until he attained the fruit of arahantship (*arahattaphala*).

The *Visuddhimagga* records this verse composed by an old sage:

> He saw the bones that were her teeth,
> And kept in mind his first perception;
> And standing on that very spot
> The elder became an Arahant.[46]

The phrase "keeping in mind his first perception [of impurity]" makes it clear that the monk had already developed well the contemplation of the impurity of the body before this event. So if one wants to follow the example of this monk, one needs to develop well one's meditation beforehand. Otherwise, one's meditation cannot be applied like this monk's to resist temptation.

One may ask, "Isn't it possible for a person with well-developed noble deeds (*pāramī*)[47] to apply this reflection of impurity, even if they have not practiced it beforehand?" That is possible, of course. The contemplation of the impurity of the body is a kind of meditation. Thus it is clear that restraint of the senses cannot be fully purified without meditation, in view of what the commentary and subcommentary clearly say regarding this type of morality: one should not let any mental defilements come in through the six sense doors.

If one wants to purify restraint of the senses before having practiced meditation, one should follow the above-mentioned methods as much as possible. But if one wants to fully purify it, one must practice meditation.

One should not delay one's meditation practice out of concern that one's restraint of the senses is not yet fully purified. Meditation will enable one to accomplish all of the kinds of restraint, including restraint of the senses.

Restraint as a prerequisite for meditation

In brief, it is only necessary for monks to fulfill two kinds of morality as prerequisites for their practice of meditation: they must observe the monastic precepts that are rules and regulations concerned with physical and verbal behavior and the monastic precepts that are rules and regulations associated with livelihood. Violation of these two kinds of morality constitutes a threat to the monk's prospects for path knowledge and fruition knowledge (*āṇāvītikkamantarāya*). Fulfilling the observation of monastic precepts automatically purifies the morality of pursuing a pure livelihood. If a monk pursues a wrong livelihood, he also spoils his observation of monastic precepts. So in order to fulfill the observation of monastic precepts, a monk necessarily must avoid pursuing a wrong livelihood.

Before taking up meditation practice, a monk should also try his best to attain restraint of the senses and to always keep in mind the purpose for using the four requisites, if possible. When one fulfills these two kinds of morality, one is free from regret or remorse. But failure to fulfill them will not harm one's practice. So do not hesitate to practice for that reason. All four kinds of morality will be fulfilled automatically when one practices meditation. This will become clearer at the end of the section on moral conduct for the laity.

The Purification of Conduct for the Laity

The practice of morality is not as exhaustive for laypeople as it is for monks. The purposes of laypeople are served by either the five precepts or the eight precepts topped with right livelihood (*ājīvaṭṭhamakasīla*). One may wonder how these two forms of morality can serve equally well when some of their precepts differ. It is because their "Dos and Don'ts" are fundamentally the same.

So if one observes the five precepts and properly follows the precept of refraining from lying, by inference one also observes the three additional verbal precepts included in the eight precepts topped with right livelihood—namely, refraining from backbiting or slander (*pisuṇavācā*), harsh or insulting words (*pharusavācā*), and frivolous speech (*samphappalāpavācā*). Likewise, if one refrains from the three bodily misbehaviors and the four verbal offenses, then one's livelihood is automatically pure, as is required by the eight precepts topped with right livelihood. Thus proper observance of the five precepts is basically the same as proper observance of the eight precepts topped with right livelihood.

On the other hand if one observes the eight precepts topped with right livelihood, by inference one is also supposed to refrain from alcoholic drink and any illegal drugs. These behaviors are considered indulgence in sensual pleasure and are therefore included in the precept concerning sexual misconduct. Thus proper observance of the eight precepts topped with right livelihood is basically the same as the five precepts. So whether one keeps one or the other of these two kinds of morality, it amounts to purification of conduct.

The five precepts are universal and exist whether or not the Buddha's teaching exists. They apply equally to all human societies regardless of time or place. To break the five precepts necessarily constitutes an offense, while observing them necessarily creates merit. That is simply the way it is. It is not something that was decided by the Buddha.

Comparisons to monastic morality

In regard to both the five precepts and the eight precepts topped with right livelihood, refraining from the three bodily misdeeds and the four verbal offenses that are not connected with one's livelihood are considered to be the lay form of observing monastic precepts. When connected with one's livelihood, refraining from the three bodily misdeeds and four verbal offenses can be considered the lay form of morality of pursuing a pure livelihood.

There is a difference, however, between a layperson and a monk's observance of the eight precepts topped with right livelihood: it is an offense for a monk not only when he seeks the four requisites in ways not approved by the code of monastic rules but also every time he uses the requisites gained in those ways. This is only a violation of right livelihood for laypeople, however, while they are committing bodily or verbal acts that are transgressions concerned with their livelihood. It is not an offense for them when they use materials they have improperly sought. This is because use alone does not involve committing any bodily or verbal misdeed, such as killing, etc. Using materials improperly sought is not a violation of a rule established by the Buddha for laypeople, as it is for monks. So it is not absolutely necessary that a layperson relinquish what he has obtained by unethical means. Simply making the determination not to continue indulging in wrong livelihood can purify a layperson's livelihood. Keeping in mind the purpose for using the four requisites pertains only to monks. Laypeople may use the requisites without considering their proper purpose. However, laypeople too may certainly enjoy the benefits of this kind of morality, thereby increasing merit and decreasing demerit.

Restraint of the senses, as explained above, is difficult to fulfill prior to practicing meditation even for monks, not to mention laypeople. In any event, the practice of meditation fulfills all four kinds of morality. This will be clarified later. There is no basis in the Pāḷi texts for the idea that these four kinds of morality should be purified for many days, months, or even years prior to taking up meditation. For monks, breaking the monastic rules interferes with their prospects for enlightenment. Therefore, for them this morality must be purified before starting meditation. However, none of the texts mention how long a monk must purify his morality before beginning to practice. So a monk can begin to practice the minute he fulfills the monastic precepts. This is also true of the moral precepts for laypeople. One can attain concentration, insight knowledge, path, and fruition the moment one's perfections are well enough developed.

The five spiritual obstacles

For laypeople, even if they have violated the precepts before, there is no barrier to path knowledge and fruition knowledge unless one or more of the five obstacles to the path knowledge and fruition knowledge hinders them. If they are hindered by any of the obstacles to path knowledge and fruition knowledge, then both laypeople and monks cannot attain path knowledge and fruition knowledge in this life. I will describe these obstacles here.

Kamma

"Kammic obstacle" (*kammantarāya*) refers to the five fatal types of misconduct: killing one's own mother, killing one's own father, killing an arahant, injuring the Buddha, and disrupting the unity of the monastic community (this last one is for monks only). These five deeds necessarily lead one to the lower world immediately after death. They jeopardize one's prospects for celestial rebirth and for path knowledge and fruition knowledge. Thus they are called "intentional acts that have immediate results (*ānantariya-kamma*)." Raping a virtuous nun is called *bhikkhunīdūsanakamma* and jeopardizes the prospect for path knowledge and fruition knowledge. These six kinds of deeds are called kammic obstacles.

Wrong views

"Defilement obstacle" (*kilesantarāya*) refers to three types of wrong views: the wrong view that there is no good or evil (*akiriyadiṭṭhi*)—the idea that actions do not become good or evil and do not lead to good or evil results; the wrong view that everything is cut off or comes to an end when a being dies (*natthikadiṭṭhi*)—the idea that no further existence will occur after death and that there are no good or evil results that come from good or evil actions; and the wrong view that volitional action does not produce good or evil results (*ahetukadiṭṭhi*)—the idea that happiness and suffering arise by themselves without causes.

Of these three views, the first denies that effects have causes, the second denies that causes have effects, and the third denies both. So the three kinds of wrong view deny the law of cause and effect.

If one holds steadfastly to any of these three types of wrong view, they are said to have steadfast wrong views (*niyatamicchādiṭṭhi*) and are bound to be reborn in the lower world immediately after death. Thus these views are an obstacle to celestial rebirth and path knowledge and fruition knowledge.

Inborn deficiency

"Obstacle of inborn deficiency" (*vipākantarāya*) refers to an inborn deficiency in spiritual intellect, called *ahetuka* or *dvihetuka*. However, this is an obstacle only to path knowledge and fruition knowledge, not to celestial rebirth. So a layperson with this obstacle can be reborn into the divine realm if he or she performs good deeds.

Insulting a noble one[48]

"Obstacle of insulting a noble one" (*ariyūpavādantarāya*) refers to the act of insulting or degrading a noble one, with or without knowledge of his or her virtues. It damages the prospect of both celestial rebirth and path knowledge and fruition knowledge. One can remove this obstacle, however, by apologizing to the noble one for the offense.

Knowingly violating the monastic code

"Obstacle of knowingly violating the monastic code" (*āṇāvītikkamantarāya*) refers to a monk's knowing violation of the code of monastic rules that are sorted into seven groups. It harms the prospects for celestial rebirth and for path knowledge and fruition knowledge. A monk can be freed from this obstacle if he atones for his offense according to regulations in the monastic code.

The Majjhima Nikāya commentary says that the violation of the monastic code is only an obstacle so long as the monk who has committed an offense meriting expulsion continues to live as a monk, or as long as a monk who has committed a minor offense does not properly atone for it. However, if the monk disrobes or atones for his offense as dictated by the code of monastic rules, it is no longer an obstacle.

The enlightenment of immoral laypeople

Given the above discussion of the five spiritual obstacles, we can conclude that for the most part moral violations by laypeople do not cause obstacles to enlightenment. This is supported by the stories of four immoral laypeople who became enlightened: the drunken minister named Santati, a fisherman named Ariya, a pickpocket, and a man of royal caste named Sarakāni.

> *The Story of Minister Santati's Enlightenment*
>
> King Kosala was once so pleased with his minister Santati's success in conquering an enemy that he conferred "seven-day kinghood" on him as a reward. The minister spent his regal week enjoying kingly life and getting drunk all the time. On the seventh day he departed the palace for the river accompanied by many royal attendants. When he met the Buddha on the way, he paid respect to him from his seat on the back of a royal elephant by nodding his head.
>
> The Buddha then predicted that on that very day the minister would become fully enlightened after listening to a single verse and then would enter *parinibbāna*.[49] Hearing this prediction,

some unbelievers sneered at the Buddha, saying that it would be impossible for a drunkard to become fully enlightened on the same day. They were sure Gotama Buddha would be humiliated by his misstatement.

That evening, however, the beautiful girl whom the minister adored most among the court ladies died under his very nose while entertaining him. He was so grief-stricken that he could find no way to console himself. He finally went to the Buddha looking for relief from his great sorrow. The Buddha spoke the following verse:

> Let past defilements wither away, do not yield to future passions,
> Do not grasp at the present—then the fires of defilement will be extinguished.[50]

The *Dhammapada-aṭṭhakathā* says that the minister became an arahant after hearing the above verse. He then flew to the height of about seven palm trees, as directed by the Buddha, in order to dispel anyone's doubts about his enlightenment. Afterward he entered parinibbāna as a layman.

The fact that the minister became an arahant after listening to just this one verse should not be taken to mean that simply listening to a Dhamma talk without practicing meditation can bring enlightenment. As the minister was listening to that verse of Dhamma, he was observing his mind and body. This brought about the insight knowledges and the attainment of the path knowledge and fruition knowledge, step by step, until he became fully enlightened.[51] The commentary to the *Satipaṭṭhāna Sutta* explains this as follows:

> Although enlightenment may occur after listening to a talk, it is impossible to bring about any insight or enlightenment without meditating on body, feelings, consciousness, and mental objects. So they[52] overcame sorrow and lamentation by taking this very path of the four foundations of mindfulness.[53]

Since the minister was drunk for the entire week before hearing this verse from the Buddha, it is clear that his morality was not purified until immediately before his enlightenment. The simple fact that he was in his final life (*pacchimabhavikā*) cannot explain this case. If he had been a monk, his violation of the monastic rules would have been an obstacle to his enlightenment, even though he was in his final life. The guideline given to the monk Uttiya, who was also in his final life, supports this:

> So, Uttiya, purify the very starting point of wholesome states. And what is the very starting point of wholesome states? Morality that is well purified[54] and view that is straight.[55] Then Uttiya, when your morality is well purified and your view is straight, based on morality, established in morality, you should develop the four foundations of mindfulness.[56]

I interpret morality here as observing the monastic code according to the *Jhāna Vibhaṅga* and the *Kaṅkhā* subcommentary. Note that although the Buddha gave the guideline to practice meditation after having fulfilled morality, he did not mention how long the morality should be purified in advance. Moreover, he prescribed the practice of the four foundations of mindfulness, but he did not specify developing only one of these four foundations nor did he specify the order of developing the four. In other words, one may develop any of the four kinds of mindfulness.

Venerable Uttiya, practicing as instructed, soon became an arahant. So clearly he was in his final life. Nevertheless he was still instructed to fulfill morality before beginning his meditation practice. Therefore it must be necessary for a monk to fulfill the morality of observing monastic precepts whether he is in his final life or not, since a moral violation is necessarily an obstacle to a monk's enlightenment. Uttiya was instructed to keep away from steadfast wrong views for a similar reason.

Given these two cases and their outcomes, it is evident that even in one's last life moral violations are an obstacle to path knowledge and fruition knowledge for a monk but not for a layperson. Therefore, one should not say that one can attain path knowledge and fruition knowledge without having purified one's morality beforehand just because it is one's final life.

> *The Story of Fisherman Ariya's Enlightenment*
> One day the Buddha returned after having collected almsfood from a village near the northern gate of Sāvatthī. He chose his

route so that on the way he would meet with a fisherman by the name of Ariya, which means "noble one."

Seeing the Buddha coming accompanied by his bhikkhus, Ariya put down his fishing pole and stood up to one side. When asked his name, he replied, "Ariya."

"A person who hurts or kills other living beings is not called Ariya," said the Buddha. "A real ariya does not behave in such a way." Then the Buddha concluded the conversation with the following verse:

Not by harming living beings
Is one a noble one.
By being harmless to all living beings
Is one called "a noble one."[57]

The commentary to the *Dhammapada* says that after hearing this talk, the fisherman Ariya became a stream enterer.

The Story of the Thief's Enlightenment

One day while the Buddha was giving a Dhamma talk in the Jetavana monastery, two pickpockets were in the audience. One of them listened carefully to the talk and became a stream enterer on the spot. The other proudly stole five coins.

Afterward at home, he laughed at his friend, saying, "You're so wise that you couldn't even get anything for your meal."

The newly reformed thief who had become a noble one reflected like this, "Out of ignorance he thinks of himself as a good and wise person." He reported this to the Buddha, who uttered the following verse:

A fool conscious of her foolishness
Is to that extent wise.
But a fool who considers himself wise
Is the one to be called a fool.[58]

If a fool knows that he or she knows nothing, he or she may approach a wise person and, listening to the wise person's admonition, become wise himself or herself. A true fool is a person who knows nothing but thinks of himself or herself as being very wise. Thinking that nobody else is as wise as oneself, one does not listen to any other person's advice, and so remains a fool for the rest of one's life.

> *The Story of Sarakāni's Enlightenment*
> Following the death of Sarakāni, a man of the Buddha's royal family, the Buddha claimed that the nobleman had become a stream enterer and was safe from rebirth in the lower realms. However, other members of the royal family disparaged the Buddha for this pronouncement, saying around the court:
>
> > "It is wonderful indeed, sir! It is amazing indeed, sir! Now who here won't be a stream enterer when the Blessed one has declared Sarakāni the Sakyan after he died to be a stream enterer, no longer bound to the nether world, fixed in destiny, with enlightenment as his destination? Sarakāni the Sakyan was too weak for the training; he drank intoxicating drink!"[59]
>
> The Buddha's cousin Mahānāma reported this gossip to the Buddha. Out of compassion, the Buddha then explained the reason why Sarakāni had become a stream enterer.[60] The Buddha gave the example of a seed: A rotten seed in poor soil will certainly not grow well. In the same way, practice that uses the wrong method will certainly not lead to enlightenment. On the other hand, a good seed in fertile soil grows well. Likewise, practicing under the Buddha's guidance, one is bound to obtain path, fruition, and nibbāna. The Buddha concluded his explanation as follows:
>
> > How much more, then, Sarakāni the Sakyan? Mahānāma, Sarakāni the Sakyan undertook the training at the time of his death.[61]

So it is clear that Sarakāni had not previously purified his morality. Only shortly before his death did he fulfill his morality and become a stream enterer.

How different types of people are suited to different trainings

Among these immoral laypeople who were enlightened, Ariya, the thief, and Sarakāni were clearly not yet in their final lives, as they only became stream enterers. It goes without saying that one could attain path and fruition without already having purified one's morality in advance if one were in one's final life. Some say that these three men were persons of quick understanding (*ugghaṭitaññū*) or persons who understand through elaboration (*vipañcitaññū*)—in other words, persons with exceptionally quick and discerning spiritual faculties—and this is why they were able to become stream enterers without purifying their morality in advance. If they had been persons to be guided (*neyya*), they would have needed to purify their morality beforehand.[62] However this line of reasoning is not consistent with the Pāḷi texts, commentaries, and subcommentaries that describe the person to be guided in this way:

> What kind of person is a person to be guided? It is a person who gradually gains a clear understanding of the Dhamma[63] by learning, discussing, applying wise attention, and associating with good companions. Such a person is called "a person to be guided."[64]

This passage explains that a person to be guided attains path and fruition by learning how to practice meditation, asking about what is not clear with regard to the instructions, properly practicing by applying wise attention, and approaching a teacher when necessary to clear up any doubts and to arouse energy, faith, and enthusiasm. Note that nowhere is it mentioned that one must purify one's morality in advance. Another teaching on this topic comes from the *Nettipakaraṇa*:

> Insight based on concentration is suitable for a person of quick understanding.
> Concentration based on insight is suitable for a person to be guided.
> Alternating concentration and insight is suitable for a person who understands through elaboration.
> Training in wisdom is suitable for a person of quick understanding.

> Training in concentration and wisdom are both suitable for a person who understands through elaboration.
> Training in morality, concentration, and wisdom are all suitable for a person to be guided.[65]

This commentary bases the suitability of practices on personality type, but these are not prerequisites for enlightenment. For example, training in morality is not mentioned as particularly suitable for persons of quick understanding and persons who understand through elaboration. But this does not mean that a monk's moral violations are not an obstacle to his enlightenment if he is a person of quick understanding or a person who understands through elaboration.

Likewise, it does not mean that a person to be guided must fulfill morality and concentration in advance. Otherwise the attainment of jhānic concentration would be a prerequisite for persons to be guided and persons who understand through elaboration, and that is impossible. The conclusion that should be drawn from the above Pāḷi reference is that the prior development of morality and concentration very much helps a person to be guided to get enlightenment, but it is not strictly necessary. Let me explain the reasoning behind the guidelines given in the above commentary.

The types of people suited to training in morality

A person to be guided requires a long time to complete his or her practice. Over the course of that time, such people will tend to reflect on their morality, and if they find deficiencies in it, their hearts will not be at peace. They tend to have a lot of remorse when remembering a past violation, even if their morality is pure at the moment. If they cannot do away with their remorse, worry and anxiety might break their insight meditation. On the other hand, when such people reflect that their morality has been pure for a long time, or at least for the time that they have been practicing meditation, they will surely feel delight, joy, happiness, calm, and tranquility. As a result of this their concentration and insight knowledge will improve. So for a person to be guided, it is very helpful to purify moral conduct over a long period of time, or at least for the period when he or she is practicing meditation.

The types of people suited to training in concentration

When a person of quick understanding listens to a short and concise Dhamma talk, they develop insight knowledge and path knowledge very quickly. So the opportunity to repeatedly attain or enter the jhānas does not present itself to them. For this reason, morality and concentration are not mentioned as particularly suited to persons of quick understanding, and morality is not mentioned as particularly suited to persons who understand through elaboration.

However concentration very much helps the insight meditation practice of a person to be guided, as described in the following commentary:

> When one's insight concentration and insight knowledge are yet immature, and one practices sitting for a long time, one grows physically exhausted. One feels a burning inside; sweat oozes from the armpits; one feels heat coming out of the head; one experiences stress; and one's mind becomes restless. Then one retires to the attainment of jhāna so as to relieve the exhaustion and stress. Then the practice of insight meditation is resumed. Sitting for a long time again produces the same feeling, and again one retires to the attainment of jhāna for relief. Thus the attainment of jhāna is very helpful to insight meditation.[66]

According to this commentary, a person to be guided who is skilled in the attainment of jhāna can retire to that attainment every time they become exhausted and restless from their insight meditation practice. This allows their concentration and insight knowledge to become mature. Then they will no longer feel exhausted and restless and may even sit tirelessly for the whole day or night. This is why the attainment of jhāna is very helpful for a person to be guided.

Nowadays most yogis frequently encounter the difficulties mentioned above. But since they have no jhāna to retire to they just continue with their regular practice of insight meditation. By doing so, exhaustion and restlessness disappear and their insight knowledge matures.

For this reason the *Nettipakaraṇa* says that all three trainings are suitable for persons to be guided. The practices of morality and jhāna concentration are very helpful to one's progress, but this doesn't mean that one needs to fulfill them for a long time in advance. In the case of Sarakāni, we can assume that he became a stream enterer by practicing during his last days. Since there is no mention in any Pāḷi text of his attaining enlightenment while listening to a Dhamma talk he should be regarded as a person to be guided, rather than a person of quick understanding or a person who understands through elaboration.

Thus it is incorrect to think that a person to be guided needs to purify his or her morality for a long time in advance in order to obtain path knowledge and fruition knowledge. In fact, even a person who is not able to realize enlightenment in this very life may experience all of the insight knowledges without having purified morality beforehand. This fact is illustrated by the story of Tambadāṭhika.

> *The Story of Tambadāṭhika*
>
> In the town of Rājagaha, there was an executioner known as Tambadāṭhika (Copper Whiskers) on account of his red moustache. Every day in service to the king he had to execute several thieves and bandits. After fifty-five years he finally retired from his post. On the day of his retirement he prepared some special rice-gruel with milk that he hadn't had the chance to eat since he had become the executioner. Then he applied perfumes to his body, adorned himself with flowers, and put on new clothes. After having dressed, he sat down to eat the rice-gruel. Just as he was about to eat, Venerable Sāriputta, out of compassion, came to his door for almsfood. When Tambadāṭhika saw the Elder, he was very delighted, invited the Elder to come in, and respectfully offered him the rice gruel.
>
> After the meal, Venerable Sāriputta gave him a discourse on the Dhamma. But Tambadāṭhika was so agitated by the memories of his unwholesome deeds of the past fifty-five years that he could not pay attention. When Venerable Sāriputta realized this, he tactfully asked Tambadāṭhika whether he killed the thieves because he wanted to or because he was ordered to do so. Tambadāṭhika replied that the king had ordered him to kill them. Then Venerable Sāriputta asked, "If that is so, are you guilty or not?"
>
> Tambadāṭhika concluded that since he was not responsible for the evil deeds, he was not guilty. With this, he calmed down and asked Venerable Sāriputta to continue his exposition. As he listened to the Dhamma with proper attention, he came very close to attaining the first stage of path knowledge, reaching

as far as insight knowledge of equanimity toward phenomena (*saṅkhārupekkhāñāṇa*), which is also known as "forbearance in conformity" (*anulomikakhantī*). After the discourse, Tambadāṭhika accompanied the Venerable Sāriputta for some distance before turning back toward home. On the way home, a cow (actually a demon in the guise of a cow) gored him to death.

When the Buddha arrived at the congregation of bhikkhus that evening, they informed him about the death of Tambadāṭhika and asked where he had been reborn. The Buddha told them that although Tambadāṭhika had committed evil deeds throughout his life, he was reborn in the Tusitā celestial realm because before he died he had comprehended the Dhamma after hearing it from the Venerable Sāriputta and had attained the insight knowledge of equanimity toward phenomena.

The bhikkhus wondered how such a great evildoer could have won such great benefit after listening to the Dhamma just once. The Buddha said that the length of a discourse is of no consequence, that one single meaningful word can produce much benefit, and spoke the following verse:

> Better than a thousand meaningless statements
> Is one meaningful word,
> Which, having heard,
> Brings peace.[67]

Now, since he could not attain path knowledge and fruition knowledge during his lifetime, we clearly cannot even regard Tambadāṭhika to have been a person to be guided, much less a person of quick understanding or a person who understands through elaboration. Nevertheless, even without pure morality, he was able to realize the insight knowledges up through the knowledge of equanimity toward phenomena, which is the insight knowledge that precedes path knowledge and the last part of the purification of knowledge and vision of the path (*paṭipadāñāṇadassanavisuddhi*).

Why was he able to do so? He was able to do so because moral violations are not an obstacle to realization for laypeople. Moral violations are an obstacle to the attainment of path and fruition for monks but not for laypeople, regardless of whether they are a person in his or her final life, a person of quick understanding, or a person who understands through elaboration.

The two reasons people fail to attain path knowledge and fruition knowledge

The two reasons that people fail to attain path knowledge and fruition knowledge in this life are bad companionship (*pāpamittatā*) and insufficient practice or instruction (*kiriyāparihāni*). We may take the case of Prince Ajātasattu as an example of bad companionship. Ajātasattu missed the opportunity for enlightenment because he followed the advice of his bad companion, Venerable Devadatta, and assassinated his own father, King Bimbisāra. Killing one's father is one of the five fatal misconducts and is necessarily an obstacle to not only path knowledge and fruition knowledge but also to insight knowledges, such as the insight knowledge of arising and passing away.

People may also fail to attain path and fruition because of inadequate practice. A man named Pessa, whose story is told in the *Kandaraka Sutta*,[68] failed in his spiritual attainment for this reason. The Buddha once gave Pessa a detailed discourse on the four types of persons. If he had listened to the discourse from the beginning to the end, he would have become a stream enterer immediately. Instead, he left before the end of the talk and missed that opportunity to attain path and fruition. Today there are also many people like Pessa: they know the method but never put it into practice or are not serious in their efforts, and so they miss out on attaining the path and fruition. This is insufficient practice.

A shortage of instruction was the difficulty when Venerable Sāriputta gave a discourse on concentration, instead of insight meditation, to the Brahmin merchant Dhānañjāni, who was lying on his deathbed. As a result, the Brahmin was reborn in the realm of Brahma's retinue after having attained the first jhāna. This was a case of insufficient instruction. If Venerable Sāriputta had given the Brahmin a discourse on insight meditation, he would have obtained path and fruition in that very life. After having been reprimanded by the Buddha, at his urging, Venerable Sāriputta later went to the realm of Brahma's retinue and taught that Brahmin insight meditation. It is said that from that point on Venerable Sāriputta never spoke on the Dhamma without teaching the Four Noble Truths. Nowadays there are also many people like the Brahmin Dhānañjāni, who lack proper instruction and therefore miss the opportunity to attain path and fruition.

Tambadāṭhika failed to realize path knowledge and fruition knowledge due to lack of practice. It can't have been due to a shortage of instruction, since he was able to realize the insight knowledges up through the insight knowledge of equanimity toward phenomena. Nor was bad companionship the reason in the case of Tambadāṭhika.

Purifying Conduct with Meditation

Moral purification is eventually necessary in order to attain the insight knowledges and path knowledge and fruition knowledge. So in cases such as that of the minister Santati and the others described above, they must have ultimately been able to purify their morality. They may have done this by forming the resolution, just before or while listening to the Dhamma talk, not to break the moral precepts any longer. That resolution itself would have affected the restoration of their morality. Otherwise nothing but their meditation itself could have restored their morality. The *Paṭisambhidāmagga* gives the following teaching on this subject:

> Morality is the abandonment of ignorance through knowledge[69] and the abandonment of the perception of permanence through contemplation of impermanence; abstinence is morality; volition is morality; restraint is morality; and nontransgression is morality.
>
> All of these kinds of morality lead to a clear conscience, delight (*pāmojja*), joy (*pīti*), tranquility, and happiness. They all lead to disenchantment, nonattachment, cessation, peacefulness, realization, enlightenment, and nibbāna.
>
> Restraint is the training in higher morality; tranquility[70] is the training in higher mind; seeing[71] is the training in higher wisdom.[72]

Morality by means of abandonment

Knowledge that discerns mental and physical phenomena (*nāmarūpaparicchedañāṇa*) abandons the delusion of a "person" or "being."

Knowledge that discerns conditionality abandons the delusion that living beings appear without any cause, or that they are all created by God, Brahma, or other divine authorities. Understanding impermanence abandons the delusion that anything in the mind or body is permanent.

"To abandon," in this context, means "to leave no place in the mind for those delusions"—just as light leaves no place for darkness in it. As a result, wholesomeness arises instead of delusion. The abandonment of the mental defilements through insight meditation is therefore considered morality, since it is a foundation or basis (*upadhāraṇa*) for wholesomeness and makes that wholesomeness firm and steadfast (*samādhāna*). This is also true for the following types of meditative morality.

Morality by means of abstinence

The commentaries and subcommentaries unanimously state that the mind that arises during insight meditation (*vipassanācittuppāda*) does not include the mental factor of abstinence from evil (*virati*). On the other hand, the mind that arises during insight meditation is directly opposed to evil behavior and wrong livelihood. It brings about abstinence or morality by temporarily removing evil behavior and wrong livelihood (*tadaṅgappahāna*), in the same way that path knowledge brings about abstinence from all evil behavior (*maggavirati*) by completely removing evil behavior and wrong livelihood (*samucchedapahāna*), although path knowledge takes nibbāna as its object.

When insight knowledges arise, such as discerning mental and physical phenomena, they leave no place in the mind for the defilement of attachment to a person or a being, to noncausality, or to the notion of permanence, satisfactoriness, and self. At such times the mental defilements that lie dormant have no chance to become active in the mind. When they are not active in the mind, there are no thoughts about a person or a being, and thus no obsessive defilements arise. And when thoughts that assume that there are persons or beings do not arise, immoral behaviors such as killing, stealing, and so on do not arise either. Since none of the defilements, whether dormant, obsessive, or transgressive, can arise, one abstains from those defilements while experiencing any of the insight knowledges, beginning with knowledge that discerns mental and physical phenomena. This is why it is called "morality by means of abstinence."

Morality by means of mental volition

Mental volition often stimulates ordinary people who have no restraint to commit evil deeds. For an insight meditator, mental volition stimulates effective awareness of meditative objects. All of one's noting involves mental volition. This mental volition is weak and mostly not obvious when one's faith, will (*chanda*), and energy are weak. Mental volition becomes obvious, however, when one's faith, will, and energy are strong. So mental volition is considered morality for an insight meditator, because it is a foundation or basis for wholesomeness and makes that wholesomeness firm and steadfast.

Morality by means of restraint

The five kinds of restraint mentioned above are called "morality by means of restraint." They are included in an insight meditator's state of mind with every noting, and they thereby block and restrain the arising of immorality, mindlessness, ignorance, impatience, and idleness. This restraint protects one from self-indulgence. In an ultimate sense, morality by means of restraint includes only mindfulness, insight, forbearance, and effort.

Morality by means of nontransgression

The noting mind, governed by mindfulness, leads to nontransgression, since it leaves no room for delusion and other defilements to arise. Volitional killing, for example, is a transgression, while refraining from killing is a nontransgression. In the same way, mindlessness is a transgression since it allows every kind of mental defilement, whether dormant, obsessive, or transgressive, to arise. The noting mind governed by mindfulness, on the other hand, is nontransgressive since it leaves no room for any defilement, whether dormant, obsessive, or transgressive. Thus the noting mind governed by mindfulness is morality by means of nontransgression.

Among these five kinds of morality, we can only directly experience morality by means of mental volition and morality by means of restraint. Morality by means of abandoning defilements is simply an absence of defilements. According to the *Visuddhimagga*, morality by means of abstinence and morality by means of nontransgression are both equivalent to the mind that arises during insight meditation. Although these two are the same in an ultimate sense, morality by means of abstinence refers to abstaining from defilements, while morality by means of nontransgression refers to avoiding transgression by not allowing defilements to arise.

Morality as remote and immediate conditions for concentration and knowledges

Laypersons can use insight meditation to fully purify the four kinds of morality, regardless of whether or not they have practiced morality for a long time beforehand. We may wonder, however, what kind of morality they must develop as a basis for their concentration and insight knowledge, given that Buddha has said on many occasions:

> A man established on morality, wise,
> Develops the mind and wisdom . . .[73]

The answer is that all meditators should develop concentration and insight knowledge based on two kinds of morality: morality that has been purified before meditation (*pubbabhāgasīla*) and morality that is purified during meditation (*sahajātasīla*). Morality that has already been observed for some time before taking up meditation practice serves as a remote condition or prior cause (*pakatūpanissāya*) for the arising of insight concentration and insight wisdom, as well as for path concentration and path wisdom. The morality that accompanied prior insight knowledges and path knowledge and fruition knowledge also serves as the remote condition for later insight concentration and insight wisdom, as well as for path concentration and path wisdom. The pure morality that accompanies each and every moment of insight knowledge and path knowledge is the immediate condition or present cause (*sahajātanissaya*) for the concentration and wisdom involved in that very moment of consciousness.

If a person has purified his or her morality before taking up meditation, then his or her concentration and wisdom are based on both remote and immediate moral conditions. If, on the other hand, a person purifies his or her morality only through insight meditation, then his or her initial concentration and wisdom are based only on the immediate moral condition, while his or her succeeding insight concentration and insight wisdom as well as path concentration and path wisdom are based on both remote and immediate moral conditions.[74]

The power of meditation to purify morality for monastics

Since the above types of morality are associated with meditation, a monk may also use insight meditation to purify two kinds of morality for monastics: the morality of observing the monastic precepts and morality of pursuing a pure livelihood. This is the case because the removal of delusion and so on does not allow for the presence of defilements, whether they are dormant or active.

In addition a monk automatically fulfills the morality of considering the purpose for the four requisites if he consumes them mindfully. The main purpose of this type of morality is to keep defilements from arising in connection with the four requisites. Actually by considering the purpose for his consumption, a monk can protect himself from active defilements but not from dormant ones. By practicing insight meditation, though, a monk can prevent defilements from lying dormant in the four requisites.

Most monks still fail to practice meditation. They think that it is more important to consider the purpose for consuming the four requisites than it is to practice meditation. They may have difficulty accepting the fact that a monk automatically fulfills the morality of keeping in mind the purpose for using the four requisites if he consumes them mindfully. In fact meditation practice is much superior to the practice of keeping in mind the purpose for using the four requisites. The Buddha said that meditation practiced for just one moment can establish good morality:

> Bhikkhus, if for just the time of a finger snap a bhikkhu develops . . . the liberation of the mind by loving-kindness, . . . he is called a bhikkhu who is not devoid of jhāna, who acts upon the teaching of the Teacher, who responds to his advice, and who does not eat the country's almsfood in vain. How much more, then, those who cultivate it!
>
> [Bhikkhus, if for just the time of a finger snap a bhikkhu] dwells contemplating the body in the body . . . the feelings in the feelings . . . the mind in mind . . . phenomena in phenomena, ardent, clearly comprehending, mindful, having removed longing and dejection in regard to the world, [he is called a

> bhikkhu who is not devoid of jhāna, who acts upon the teaching of the Teacher, who responds to his advice, and who does not eat the country's almsfood in vain. How much more, then, those who cultivate it!][75]

"Loving-kindness" refers to the ordinary loving-kindness that anybody can develop. It does not refer specifically to absorption (*jhāna*) or access concentration (*upacāra*) of loving-kindness. The Aṅguttara Nīkaya commentary says:

> Loving-kindness here refers neither to absorption nor access concentration gained by practicing loving-kindness but to ordinary loving-kindness, wishing for the well-being of creatures.[76]

Thus if a monk develops loving-kindness or any other type of meditation, whether concentration or insight, just for one moment, he can be counted as a trainee (*sekkha*). His consumption of public almsfood is therefore beneficial to himself and his donors. Of course, this also goes without saying for those who uninterruptedly develop meditation. The Aṅguttara Nikāya commentary explains this as follows:

> If a bhikkhu develops loving-kindness for just one moment, his consumption of public almsfood is not in vain but beneficial both to himself and to his supporters (*amoghaparibhoga*). How is it beneficial to himself? Since he develops loving-kindness, his consumption is his own (*sāmiparibhoga*), debt-free (*āṇaṇyaparibhoga*), passed by inheritance (*dāyajjaparibhoga*). Even if he consumes the food without considering its purpose, he is not liable for any debt, since he has given the full benefit to his supporters. The development of loving-kindness itself is, of course, also beneficial to him. This is how a moment's practice of loving-kindness is beneficial to the bhikkhu himself.
>
> The alms donors can also enjoy great benefits in this case, since they have offered their alms to a bhikkhu who is one of the eight worthy recipients: one who is making an effort to attain the fruition of the first stage of enlightenment.[77] As both sides derive much benefit we say that it is "beneficial both to himself and to his supporters." Thus both the bhikkhu and the donors

> can benefit from just a single moment of loving-kindness, to say nothing of when it is uninterruptedly developed.[78]

This commentary very directly expresses how rewarding the development of loving-kindness is. The same is true of any other meditations, whether concentration or insight, according to the Pāḷi canon. The commentary does not mention other concentration or insight meditations specifically, because having explained one meditation the others can be understood analogously. Therefore, insight knowledge fulfills the morality of keeping in mind the purpose for using the four requisites.

Nota bene: the practice of morality is essential

My purpose in explaining that the practice of meditation alone can purify morality is not to downplay the importance of practicing morality but to overcome the mistaken notion that meditation should only be taken up after morality has been fulfilled for a long time, and to refute the idea that morality as an immediate condition is not an adequate foundation for meditation. Such notions may prevent you from beginning meditation sooner rather than later. They may also lead you to deprecate those who properly practice meditation.

In fact, morality should be regarded with the greatest honor and respect. Perhaps ninety-nine percent of the time, lower rebirth is the result of moral violations. More than half of those who enjoy human or celestial births may only be able to do so because they have practiced pure morality. Most of those who obtain path and fruition have probably purified their morality in advance. People like the minister Santati, who was able to obtain path and fruition without developing morality beforehand, are certainly few and far between.

So you should protect your morality with great care, just as you would protect your very life. You should not be negligent about your behavior, thinking that you can correct it later. You might die at any time and be immediately reborn in the lower worlds if your morality is deficient. Morality is especially important for those who are practicing meditation. They should even honor and respect it more than their lives and keep it fully purified.

Therefore, if you wish to practice meditation, you should observe in advance the five precepts or the eight precepts topped with right livelihood in order to strengthen the development of concentration and insight knowledge, even if your morality is already generally pure. If you plan to participate in an intensive meditation retreat, leaving all worldly responsibilities behind, you should observe the eight or ten precepts.

If you purposely and properly purify morality, then you will have a clear conscience every time you reflect about morality during your meditation practice. You will experience joy and delight, tranquility, happiness, and peace. By observing the physical and mental processes every time they arise, you will see things as they really are and gain further insight knowledge.

Here ends chapter 1 regarding the Purification of Conduct.

Purification of Mind

2

Mental Purification

"Purification of mind" or "mental purification" are translations of the Pāḷi word *cittavisuddhi*. The preeminent element of *cittavisuddhi* is *citta* or "mind." When one cultivates strong concentration by means of tranquility or insight meditation, the mind is no longer distracted by thoughts and other hindrances. Such pure concentration, continuously focused on an object for either tranquility or insight, is considered mental purification. A mind associated with such concentration is also purified of hindrances due to the power of the concentration.

Three types of mental purification

There are three types of concentration that entail purification of mind: access or neighborhood concentration (*upacārasamādhi*), absorption concentration (*appanāsamādhi*), and momentary concentration (*khaṇikasamādhi*).

Access concentration

One develops access concentration by contemplating a conceptual object of meditation (*paṭibhāganimitta*) in order to block hindering thoughts. It is called "access" or "neighborhood" concentration because it nears absorption concentration. True access concentration can be aroused by contemplating: a visual object, such as a colored disk (*kasiṇa*); the impurities of the body (*asubha*); mindfulness of the body (*kāyagatāsati*); the in- and out-breaths (*ānāpāna*); the four divine abodes (*brahmavihārā*);[79] or immateriality (*ārupa*).

Contemplating the eight kinds of recollection (*anussatī*), the perception of impurity (*pāṭikūlasaññā*), or the analysis of the four elements (*catudhātuvavatthāna*) cannot arouse true access concentration. Concentration aroused using these three objects cannot be considered true access concentration because it does not have the potential to lead to absorption concentration. It is, nevertheless, typically referred to as access concentration because it produces similar results in terms of suppressing hindrances.

Absorption concentration

Absorption concentration is quite unshakable, as if the mind has been absorbed into the meditation object. There are a total of either eight or nine absorptions: the material absorptions (*rūpajjhānā*), divided into four or five stages, and the immaterial absorptions (*arūpajjhānā*), divided into four stages.

Momentary concentration

When an insight meditation practitioner's faith, effort, mindfulness, concentration, and wisdom have become strong and balanced, the process of meditation continues with uninterrupted purity. Thoughts or other hindrances do not interfere in the process. At such times each and every noting produces a strong and clear concentration on the physical or mental phenomenon that is the object of meditation. This is momentary concentration aroused by moment-to-moment observation.

Two vehicles for going to enlightenment

One who develops insight based on a foundation of access or absorption concentration is called "one who takes the vehicle of tranquility to nibbāna" (*samathayānika*). A person who takes the vehicle of tranquility uses access and/or absorption concentration to bring about the necessary mental purification. His or her insight meditation practice is then based on that mental purification.

One who practices pure insight meditation without first laying a foundation of access or absorption concentration is called "one who takes the pure vehicle of insight to enlightenment" (*suddhavipassanāyānika*). A person who takes the vehicle of insight uses only momentary concentration to bring about the necessary mental purification, and his or her insight practice is then based on that mental purification.

According to the *Visuddhimagga*:

> Purification of mind includes the eight jhānas and access concentration.[80]

Although momentary concentration is not explicitly identified as mental purification in this commentary, it is described in the Pāḷi texts that follow. Access and absorption concentration are specifically mentioned because they must be developed in advance. However, momentary concentration develops naturally in the course of insight meditation practice.

Momentary concentration may also be considered to fall under the umbrella of access concentration, since it is similar in terms of being free of hindrances. According to the commentary on the *Satipaṭṭhāna Sutta*:

> The other twelve are also access meditation.[81]

So this consideration is in accordance with the Pāḷi texts.

Consider well the following passage from a subcommentary on the *Visuddhimagga*:

> If tranquility meditation is the vehicle that takes one to enlightenment, then one is called "one who takes the vehicle of tranquility to enlightenment." This person practices insight based on absorption or access concentration; he or she develops insight after having practiced tranquility meditation. One who practices pure insight without those two concentrations is called "one who takes the vehicle of insight to enlightenment." This is the definition of a practitioner of pure insight.[82]

It is clear from this passage that one who practices insight after developing access or absorption concentration is called "one who takes the vehicle of tranquility to enlightenment," while one who practices pure insight without depending on either of those two kinds of concentration is "one who takes the vehicle of insight to enlightenment." Based on the statement "Devadatta, who is growing fat, does not eat during the day," we can infer that Devadatta eats at night. Likewise, we can also infer, based on the statement "Insight knowledge can be aroused without depending on access or absorption concentration," that insight knowledge must be aroused based on momentary concentration. This point is explicitly spelled out in the following passage:

> It is impossible for one who takes the vehicle of tranquility to enlightenment to become enlightened without access or absorption concentration, and it is impossible for one who takes the vehicle of insight to enlightenment to become enlightened without momentary concentration. Neither can one attain enlightenment without the gateway to liberation (*vimokkha-mukha*).[83] Hence, "develop both concentration and insight."[84]

The text on which the above passage from the subcommentary bases itself is:

> A man established in morality, wise,
> Develops the mind and wisdom;
> A monk ardent and discreet:
> He can disentangle this tangle.[85]

The phrase "he can disentangle this tangle" should be interpreted to mean "he is able to solve the problem of attachment." The phrase is not clear on its own, but the Buddha indicates that he is able to solve the problem if "he develops the mind and wisdom." In this context, "mind" refers to concentration and "wisdom" refers specifically to insight knowledge. Thus the above commentary cites the advice to "develop both concentration and insight."

The overall meaning of this canonical passage is that if one develops both concentration and insight knowledge one will solve the problem of attachment—that is, one will become a fully enlightened being, an arahant fully liberated from attachment. The commentary itself does not explain who should develop which kind of concentration, or why both concentration and insight should be developed. The subcommentary makes these points clear.

As it says, one who takes the vehicle of tranquility to enlightenment can only realize path knowledge and fruition knowledge after developing either access or absorption concentration, and not otherwise. One who takes the vehicle of insight to enlightenment can only be enlightened after developing momentary concentration, and not otherwise. Both those who take the vehicle of tranquility to enlightenment and those who take the vehicle of insight to enlightenment must achieve path knowledge and fruition knowledge through the gateway to liberation, that is, by developing insight into the three universal characteristics of impermanence, unsatisfactoriness, and not-self. Only a person who develops one of the three kinds of concentration and insight knowledge of the three universal characteristics can attain arahantship and solve the problem of attachment. The commentary alludes to these points with the phrase "develop both concentration and insight."

It is clear, following the above subcommentary, that those who take the vehicle of insight to enlightenment need not develop access or absorption concentration. Momentary concentration alone is enough for them to bring about the mental purification required for path knowledge and fruition knowledge.

Methods for taking the two vehicles to enlightenment

Since this point of view is only in accord with the commentary, let's consult the following text where two kinds of meditation are explained in order to strengthen your confidence in it.

The method for taking the vehicle of tranquility to enlightenment

> This is how to develop the noble path:[86] one develops tranquility prior to insight and then practices insight based on tranquility. How?
>
> One develops access or absorption concentration. This is tranquility. One practices insight by observing the concentration itself, and its mental constituents, in terms of impermanence, unsatisfactoriness, and not-self. This is insight.
>
> Thus tranquility precedes insight. Therefore, one who practices tranquility before insight is called "one who takes the vehicle of tranquility to enlightenment." One who takes the vehicle of tranquility to enlightenment realizes the noble path in this way.[87]

This is how one who takes the vehicle of tranquility to enlightenment gains the noble path according to the subcommentary: one meditates on concentration itself and its mental constituents in terms of impermanence, unsatisfactoriness, and not-self. Most of those who take the vehicle of tranquility to enlightenment follow this procedure.

Note that the commentary says that one first develops concentration and then meditates on that very concentration in terms of impermanence and so on. This description might give the impression that one realizes the insight knowledge of impermanence, unsatisfactoriness, and not-self without developing the two preliminary knowledges that discern mental and physical phenomena and conditionality. But insight knowledge cannot be aroused without first attaining these two preliminary knowledges, and it is not reasonable to assume that the two preliminary knowledges can arise before the development of concentration.

So the verse should be interpreted to mean that one develops concentration first, then the two preliminary knowledges, and then the insight knowledge of impermanence and so on. Here the phrase "seeing phenomena in terms of impermanence and so on" is used figuratively (*padhāna-naya*) to refer to a set of related things by only explicitly mentioning the most important. For example, the phrase "the king arrives" only explicitly refers to the arrival of the king himself, yet we can safely assume that the king does not travel alone but with a retinue of attendants, bodyguards, and so on. In the same way, although the subcommentary only explicitly mentions the insight knowledge of impermanence and so on we can take this statement to imply inclusion of the two preliminary knowledges as well. Otherwise, the statement would not be in harmony with the Pāḷi texts that explain the process of developing insight knowledge.

The method of those who take the vehicle of insight to enlightenment

> Here in this Holy Order, one who practices the method of insight prior to tranquility does not develop the two kinds of concentration, namely access and absorption, as one does using the method of tranquility preceding insight. One sees phenomena in terms of impermanence and so on without developing the two kinds of concentration. This is insight. When one's insight meditation practice grows strong enough, penetration of the objects [of insight] produces concentration. This is tranquility.
>
> Thus insight comes first and tranquility later. By developing tranquility based on insight, one brings about the noble path.[88]

This is how one who takes the vehicle of insight to enlightenment gains the noble path according to the subcommentary: "The second one describes one who takes the vehicle of insight to enlightenment."[89] The phrase "without developing the two kinds of concentration" makes it clear that insight is initially developed without access or absorption concentration. As was the case for those who take the vehicle of tranquility to enlightenment, the phrase "one sees phenomena in terms of impermanence and so on" implies that one has already developed the two basic knowledges that discern mental and physical phenomena and conditionality. The sentence "When one's insight meditation practice grows strong enough, the penetration of the objects of insight produces concentration" indicates that insight meditation produces concentration when it becomes strong enough. The subcommentary says that the term "insight" in this passage refers specifically to the very clear insight knowledge that leads to emergence (*vutthānagāminīvipassanā*), which occurs just prior to path knowledge. It also says that the term "tranquility" refers to the concentration associated with path knowledge itself.

The word "path" in the phrase "one brings about the noble path" refers to the first noble path, as illustrated by the following passages from Pāḷi texts:

> "Path arises" means the first supramundane path occurs.[90]
>
> He pursues this path, develops it, and cultivates it.[91]
>
> It is impossible to pursue a path that lasts for only a single mind-moment. Thus the phrase "He pursues this path, develops it, and cultivates it" means that he brings about the second path and so on.[92]
>
> Thus, by pursuing, developing, and cultivating this path, one removes the fetters (*saṃojanāni*) and roots out latent defilements (*anusayā*).[93]

Yet the original commentary simply says that one develops concentration based on insight, which does not necessarily indicate a path-related concentration. The commentary also says that one who develops concentration gives rise to the first supramundane path. It does not make sense that one would bring about path knowledge by developing path-related concentration, because that would be like saying "one turns gold into gold," since path-related concentration is a factor of path itself.

In the method of insight practice based on tranquility, both practices of insight and tranquility are mundane. Given the parallel structure used to describe the two methods, in this method of tranquility based on insight both practices must also be mundane. For these reasons, "tranquility" here should be taken to mean "the momentary concentration associated with insight."

Insight with momentary concentration

We can classify the strong insight concentration associated with momentary concentration as either basic, intermediate, or advanced insight with concentration.

Basic insight with concentration

The basic level of insight with momentary concentration begins with knowledge that discerns mental and physical phenomena. At this level of concentration, thoughts and hindrances cannot interfere with one's practice. As a result of this the mind is free of hindrances, and so realizes the specific characteristics (*sabhāvalakkhaṇā*) of mental and physical phenomena, which in turn gives rise to the knowledge that discerns mental and physical phenomena. This momentary concentration creates a unification of mind comparable to access concentration—the neighborhood concentration developed by one who takes the vehicle of tranquility to enlightenment. It is impossible to be aware of the true nature of mental and physical phenomena without this basic level of concentration. This momentary concentration constitutes a purification of mind that aids the development of insight knowledge, such as the knowledge that discerns mental and physical phenomena.

The *Paṭisambhidāmagga* describes this basic level of concentration as follows:

> The process of "training in the higher mind" (*adhicittasikkha*) is devoid of mental restlessness (i.e., it is concentrated).[94]

According to the following Pāḷi passage, knowledge that discerns mental and physical phenomena (*nāmarūpaparicchedañāṇa*) and knowledge that discerns conditionality (*paccayapariggahañāṇa*) are considered insight:[95]

> Each type of insight knowledge dispels a hindrance associated with it, just as bright light dispels darkness. For example, knowledge that discerns mental and physical phenomena helps to dispel the idea of a "self" associated with mind and body. Knowledge of conditionality helps to dispel erroneous beliefs in causelessness and fictitious causes. The illusion of objects is dispelled by means of change-of-lineage consciousness (*gotrabhū*).[96] These are temporarily eliminated (*tadaṅgappahāna*).[97]

Intermediate insight with concentration

The intermediate level of insight with momentary concentration begins with insight knowledge of arising and passing away (*udayabbayañāṇa*). The *Visuddhimagga* considers this insight knowledge to be "fledgling insight" (*taruṇavipassanā*) and calls one who reaches this stage an "energetic meditator" (*āraddhavipassaka*). In many Pāḷi texts, this insight knowledge is described as an element of exertion (*padhāniyanga*) to attain the path and its fruit, and is the first of the well-developed insight knowledges.

Advanced insight with concentration

The advanced level of insight begins with insight knowledge of dissolution (*bhaṅgañāṇa*). The advanced level of momentary concentration also begins at that point. This will be further explained at the end of this chapter in accordance with the explanations of the insight knowledge of dissolution in the *Paṭisambhidāmagga* and *Visuddhimagga*.

Strong momentary concentration

Momentary concentration can grow as strong as if the mind were concentrated on a single object. Although it moves between different objects, the preceding and succeeding mind-moments are equally concentrated on one object after another. When this happens, the strength of the momentary concentration is comparable to that of absorption in tranquility meditation. The difference is that the object of absorption in tranquility is always the same and thus cannot help one to clearly see mental and physical phenomena, their impermanence, and so on. The object of insight concentration constantly changes, which helps one to clearly see mental and physical phenomena, their impermanence, and so on as the insight knowledge matures. This is the only difference between the objects for the two kinds of concentration. The mind can grow equally concentrated with either type of object. As the *Mahāṭīkā* says:

> Momentary single-pointedness of mind (*khaṇikacittekaggatā*) is momentary concentration. When it continuously dwells on an object [of insight] over a long period, opposing hindrances cannot overwhelm it, and it is able to make the mind as strong and steadfast as jhāna or absorption concentration.[98]

This subcommentary supports the commentary to the *Ānāpāna Gathā*,[99] which says "the mind is concentrated" (*samādahaṃ cittaṃ*). This means that access and absorption concentration are not the only concentrations that can keep the mind steady on an object; momentary concentration associated with insight can also be steadfast.

How strong should this momentary concentration be? The phrase "when it continuously dwells on an object over a long period . . ." (*ārammaṇe nirantaraṃ ekākārena pavattamāno*) indicates that it should be strong enough to be focused for a long time without hindering thoughts, as is the case with access concentration. Then the noting mind is said to be steadfast.

The phrase "opposing hindrances cannot overwhelm it . . . it is . . . as strong as . . . concentration" (*paṭipakkhena anbhibhūto appito viya*) indicates that the concentration associated with insight knowledge of arising and passing away, insight knowledge of dissolution, and so on is even stronger: this concentration can become as steadfast as absorption concentration without being disturbed by opposing phenomena.

Two interpretations of a key term

It is possible to interpret the Pāḷi word *vosagga* (penetration) that the commentary[100] uses in the compound word *vosaggārammaṇato* (penetration of the objects [of insight]) in two ways: it can mean either "to relinquish or give up" or "to penetrate or rush into." Both are viable meanings. If we read *vosagga* in this compound as "to relinquish," we must interpret the compound to mean "relinquishing, i.e., abandoning, objects" (*ārammanānaṃ vosaggo pariccāgo*), where the objects intended are external. In the context of insight meditation, any object that one fails to observe is regarded as an external object. According to the Satipaṭṭhānasaṃyutta, "mind distracted outwardly" (*bahiddhā vā cittaṃ vikkhipati*) means the mind wanders outside the range of insight.[101]

If we read *vosagga* as "to penetrate," we must interpret the compound to mean "penetrating, i.e., rushing into, objects" (*arammane vossaggo pakkhandanaṃ*), where the objects intended are internal. Any object that one successfully observes is regarded as an internal object. As the Satipaṭṭhānasaṃyutta says, ". . . internally mindful, I am happy" (*ajjhattaṃ satimā sukhamasmi*).[102] Any object of insight is considered an internal object, an object that falls within the scope of insight. They are also called "the internal field" (*gocarajjhatta*).

The meanings of both of these interpretations are actually the same, differing only in the grammatical sense. "To relinquish external objects" means to have a mind that does not wander, which by extension also means to have a mind that penetrates internal objects. The important point here is that one who takes the vehicle of insight to enlightenment begins his or her insight practice without any access concentration or absorption concentration. However, they attain those concentrations by first developing insight knowledge.

The commentary explains these two methods of development with reference to the Pāḷi canon, only adding a few words to the passage from the Pāḷi canon for the sake of clarity. As its explanation follows the passage from the Pāḷi canon nearly verbatim, there should be no doubt as to whether it accords with the canon. For reference consult the *Aṅguttara Nikāya* and the *Paṭisambhidāmagga*. The passage from the *Paṭisambhidāmagga* reads:

> Seeing physicality as impermanent is insight. Seeing physicality as unsatisfactory and not-self is insight. At the moment of insight, the mental state of relinquishing external objects, or penetrating internal objects, or one-pointedness of that insight mind is concentration. Thus insight comes first and concentration afterwards and so one is said to develop concentration based on insight.[103]

However, the *Mūlapaṇṇāsa* subcommentary says that it should be interpreted as follows:

> At the moment of the noble path (*ariyamagga*), the mental state that has nibbāna as its object, or one-pointedness of that path mind, is path concentration. Thus insight comes first and concentration afterward and so one is said to develop concentration based on insight.[104]

Methods for developing insight

Four methods for developing insight are mentioned in the Pāḷi canon, two of which are the pairing method and the elimination of practice-related agitation method. The commentary, however, only mentions these two methods, because the others can be subsumed within them. This is how they are included:

The pairing method

In the pairing method (*yuganaddhanaya*), one who has cultivated the jhānas becomes absorbed in the first jhāna and then practices insight by contemplating that very jhāna. In the same way, one practices the second jhāna, third jhāna, and so on paired with insight until one attains path knowledge. And so this method is subsumed within the method of developing tranquility prior to insight (*samathapubbaṅgama*).

The elimination of practice-related agitation method

At the stage when insight knowledge of arising and passing away arises, a practitioner is likely to encounter obstacles to insight (*vipassanupakkilesa*), such as bright light, knowledge, rapture, tranquility, and so on.[105] Such obstacles can occur regardless of whether one practices tranquility on the basis of insight or insight on the basis of tranquility. If one mistakes these phenomena for some kind of enlightenment or for special results from enlightenment, one may waste time thinking about or reflecting on the experience.

This kind of restlessness is called "practice-related agitation" (*dhammuddhacca*). When a practitioner succumbs to such restlessness, he or she may not see objects clearly, and his or her practice may become stagnant or decline. One should overcome this kind of practice-related agitation by ignoring the lights and so on and paying greater attention to noting. By noting in this way, practice-related agitation will automatically disappear and mental and physical phenomena will grow even clearer. The noting mind focuses steadily only on the internal field.[106]

From this point on insight knowledge gradually develops until the practitioner attains path knowledge. This method of developing the path is applicable to both those who develop tranquility prior to insight and those who develop insight prior to tranquility, so it is subsumed within both of them. This is why the commentary only mentions these two methods of development.

Mental Purification for Those Who Take the Vehicle of Insight to Enlightenment

The Pāḷi texts examined above make it clear that those who take the vehicle of insight to enlightenment need not develop tranquility in advance in order to purify the mind, but they may begin with pure insight. The momentary concentration that arises when their insight practice grows strong enough then serves as mental purification.

The principal emphasis of this book is to explain precisely this point: how those who take the vehicle of insight to enlightenment practice—that is, how to develop pure insight without a foundation of tranquility concentration. So there is no need to extensively explain mental purification here.

However, it will be beneficial for those who take the vehicle of insight to enlightenment and develop insight based on momentary concentration to learn something regarding the following points: the eightfold liberation (*niyyāna*) and the eight hindrances to liberation (*niyyānāvaraṇa*), the six enemies of concentration and the ways of evading them, and the unification of mind (*ekatta*) or seclusion from mental defilements.

Liberations and hindrances

> The wholesomeness that arises from insight (*nekkhamma*) is a cause of liberation for noble ones. Noble ones gain liberation from the cycle of suffering by developing it. Attachment or desire is a hindrance to liberation. When present, it hinders a noble one's realization of the wholesomeness that arises from insight on the path to liberation. For this reason, attachment is called a hindrance to liberation.[107]

As the following verse explains, the word *nekkhamma* has multiple meanings.

> Going forth, the first jhāna, insight, and nibbāna—all wholesome mental states are called renunciation (*nekkhamma*).[108]

Depending on the context, renunciation may mean giving charity, attaining the first jhāna, practicing insight, realizing nibbāna, or performing any meritorious deed. The *Mahāṭīkā* defines renunciation as any meritorious deed that is performed without attachment. In this case, however, renunciation should be understood to mean insight concentration. When used in describing the following liberations, it will likewise be used only in relation with insight concentration.

Insight and attachment

If one does not observe mental and physical phenomena every time they arise at the six sense doors, one cannot realize that there is nothing to them but mind and body, which are conditioned, impermanent, unsatisfactory, and not-self. As a result one will develop an attachment to the objects that one fails to observe. If, on the other hand, one observes mental and physical phenomena the moment they occur, one will realize that there is nothing to them but mind and body, which are conditioned, impermanent, unsatisfactory, and not-self. As a result one will be free from attachment to objects that one is able to observe. Thus the wholesome (*kusala*) action of insight liberates one from attachment and thus is considered renunciation. This renunciation, in turn, liberates noble ones from the cycle of suffering (*saṃsāra*) by developing insight step by step until nibbāna is attained. And so the wholesome act of insight is called "the great liberation of noble ones" (*ariyanaṃ niyyanaṃ*) because of its liberating effect.

Attachment, or sensual desire (*kāmacchanda*), is called a hindrance because it obstructs insight practice. We must do uncountable things for the sake of ourselves, our spouses, children, relatives, friends, devotees, supporters, teachers, and so on in order to achieve happiness and comfort in this life. These activities are all driven by the desire for happiness and comfort. We constantly seek what we have not yet gained, while trying to maintain what we have already gained. Since we must make so much effort to satisfy our desires, we cannot find time for practice, and we may not even think of it. And even if we do think about practicing, we may never get around to it. At worst, we remain content to let the mind wander at will and enjoy ourselves, saying or doing whatever we please.

Then when we think about practicing meditation, we are worried that the little happiness and comfort we enjoy at present might be destroyed. The end result is that we fail to practice and have no way to enjoy the benefits of insight. It is impossible to escape the cycle of suffering without insight practice, so it is clear that sensual desire is the source of our bondage. Sensual desire hinders insight practice and prevents us from attaining liberation. Some people cannot practice insight because they want to continue to enjoy sensual pleasures even in their future lives. These are the ways that sensual desire obstructs the path to liberation.

Sensual desire often obstructs insight during practice as well. There are a number of ways this may occur. Sensual desire often takes the form of thinking about sense objects, which is a distraction. There may also occur a mild desire connected with the practice itself. We may come to enjoy the ease of practice or the unusual experiences that one has therein. We may then feel proud of these experiences and reflect on them time and again. We may encourage close friends to take up practice. Or we may long for better and smoother practice, or for more and different unusual experiences. We may even long for the path, fruition, and nibbāna!

Some scholars say that desire for the path, fruition, and nibbāna is not craving (*taṇhā*) but a wholesome wish, and that craving cannot take a supramundane state (*lokuttarā*) as an object. We should consider whether or not an ordinary person is able to take as his or her object the genuine path, fruition, and nibbāna. An ordinary person can take genuine nibbāna as an object of consciousness only at the moment when change-of-lineage consciousness matures. This occurs immediately before the arising of the path of stream entry, the first path knowledge. In the case of an ordinary person, no other mental state can take nibbāna as its object. Moreover, it is impossible for an ordinary person to take the path and fruition as an object.

According to these explanations from the Pāḷi texts, an ordinary person's notions of the path, fruition, and nibbāna are not accurate representations of absolute reality (*paramattha*) but simply ideas based on hearsay, inference (*anumāna*), and other mental concepts. Such ideas are merely conventional realities (*paññatti*) defined by name (*nāmapaññatti*), manner (*ākārapaññatti*), or appearance (*saṇṭhānapaññatti*). Such conventional understandings of the path, fruition, and nibbāna can become the objects, not only of wholesome aspiration, but also of unwholesome, worldly desire.

The *Saḷāyatanavibhaṅga Sutta* says, "one generates a longing for the supreme liberations,"[109] which we can understand to mean "one arouses the desire for the supramundane liberation that is the fruit of arahantship (*arahattaphala*)." The subcommentary clarifies this passage, saying that the fruit of arahantship mentioned here is not the genuine attainment but the idea of it based on hearsay and inference. The subcommentary to the *Sakkapañha Sutta* says the same thing.[110] The genuine supramundane state cannot be the object of craving. Instead, the desire is aimed at an idea of the fruit of arahantship based on hearsay.

The insight process flows smoothly if sensual desires do not arise. If they do arise, however, they obstruct the flow of insight. They appear as rivals to insight, as if saying, "It is our turn; stay away insight!" Once this kind of desire takes hold, one's concentration and insight may decline, and one may feel regret. This is how sensual desire acts as a hindrance during practice. It is said that the hindrance of sensual desire prevents one from realizing the wholesome act of insight as the cause of the noble ones' liberation. This means that it prevents one from gaining personal, empirical knowledge (*bhāvanāmayañāṇa*) but not from gaining theoretical knowledge (*sutamayañāṇa*). Thus the sensual desire that hinders the arising of insight as the cause of the noble ones' liberation is called "a hindrance to liberation" or "a hindrance" (*nīvaraṇa*).

In summary the wholesome act of insight, called renunciation, is considered liberation because it leads noble ones to liberation. Whoever wishes to escape the cycle of suffering must develop insight, which is the cause of the noble ones' liberation. Because sensual desire hinders or obstructs insight from being a cause for liberation, it is called a hindrance to liberation. It must be avoided when possible and eliminated by noting it when it occurs.

Nonaversion and aversion

> Nonaversion[111] is a cause of liberation for noble ones. Noble ones gain liberation from the cycle of suffering by developing it. Aversion is a hindrance to liberation. When present, it hinders a noble ones' realization of nonaversion on the path to liberation. For this reason, aversion is called a hindrance to liberation.[112]

The absence of aversion or frustration associated with the noting mind in insight practice is called "nonaversion" (*abyāpāda*). This quality allows one to continue noting without frustration when unpleasant objects, unbearable pain, or other difficulties arise during practice, until one attains nibbāna and is released from the cycle of suffering. For this reason, nonaversion is called a cause of liberation for noble ones and should be cultivated in practice.

Aversion to someone or something, or frustration with hardships in practice, is called "aversion" (*byāpāda*). One cannot attain liberation if this aversion is present. If aversion arises one cannot realize those phenomena that are a cause for liberation when noted with nonaversion. Aversion is a hindrance to liberation and must be eliminated. Aversion may manifest as feeling angry or quarrelling with someone, or feeling angry about hardships and pains that arise or at what one sees or hears, and so on. We must eliminate these forms of aversion by noting them. Afterward we should return to the primary object. If aversion continues after noting it two or three times, one should note it repeatedly and finally the aversion will disappear altogether.

Brightness and sloth and torpor

> Observing light is a cause of liberation for noble ones. Noble ones gain liberation from the cycle of suffering by developing it. Sloth and torpor are hindrances to liberation. When present, it hinders the observation of light. For this reason, sloth and torpor are called hindrances to liberation.[113]

Contemplation of sunlight, moonlight, starlight, and light that arises in meditation is called "observing light" (*ālokasaññā*). It can overcome fatigue or sleepiness (*thinamiddha*). Contemplation of bright light overcomes dullness and sleepiness and one can continue practicing insight. With this practice one attains nibbāna and is therefore liberated from the cycle of suffering. Hence, the contemplation of light is called a cause of liberation for noble ones.

In the context of insight practice, contemplating mental and physical phenomena in such a way that they are vividly known is also called observing light. When one can observe objects vividly, sleepiness, dullness, and laziness disappear. Day or night, the mind is always clear without being sleepy or dull. Even if one stops meditating and goes to bed, one may continue to contemplate objects automatically, every time they arise. Also, we are able to overcome sloth and torpor by contemplating objects vividly. We gradually attain insight and path knowledges, and we are thereby able to be liberated from the cycle of suffering. Hence, contemplating objects vividly is called a cause of liberation for noble ones.

Laziness, whether or not it results in sleepiness, is also called fatigue. It is called a hindrance to liberation, because it hinders one from contemplating vividly. One should take great care to overcome it when it occurs.

Momentary concentration and restlessness

> Nondistraction is a cause of liberation for noble ones. Noble ones gain liberation from the cycle of suffering by developing it. Distraction[114] is a hindrance to liberation. When present, it hinders the noble ones' realization of nondistraction on the path to liberation. For this reason, distraction is called a hindrance to liberation.[115]

Momentary concentration that focuses on mental or physical objects from moment to moment is called nondistraction (*avikkhepa*), a mental state that is the opposite of restlessness. When momentary concentration becomes strong, the mind seems to penetrate its object every time an object is noted.

Often the noting mind and object it notes seem to be bound together, like a heavy rice bag that stands still on the very place where it is set, or a sharply pointed spear that stands firmly where it is stuck, or something sticky that sticks to the part of the wall where it is thrown. Similarly, although mental and physical objects continuously change, one's mind becomes firmly focused on each and every object as it is noted by means of momentary concentration. This momentary concentration leads to insight knowledges, path, and fruit, liberating noble ones from the cycle of suffering. For this reason, nondistraction, or momentary concentration, is called a cause of liberation for noble ones and should be cultivated and developed.

A restless state of mind that wanders away from an object while observing it is a mental state called restlessness (*uddhacca*). It flies away from the object. Due to restlessness the mind cannot remain very long with an object but often wanders elsewhere. The stronger the restlessness becomes, the longer the mind wanders. The weaker the restlessness becomes, the more briefly the mind wanders.

Sometimes the mind may wonder about practice itself. For example, the mind may wander off into analyzing whether an object was noted effectively, or sequentially, or vividly. The mind may wander off into thinking about how one is going to note an object. Under these circumstances, insight concentration cannot arise. When our mental state is restless, any concentration that arises cannot become well established. Hence restlessness of mind is called a hindrance to liberation. When restlessness arises it should be abandoned by noting it. At such times, note the usual object with extra care.

Discriminating knowledge and skeptical doubt

> Knowledge that discriminates phenomena[116] is a cause of liberation for noble ones. Noble ones gain liberation from the cycle of suffering by developing it. Skeptical doubt is a hindrance to liberation. When present, it hinders the noble ones' realization of discriminating knowledge on the path to liberation. For this reason, skeptical doubt is called a hindrance to liberation.[117]

The type of knowledge that distinguishes between wholesomeness and unwholesomeness is called knowledge that discriminates phenomena (*dhammavavatthānañāṇa*). By correctly discerning the wholesomeness and unwholesomeness of phenomena, noble ones abandon what is unwholesome and develop what is wholesome until they experience nibbāna and are liberated from the cycle of suffering. Hence this discriminating knowledge is called a cause of liberation for noble ones.

Uncertainty about what is wholesome and unwholesome is called skeptical doubt (*vicikicchā*). It is considered a hindrance to liberation as it hinders the arising of discriminating knowledge. A person who has doubts about the wholesomeness and unwholesomeness of phenomena is unable to abandon what is unwholesome, develop what is wholesome, and escape the cycle of suffering.

In insight practice, it is very important to be able to distinguish between insight and noninsight and between wholesome phenomena that are supportive and unsupportive of insight. These two kinds of knowledge should be considered causes for liberation.

The means of distinguishing between insight and noninsight will be explained in detail below.[118] In brief: the moment-to-moment observation of mental and physical phenomena is called personal insight knowledge (*paccakkhavipassanā*). When this personal knowledge (*paccakkhañāṇa*) matures, one may also develop inferential understanding about past, future, and external phenomena. Both types of insight knowledge, personal and inferential, are insight wholesomeness. However, ordinary reasoning that is not based on personal insight knowledge cannot be considered true insight wholesomeness. Because they understand this distinction, noble ones develop true insight until they attain nibbāna and are liberated from the cycle of suffering. Understanding that moral conduct, ascetic exercises (*dhutaṅga*), tranquility meditation, and the right mental attitude are wholesome actions that support insight is also a cause of liberation. So both these causes of liberation should be cultivated through learning, listening, and discussing.

Doubt about the fact that insight wholesomeness consists of simply observing the presently arising mental and physical phenomena is also skeptical doubt. This doubt is so subtle that it is rarely detected but is instead mistaken for investigation. This doubt masquerades as analytical knowledge. The commentary on *Netti Yuttihāra* explains as follows:

> Doubt appears in the guise of investigation.[119]

Poorly informed people rarely have this kind of skeptical doubt. Since they depend on their teachers for guidance, they are likely to follow the practice instruction strictly. However, it is impossible for them to practice without a teacher. On the other hand well-informed people may practice without a teacher if they have learned the correct method of practice. But just as those who travel to a new place for the first time may feel uncertain about the road, and thus delay their progress, so also a well-informed person, having learned much, may suffer from doubt and procrastination.

The *Vammika Sutta*[120] likens skeptical doubt to a fork in the road. Say a traveler who is carrying many valuables arrives at a fork in the road; if he lingers there unable to decide which way to take, robbers may catch and possibly kill him. In the same way, a doubtful meditator who falls prey to wavering and procrastination cannot continue on with practice. He or she will then become a victim of mental defilements and be unable to escape the cycle of suffering. Only when he or she abandons doubt by noting it and uninteruptedly continues the practice can he or she be liberated from the cycle of suffering.

Skeptical doubt can arise regarding eight subjects: Buddha, Dhamma, and Saṅgha, the threefold training,[121] one's past lives, future lives, and present life, and dependent origination (*paticcasamuppāda*). These days, people tend to have doubts about four other points as well: their teacher, the method of practice, individuals who have become enlightened by practicing the method, or their own practice. I have included many examples in this book, beginning with how moral purification is fulfilled, and the hope that one may speedily attain the path, fruition, and nibbāna by practicing insight smoothly after having abandoned skeptical doubt. I will give further explanation of these points below.[122]

According to the method I will describe in chapter 5, observation of walking, standing, sitting, reclining, bending, stretching, and so forth is purely wholesome. There should be no doubt about whether or not these observations are wholesome deeds. For example, the moment that one notes a movement, insight into the mental and physical phenomena involved in moving arises together with awareness, faith, nonattachment, and nonaversion. These are all wholesome mental states. Because only wholesome states arise with each noting, one only develops insight wholesomeness and nothing else. Similarly, one who practices tranquility meditation using the earth kasiṇa (*pathavīkasiṇa*) as a meditation object arouses wholesomeness in every moment that one notes, "earth, earth . . ." This is a brief explanation in order to remove any doubt about one's practice. I will go into this in more detail below.[123]

If one suffers from doubt, one cannot develop discriminating knowledge and confirm for oneself that the observation of mind and body constitutes insight wholesomeness. If one lacks this knowledge as a cause for liberation, one cannot be liberated from the cycle of suffering while practicing insight. Thus skeptical doubt is called a hindrance to liberation. Be careful not to mistake doubt for analytical knowledge. Please make an effort to abandon it every time it arises. Otherwise it will hinder your liberation from the cycle of suffering. Please take extra care.

Knowledge and ignorance

> Knowledge (*ñāṇa*) is a cause of liberation for noble ones. Noble ones are liberated from the cycle of suffering by developing it. Ignorance (*avijjā*) is a hindrance to liberation. When present, it hinders the noble one's realization of knowledge on the path

to liberation. For this reason, ignorance is called a hindrance to liberation.[124]

We read this passage according to the *Visuddhimagga-mahāṭīkā*, which says that "knowledge" includes knowledge that discerns mental and physical phenomena and knowledge that discerns conditionality. However, it is reasonable to consider all kinds of insight and path knowledge to be knowledge, rather than only these two.

The *Mahāṭīkā* also says that "ignorance" includes the wrong belief in a person, being, or self, the wrong belief that God, Sakka, or Brahma creates beings,[125] and the wrong belief that there is no cause for living beings. However, all kinds of ignorance, the corresponding opposites of insight knowledge, should be considered to be ignorance. So, in the context of insight practice, we will consider all kinds of insight to be knowledge and all kinds of delusions to be ignorance. These two are mutually exclusive phenomena.

By observing mental and physical phenomena every time they occur, one begins to realize that there is nothing but mental phenomena that experience objects and physical phenomena that cannot experience objects. As insight matures one realizes that certain causes produce mental and physical phenomena, and that mental and physical phenomena are effects of certain causes; there is nothing but cause and effect. When insight knowledge gradually matures still further, one realizes that phenomena are impermanent, unsatisfactory, and not-self; phenomena disappear immediately after they appear, and they continuously disappear, moment after moment. All of these realizations that arise from observation are called insight knowledge. Noble ones are liberated from the cycle of suffering by developing all of the stages of insight knowledge and experiencing nibbāna. So each of these kinds of insight knowledge is called a cause of liberation for noble ones. Thus, we should develop insight.

One who fails to observe mental and physical phenomena every time they arise cannot see them as merely mental and physical phenomena. Furthermore, one does not realize their causality, impermanence, unsatisfactoriness, not-self, or their immediate disappearance upon arising and their continuous disappearance thereafter. Therefore, one mistakenly identifies these mental and physical phenomena with a personal entity, a person who is either born without any cause or created by a creator. One mistakes them for someone or something permanent and pleasant, everlasting, and unchanging. Although one doesn't reflect in this way at that very moment, upon later reflection one will certainly come to have such wrong beliefs. For this reason, it is said that any phenomenon unobserved leads to ignorance.

Knowledge is called *ñāṇa* or *vijjā* in Pāḷi, and ignorance, the mental state opposite to it, is called *moha* or *avijjā*. All of the above-mentioned varieties of delusion or ignorance are called *avijjā* in Pāḷi. Ignorance continuously occurs, from moment to moment, in a person who fails to observe. Ignorance often gets the upper hand on a practitioner during his or her initial period of practice. Although a meditator practices observing at the beginning of his or her practice, one cannot discern mental and physical phenomena. His or her comprehension is still quite ordinary: he or she sees the object in a conceptual way. For example, at the moment of seeing one immediately mistakes the seeing process or the form that is seen as "I see" or "someone or something is seen," before realizing it in its true nature.

Although ignorance literally means "not knowing," in this context it means "not knowing ultimate reality." Ignorance immediately knows things in an ordinary, conceptual way. Because ignorance and its accompanying mental states arise first, wrong beliefs ensue. Therefore the texts say, "Ignorance conceals the true nature of objects." Every time an object of insight, such as the six sense doors, the six sense objects, the six kinds of consciousness, and so on arises, we have a deluded notion about these objects because ignorance arises first. Due to this, insight knowledge cannot arise as a cause of liberation, and so ignorance is called a hindrance to liberation.

In summary, the observation of every object as it occurs is considered liberation through knowledge (*ñāṇaniyyāna*). Each and every noting amounts to the development of liberation. On the other hand failure to note and wandering thoughts are considered ignorance and are a hindrance to liberation (*avijjāniyyānāvaraṇa*). One abandons ignorance by noting every time one fails to observe an object, noting it as "forgetting, forgetting" or "thinking, thinking." In this case, its mental factors are also regarded as ignorance.

Delight and laziness

> Spiritual delight (*pāmojja*) is a cause of liberation for noble ones. Noble ones gain liberation from the cycle of suffering by

> developing it. Laziness[126] is a hindrance to liberation. When it is present, it hinders the noble ones' realization of spiritual delight on the path to liberation. For this reason, laziness is called a hindrance to liberation.[127]

The *Mahāṭīkā* says that the delight leads to jhāna in certain cases. However, this does not mean that it cannot also give rise to insight concentration. Some Pāḷi texts explicitly mention that spiritual delight leads to the wholesome arising of other mental states such as rapture, calm (*passaddhi*), happiness (*sukha*), concentration, and knowledge of things as they really are (*yathābhūtañāṇa*). In the context of insight practice, every time one notes an object well it gives rise to delight. As a result of this, practice becomes enjoyable. This enjoyment in turn supports the progress of insight knowledge, step by step, until noble ones are liberated from the cycle of suffering. This is why delight is regarded as a cause of liberation for the noble ones.

Delight tends to arise more often in softhearted persons and less often in those with stronger powers of reason. This is similar to how a child is satisfied with a few cents of pocket money, while an adult will only be satisfied with a hundred dollars or more. But however mature one may be, delight will arise at the insight knowledge of arising and passing away or any time that one's noting goes well. As the *Dhammapada* says:

> Fully knowing
> The arising and passing of the khandhas
> One attains joy and delight.
> For those who know, this is the deathless.[128]

As I will explain below,[129] delight will arise spontaneously when one's mindfulness, concentration, and insight mature. There is generally no need to try to deliberately develop it. However, when laziness is an obstacle, one should arouse delight by contemplating the virtues of the Triple Gem, the benefits of insight, how much one has purified one's moral conduct since beginning to practice, or the pure and noble quality of the noting mind.

Laziness in insight practice is called discontent (*arati*). Laziness prevents many from practicing, so that those who practice are greatly outnumbered by those who do not practice. So we shouldn't complain about the great suffering we face. As the *Dhammapada* says:

> Blind is the world;

Few see clearly here.
As birds who escape from nets are few,
Few go to heaven.[130]

Even among those few who practice, some become lazy when noting is not going well or when they cannot get any special insights. Being lazy, their delight wanes or they are unable to follow through with practice. Then there is no way to escape the cycle of suffering. This is why laziness in insight practice is called a hindrance to liberation. To overcome this hindrance, one should contemplate the virtues of the Triple Gem and so forth, as described above, or the eight sources of spiritual urgency.[131]

Wholesome[132] and unwholesome[133]

> "All kinds of wholesomeness are the noble ones' causes for liberation. By developing them, noble ones gain liberation from the cycle of suffering. All kinds of unwholesomeness are hindrances to liberation. When they are present, they hinder the noble ones' realization of all kinds of wholesomeness on the path to liberation. All profitable [*dhammas*] are an outlet for the noble ones, and noble ones are let out by all profitable dhamma; all unprofitable ideas block that outlet, and because one is hindered by all unprofitable ideas one does not understand the noble ones' outlet consisting in all profitable [*dhammas*]."[134]

All kinds of wholesomeness—such as generosity, moral conduct, meditation, and voluntary service—are causes for liberation. The emphatic particle *pi* when attached to the Pāḷi word *sabba* (all), as in the phrase *sabbepi kusalā dhammā*, means "each and every kind of wholesome action." In other words, every kind of wholesomeness contributes to the cause of liberation; any activity, if its purpose is to aid liberation, is considered a wholesome action. A passage in Pāḷi says:

A well-directed mind . . .
With a well-directed view . . .[135]

Noble ones realize nibbāna and escape from the cycle of suffering through all kinds of wholesome actions that they have cultivated. So if one wishes to escape the cycle of suffering, one should do one's best to perform as much and as many kinds of wholesome acts dedicated to liberation from the cycle of suffering as possible: generosity, moral conduct, meditation, voluntary service, and so on. No wholesome action should be overlooked.

However, when intensively practicing insight, your first priority should be given to it, with the understanding that insight is the essential cause of liberation. Therefore, you should give special consideration to insight. You should not interrupt it for a minute or even a second. Insight is the noblest among worldly wholesome acts, as it is the cause for liberation when nibbāna becomes one's object with the attainment of path knowledge. During intensive insight practice, one should not take a break to perform any other wholesome act, even tranquility meditation, much less any other demanding wholesome act that interferes with insight. The *Dhammapada-aṭṭhakathā* tells the story of a monk called Attadattha to elaborate on this point:

> *The Story of Venerable Attadattha*
> In the final months before the Buddha passed away, there was a certain bhikkhu who wished to become enlightened before the Buddha passed away. He decided to practice intensively until he became an arahant in the presence of the Buddha. He was so committed to this aspiration that he did not even leave his meditation to attend the periodic gathering of the Saṅgha. Thus he came to be called by the nickname Attadattha, "Mr. My Own Welfare."
>
> Some monks who lacked any attainments of the path and fruition eventually complained to the Buddha, saying that Attadattha did not respect the Buddha. They said that as the Buddha's demise grew closer, he did not even bother to attend the Saṅgha meeting, and that he was very cold and distant. The Buddha called this bhikkhu to him and, after listening to his answer, said, "Well done!" After praising Attadattha, the Buddha admonished the other bhikkhus, saying:
>
> > O bhikkhus, anyone who reveres me should follow the example of Attadattha. Offering me fragrances and so on does not pay homage to me, but practicing in harmony with the Dhamma amounts to reverence of me. So others should imitate Attadattha.[136]
>
> Then, the Buddha spoke this verse:

Don't give up your own welfare
For the sake of others' welfare, however great.
Clearly know your own welfare
And be intent on the highest good.[137]

In worldly affairs one shouldn't give up one's own welfare, no matter how little, so that others may reap the benefit, no matter how large. Likewise, in spiritual affairs, one should not sacrifice the attainment of stream entry even in order for another person to be able to realize the fruition knowledge of arahantship. Benefit gained by others, even if enormous, may not bring one any happiness. But benefit to oneself, however small, is sure to bring one some amount of happiness. Keeping this point in mind, one should make every effort possible to secure one's own benefit. In working for one's own benefit, one should choose those opportunities that are good and beneficial, not those that are evil and detrimental. For example, someone working for a hundred dollars a day should not take a job that pays one dollar a day. The commentary explains this example as follows:

> "Not to sacrifice one's own welfare" means that a bhikkhu should not fail to carry out Saṅgha assignments, such as repairing a pagoda or taking care of one's ordination preceptor, that will help one to realize the path, fruition, and nibbāna. Performing these meritorious services is also in the best interest of one's own welfare. However, a bhikkhu who is practicing intensively, with the aspiration of realizing the path, fruition, and nibbāna as soon as possible, should keep exclusively to one's practice without caring for any other duties or assignments.[138]

It is implicit in the above commentary that it is necessary for a monk to fulfill the duty to care for one's ordination preceptor and so on. Failure to do so is an offense referred to as "breach of the rules concerning one's duty" (*vaṭṭabhedakadukkatā*), which is a threat to prospects for celestial rebirth as well as path knowledge and fruition knowledge. For the sake of one's insight practice, however, one should give up even such serious duties, not to mention lesser Saṅgha assignments, such as repairing a pagoda, that are not connected with an offense according to monastic rules. In such cases, though, a monk with the intention to intensively practice insight should ask his preceptor for permission not to take care of him so that the monk will be free from offense.

The noblest offering

When the Buddha was lying on his deathbed in the Sāla park of the Malla princes in Kusinārā, celestial beings and brahmās came from ten thousand worlds filling every corner of the universe. They surrounded the Buddha, paying their final homage to him with various kinds of flowers and fragrances and different kinds of celestial music. On that great occasion, the Buddha addressed the assembly as follows:

> "Ānanda, humans and celestial beings do not honor, revere, esteem, worship, or adore the Tathāgata with offerings of things like fragrances and divine music.
>
> "Ānanda, whatever bhikkhu, bhikkhunī, male or female lay follower practices the Dhamma properly in accordance with the Dhamma that leads to enlightenment, he or she honors the Tathāgata, reveres and esteems him, and pays him the supreme homage.
>
> "Therefore, Ānanda, 'We will live practicing the Dhamma properly in accordance with the Dhamma that leads to enlightenment'—this must be your watchword."[139]

Actually, paying obeisance to the Buddha or offering flowers and fragrances to him develops wholesomeness and is even a cause of liberation for noble ones. The Buddha, however, said that such forms of adoration did not yet amount to doing him honor. The commentary explains his meaning as follows:

The Buddha went to great trouble for four eons and one hundred thousand world cycles to fulfill the prerequisites of Buddhahood—namely the noble deeds (*paramī*), generosity (*cāga*), and conduct (*cariya*)—for the purpose of helping celestial and human beings gain knowledge of both the path and fruition, and nibbāna, and not to be honored with flowers and fragrances. If one is satisfied by simply honoring the Buddha materially, and regard it as great wholesomeness, then one may fail to fulfill the nobler wholesome practices of morality, concentration, and insight, which are the causes of liberation, and one cannot realize the path, fruition, and nibbāna in this very life, nor will one yet be able to escape from the cycle of suffering. Moreover, one cannot help the Buddha's teachings (*sāsana*) to endure for one day or even for the short time necessary to finish one's breakfast rice gruel with that kind of devotional offering. Even if one had one thousand monasteries or pagodas built, that wholesome action would only serve as a source of great merit for the supporter, but it would not be a devotional offering that helps the Buddha's teachings to endure. Only the practices of morality, concentration, and insight are called worthy and suitable offerings or reverences to the Buddha. These practices will help the Buddha's teaching to endure for a long time. This is why the Buddha gave the above-mentioned teaching: because he wants people to honor him only by means of personal practice.

This is the basic meaning of the commentary's explanation, though not a direct translation.

Heirs in the Dhamma

The following passage is from the *Dhammadāyāda Sutta* in the Majjhima Nikāya of the Pāḷi canon:

> "Bhikkhus, be my heirs in the Dhamma, not my heirs in material things. Out of compassion for you I have thought, 'How shall my disciples be my heirs in the Dhamma and not my heirs in material things?'"[140]

The four requisites—robes, food, shelter, and medicine—that are allowed to monks by the Buddha are lowly, material inheritances. A monk who enjoys this type of inheritance is an inferior heir. Any wholesome act that is performed with the wish for a better rebirth is also regarded as an inferior inheritance. Any monks, novices, or laypeople who engage in these are regarded as inferior heirs. Those who only enjoy this inferior material inheritance cannot escape from the cycle of suffering, even though they have had the rare chance to encounter the Buddha's teaching. Like a mother whose heart is full of compassion and quivers at the prospect of the great suffering of her dearly beloved child, the Buddha, seeing beings stuck in the cycle of suffering and experiencing so much suffering, felt great compassion for them. Therefore, the Buddha admonished his disciples to not be satisfied with inferior material inheritance alone. The most valuable and true Dhamma inheritance is the path, fruition, and nibbāna.

Morality, concentration, and insight are indirectly true Dhamma inheritances because they are indispensable for realizing the path, fruition, and nibbāna in this life. All the wholesomeness gained from practicing generosity, observing moral conduct, and so on aimed at attaining nibbāna is also regarded as a Dhamma inheritance. However it is called an "imitation Dhamma inheritance," because this wholesomeness is merely the basis for the realization of the path, fruition, and nibbāna in future existences.[141]

So one must strive to get both kinds of Dhamma inheritance—the true Dhamma inheritance and the one that seems to be it. Moreover, between these two kinds of inheritance one needs to strive to get the true Dhamma inheritance of the path, fruition, and nibbāna in this very life by practicing and developing the morality, concentration, and insight that are its causes. Regarding this matter the Buddha made it very clear in his admonition to the Venerable Potthila Mahāthera that one needs to strive to attain the path, fruition, and nibbāna in this very life. A brief account of the story will be given below.[142]

The Buddha's purpose in teaching was very sublime and noble. He was not yet satisfied with one who attained only the lowest stages of the path and fruition. He was only satisfied with one who achieved fruition knowledge of an arahant. In the *Dhammapada* the Buddha said:

> Not with
> Virtue or religious practice,
> Great learning,
> Attaining samādhi,
> Dwelling alone,
> Or [thinking], "I touch the happiness
> Of renunciation unknown by ordinary people,"
> Should you, monk, rest assured,
> Without having destroyed the toxins.[143]

This teaching is meant for monks who have good moral conduct and the other attainments mentioned here. Some monks may feel content with their good morality, thinking that since they are pure in moral conduct they may become an arahant at any time without practicing. Others may feel content with having fulfilled ascetic practices, being very learned, having attained eightfold jhānic absorption, leading a secluded life, or having attained the fruition of a nonreturner. They think that it will not be difficult to attain the fruition of full enlightenment as an arahant, and being content they do not practice insight in order to attain the fruition of full enlightenment as an arahant. It was to these kinds of monks that the above admonition was given. In fact, one should not be content as long as one has not become an arahant. One should continue to make great effort until one becomes an arahant. The Buddha's innate desire is indeed a very noble and sublime one.

According to these words of the Buddha, insight is the most important among the tasks one should do. One who practices insight is one who honors the Buddha in the noblest way and is heir to the noble Dhamma. He or she is one who is following the Buddha's instruction not to be content with lesser attainments. During a period of intensive retreat, priority should be given to insight practice. There is no need to perform other kinds of wholesome actions. However, if hindrances such as sensual desire interfere with one's practice, there are some other objects that one may contemplate to abandon these thoughts. The following section gives a brief explanation of these, according to the *Vitakkasaṇṭhāna Sutta*.

Helpful contemplations to dispel hindrances

Apply a specific antidote

This first set of helpful contemplations is suitable for knowledgeable persons and those proficient in tranquility meditation:

> To overcome sexual desire, develop contemplation on the loathsomeness of the human body.
>
> To overcome attachment to material objects, arouse understanding of impermanence by considering that objects are ownerless and temporary.
>
> To conquer hatred or aversion, develop loving-kindness.
>
> When angry, reflect on the elements that comprise a human being.[144]
>
> When delusions connected with doubt and a wavering mind arise, remove it by listening to and discussing the Dhamma.
>
> When feeling regret about any of the bhikkhu's moral precepts, alleviate it by confessing the offense to a fellow bhikkhu.

To overcome any mental defilement, apply any of the types of tranquility meditation.
To deal with exhaustion from long periods of practice, one may shift to a tranquility practice that he or she has fully mastered. One who has no such mastery of tranquility meditation should continue to practice insight in such a way that one feels at ease.[145]

Consider the disadvantages

When lustful thoughts arise, one should consider their disadvantages as follows: If lust increases, it can ruin one's moral conduct and lead to an unfortunate rebirth. Lust often prevents one from attaining higher rebirth and liberation from the cycle of suffering. If one cherishes one's physical body by constantly satisfying its demands, one suffers greatly throughout the cycle of suffering.

By reflecting in this way, one should overcome such unwholesome thoughts. The old sages composed the following verse regarding this contemplation:

O body, center of unwholesome thoughts,
I am no longer your slave or your servant.
Being taught by the Buddha, I won't humor you any longer.
Looking after you, I suffered greatly throughout the cycle
of suffering.[146]

Do something wholesome

This approach is most suitable for those whose insight knowledge of equanimity toward formations has matured but who are not able to reach path knowledge due to longing or too much effort. In this case if observing objects often arouses unwholesome thoughts, one should not continue to observe those objects. One may even need to take a complete break from observation if such thoughts arise frequently. The Pāḷi texts say that in such cases one "should try to forget those thoughts and should not give attention to them."[147] Such a break can be very helpful for those who have too much longing or energy.

During such times one should completely cease practicing and chat with one's companions for about two or three hours, half a day, or even a whole day or night. Or one should go to a pagoda to pay obeisance, take a shower, wash some clothes, or do other such things. One should have a good sleep, if one wishes. In due time, one should resume practice.

In the commentary to the Majjhima Nikāya, too, we find the following recommendations. If these thoughts cannot be overcome by not paying attention, one should chant a text that has been memorized, or do some reading. One is also advised to repeatedly identify simple things just as they are. For example: "This is a match box. This is a matchstick. This is a needle. This is a razor. This is a nail clipper. This is a pin, and so on." This commentary also tells the story of a monk who successfully eliminated unwholesome thoughts by building a monastery.

Note inattentiveness

When a wandering thought occurs, one should look for its cause. Before a wandering thought has fully manifested, it begins to take shape due to inattentiveness when it comes in contact with an object. When one can note this inattentiveness immediately, the thought cannot fully develop and will disappear.

Wandering thoughts tend to last a long time only for those who indulge them. If such thoughts are noted every time they arise, without indulging them, they tend to pass away as soon as they are noticed, or a few moments after. If the thought does not pass away when noted, trace it back to the previous thoughts from which it originated. When the source is found, one should make the firm resolution, "I will not allow this source to lead to such thoughts," and continue with practice.

Note more persistently

Noting more persistently is not actually a special type of contemplation but simply the exercise of strong persistence in the usual method of noting. Whatever mental defilements may occur, one should be resolute and persistent in noting them without any interruption, as if one is threatening them: "You! Defilements! What are you up to? Wait, I will conquer you!" This is why the Buddha said:

> If, while he is giving attention to stilling the thought formation of those thoughts, there still arise in him evil unwholesome thoughts connected with desire, with hate, and with delusion,

> then, with his teeth clenched and his tongue pressed against the roof of his mouth, he should beat down, constrain, and crush mind with mind.[148]

You will surely overcome wandering thoughts with this approach. It is called developing insight by continuously observing the usual meditation object without letting the mind incline elsewhere (*appanidhāyabhāvanā*). This method is most suitable for beginning practitioners and persons with little knowledge. Thus, insight practitioners should especially make use of this approach.

The first four contemplations described above are called developing insight by directing the mind toward and observing alternative objects of meditation (*panidhāyabhāvanā*). They are more suitable for long-term practitioners and knowledgeable persons. Both of these types of contemplation are explained in the Satipaṭṭhānasaṃyutta.[149] The methods of contemplation for removing hindrances and developing the factors of enlightenment (*bojjhaṅgā*) are explained in texts such as the commentary on the *Satipaṭṭhāna Sutta*. Most of them are also included in the development of insight by focusing the mind on different objects of meditation.

All types of wholesome acts support the causes of liberation for noble ones and are worth doing. During intensive insight practice, however, one must give priority solely to insight meditation. Alternative methods of contemplation should only be used when one's mind wanders too much and one is not able to continue with insight. As soon as wandering thoughts have subsided, one should immediately return to insight. The teacher should properly guide persons with little knowledge when needed.

All types of unwholesome acts are hindrances to liberation. In the context of insight practice, all kinds of wandering thoughts are hindrances to insight. Therefore, one must eliminate wandering thoughts by noting them whenever they occur.

Obstacles to concentration and the methods to overcome them

Thoughts of past and future

> Returning to the past, the mind grows restless. Not thinking of the past, the mind settles on objects in the present. Then the mind does not become restless.

> Anticipating the future, the mind becomes restless. Not thinking of the future, the mind settles on objects in the present. Then the mind does not become restless.[150]

Things that one has previously seen, heard, smelled, tasted, touched, or thought about are called objects in the past. Remembering them makes the mind restless. This is called a restless mind. The past may distract one in various ways during insight practice: one may simply remember objects that one once experienced; one may think about whether or not one's practice was going well; one may wonder whether one's contemplation was effective; one may wonder whether or not one's previous noting was distinct; one may wonder whether one experienced mind or body; and so on.

When the mind wanders back to the past in this way, we say that the mind is restless, and this creates an obstacle to insight concentration. Therefore, every time this restless mind has been noted, the mind should be placed again on an object in the present. This means that one must note only objects that arise from moment to moment. In connection with insight concentration, this means the present object. In connection with concentration practice, it means that the mind must be kept on the object of concentration. By contemplating phenomena in the present from moment to moment, the mind remains concentrated on objects in the present.

Things that one may later see, hear, smell, taste, touch, or think are all called objects in the future. Anticipating and hoping for such things in the future makes the mind restless. One may contemplate the future in many ways: one may anticipate objects that one is going to see, hear, and so on; daydream about future prosperity; imagine meeting someone one wishes to see; plan how to carry out a successful business project; fantasize about enjoying celestial rebirth; think about how or what objects to note in the future; anticipate good developments in practice; dream of enlightenment or some special experience; wonder whether one will do as well as others; and so on.

A mind that anticipates or longs for objects that have not yet come into existence is by nature wavering, restless, and unsteady. This is an obstacle to insight concentration. Therefore, one should note every time the mind grows restless and then direct the mind to objects in the present. Then the mind will no longer wander but will be well focused on objects in the present.

In short, do not return to the past or dream of the future, but note all mental and physical phenomena in the present without fail.

Laziness and restlessness

> Shrinking and lax, the mind grows lazy. Encouraging the mind, laziness is overcome. Then the mind does not become restless.
>
> When overactive, the mind becomes fidgety. Reducing exertion, fidgetiness is overcome. Then the mind does not become restless.[151]

Laziness and idleness often occur due to a mind that shrinks and is lax when practice does not go smoothly, when special insight knowledge cannot be aroused, or when progress cannot be made. This laziness or unwillingness to practice is an obstacle to insight concentration. So laziness should be removed by noting it closely. If this does not work, the mind must be encouraged in some other way. The Dīgha Nikāya commentary[152] gives eleven ways of developing the enlightenment factor of effort (*vīriya-bojjhaṅga*), such as reflecting on the suffering of the hell realms, the benefits of practice, the nobility of practice, and so on.[153] Here I will describe a few of these reflections.

Reflecting on the dangers of the lower realms

A victim in the hell realms is about three furlongs tall.[154] The wardens of hell push the victim down onto the flaming iron ground, forcing him or her to lie in a supine position. Then they drive nails as big as palm trees into the right and left hands, right and left feet, and waist. After that, the victim is forced to lie face down or on the side and is tortured again in the same way. As long as his or her unwholesome kamma has not yet been exhausted, the victim cannot die. To even see the flaming iron ground and hear the cruel and ruthless shouts of the wardens of hell provokes incredible agony. But to be staked to the ground and consumed by flames, to see huge nails and be cruelly pierced by them, causes mental and physical suffering that cannot be fathomed. In hell there is no one who is kind or who rescues the victims of hell, even though they cry for mercy with cheeks streaked with tears. Being separated from their mothers, fathers, relatives, and intimate friends, being completely alone, they wail despondently as they experience this great suffering without relief for even one second. During this time there is no chance to practice insight.

If the victim has not perished after the first round of torture, the wardens slice his or her body into various shapes with scythes as big as the roof of a house, until blood flows like a river. Huge flames leap up from the blood, burning the sliced parts of the body. Again, the victim suffers immeasurably and has no opportunity at all to practice insight.

If this doesn't finish the victim off, the wardens hang him or her upside down and shave off his or her flesh with an adze, slice by slice. If the victim has still not died, they harness him or her to a flaming cart, like a cow or a horse, and force the victim to pull the cart up a mound of burning coals. If the victim does not climb up, he or she is goaded on, being repeatedly beaten with burning iron bars. After reaching the top, the wardens force the victims to go down again. In this way, the victims are forced to go up and down the mound.

If they have not died after that, the wardens plunge them into a huge pot full of red-hot liquid iron called Lohakumbhī. The victim sinks down through the bubbling hell pot for thirty thousand years, until he or she finally hits the bottom. From there, another thirty thousand years pass before the victim floats back up to the surface, bobbing around like a grain of rice in boiling water. The victim suffers inconceivable anguish, and there is no way at all to practice.

If the victim's misfortune has still not been exhausted, and he or she has not yet died, the wardens pull the victim from the hell pot and throw him or her into the huge blazing hell. This hell is one hundred yojanas[155] in length, width, and height, and resembles a huge iron box. If the flames that originate from the eastern wall were to bore a hole through the western wall, the heat would expand up to one hundred yojanas on the outside. And the same would happen with flames that originate from the western, southern, and northern walls, as well as from the ceiling and floor. The victims in this hell scramble and are tossed around, screaming and shouting, and thereby experience incredible suffering. It sometimes happens that after many years one of the doors of this hell will open. The inmates run desperately toward it in order to escape. Some grow exhausted on the way, some make it to the door, and some actually pass through to the outside. After many hundred thousands of years the door is closed again.

Those who manage to escape and step outside immediately fall into the hell of excrement. Immersed in excrement, they are bitten by maggots as big as the neck of an elephant or a small boat. If they escape from the hell of excrement, they fall into a hell of hot ash, where red-hot coals as big as houses scorch them. Again they have to experience immense suffering. If they escape the hell of ash, they fall into a hell of thorn-trees, whose flaming thorns are sixteen inches long. The hell wardens beat them and force them to climb up and down the trees. The thorns of the trees point downward when the victims climb up and upward when they climb down. So the victims climb up and down in a clumsy panic, as their bodies are pierced and torn by the thorns. When they escape from that hell, they move into the hell of trees that have double-bladed swords for leaves. As soon as they arrive there, the leaves fall on the body of the victims, cutting off body parts such as arms, legs, ears, and noses. If the victims flee, they have to cross sharp blades protruding from the ground and iron walls that obstruct their passage.

If they escape this hell, they come to the hell of the stream called Vettaranī. This stream is full of bubbling, liquid iron that has reeds and lotuses floating in it whose leaves are as sharp as razor blades. The riverbed is covered with sharp razor blades, and the banks of the stream are also overgrown with grasses and reeds whose leaves are also as sharp as razor blades. If the victims happen to go into the stream, they fall down with a thud as they cut themselves on the sharp razor blades on the ground, and they are burned by the hot molten iron. And after falling down, they float in the bubbling hot molten iron, going upstream and down. As there are the sharp razor blade–like grasses and reeds on the banks of the stream and razor-like leaves on the lotuses and reeds in the molten iron, the victim's body becomes torn and tattered. Here too, they have no opportunity at all for practice.

When the wardens of hell see these victims experiencing extreme suffering floating up and down the stream, they pull them onto the bank with big iron hooks and ask them what they want. When the victims reply that they are hungry, the hell wardens bring baskets full of red-hot iron morsels. The victims clamp their mouths shut in fear, but the hell wardens pry them open with an ax and pour in the scorching iron morsels. After having burnt the lips, tongue, palate, throat, and bowels, the morsels leave the body through the anus. If the victims are thirsty, they are given hot bubbling molten iron that leaves the body through the urethra. The victim, without being able to move, experiences horrendous suffering.

If their kamma is still not exhausted and they have still not yet died, the victims are thrown again into the big hell. The terrible suffering of these hell realms is extensively described in discourses like the *Balapaṇḍita Sutta*[156] and the *Devadūta Sutta*.[157] Being faced with such horrible sufferings as these, beings in the hell realms have no chance at all to practice insight. This consideration should motivate one to practice seriously.

O virtuous people, you who are practicing insight meditation! Don't be forgetful! Don't be lazy! If you are, you cannot escape the cycle of suffering. And being unable to escape, you will sometimes be reborn in hell and experience enormous suffering. In fact, you have undoubtedly suffered there in the past. Once you land in hell, it is too late; there is no chance to practice, even if you try with tears rolling down your cheeks. Now is the time for you to seize the opportunity to practice. So don't be lazy; don't be forgetful! Practice insight intensively and diligently, following the instruction given by the Buddha:

> *Bhikkhu*, be absorbed in meditation;
> Don't be negligent;
> Don't let your mind whirl about
> In sensual desire.
> Don't be negligent and swallow a molten iron ball,
> And then, being burnt, cry out,
> "This is suffering!"[158]

In the animal world one has no chance to practice because one is always in danger of being caught in a trap or net. It is impossible for domesticated animals, such as horses and cattle, to practice since they are constantly forced to pull carts or carriages, to carry heavy loads, and to suffer being beaten or pierced with sticks and goads. In the world of the hungry ghosts there is no chance to practice because one incessantly suffers from severe hunger and thirst during the hundreds of thousands of years that pass between the lives of the buddhas. Moreover, it is impossible for the *asura*s called Kālakañcika to practice at all. Their bodies are more than a hundred feet tall and consist only of bones and skin. They constantly suffer from severe hunger and thirst in the open air under a hot sun. And even if the animals, hungry ghosts, and asuras were able to practice, they could not realize any insight or path knowledge.

O virtuous people! Only at a time when you are a human being can you practice insight. Don't be lazy! Don't be forgetful! Practice seriously! This is how to be encouraged and motivated by reflecting on the dangers of the lower realms.

Reflecting on the benefits of practice

Insight practice leads one to enlightenment through the path, fruition, and nibbāna, and brings liberation from both the suffering of the lower realms and the cycle of suffering. The benefits that it bestows are so great that there is no way that they will be realized with a half-hearted practice.

In this world, one has to work very hard to earn even a very small amount of money. If one had the opportunity to earn enough money to last for an entire year from a single day of work, one would naturally take that job and do it with great zeal. One would take and perform a job with even greater enthusiasm if it would earn one lifelong prosperity in only a month.

Wouldn't it be a good investment, then, to devote two weeks, a month, or even two to intensively practicing insight, and bear whatever hardships are involved, when the payoff is gaining freedom from the entire cycle of suffering? One should take up insight practice even more zealously than a lucrative job, since just a few weeks or months of hard work in the practice can gain one freedom from the unsatisfactoriness of the endless cycle of saṃsāra.

O virtuous people! Intensively practice insight! It will surely bring you the great benefits of the path, fruition, and nibbāna. Arouse enthusiasm for practice by considering these great benefits.

Reflecting on the nobility of the lineage

This practice of insight is not a path that can be followed by ordinary people but one that has been followed by all the buddhas, silent buddhas (*paccekabuddha*), and noble disciples. Lazy and bad-mannered people cannot walk this path. Therefore, those who follow this path can be compared with buddhas and other noble beings in terms of the quality and virtue of their practice.

O virtuous people! Are you indifferent to these noble virtues? Don't you wish to possess them yourself? Follow the noble path effectively. Encourage yourself in the practice by considering the nobility of this path.

Respect and appreciation for requisites received

Only monks can use this line of reasoning to arouse motivation for practice.

Lay supporters have to work day and night, even risking their lives at times, to earn their living. However, they only use an appropriate part of their earned resources for themselves and offer any surplus to monks. This offering is not made to relatives, out of gratitude, or with the hope of increasing prosperity. The offering is made because monks are endowed with morality, concentration, and wisdom, and offering to them can bring immeasurable worldly and celestial happiness and the happiness of nibbāna as well.

The donation of a banyan seed brings even greater benefits than the donation of just a banyan tree. The donation of a spoonful of rice, a dish of curry, a fruit, a cake, a robe, a cottage, or a glass of medicine can lead to countless lives blessed with worldly or celestial prosperity. It can even lead to nibbāna. Wishing to get these kinds of benefits, lay supporters make offerings using some of their own resources. Of course, lay supporters must make the offerings without defilements in order to bear wholesome fruit.

But even if the offering is made with pure intention, it will not be as beneficial as it could be if the monks offered to are not fully endowed with morality, concentration, and wisdom. So a monk who wishes that his supporters will enjoy the greatest possible benefit from their offerings should develop morality, concentration, and wisdom. He should not be lazy. Any laziness amounts to being unkind to his supporters. Therefore, the *Ākaṅkheyya Sutta* says:

> If a bhikkhu should wish, "May the services of those whose robes, almsfood, resting place, and medicinal requisites I use bring them great fruit and benefit," let him fulfill the precepts, [be devoted to internal serenity of mind, not neglect meditation, be possessed of insight, and dwell in empty huts.][159]

So a monk should encourage himself by reflecting in this way: Lay supporters provide me with the four requisites out of strong faith. They do this with hopes of gaining the three types of happiness from their offering—human happiness, celestial happiness, and the happiness of nibbāna. They expect nothing in return from me. Thanks to their support, I do not suffer from hunger, heat, cold, and so on. I am able to practice according to the Buddha's guidance without having to worry about material sustenance.

They provide me with tremendous assistance. If I am lazy and negligent in developing morality, concentration, and insight knowledge, my faithful supporters won't be able to enjoy the full benefits of the assistance they have given me. In order to repay them, I should be diligent in my insight practice.

This is how a monk should encourage himself in his practice by arousing a sense of gratitude toward his lay supporters. As shown in the commentaries with this kind of inspiration, a monk can arouse the four factors of great effort in practice and arrive at the fruit of arahantship, like the monks named Mahāmitta and Piṇḍapātika Tissa.[160] In the Saṃyutta Nikāya, we find this passage:

> When . . . a clansman who has gone forth out of faith to arouse his energy thus . . . it is enough to strive for the goal with diligence.[161]

We can interpret this passage to mean that a monk who has joined the order out of faith, with the goal of attaining the path, fruition, and nibbāna, should make a heroic effort with the resolution:

> "Willingly, let only my skin, sinews, and bones remain, and let the flesh and blood dry up in my body,[162] but I will not relax my energy so long as I have not attained what can be attained by manly strength, by manly energy, by manly exertion."
>
> It is not by the inferior that the supreme is attained; rather it is by the supreme that the supreme is attained . . . Therefore, bhikkhus, arouse your energy for the attainment of the as-yet-unattained, for the achievement of the as-yet-unachieved, for the realization of the as-yet-unrealized, with the thought: "in such a way this going forth of ours will not be barren, but fruitful and fertile; and when we use the robes, almsfood, lodgings, and medicinal requisites offered to us by others, these services they provide for us will be of great fruit and benefit to them." Thus, bhikkhus, you should train yourselves.
>
> Considering your own good, bhikkhus, it is enough to strive for the goal with diligence; considering the good of others is enough to strive for the goal with diligence, considering the good of both is enough to strive for the goal with diligence.[163]

Other reflections

One may also find inspiration through other reflections that may cause the enlightenment factor of rapture (*pītisaṃbojjhaṅga*) to arise: thinking about being an heir to the noble ones, thinking about having a noble teacher, reflecting on the attributes of the Triple Gem, considering the heroic efforts made by Sona Mahāthera and others, contemplating one's own purification of morality, remembering inspiring discourses, and so on. These reflections, whether you take up just one or several of them, will provide encouragement to you. When the mind is inspired, it will stop wandering and grow focused and stable. Then you will be able to note very well.

Overzealousness

Sometimes one's mind may become overzealous and overenergized. This can manifest in various ways, such as: making a determination to effectively note every single object, however delicate or subtle it may be; spending time checking whether or not one was successful in noting an object, or which objects were missed or caught; making a resolution not to miss any object ever again, when one finds one has missed an object; reflecting that one has made the utmost effort and that one cannot do more than this; or experiencing physical tension such as clenching the jaw, gritting the teeth, clenching the hands, or making fists.

As one is often caught in such thoughts, the overzealous mind grows restless, and because of this restlessness the noting mind is not well focused on the object. This is like overshooting the object that should be noted. Therefore, an overzealous mind is an obstacle for insight concentration.

The words "restless" (*vikkhepa*) and "fidgety" (*uddhacca*) used in connection with the first obstacle to concentration both share the same general meaning of "restlessness." However, here "restless" has the specific sense of thought about past objects that draws the mind far away from present ones, whereas "fidgetiness" has the sense of excessively striving after objects of meditation, such that the mind overshoots them and cannot get close to them. When one is overzealous, one may not be able to note the wandering thoughts that result from excessive striving. Objects being observed may then seem unclear, and one may experience difficulty with the practice.

In such situations one should relax and think: "There is no soul or self that can arrange things as I would like. No matter how hard I try, insight knowledge may still not arise. Let me just allow things to follow their natural course. It doesn't matter if I miss some objects here and there. I'll just keep on noting the best I can." Then the restless or wandering mind will automatically subside. Some people even find that with relaxation the mind immediately settles down and the noting becomes very good. Hence overexertion is oppressive; when relaxed the mind does not wander and becomes stable.

In short:

> When effort is slack, encouragement is needed;
> When tension is excessive, relaxation is needed;
> When neither slack nor tense, and when noting is balanced,
> The mind becomes focused.

Lust and aversion

> Gratified, the mind grows lustful. Being aware of it, lust is overcome.
> Then the mind does not become restless.
>
> Frustrated, the mind becomes averse. Being aware of it, aversion is overcome. Then the mind does not become restless.[164]

The mental state of feeling pleased and glad with smooth practice, or of awaiting special insight knowledge or path knowledge and fruition knowledge, and nibbāna, is called a gratified mind. This mental state is connected with attachment and is an obstacle to insight concentration, as explained in the section "Insight and attachment" above. So this mental state of gratification must be noted without fail. If one clearly recognizes it by noting it, one has already abandoned lust, as it does not subsequently arise. Thus the mind is free from lust. How lust and other defilements can be abandoned by simply recognizing them will be clarified below under the discussion of the commentaries to the Saṃyutta and Majjhima Nikāyas.[165] When freed of this lust by simply noting it, the mind does not wander and becomes focused.

Although you have already practiced for many days or months, you may want to give up, thinking that you are not going to make it. This mental state leads one away from the path of insight and from the prospect of higher insight knowledges and path knowledge and fruition knowledge. You may even think about running away from the meditation center. This mental state is connected with aversion or frustration. When it is present, concentration cannot arise at all, and there is no way to progress. This is why frustration is such a great obstacle to insight concentration. Therefore, you should abandon this mental state by noting it. Note the desire to give up, the wish to leave the meditation center, or the frustration. Even if it has not disappeared after noting it once or twice, do not give up but keep noting it every time it arises. Afterward note the usual objects again. In the end, the frustration will completely disappear and you will be able to note calmly. This is why the Buddha said, "Being aware of it, aversion is overcome. Then the mind does not become restless."

In short:

> Don't long for anything.
> Don't be frustrated by anything.
> Note liking and longing every time they occur.
> Observe frustration or disappointment whenever it arises.

States of one-pointedness[166]

When the obstacles to concentration have been overcome with the aforementioned six remedies,[167] one's mind no longer returns to the past or anticipates the future. It is no longer shrinking or overactive. Rather, it is only noting the mental and physical phenomena that arise in the moment. The mind is completely purified of the hindrances in insight. This is called one-pointedness. When concentration is good, defilements cannot enter the noting mind, so the meditating mind does not mingle with any companions—that is to say the defilements. Therefore, this kind of concentration is called one-pointed (*ekattagata*): it is comprised of only the meditating mind devoid of any defilement. The one-pointed mind is established in concentration and not rooted in any of the defilements.

> The mind is fully purified by overcoming these six obstacles and becomes one-pointed.
>
> What are the states of one-pointedness? One-pointedness based on contemplation of generosity, one-pointedness based on tranquility meditation, one-pointedness based on knowledge of dissolution, and one-pointedness based on knowledge of cessation.
>
> One-pointedness based on contemplation of generosity is

> for those contemplating generosity. One-pointedness based on tranquility meditation is for those who practice tranquility meditation. One-pointedness based on insight knowledge of dissolution is for those who develop insight; one-pointedness based on knowledge of cessation is for those noble persons who realize nibbāna.[168]

One-pointedness based on contemplation of generosity

One has attained this form of one-pointedness if, when contemplating one's acts of generosity, one's concentration becomes so strong that one can turn the mind to nothing other than the offering one has performed. The noting mind no longer suffers interference from the mental defilements and becomes well established in one-pointedness based on contemplation of generosity (*dānavosaggupatṭṭhānekatta*).

One-pointedness based on tranquility meditation

One has attained this type of one-pointedness if, when developing tranquility meditation, one's concentration becomes so strong that it experiences nothing other than the object of meditation. One's noting mind is no longer disturbed by the mental defilements and becomes well established in one-pointedness based on tranquility meditation (*samathanimittupaṭṭhānekatta*). Since the mind is solely focused on the object of concentration, this one-pointedness is a form of access concentration or absorption concentration.

One-pointedness based on insight knowledge of dissolution

Once one, as an insight meditator, attains insight knowledge that discerns mental and physical phenomena, and one's concentration is well established, one begins to experience nothing but those mental and physical phenomena to the exclusion of other objects, such that other objects do not appear. One's noting mind becomes one-pointed and continuous, without interference from hindering thoughts. From that time on the noting mind is one-pointed and free from hindrances.

From the stage when one attains insight knowledge of dissolution up to the stage of knowledge of adaptation, a meditator especially experiences only phenomena's characteristic of disappearance every time one notes them. At this point, every noting mind is free from defilements and well established in one-pointedness based on insight knowledge of dissolution (*vayalakkhaṇupaṭṭhānekatta*). In other words, momentary concentration is well established because one experiences only the dissolution of phenomena. This is why Pāḷi scriptures say that momentary concentration is fully mature at this stage of knowledge. This is very clear to yogis who have attained insight knowledge of dissolution.

One-pointedness based on knowledge of cessation

At the peak of insight practice, a meditator realizes path knowledge and fruition knowledge. At that moment, the meditator experiences nothing but nibbāna. All other conditioned mental and physical phenomena cease. For this reason, we say that the mind that experiences path knowledge and fruition knowledge is well established in one-pointedness based on knowledge of cessation (*nirodhupaṭṭhānekatta*). This is perfectly clear to those who have experienced it.

Using these explanations, one can clearly understand how an insight meditator must practice in order to fulfill the purification of mind, and how this purification arises.

Here ends chapter 2 regarding mental purification.

Absolute and Conventional Realities[169]

3

What Is Reality?

Ultimate reality

We cannot say that conditional, relative realities are "ultimate." Only timeless, immutable realities should be accepted as "ultimate." Ultimate reality (*paramattha*) consists only of the following elements, because they are absolute and immutable facts of experience: mind, mental factors, matter, and nibbāna.

> An ultimate, irreducible phenomenon is called an "ultimate reality."[170]

What we learn from others is also not necessarily true, so it should not be considered ultimate reality. On the other hand, what we empirically experience ourselves is never false but always true. Therefore, mind, mental factors, matter, and nibbāna are called "ultimate reality," because they can be empirically experienced. As the Abhidhamma commentary says:

> An ultimate, personally experienced phenomenon is called an "ultimate reality."[171]
>
> The expression "empirically experienced" (*saccikaṭṭha*) refers to ultimate realities, not to illusions like magic and mirages that should not be accepted. The word "ultimate reality" refers to an ultimate reality that should not be accepted by hearsay and so on.[172]

Phenomena that we can personally experience are called "empirically experienced," "what truly exists," as well as "ultimate truth." There are fifty-seven of these ultimately real phenomena: the five aggregates, the twelve sense bases, the eighteen elements, and the twenty-two mental faculties.

According to the commentary these fifty-seven classes of phenomena are called "empirically experienced" or "ultimate reality." They can be summarized into the four ultimate realities of mind, mental factors, matter, and nibbāna—or mind and matter, in brief. For simplicity's sake, I will refer to them here as mind and matter.

Conceptual illusions

When a magician conjures gold, silver, or gems out of a brick, a piece of paper, or a stone, people are under the illusion that these are genuinely gold, silver, or gems. Such imaginary things are said to be "not genuinely existing" (*abhūtattha*) or "not personally experienced" (*asaccikaṭṭha*), since they are mistaken for something genuine, just as a thirsty deer mistakes a mirage for water from a distance. Concepts such as woman, man, hand, foot, and so on have this kind of illusory nature. On the other hand, mind and matter can be experienced as they really are, so they are said to be "ultimate reality," "personally experienced," and "genuinely existing" (*bhūtattha*).

For example, when people see a visible form with their eyes they know, "I see a visible form" or "The visible form that is seen exists." This visible form is what really exists and what is genuinely known at the moment of seeing; it is not an illusion like the gold, silver, or gems created by a magician or a mirage mistaken for water. Seeing would not be possible without a visible form. Therefore, a visible form that can be seen with the eyes is called a reality that genuinely exists or that is personally experienced. If a form is personally experienced, it is also called an ultimate reality.

The experience of seeing a visible form is followed by a mental process that investigates and determines it to be of a certain shape: tall or short, spherical or flat, square or round, woman or man, face or arm, and so on. This mental process of investigation can only be experienced in an obvious way when one encounters an especially novel object, since the investigation of new objects takes time. This type of investigation is not usually apparent since it doesn't take much time to investigate an object that one has seen before and that one is familiar with. Thus ordinary people are under the illusion that they actually see the forms or shapes that they imagine, because they cannot distinguish between prior and subsequent processes of seeing and investigation. According to the Abhidhamma subcommentary:

> The function of eye-consciousness is only to see visible forms, not to ascertain physical gestures or movements. However, succeeding mental processes follow so quickly that ordinary people think that they see, as if with their real eyes, the movement known by the succeeding mental process of investigation.[173]

For example, when we see a hand moving, our eye-consciousness sees only the visible form. It is not able to know that it is a hand or that it is moving. The mind is very fast, however, so the movement that the succeeding mind of investigation knows is taken to have been seen with the eyes. Ordinary people cannot distinguish between preceding and succeeding mental processes. On the other hand, a meditator who has practiced insight proficiently can recognize the mental process of seeing visible form as distinct from the subsequent mental processes that know it as a hand and movement.

The Pāḷi texts give the example of a swinging torch to clarify this point. If a lit torch is twirled in the darkness, it will appear as a solid ring of fire to anyone watching. If it is swung in a linear or triangular pattern, then it will appear as a line or triangle. In reality, there is no circular, linear, or triangular shape to the fire, only the red visible form that can be seen moving from place to place where the fire passes. In reality, it is the succeeding mental processes that merge the visible forms that appear in different places and interpret them as a circle of fire and so on. This is the actual example from Pāḷi texts.

Another example of this is found in people who cannot read well. They must read slowly to comprehend a piece of writing from the context, carefully reading word by word. The mental process of investigation is apparent to them because it proceeds so slowly. On the other hand, for those who read well, the mental process of investigation is much faster and therefore cannot be clearly detected. It seems as if they can read just by seeing the words. Similarly, when we see a novel object, we can experience the processes of seeing and investigating separately because they proceed more slowly. On the other hand, when we see a familiar object, the mental process of investigation goes unnoticed because it occurs so quickly.

So it seems to us as if we know a familiar woman or man as soon as we see them. But in reality, after we see them, investigation immediately follows. It is only due to this investigation that we can determine whether it is a woman, a man, and so on. Thus, as with the circle of fire, woman and man are not considered to be absolute realities, realities that genuinely exist, are personally experienced, or are ultimately true, but are instead merely conventional realities (*sammutipaññatti*) consisting of concepts. We can understand this by thinking thusly: If we subtract all of the clearly visible forms or shapes from the matter or substance that we take to be a woman, a man, and so on, no such woman or man would be left to be seen. What we actually see is only visible form, and not a woman, a man, and such. We see only a collection of visible forms; we cannot see a woman, man, and such. The seeing of a woman, man, and such is a concept; it does not truly exist as imagined.

You may ask, "Can't we touch a woman or man, even though they lack any visible phenomena by which they can be seen?" In this case too, what we touch is not a woman or man but simply phenomena that can be experienced by touch. One can only touch a tangible object (*phoṭṭhabba*); there is not any woman or man we can touch. If we subtract all the tangible phenomena that we can clearly touch, there would be no woman or man to be touched. Therefore, the concepts of woman, man, and so on are called "realities that do not genuinely exist" and "are not personally experienced." The woman or man that we think we see or touch is not what really exists. Because it is not personally experienced it is not ultimately real, meaning that it is not an ultimate reality.

What really exists is referred to as "eye-sensitivity" (*cakkhupasāda*). Eye-consciousness occurs because eye-sensitivity sees visible forms. We could not see visible forms if there were no eye-sensitivity. How could we see then? For example, if a mirror is clear, we can see reflections of form in it. If the mirror were not clear, we could not see reflections of form in it because the reflections would not appear. Therefore, in order for there to be seeing, there must be eye-sensitivity, and there must be visible forms that really exist, are realities that genuinely exist, are personally experienced, and are ultimate reality. Thus, seeing really exists. And thanks to its existence we can see a great variety of forms. If seeing did not exist, we could not know what we see, let alone say what it is. Therefore, eye-consciousness is also called "a reality that genuinely exists," "is personally experienced," and "ultimate reality." The same is true of sound, ear-sensitivity, and ear-consciousness in the case of hearing, and likewise for the other senses.

Hearsay and such

Things learned through hearsay and such may be true or false. So such truths are not regarded as higher reality (*uttamattha*) or ultimate reality (*paramattha*). On the other hand, what can be empirically experienced really exists and is regarded as higher reality and ultimate reality. The term "and such" in the phrase "hearsay and such" refers to realities that are accepted on the basis of tradition, scripture, logic, method, reason, or personal opinion. Realities that are accepted on the basis of these, rather than through personal experience, cannot be regarded as ultimately real.

What is handed down through tradition by our teachers and forefathers (*paramparā*), as well as what we receive through hearsay (*itikirā*), are sometimes true and sometimes not. So they should not be considered ultimate realities. Also the validity of what is considered to be in accord with scripture (*piṭakasampadā*) depends on the quality of the scripture. Even when a scripture is reliable, it is still necessary to correctly interpret it in order to extract genuine truth from it. So such truths are not yet considered ultimate realities. Ideas arrived at through logic (*takkahetu*) are not always true, and therefore they should not be considered to be ultimate realities. Ideas that are arrived at methodically (*nayahetu*) may be true or not, depending on the rationality of the method, and so they should not be considered to be ultimate realities. Ideas that are accepted based on reason (*ākāraparivitakka*) or personal opinion (*diṭṭhinijjhānakhanti*) are also not always true, and thus they cannot be considered to be ultimate realities.

For all these reasons, in the *Kālāma Sutta*[174] and elsewhere the Buddha discouraged us from holding views based on hearsay, tradition, and so on. A truth accepted by any of these means is not reliable. Instead, he instructed us to experience the truth empirically for ourselves through practice. It is only through empirical knowledge that we can experience mental and physical phenomena.

A person who is born blind cannot, by any means, know the colors white, red, yellow, or blue, no matter how others may describe those colors. He or she is simply not able to comprehend the experience of seeing. Similarly, someone with a deficient sense of smell cannot know the difference between fragrant and putrid odors, regardless of how others may explain them. One cannot truly know the flavor of a food that one has never tasted, no matter how it is described. And one cannot understand the pain of a headache, toothache, or stomachache if one has never had them.

Likewise, one cannot really know insight knowledge, jhāna, or the path and fruition if one has not yet attained them, regardless of how they may be explained in accordance with scripture. We cannot say that understanding an object by means of hearsay, tradition (*anussava*), or inference (*anumāna*) is to know its ultimate truth. Real, empirical knowledge belongs only to insight meditators, those who achieve jhāna, and noble ones. Therefore, whatever is known through hearsay and such is merely conceptual and not a real, ultimately existing mental or physical phenomenon.

Since we can see visible objects, they can be empirically known, and since it is obvious that the continuum of life possesses eye-sensitivity and eye-consciousness, they too can be empirically known. The same is true for the mental and physical phenomena of sound, the ear-sensitivity, and ear-consciousness, and similarly for the other senses of smell, taste, touch, and thought. We can clearly experience these mental and physical phenomena by means of insight knowledge, path knowledge and fruition knowledge, and reviewing knowledge (*paccavekkhaṇañāṇa*). Because we can empirically know them, these truly existing mental and physical phenomena are called empirical reality, higher reality, and ultimate reality.

Because we know that these phenomena truly exist through personal experience, they are real. And because they are not accepted through hearsay or on the basis of scripture, they cannot be incorrect realities. Therefore they are also said to genuinely exist and are empirically experienced.

Description vs. experience

Subcommentaries on the Abhidhamma say:

> Knowledge that is based on hearsay and such may or may not be true, so it is not ultimate reality. Only empirical facts are ultimate realities. To communicate this point, it is said that "They cannot be experienced by hearsay; they are higher realities (*uttamattho*)."[175]

> Being ultimate, genuine realities are called "ultimate realities." Mental and physical phenomena that can be empirically known are phenomena that cannot be pointed out. Therefore, they are called "higher realities."[176]

Because genuinely existing mental and physical phenomena are irreducible, they are ultimately real and are therefore called ultimate realities. Insight knowledge of reobservation, insight knowledge, and so on clearly experiences these ultimate realities, but these realities cannot be pointed out on the basis of having heard about them from somebody else. They are the intrinsic characteristics (*sabhāvalakkhaṇā*) of mental and physical phenomena.

The phrases "cannot be experienced by hearsay" (*anussavādivasenaggahetabbo*) and "cannot be pointed out" (*aniddisitabbasabhāvo*) that the Abhidhamma commentary and subcommentary use above have essentially the same meaning. The commentary says that ultimate realities cannot be experienced by means of hearsay and such, while the subcommentary further explains that descriptions of ultimate realities cannot help others understand them. Both phrases, however, refer to the fact that one can only know ultimate reality through empirical knowledge.

Since it may be difficult to understand why ultimate reality "cannot be pointed out," I will explain it further. I will begin by asking, "Why are true phenomena said to be indescribable?" It is certainly possible to describe the true characteristics of phenomena. For example, the earth element has the characteristic of hardness, mind has the characteristic of cognizing the object, contact has the characteristic of touching the object, and so on. So why are the intrinsic characteristics of mental and physical phenomena said to be indescribable?

It is true that we can describe mental and physical phenomena in terms of their characteristics. This is why Pāḷi texts, commentaries, and subcommentaries provide descriptions of them. However, what we understand by recourse to scriptural descriptions is not ultimate reality but simply names and concepts like earth element (*pathavīdhatu*), mind (*citta*), and contact (*phassa*). These names do refer to ultimate realities, and thus they are called "concepts that refer to what ultimately exists" (*vijjamānapaññatti*) or "concepts that refer to ultimate reality" (*tajjāpaññatti*). But if their manner is learned—that is, the way the earth feels hard, the way the mind cognizes objects, the way that mental contact connects with objects, and so on—then what is known is simply concepts about the manner (*ākārapaññatti*) of these phenomena. If one knows them as solid forms or powder, then what one knows are concepts of form or shape (*saṇṭhānapaññatti*).

A learned person knows the descriptions of the path, its fruition, and nibbāna from the Pāḷi texts and can also talk about them. However, unenlightened persons can never take the genuine path and fruition as objects; they can never experience them. And before attaining knowledge of change-of-lineage (*gotrabhū*) they can never take nibbāna as their object; they can never experience it. Therefore, unenlightened persons do not understand path, fruition, and nibbāna through personal experience, and so these are not yet ultimate realities for them. Since they know these realities only through oral tradition, lineage, or in accordance with the scripture and reasoning, they only have a conceptual understanding of them. Such understanding is either a concept of name (*nāmapaññatti*), a concept about the manner, or a concept of form or shape.

In fact, even the mundane phenomena that we believe we understand are still only conceptually known unless personally experienced. Ordinary people can experience the mental and physical phenomena that belong to the domain of the senses (*kāmāvacara*), since they obviously occur in the continuum of life. They can also experience phenomena when they appear at the six sense doors and by practicing insight. Those who have achieved jhāna can experience jhānic phenomena as well. We can realize that such-and-such is called "the earth element," such-and-such is called "consciousness," and such-and-such is called "mental contact" by checking our own experience against Pāḷi texts and Dhamma talks.

For example, a person who has never eaten grapes doesn't yet know the actual taste of grapes, although he or she has learned about it from somebody else. Only when he or she actually eats them does he or she know how grapes really taste. People usually think that supramundane phenomena are so profound that ordinary people cannot understand them but that anyone can understand mundane phenomena. I have already mentioned the example of a person who is born blind and cannot know forms.

To explain the fact that the intrinsic characteristics of mind and body cannot be described, the Abhidhamma subcommentary says:

> Phenomena cannot be described in an ultimate sense.[177]

This means that we cannot understand the intrinsic characteristics of mental and physical phenomena based on descriptions but only based on our own experience. Only what we experience personally is ultimate reality. How profound that is! Reflect on this repeatedly until you understand it.

The correct definition of ultimate reality

In the *Abhidhammatthavibhāvinī*,[178] ultimate reality (*paramattha*) is defined in accordance with the Anuṭīkā as "the highest" (*uttama*), "not false" (*aviparīta*), "truth" (*attha*). "Highest" and "ultimate" have the same literal meaning, while "not false" is a synonym of ultimate. Other synonyms for ultimate include: "existence" (*bhūta*), "real existence," or "things as they are" (*yathābhūta*), "true" (*tatha*), "real" (*taccha*), and "not untrue" (*avitatha*).

Following the explanations given in the commentaries and subcommentaries, we should correctly understand ultimate reality in this way: the four realities—mind, mental factors, matter, and nibbāna—that can be personally experienced, are immutable, and really existing are called "ultimate realities." We should always keep this correct definition of ultimate reality in mind.

There is a misapprehension that ultimate realities are eternal and unchanging while conventional realities (*paññatti*) are transitory and changing. Accordingly it is explained that ultimate realities are eternal in several ways: in terms of characteristics or with regard to consequences. Matter (*rūpa*), for instance, is defined as malleable or transformable and subject to alteration by cold, heat, and so on. However it is also said that it is characteristically perpetual. This contradiction is actually rooted in confusing the words *aviparīta* (not false) and *aviparinaṇāta* (unchanging), thinking that they have the same meaning.

The word *aviparinịāta* is composed of the root √*namu* with the prefixes *vi-* and *pari-*. The literal meaning of this word is "unchanging." By extension it can be read as "enduring" or "perpetual." On the other hand, the word *aviparīta* is composed of the root √*i* with the same prefixes, *vi-* and *pari-*. The literal meaning of this word is "not false," or, in other words, "true." The subcommentary to the *Paramatthavibhāvinī*[179] defines ultimate reality as "not false (*aviparīta*); truth (*attha*)." This explanation should resolve the confusion mentioned above.[180] Keep these correct definitions in mind to better understand what is meant by the term "ultimate reality."

Transience

The notion that concepts are transitory is completely wrong. In fact, concepts do not appear, exist, or disappear at all. Since they do not have any real existence in an ultimate sense, it is impossible to say that they arise or pass away. It is impossible for conventional truths to arise, exist, and pass away, because they are not what really exists but are merely imaginary constructs.

Take a person's name, for example. When does that name come into existence? Where does it exist: in one's head, or body, or somewhere else? When does it pass away? Actually, a name cannot be said to come into being, to exist anywhere, or to disappear. It is purely imaginary, isn't it? It seems to disappear when people forget it or no longer use it, but it is impossible for it to vanish. That is why today we still know the name of the hermit Sumedhā,[181] who lived four incalculable eons and a hundred thousand world-cycles ago. The same is true of names like "woman," "man," "pot," "sarong," and so on. All conceptual designations, like "woman," "man," "pot," and "sarong," are like a person's name; they do not arise, exist, or disappear. Ultimately, such persons or things do not exist anywhere.

Instead, the collection of visible forms that one sees, all the sounds that one hears, all the tangible objects that one touches, and so on are considered to be the solid substance of a woman, man, and so on, and we think that they really exist. As explained before, such conceptual ideas are formed by the failure to distinguish between the preceding mental processes of seeing, hearing, touching, and so on and the succeeding mental processes that imagine solid forms. Just as we cannot find a cart that exists apart from its component parts, such as wheels, axles, and so on, so also we cannot find a man or a woman that exists apart from mental and physical phenomena.

Here are some examples that the Pāḷi texts mention to illustrate this point:

> *A Line of Termites*
> From a distance, a line of moving termites looks like a continuous line. However, there is no line apart from the individual termites that comprise it. In the same way, there is no person or solid substance apart from the mental and physical phenomena that comprise him or her.

A Sand Bag

When a sand bag is hung up and punctured, a constant stream of sand flows out of it. When the bag is pushed back and forth, the stream of sand seems to move back and forth. We conceive of the stream of falling sand as something that flows down. In fact, there is neither a stream nor its movement but only successive grains of falling sand. When the hole in the bag is sealed, or all of the sand has emptied out, the stream no longer appears to exist or to move. But we cannot say that the stream disappears, because there wasn't actually any inherently existing stream apart from the individual grains of sand. In reality, to say that the stream no longer exists means that the grains of sand are no longer falling in succession. In the same way, there is no person apart from mental and physical phenomena, and there is no moving hand or foot apart from the physical phenomena that arise in successive movements. There is also no death of a person apart from the absence of new mental and physical phenomena arising.[182]

Rope

A rope appears to be a solid entity. However, there is no rope apart from the individual strings that comprise it. The thickness or length of a rope depends on the number and length of the strings that comprise it. A long rope does not inherently exist. In the same manner, there is no inherently existing form of a person apart from mental and physical phenomena that have no solid substance. There is no inherently existing person who lives for one hour, one day, one month, one year, and so on apart from mental and physical phenomena that don't even last for the blink of an eye.

A River

A river seems to flow continuously because the water that flows downstream is constantly being replaced with new water. However, if one gazes at the river in one spot, one will find that the water that one sees at present is different from the water one saw only a moment ago. In the same way, a man or a woman seems to be the same person all the time because passing phenomena

> are continuously replaced with new ones. This is a concept of continuity (*santatipaññatti*).
>
> *A Tree*
>
> A tree is composed of its parts: the trunk, branches, twigs, leaves, and so on. Actually, there is no inherently existing form of a tree apart from these parts. Some kinds of evergreen trees never appear to shed their leaves, because the leaves they shed are continuously replaced with new ones. This gives the impression that these trees are always green and lush. However, by observing the old leaves that are shed and new buds that sprout, we can know their impermanence. This example shows that solidity (*samūhapaññatti*), form or shape, and unending processes exist only in a conceptual sense, not in an ultimate sense.

By repeatedly reflecting on these examples, we can all come to realize that the conceptual realities of woman, man, and so on are like a person's name: they do not appear and disappear, and they do not exist anywhere. They are only objects of our imaginations. We can conclude that conceptual realities do not change.

Among the ultimate realities, nibbāna is called an unconditioned reality (*asaṅkhataparamattha*). It is subject to nothing and does not arise and disappear, and so it is said to be permanent (*nicca*) and stable (*dhuva*). All the other ultimate realities are conditioned realities (*saṅkhataparamattha*). Being subject to relevant conditions, they actually appear and disappear, and so they are said to be impermanent (*anicca*) and unstable (*adhuva*). These conditioned ultimate realities, internal or external, are what really exist in the present, really happened in the past, and will come into existence in the future. Aside from conditioned phenomena and unconditioned nibbāna, all other objects that we imagine in our mind are conceptual things.

Names or words, for example, are concepts of name. The persons or things indicted by these words are concepts of things (*atthapaññatti*). Names or words, such as the Pāḷi word *rūpārammaṇā*, which means "[visible] form object" in English, are all imaginary things. They do not arise in the present, have not arisen in the past, and will not arise in the future internally or externally. They cannot be experienced anywhere. Thus they are regarded as concepts of name and not as ultimate realities.

On the other hand the phenomenon indicated by the words "visible object" is a genuinely visible object that can be experienced the moment that one sees it, or reflects upon it later. What one experiences in this way is ultimate reality, while the things that one does not really see or experience are only imaginary visible objects. They may be concepts of names or words, concepts of gesture or manner, or concepts of solid forms.

They are not real ultimate realities because they do not exist, have never existed, and will never exist as objects, neither internally nor externally. And because they do not exist anywhere, they cannot be experienced. We can compare these imaginary objects to ghosts that timid people imagine, or to objects that appear in dreams. All such objects seem real, but they do not actually exist; they merely appear in our imagination. Thus all of the objects that the mind creates are conventional realities. The same is true with regard to all other aspects of our other senses—eye-sensitivity, eye-consciousness, sound, ear-sensitivity, ear-consciousness, and so on. These names or words are conventional realities, while the objects that we can empirically experience are genuine ultimate realities (*nibbatthitaparamattha*).

The Two Meanings of Activity

Verbs such as "going," "standing," "sitting," "sleeping," "bending," "stretching," and so on are all concepts. Since these words indicate real actions and intentions, they are called "concepts that refer to what ultimately exists" (*vijjamānapaññatti*) or "concepts that refer to ultimately real phenomena" (*tajjāpaññatti*). Recall that the actions indicated by these verbs are ultimately constituted of mind, mental factors, and matter. The meaning that concepts indicate is twofold: the meaning that ordinary people know and the meaning that insight meditators know.

The meaning that ordinary people know

When ordinary people move, stand, sit, sleep, bend, and so on, their experience of doing so is mingled with notions of "I," "hand," "foot," and "bodily shape." Their experience is actually a concept of person (*puggalapaññatti*), or a concept of form or shape. Their experience is not an ultimate reality, because there is no inherently existing personal identity or form apart from the intention to move, the physical process of moving, and so on. So knowledge and so on cannot find them.

You may ask, "Why shouldn't the realities indicated by concepts that refer to things with actual existence be considered ultimate realities?" It is because what we understand depends on how we think. For example, prior to the Buddha's appearance, words like matter, feeling (*vedanā*), earth (*pathavī*), and so on were used without any empirical knowledge of their meaning. What was understood when using those words at that time was not ultimate reality but merely concepts of form, feeling, the earth element, and so on. Even today, due to how they think, some learned Buddhists still only know the concepts of form and so on that these words indicate. It is not necessarily the case that we will know ultimate reality just because words refer to empirical facts.

The meaning that insight meditators know

When a meditator's insight knowledge matures by constantly observing mind and body, he or she becomes aware of both the intention to move and the subsequent gradual process of movement. A meditator also perceives that as soon as preceding phenomena disappear, subsequent ones replace them. Thus he or she realizes that there is no self that moves, as the sentence "I move" would suggest. Through his or her own insight knowledge, a meditator knows that what really occurs is the intention to move, followed by the gradual physical process of movement. When standing, a meditator can experience the intention to stand and the resulting sequence of moments of stiffness that support the standing posture. Insight meditators comprehend that the phenomena involved in the process of standing appear and disappear from moment to moment and that the sentence "I stand" is merely a concept. In actuality, they know through their own insight knowledge that there is no self who stands but only the sequential processes of intention and stiffness.

In the same way, we can see bending as a process caused by the intention to bend, followed by an inward movement that progresses in separate little movements. We can see that the phenomena involved in bending arise and pass away moment by moment. So the sentences, "The arm is bending," "The leg is bending," or "I am bending" are just words; there is no arm, leg, or person that bends. Meditators know through their own insight knowledge that there is only the intention to bend and the gradual movement of bending. The processes of sitting, lying down, stretching, and so on should be understood in the same way. The realities that one knows in this way are regarded as ultimately real phenomena because these are realities that can be known as they really are by means of empirically observed insight knowledge. This is how to distinguish between conventional and ultimate realities.

English words such as "woman," "man," "hand," "foot," "pot," "sarong," and so on are all concepts of name. They refer to forms or entities that cannot be directly experienced because they do not exist in an ultimate sense. As explained previously, what one regards as a man or woman is only an interpretation of mental and physical processes. There is no person, only the processes of mind and body. The moment we see something or someone, what we truly see is only visible form. The moment we hear something, what we truly hear is only sound. The same is true for smell and taste. The moment we touch something, what we truly touch are the earth element (*pathavīdhātu*), characterized by softness or hardness, the fire element (*tejodhātu*), characterized by warmth, heat, or coldness, or the air element (*vāyodhātu*), characterized by tension, tightness, or looseness.

We touch no man or woman apart from these bodily sensations. We cannot empirically know the form or shape of a woman or man. When eye-consciousness of a woman has ceased, for example, we can only know the woman by means of the subsequent, third mental process (*vīthi*) of investigation.[183] Although we know her, our knowledge is not an empirical knowledge, but only a conclusion based on previous encounters. So we can empirically know, in ourselves, what is arising and what has arisen by reflecting about it through thoughtful reconsideration (*paṭisaṅkhānañāṇa*). We can also empirically know this through insight knowledge. With thoughtful reconsideration and insight knowledge, we can determine that these conventional realities do not clearly exist, because we cannot empirically find a "woman." We cannot empirically experience a person through insight knowledge. When our insight knowledge grows sharp and mature enough, however, we are able to experience the genuine phenomena that underlie such concepts. As the saying goes:

> As ultimate reality emerges, concepts submerge.

This means that we simultaneously know the real, ultimate realities of mind and body, as well as the illusory nature of concepts. It is the opposite for those who have not yet attained any insight knowledge, however:

> As concepts emerge, ultimate reality submerges.

This means that only concepts clearly arise, whereas the ultimate realities of mind and body submerge. So for ordinary people, the conceptual form and shape of a so-called man or woman prevail, while mental and physical phenomena such as colors, sounds, and so on become apparent only when they are deliberately considered. This is because ordinary people cannot distinguish between preceding and succeeding processes of mind. This is how to differentiate ultimate reality from concepts.

Two Kinds of Insight

There are two kinds of insight, empirical (*paccakkha*) and inferential (*anumāna*). Knowledge that is cultivated by empirically meditating on mental and physical phenomena is called empirical insight. One can be clearly aware of the unique characteristics and impermanence of phenomena via empirical insight. Insight meditators should develop empirical insight from the beginning up to the peak insight knowledge of adaptation (*anulomañāṇa*).

Every empirical insight, when it matures, is followed by inferential insight that extrapolates to phenomena that are not directly experienced from insight based on experiential phenomena. The objects of this inferential insight include all mundane phenomena, internal and external, past, future, and present. However, insight that is inferential, rather than empirical, is unable to experience the unique characteristics of phenomena. It is not necessary to deliberately develop inferential insight, since it always arises by itself following every mature empirical insight. So from here on I will only explain objects of empirical insight.

Appropriate objects for meditation

In order to develop true insight knowledge, starting with knowledge that discerns body and mind, one should observe ultimate mental and physical phenomena and not conceptual objects. In addition, among ultimate mental and physical phenomena, only those that are mundane should be taken as the objects of insight meditation and not those that are supramundane. The reason for this is, as the *Visuddhimagga* says, ordinary people cannot observe supramundane phenomena that they have not yet realized (*anadhigatattā*).[184] However, even if one has realized them, observing supramundane phenomena does not serve the purpose of insight meditation,[185] because the illusions of permanence, satisfaction, and personality are only connected with mundane phenomena and not with supramundane ones. These illusions can only be eradicated by observing mundane phenomena and not by observing supramundane ones. For example, if a person wants to level the ground, they must remove places that are too high and fill in places that are too low. Doing so serves the purpose of leveling the ground, but if the ground was already level, doing so would serve no purpose.

Among mundane phenomena, beginners cannot meditate on the highest jhāna, "neither perception nor nonperception" (*nevasaññānāsaññāyatana*). It is so extremely subtle that even Venerable Sāriputta was unable to observe it directly.[186] So, although they are mundane, sublime types of consciousness experienced with the attainment of jhāna cannot be observed if one has not attained them. Thus the subcommentary says that the sublime types of consciousness (*mahaggatacittāni*) can be observed or experienced only by those who have achieved jhāna.

> Only for *jhāna* achievers is *jhānic* consciousness obvious enough to be observed and experienced.[187]

The phrase "obvious enough" means that the sublime types of consciousness can be empirically observed. Phenomena that are not obvious enough can only be inferentially known. So only those who have achieved jhāna can empirically observe the unique characteristics of jhānic phenomena; those who have not attained jhāna may only know them inferentially. Therefore, one who has not attained jhāna should not contemplate jhānic phenomena but only sensual phenomena. However, one can inferentially perceive jhānic phenomena when one's empirical insight based on sensual phenomena matures. So do not think that there are some worldly phenomena that a yogi cannot perceive.

In the case of sensual phenomena (*kāmāvacara*), one should only note the obvious mental and physical phenomena. One should not note vague objects by imagining them based on scriptures. To confirm this point, the *Visuddhimagga* says:

> Even among distinct, mundane objects, one should make effort to contemplate objects that are obvious and easy enough to observe.[188]

Among the twenty-eight kinds of physical phenomena, one should only meditate on the eighteen kinds[189] that are referred to in the following ways: physical matter (*rūpārūpa*), i.e. real, ultimate matter; concretely produced matter (*nipphannarūpa*), i.e. matter that is produced by kamma, consciousness, temperature, and nutrition; matter possessing real characteristics (*salakkhaṇarūpa*), i.e. matter that is marked by the three characteristics of appearance, existence, and disappearance; and matter to be comprehended by insight (*sammasanarūpa*).

The remaining types of nonconcretely produced matter (*anipphannarūpa*) should not be noted. As the subcommentary says:

> Discern only concretely produced matter, not matter characterized as mutable.[190]

This should be understood as follows: one should only observe concretely produced matter, matter possessing real characteristics, and matter to be comprehended by vipassanā—all of these are collectively referred to as the eighteen kinds of physical matter. One should not observe the space element and the five types of mutable material phenomena (*vikārarūpa*), which consist of bodily intimation manifested as bodily movement, (*kāyaviññattirūpa*), verbal intimation manifested as verbal expression (*vacīviññattirūpa*), lightness (*lahutā*), malleability (*mudutā*), and wieldiness (*kammaññatā*). Nor should one observe the four characteristics of material phenomena (*lakkhaṇarūpa*), which consist of production (*upacaya*), continuity (*santati*), decay (*jaratā*), and impermanence (*aniccatā*).

Among mental phenomena, ordinary people and noble trainees (*sekkha*) at the first seven stages of enlightenment cannot observe the mental states that belong only to arahants, who are fully enlightened beings at the eighth stage. So appropriate objects of contemplation for ordinary people, those who take the vehicle of insight to enlightenment, and noble trainees are limited to the eighteen kinds of concretely produced matter, and the forty-five sense-sphere consciousnesses (*kāmāvacaracitta*) and their fifty-two constituent mental factors (*cetasika*).[191]

The Eighteen Kinds of Concretely Produced Matter

1–5. Five sensitivities of eye, ear, nose, tongue, and body
6–12. Seven sense objects of visible form, sound, smell, taste, and touch that are characterized by earth element, fire element, and air element
13–14. Two genders
15. Water element
16. Physical basis of mind called "heart"
17. Nutrition
18. Vitality

The Forty-Five Sense-Sphere Consciousnesses

1–12. Twelve unwholesome consciousnesses
13–29. Seventeen rootless consciousnesses
30–37. Eight great wholesome consciousnesses
38–45. Eight great resultant consciousnesses

Among these mental and physical phenomena, one should essentially observe a single, distinct object.

The phenomena we can experience the moment we see are eye-sensitivity, visible forms, eye-consciousness, and its mental factors. Most often, however, only one of these is obvious enough that we can experience its characteristics. The complete mental process of seeing is composed of thirty-eight units of cognition:[192]

1. One mind-moment that adverts one of the five sense doors to an object (*pañcadvārāvajjana*)
2–3. Two mind-moments that receive a sense impression of the object (*sampaṭicchana*)
4–6. Three mind-moments that investigate the object (*santīraṇa*)
7. One mind-moment that determines the object (*votthapana*)
8–27. Twenty mind-moments that are kammic impulsions that fully perceive or move toward the object (*javana*)

28–38. Eleven mind-moments that register the object (*tadārammaṇa*)

Similarly, we can clearly experience phenomena for the other physical senses as well. We can experience ear-sensitivity, sound, ear-consciousness, and its mental factors with respect to hearing, nose-sensitivity, odor, nose-consciousness, and its mental factors with respect to smelling, tongue-sensitivity, flavor, tongue-consciousness, and its mental factors with respect to tasting, and body-sensitivity, bodily sensation characterized by softness, hardness, cold, warmth, heat, motion, tension, pressure, tightness, or looseness, body-consciousness, and its mental factors with respect to touch.

We can experience our own genders when we are aware of our masculine or feminine appearance. We can experience the water element (*āpodhātu*) when we swallow or spit saliva, or feel the flow of tears, phlegm, or sweat.

During a moment of thinking or observing we can clearly experience the phenomena of the thinking or observing mind, and its physical basis, called the heart-base (*hadayavatthu*). There are thirty-two possible units of mind[193] involved in thought:

1. One mind-moment that adverts the mind to a mental object (*manodvārāvajjana*)
2–9. Eight mind-moments that are wholesome kammic impulsions
10–21. Twelve mind-moments that are unwholesome kammic impulsions
22–32. Eleven mind-moments that register the mental object

In the case of a meditating mind, twenty mind units[194] are represented:

1. One mind-moment that adverts the mind to a mental object
2–9. Eight great wholesome kammic impulsions
10–20. Eleven mind-moments that register the mental object

It should be noted here that wholesome ethical impulsion to insight can sometimes occur without one consciously knowing it (*ñāṇavippayutta*), as reported in the following Pāḷi texts:

> When practicing, a yogi may develop insight through one of the wholesome impulsions, with or without knowing.[195]
>
> Sometimes, being skillful, one may develop insight without realizing it.[196]
>
> From time to time, practicing tranquility or insight meditation over and over again, one may develop insight without realizing it.[197]

We can experience nutrition when our strength increases or decreases depending on nutrition or malnutrition. We can clearly experience the vitality that depends on continuously arising sensitivity, gender, and heart-base when these phenomena are clear. As stated above, you should essentially note the most obvious object among them.

Should we observe internal or external phenomena?
One should note both internal and external objects. However, one should empirically observe internal phenomena as they arise according to one's acquired perfections and understanding. When one's empirical knowledge matures, one can inferentially contemplate external objects as a whole using inferential insight, without distinguishing between them. These are the two ways of the Buddha's disciples. One should mainly note internal objects, the phenomena of one's own experience. The following passage from the subcommentary on the *Anupada Sutta*[198] shows how the Venerable Moggallāna became fully enlightened by meditating on only some of the objects that Buddhist disciples usually observe:

> The phrase "only some of the objects" (*ekadesamevā*) means that, as he was unable to observe the entirety of phenomena, he contemplated only some of the objects according to his acquired perfections. So he observed his own phenomena, and then he observed others' as a whole, without distinguishing them individually. This is the way the Buddha's disciples do it.[199]

One should not seek external objects for insight meditation, because doing so often causes a restless mind. Restlessness, in turn, results in a slower development of concentration and insight knowledge. Even after two weeks or a month, one may gain nothing special. Because those who engage in reflection and thinking based on their general knowledge do not acquire empirical insight, neither do they develop concentration and insight knowledge. This is why external objects should only be noted when they arise at the six sense doors of their own accord. One should strive to continuously observe internal objects. Only by observing one's own internal objects can one's purpose be fulfilled. That is why the *Visuddhimagga-mahāṭīkā* says:

> Initially, one practices insight meditation by contemplating internal or external objects. However, when insight is accomplished by observing internal phenomena, all mental and physical phenomena are also said to have been fully noted in terms of their characteristics.[200]

Should we observe past, future, or present phenomena?

One should only observe present phenomena. When empirical knowledge matures, one understands past and future phenomena using inferential insight. One shouldn't bother with past and future objects, since they cannot be accurately experienced in terms of their unique characteristics and so on. Is it possible, for example, to experience the mental and physical phenomena that occurred in past lives? Can one know whether one had a fair or dark complexion, was able or disabled, male or female? Can one truly know the physical phenomena that happened in the past? Can one know which mental states were experienced at different moments in the past and so on? Can one truly know the mental phenomena that happened in the past? Even in this present life, can one experience accurately what occurred last year, last month, or even yesterday? Indeed, it is impossible to accurately experience the mental and physical phenomena that took place even an hour or a few minutes ago. Even if one does not believe this point, once present objects are observed in practice at the moment they arise, then one can admit that it is so.

There are no means by which to experience future phenomena. We cannot be aware, the moment we lift our right foot, of what will happen when lifting our left foot in the next moment. Although we expect a wholesome mental state, it may be unwholesome; despite our hope for happiness, sadness may arise. While dreaming of pleasure, we may suffer accidents and disasters, such as being attacked with a weapon, having a building collapse around us, taking a nasty fall, fire, drowning, snakebite, stumbling, and so on. We may hope for a long life and happiness, even on our deathbeds. If it were possible to accurately predict the future, astrologers and clairvoyants would be out of work. Predictions about the future may prove to be accurate in some cases, but this is likely just coincidence. We are likely to be right sometimes, after all, when guessing "heads or tails."

Present phenomena are those that occur within the continua of our lives, that is, within our bodies and minds, as well as those that occur at the six sense doors. If one mindfully and attentively observes, one can experience the unique characteristics and so on of a distinctly appearing mental or physical phenomenon. For example, if one is watching the moment a bolt of lightning strikes, one can accurately see where and how it strikes, but if one looks afterward, one cannot perceive exactly where it struck, let alone how it struck. It is also completely impossible to know where and how lightning will strike beforehand. Likewise, one cannot be accurately aware of past and future phenomena. We can only know present phenomena exactly. So don't bother with past and future objects. Empirically observe only the present.

Latent defilements dwell in present phenomena that we have not yet noted. These are called "defilements that lie dormant in sense objects" (*ārammaṇādhiggahita-kilesā*) or "defilements that arise when sense objects are not observed" (*ārammaṇādhiggahituppanna*). Such defilements do not dwell in a phenomenon that has been noted. By observing present objects, we can temporarily remove mental defilements (*tadaṅgappahāna*), and as a result of this, the creation of unwholesome kamma and the negative consequences under the influence of that defilement becomes impossible. I will explain this further below in the section dealing with contemplation of impermanence (*aniccānupassanā*).[201]

As soon as we fail to observe phenomena, that omission leaves defilements dormant in our mental processes. In other words, the concept of solid form (*ghanapaññatti*) has already been impressed on our mental processes, like a picture that has been developed. So whenever we happen to think about what we have seen, heard, smelled, tasted, touched, and thought about in the past, the concept of solid form emerges, and belief in permanence, happiness, and personality follow in its wake. As a result, this concept of solid form is firmly stuck in the mind and cannot be removed, even though we repeatedly reflect on the fact that objects are merely mental and physical phenomena and are impermanent, unsatisfactory, and not-self. We cannot get rid of defilements that believe in permanence, happiness, and personality.

Children who are taught to be unafraid of ghosts will not be scared, even if they see one. They would simply think that they have encountered something strange. In the same way, phenomena that are observed the moment they occur cannot arouse mental defilements, even if one recollects them, since they were not impressed on one's memory as solid persons or things. On the other hand, Burmese children who are taught that a ghost is something dreadful are usually unreasonably frightened of them. It is almost impossible to reeducate them not to be afraid, because the concept of "ghost" has already become deep-seated in their minds. Similarly, it is too late to root out the delusory sense of forms, i.e., the delusory sense of persons or things that have already formed due to our failure to observe them the moment they took place. So it is useless to observe past phenomena, because doing so cannot help to arouse insight knowledge and remove mental defilements.

Future phenomena have yet to come into existence, so observation of them will not help us escape from the delusory sense of solid forms either, if we fail to be aware of them the moment they actually occur. Observing future phenomena will in no way serve the purpose of being aware of their characteristics or remove mental defilements.

Therefore, you should not make great effort to observe past and future phenomena, although you can be aware of them by means of inferential knowledge once your empirical knowledge matures. By observing present phenomena you not only know the true nature of mental and physical phenomena as they arise and disappear, you can also remove defilements. It is reasonable that we should observe only the present. The following verses from the Pāḷi texts prove this point:

> Let not a person revive the past
> Or on the future build his hopes;
> For the past has been left behind
> And the future has not been reached.
> Instead with insight let him see
> Each presently arisen state;
> Let him know that and be sure of it,

Invincibly, unshakeably.
Today the effort must be made;
Tomorrow Death may come, who knows?
No bargain with Mortality
Can keep him and his hordes away,
But one who dwells thus ardently,
Relentlessly, by day, by night—
It is he, the Peaceful Sage has said,
Who has had a single excellent night.[202]

The Buddha explained that when we remember the past, "We becomes attached to the past, recollecting how we used to look." The commentary explains further, "We remember favorably that our complexions had the color of a precious stone." In view of these explanations, it is reasonable to assume that "the past" mentioned here refers to the past in general and not to past lives (*addhātīta*), which only those who achieve jhāna can recall. This discourse was intended not only for those who achieve jhāna but also for ordinary people.

I will now explain how to recall the past and imagine the future from the perspective of ordinary people.

All phenomena that have occurred in the past are gone, so we should not recall them with attachment and wrong view. Phenomena associated with seeing that arose in the past, for example, have ceased to exist; they do not exist now. We might be attached to our past sights, thinking: "My eyes were very clear. I had very good eyesight. I used to be able to see even the smallest things." Or "My face used to be pretty and attractive. My eyes, eyebrows, arms, and legs were beautiful. My complexion was very clear." Or, "I had so many beautiful clothes and so many different things." Or, "I once met such-and-such a person. I had a very good time with him or her." In this way, being attached to something or someone we have seen in the past, happy memories arise. We develop a wrong view of the past if we have the delusion that there is an "I" or a being that sees, that he or she saw someone, or that a person he or she saw has died, was reborn, or is no longer reborn. So we should not recall past seeing with attachment and a wrong view. The same is true for the rest of the senses: hearing, smelling, tasting, touching, and thinking. As for a meditator, he or she should not recall good or bad times he or she had during previous practice.

Do not dream of the future. Future phenomena have not yet come into existence; they do not yet exist now. Spending one's time imagining the future is like wasting time pondering what one would do if one won the lottery. So we should not dream of the future, thinking with regard to future seeing: "May my eyes remain good for the rest of my life. May my eyesight never become poor." Or, "May I remain attractive forever." Or, "May I see beautiful people and things." Or, "May I always have eyesight" and so on. The same is true for the rest of the senses, such as hearing and so forth. As for a meditator, he or she should not look forward to attaining something special during practice, such as insight knowledge or path and fruition.

The present moment

Whether seeing, hearing, smelling, tasting, touching, walking, standing, sitting, sleeping, bending, stretching, or thinking, whenever one of these phenomena arises in the present, we must observe it in order to realize that it is just a mental and physical phenomenon, and to see its impermanent, unsatisfactory, and impersonal nature. Otherwise, we will become attached to such phenomena and believe that they are permanent, pleasing, favorable, beautiful, and obey our wishes. As a result of doing so, we will develop wrong views. This is how unwholesome thoughts that spring up from attachment and wrong views come about.

When we see a person, we are likely to identify who it is, whether it is a man or a woman, whose son or daughter it is, whose mother or father it is, why this person is here, what type of personality he or she has, how this person behaves, and so on. Furthermore, if we find that person attractive, we will become attached to him or her, thinking lustfully: "How lovely they look! How polite they are! How gentle their behavior is! How nice it would be if I could have a conversation with them! How wonderful it would be if I got a chance to be friendly with them!" On the other hand, if we find that person objectionable, we will regard him or her with disgust, thinking: "How terrible they look! What an unpleasant personality they have! How badly they treat me! How nice it would be if they got in trouble, or were tortured, or died!" This kind of mental state "yields to temptations of attachment and wrong view" (*saṃhīra*) and is "ruined by attachment and wrong view" (*saṃkuppa*). The same is true of the mind when it yields to the temptation of, or is ruined by, attachment and wrong view due to a failure to note the phenomena involved in hearing and so on, the moment they take place.

On the other hand, when we are able to note, each time one notes, no sensual thoughts spring up from attachment and wrong view. Such a noting mind "does not yield to temptations of attachment and wrong view" (*asaṃhīra*) and "is not ruined by attachment and wrong view" (*asaṃkuppa*). By observing present objects, we should develop insight until reaching the phase called "contemplation of relinquishment" (*paṭinissaggānupassanā*), which includes insight knowledge of equanimity toward formations (*saṅkhārupekkhāñāṇa*), insight knowledge of adaptation (*anulomañāṇa*), knowledge of change-of-lineage (*gotrabhūñāṇa*), path knowledge (*maggañāṇa*), and fruition knowledge (*phalañāṇa*).

Then and there

As mentioned in the *Visuddhimagga*, we may ask here, with regard to a remark made by Venerable Mahākaccāyana, "Doesn't the word "the present life" (*addhāpaccuppanna*)[203] refer to the period between birth and death?"

That is true only in the case of mental states that do not yield to the temptations of attachment and wrong view and are not ruined by attachment and wrong view. However, it is not possible to develop insight by observing, in general, all phenomena arising between birth and death by conjecture, by imagining them before they take place, or by reflecting about them long after they have passed. Rather, we must develop insight by observing phenomena the moment they take place. To make this point clear, the commentary explains a passage from the *Khuddaka Nikāya*:

> The phrase "then and there" (*tattha tattha*) means that even though a phenomenon occurs in the present life, one should observe it right then and there by means of the seven contemplations,[204] beginning with contemplation of impermanence (*aniccānupassanā*).[205]

The word "even" (*pi*) in this commentarial passage indicates that even though phenomena that occur between birth and death are considered "the present," it is not possible to observe them all as a whole. All one needs to do is note present phenomena as soon as they arise. The phrase "then and there" means that one should observe an object the moment it takes place, and not before or after.

So objects of insight meditation must be phenomena of the serial present (*santatipaccuppanna*), limited to a single mental process, and phenomena of the momentary present (*khaṇapaccuppanna*), restricted to a single mind-moment, and not phenomena of "the present life," which spans from birth until death. As is the case for insight meditation, the supernormal ability to read others' thoughts (*cetopariya abhiññāṇa*) also observes only phenomena of the serial present. That is why the *Visuddhimagga* and its commentary say:

> Here, the Saṃyutta commentary says that "the present life" is restricted to a single process of mind. That is well said.[206]

> "The present life" is defined as the limited period of a single mental process, not the entire period between birth and death. This is the explanation from the commentary.[207]

According to these Pāḷi texts, it is quite clear that the phenomena that are experienced through the supernormal ability to read others' thoughts and through empirical insight are those associated with a single mental process, not those associated with an entire life. However, all phenomena from birth to death are taken into consideration in the process of inferential insight. In conclusion, according to the *Bhaddekaratta Sutta* and the commentaries, the objects of empirical insight are only present phenomena at the time of their arising.

The teaching of the *Satipaṭṭhāna Sutta*

The *Satipaṭṭhāna Sutta* and its commentaries also explicitly state that only present phenomena should be noted. In the section on contemplation of the body, we are instructed to observe the present matter thusly:

> When walking, a bhikkhu understands: "I am walking"; . . .[208]

We are never directed to note past and future objects along the lines of: "After having walked, a bhikkhu knows, 'I have walked,'" or "When about to walk, a bhikkhu knows 'I will be walking.'"

In the section on feeling (*vedanā*), we are instructed to note present feelings thusly:

> When feeling a pleasant feeling, a bhikkhu understands, "I feel a pleasant feeling"; . . .[209]

We are not instructed to note past and future feelings, along the lines of: "After having felt a pleasant feeling, a bhikkhu knows, 'I felt a pleasant feeling,'" or "When about to feel a pleasant feeling, a bhikkhu knows, 'I will feel a pleasant feeling.'"

Also in the section on the contemplation of mental objects, the Buddha instructs us to note present objects thusly:

> There being sensual desire in him, a bhikkhu understands: "There is sensual desire in me"; . . .[210]

He does not instruct us to observe past and future desire, along the lines of: "Be aware of sensual desire that arose," or "Be aware of sensual desire that will arise."

The section on the contemplation of mind explains that we should meditate on our minds thusly:

> Here a bhikkhu understands mind affected by lust as mind affected by lust . . .[211]

In this case, the statement is vague with regard to the time when we are to note the object. To clarify this point the commentaries explain:

> The moment a state of mind arises one observes either one's own mind or another's mind; or sometimes one's own mind and sometimes another's mind. This is called "contemplating mind as mind."[212]

The point of this commentary is that contemplation of mind (*cittānupassanā*) is noting the mind the moment it arises. Here I translate the word *sallakkhento* as "one observes," in other words, "a person notes." The terms "to note," "to observe," and "to bear in mind" are all synonyms for the purposes of insight practice.

Some disregard this commentarial explanation and misinterpret the passage as an indication of how to meditate on the mind. According to these people, contemplating mind consists of reflecting in this way: "These eight kinds of consciousness rooted in greed are called a mind affected by lust (*sarāgacitta*). Mundane wholesome or indeterminate (*abyākata*) kinds of consciousness are called a mind not affected by lust." These people hold this opinion because they do not pay attention to the commentary, or their misunderstanding arises because they do not grasp the commentator's point, and neither do they understand the right method of insight meditation, nor its true nature.

It is obvious that observing the mind the moment it arises is contemplation of mind. It is impossible to really observe the mind, whether one's own or another's, in the past, present, or future by reflecting on the eight kinds of consciousness rooted in greed that are called "mind affected by lust." The same applies for minds not affected by lust. All that one would perceive with that kind of reflection would be conceptual ideas, such as the names and numbers of the classes of mind affected by lust and so forth. Contemplation of mind cannot be developed in the least in that manner, and the notion that it can be is simply a misinterpretation.

This misinterpretation becomes especially obvious when applied to the case of the supernormal ability to read others' thoughts. The Buddha explains that in this case, others' thoughts should be experienced in exactly the same way as one experiences one's own when contemplating mind:

> He understands a mind affected by lust as affected by lust . . .[213]

And the commentary explains it in the same way.

If one believes the view of such people, then when one reflects, "The eight kinds of consciousness rooted in greed are called a mind affected by lust," one would have attained the supernormal ability to read others' thoughts. But this is not the case. So it is obvious that the commentary only uses the line "He understands a mind affected by lust as affected by lust . . ." as an illustration. Only when someone definitely knows another's mind the moment it arises can we say that he or she has the supernormal ability to read others' thoughts. Likewise, the explanation regarding contemplation of mind is only used as an illustration and not as an example of how to practice contemplation of mind.

Thus evidence from Pāḷi texts and their commentaries is good enough to confirm that we can only develop empirical insight by observing present phenomena the moment they take place. If you still have doubts on this point, further evidence will be provided in the section below on lessons to learn from those who take the vehicle of tranquility to enlightenment and in chapter 6. If you are still confused after reading those, then you may have deep-seated doubt that will prevent you from realizing the causes of liberation for noble ones in this life.

Preaching order and practice order

> Any physical phenomenon, whether past, future, or present, internal or external, obvious or subtle, base or exalted, far or near, should be observed entirely in terms of impermanence. That is one type of comprehension (*sammasana*) of mind and body.[214]

One may wonder, "Shouldn't one observe past phenomena first?" The answer to this question is "no." The order given to the categories of phenomena in the above passage is the order used for preaching, not for practice. Moreover, the insight knowledge mentioned here that comprehends (*sammasana*) phenomena in terms of impermanence and so on is not empirical insight but inferential insight. So this Pāḷi passage cannot be used to prove that one should observe past phenomena first.

Insight meditation is an uninterrupted observation of all phenomena as they arise at the six sense doors, such that one can realize the unique characteristics and so on of mental and physical phenomena as they really are. So if one observes in the sequence mentioned in the Pāḷi text, would one be noting the phenomena as they arise? After the past, the present arises, not the future. After the future, the present does not arise; it arose before. It is not that phenomena that are external, subtle, and so on arise only after phenomena that are internal, obvious, and so on. So if one observes future phenomena after having observed past phenomena, one misses the present phenomena that come in between. If one observes the present after the future, that would be in reverse. At the moment of lifting the right foot, one cannot note the subsequent lifting of the left foot in the future and then return to the present lifting of the right foot. Even if such a thing were possible, it would not help one to develop insights, such as arising and passing or dissolution (*bhaṅga*), which can only be cultivated by observing present objects.

The passage above also uses the phrase "internal or external," but that doesn't mean that one should observe internal objects first. It is quite possible to observe an external object first and then an internal one. This is why the commentary says:

> After having observed external objects, one arrives at (path knowledge while noting) internal ones.[215]

As explained above, it is impossible to understand the unique characteristics of individual mental and physical phenomena by observing past phenomena that no longer exist, or future phenomena that have not yet come into existence. Since we do not even experience the unique characteristics of these past and future phenomena, it is impossible to understand their conditioned characteristics (*saṅkhatalakkhaṇā*) of appearance, existence, and disappearance, let alone their universal characteristics (*sāmaññalakkhaṇā*) of impermanence, unsatisfactoriness, and not-self. So, to reiterate, the elements of the Pāḷi passage above are organized according to the preaching order (*desanākkama*) and not practice order (*paṭipattikkama*).

Inferential insight: knowledge by comprehension

As mentioned above, the insight knowledge mentioned here that comprehends phenomena in terms of impermanence and so on does not refer to empirical insight but to inferential insight. It means that one observes all physical phenomena as a group, rather than individually, one by one. For example, one may observe the entire range of feelings taken as a whole, rather than noting individual feelings from moment to moment. It is not possible, when one does this, to experience the unique characteristics of feelings, so one develops only inferential insight.

Inferential insight follows mature empirical insight and considers all phenomena as a group in terms of impermanence and so on. There is no limit to the worldly objects that one may consider using inferential insight. Those with sharp intellects or with good general knowledge can reflect on a wide range of objects. This is why the *Paṭisambhidāmagga* and *Visuddhimagga* describe a wide range for this type of insight. While empirical knowledge that comprehends phenomena in terms of impermanence and so on takes place only before the insight knowledge of arising and passing away (*udayabbayañāṇa*), this type of inferential insight knowledge that comprehends phenomena in terms of impermanence and so on can be developed not only before but also after the insight knowledge of arising and passing away and the insight knowledge of dissolution. The Pāḷi references to support this will be given later in the sections on those types of insight.

Inferential insight is referred to by several names: "knowledge that comprehends all phenomena as a whole" (*kalāpasammasana*), since it comprehends the entirety of phenomena as a group, and "inferential insight" (*nayavipassanā*), "inferential observation" (*nayadassana*), or "inferential attention" (*nayamanasikāra*), since it perceives phenomena following empirical insight. The following Pāḷi passage makes clear the reason for referring to this knowledge as inferential observation and inferential attention:

> Even if one empirically sees even a single conditioned phenomenon to be impermanent, one can inferentially understand that all other conditioned phenomena are also impermanent. Thus the phrase "when one realizes all conditioned phenomena to be impermanent" refers to inferential, rather than empirical, insight.[216]

This commentary uses the word "even" (*pi*) to mean that if through empirical insight one finds just a single conditioned phenomenon to be impermanent, let alone many, inferential insight will spontaneously follow. This inferential insight is also called "inferential attention." The phrase "sees . . . to be impermanent" is explained as referring to understanding through empirical insight, and "one can inferentially understand" refers to inferential insight, also known as "inferential attention," "inferential observation," and "inferential insight." Since this comprehension of phenomena is done as a whole, the *Visuddhimagga* calls it "knowledge that comprehends all phenomena as a whole."

The phrase "refers to inferential, rather than empirical, insight" indicates other passages in the Pāḷi scriptures, like "All conditioned phenomena are impermanent . . . all conditioned phenomena are suffering . . . all phenomena are not self. A Tathāgata awakens to this and breaks through to it . . ."[217] This shows that after empirical insight has taken place, one realizes all conditioned phenomena by observing them as a whole by means of inferential insight. So all these passages from the discourses were aimed at explaining how to observe only by means of inferential insight and not by means of empirical insight. Thus we can conclude that inferential insight is not a kind of insight that is developed first. Rather, it spontaneously happens following empirical insight.

What should be emphasized is this: whatever method one uses, the mental and physical phenomena that one takes as objects are all present ones. The section of the *Visuddhimagga* that explains how to develop insight knowledge that comprehends phenomena in terms of impermanence and so on describes this.[218]

Lessons to Learn from Those Who Take the Vehicle of Tranquility to Enlightenment

Now, as an example, I will show the method of practicing insight meditation of those who take the vehicle of tranquility to insight. The method described here is both directly based on the *Satipaṭṭhāna Sutta* and also strongly supported by many other Pāḷi texts. Some people, however, may need more evidence to overcome their doubt and accept the right method.

> Here, quite secluded from sensual pleasures, secluded from unwholesome states, a bhikkhu enters upon and abides in the first jhāna, which is accompanied by applied and sustained thought, with rapture and pleasure born of seclusion.
>
> Whatever exists therein of material form, feeling, perception, formations, and consciousness, he sees these states as impermanent, as suffering, as a disease, as a tumor, as a barb, as a calamity, as an affliction, as alien, as disintegrating, as void, as not-self.[219]

This Pāḷi passage explicitly states that one who achieves jhāna enters the first jhāna as a precondition for practicing insight. After one emerges from jhāna, one immediately practices insight by observing only those phenomena that are present in the first jhāna. The same is true for the other fine-material and immaterial absorptions. Many other Pāḷi texts describe this same method of practicing insight for those who take the vehicle of tranquility to enlightenment. They agree that one who achieves jhāna practices by first entering any of the jhānas, and then, after emerging from the absorption, observing the phenomena present in that jhāna.

On the other hand, no Pāḷi text says that anyone practices insight by considering, pondering, or imagining phenomena. Keep this point in mind as a guideline. The phrase "as impermanent" (*aniccatā*) in the above passage should not give anyone the false notion that it is possible to develop the first two types of knowledge—knowledge that discerns mental and physical phenomena and knowledge that discerns conditionality—by simply considering or pondering phenomena without seeing phenomena as impermanent and so on. Instead, one should infer that one cannot develop these first two insights without directly experiencing the characteristics of phenomena. The *Visuddhimagga*, in accord with Pāḷi texts, says the following:

> Purification of view (*diṭṭhivisuddhi*) means to see mental and physical phenomena as they really are. In order to develop it, those who achieve jhāna and practice insight by observing jhānic phenomena must emerge from any fine material or immaterial jhāna, except neither perception nor nonperception, and then observe the jhāna factors, such as initial application of mind, and their mental factors, such as mental contact, perception (*saññā*), intention (*cetanā*), mind, and so on, in terms of their unique characteristics, functions, and such.[220]

According to the subcommentary, an inexperienced meditator who has attained jhāna and who practices insight by observing jhānic phenomena has to omit observing the highest jhāna, called "neither perception nor nonperception," as it is beyond his or her reach. This will be particularly obvious when we look at the *Anupada Sutta* below.

The phrase "in terms of their unique characteristics, functions, and such" (*lakkhaṇarasādivasena*) indicates that those who achieve jhāna and practice insight by observing jhānic states should observe the characteristics, functions, and so on of the jhāna factors and their mental constituents, as opposed to their names, forms, shapes, numbers, and so on. When we say "I see the moon from below" (*candaṃ heṭṭhimatala vasena passāmi*), the word "from" (*vasena*) indicates the particular perspective from which one sees the moon—that is, in terms of being below it. This implicitly excludes the possibility of seeing it from above at the same time. Likewise, when the above passage says "observe . . . in terms of their unique characteristics, functions, and such" (*lakkhaṇarasādi vasena pariggahetabbā*), the phrase "in terms of" (*vasena*) indicates that one should make an effort to see phenomena from the particular perspective of their characteristics, functions, and so on.[221] In this case, characteristics, functions, and so on of phenomena are their ultimate reality, and to perceive their unique characteristics and so on means to completely, not partially, perceive ultimate reality. Mental contact, for example, has the characteristic of mind being in contact with its object. To directly experience this characteristic is not a partial knowledge but a complete one. So it is important that we interpret the Pāḷi word *vasena* correctly in this case.

Furthermore, the reason the subcommentary does not mention observation of physical objects is that the first things to appear to those who achieve jhāna are often the jhāna factors and their mental constituents. So one mostly observes mental phenomena at first. Another possible reason for the omission is that the way in which physical phenomena should be observed is included later in the section of the commentary that describes methods of observation for pure insight practitioners. So only a general explanation is given with regard to this topic. It may also be because priority should be given to the observation of mind, or because mind and body cannot be observed at the same time. For these reasons, the text later explains how to observe the material phenomenon of the heart (*hadayarūpa*) that is the basis for jhāna.

So the passage from the *Visuddhimagga* accords with the above passage from the *Aṅguttara Nikāya*. The following three passages drawn from subcommentaries show that we should not consider the Pāḷi text to be incomplete because it doesn't mention the attainment of the highest immaterial jhāna or physical phenomena. The subcommentaries explain this as follows:

> Mental and physical phenomena, being diametric opposites of each other, cannot be observed at the same time.[222]

Mental phenomena are able to know objects, while physical ones are not able to know objects. Thus they are diametrically opposed and cannot be observed together:

> Most of those who have achieved jhāna and who practice insight by observing jhānic phenomena begin practicing insight by mainly observing mental phenomena. On the other hand, most practitioners who take the vehicle of insight to enlightenment mainly observe physical phenomena.[223]

I will explain how to begin by observing physical phenomena first in chapter 5 below.

> When observing mainly physical phenomena, one observes the in- and out-breath. When observing mainly mental phenomena, one observes the jhāna factors.[224]

The phrase "mainly mental phenomena" (*arūpamukhena*) means that among simultaneously arising mental and physical phenomena one only observes distinctly mental phenomena. One doesn't observe physical phenomena. However, even if one's main focus is on mental phenomena, both mental and physical phenomena must be observed. The same applies in terms of mainly observing physical phenomena.

Observation of the in- and out-breath

The quote from the Dīgha Nikāya subcommentary says that those who have achieved jhāna and who practice insight by observing jhānic states observe the in- and out-breath when observing a physical object. This is because it is specifically explaining practice with the in- and out-breath (*ānāpāna*). Actually, those who have achieved jhāna and who practice insight by observing jhānic phenomena may observe other physical objects as well when observing physical objects, not only the in- and out-breath.

When considering these Pāḷi texts, we should be careful not to develop erroneous ideas. For example, it is incorrect to say that the observation of the in- and out-breath can only be used for tranquility (*samatha*) but not for insight (*vipassanā*). It is also incorrect to say that only one who has achieved jhāna can develop insight by observing the in- and out-breath, owing to the fact that he or she has just emerged from the jhāna. There is not any Pāḷi text, commentary, or subcommentary that says, "Among sensual phenomena,[225] such-and-such objects are only for those who have achieved jhāna and who practice insight by observing jhānic phenomena, and such-and-such are only for those who take the insight vehicle." Any sense-sphere phenomena that one who has achieved jhāna and who practices insight by observing jhānic phenomena uses to develop insight can also be used by a practitioner of pure insight. The only difference is that observation of the conceptual form of the breath produces tranquility, while attention to its touch and movement produces insight.

This is why, in the *Ānāpānasati Sutta*, the Buddha says:

> I say that this is a certain body among the bodies, namely in-breathing and out-breathing (*assāsapassāsa*).[226]

This statement indicates that the breath is not merely a concept but is something that ultimately exists and can be empirically experienced. According to the commentary, the in- and out-breath is a manifestation of the air element that is one of four empirical physical bodies or dimensions: earth, water, fire, and air. It is also associated with the dimension of air pressure, a tangible sense base (*phoṭṭhabbāyatana*) in the model that enumerates twenty-five physical bodies. This enumeration of twenty-five is found in the commentaries to the *Mahāgopālaka Sutta*[227] contained in the Mūlapaṇṇāsa section of the Majjhima Nikāya, and in the Aṅguttara Nikāya.

According to Pāḷi texts,[228] those who have achieved jhāna and who practice insight by observing jhānic phenomena should observe an object that is obvious in the present moment, such as jhāna consciousness, its physical basis, or physical phenomena that have arisen based on that mind. So taking the example of one who has achieved jhāna and who practices insight by observing jhānic phenomena, a practitioner of pure insight should know to observe a phenomena that is distinct in the present moment. The only difference between the two is that those who have achieved jhāna are able to clearly observe phenomena related to jhāna, while practitioners of pure insight must note other phenomena since phenomena related to jhāna are not accessible to them. This is the only difference; the way of observing phenomena does not differ. Therefore, in a moment of seeing, a practitioner of pure insight should observe eye-consciousness and its mental factors, their physical basis, or the visible object. The same is true for the other physical senses: hearing, smell, taste, and touch. In a moment of thought, one can observe the thinking mind and its mental factors, the observing mind and its mental factors, the mind's physical basis, the object one is thinking about, or physical phenomena that arise due to that mind.

It isn't necessary, however, to observe all mental and physical phenomena in great detail, considering them as they are expounded in the Abhidhamma. One should only observe one of these phenomena: the one that is most distinct. It is impossible to be empirically aware of two or more phenomena at the same time. For example, the unique characteristics of the earth element and mental contact are different from those of the water element and feeling. One cannot empirically experience these different unique characteristics at the same time. However, if one notes and realizes one of these mental and physical phenomena that happen at the same time, the purpose of noting and understanding is fulfilled.

To what extent must insight be purified?

One might imagine that all enlightened persons experience phenomena in the same way, or that they became enlightened only after experiencing all phenomena in detail as they are described in the Pāḷi texts and commentaries. But in practice, the depth of one's realization varies according to the perfections that one has acquired. A person who is fit for liberation and is of sharp intelligence (*tikkhabhabba-puggala*) can have the most complete and detailed understanding available within a disciple's (*sāvaka*) range of understanding. However, that person's understanding is still not as comprehensive as explained in the Abhidhamma and the discourses. This will become obvious when we deal with the *Anupada Sutta*.

If a person is of dull intelligence but fit for liberation (*mandabhabba-puggala*), with only the minimum insight needed to become enlightened he or she will attain understanding of the path and its fruit. It says in the Majjhima Nikāya commentary:

> Disciples may become enlightened by experiencing only some of the primary material elements.[229]

A similar point is made by the answers of four arahants questioned in the *Kiṃsukopama Sutta*.[230] The question raised there is:

> "To what extent should one's vision be purified to become an arahant?"[231]

The first answer

> "When, friend, a bhikkhu understands as they really are the origin and passing away of the six bases for contact, in this way his vision is well purified."[232]

A monk who had become an arahant by observing only the six internal sense bases gave this answer. His answer implies that he did not observe any external phenomena at all. He observed only the six internal sense bases that include the mind and the five sensitivities of the eye, ear, nose, tongue, and body. He did not observe any other physical phenomena nor did he observe any mental factors. Nevertheless, this method led him to the fruition of an arahant, so who would dare to contradict it? As he was basically observing the six internal sense bases, the purpose of noting and understanding the six external sense bases was also fulfilled at the same time. This is in agreement with the detailed explanations given in the Pāḷi texts and commentaries, because observing the six internal sense bases is said therein to be "noting and understanding all mental and physical phenomena."

The second answer

> "When, friend, a bhikkhu understands as they really are the origin and passing away of the five aggregates subject to clinging, in this way his vision is well purified."[233]

This answer is complete as stated.

The third answer

> "When, friend, a bhikkhu understands as they really are the origin and passing away of the four great elements, in this way his vision is well purified."[234]

This answer implies that this arahant meditated on nothing but the four fundamental elements. He did not observe any other physical phenomena nor did he observe any mental phenomena. Nonetheless, his method was also effective. As he was basically observing the four primary material elements, the purpose of noting and understanding the other mental and physical phenomena occurring simultaneously was also fulfilled at the same time. This does not contradict the detailed explanations given in the Pāḷi texts and commentaries. These texts only give an abridged explanation of how different people observe and understand phenomena. It doesn't mean that every person has to observe and understand the whole range of phenomena.

The fourth answer

> "When, friend, a bhikkhu understands as it really is: 'Whatever is subject to origination is all subject to cessation,' in this way his vision is well purified."[235]

This answer is also complete as stated.

On this occasion, the monk who asked the question had the idea that all arahants have the same experience and that they know all mental and physical phenomena. He was dissatisfied with the arahants' answers, not only because none of them mentioned the whole range of experiences by observing mental and physical phenomena, but also because their answers differed.

He then asked the Buddha to explain the reason for this, and the Buddha replied thusly:

> ". . . those superior men answered as they were disposed, in just the way their own vision had been well purified."[236]

This means that each of the arahants answered according to how he had noted until becoming an arahant and that all four of these ways are correct ways for attaining arahantship.

Venerable Sāriputta's method

According to the Pāḷi texts and commentaries mentioned above, it is perfectly clear that one cannot observe all the mental and physical phenomena that simultaneously arise in the detailed way they are explained in the scriptures of the Abhidhamma. When one observes one distinct physical or mental object at the moment of seeing, one fulfills the purpose of observing and understanding all the other mental and physical phenomena that are happening at the same time, and one can attain the fruition of an arahant.

Here I will explain the remarkable way in which the Venerable Sāriputta meditated, as mentioned in the *Anupada Sutta*:

> "During half a month, bhikkhus, Sāriputta had insight into states one by one as they occurred. Now Sariputta's insight into states one by one as they occurred was this:
>
> "Here Bhikkhus, quite secluded from sensual pleasures, secluded from unwholesome states, Sāriputta entered upon and abided in the first jhāna, which is accompanied by applied and sustained thought, with rapture and pleasure born of seclusion.
>
> "And the states in the first jhāna—the applied thought, the sustained thought, the rapture, the pleasure, and the unification of mind; the contact, feeling, perception, volition, and mind; the zeal, decision, energy, mindfulness, equanimity, and attention[237]—these states were defined by him one by one as they occurred; known to him those states arose, known they were present, known they disappeared. He understood thus: 'So indeed, these states, not having been, come into being; having been, they vanish.'"[238]

Insight into states one by one as they occur

Venerable Sāriputta became an arahant by observing the states of attainment one by one as they occurred for fifteen days. In short, this is how he practiced: entering the first jhāna he could distinguish each of the sixteen phenomena contained in that jhāna.[239] Venerable Sāriputta clearly perceived the beginning, middle, and end of these phenomena—that is to say, their appearance, existing, and the disappearance. Thus Venerable Sāriputta understood, "These phenomena, which did not exist before I entered the jhāna, have now appeared. After having appeared, they disappear again." He observed all the other fine-material and immaterial jhānas up to the third immaterial jhāna in the same way. Among the phenomena observed were a few changes: some jhāna factors were not present anymore while others were present.

To explain this in more detail: Venerable Sāriputta entered the first jhāna and then observed that jhāna itself. After that he entered the second jhāna and observed that jhāna itself. In the same way, he entered the eight attainments one after the other and also practiced insight by observing the jhāna itself. This is called "insight into states one by one as they occur" (*anupadadhamma-vipassanā*). According to another definition in the Pāḷi texts, insight knowledge that observes the attainments one by one as they occur means that, when one has entered one of the jhānas, one observes the various jhāna factors of that state of jhāna consciousness one by one as they occur. It means "insight that observes phenomena contained in a jhāna consciousness one by one as they occur."

The commentary defines insight into states one by one as they occur as follows:

> He practices insight in the order of attainment (*samāpatti*),[240] or of the jhānic factors.[241]

According to the second definition it seems that after having entered the jhāna only one time, one continuously observes it sixteen times. However, the *Paṭisambhidāmagga* states that after observing an object vanish, one should immediately meditate on the observing mind itself.[242] The *Visuddhimagga* also says that the first mind should be observed by a second one, and that, in turn, should be observed by the third one.[243] Thus these texts explain a method of "one mind per observation." Thus, after having entered a jhāna the first time, one observes initial application of mind; after having entered a jhāna the second time, one observes sustained application of mind. It is reasonable to accept that, using this method, one enters the jhāna sixteen times and observes its factors one by one sixteen times. Venerable Sāriputta became an arahant by practicing both kinds of insight one by one for fifteen days.

How Sāriputta developed insight one by one

Venerable Sāriputta entered the jhānas one by one in order. Immediately after emerging from each jhāna, he observed initial application and so on, and understood their unique characteristics. So he understood the unique characteristics of these states:

1. Initial application of mind (*vitakka*) characterized by initial application
2. Sustained application of mind (*vicāra*) characterized by sustained application

3. Rapture (*pīti*) characterized by rapture
4. Pleasure (*sukha*) characterized by pleasure
5. One-pointedness of mind, that is to say, concentration (*citte-kaggatā*) characterized by one-pointedness of mind
6. Mental contact (*phassa*) characterized by mental contact
7. Feeling (*vedanā*) characterized by feeling
8. Perception (*saññā*) characterized by perception
9. Intention or urging (*cetanā*) characterized by intention
10. Cognition (*citta*) characterized by cognition
11. Desire to act (*chanda*) characterized by the desire to act
12. Determination (*adhimokkha*) characterized by determination
13. Exertion (*vīriya*) characterized by exertion or effort
14. Mindfulness (*sati*) characterized by mindfulness
15. Balanced equanimity (*tatramajjhattupekkhā*) characterized by balanced equanimity and balanced observation
16. Attention (*manasikāra*) characterized by attention

In this way, he distinguished and understood these sixteen states one by one. They were clearly perceptible as they appeared, existed, and disappeared; he understood that they freshly arose and immediately vanished. However, one should not get the wrong idea that he realized their appearance, existence, and disappearance by means of the jhāna consciousness itself, or that the jhāna and other perceptions arose simultaneously. To clarify this, the commentary says:

> It is impossible for a fingertip to touch itself. In the same way, a particular consciousness cannot understand its own appearance, presence, and disappearance. It is impossible for a particular jhāna to understand itself. If two consciousnesses were to occur at the same time, one could understand the appearance, existence, and disappearance of the other. But it is impossible for two contacts, feelings, perceptions, intentions, or consciousnesses to occur at the same time. They only happen one by one. Different consciousnesses cannot happen at the same time.[244]

Because Venerable Sāriputta could distinguish and understand the physical base and objects that were the bases of those sixteen phenomena, when he emerged from the jhāna and began to observe it, he clearly knew the appearance of those phenomena, as if it were happening right at that moment. Likewise, he clearly knew their existence and disappearance as if they were happening right at that moment.

Observing and understanding such distinct phenomena is referred to "observing and understanding a period limited to a single mind-moment," as in the case of insight knowledge of arising and passing away and insight knowledge of dissolution. This is why in the passage above the Buddha said, "known to him those states arose," and so on. Understanding "not having been, they come into being" is knowledge that understands arising or appearance (*udaya*). Understanding "having been, they vanish" is insight knowledge that understands passing away or disappearance (*vaya*). This broad explanation of the meaning accords with the commentary.

Venerable Moggallāna's method

Venerable Sāriputta practiced in this way for fifteen days and became an arahant. However, it took Venerable Moggallāna only seven days to become an arahant. It took Venerable Sāriputtā, who had greater knowledge, a week more than it took Venerable Moggallāna to complete his practice because he practiced on a wider scale. That is, he practiced by means of insight knowledge that observes the states of attainment one by one as they occur. Venerable Moggallāna's practice only took him seven days because it was not as all encompassing. The commentary relates:

> By meditating on only a few of the phenomena within a disciple's reach, like touching only a few spots of ground with a walking stick, it took Venerable Moggallāna only seven days to become fully enlightened.
>
> On the other hand, Venerable Sāriputtā contemplated all phenomena, aside from those that only buddhas and silent buddhas (*paccekabuddha*) can know. So it took him half a month to attain arahantship and he knew that it would be impossible for any other disciple to understand the wisdom he had gained.[245]

The subcommentary says:

> What is contemplated is called a "meditative object," and is the domain of insight.[246]

Internal phenomena that are known empirically and external phenomena that are known inferentially are the domain of insight disciples. Consider well the phrase "touching only a few spots of ground with a walking stick" in the passage above. The spots of ground touched by a walking stick as one walks are quite small compared to the surrounding areas of ground that go untouched. Likewise, what disciples observe is very small compared to the phenomena that go unobserved. There were wide gaps even in the practice of the second chief disciple, which justified this comparison of the objects he observed to the spots of ground that a walking stick touches. Imagine how much greater the gaps in the practice would be for "ordinary" fully liberated beings (*arahant*), nonreturners (*anāgāmī*), once returners (*sakadāgāmī*), stream enterers (*sotāpannā*), and ordinary persons.

A note of caution

The Pāḷi texts and commentary say that, in the case of insight, Venerable Sāriputta—who was able to observe the entire range of states possible for a disciple—clearly knew at most only the sixteen states that he observed one by one. But he actually only knew fifteen states, because among those sixteen states, pleasure (*sukha*) and feeling (*vedanā*) are the same in terms of experience. It is stated in the Abhidhamma that the first jhāna contains thirty-five mental factors. Even if one takes out compassion (*karunā*) and sympathetic joy (*muditā*), which only arise sometimes, one is still left with thirty-three factors. So in the first jhāna there are thirty-four states, including the jhāna consciousness.

In the above discourse and commentary, it was made obvious that he observed only fifteen among these thirty-four states; it is not obvious that he observed the remaining nineteen. The subcommentary mentions two views: "the ācariya's position" (*ācariyavāda*) says, "Only those sixteen states were clear, and therefore only those were observed," whereas "the position of others" (*aparevāda*) is that one should not say that the remaining states were not clear.[247] Although he could only observe sixteen states, Venerable Sāriputta's wisdom is indeed praiseworthy because he could empirically distinguish and observe sixteen states contained in the mind at one time. As this was a great and noble act, those who have systematically practiced insight meditation limitlessly venerate and are amazed by it. But those who have yet to attain true insight knowledge will erroneously think that observing only sixteen states is not yet complete or that it is not difficult. So be especially careful not to have a low opinion of those who can "only" observe these sixteen states.

Some think that insight practice, which is the observation of mental and physical phenomena, is done and complete merely by reflecting on these phenomena based on understanding what one has learned and memorized about their characteristic, function, manifestation, approximate cause, sequence, and so on. The above-mentioned Pāḷi texts, commentaries, and subcommentaries do not approve of this notion. They emphasize repeatedly that insight can only be accomplished when one understands mind and body internally or externally as they really are, whereas academic knowledge accomplishes nothing.

Any objects perceived through reflection and speculation are concepts and not ultimate reality, because they do not really exist either internally or externally. It is equally easy to intellectually understand any phenomena, whether they are the extremely subtle experiences of jhāna, path, fruition, and nibbāna or very gross, sensual objects. One cannot clearly know the sweet call of a Karaviko bird that one has never heard before in the way that one can clearly know the call of parrots that one has heard before. Likewise, one cannot clearly know the jhāna, path, or fruition that one has never experienced in the way that one can see an object that one can experience. The experience of jhāna is very subtle, whereas sensual objects are very gross. Jhāna cannot be as clearly known as sensual objects are.

This being so, how could the way of clearly knowing by reflection be the same? The object of one's reflection that is based on general knowledge is not an object that can be personally experienced. It is not an ultimate reality but only a concept, and thus it does not amount to real insight. Regarding real insight: because the highest formless jhāna was extremely subtle, Venerable Sāriputta also did not know it as clearly as the other jhānas. So he could not observe the states one by one as they occurred. Based on the other jhānas, he had to observe it inferentially by means of knowledge that comprehends all phenomena as a whole (*kalāpasammasana*). The following passage from the Pāḷi illustrates how he observed:

> "Again, bhikkhus, by completely surmounting the base of nothingness (*ākiñcaññāyatana*), Sāriputta entered upon and abided in the base of neither perception nor non-perception.

> "He emerged mindful from that attainment. Having done so, he contemplated the past states, which had ceased and changed, thus: 'So indeed, these states not having been, come into being; having been, they vanish.'"[248]

In the cases of the other jhānas, the Buddha explains in detail how Venerable Sāriputta distinguished and observed initial application, sustained application, and so on of the jhānas one by one as they occurred and how he understood their appearance, existence, and disappearance. In the case of the base of neither perception nor nonperception, however, the Buddha merely gives the general explanation that Venerable Sāriputta "contemplated the past phenomena, which had ceased and changed."

The commentary explains the reason for this as follows:

> The phrase "he contemplated the past phenomena"[249] indicates that the observation of the base of neither perception nor nonperception and its states one by one is a domain of insight only for buddhas. It is not a domain for any disciple [because the states of this jhāna are too subtle for disciples to individually and empirically observe]. This is why [the Buddha explains that Venerable Sāriputta] inferentially observed them as a whole.[250]

In the case of this highest jhāna, only buddhas can distinguish and observe states such as perception, one-pointedness of mind, contact, feeling, and so on one by one as they occur. Disciples like Venerable Sāriputta and others cannot distinguish and observe them one by one. The reason is that this jhāna is extremely subtle, just like the last mental state immediately preceding sound sleep, unconsciousness, or death. Because of its subtlety, disciples cannot clearly know this jhāna. As a result, they cannot observe the phenomena contained in this jhāna one by one and distinguish them by their unique characteristics.

So Venerable Sāriputta had to emerge from that jhāna and observe it as a whole. Like the phenomena of the previous jhānas, the phenomena of this jhāna not having been came into being, and those having been vanished. So he observed it with inferential insight based on the way he had observed the previous jhānas. The Buddha described this jhāna in a general way by explaining inferential insight. "Insight that observes all phenomena as a whole" (*kalāpavipassanā*), "knowledge that comprehends all phenomena as a whole" (*kalāpasammasana*), "inferential insight" (*nayavipassanā*), and "inferential attention" (*nayamanasikāra*) all share the same meaning.

One cannot differentiate the highest jhāna from the lower jhānas through speculation based on general knowledge. This being so, Venerable Sāriputta only had insight into phenomena one by one as they occurred in the lower jhānas that he clearly knew. In the case of the highest jhāna, insight knowledge that observes the phenomena of the attainment one by one as they occur could not happen; instead what took place was the insight that observes all phenomena as a whole. Why was this so?

The reason is as follows: Venerable Sāriputta's observation was neither theoretical (*sutamayañāṇa*) nor analytical knowledge (*cintāmayañāṇa*), but rather it was meditative knowledge (*bhāvanāmayañāṇa*) or a genuine meditative insight that observed actually arising phenomena as they really were. If it were possible for genuine insight to occur by means of reflection based on general knowledge, then Venerable Sāriputta could have practiced insight that observes the states of attainment one by one as they occur by reflecting on the states of the highest jhāna one by one based on general knowledge. But reflection or speculation based on general knowledge does not produce genuine insight. Therefore, I hope you will be able to discard the wrong notion that insight can be produced by merely reflecting on on ideas about mental and physical phenomena, without observing and understanding genuinely existing mental and physical phenomena as they appear and disappear.

> "Others will adhere to their own views, hold on to them tenaciously, and relinquish them with difficulty; we shall not adhere to our own views or hold on to them tenaciously, but shall relinquish them easily": effacement should be practiced thus.[251]

The method of practicing insight used by those who have achieved jhāna and who practice insight by observing jhānic phenomena is directly explained in the Pāḷi texts mentioned here. There are other discourses in which the same method is explained. One should take the method of those who achieve jhāna and who practice insight by observing jhānic phenomena as an example, and then get to know the method of those who practice pure insight. One who has achieved jhāna and who practices insight by observing jhānic phenomena observes the mental and physical phenomena presently arising in his or her continuum. Likewise, a practitioner of pure insight should also observe either the mental and physical phenomena that are presently arising in his or her continuum or the mental and physical phenomena that are presently arising at his or her six sense doors. It is the objective of insight knowledge that observes phenomena of attainment one by one as they occur to be concerned with only one distinct object. It is likewise the objective of empirically observed insight to distinguish and observe the unique characteristics and so on of only one distinct object.

The highest jhāna is the domain of inferential insight for those who have achieved jhāna and who practice insight by observing jhānic phenomena. Likewise, phenomena that do not happen within his or her continuum, that are not distinct, or that are so subtle that their unique characteristics and so on cannot be known, are the domain of inferential insight for practitioners of pure insight. So you shouldn't observe phenomena that are not distinct by deliberately thinking about them. If you were to do this as a beginner, the phenomena would not become apparent. Even so, you shouldn't observe the highest jhāna as a beginner either. Only when the insight gained through empirically observing distinct phenomena has become mature and purified will you will be able to observe those phenomena that are not distinct by means of inferential insight. So only when Venerable Sāriputta's empirical insight had been purified by observing the distinct lower jhānas did he observe the highest jhāna by means of inferential insight.

Here ends chapter 3 regarding Absolute and Conventional Realities.

The Development of Mindfulness 4

In this chapter I will explain the way in which to meditate and the way of correct seeing and understanding based on the Pāḷi texts, commentaries, and subcommentaries.

In the last chapter, I explained that a person who takes the tranquility vehicle meditates on the jhāna consciousness that he or she has entered, the physical basis of that jhāna consciousness, or physical phenomena that have arisen due to that jhāna consciousness. Similarly a person who takes the vehicle of insight observes presently arisen consciousness of seeing, hearing, smelling, tasting, touching, or thinking, the physical bases of these kinds of consciousness, physical phenomena arisen due to these kinds of consciousness, or physical phenomena arisen due to the objects of these kinds of consciousness. Moreover I explained that, according to the Pāḷi texts, commentaries, and subcommentaries, "seeing" refers to the entire mental process of seeing, not to each individual mental moment of it. Further explanation on this point will also be given in chapter 6 when we deal with the insight knowledge of dissolution.

Checking Meditation against the Pāḷi Texts

Five kinds of phenomena

One should note seeing as "seeing" at the very moment of seeing. The same applies for hearing, and so on. When one notes "seeing," one experiences any of the following five kinds of phenomena: (1) eye-sensitivity (*cakkhupasāda*), (2) form base (*rūpāyatana*), (3) eye-consciousness (*cakkhuviññāṇa*), (4) the mental contact (*phassa*) between eye and object, (5) feelings (*vedanā*) that are pleasant, unpleasant, or neither unpleasant nor pleasant.

For example when the clarity of a meditator's eyesight becomes obvious to him or her, the meditator is mainly experiencing eye-sensitivity. When the visible form that has been seen draws one's attention, one is mainly aware of the visual object. If one notices the mental state of seeing, then one is realizing eye-consciousness. If the contact between one's eye and the visual object is clear, then one is experiencing mental contact. If one finds the object to be pleasant, unpleasant, or neither unpleasant nor pleasant, then one is mainly aware of feeling.

You may ask, "If this is so, then rather than noting seeing as 'seeing,' shouldn't one note it as 'eye-sensitivity,' 'the visual object,' 'eye-consciousness,' 'mental contact,' or 'feeling,' according to what one clearly experiences, so that the labels will be in harmony with what they indicate?"

This sounds very reasonable. In practice, however, it would keep the meditator so busy thinking about exactly which object they were experiencing in a moment of seeing that there would be many gaps between notings. In other words, one would not be able to focus on present objects. In addition, one would fail to note the thinking and analyzing, so one's mindfulness, concentration, and insight knowledge would not be able to mature in a timely manner. Therefore, you should not note while simultaneously trying to find a word that perfectly matches the label with the experience. Instead, you should simply note seeing as "seeing" every time you see. In this way you will avoid such difficulties.

The term "seeing" should be understood to refer to all of the phenomena involved in the mental process of seeing. For this reason it is called a concept that refers to what ultimately exists (*vijjamānapaññatti*). It is also called a concept that refers to ultimately real phenomena (*tajjāpaññatti*). So words such as "earth" (*pathavī*), "mental contact" (*phassa*), and so on are all concepts that refer to ultimately real phenomena. I also covered this in the last chapter. Still, the question may be raised, "Won't my attention be drawn to the concept of the word being used, instead of connecting with the ultimately real phenomena that it indicates?"

This is true in the immature stages of meditation. However, when first beginning practice, one can accurately focus one's mind on objects only when one notes them by labeling them one by one. Eventually, though, one learns to experience the ultimately real phenomena that lie beyond names or concepts. In this way, the perception of the solidity and continuity of phenomena (*santatighana*) vanishes and one is able to understand the three universal characteristics. This is confirmed by the following passage from the *Mahāṭīkā*:

> Should one observe ultimately real phenomena in terms of concepts that refer to ultimately real phenomena?[252]
>
> Yes, in the beginning of the practice one should. However, when one's practice is mature, one's mind will reach the ultimately real phenomena beyond the concepts that refer to them.[253]

This passage refers specifically to meditation on the Buddha's attributes, but it can serve as good guidance in the case of insight meditation, as well. During certain stages, such as the insight knowledge of arising and passing away, phenomena arise so rapidly that it is not possible to label them individually, and one must simply be aware of their characteristics. This will be explained in detail in chapter 5. However, one will realize it for oneself when one attains those knowledges. So one shouldn't waste one's time deciding what to note. One just notes "seeing" every time one sees. Then one experiences objects in terms of their characteristics, functions, manifestations, or proximate causes. Then one understands these phenomena as they really are.

Four aspects of phenomena

Some may wonder whether it is possible to experience phenomena accurately without an education in theory. It is possible if we mindfully observe mental and physical phenomena the moment they occur. Ultimately real phenomena are made up of nothing but the particular aspects of their (1) characteristics (*lakkhaṇā*), (2) function (*rasā*), (3) manifestation (*paccupaṭṭhānā*), and (4) proximate cause (*padaṭṭhānā*).

So if we directly experience an ultimately real phenomenon, we understand it in terms of one of those four factors—in other words, we can only experience an ultimately real phenomenon in terms of these four factors. If we perceive an object in any other way, the object we perceive is not a genuine, ultimately real phenomenon but a concept of something such as its manner, identity, image, solid form, and so on.

We can experience a phenomenon as it really is if we observe it the moment it takes place. This type of experience is neither imagination nor reasoning, but awareness of a phenomenon in terms of its characteristic and so on. If we observe a lightning bolt the moment it strikes, for example, we will certainly be aware of its unique characteristic (brightness), its function (to remove darkness), its manifestation (whether it is straight, branched, or arcing), or its proximate cause (a cloud and so on). It is impossible, on the other hand, to perceive the lightning bolt as it really is if we imagine or analyze it after it has disappeared. Likewise, if we observe phenomena the moment they occur, we can understand the characteristics and such of these truly arising mental and physical phenomena just as they really are, even without any theoretical knowledge of them.

We cannot understand the characteristics and such of these truly arising mental and physical phenomena as they really are by merely thinking or reflecting on them, without noting them as they arise in the present moment, even if we have theoretical knowledge of them. For example, if you note an unpleasant feeling, you can understand its characteristic (unpleasantness), its function (stress), its manifestation (discomfort), or its proximate cause (contact between the mind and an unpleasant object), as it really is with personal experience.

Actually, the proximate cause of an object is distinct from the observed object itself. So during the early stages of meditation[254] you should not pay attention to it. This is why the *Abhidhammatthavibhāvinī* subcommentary only says that one should be mindful of an object in terms of its characteristic, function, and manifestation, and that this understanding is considered purification of view (*diṭṭhivisuddhi*). The *Mahāṭīkā*[255] explains that the proximate cause is not mentioned because it is a separate phenomenon. In the case of meditation on the four fundamental elements, for example, when one observes any of the four primary material elements, it is not necessary to pay attention to the remaining elements that are its proximate causes. Otherwise one would be observing objects different than that which one intended to note.

In the same way, in the case of knowledge that discerns mental and physical phenomena, we need only be aware of present mental and physical phenomena the moment they occur; we needn't yet be concerned with their causes. If we were to observe objects in terms of their proximate causes, then, when observing a primary material element, we would first need to be aware of the other three elements. When observing eye-sensitivity, we would first need to observe the primary material elements that are its proximate causes. Or the moment a feeling became obvious, we would first need to note the mental contact that was its proximate cause. Or the moment contact became obvious, we would first need to observe the object.

Thus when one object is most obvious, we would have to be aware of a different one. In other words, we would have to note the first object later. This might make it seem like we could gain knowledge that discerns conditionality (*paccayapariggahañāṇa*) by skipping knowledge that discerns mental and physical phenomena. It is significant that the *Visuddhimagga* and Abhidhamma subcommentaries[256] do not include observation of proximate causes in their instructions for the first level of knowledge. The reason that the *Abhidhammattha Saṅgaha* includes proximate causes is because the proximate cause becomes obvious and can be observed at later stages of purification of view when one is about to attain knowledge that discerns conditionality.

A person can only realize one of the four aspects of characteristic, function, manifestation, and proximate cause at a time. When a person is noting a mental or physical phenomenon in a given moment, only one of these four aspects is obvious, so he or she can only observe one of them at a time. Since two, three, or four aspects are not obvious at the same time, a person cannot be aware of all of them at once. Fortunately it's not necessary to be aware of an object from all aspects at the same time in order to accomplish one's aim. Indeed, understanding an object from a single aspect serves the purpose. As the *Mahāṭīkā* says:

> Why are both characteristic and function mentioned here [in the case of the four primary material elements]? Because they are intended for meditators of different dispositions. When meditating on a primary material element, one person may experience it in terms of its characteristic and another in terms of its function.[257]

If a person observes one of the four primary material elements solely in terms of its characteristic or solely in terms of its function, it fully serves the purpose. One cannot simultaneously observe both its characteristic and its function. The reason why the commentary explains both its characteristic and its function is because people have different dispositions and inclinations. Let me elaborate: when observing one of the four primary material elements, the specific characteristic is obvious for some people and therefore they can only observe and realize the specific characteristic; for others its function is obvious and therefore they can only observe and realize the function.

Contemplation of the Body

The case of seeing

When noting "seeing," a person can experience any one of the five factors of seeing from any of its four aspects. I will explain each of these cases in order:

Eye-sensitivity

When we experience our eye as clear or sufficiently clear that a visual object appears to it, the eye-sensitivity is understood in terms of its unique characteristic (*sabhāvalakkhaṇā*).

When we experience eye-sensitivity carrying our attention to an object or allowing us to see an object, the eye-sensitivity is understood in terms of its function.

When we experience the eye-sensitivity as the basis for seeing or the starting point of seeing, it is understood in terms of its manifestation.

When we are aware of the solid, bodily eye, the eye-sensitivity is understood from the aspect of its being a proximate cause.

The visual object

When we accurately understand a visual object, we know that it appears to the eye (its characteristic), that it is seen (its function), that it is an object of sight (its manifestation), and that it is based on the four primary material elements (its proximate cause). This explanation accords with the Pāḷi texts explanation that ". . . understands the eye, understands forms . . ."[258] means that "the eye-sensitivity and visible form are understood in terms of characteristic and function."[259]

"Deconstructing attention" (*cuṇṇamanasikāra*) is a type of tranquility meditation on the four primary material elements that mentally deconstructs them into particles. Some apply this methodology in insight meditation, contemplating the physical body by breaking it into parts. But this method is not suited to insight meditation because it makes it impossible to be aware of objects in terms of their characteristics and so on.

Eye-consciousness

When we accurately understand eye-consciousness, we know that it occurs in the eye, or sees visible forms (its characteristic), that it takes only visible form as its object or that it simply sees (its function), that it is directed toward the visible form (its manifestation), and that it occurs due to attention, the conjunction of functioning eyes with visual objects, or good or bad kamma (its proximate cause).

Mental contact between eye and object

When we accurately understand visual contact, we know that it contacts a visual object (its characteristic), that it encounters visual objects (its function), that it is a meeting of the eye, a visual object, and sight (its manifestation), and that visual objects give rise to it (its proximate cause).

Feelings that are pleasant, unpleasant, or neither unpleasant nor pleasant

When we accurately understand a pleasant feeling, we know that it is pleasant (its characteristic), that it feels pleasant (its function), that it arouses pleasure in the mind (its manifestation), and that it is caused by contact with a pleasant or desirable object, or a peaceful mind (its proximate cause).

When we accurately understand an unpleasant feeling, we know that it is unpleasant (its characteristic), that it feels unpleasant (its function), that it arouses displeasure in the mind (its manifestation), and that it is caused by contact with an unpleasant or undesirable object (its proximate cause).

When we accurately understand a neither-unpleasant-nor-pleasant feeling, we know that it is neither unpleasant nor pleasant (its characteristic), that it feels neither amusing nor boring (its function), that it is tranquil (its manifestation), and that a balance between pleasure and displeasure causes it (its proximate cause).

Note that eye-consciousness itself is associated only with neutral feeling. According to canonical discourses that deal with insight, however, we should observe all six senses in terms of these three types of feeling. The reason for this is that the complete mental processes for the six senses include units of mentality that are directly associated with pleasant or unpleasant feelings, as well—namely, investigation (*santīraṇa*), impulsion (*javana*), and registration (*tadārammaṇā*). This will become obvious below when we deal with the *Abhiññeyya Sutta* and the *Pariññeyya Sutta*.

I will elaborate in order to broaden our understanding. The subcommentaries say:

> An unwholesome resultant feeling that is neither unpleasant nor pleasant (*upekkhā*) can be considered an unpleasant feeling since it is disagreeable; a wholesome one can be considered a pleasant feeling since it is agreeable.[260]

Based on the use of the words "agreeable" and "disagreeable" in the above passage, it is reasonable to assume that if an object is neither agreeable nor disagreeable, the feeling involved should be regarded as neither-unpleasant-nor-pleasant. Although sense consciousness itself is associated with neither unpleasant nor pleasant feelings, we are likely to feel pleasure when encountering a pleasant sight, a sweet sound, a fragrant odor, or a delicious flavor. When we experience the fragrant smell of flowers or perfume, or consume tasty food and drink, the feeling of pleasure is obvious. On the other hand, we feel displeasure when we encounter unpleasant sights, sounds, odors, or flavors, such as the smell of something rotting or burning, the taste of bitter medicine, and so on. Body-consciousness is of two kinds as well: pleasant and unpleasant. It would seem that when an object is neither unpleasant nor pleasant, it should be possible to feel not only pleasant or unpleasant feelings but also feelings that are neither unpleasant nor pleasant. Such neither-unpleasant-nor-pleasant feelings, however, should be considered a lesser form of pleasure.

As mentioned above, eye-sensitivity, visible form, eye-consciousness, mental contact between the eye and the object, and feelings that are pleasant, unpleasant, or neither unpleasant nor pleasant are the five factors that constitute sight. At the moment of seeing, we note "seeing, seeing," and, as explained before, come to know its characteristic, function, or manifestation according to our disposition and inclination. At the mature stages of purification of view we may also be able to know its proximate cause. With this purpose in mind, the Saṃyutta Nikāya[261] and *Paṭisambhidāmagga* say:

> Bhikkhus, the eye should be fully understood, forms should be fully understood, eye-consciousness should be fully understood, mental contact between eye and form should be fully understood, and whatever feeling arises with mental contact—

> whether pleasant or painful or neither painful nor pleasant—should be fully understood.[262]

Learning and logical thought

Knowledge gained through learning and logical thought is not insight. Mental and physical phenomena are understood as they really are by being aware of them in terms of their characteristics and so on the moment they occur. This understanding or insight knowledge is superior to learning and logical thought. It is superior even to knowledge derived from tranquility meditation (*samathabhāvanāmaya*). The textual reference on this point is:

> "Wisdom of full understanding" (*abhiññāpaññā*) is a knowledge that understands ultimately real phenomena by noting them in terms of their characteristic and so on.[263]

In the ultimate sense, this is knowledge that discerns mental and physical phenomena and knowledge that discerns conditionality.

> Full understanding (*abhiññātā*) is an understanding of [ultimately real phenomena] derived from knowledge [that discerns mental and physical phenomena and conditionality] and is superior to knowledge derived from learning, logical thought, and even to some derived from tranquility meditation.[264]

This passage makes it clear that learning and logical thought do not even belong to the realm of basic knowledge, let alone to that of higher insight knowledges.

The *Abhiññeyya Sutta*[265] says that one must fully understand the eye, one must fully understand visible form, and so on, in this way generally exposing different points one after the other in due order. If a person were to note one object five different ways, many other objects would pass by unobserved. In any event, one's mind cannot note quickly enough to notice all five factors in every instance of sight. Such an approach would also contradict the *Paṭisambhidāmagga*, a text in the Pāḷi canon, which says that a person who has reached the stage of insight knowledge of dissolution can be aware of both the disappearance of an object and of their awareness of its disappearance itself. So a person should observe only one object for each instance of sight. One's purpose of noting and understanding is fulfilled when one observes and understands one distinct phenomenon among these five.

The *Pariññeyya Sutta*[266] explains how it is fulfilled. At the mature stages of the first two knowledges, whenever one notes "seeing," one comes to know that the seeing did not exist before and that it has now appeared. Thereby one also understands the appearance of these five phenomena. One further understands the disappearance of these phenomena, seeing them vanish after they have arisen—using sharp mindfulness one sees them instantly disappear. When one begins to see arising and disappearance, one understands the characteristic of impermanence (*aniccalakkhaṇā*). Because phenomena are not exempt from arising and disappearance, they are unsatisfactory: this is understanding the characteristic of unsatisfactoriness (*dukkhalakkhaṇā*). And because they arise and disappear even though one doesn't wish them to, there is no self that has any control over them: this is understanding the characteristic of not-self (*anattālakkhaṇā*). Thus one fully understands the general characteristics of impermanence and such of all five of these phenomena that are present in each moment of sight.

The *Abhiññeyya Sutta* and *Pariññeyya Sutta* both explain all six of the sense doors in the very same way. According to the *Pariññeyya Sutta*, when a person understands the general characteristics of impermanence and such by observing one distinct phenomenon among the five phenomena, one fulfills the aim of fully understanding these phenomena at the moment of seeing them. When one accomplishes this understanding, the phenomena cannot give rise to defilements.

The arising and nonarising of mental defilements

When a defilement arises in connection with sight, it arises at the moment of seeing based on a distinct object that you see. When there is no distinct object and it is not known, the defilement does not arise. Affection or hate for a certain person only arises because you have previously met or seen that person. It may also happen due to hearing about that person from somebody else. Let's assume that you have neither met this person nor heard about him or her; you don't even know that this person exists on the planet. Because this person is neither distinct to your mind nor do you know him or her, it is impossible for affection or hate to arise in your mind with respect to him or her. The same follows for a form that you have neither seen in the past or presently, nor have ever imagined. Such a visible form is like a woman or man that lives in a village, town, country, celestial realm, or different universe that you have never visited before. Because there is no such visible form obviously present in your mind, greed, hatred, and other defilements cannot arise with respect to it. This is why, at the request of a monk named Māluṅkyaputta, the Buddha gave meditation instructions by raising questions as follows:

> "What do you think, Māluṅkyaputta? Do you have any desire, lust, or affection for those forms cognizable by the eye that you have not seen and never saw before, that you do not see and would not think might be seen?"
>
> "No venerable sir."[267]

With this first question, the Buddha explicitly states that visible objects that are not apparent cannot arouse mental defilements. In other words, it isn't necessary to make any effort to prevent mental defilements from arising with respect to such objects. On the other hand, this implies that mental defilements can arise from distinct objects that one can actually see. So if one can use insight meditation to prevent affection or hatred from arising, then defilements cannot arise even with apparent visible objects, just as is the case with visible objects that are not apparent. The point is that one should observe the objects one sees so that the defilements are abandoned by means of insight meditation, just like the objects that one does not see. Such implied meanings are called *neyyatthanaya* ("the implicit method"), *avuttasiddhinaya* ("the method established without being said"), or *atthāpannanaya* ("the deductive method") in Pāḷi.

What makes us love or hate someone when we see him or her? In an ultimate sense, it is the visual phenomenon, the visible form delineated by the skin. Based on this visible form we think about the person and come to regard the whole of his or her body as what we like or dislike. If we didn't see the external visible form of the person, we wouldn't think of the whole of his or her body as what we like or dislike. Since, consequently, attachment would not arise when the person is seen, it naturally follows that defilements do not arise and therefore would not need to be abandoned. On the other hand, an object that we become attached to the moment we see it can arouse mental defilements any time we think about it. Therefore we must observe the objects that we see so that they do not lead to love or hate, just as objects we don't see do not lead to love or hate.

Buddha gives the same question and answer with respect to the other senses of hearing, smelling, tasting, touching, and thinking.

> "Here, Māluṅkyaputta, regarding things seen, heard, sensed, and cognized by you: in the seen there will be merely the seen; in the heard there will be merely the heard; in the sensed there will be merely the sensed; in the cognized there will be merely the cognized.
>
> "When, Māluṅkyaputta, regarding things seen, heard, sensed, and cognized by you, in the seen there will be merely the seen, in the heard there will be merely the heard, in the sensed there will be merely the sensed, in the cognized there will be merely the cognized, then, Māluṅkyaputta, you will not be 'by that.' When, Māluṅkyaputta, you are not 'by that,' then you will not be 'therein.' When, Māluṅkyaputta, you are not 'therein,' then you will be neither here nor beyond nor in between the two. This itself is the end of suffering."[268]

In the *Udana-aṭṭhakathā*,[269] the sentence "When you are not 'therein'" is said to mean that one is neither in the six internal sense bases (eye, ear, nose, tongue, body, and mind) nor in the six external sense bases (visible forms, sounds, odors, tastes, touch, and thoughts), nor in the six kinds of consciousness that are between the two of them. When one is not in the six internal sense bases, the six external sense bases, or the six kinds of consciousness, it is the end of suffering.

The explanation of this verse is as follows: when you see a visual object, just let seeing be seeing; do not let mental defilements intrude by thinking about the form that has been seen. You should observe the visible form that you see so that the defilements have no chance to arise. Being mindful of the visible form, you will know its true nature: you will understand it as having the nature of just being seen, disappearing after it has arisen, and disappearing even while being noted. Thus you will realize that it is impermanent, unsatisfactory, and not-self. Even though you see this visible form, it is the same as an object that you do not see, so you don't mentally grasp it as something to be loved or hated, or as solid matter. Even if you happen to think of it, you will not reflect on it with delusion. You will remember it as impermanent, unsatisfactory, and not-self, just as you found it to be when you first noted it. Thus defilements of love or hate will be unable to arise based on thoughts connected with that visible form.

In other words, every time you see, you must observe so that no defilements can arise. When hearing a sound, smelling an odor, experiencing a taste, touching any kind of tangible object, or thinking a thought, you must observe so that ensuing thoughts and defilements have no chance to arise. You just let hearing be hearing, and likewise with the rest. As you just let seeing be seeing, hearing be hearing, and so on, and uninterruptedly continue to note, you gradually develop the moral conduct, concentration, and understanding that are developed hand in hand with the practice of insight meditation. Finally, this leads to moral conduct, concentration, and wisdom associated with path knowledge.

The *Udāna-aṭṭhakathā* elaborates still further on this verse.[270] When you continuously note a visible form as "seeing," for example, seeing is just seeing. When noting a visible form, the nature of "just seeing" is obvious, as is the nature of impermanence, unsatisfactoriness, and not-self, but it is not obvious that the visible form is something to be loved or hated or a so-called person. These objects are seen like objects that are not apparent: they do not become objects based upon which defilements arise, and given that you have no attachment to these objects, defilements cannot arise. This is why the Pāḷi texts, commentaries, and subcommentaries say that such objects do not leave behind dormant defilements (*ārammanānusaya-kilesā*). Insight meditation temporarily removes defilements and so is described as "temporary seclusion" (*tadaṅgaviveka*), "nonattachment" (*virāga*), "cessation" (*nirodha*), and "release" (*vosagga*). An insight practitioner is considered "a person who is temporarily liberated from defilements" (*tadaṅganibbūta*), as stated in the Saṃyutta Nikāya. One is not carried away by defilements connected with seeing and so on; one is not attached to the object one sees, nor is one averse to it; and one also does not entertain thoughts of taking things to be permanent, satisfying, and self.

Because such persons can abandon the perception of permanence and so on, their understanding is called "full understanding by abandoning" (*pahānapariññā*). Understanding the disappearance of the visible form that is seen is "insight full understanding by abandoning" (*vipassanāpahāna-pariññā*). Understanding the complete cessation of all conditioned phenomena that include the visible form that is seen together with the noting mind is "path full understanding by abandoning" (*maggapahānapariññā*). That is immediately followed by fruition (*phala*). Both path knowledge and fruition knowledge take nibbāna as their only object. At that point, "you will not be therein" with sense objects. That is, you will no longer have attachment (*taṇhā*), pride (*māna*), or wrong view (*diṭṭhi*).[271]

The commentary on the passage above explains that path and fruition refer to the arahant path (*arahattamagga*) and the fruit of arahantship (*arahattaphala*). We cannot say of a fully enlightened being, an arahant, that he or she is here in this life or world because he or she does not have any attachment. Likewise, we cannot say that he or she is "there" (in the next life or another world), as he or she will not be reborn after death. Therefore, not being "here or there" (in this world or the world beyond) means the complete cessation of the cycle of unsatisfactoriness as there is no more attachment and no more arising of any new mental and physical phenomena; this is called "nibbāna without residue" (*anupādisesanibbāna*).

Some scholars interpret this line in this way: at the moment of path and fruition, the six internal sense bases (eye, ear, nose, tongue, body, and mind) do not appear to the mind and therefore one cannot observe them. The six external mundane sense objects (visible form, sound, smell, taste, touch, and mental objects) do not appear to the mind and, therefore, one cannot observe them. The six kinds of consciousness (seeing, hearing, smelling, tasting, touching, and thinking consciousness) do not appear to the mind and, therefore, one cannot observe them. Path knowledge and fruition knowledge arise by taking the cessation of the sense bases, sense object, and consciousness as their object. Realizing the nature of cessation with the attainment of path and fruition is called nibbāna, the end of unsatisfactoriness.

The Venerable Māluṅkyaputta responded to the Buddha by interpreting the Buddha's brief discourse in his own words as follows:

"Having seen a form with mindfulness muddled,
Attending to the pleasing sign,
One experiences it with infatuated mind,
And remains tightly holding to it.

"Many feelings flourish within,
Originating from the visible form,
Covetousness and annoyance as well
By which the mind becomes disturbed.
For one who accumulates suffering thus,
Nibbāna is said to be far away."[272]

This verse explains that one cannot attain nibbāna if one lacks mindfulness at the time of seeing. The phrase "attending to the pleasing sign" indicates that unwise attention leads to desire. The phrase "with mindfulness muddled" means that one fails to be mindful of visible forms as they really are: impermanent, unsatisfactory, and not-self. The phrase "one experiences it with infatuated mind" implies also the cases that he hates it if it is undesirable and ignores it in delusion if it is neutral.

> "When fully mindful, one sees a form,
> One is not inflamed by lust for forms;
> One experiences it with dispassionate mind
> And does not remain holding it tightly.
>
> "One fares mindfully in such a way
> That even as one sees the form,
> And while one undergoes a feeling,
> [Suffering] is exhausted and not built up.
> For one dismantling suffering thus,
> Nibbāna is said to be close by."[273]

This verse explains that one can attain nibbāna, if one possesses mindfulness at the time of seeing. The Buddha presented the same instructions for the remaining senses of hearing, smelling, tasting, touching, and thinking. Then the Buddha confirmed Māluṅkyaputta's interpretation of the instructions by saying: "Well spoken, Māluṅkyaputta!" The Buddha then told Māluṅkyaputta that the meaning of the brief instructions for insight meditation should be retained in detail. Thereafter, the Buddha repeated the above verses again. The Venerable Māluṅkyaputta practiced insight meditation according to this summary, and before long he became one of the arahants.

The *Māluṅkyaputta Sutta* conveys three main points: phenomena that are not apparent and not perceived through one of the six kinds of consciousness naturally do not arouse defilements, so one should not try to note them; phenomena that are apparent and perceived through one of the six kinds of consciousness and that are not being noted do arouse defilements, so one should note them—defilements that arise when one is not mindful are abandoned by noting them; and if one is mindful of an apparent phenomenon, defilements do not arise from phenomena that are either apparent or not apparent, so when one notes one apparent phenomenon, then the purpose of noting and understanding is fulfilled for all phenomena.

Thus if one understands the arising and passing away and sees the impermanent nature and such of one phenomenon by noting it each time one sees it, then the aim of understanding the five factors involved at the moment of seeing is fulfilled.

The complete discourse can be found in the Saḷāyatanasaṃyutta.[274]

Defilements

Although one tries to constantly note seeing as "seeing," defilements will often intrude when insight knowledge is still immature. However, you should not feel disappointed. You should not give up. You can overcome defilements by noting them over and over again, just as a person hand-washing clothes gets them completely clean by repeatedly beating and squeezing them. The difference is that a person can easily see how clean the clothes are getting, but a meditator has no way of knowing how many defilements he or she is eradicating every day. Only when we reach path knowledge and fruition knowledge can we know how many defilements we have eradicated. To illustrate this point, the Buddha gave the example of a carpenter who doesn't notice the wooden handle of his axe being worn down by use until the impression of his fingers appears on it after months or years. This discourse can be found in the Khandhavagga of the Saṃyutta Nikāya.[275] In the same way, a meditator cannot know exactly how many defilements he or she has overcome until he or she attains path knowledge and fruition knowledge.

However, as insight matures defilements arise less and less often and disappear once they are noted. They no longer persist. Instead, the noting mind flows continuously most of the time. Later one's insight knowledge becomes so powerful that it prevents unwholesome impulsion from arising. Instead, wholesome impulsion arises during the mental process of seeing, even with regard to a visual object that is likely to arouse attachment. At that point, the mental process of seeing may even stop with determining (*votthapana*), the mind-moment that determines an object prior to impulsion. Then one clearly sees that defilements are extinguished during the practice of insight meditation. According to the commentary on the Saḷāyatanasaṃyutta of the Saṃyutta Nikāya:

> The statement "bhikkhus, . . . slow might be the arising of his mindfulness"[276] means that mindfulness is slow to progress. But

> once it develops, some defilements are suppressed; they can no longer persist. For example, if attachment enters through the eye door, one notices this defilement occurring in the second mental process. In this way, one causes wholesome impulsions to arise in the third mental process. It is not surprising that a meditator can suppress defilements by the third mental process. One can even replace unwholesome impulsions in the mental process of seeing with wholesome impulsions after seeing-related mind-moments, from the life-continuum (*bhavaṅga*) and adverting (*āvajjana*) up to determining (*votthapana*),[277] even when the visual object is desirable and conducive to attachment. This is the benefit an intensive meditator can get from insight practice, which becomes strong and develops the mind.[278]

This passage shows that a meditator at intermediate levels of insight knowledge may have defilements at the moment of seeing, but he or she can transform them into wholesome states by the third mental process. The sentence "It is not surprising . . ." shows that no defilements arise in a meditator at higher levels of insight knowledge; instead, pure observation continuously flows. This passage also implies that the subsequent mental process can perceive the mental process of sight.

Sense experience without impulsion

The following section is included to show that the mental process of seeing may even stop at determining.

> For a mature (strong) meditator, if there is unwise attention when an object enters through the eye door or any other door, his or her mind will fall into life-continuum without arousing any defilements after subsisting for two or three determining mind-moments. This is how it is for a meditator at the peak of practice.
>
> For another type of meditator in this situation, a mental process accompanied by defilement arises. At the end of that mental process he or she realizes that the mind is accompanied by defilement and so starts to note it. Then, during the second mental process, the mind is free from the defilement.
>
> For yet another type of meditator, only at the end of the

> second mental process does he or she realize that the mind is accompanied by defilement and so starts to note it. Then, during the third mental process, the mind is free from the defilement.[279]

The three types of meditators described here are a first-class meditator (one at the highest level of mature insight meditation), a second-class meditator (one at an intermediate level of mature insight meditation), and a third-class meditator (one at the lower level of mature insight meditation).

Regarding the second and third types of meditators, the translation of the original Pāḷi passage is clear enough and no additional explanation is needed. For the first type of meditator, due to repeated insight practice, even if the mind-moment that adverts to a sense object arises with unwise attention, it will not be strong enough to take the object clearly. This is also the case for the subsequent mind-moments of the five physical sense consciousnesses (*pañcaviññāṇa*), that which receives (*sampaticchana*) the sense object, and that which investigates the sense object. As a result, the determining mind-moment that is also called the mind-door-adverting consciousness (*manodvārāvajjana*) is not able to determine the sense object clearly. It occurs two or three times, repeatedly considering the sense object that is referred to in this verse as "after subsisting for" (*āsevanaṃ labhitvā*). However, because the sense object cannot be determined after two or three times, the mental units of impulsion do not arise and life-continuum arises.

This type of mental process is called "a mental process that ends with determining" (*votthapanavāravīthi*). It can occur not only in the case of sense objects but also for mental objects. Objects are not experienced clearly in this kind of mental process. One just experiences a general sense of seeing, hearing, or thinking. After emerging from the life-continuum (*bhavaṅga*), there arises at the mind door an insight-based mental process that notes the not very distinct seeing. For such a meditator wholesome and unwholesome mental processes do not occur at all by way of the five sense doors. Mental processes of insight impulsion arise only at the mind door.

Sixfold equanimity

This type of mental process can be experienced very clearly at the level of the insight knowledge of equanimity toward phenomena (*saṅkhārupekkhāñāṇa*), where equanimity prevails and one remains balanced. One verifies this point with one's own experience at that level and is said to possess sixfold equanimity (*chaḷaṅgupekkhā*) like an arahant. As the Pañcaṅguttara Tikaṇḍhakīvagga of the *Manorathapūraṇi* says:

> It is good for a bhikkhu from time to time to dwell equanimous, mindful and clearly comprehending, having turned away from both the repulsive and the unrepulsive.[280]

The commentary explains this as follows:

> This part refers to sixfold equanimity, which is comparable to an arahant's mental state. However, it is not really the equanimity of an arahant. In this discourse, the Buddha refers only to insight. An accomplished meditator (who has attained knowledge of arising and passing away) can have this kind of equanimity.[281]

Another commentary, on the *Mahāhatthipadopama Sutta*,[282] says:

> Here, upekkhā refers to sixfold equanimity. This is the type of equanimity possessed by an arahant that gives one a balanced attitude toward both pleasant and unpleasant objects. However, a monk may take his success at insight practice for arahantship, since he experiences this type of equanimity through the strength of his intensive practice. Thus insight itself can be called sixfold equanimity.[283]

The following story of the Venerable Potthila deals with this kind of mental process. Using the simile of catching a reptile, a remarkable young novice instructed Venerable Potthila to practice insight until impulsion was eliminated at the five sense doors.

> *The Story of Venerable Potthila*
> In the time of the Buddha, there lived a monk by the name of Potthila. He had learned and taught the complete canonical texts during the lives of six past buddhas, including Buddha Vipassī. He did the same in the time of our Buddha. However, he did not practice meditation. Thus the Buddha deliberately

called him "Empty Potthila" (*Tuccha Potthila*)[284] whenever he met him.

As a result, a feeling of spiritual urgency arose in Venerable Potthila. So he thought: "I have learned the entire canonical text together with the commentaries by heart and I am teaching it to five hundred monks. Yet the Buddha calls me 'Empty Potthila.' This must be because I have no spiritual attainment like the jhānas or path and fruition."

He then left for a place 120 yojana[285] away, with the aim of practicing meditation. In that forest monastery he met thirty arahants and humbly asked the eldest monk to give him guidance on how to practice meditation. However, the eldest monk, wishing to suppress Venerable Potthila's pride in his canonical knowledge, sent him to the second most senior monk. That monk, in turn, sent him to the third most senior monk, and so on. In the end, Venerable Potthila was compelled to meet with the youngest arahant of the group, who was a seven-year-old novice.

By then Venerable Potthila was not showing any more pride in his canonical knowledge. Instead, he paid respects to the novice with his hands folded together and humbly requested that the young arahant give him guidance in meditation. How admirable! A senior monk is not allowed to bow down to a junior one, but he may fold his hands together in respect (*añjalīkamma*) when requesting guidance, pardon, and so on. It is really admirable that such a highly learned, senior monk was able to show such humble respect for the Dhamma, rather than arrogantly thinking, "I will practice as I have learned rather than accepting guidance from anybody."

But the novice rejected his request, saying, "Venerable sir, I am still young and not very knowledgeable. I am the one who should learn from you." Yet Venerable Potthila persisted in his request.

"Well, if you follow my instructions meticulously," said the novice, "I will teach you how to practice meditation."

Venerable Potthila promised, "Even if you ask me to walk into the fire, I will do exactly as you say." In order to test his sincerity, the novice then asked him to get into a nearby pond.

> Without a second thought, the senior monk immediately began walking into the pond.
>
> However, just as the edge of his robe got wet, the novice called him back and taught him to practice as follows: "Venerable sir, suppose there were an anthill with six openings and a lizard inside. If you wanted to catch the lizard, you would have to close off five of the openings first and then wait at the sixth one. In the same way out of the six sense doors, you must work only at the mind door, leaving the other five sense doors closed."

Here, "leaving the other five sense doors closed" means not to allow the sensory mental process to reach kammic impulsion. It does not mean to literally close one's eyes, ears, and so on. This would actually be impossible, as there is no way to "close" the tongue or the body. But, even if it were possible to do so, it would not serve any purpose. That is why the Buddha said in the *Indriyabhāvanā Sutta*:

> "If that is so, Uttara, then a blind man or a deaf man will have developed mental faculties, according to what the brahmin Pārāsariya says. For a blind man does not see forms with the eye, and a deaf man does not hear sounds with the ear."[286]

Moreover, the Buddha teaches us to be mindful of the senses by experiencing them, not by avoiding them. This is consistent with many canonical texts, such as:

> Here, having seen a form with the eye, a bhikkhu is neither joyful nor saddened, but dwells equanimous, mindful, and clearly comprehending.[287]

The Buddha never taught to protect oneself by preventing sense experiences from occurring. So we can conclude that "to close the sense doors" means to not allow the sensory mental processes to continue through to impulsion. The phrase "to work only at the mind door" means to develop insight just by working at the mind door. The point here is to practice until one develops sixfold equanimity.

Since Venerable Potthila was a highly learned monk, he fully understood the young arahant's meaning, as if a light had been turned on in the darkness. While the senior monk was practicing as instructed, the Buddha emitted rays of light and encouraged him with the following guidance:

> Wisdom arises from [spiritual] practice;
> Without practice, it decays.
> Knowing this two-way path for gain and loss,
> Conduct yourself so that wisdom grows.[288]

The *Dhammapada-aṭṭhakathā* says that at the end of this verse, Venerable Potthila became fully enlightened, an arahant. This is how to develop insight to the level of sixfold equanimity: by noting seeing as "seeing" the moment it occurs, and so on for the rest of the senses.

More evidence

From the evidence already provided, it is clear that the aim of understanding is fulfilled by understanding one phenomena at the moment a mental process arises. However, I will provide here some additional references from the commentaries and subcommentaries to more strongly substantiate the above-mentioned points.

> Having realized physical phenomena very well, three aspects of mental phenomena—mental contact, feeling, and consciousness—appear.[289]

If a person is able to note physical objects very well, then each time he or she notes a physical object, the noting mind as a mental phenomenon appears on its own. While one is taking a physical phenomenon as one's object, the mental phenomena at the five sense doors like the body-consciousness, the eye-consciousness, and so on appear on their own. They do not, however, appear all together as a group: when mental contact is distinct, it appears; when feeling is distinct, it appears; when consciousness is distinct, it appears.

Either mental contact, feeling, or consciousness will become apparent to a beginning meditator. For example, when you are experiencing hardness or softness (the earth element) you note it as "touching, touching," "hard, hard," or "soft, soft." For some, the mental contact that strikes against hardness or softness is distinct. For some, the feeling that experiences hardness or softness is distinct. For some, the consciousness that merely cognizes hardness or softness is distinct.

Thus when mental contact is distinct, one can only empirically observe the true nature of mental contact. However, mental contact never arises alone. Besides mental contact, mental factors like feeling, perception, volition, as well as consciousness also arise. It is not possible for mental contact to be split apart. Therefore, when mental contact, being the distinct phenomena, is understood, then the feeling, perception, other mental factors, and consciousness that arise together with it are said to be apparent and are also said to be understood. But this doesn't mean that they aren't understood if they aren't apparent.

Imagine that five ropes are tied together and four of them are immersed in water. You can only see one rope. If you pull this rope, you not only pull this single rope but pull all five ropes that are tied together. In this example, the rope that you can see is like the mental contact that is apparent. The ropes that are immersed in water are like the feeling, perception, and so on that are not apparent. Pulling the rope that you see and thereby pulling the ropes immersed in water is like noting and understanding the apparent mental contact and thereby including the nonapparent feeling, and so on. When feeling or consciousness is apparent, it can be understood in the same way. As the *Mahāṭīkā* says:

> The commentary explicitly mentions the realization of mental contact (*phassa*) as mental contact. However, when mental contact is realized, the other mental phenomena are also apparent, i.e., feeling (*vedanā*) as feeling, perception (*saññā*) as perception, volition (*cetanā*) as volition, and cognition (*viññāṇa*) as cognition.[290]

In this subcommentary, it is shown that when mental contact is apparent, one can observe it in terms of its unique characteristics. However when mental contact is apparent, the other accompanying phenomena of feeling, perception, volition, and consciousness are also apparent. This means that being apparent fulfills their purpose.

The commentaries to the *Sakkapañha Sutta*[291] and the *Satipaṭṭhāna Sutta*,[292] and the Satipaṭṭhānavibhaṅga of the *Vibhaṅga-aṭṭhakathā*, an Abhidhamma commentary, say:

> When mental contact is apparent to a person, not only is this mental contact apparent, but also feeling that feels, perception that perceives, volition that wills, and consciousness that cognizes. Therefore, it is said that all five phenomena are noted.[293]

You should understand the meaning of the two passages from the commentaries cited above as follows: For that person mental contact is distinct, and so one only observes mental contact in terms of its unique characteristic, and so on. However, it is said that he or she observes the five "contact-led" phenomena (*phassapañcamaka*), because mental contact never arises alone. It always occurs together with feeling, perception, volition, and consciousness.

You should not interpret the passages as follows: When mental contact is distinct to a person, he or she observes the five contact-led phenomena by reflecting about them based on his or her knowledge learned or heard from others, because he or she knows that mental contact never occurs alone but is always accompanied by feeling and so on. Nowhere do the Pāḷi texts, commentaries, or subcommentaries explain that one should observe by means of reflection based on knowledge learned or heard from others. They always explain that the noting must only be done with empirical knowledge.

For example, the moon is only apparent to people by way of its visible form. People can only see that visible form. Its smell, taste, and touch are not apparent. However, we can say that they see and understand the moon by way of seeing its visible form. Likewise, when mental contact is apparent and observed, we can say that other accompanying phenomena are also apparent. I have already explained this point several times before, but here is more textual support for it:

> Eye-consciousness is associated with three aggregates: feeling, perception, and mental formations. These aggregates can be experienced along with eye-consciousness. Thus they are called mental phenomena that can be perceived along with eye-consciousness (*cakkhuviññānaviññātabbā*).[294]

> If mental contact is understood in three ways—namely, with full understanding of the known, full understanding by investigation, and full understanding by abandoning—three kinds of

> feeling are also understood, since they are rooted in contact or associated with contact.[295]

Here, the Pāḷi terms are understood as follows: "full understanding of the known" (*ñātapariññā*) refers to insight knowledge that discerns mental and physical phenomena and insight knowledge that discerns conditionality.[296] "Full understanding by investigation" (*tīraṇapariññā*) refers to insight knowledge by comprehension and insight knowledge of arising and passing away.[297] "Full understanding by abandoning" (*pahānapariññā*) refers to the remaining insight knowledges up to path knowledge.[298]

> When a particular type of consciousness is understood, the associated phenomena, whether mental or physical, are also understood, since they are rooted in or come along with that consciousness.[299]

It is clear from these passages that if one understands any constituent of an obvious object, the aim of understanding not only the five contact-led phenomena but all other phenomena involved in that single mental process are fulfilled. Moreover, given the term "come along with" (*sahuppannattā*), it is reasonable to assume that if one observes and understands any part of an obvious object, whether mental or physical, the aim of understanding all associated mental and physical phenomena is fulfilled.

The following passages are from the *Bahudhātuka Sutta*[300] in the Pāḷi canon and its commentary:

> "There are, Ānanda, these six elements: the earth element, the water element, the fire element, the air element, the space element, and the consciousness element. When he knows and sees these six elements, a bhikkhu can be called skilled in the elements."[301]

> Here, "knows and sees" refers to path (*magga*) and insight (*vipassanā*).[302] The terms "the earth element, the water element . . ." show that we are not a being but only elements. Moreover, other elements should be added to these six so that there is a total enumeration of eighteen elements. When this enumeration is made, one should break down the consciousness element

> into its six varieties—that is, the eye-consciousness element and so on. When the eye-consciousness element is noted, the noting of the eye that is its base and the physical matter that is its object is also fulfilled. It is the same for the other kinds of consciousness elements. When the mind-consciousness element is noted, the noting of the two other elements, the mind element and mind-object element, is also fulfilled. The Buddha mentioned these six elements in the discourse because he wanted the bhikkhu's practice for liberation to lead him all the way to the goal.[303]

To explain the quote above: A monk can be called "skilled in the elements" when he sees and understands them by means of insight knowledge and path knowledge. One who understands the six elements can fully understand the tangible element and the mind-consciousness element.

In the mental-object element, only the water element and the space element can be understood. The remaining elements of the mental-object element and the eye element, the ear element, the nose element, the tongue element, the body element, the visible form element, the sound element, the smell element, and the taste element cannot be understood. So doubts can arise with regard to the statement that one can understand the eighteen elements. In order to dispel these doubts, the Majjhima Nikāya commentary states, "Moreover, other elements (*tāpi purimāhi*). . . ," which it explains as follows: There are six kinds of consciousness elements—the eye-consciousness element, ear-consciousness element, nose-consciousness element, tongue-consciousness element, body-consciousness element, and the mind-consciousness element.

If one understands the eye-consciousness element (seeing), then understanding the eye element (the physical basis of the eye) and the visible form element (the form that is seen) is fulfilled. If one understands the ear-consciousness element (hearing), then understanding the ear element (the physical basis of the ear) and the sound element (the sound that is heard) is fulfilled. If one understands the nose-consciousness element (smelling), then understanding the nose element (the physical basis of the nose) and the smell element (the smell that is smelled) is fulfilled. If one understands the tongue-consciousness element (tasting), then understanding the tongue element (the physical basis of the tongue) and the taste element (the taste that is tasted) is fulfilled. If one understands the body-consciousness element (touching), then understanding the body element (the physical basis of the body) and the tangible element (the touch that is felt) is fulfilled. The Pāḷi texts directly mention this tangible element. At the moment of touching, one can empirically observe and understand hardness, softness, heat, warmth, cold, stiffness, and suppleness. If one understands the mind-consciousness element (thinking), then understanding the mind element (comprised of receiving [*sampaṭicchana*] and five-sense-door-adverting [*pañcadvārāvajjana*] consciousnesses) and the mental object element (the thought that is thought) is fulfilled. Thus as the aim of understanding the remaining elements is fulfilled, although one essentially understands only the six elements, all eighteen elements are understood.

In conclusion, it is clear from this Pāḷi text and its commentary that by understanding one of the consciousness elements one fulfills understanding of its physical basis and its mental or physical object as well. Therefore, based on the term "come along with," if one observes and understands any distinct mental or physical phenomena, one also fulfills the aim of understanding all of the other mental and physical phenomena that occur at the same time.

The case of hearing

As was explained above for the case of seeing, when we note hearing as "hearing" (smelling as "smelling," tasting as "tasting," touching as "touching"), one of the five phenomena that are distinct at the moment of hearing (smelling, tasting, or touching) becomes apparent in terms of its characteristic and so on. Thus we see and understand that phenomenon as it really is; this is "full understanding of the known." We also see and understand the characteristics of impermanence and so on, and see and understand the phenomenon as arising and passing away. These are "full understanding by investigation" and "full understanding by abandoning."

Ear-sensitivity

When one correctly understands the ear-sensitivity (*sotapasāda*), one knows that: it is sensitive or functional enough to detect a sound (characteristic); it brings a person or allows a person to hear a sound (function);

it is the basis for hearing, the basis from which hearing results (manifestation); and its proximate cause is the kamma-generated solid ear (proximate cause). This is what "he understands the ear" (*sotañca pajānāti*) means in the *Satipaṭṭhāna Sutta*.[304]

Sound base

When one correctly understands the sound base (*saddāyatana*), one knows that: it becomes apparent in the ear (characteristic); it is heard (function); it is an object of hearing and experienced through hearing (manifestation); and it is based on the four primary material elements (proximate cause). This is what "he understands sounds" (*sadde ca pajānāti*) means in the *Satipaṭṭhāna Sutta*.

Ear-consciousness

When one correctly understands ear-consciousness (*sotaviññāṇa*), one knows that: it arises in the ear or hears a sound (characteristic); it only takes sound as its object, or it is simply hearing (function); it is directed toward the sound (manifestation); and it is caused by paying attention, by the conjunction of the ear with sound, or by good or bad kamma (proximate cause).

The case of smell

Nose-sensitivity

When one correctly understands nose-sensitivity (*ghānapasāda*), one knows that: it is sensitive or functional enough to detect a smell (characteristic); it brings a person or allows a person to smell an odor (function); it is the basis for smelling, the basis from which smelling results (manifestation); and its proximate cause is the kamma-generated solid nose (proximate cause). This is what "he understands the nose" (*ghānañca pajānāti*) means in the *Satipaṭṭhāna Sutta*.

Odor base

When one correctly understands the odor base (*gandhāyatana*), one knows that: it becomes apparent in the nose (characteristic); it is smelled (function); it is an object of smell and experienced through smelling (manifestation); and it is based on the four primary material elements (proximate cause). This is what "he understands odors" (*gandhe ca pajānāti*) means in the *Satipaṭṭhāna Sutta.*

Nose-consciousness

When one correctly understands nose-consciousness (*ghānaviññāṇa*), one knows that: it arises in the nose or smells an odor (characteristic); it only takes odor as its object or it is simply smelling (function); it is directed toward the odor (manifestation); and it is caused by paying attention, by the conjunction of the nose with odor, or by good or bad kamma (proximate cause).

The case of taste

When we consume food, we experience the quality of its flavor—sweet, sour, hot, bitter, salty, and so on. Thus when we eat something, we should note it as either "eating" or as "sweet," "sour," and so on, according to its flavor.

Tongue-sensitivity

When one correctly understands tongue-sensitivity (*jivhāpasāda*), one knows that: it is sensitive or functional enough to detect a flavor (characteristic); it brings a person or allows a person to taste a flavor (function); it is the basis for tasting, the basis from which tasting results (manifestation); and its proximate cause is the kamma-generated solid tongue (proximate cause). This is what "he understands the tongue" (*jivhañca pajānāti*) means in the *Satipaṭṭhāna Sutta.*

Flavor base

When one correctly understands the flavor base (*rasāyatana*), one knows that: it becomes apparent on the tongue (characteristic); it is tasted as something sweet, something sour, and so on (function); it is an object of taste, experienced through tasting (manifestation); and it is based on the four primary material elements (proximate cause). This is what "he understands flavors" (*rase ca pajānāti*) means in the *Satipaṭṭhāna Sutta.*

Tongue-consciousness

When one correctly understands tongue-consciousness (*jivhāviññāṇa*), one knows that: it arises on the tongue or tastes a flavor of sweetness, sourness, and so on (characteristic); it only takes flavor as its object, or it simply tastes (function); it is directed toward the flavor (manifestation); and it is caused by paying attention, by the conjunction of the tongue with flavor, or by good or bad kamma (proximate cause).

Note that when we have a meal the sight of the food is seeing, the odor of the food is smelling, the touch of the food at our fingers, lips, tongue, throat, and so on is touching, as is moving the hands, opening and closing the mouth, chewing the food, and so on. Examining the food is considered thinking.

In this way, when noted as shown above in the case of seeing and such, we can understand all movements and activities in their true nature. Moreover we can understand the mental constituents, such as contact, feeling, and so on, that are involved in moments of hearing, smelling, and tasting, in terms of their characteristics and such as well.

The case of touch

We can experience touch throughout the whole body. The feet touch one another, the hands touch one another, and the hands touch the feet. The hands, feet, and hair touch the body, and the tongue touches the teeth and the palate. Mucus, saliva, food, and water touch the throat and the palate. Many organs and substances inside the body touch one another, such as food and internal air that touch the intestines. Blood, internal air, flesh, sinews, and bones touch each other. We are also always coming into physical contact with external things such as our clothes, shoes, bed, pillow, blanket, the floor or ground, the wall, our umbrella or walking stick, stones and plants, the wind, sunlight and water, tools and furniture, and so on. Animals and insects, such as mosquitoes and horseflies, touch us too. Aside from specific sensations, all touch must be noted as "touching" every time one notices it.

If the touching sensation is distinct as a pleasant or unpleasant feeling, then we should note it as it is. If it feels hot, note it as "hot, hot." If cold, note it as "cold, cold." If warm, note it as "warm, warm." If chilly, note it as "chilly, chilly." If lying down, note it as "lying, lying." If tired, note it as "tired, tired." If painful, note it as "pain, pain." If numb, note it as "numb, numb." If aching, note it as "aching, aching." If itchy, note it as "itching, itching." If stiff, note it as "stiff, stiff." If dizzy, note it as "dizzy, dizzy." If pleasant, note it as "pleasant, pleasant." In this way, we should note touch from moment to moment. Note the nature of these sensations of touch clearly, precisely, and accurately using everyday language and words that indicate ultimate realities.

Body-sensitivity

When one correctly understands body-sensitivity (*kāyapasāda*), one knows that: it is sensitive or functional enough to detect physical sensation (characteristic); it brings a person or allows a person to touch a tangible object (function); it is the basis for touch, the basis from which touch results (manifestation); and its proximate cause is the kamma-generated solid body (proximate cause). This is what "he understands the body" (*kāyañca pajānāti*) means in the *Satipaṭṭhāna Sutta.*

Tangible object base in general

When one correctly understands the tangible object base (*phoṭṭhabbāyatana*), one knows that: it becomes apparent in the body (characteristic); it is felt as touching (function); and it is an object of touch, experienced through touch (manifestation).

Tangible object base in particular: the primary material elements

When one correctly understands the earth element, one knows that: it is hard or rough, or soft or smooth (characteristic); it is the basis or foundation for all other physical matter (function); it receives or bears other physical matter (manifestation); and it is hard or soft because of the other three primary material elements—namely, it is hard due to solidity, cold, and pressure, and soft due to moisture, fluidity, and warmth (proximate cause).

Awareness of weight, whether heavy or light, is awareness of the earth element. However, pleasant and unpleasant physical sensations can be associated with any of the three elements of earth, fire, and air. The Abhidhamma commentary called *Aṭṭhasālinī* says:

> The earth element is defined by six qualities: hardness, softness, smoothness, roughness, heaviness, and lightness. On the other hand, the two qualities of pleasant and unpleasant (touch) are defined in terms of the three (discernable) primary material elements.[305]

When one correctly understands the fire element, one knows that: it is hot, warm, or cold (characteristic); it matures, or ripens matter (function); it softens matter (manifestation); and it is hot, warm, or cold because of the other three primary material elements (proximate cause).

When one correctly understands the air element, one knows that: it is supporting, stiff, loose, or flabby (characteristic); it moves or shifts matter (function); it conveys to other places (manifestation); and it is stiff or loose because of the other three primary material elements (proximate cause); This is what "he understands tangibles" (*phoṭṭhabbe ca pajānāti*) means in the *Satipaṭṭhāna Sutta.*

Body-consciousness

When one correctly understands body-consciousness (*kāyaviññāṇa*), one knows that: it arises in the body or experiences touch (characteristic); it only takes touch as its object, or it is simply touch (function); it is directed toward the tangible (manifestation); and it is caused by paying attention, by the conjunction of the body with a tangible, or by good or bad kamma (proximate cause).

Physical pain

When one correctly understands physical pain (*kāyikadukkha*), one knows that: it is the feeling of an unpleasant tangible object (characteristic);[306] it withers or weakens its associated mental states (function);[307] it is painful or irritates the body (manifestation);[308] and it is painful because of body-sensitivity, the fine fleshy tissue, or an unpleasant touch (proximate cause).[309]

Physical pleasure

When one correctly understands physical pleasure (*kāyikasukha*), one knows that: it is the feeling of a pleasant tangible object (characteristic); it intensifies associated mental states (function); it is pleasant and enjoyable (manifestation); and it is pleasant because of body-sensitivity, the fine fleshy tissue, or a pleasant touch (proximate cause).

Mindfulness of breathing

> . . . mindful he breathes in, mindful he breathes out.[310]

According to this quote from the Pāḷi canon, every time we note the breath moving in and out as "in, out," we feel the touch of the air and are aware of the body-consciousness. Thus awareness of the breath amounts to an awareness of touch. In chapter 3 I explained how the observation of the in- and out-breath can serve as insight meditation.

If we observe the breath, we experience it as distention inside the nose. This is correct understanding of the characteristic of the air element, the characteristic of distension (*vitthambhanalakkhaṇā*). If we feel moving, movement, or motion, this is correct understanding of the function of the air element, the function of movement (*samudīraṇarasa*), and if we feel conveying, this is correct understanding of its manifestation, the manifestation of conveying (*abhinīhārapaccupaṭṭhāna*).

If we see the separate units of movement of the in- and out-breath as caused by the existence of the physical body, the nose, and the intention to breathe, this is correct understanding of the cause of its arising, referred to as:

> . . . he abides contemplating in the body its nature of arising . . .[311]

If we see the separate units of movement of the breath disappear or that the breath cannot appear without the physical body, the nose, and the intention to breathe, this is correct understanding of the cause of its vanishing, referred to as:

> . . . or he abides contemplating in the body its nature of vanishing . . .[312]

When we note "in, out" with each breath, we do not take this process to be a person, a being, a woman, a man, me, or mine, but we see and understand it as a mere collection of movements that are felt. Or, as it is said:

> Or else mindfulness that "there is a body" is simply established in him . . .[313]

The abdomen rises and falls as a result of the in- and out-breath. By noting this as "rising" and "falling," we are aware of tightening, loosening, or distending. This is correct understanding of the characteristic of the air element. If we are aware of movement and conveyance, this is correct understanding of the function and the manifestation of the air element. If we see that the rising and falling movements of the abdomen appear and disappear in separate units, this is correct understanding of arising and vanishing. In other words, we should perceive the actions and movements of our bodies in accord with the Pāḷi passage:

> . . . he understands accordingly however his body is disposed.[314]

In an ultimate sense the rise and fall of the abdomen characterized by tension, pressure, or movement is the air element. It is considered part of the physical aggregate (*rūpakkhandhā*), a tangible object (*phoṭṭhabbāyatana*), a tangible object element (*phoṭṭhabbadhātu*), and the truth of suffering (*dukkhasacca*). Thus the rise and fall of the abdomen is clearly an appropriate object of meditation for the development of insight.

Moreover, it is obvious from the last verse above that any bodily action or movement can be taken as an object for insight meditation. There is no way that this view can be considered incorrect. In fact, it is in accord with the Buddha's teaching and is highly beneficial in a variety of ways. By practicing insight meditation one acquires right view (*sammādiṭṭhi*) and true knowledge (*vijjā*), the defilements based on ignorance can be abandoned, and one can attain the end of unsatisfactoriness, that is, the fruit of arahantship (*arahattaphala*) and nibbāna.

I mention this point here, not because the observation of the rise and fall of the abdomen is part of practice with the in- and out-breath (*ānāpāna*), but because the in- and out-breath itself produces the rise and fall of the abdomen. Actually, perception of the rise and fall of the abdomen constitutes contemplation of the body (*kāyānupassanā*) since it is both a physical movement and one of the elements. It can also be considered awareness of mental objects (*dhammānupassanā*) since it is included in the physical aggregate, the basis of the physical sense, and the truth of suffering.

The four primary material elements

We can experience any one of forty-two parts of the body when sitting, standing, walking, or lying down. These include twenty parts that are dominated by earth element,[315] twelve dominated by the water element,[316] four dominated by the fire element,[317] and six dominated by the air element.[318]

Each time a person touches one of these parts of the body, he or she notes it as "touching, touching," and so correctly understands that: the earth element is experienced via the characteristics of hardness, softness, or smoothness (*kakkhaḷalakkhaṇā*); the fire element is experienced via the characteristics of heat, warmth, or cold (*uṇhattalakkhaṇā*); the air element is experienced via the characteristics of firmness, stiffness, or looseness (*vitthambhanalakkhaṇā*); and the air element is experienced via the function of movement, pushing, or pulling (*samudīraṇarasa*), and the manifestation of conveying (*abhinīhārapaccupaṭṭhāna*).

In reality we cannot directly experience the water element with the sense of touch. But given the power of this element, we can know its true nature with mind-consciousness based on bodily sensations of the earth, fire, and air elements that arise in conjunction with the water element. Thus the water element is understood by noting touch. The water element is experienced via the characteristics of flowing or melting (*paggharaṇalakkhaṇā*). This type of sensation is especially noticeable when sweat, mucus, or tears flow, when spitting or swallowing phlegm or saliva, or when urinating. The function of the water element is experienced via expansion or dampening (*brūhanarasa*). We feel it mainly when we take a bath, have a drink, and so on. The manifestation of the water element is experienced via cohesion or holding together (*saṅgahapaccupaṭṭhāna*).

Thus every time we note a bodily sensation, we will be aware of the four primary material elements. We will understand that there is no person, being, woman, man, "I," or "mine," but only a collection of physical elements such as hardness, softness, heat, warmth, cold, tightness, looseness, movement, pulling, pushing, flowing, melting, wetness, expansion, and cohesion. This understanding is in accord with the following canonical passage:

> . . . a bhikkhu reviews this same body, however it is placed, however disposed, by way of elements thus: "In this body there are the earth element, the water element, the fire element, and the air element."[319]

Note that awareness of the rise and fall of the abdomen is naturally in accord with this Pāḷi quote. Mindfulness of walking, bending, and other movements is also covered under this awareness of touch. However, the intention to walk, intention to bend, and so on are awareness of mind, so they will be explained in the upcoming sections on posture and clear comprehension.

How to observe thought

I have previously explained that mental activities, such as thinking, considering, examining, reflecting, and so on, are referred to as mind door processes. When one notes them as "thinking," "considering," "examining," "reflecting," and so on, one phenomenon, such as the mind door (*manodvāra*), mental object (*dhammārammaṇā*), mind-consciousness (*manoviññāṇa*), mental contact, or feeling will be apparent in terms of its characteristic and so on. Thus one will see and understand one of these phenomena as it really is. This is full understanding of the known (*ñātapariññā*). One will also see and understand the characteristic of impermanence and so on, and will see and understand it as arising and passing away. These are full understanding by investigation (*tīraṇapariññā*) and full understanding by abandoning (*pahānapariññā*).

The commentaries and subcommentaries explain that "mind door" refers to both the life-continuum and the mind-unit that adverts to mental objects. Since the mind-sensitivity of the heart is the basis for these, it is also figuratively called the mind door (*manodvāra*). Mental objects include the five sensitivities—the eye, ear, nose, tongue, and body sensitivities; the six kinds of subtle matter (*sukhumarūpa*)—the water element, femininity (*itthibhāvā*), masculinity (*pumbhāva*), the mind-sensitivity of the heart (*hadaya*), vitality (*jīvita*), and nutrition (*āhāra*); and all mundane mental states, all mundane mental factors. These are all mental objects to be observed for the development of insight. Mind-consciousness includes both wholesome and unwholesome thoughts, as well as registration (*tadārammaṇa*). The mental contact and feeling included here are those associated with mind-consciousness.

The mind door

When insight knowledge becomes extremely keen and pure, there are gaps between two consecutive notings. For example, when one bends the arm, each separate little movement of bending has to be noted as "bending, bending." When one is aware like this gaps between the previous noting, the following intention, and the following bending movement become apparent. Over time it will seem as if fewer and fewer objects are noted or that there are gaps in one's noting. In fact, objects will not have become fewer and there are not gaps in one's noting. Instead, given the quickness of one's noting, the life-continuum consciousness that falls between successive mental processes becomes apparent. Seeing the gap between two successive mental processes at that moment is called "understanding the life-continuum consciousness or the mind door."

Another mind door is the mind-moment that adverts to an object. When one correctly understands adverting consciousness, one knows it as initial attention (characteristic), initial investigation (function), initial examination (manifestation), and the first moment of full consciousness following the life-continuum consciousness (proximate cause).

As mentioned before, the mind-sensitivity of the heart is also metaphorically regarded as a mind door, since it serves as the basis for the mind. When one correctly understands the mind-sensitivity of the heart, one knows that: it is the basis of the thinking or noting mind (characteristic); it supports the existence of the thinking mind or noting mind (function); it receives or bears the thinking mind (manifestation); and it is caused by the four primary material elements (proximate cause). This is what "he understands the mind" (*manañca pajānāti*) means in the *Satipaṭṭhāna Sutta*.

Mental objects

Many varieties of mentality (*citta*) and mental constituents (*cetasika*) fall into the category of mental objects. I have already explained awareness of certain mental objects, such as the five sensitivities of eye, ear, nose, tongue, and body, the water element, and the mind-sensitivity of the heart. Certain other mental objects will be explained later, so I will not elaborate on them in detail here.

Gender

When one smiles or thinks with awareness of one's own gender, one experiences one's femininity or masculinity. When one correctly understands it, one knows that: it has the nature of femininity or masculinity (characteristic); it shows femininity or masculinity (function); it manifests as the female or male structure of the body, its feminine or masculine features, the typical feminine or masculine occupations, and the typical feminine or masculine deportment (manifestation); and it is caused by the four primary material elements (proximate cause).

Vitality

A physical phenomenon called vitality (*jīvīta*) enlivens the five senses, the mind-sensitivity of the heart, and gender. It becomes apparent along with these when one notes a sight, a sound, and so on, since it appears and disappears along with them. Before it disappears, it performs the function of enlivening the physical constituents, such as the eye-sensitivity and so on. The process by which the eye-sensitivity continuously generates new instances to replace old ones until one dies occurs due to and is sustained by vitality. When one correctly understands vitality, one knows that: it maintains the physical constituents of the eye-sensitivity and so on (characteristic); it makes the physical constituents of the eye-sensitivity and so on, occur (function); it supports the existence of the physical constituents of eye-sensitivity and so on (manifestation); and it is caused by the four primary material elements (proximate cause).

Nutrition

When one feels physically strong and mentally alert after having eaten, nutrition becomes apparent. When one correctly understands nutrition, one knows that: it has nutritive essence (*ojā*) (characteristic); it sustains the physical body (function); it strengthens the body (manifestation); and it is caused by food (proximate cause).

Thinking consciousness

When one correctly understands mind-consciousness, one knows that: it appears as thought, reflection, consideration, knowing, wandering, and so on (characteristic); it only takes mental objects as its object, or it is simply cognizing (function); it is directed toward mental objects (manifestation); and it is caused by attention or the combination of the mind-sensitivity of the heart and mental objects (proximate cause).

Mental contact

When one correctly understands mental contact, one knows that: it is mental contact between an object and the mind (characteristic); it strikes the object (function); it is the concurrence of the mind-sensitivity of the heart, consciousness, and an object (manifestation); and it is caused by the appearance of an object (proximate cause).

Feeling

When one correctly understands the feeling of joy (*somanassavedanā*), one knows that: it experiences a pleasant object or is delightful (characteristic); it partakes in pleasure (function); it is mental pleasure and enjoyment (manifestation); and it is caused by pleasant objects or mental peace and calm (proximate cause).

When one correctly understands the feeling of distress (*domanassavedanā*), one knows that: it experiences an unpleasant object, is an unpleasant or frustrating mental activity, or is mental distress, sadness, sorrow, or worry (characteristic); it partakes in displeasure, dislike, or disgust with respect to an object (function); it is mental affliction, displeasure, or suffering (manifestation); and it is caused by the mind-sensitivity of the heart and unpleasant objects (proximate cause).

When one correctly understands the feeling of neither displeasure nor pleasure (*upekkhāvedanā*), one knows that: it is felt as neutral, neither unpleasant nor pleasant, neither happy nor unhappy (characteristic); it keeps the mind balanced between pleasure and pain (function); it is subtle or calm (manifestation); and it is caused by a consciousness without rapture or an object that is neither unpleasant nor pleasant (proximate cause).

Perception

Perception, also called the aggregate of perception (*saññākkhandhā*), is the recognition, remembrance, and identification of an object so as not to forget it. It is especially obvious when one encounters a novel object or pays particular attention to someone or something. When one correctly understands perception, one knows that: it perceives an object so as not to forget it (characteristic); it recognizes objects one has encountered previously (function); it is retained in one's memory the way it has been apprehended (manifestation); and it is caused by all apparent objects (proximate cause).

Mental formations

The fifty mental factors other than feeling and perception[320] are included in the aggregate of mental formations (*saṅkhārakkhandhā*). It includes all the mental phenomena that make things happen, such as seeing, hearing, and such, or going, standing, sitting, lying, or bending, and such.

Among these fifty factors, I will only explain mental volition (*cetanā*) here, since it directs all the others. In this respect, mental volition is like a foreman who both performs his or her own duties while simultaneously directing his or her co-workers in theirs. Another analogy is that volition is like a farmer who does his own work on the farm while also supervising his or her workers. In the same way, volition makes the other mental constituents do their tasks as well. Volition is especially obvious when an urgent situation needs to be acted upon very quickly and one feels as if one is urged and pushed to act.

When one correctly understands volition, one knows that: it activates or stimulates the mental factors (characteristic); it acts, works, and accomplishes (function); it coordinates activities like a ruler who sentences someone to death or a donor who allows the goods he has offered to be taken away (manifestation); and it is caused by a wholesome or unwholesome attention or attitude (*manasikārapadaṭṭhānā*), ignorance of true happiness and suffering (*avijjāpadaṭṭhānā*), the sense bases and sense objects (*vatthārammaṇapadaṭṭhānā*), or consciousness (*viññāṇapadaṭṭhānā*) (proximate causes).

How to note general activities

When walking, you should note each and every step as "walking, walking" or "stepping, stepping" or "right, left" or "lifting, moving, dropping." When your mindfulness and concentration grow strong, you will be able to note the intention to walk or the intention to move before starting to walk or move. At that point you will come to personally and thoroughly understand that the intention to walk occurs first, and that as a result of this intention, a sequence of movements happens, and that as these movements happen everywhere, all the physical phenomena that are called "body" move in separate little movements, arising and disappearing one after the other. This is called "walking." This is referred to in the following Pāḷi passage from the *Mahāsatipaṭṭhāna* and *Satipaṭṭhāna Sutta*s:

> . . . when walking, a bhikkhu understands "I am walking."[321]

And from the commentary to the Dīgha Nikāya:

> One understands that the intention to walk arises. This (intention) causes movement (i.e., the air element) to arise. This movement causes intimation to arise. Because these movements happen everywhere, all the physical phenomena that are called

"body" move in separate little movements to the intended place. This is called "walking."[322]

This is not common knowledge. Those who have never practiced in this way or gained any knowledge may be dubious about the instruction: "When walking, a bhikkhu understands 'I am walking.'" I will explain this point here in accordance with the commentary.

One may wonder: "Doesn't even a dog or a fox understand it is walking when it is walking?" That is true. But the Buddha was not at all referring to this kind of common knowledge. Actually dogs, foxes, and ordinary people do not know their intention to walk or the movement that happens in separate little movements. They can't distinguish between mind and body and do not understand that the intention causes the movement to happen. They do not understand that there is only a sequence of successive intentions and successive movements that disappear and vanish one after the other. In fact, dogs, foxes, and ordinary people only know some of the time that they are walking, and this may be either in the beginning, the middle, or at the end of it; most of the time their minds wander elsewhere while they are walking.

Even when ordinary people occasionally know they are walking, they perceive it as an individual person who is walking, and they take that person to be unchanging. They think that they are the same person before, during, and after the walk. Even after walking a hundred miles, they think that they are certainly the same individual that they were before they left, even after having arrived at a different location. They think that they stay exactly the same as before. One cannot abandon the wrong view of a being, rid oneself of attachment to such a view, nor produce the insight knowledges with such an ordinary understanding. Making this kind of understanding the object of one's meditation or meditating based on such an understanding does not amount to practicing insight. So this ordinary understanding is not meditation (*bhāvanākamma*). And since it is not a basis of insight meditation (*vipassanākamma*), this ordinary understanding cannot be called a basis or foundation for practice (*kammaṭṭhānā*). Since this understanding is not based on insight and mindfulness, it is not meditation on the foundations of mindfulness (*satipaṭṭhānabhāvanā*). One should understand that in the above passage, the Buddha did not intend the ordinary understanding that is common to dogs, foxes, and ordinary people.

However, if you note "intention" and "walking" whenever one walks, the intention that arises in the mind and the bodily movement that take place will be very distinct. Then you will not mix the mental process of intention with the body but will understand them as different processes. Likewise, you will not mix the bodily movements with the mind but will understand them as different processes. You will understand that the intention to walk causes the separate units of little movements to happen, and, thereby, you will understand that there are only separate units of intention and movement. Further, the intentions will not merge into the movements and the little separate movements will not merge into the next little movement, but they will disappear one after the other. As the commentaries explain, you can see six or even more separate little movements in one pushing movement of the foot.

Based on this you will realize that saying "I am walking" or "he is walking" is purely conventional. There is in fact no individual person who walks; there is only the intention, followed by the movement of a collection of physical phenomena. No physical phenomenon lasts even for the twinkling of an eye. Everything is subject to impermanence, and because everything instantly arises and disappears, it is just a mass of unsatisfactoriness. You can judge it to be unsatisfactory based on personal experience. This understanding is called "clear comprehension without delusion" (*asammohasampajañña*), and it is one of the four kinds of clear comprehension. The understanding that arises from noting "intention" or "walking" belongs to clear comprehension of the domain (*gocarasampajañña*). The latter clear comprehension is the cause for the former. You should repeatedly cultivate and accomplish clear comprehension of the domain so that clear comprehension without delusion can spontaneously arise.

This is how one can abandon the view of a being and get rid of the attachment to that view by means of the insight knowledge developed by observing intention and bodily movements. In addition to becoming an object for counter-insight (*paṭivipassanā*), this causes insight knowledge to powerfully arise, so it is also called "a basis or foundation of practice." And since one's understanding is developed with mindfulness, it is called "meditation on the foundations of mindfulness." There is no doubt that the instruction "when walking, a bhikkhu understands, 'I am walking'" is the authentic word of Buddha.

> This meditator's understanding helps him abandon the wrong view of a being and to eradicate the belief in self. Thus it is a

> basis or foundation (of practice) and also meditation on the foundations of mindfulness.[323]

According to this passage from the commentary, the phrases "the basis or foundation of practice" and "meditation on the foundations of mindfulness" are synonymous in an ultimate sense. But they are different in a technical sense. The mindfulness that penetrates objects such as the intention or the physical process of walking, for example, is called "a foundation of mindfulness" (*satipaṭṭhāna*). It is also called "meditation" (*bhāvanā*), since it must be developed. For these two reasons it is called "meditation on the foundations of mindfulness": it is mindfulness that must be developed and that penetrates objects.

Insight knowledge is necessarily associated with mindfulness. There is no insight knowledge without mindfulness. In this regard we should only call it "meditation on the foundations of mindfulness" when one's understanding is guided by mindfulness. This understanding is also called "the basis or foundation of practice," since it helps successive insight knowledges to powerfully arise, and "counter-insight," since it serves as a meditative object for the practice that follows. When the intention is noted, that very noting mind is noted in turn as "noting" or "perceiving." After that, one notes the resulting movement and then notes that noting mind. This is called "counter-insight meditation" (*paṭivipassanābhāvanā*).

In this way, beginning with the stage of insight knowledge of dissolution, insight grows stronger and stronger by taking the noting mind itself as an object to be noted. That is why the understanding that arises due to mindfulness of the mental and bodily processes involved in walking is called both "a basis or foundation for practice" and "meditation on the foundations of mindfulness."

Clear comprehension

In walking

This Pāḷi instruction explains how clear comprehension without delusion (*asammohasampajañña*) arises:

> . . . a bhikkhu is one who acts in full awareness when going forward and returning; . . .[324]

The commentaries explain this as follows:

> Clear comprehension without delusion or clear comprehension of reality is the knowledge that there is no "I" or "self" behind activities. Understand it in the following way: ordinary people have deluded views about going forward and so on, such as "the self goes forward," "the self makes a forward movement," "I go forward," or "I make a movement." On the other hand, a bhikkhu (monk or meditator) who is going forward or backward understands that, when one intends to go forward, the intention and the movement it causes make movement to another place happen. As the movement instigated by the mind spreads everywhere, the collection of physical phenomena, the so-called body,[325] moves forward. While going forward, every time one lifts a foot, the earth and water elements become weak and ineffectual and the fire and air elements become strong and powerful. The same is true when pushing the foot down. When one releases momentum from pushing the foot forward, the fire and air elements become weak and ineffectual, and the earth and water elements become strong and powerful. This continues while dropping and pressing the foot.[326]

According to the subcommentary, lifting consists of dominant fire element followed by air element, moving forward and pushing consist of dominant air element followed by fire element, and releasing consists of dominant water element followed by earth element. Here, we can say that the water element is heavier than the earth element, which is consistent with the *Atthasālinī*, a commentary on Abhidhamma. Dropping and pressing consist of dominant earth element followed by water element. Thus when we are aware of lifting, the fire element is understood; when we are aware of moving forward and pushing, the air element is understood; when we are aware of releasing, the water element is understood; and when we are aware of dropping and pressing, the earth element is understood.

> While lifting, the mental and physical phenomena consisting of the intention to lift and the lifting movement do not carry over into the process of pushing. Likewise, the mental and physical phenomena happening while pushing do not carry over into

> the process of moving forward. Those happening while moving forward do not carry over into the process of releasing. Those happening while releasing do not carry over into the process of dropping. Those happening while dropping do not carry over into the process of pressing. They arise and disappear one after the other. Their distinct arising and disappearance are like sesame seeds bursting in a heated frying pan that make a sound like *pata-pata*. So who is going forward? Whose movement is it? In an ultimate sense, only selfless elements go forward, only elements stand, only elements sit down, only elements lie down. Thus along with the physical phenomena . . .
>
> > The preceding mind vanishes and the subsequent mind appears,[327] like the current of a river that ceaselessly flows forever.
>
> Thus is clear comprehension of reality when going forward and so on.[328]

Passages from the above commentary, such as "when one intends to go forward, the intention and the movement it causes make movement to another place happen" and "While lifting, the mental and physical phenomena consisting of the intention to lift and the lifting movement do not carry over into the process of pushing," are clearly not referring to the tranquility meditation of determining the four primary elements (*dhātu-vavatthāna*) but to the practice of insight meditation. This is so because such understanding can only belong to insight meditators, not to tranquility meditators. The above passages from the commentary explain how when insight knowledge is strong, which is the clear comprehension of the domain, insight knowledge of clear comprehension of reality arises.

The word "element" here is opposite in meaning to "being" or "soul" (*jīva*). It refers to the mental and physical phenomena, the four primary material elements that are dominant during movement. Although all of the commentaries concerned with this instruction use the term "mass of bones" (*aṭṭhisaṅghāto*), it is unreasonable to conclude from this that the skeleton becomes apparent to an insight meditator. It is also unreasonable to conclude that a tranquility meditator who is contemplating the skeleton would gain insight knowledge of phenomena such as the intention to go forward and so on. So the correct phrase to use here would be "mass of physical phenomena" (*rūpasaṅghāto*), rather than "mass of bones." But even if one takes "mass of bones" to be the correct term, one must interpret it as an idiomatic reference to the repulsiveness of the body, rather than as a literal reference to the physical skeleton.

Some teachers who use the tranquility method of meditating on particles instruct that one should observe the foot moving forward and so on by imagining it as particles of dust. But this is not correct, since the text instructs us to be aware of the air element that is dominant at the moment of moving the foot forward. When one is aware of this air element, one will experience it in terms of its ultimate characteristics of tension or pressure, its function of motion, or its manifestation as conveyance. If one understands any one of these aspects, one's awareness of the air element is accurate. Knowing the form of the foot to be particles is actually a concept, not an ultimate reality.

When you stand, sit, or lie down, note it as "standing," "sitting," or "lying down" in accordance with the Pāḷi texts.[329] When your mindfulness, concentration, and insight knowledge become powerful, you will be able to clearly understand the intention to stand and the air element that holds the standing posture by supporting it. This is also true for sitting. When you lie down, you will be able to clearly understand the intention to do so and the air and earth elements that manifest as the process of lying down. In this respect there is a difference between a meditator's understanding and that of ordinary people. As the *Vibhaṅga-aṭṭhakathā* says:

> One bhikkhu walks with a wandering mind, thinking of something else, while another walks without abandoning the subject of meditation. The same is true of standing, sitting, or lying down. One bhikkhu does so with a wandering mind, while another does so without abandoning the subject of meditation.[330]

So in keeping with the Pāḷi line "a bhikkhu is one who acts in full awareness when going forward and returning," you should be aware of going forward, backward, or sideways or of bending or curling up when you do these things. When your practice becomes powerful, you will also become aware of the intention and the air element involved in moving forward, backward, or sideways, and so on.

In seeing

> . . . who acts in full awareness when looking ahead and looking away; . . .[331]

According to this line of Pāḷi, one should be mindful when one looks ahead, to the side, down, up, or back. When one looks one should note it as "looking." Thus one maintains one's awareness and does not abandon the subject of insight meditation. This is clear comprehension of the domain (*gocarasampajañña*).

> Not abandoning the subject of meditation is clear comprehension of the domain. It means understanding the domain of the object. When meditating on (the phenomena of the) aggregates, elements, or sense bases, one should do the looking ahead or sideways only in accordance with one's insight practice. However, when contemplating kasiṇa-objects and so on, one should give first priority to one's tranquility meditation practice when looking ahead or sideways.[332]

So if a meditator practicing tranquility meditation wants to look at something or someone, he should do so without abandoning the subject of his meditation, like a cow that gives first priority to protecting her calf, even while she is eating. For an insight meditator, however, any object can serve as an object of insight meditation. So by noting the intention to look, insight knowledge of the four mental aggregates, two mental sense bases, and two mental elements can arise. Then by noting the movements caused by intention, such as opening the eyes, moving the eyes, or turning of the head, insight knowledge of the physical aggregate, the physical sense bases, and the physical elements can arise. By noting the seeing consciousness, insight knowledge of the five aggregates, four sense bases, and four elements can arise. If thinking arises, similar insight knowledge can arise by noting this thinking.

Thus the objects of insight meditation are none other than the intention to look and so on. For this reason it is said that one should deal with the act of seeing in accordance with one's foundation of practice. A meditator practicing tranquility meditation does not need to deal with the act of seeing in a special way; he just changes the focus of his meditation object to seeing for a moment. The insight meditator, however, has to note whatever mental or physical phenomena are arising. By noting in this way, the intention to look and the air element (that manifests as movements of the eyes or head) will be clearly understood when one's insight knowledge becomes strong.

In bending and stretching

> . . . who acts in full awareness when flexing and extending his limbs; . . .[333]

According to this Pāḷi passage, when one stretches, one should note it as "stretching." When shaking one's hands, when pushing and pulling, or when lifting, raising, and putting down, one notes them as "shaking," "pushing," "pulling," "lifting," "raising," or "putting down." When one's insight knowledge becomes strong one will clearly understand the intention to bend or to stretch and the air element that manifests in the bending or stretching movement. The commentary on the Mūlapaṇṇasa of the Majjhima Nikāya relates the following story of an elderly monk to explain the clear comprehension of the domain:

> Once, an elderly bhikkhu who was speaking with his pupils bent his arm abruptly. He then returned his arm to its original position and bent it again slowly. His students asked the reason for this peculiar behavior, and he explained, "Since I began meditating, I've never bent my arm without mindfulness. But as I was speaking with you now, I forgot to do it mindfully. That's why I put my arm back and bent it again mindfully." His pupils were filled with admiration for his great mindfulness and said: "Well done, sir! You are a true bhikkhu!"

If, like this elderly monk, one bends and stretches one's limbs without abandoning the meditation subject by noting it as "bending" or "stretching," one understands the intentions and the movements of bending or stretching as separate little movements that happen one after the other. This is clear comprehension of the domain. When this comprehension becomes sharp, the understanding arises that it is not a self within this body that makes it bend or stretch, but it is the intention that causes tiny little separate movements to arise. Moreover, one sees that the intention to bend disappears before the actual bending movement takes place and that the bending movements also appear and disappear one after the other. Thus one understands that all phenomena are impermanent, unsatisfactory, and not-self. This is clear comprehension of reality.

You may wonder: "When noting 'bending' or 'stretching,' am I not simply seeing the conceptual name and form of my limb being bent and stretched?" In the beginning you will happen to note the conceptual names and forms of objects, but you will also see the movement as a manifestation of the air element. So, at first, your understanding will be mixed with concepts. However, when your mindfulness, concentration, and insight knowledge grow powerful and strong, you will no longer focus on concepts. Since you will only see the intentions and movements appearing and disappearing one after the other, clear insight knowledge can arise. I have explained this at the beginning of this chapter.

In carrying or wearing

> . . . who acts in full awareness when wearing his robes and carrying his outer robe and bowl; . . .[334]

When one wears robes one notes it as "wearing." When one uses the alms bowl, cup, plate, or spoon, one notes it as "touching," "holding," "lifting," "putting down," and so on as appropriate. When one's insight knowledge becomes strong, mainly intentions and their resulting movements (that manifests as the air element), as well as the sensations and body-consciousness, will become obvious.

In eating, drinking

> . . . who acts in full awareness when eating, drinking, consuming food and tasting; . . .[335]

When one eats, drinks, chews, licks, or swallows, one notes it as "eating," "drinking," chewing," "licking," and "swallowing." When one's insight knowledge becomes strong, mainly the intention to eat and the resulting movement of eating (that manifests as the air element), as well as the sensation and tongue-consciousness, will become obvious.

Some suggest that one should meditate on eating by contemplating the repulsiveness or foulness of food in accord with the commentary that explains how to develop clear comprehension of reality. But that is actually a tranquility meditation—namely, contemplating ten aspects of the foulness of food, such as the trouble involved in obtaining it, the process of consuming it, the foulness of it in the stomach when mixed with bile, phlegm, blood, and so on.

On the other hand, when one's clear comprehension of the domain matures through the practice of noting eating, chewing, swallowing, savoring, and so on every time one eats, one will also understand the repulsiveness of food. For some meditators the repulsiveness and foulness of food becomes apparent as they note while preparing or eating food. Such meditators grow very disgusted, stop eating, and remain seated there, noting, even though they have not yet eaten enough. This kind of experience is quite common among meditators even nowadays. Some meditators even have this kind of experience while eating when their practice has not yet matured. If, in such cases, one feels extremely disgusted by one's food, as if it were human waste, it isn't actually clear comprehension but merely aversion. The commentary presumably mentions comprehension of the foulness of food in connection with clear comprehension of reality because it often arises spontaneously when one's clear comprehension of the domain matures.

In defecating and urinating

> . . . who acts in full awareness when defecating and urinating; . . .[336]

When one defecates or urinates, one notes it as "defecating," and so on. No object is regarded as good or bad in insight meditation. One must simply be aware of every phenomenon as it is. When one's insight knowledge becomes strong, primarily the intention to defecate or urinate and the resulting movements (that manifests as the air element), as well as the unpleasant sensations and body-consciousness and so on, will become obvious.

In walking, standing, sitting, falling asleep, waking, speaking, and keeping silent

> . . . who acts in full awareness when walking, standing, sitting, falling asleep, waking up, talking, and keeping silent.[337]

The method of comprehension for walking, standing, and sitting has already been explained above. Regarding awareness of falling asleep, when one feels sleepy, one notes it as "sleepy," "nodding," "drowsy," "heavy," and so on. When one feels very sleepy, one lies down and while lying notes "lying, lying," and all other distinct mental and physical phenomena. When one wakes one tries to note that very mental state.

This can be difficult for the beginner. If you cannot note it yet, you should start noting the moment you remember to be mindful. Eventually, when your mindfulness strengthens, you will be able to catch the moment of waking. Then you will understand that the mental and physical phenomena that occur just prior to falling asleep do not carry over into sleep. The arising of those kinds of consciousness that cannot (consciously) think, note, see, hear, touch, and so on is called sleep. Likewise, the phenomena that occur during sleep do not carry over into waking. Here "waking" indicates the reemergence of fully conscious activities, such as thinking, noting, and so on. There is no self or "I" that falls asleep or wakes up. You will understand that there are no permanent or pleasing phenomena. This understanding is called clear comprehension of reality.

When one speaks, one notes "wanting to speak," and "speaking." It is quite difficult to note speaking thoroughly, so it's better not to speak unless it's really necessary. When one's mindfulness becomes strong, mainly the intention to speak and the resulting movements (that manifests as the air element), as well as the sensations of touch (that manifests as the earth element) will become obvious. When one stops speaking, note it as "wanting to stop," "stopping," and "being quiet," and then continue noting other obvious objects. When one's mindfulness becomes powerful, one understands that the phenomena in a moment of speech are gone the moment one is quiet and that the intention to stop speaking and the physical phenomena of not talking anymore vanish at that very moment. This understanding is clear comprehension of reality.

Internal and external phenomena

When clear comprehension of the domain becomes strong and grows keen, one understands that in going there is only the intention and a collection of physical phenomena that are moving in separate little movements one after the other. There is no self that goes. "I go" is actually a concept that people use out of convenience, just as people address strangers as "nephew," "grandchild," "auntie," or "grandfather" in order to be polite.[338]

When clear comprehension of reality arises, one understands that phrases like "he goes," "a woman goes," or "a man goes" are merely conventional expressions and that there is no being or self that goes. One comes to see that existence is the same for others as it is for oneself, in that it consists only of the intention to go and separate segments of bodily movements. This understanding is consistent with the Pāḷi passage:

> . . . he abides contemplating the body as a body . . . externally . . .[339]

I explained in chapter 3 that there is no need to observe phenomena in the continua of others by distinguishing them as separate continua. It sometimes happens that by noting "intention" and "going" in one's own continuum, clear comprehension of reality arises and one observes that the same is true in the continuum of another. So one alternates between observing internal and external phenomena. This accords with:

> . . . he abides contemplating the body as a body . . . both internally and externally.[340]

Appearance and disappearance

Both the intention to go and its resulting physical movement appear and disappear instantly. This is understanding appearance and disappearance. While one notes one understands: These physical phenomena arise due to a cause; they could not arise if there were no cause. These physical phenomena arise due to the mind; they could not arise if there were no mind. These physical phenomena arise due to previous kamma; they could not arise if there were no kamma. These physical phenomena arise due to ignorance; they could not arise if there were no ignorance. These physical phenomena arise due to attachment; they could not arise if there were no attachment.

These physical phenomena arise due to nutrition; they could not arise if there were no nutrition. Thus one understands the appearance and disappearance of phenomena on the basis of what one sees and observes oneself and what one has learned. This accords with:

> . . . he abides contemplating in the body its nature of both arising and vanishing.[341]

Accurate awareness

With each noting of "intention" and "going" one is aware that what exists is only physical phenomena that are moving, and not a being, person, self, woman, or man. It means that what appears to one's awareness is the uninterrupted and continuous occurrence of intentions and movements without the concept of a solid form or shape. When awareness begins to become very keen and sharp, some meditators examine and reflect on whether or not they still have a body, head, arms, or legs. Their awareness and insight knowledge progress step by step and grow increasingly keen and sharp due to their accurate awareness. Each noting is free from attachment. This accords with:

> . . . he understands accordingly however his body is disposed.[342]

Thus is contemplation of the body (*kāyānupassanā*).

Contemplation of Feeling

Pleasant feeling

> . . . when feeling a pleasant feeling, a bhikkhu understands: "I feel a pleasant feeling";[343]

According to this passage from the *Satipaṭṭhāna Sutta*, pleasant bodily or mental feelings (*sukhavedanā*) should be noted as "pleasant," "comfortable," "good," or "happy." Then one will understand pleasant feeling as it is. I have fully explained how this understanding arises in the sections on how to note while seeing, touching, or thinking. The commentary on the Mūlapaṇṇasa of the Majjhima Nikāya dispels skeptical doubt on this point for those who lack any distinctive insight knowledge. I will present the following explanation based on this commentary.

You may wonder: "Even a baby suckling its mother's milk understands the pleasantness of it, doesn't it?" This is true, but the Buddha is not referring to that kind of understanding at all. Like babies, ordinary people are usually not aware of their pleasant feelings. Most of the time their minds wander off and they are unaware of the feeling they are experiencing. Even when they do occasionally become aware of it, they know it on the basis of the "I" that feels pleasure. Not seeing its momentary nature, they take it to be something permanent and lasting. They cannot abandon the view in a being or self based on this kind of understanding. Consequently, when they focus on an object with this kind of understanding, insight knowledge does not arise. Thus this understanding is not an object of insight meditation and is therefore also not called "a basis or foundation of practice." Since it is not an understanding based on mindfulness, it also does not give rise to the meditation on the foundations of mindfulness. So you should understand that the Buddha was not referring to the kind of understanding that babies and ordinary people have.

A meditator who uninterruptedly observes is aware of a pleasant feeling every time it arises, and so he or she understands it as just another phenomenon in terms of its characteristics and so on. He or she also sees that successive moments of pleasantness do not continue, but rather disappear one after the other. Because of seeing things in this way, the concept of continuity cannot continue to conceal the fact that feelings are impermanent, unsatisfactory, and not-self. With this kind of understanding, one can abandon the view of a being or self. As I explained in the section on how to note the postures, this is called "a basis or foundation of practice," and amounts to "meditation on the foundations of mindfulness." It was only with reference to this kind of understanding that the Buddha said, "When feeling a pleasant feeling, a bhikkhu understands: 'I feel a pleasant feeling.'"

When one's mindfulness becomes strong, one understands from one's own experience that expressions such as "I'm comfortable" and "I'm happy" are just conventional expressions. There is not really any "I" or a "being" who feels comfortable or happy. All that exists are momentary mental states of comfort or happiness. That is why the commentary says:

> A person who, by focusing on an object that causes pleasure to

arise, observes feeling only as feeling is one who knows that he is observing a pleasant feeling.[344]

Unpleasant feeling

Unpleasant physical feelings (*dukkhavedanā*), such as cramps, stiffness, aching, dizziness, heat, cold, numbness, pain, itchiness, and tiredness, are all classified as physical pain (*kāyikadukkha*). One should note them precisely and accurately as "cramp, cramp" and so on. Unpleasant mental experiences, such as sadness, frustration, worry, and fear, are classified as mental pain (*cetasikadukkha*) or distress (*domanassa*). These feelings should be noted by using ordinary language such as "sad, sad," "frustration, frustration," and so on. I have fully explained the way it is experienced and understood in the sections on how to note while seeing, touching, or thinking.

Some people think that one can only understand ultimate reality when using technical Pāḷi terms such as *rūpa, nāma, pathavī, āpo, phassa, vedanā, sukha, somanassa*, and so on. This is wrong. What matters most is to perceive the arising and passing away of mind and body as it really is. Technical terminology is not important. Pāḷi terms can be useful for Pāḷi scholars but not for other people. For the Burmese the Burmese terms will serve their purposes best. English speaking people should use English words.

If a Burmese person accurately notes pain as *narde* in Burmese, for example, he or she is bound to become aware of its true characteristic. What does it matter if one doesn't know the Pāḷi term for it? Will the insight knowledge one has gained be lost due to a lack of knowledge of Pāḷi? Not at all. Would knowledge of the correct Pāḷi term help improve one's insight knowledge? That is not possible. In actuality, when a meditator's insight knowledge matures, he or she will be aware of the instantaneous arising and passing away of mental and physical processes such that there will not even be time to note by labeling or naming. At that point, one's insight knowledge improves; it does not decline. So it is completely incorrect to think that one will only understand ultimate reality when one notes an object using a Pāḷi term.

Neither-unpleasant-nor-pleasant feeling

It is quite difficult to clearly experience neutral feelings (*upekkhavedanā*), as they are neither unpleasant nor pleasant. The commentaries on the

Cūḷavedalla Sutta[345] and the *Saṅgīti Sutta*[346] compare neither-unpleasant-nor-pleasant feeling (*adukkhamasukhavedanā*) to ignorance, since it too is too subtle to be noticed. And the commentary to the *Bahudhātuka Sutta*[347] also says that neutral sensation is like ignorance because it is not distinct. Both neither-unpleasant-nor-pleasant feeling and ignorance seem to be clear and easy to perceive with knowledge derived from scripture but not with empirical knowledge.

It is not as easy to notice ignorance as it is to notice attachment and aversion. In the same way, neither-unpleasant-nor-pleasant feelings are not as obvious as pleasant and unpleasant ones. We only say that neither-unpleasant-nor-pleasant feeling and ignorance are difficult to understand and not distinct in reference to how difficult it is to experience them empirically. With reference to these points, the commentaries on the *Sakkapañha Sutta*[348] and the *Satipaṭṭhāna Sutta*[349] say:

> Neither-unpleasant-nor-pleasant feeling is barely obvious, like an object in the dark. However, when both pleasant and unpleasant feelings are absent one can find the feeling to be neither. Thus one can inferentially know it as the opposite of those pleasant and unpleasant feelings.[350]
>
> "Barely obvious" here means that it is difficult to clearly see (neither-unpleasant-nor-pleasant feeling) with empirical knowledge. That is why the commentary says, "like an object in the dark."[351]

Although neither-unpleasant-nor-pleasant feeling is quite subtle, it can be an obvious contrast to pleasant and unpleasant feeling the moment they disappear. This type of realization is called "inferring a deer's footprint" (*migapadavalañjananaya*). The term comes from the example of inferring that a deer has stepped on a flat rock even though its footprint cannot be found there, because one sees its footprints on either side of the rock. Even though the deer's footprints cannot be found on the rock itself, we can draw the conclusion that the deer did indeed pass over it.

In the same way, as a meditator clearly experiences an unpleasant feeling and notes it as "pain, pain" and so on, the painful feeling may fade away. At that point the unpleasant feeling is no longer apparent, but neither is a pleasant feeling yet apparent. But there will be another distinct object that the meditator continues to note. After a few minutes, a pleasant or unpleasant feeling may occur again, and the meditator will note it. Then the meditator will perceive that a neither-unpleasant-nor-pleasant feeling occurred during the interval between the preceding and succeeding feelings of pain or pleasure.

From experiences like this, one realizes that the neither-unpleasant-nor-pleasant feeling is very difficult to perceive in an obvious way. Since no mental phenomenon occurs without feeling, one can conclude that there must be neither-unpleasant-nor-pleasant feeling present when pleasant and unpleasant feelings are not apparent. This conclusion is reached via the method of "inferring a deer's footprint." Although neither-unpleasant-nor-pleasant feeling will not be obvious to beginning meditators, more sharp minded or mature meditators can experience it empirically. I have shown how it can be experienced and understood when I dealt with how a meditator notes seeing or thinking.

Worldly pleasure

The happiness associated with external things that one loves or is fond of—one's spouse, children, clothing, property, estate, animals, gold, silver, and so on—or with internal things that one loves—one's eyesight, comfort, talents, skills, and so on—is called "worldly pleasure" (*sāmisasukha*). The Pāḷi term literally means "happiness that feeds on sensual pleasure," that is, happiness associated with sensual objects. It is also called "home happiness" (*gehassitasomanassa*), that is, happiness that dwells in the home of sensual satisfaction.

When one enjoys the beauty or sweet voice of one's spouse, for example, that visual object or sound arouses happiness. Or one may feel happy when thinking about a good time one had in the past. One should note all of these kinds of happiness as "happy, happy," according to the instruction:

> When feeling a pleasant feeling associated with a sensual object, one understands "I feel a pleasant feeling associated with a sensual object."[352]

Unworldly pleasure

A meditator whose awareness is constant and uninterrupted and whose insight knowledge is mature experiences the arising and passing away of the six sense objects arising at the six sense doors, and so understands their impermanent nature. Equating or relating this present object to other present objects or objects of the past, he or she then comes to understand that they are impermanent, unsatisfactory, and changing all the time. This realization arouses a type of happiness called "unworldly pleasure" (*nirāmisa-sukha*), happiness not associated with sensual objects. It is also called "happiness associated with renunciation" (*nekkhammassitasomanassa*). Regarding this kind of happiness, the Buddha says in the *Saḷāyatana-vibhaṅga Sutta*:

> When, by knowing the impermanence, change, fading away, and cessation of forms, one sees as it actually is with proper wisdom that forms both formerly and now are all impermanent, suffering, and subject to change, joy arises. Such joy as this is called joy based on renunciation.[353]

The Buddha then repeats this same statement for all the other sense objects. Such happiness may grow so strong at the early stage of insight knowledge of arising and passing away that you cannot restrain it. In that case, simply be aware of it as it is by noting it as "happy, happy," in accord with this Pāḷi passage:

> . . . when feeling an unworldly pleasant feeling, he understands "I feel an unworldly pleasant feeling"; . . .[354]

Worldly displeasure

When we do not get the desirable objects we want, we feel disappointed and frustrated and think that we are unfortunate. Sometimes we may suffer distress when we think of our lack of sensual pleasures in the present or in the past. Such distress, sadness, frustration, worry, and so on is called "worldly displeasure" (*sāmisadukkha*), unsatisfactoriness associated with sensual objects. It is also called "home distress" (*gehassitadomanassa*), that is, the distress that dwells in the home of sensual dissatisfaction. Every time this sadness occurs, note it as "sadness," as this Pāḷi passage says:

> . . . when feeling a worldly painful feeling, he understands "I feel a worldly painful feeling;" . . .[355]

Unworldly displeasure

When a meditator has reached the insight knowledges beginning with knowledge of arising and passing away, and has spent quite a long time meditating, he or she may long to become a noble person (*ariya*) endowed with path knowledge and fruition knowledge (*maggañāṇa*; *phalañāṇa*). But the meditator may feel disheartened, having not achieved what he or she wanted to achieve and thinking that he or she will be unable to attain path knowledge and fruition knowledge in this life. This distress is called "unworldly displeasure" (*nirāmisadukkha*), unsatisfactoriness not associated with sensual objects, or "distress associated with renunciation" (*nekkhammassitadomanassa*). Every time this kind of distress or dissatisfaction arises, note it as it is, according to this Pāḷi passage:

> . . . when feeling an unworldly painful feeling, he understands "I feel an unworldly painful feeling;" . . .[356]

Regarding unworldly displeasure, the commentary illustrates it with the story of the erudite monk Mahāsīva. I will relate the story here briefly.

> *The Story of Mahāsīva*
> Venerable Mahāsīva was a great teacher who taught the Buddhist scriptures to eighteen Buddhist sects. It is said that under his guidance as many as thirty thousand monks were enlightened by attaining the path knowledge and fruition knowledge of arahantship.
>
> One of these reflected on his spiritual achievement and found that it had innumerable virtues. He then investigated his teacher's virtues, using his psychic powers, thinking that they would be much superior. However, to his surprise, he found that his teacher was still an ordinary, unenlightened person. Then and there he flew to his great teacher by means of his

psychic powers. His purpose was to remind his teacher that although the teacher was a refuge for many, he was not a refuge for himself.

He came down near his teacher's monastery and approached him. When asked the purpose of his visit, he said that he had come to hear a sermon from the teacher. However the great teacher replied that he had no time to teach him just then.

He then asked the great teacher if he would teach him while he was waiting to go for almsfood in the entranceway of the monastery. Again the teacher refused, saying that he would be busy with some other monks who were studying with him. The monk then asked if he could be taught while the great teacher was on his way to the village for alms. The great teacher again gave the same response.

The monk humbly continued to ask if he could be taught while the great teacher was adjusting his robes, taking his alms bowl out of the bag, or having rice gruel. Each time he received the same response. He asked if he could be taught while the teacher was on his way back from the village, after his lunch, during the afternoon rest, while preparing for bed, while getting up from bed, before washing his face, or while sitting in his room. On each of these occasions the teacher said that he would be busy.

The monk then made a pointed comment about his teacher's lifestyle, saying: "Venerable sir, you should take the time to practice meditation in the morning after having washed your face, when you go into your room to warm up your body. At the moment, you do not even seem to have time to die! Like a chair, you have been supporting others but not yourself. So I give up my hope of hearing a sermon from you." So saying he flew off into the sky.

The great teacher then realized that the monk had come, not to learn anything from him, but to remind him of what he should do. Early in the morning the next day, the teacher left the monastery to practice, taking his alms bowl and robes with him. He did not inform any of his disciples about his journey, thinking: "For a person like me, it will not be difficult to attain the fruit of arahantship (*arahattaphala*). It will probably take two or three days to become fully enlightened."

The great teacher began practicing in a valley near a village two days before the full moon day in July. However he did not succeed in realizing enlightenment on the full moon day as he had expected. Still he continued to practice, considering: "I thought it would take two or three days to attain the fruit of arahantship, but it did not. So be it. I will continue to practice during the three months of the annual rains retreat (*vassa*). After the annual rains retreat, I will show them who I am."

By the end of the annual rains retreat, however, he had still not attained any path knowledge and felt ashamed, thinking: "I intended to reach the goal in two or three days, but even after three months I have not achieved anything. My fellow monks may conduct *pavāraṇā*[357] as arahants, but not I." As he thought about this, tears rolled down his cheeks.

From then on he put his bed away and spent all of his time practicing intensively using the three postures of sitting, walking, and standing. He did not lie down at all, thinking that it was a waste of time to lie down. Even so, after twenty-nine years, he still had not attained enlightenment. On every *pavāraṇā* day for twenty-nine years tears rolled down his cheeks. On the thirtieth *pavāraṇā* day, he again found himself without any experience of path knowledge and fruition knowledge, and again wept over his failure to gain enlightenment, regretting that he could not yet join his fellow monks as an arahant at the *pavāraṇā* ceremony. However this time he also heard someone else crying nearby and called out to know who it was.

"It is I," answered a celestial being, "a deva, venerable sir."

"Why are you crying here?" asked the monk.

"Because I hope, sir," replied the deva, "to attain two or three stages of path knowledge and fruition knowledge just by crying."

Feeling humiliated the great monk admonished himself, "Even devas are laughing at me! This is not the way to behave." He then set aside his regret, calmed his mind, and developed

> insight knowledge, stage by stage, until finally attaining enlightenment, the fruit of arahantship.

Venerable Mahāsīva presumably took so long to complete his practice because he practiced insight by contemplating phenomena on a large scale, the same reason it took Venerable Sāriputta longer to attain arahantship than Venerable Moggallāna. The subcommentary says that it took that long for his insight to mature. This must refer to the development of insight knowledge over a wider range of phenomena than what is strictly necessary for the attainment of arahantship.

Venerable Mahāsīva was so learned that he had memorized the entirety of the canonical texts, so it is reasonable to conclude that his noble deeds (*pāramī*) and insight knowledge were more than sufficient to realize arahantship on a small scale, as was the case with the hermit Sumedha, the Buddha-to-Be, whose noble deeds and insight knowledge were sufficient to have become an enlightened disciple under Dīpaṅkarā Buddha.

Worldly neither displeasure nor pleasure

Ordinary, spiritually blind people (*andhaputthujjana*) often feel neither happy nor unhappy when they encounter a sensual object that is neither unpleasant nor pleasant. However, they are not aware of this, cannot give up the object, and relate to it with attachment. This kind of feeling is called "worldly neither displeasure nor pleasure" (*sāmisa-adukkhamasukha*), "home equanimity" (*gehassita-upekkhā*), or "equanimity associated with delusion" (*aññāṇupekkhā*). Insight practitioners often experience it, but it is difficult to notice since it is not distinct. When you notice it, note it according to the following Pāḷi passage:

> . . . when feeling a worldly neither-painful-nor-pleasant feeling, he understands "I feel a worldly neither-painful-nor-pleasant feeling;" . . .[358]

Unworldly neither displeasure nor pleasure

When one's insight meditation practice is purified from the corruptions of insight, any of the six sense objects that arise will become very distinct and neither-unpleasant-nor-pleasant feeling becomes very distinct in the face of penetrating insight knowledge. At the stage of insight knowledge of equanimity toward formations it becomes even more distinct. This neither-unpleasant-nor-pleasant feeling is called "unworldly neither displeasure nor pleasure" (*nirāmisa-adukkhamasukha*). It is also called "neutral feeling associated with renunciation" (*nekkhammassita-upekkhā*). Note it accordingly, based on the following quote:

> . . . when feeling an unworldly neither-painful-nor-pleasant feeling, he understands "I feel an unworldly neither-painful-nor-pleasant feeling."[359]

Realizing feelings

The method for contemplating feelings is the same as the method for contemplating external and internal phenomena previously explained in the section on contemplation of the body.

When one notes feelings, one sees that they instantaneously arise and pass away. This is realization of the arising and passing away of feelings. One also realizes that one feels happy, unhappy, or neutral due to pleasant, unpleasant, or neither-unpleasant-nor-pleasant objects, respectively, and that one does not have those feelings in the absence of such objects. One further realizes that a feeling arises due to a previous action, ignorance, and attachment, and that in the absence of a previous action, ignorance, and attachment no feeling arises. Therefore one realizes the causes of arising, disappearance, and nonarising of feelings as described by the Pāḷi passage:

> . . . he abides contemplating in feelings their nature of both arising and vanishing.[360]

Every time one notes a feeling accurately, one realizes that there is no person or being, no "I" or "mine," and no woman or man that feels, but simply a feeling that is pleasant, unpleasant, or neither unpleasant nor pleasant. In other words one is able to perceive the feeling independent of any conceptual forms or shapes—that is, free from conditioned solid images. In this way one's mindfulness and insight knowledge improve and attachment weakens, as stated in the Pāḷi passage:

> . . . mindfulness that "there is feeling" is simply established in him . . .[361]

This is the contemplation of feelings (*vedanānupassanā*).

Contemplation of Mind

Mental states

Craving, lust, and desire are called "mind affected by lust" (*sarāgacitta*). When this state of mind occurs, note it as "desire, desire." It may disappear when you note it just once or twice. If it persists, continue to note it repeatedly until it finally fades away. When the mind is free from wanting and liking, it becomes pure and clear, a mind unaffected by lust (*vītarāgacitta*). You should note this state of mind as it is, as described in the Pāḷi passage:

> Here a bhikkhu understands mind affected by lust as mind affected by lust, and mind unaffected by lust as mind unaffected by lust.[362]

Anger, frustration, hate, hostility, and cruelty are called "mind affected by hate" (*sadosacitta*). When one of these occurs, note it as "angry" and so on. It may disappear when you note it just once or twice. If it continues, note it repeatedly until it disappears. Eventually it will vanish completely and then the mind becomes pure and clear, a mind unaffected by hate (*vītadosacitta*). You should also note this state of mind as it is, according to the Pāḷi passage:

> He understands mind affected by hate as mind affected by hate, and mind unaffected by hate as mind unaffected by hate.[363]

The mind that is simply confused or restless, in the grip of ignorance or delusion, is called "mind affected by delusion" (*samohacitta*). Sensual thoughts, hypocrisy, and delusions of identity are considered states of mind rooted in desire and affected by delusion (*lobhamūla samohacitta*). Unpleasant states of mind, such as fear, worry, grief, sadness, aversion, jealousy, and regret, are all states of mind rooted in hate and affected by delusion (*dosamūla samohacitta*). When any of these states of mind occur, note them as they really are. When these states of mind have come to an end, the mind becomes pure and clear, a mind unaffected by delusion (*vītamohacitta*). You should also note as it is, according to the Pāḷi passage:

> He understands mind affected by delusion as mind affected by delusion, and mind unaffected by delusion as mind unaffected by delusion.[364]

When experiencing any of these other states of mind, a meditator should also note them accordingly: an indolent state of mind (*saṃkhittacitta*), a distracted state of mind (*vikkhittacitta*), a concentrated state of mind (*samāhitacitta*), an unconcentrated mind (*asamāhitacitta*), a liberated state of mind, when the noting mind is temporarily liberated from mental defilements (*vimuttacitta*), and an unliberated mind, when there is no awareness and the wandering mind is subject to mental defilements (*avimuttacitta*).

The following four states of consciousness occur only to those who have achieved jhāna, so they are not relevant for a practitioner of pure insight meditation: a developed state of mind (*mahaggatacitta*), an undeveloped state of mind (*amahaggatacitta*), an inferior state of mind (*sa-uttaracitta*), and a superior state of mind (*anuttaracitta*).

The observation of states of mind as they are from moment to moment is called contemplation of mind (*cittānupassanā*). If one focuses on the enumeration or itemization of states of mind, considering that there are eight types of mind rooted in lust, that they are called mind affected by lust, and so on, this is not true contemplation of the mind but only conceptualization. This is why the commentary says:

> The moment a state of mind arises one observes either one's own mind or another's mind, or sometimes one's own mind and sometimes another's mind. This is called "contemplating mind as mind."[365]

If one notes a state of mind the moment it occurs, one understands: it has the characteristic of knowing an object (*vijānanalakkhaṇā*); it sees, hears, smells, tastes, or touches, and although it appears and disappears along with its mental factors, it is like a forerunner to perceive the object—it has the function of leading its mental factors (*pubbaṅgamarasa*); it manifests continuously, one moment after the other (*sandahanapaccupaṭṭhāna*); and its proximate causes are a physical basis, an object, mental contact, feeling, and so on (*vatthārammanapadaṭṭhāna*; *nāmarūpapadaṭṭhāna*).

Realizing mind

The method for the contemplating of mind is the same as the method for awareness of external and internal phenomena previously explained in the section on contemplation of the body.

When one notes a state of mind, one sees that it instantaneously arises and passes away. This is realization of the arising and passing away of mind. One also realizes that a particular state of mind arises only in the presence of such conditions as its specific mental factors, a physical basis, past actions, delusion, and attachment. Without these conditions, that state of mind does not arise. This is realization of the cause of states of mind that are arising and passing away, as described in the Pāḷi passage:

> . . . he abides contemplating in mind its nature of both arising and vanishing.[366]

Every time one notes a state of mind, one realizes that there is no person or being, no "I" or "mine," and no woman or man that knows, but only awareness of an object. In other words, one is able to perceive the mind independent of conditioned conceptual images. Thus one's mindfulness and insight knowledge improve and attachment weakens, as stated in the Pāḷi passage:

> Or else mindfulness that "there is mind" is simply established in him . . .[367]

This is contemplation of the mind (*cittānupassanā*).

Contemplation of Mental Objects

The five hindrances

The desire for and enjoyment of sensual pleasures is called "the hindrance of sensual desire" (*kāmacchandanīvaraṇa*). It also includes desire for attainment of jhāna or for realization of path, fruition, and nibbāna. In chapter 2 I explained why the desire for spiritual attainment can become sensual desire. When sensual desire arises, note it as it is.

> [. . . there being sensual desire in him, a bhikkhu understands:] "There is sensual desire in me."[368]

Anger, frustration, hatred, cruelty, and hostility are included in what is called "the hindrance of aversion" (*byāpādanīvaraṇa*). One should be aware of these, as they truly are, the moment they occur. The hindrance caused by the sluggishness, dullness, and lack of energy of the mind and mental factors is called "the hindrance of sloth and torpor" (*thinamiddhanīvaraṇa*). Be aware of these, as they truly are, the moment they occur. Mental restlessness is called "restlessness" (*uddhacca*). Note it as it is the moment it occurs. Regret and remorse are called "regret" (*kukkucca*). Note it as it is the moment it occurs. This is the way to note, according to the Pāḷi passage:

> [There being ill will in him . . . There being sloth and torpor in him . . . There being restlessness and remorse in him, a bhikkhu understands] "There is ill-will . . . sloth and torpor . . . restlessness and remorse in me."[369]

Skeptical doubt about the Buddha's omniscience, the attainments of path, fruition, and nibbāna, the enlightenment of disciples, or about the fact that there is no person or being but only the law of cause and effect,[370] or doubts about whether one is practicing the correct method, whether the practice will lead to path, fruition, and nibbāna, whether one's teacher's instructions are correct, or whether anyone has ever become enlightened using this method is called "doubt" (*vicikicchā*). When you experience such doubt, note it as it is the moment it takes place, according to the following Pāḷi passage:

> [There being doubt in him, a bhikkhu understands:] "There is doubt in me."[371]

These mental hindrances may disappear when you note them once, twice, or several times.

You should also note mental states free from hindrance as they are:

> [There being no sensual desire in him, a bhikkhu understands:] "There is no sensual desire in me."[372]

Sensual desire arises out of unwise attention. You will be able to note it when your insight knowledge matures. You will also experience the disappearance of sensual desire when you are aware of it. This awareness is wise attention. You may sometimes also become aware of unwise attention soon enough to prevent sensual desire from arising. The same applies for the other hindrances. When you note sloth and torpor, for example, and they disappear, you may feel alert for the rest of the day and night. Thus you will come to see the cause of mental hindrances. You will realize that unwise attention is what arouses sensual desire and the other hindrances, and wise attention is what dispels them.

Wise attention

As I explained in chapter 1, any awareness that arouses wholesomeness should be regarded as wise attention or right attitude (*yoniso manasikāra*). Here I will elaborate on wise attention as it relates specifically to insight meditation.

In the case of insight meditation, wise attention consists of noting or observing mental and physical phenomena the moment they take place, in terms of their specific and general characteristics. When one's empirical knowledge of mental and physical phenomena matures, one will then inferentially realize the nature of phenomena that one has never experienced by comparing them with those one has. This is also wise attention. Therefore, wise attention is attention that leads to the attainment of higher insight knowledges and path knowledge and fruition knowledge. As the commentaries say:

> Wise attention is the (right) method and the (right) way of attention; wise attention is seeing what is impermanent as impermanent, seeing what is unsatisfactory as unsatisfactory, seeing what is not-self as not-self, and seeing what is unappealing as unappealing.[373]

Insight knowledges, path, fruition, and nibbāna are the true prosperity that an insight meditator hopes to gain. Thus "wise attention" is awareness of phenomena as they truly are, contemplation of the characteristics, impermanence, and so on of mental and physical phenomena.

An insight meditator need only know distinct mental and physical phenomena as they really are; he or she needn't experience a person, a being, an "I," a woman, or a man. A meditator needs to understand the general characteristics of impermanence, and so on that help remove mental defilements; he or she needn't experience the appearance or apparent existence of permanence, satisfaction, self, and attractiveness. When a meditator experiences any of the six sense objects through the six sense doors, the mind units called "the five-sense-door-adverting" (*pañcadvārāvajjana*) or "the mind-door-adverting" (*manodvārāvajjana*) arise and are aware of those sense objects in such a way that they are only perceived as impermanent mental and physical phenomena. This type of "adverting mind" is then followed by an insight impulsion. Both of these are regarded as wise attention, since they lead toward right understanding of mental and physical phenomena and path knowledge and fruition knowledge. As the subcommentary on the *Satipaṭṭhāna Sutta* explains:

> Wise attention is a state of mind guided by wisdom that rightly understands the specific and general characteristics, function, and so on of wholesome mental states. It is called "wise attention" because it is the right way of paying attention. The adverting mind is also considered wise attention like that (wisdom-guided) state of mind.[374]

According to this subcommentary, both the adverting mind and the insight impulsion that arise in preceding mental processes should be considered wise attention, since they produce wholesome states of mind in the mental processes that follow.

Unwise attention

> Unwise attention (*ayoniso manasikāra*) is not the (right) method and is not the (right) way of attention; unwise attention is seeing what is impermanent as permanent, seeing what is unsatisfactory as satisfactory, seeing what is not-self as self, and seeing what is unappealing as appealing.[375]

Taking the mental and physical phenomena that appear at the six sense doors to be permanent, satisfactory, self, and attractive is unwise attention. In fact any instance of unmindfulness should be regarded as unwise attention, because it may lead to notions of permanence and so on.

Let's say, for example, that we fail to note an instance of seeing the moment it occurs. Because we do not stop with the mere process of seeing, we begin to think about who it is that one sees or about the fact that we have seen the person before. Or a bit later we reflect: "That person was in that place a moment ago, and now he is in this place," or "It is I who am thinking about that person after having seen him." Having these kinds of thoughts indicates that we harbor a perception of permanence. Or we may happily consider: "I see a woman. I see a man. He is well. It is nice to meet her." Or we may take the object and our eye-consciousness to be a person, a being, or an "I." Or we may take it to be nice and attractive. It is unlikely that we will see impermanence and the other characteristics at such times, and even if we were to pay attention, impermanence and so on would not clearly appear to us. It goes without saying that we would stand no chance of attaining path and fruition under such circumstances. Any state devoid of mindfulness is considered to be unwise attention because it bears no benefit and doesn't result in attainment of insight knowledge or path and fruition. Unwise attention is the cause for any kind of unwholesomeness.

We should also consider both the adverting mind and all unwholesome impulsions that arise in preceding mental processes to be unwise attention in such cases, since they produce unwholesome states of mind in the mental processes that follow. Within a single mental process, the adverting mind should be considered unwise attention when it leads to unwholesomeness.

Ordinary people are generally inclined toward sense objects that arouse mental defilements. As soon as the object appears at one of the six sense doors, the adverting mind arises based on unwise attention, as if it wonders whether the object is lovely or terrible. This kind of adverting mind is comparable to someone who is afraid of ghosts and jumps at any noise in the night, or to someone who is so eager to meet a dear friend that one mistakes a random passerby for that friend. In the case of the process at the five sense doors,[376] after consciousness adverts, receiving and investigating moments of consciousness arise, followed by a determining consciousness that decides whether the object is lovely or terrible. This is how kammic impulsions arise based on greed, hatred, and delusion. Also in the case of the process at the mind door, unwholesome kammic impulsions arise depending on the attention paid to the object when consciousness adverts to it and takes it to be something lovely or terrible. This is how unwholesome mental states arise due to unwise attention.

In brief, wise attention refers to mindfulness in the case of insight meditation. Attention that supports mindfulness is also considered wise attention. The wandering mind is unwise attention and produces mental hindrances. One should be aware of these two kinds of attention, according to the Pāḷi passage:

> . . . he also understands how there comes to be the arising of unarisen sensual desire, and how there comes to be the abandoning of arisen sensual desire, and how there comes to be the future non-arising of abandoned sensual desire.[377]

Regarding future nonarising of abandoned hindrances: the first path knowledge uproots skeptical doubt; the third path knowledge uproots aversion and regret; and the fourth path knowledge completely removes sensual desire, sloth and torpor, and mental restlessness.

The various knowledges of the path that cause the complete uprooting of their respective hindrances can only be known at the moment of reviewing knowledge that occurs only after attaining the respective path knowledge. Before that, one can only understand them based on scriptural knowledge. Using scriptural knowledge one can determine that one has not yet attained a particular path knowledge because its hindrances still arise. This helps one to make greater efforts to attain the various path knowledges.

The five aggregates

There is no particular method for contemplating the aggregates. As mentioned before, those for whom the noting of materiality is suitable are able to thoroughly understand them when they note "seeing," "hearing," and so on. But those for whom the contemplation of the sense bases (*āyatana*) or elements (*dhātu*) is suitable will understand them when they note "seeing" and so on. This will also serve the purpose of those for whom contemplation of mental and physical phenomena is suitable.

If one notes "seeing, seeing" at the moment of seeing and is aware of one's eye-sensitivity or the visual object, then one is aware of the physical aggregate. If one is aware of a pleasant, unpleasant, or neither-unpleasant-nor-pleasant feeling connected with the visual object, one is aware of the aggregate of feeling. If one is aware of recognizing the visual object, one is aware of the aggregate of perception. If one is aware of mental formations arising, such as mental contact with the visible object, the volition to see it, greed, faith, and so on, one is aware of the aggregate of mental formations. If one is aware of eye-consciousness, one is aware of the aggregate of consciousness. Being aware of the aggregates in these ways is consistent with the Pāḷi passage:

> [Here a bhikkhu understands:] "Such is material form . . . such is feeling . . . such is perception . . . such are the formations . . . such is consciousness."[378]

The same applies to hearing and so on. If one notes "bending" while bending a limb, one is aware of the physical aggregate in the form of the bending movement, the mental aggregate of consciousness in the form of the intention to bend, and mental formations connected with bending, such as the contact between the mind and the physical process and the volition that drives the physical process. The aggregates of feeling and perception are only obvious some of the time. When they are, one is aware of the pleasant or unpleasant nature associated with the intention to bend and of the perception that recognizes the experience. The same applies for stretching, walking, and so on.

In this way knowledge that discerns mental and physical phenomena arises. One thoroughly understands that the physical aggregate is just this: changing for the worse. Feelings are just feeling, perception is just perceiving, mental formations are just performing their functions, and consciousness is just knowing the object. This is not merely an enumeration or itemization of the five aggregates but an empirical realization based on moment-to-moment awareness, consistent with the Pāḷi passage above, "Such is material form, such is feeling . . ." The commentary gives the following explanation:

> "Such is material form" indicates (realization of physicality in this way): "Such is material form. It consists of this much and no more." One understands material form based on its unique characteristics. The same applies for feelings, and so on.[379]

The appearance and disappearance of physical phenomena

Every time one notes physical phenomena, one sees that they are instantaneously appearing and disappearing. For example, when seeing, we see that eye-sensitivity and the visible object momentarily appear and disappear. This is the insight knowledge of arising and passing away that realizes the characteristic of arising (*nibbattilakkhaṇā*) and the characteristic of disappearance (*vipariṇāmalakkhaṇā*).

People believe that mental and physical phenomena are good and beautiful. They cannot see that they are unsatisfactory, bad, and unattractive. They do not understand that the complete cessation of these mental and physical phenomena is peaceful and good. This not knowing is ignorance. Because of this ignorance people were attached to mental and physical phenomena in past lives and committed wholesome or unwholesome deeds in an attempt to make them pleasant. These wholesome and unwholesome actions are kamma. Wholesome kamma is the cause of this human life. An insight meditator has already accepted the law of kamma after having learned that kamma brings both mental and physical good or bad results. One also empirically realizes the causes of mental and physical phenomena and their appearance and disappearance while practicing insight. Thus a meditator's understanding is a combination of empirical and scriptural knowledge.

By way of reflection one understands: "This physical body has arisen in this life because ignorance was present in a past life; it could not have arisen without ignorance; this physical body has arisen in this life because attachment and craving were present in a past life; it could not have arisen without attachment and craving; this physical body has arisen in this life because wholesome and unwholesome deeds were performed in a past life; it could not have arisen without wholesome and unwholesome deeds; this physical body has arisen in this life because of nourishment in this life; it could not have arisen without nourishment."

According to the *Paṭisambhidāmagga*, this realization is regarded as inferential knowledge of the arising and passing away of phenomena. One will also realize the immediate causes of physical phenomena in one's present existence—that the physical process of bending the hand is caused by the intention to do so, for example. The bending would not occur without the intention. Also, physical sensations of heat or cold are caused by environmental conditions of heat or cold. The physical experience of being hot or cold would not occur without those conditions. As the Pāḷi text says:

> Such is material form, such its origin, such its disappearance; . . .[380]

Feeling, perception, and formations

Comfort, pleasure, and happiness are called "pleasant feeling" (*sukhavedanā*). Discomfort, unpleasantness, and sadness are called "painful feeling" (*dukkhavedanā*). A feeling that is neither unpleasant nor pleasant is called "neutral feeling" (*upekkhāvedanā*). When one notes these feelings, one sees that they instantaneously arise and disappear. This is the insight knowledge of arising and passing away that realizes the characteristics of appearance and disappearance of phenomena.

By way of reflection one understands: "These feelings have arisen in this life because ignorance was present in a past life; they could not have arisen without ignorance; these feelings have arisen in this life because attachment and craving were present in a past life; they could not have arisen without attachment and craving; these feelings have arisen in this life because wholesome and unwholesome deeds were performed in a past life; they could not have arisen without wholesome and unwholesome deeds; these feelings have arisen in this life because of nourishment in this life; they could not have arise without nourishment.

This realization is regarded as inferential knowledge of the arising and passing away of feelings. The same is true for the aggregates of perception and mental formations. As the Pāḷi text says:

> . . . such is feeling, such its origin, such its disappearance; . . .[381]

Consciousness

When one notes consciousness as "seeing," "hearing," "intention to bend," "intention to stretch," "knowing," and so on, one sees that it instantaneously arises and disappears. This is the insight knowledge that realizes the characteristic of the arising and the characteristic of the disappearance or passing away of phenomena.

By way of reflection one understands: This consciousness has arisen in this life because ignorance was present in a past life; it could not have arisen without ignorance; this consciousness has arisen in this life because attachment and craving were present in a past life; without attachment and craving, it could not have arisen; this consciousness has arisen in this life because wholesome and unwholesome deeds were performed in a past life;

it could not have arisen without wholesome and unwholesome deeds; this consciousness has arisen in this life because of nourishment in this life; it could not have arisen without nourishment.

This realization is regarded as inferential knowledge of the arising and passing away of consciousness. Because there is an object, consciousness arises; without it consciousness would not arise. Because there is a preceding consciousness, the following consciousness arises; without it consciousness would not arise. As the Pāḷi text says:

> . . . such is consciousness, such is its origin, such is its disappearance.[382]

According to the commentary, insight knowledge of arising and passing away arises in fifty ways: each aggregate is realized in terms of its appearance, disappearance, four causes of appearance, and four causes of disappearance,[383] making ten ways for each aggregate. Therefore, the five aggregates are realized in fifty ways, altogether. But what is most important is realizing this understanding in ten ways—that is, seeing each of the five aggregates in terms of its appearance and disappearance.

The six senses

Seeing

At the moment of seeing we can experience various sense bases and elements and mental and physical phenomena, such as the eye-sensitivity that is the eye base (*cakkhāyatana*) and the eye element (*cakkhudhātu*), the visual object that is the form base (*rūpāyatana*) and the form element (*rūpadhātu*), and the mind base (*manāyatana*).

We can also experience bases and elements associated with the mental process of sight. These arise in the following order: the element of eye-consciousness (*cakkhuviññāṇadhātu*), the mind element (*manodhātu*) comprised of a mind-moment that adverts to the object (*āvajjana*) and a mind-moment that receives the sense object (*sampaṭicchana*), followed by the mind-consciousness element (*manoviññāṇadhātu*) comprised of a mind-moment that investigates the sense object (*santīrana*), a mind-moment that determines the sense object (*votthapana*), mind-moments of kammic impulsion (*javana*), and a mind-moment that registers the sense object (*tadārammaṇa*).[384]

All the mental factors are called the mental object base (*dhammāyatana*) and the mental object element (*dhammadhātu*). Some of these are: mental contact (*phassa*) with a visual object, feeling (*vedanā*), perception (*saññā*), volition (*cetanā*), desire (*lobha*), aversion (*dosa*), and faith (*saddhā*).

Consciousness and the mental factors are called *nāma* because they "go" or "bend" toward the visual object.[385] The eye-sensitivity and the visual object cannot bend toward the object. They are called *rūpa* because they undergo alteration and are deformed when they meet with adverse physical conditions.[386] Thus, depending on one's disposition, every time one notes seeing as "seeing," one understands phenomena in terms of either the four bases, the six elements, or in terms of being mental (*nāma*) and physical (*rūpa*).

Hearing, smelling, tasting, touching

At the moment of hearing, the bases and elements and mental and physical phenomena that we can experience are: the ear-sensitivity that is physical, the ear base (*sotāyatana*), and is the ear element (*sotādhātu*); the sound that is physical, the sound base (*saddāyatana*), and is the sound element (*saddādhātu*). The mental process of hearing is mental and can be subdivided in terms of bases into its mind base and mental object base, or in terms of elements into its ear-consciousness element (*sotāviññāṇadhātu*), its mind element, its mind-consciousness element, and its mental object element.

At the moment of smelling we can experience: the nose-sensitivity that is physical, the nose base (*ghānāyatana*), and the nose element (*ghānadhātu*); the odor that is physical, the smell base (*gandhāyatana*), and is the odor element (*gandhādhātu*) The mental process of smelling is mental and can be subdivided in terms of bases into its mind base and mental object base, or in terms of elements into its nose-consciousness element (*ghānaviññāṇadhātu*), its mind element, its mind-consciousness element, and its mental object element.

At the moment of tasting we can experience: tongue-sensitivity that is physical, the tongue base (*jivhāyatana*), and the tongue element (*jivhādhātu*); the flavor that is physical, the flavor base (*rasāyatana*), and is the flavor element (*rasadhātu*). The mental process of tasting is mental and can be subdivided in terms of bases into its mind base and mental object base, or in terms of elements into its tongue-consciousness element (*jivhāviññāṇadhātu*), its mind element, its mind-consciousness element, and its mental object element.

At the moment of touching we can experience: body-sensitivity that is physical, the body base (*kāyāyatana*), and the body element (*kāyadhātu*); the bodily sensation that is physical, the tangible object base (*phoṭṭhabbāyatana*), and is the tangible object element (*phoṭṭhabbadhātu*); the mental process of touching that is mental and can be subdivided in terms of bases into its mind base and mental object base, or in terms of elements into its body-consciousness element (*kāyaviññāṇadhātu*), its mind element, its mind-consciousness element, and its mental object element.

Thus, depending on one's disposition, every time one notes hearing as "hearing," and so on, one understands the phenomena in terms of the four bases or six elements, or in terms of being physical and mental.

Thinking

At the moment of thinking we can experience the following bases and elements, or physical and mental phenomena: the mental process of simply taking an object that is mental, the mind base (*manāyatana*), and is the mind-consciousness element (*manoviññāṇadhātu*).

We can also experience mental factors that are comprised of mind objects and mind bases, such as: mental contact with the object, feeling, perception, volition, concentration, initial application, sustained application, determination, energy, rapture, will, desire, aversion, delusion, wrong view, pride or conceit, jealousy, regret, sloth and torpor, restlessness, skeptical doubt, nongreed, goodwill or benevolence, compassion, sympathetic joy, faith, mindfulness, moral shame and fear of consequences, wisdom, calm or tranquility, lightness and agility, and so on.

There are also physical phenomena associated with thinking that are mental object bases and mental object elements, such as: the heart-base (*hadayavatthu*) that is the physical base for thoughts, and the feminine faculty (*itthindriya*) and masculine faculty (*purisindriya*) that bring about male and female traits, respectively.

Thus, depending on one's disposition, when one notes the thinking mind—the intention to bend or stretch one's limbs, thinking, wandering, considering, noting, observing, and so on—one understands phenomena in terms of the two bases, or two elements, or in terms of being mental and physical. A mental object can be either conceptual or ultimate. If it is ultimate one can understand it in terms of its bases, elements, or in terms of being mental and physical.

The ten fetters

There are ten fetters: (1) lust (*kāmarāga*), the desire for internal or external sensual objects, (2) anger (*paṭigha*), frustration, hatred, wanting someone to die, (3) arrogance (*māna*), thinking highly of oneself, and competing with others, (4) wrong view (*diṭṭhi*), the view of a "self" or personal identity that either lasts forever or is annihilated after death, (5) doubt (*vicikicchā*), (6) wrong belief (*sīlabbataparāmāsa*), the belief that rituals or ritualistic behavior can lead to liberation, (7) desire for existence (*bhavarāga*), the desire for and enjoyment of a good life, (8) envy (*issā*), (9) stinginess (*macchariya*), not wanting others to have the same prosperity and reputation as oneself, and (10) ignorance (*avijjā*), not knowing the true nature of mind and body—this fetter accompanies all the others.

When any of these ten fetters are present in a person, he or she will assume a new existence following death in the previous one and cannot be freed from the unsatisfactoriness of repeated existences. This is why they are called fetters: they bind us to the unsatisfactoriness of repeated existences. The ten kinds of fetter arise in our minds if in a moment of seeing we fail to be aware of the eye-sensitivity, the visual object, or eye-consciousness, or if in a moment of hearing we fail to be aware of the ear-sensitivity, sound, or ear-consciousness, and so on. When a fetter occurs, we should note it as it is.

If sensual desire arises and one notes it as it is, for example, one will become aware of the unwise attention that is arousing that sensual desire. By noting it as it is, one will then become aware of the wise attention that dispels that sensual desire. When one's practice matures, there are times when one will become aware of unwise attention as soon as it occurs and, by noting it, the sensual desire will disappear without having been fully developed. This is why the Pāḷi text says:

> Here a bhikkhu understands the eye, he understands forms, and he understands the fetter that arises dependent on both; and he also understands how there comes to be the arising of the

> unarisen fetter, and how there comes to be the abandoning of the arisen fetter, . . .[387]

Reviewing knowledge (*paccavekkhaṇañāṇa*) is the knowledge that arises immediately after path and fruition, and it reflects on the five factors of path, fruition, nibbāna, mental defilements that have been uprooted, and those that have not yet been uprooted. One can only reflect on path and fruition that uproot the fetters in a moment of reviewing knowledge, according to the Pāḷi phrase:

> . . . and how there comes to be the future non-arising of the abandoned fetter.[388]

For general knowledge, however, one should know that: the first path knowledge uproots the view of personality (*sakkāyadiṭṭhi*), skeptical doubt regarding the Buddha's teachings (*vicikicchā*), belief in rites and rituals as a path to liberation (*sīlabbataparāmāsa*), envy or jealousy (*issā*), and avarice or stinginess (*macchariya*); the second and third path knowledges uproot the gross and subtle forms, respectively, of sensual desire (*kāmarāga*) and aversion (*paṭigha*); and the fourth and final path knowledge eradicates pride or conceit (*māna*), desire for existence (*bhavarāga*), and ignorance (*avijjā*).

Note that not every apparent instance of stinginess is necessarily a sign of the fetter of stinginess. Even though the first path knowledge uproots stinginess, this doesn't mean that a stream enterer becomes so generous that he or she will give away anything he or she has. Apparent stinginess can occur due to attachment to belongings, as well as due to stinginess. Stinginess is the kind of stinginess or avarice that is so strong one cannot bear the thought of or approve of another person possessing or using one's belongings. A stream enterer is free from this kind of stinginess but not from attachment to property.

Remember that there were wealthy laymen and laywomen as well as kings and queens during the Buddha's time who attained the first three stages of enlightenment: stream enterer, once returner, and nonreturner. There surely must have been thieves or those holding opposing views to the Buddha's teaching who demanded property from such people under threat of force. If these noble persons had given whatever was requested, they would have lost all their wealth. Even the household of the merchant Anāthapiṇḍika experienced theft. If the merchant had always given whatever was asked of him, no one would have had cause to commit such a crime. So unwillingness to give is not necessarily the fetter of stinginess. On the other hand feeling jealous at the thought that another person would possess or use one's own possessions is considered stinginess. Simply being attached to one's own property is not stinginess but rather desire.

Moreover, not giving what one shouldn't give to anyone is neither stinginess nor attachment to one's belongings. The female arahant Uppalavannā, for example, refused bhikkhu Udāyī's request for her underrobe. Uppalavannā was not only free from desire and stinginess but from all defilements. She simply refused the request because her underrobe was not something fit to be given away.

The seven factors of enlightenment

Mindfulness

Beginning with the stage of insight knowledge of arising and passing away, one's practice is less and less disturbed by the hindrances, and one firmly establishes mindfulness of objects to be noted. It seems as if mental and physical objects that instantaneously arise and disappear spontaneously present themselves to the noting mind. Immediately after one object has been noted another object appears. The noting mind seems to sink into the object, and the object seems to sink into the noting mind. The commentary says that this noting is characterized by a mental state that "dips" its mental constituents into the object. This quality of mindfulness is the enlightenment factor of mindfulness (*satisaṃbojjhaṅga*), since it leads to path knowledge.

Investigation

When one notes an object, one understands the characteristics of the mental or physical phenomena associated with it. One also sees the sudden arising and disappearance of these mental and physical phenomena. Furthermore, one clearly sees their characteristics of impermanence, unsatisfactoriness, and not-self. This understanding is the enlightenment factor of investigation (*dhammavicayasaṃbojjhaṅga*).

Energy

When one notes an object, one should apply moderate effort or energy. If one begins one's practice with too much energy, one will later become overzealous and restless, and one's noting will not be as good as it could be. On the other hand, if one begins one's practice with too little energy, one's effort will not be strong enough for one's noting, and the mind will become lethargic and dull. So one should apply moderate effort in practice, reducing the effort when it's too strenuous, and boosting energy when it's too weak. Then one will be neither restless due to excessive effort nor lethargic due to deficient energy. One will be mindful of each object that arises without missing any objects. This kind of energy is considered the enlightenment factor of energy (*vīriyasaṃbojjhaṅga*).

Delight and calm

Experiencing delight with every noting mind is the enlightenment factor of delight (*pītisaṃbojjhaṅga*). The mental calm or tranquility that results from effortless practice is the enlightenment factor of tranquility (*passaddhisaṃbojjhaṅga*). These qualities of delight and calm are very obvious, especially at the beginning of insight knowledge of arising and passing away, at which point one feels greater delight and tranquility than one has ever felt before, verifying the Buddha's statement:

> The delight in Dharma surpasses all delights.[389]

In all activities such as walking, standing, sitting, lying down, bending, stretching, and so on, one will feel well in body and mind. Due to delight one may feel as if swaying back and forth in a hammock. Due to calmness one may not note any object, feeling as if one is gazing at it or just sitting calmly. These mental states of delight and tranquility only occur occasionally beginning with insight knowledge of dissolution, but they often gain momentum with insight knowledge of equanimity toward formations.

Concentration

The mind focuses on each object as one notes it, sticking to it without wandering off, firmly concentrated on it. This type of concentration enables one to understand mental and physical phenomena in terms of both their unique characteristics and their universal characteristics of impermanence and so on. This kind of "momentary concentration" involved in each and every moment of noting is considered the enlightenment factor of concentration (*samādhisaṃbojjhaṅga*).

Equanimity

The mind is balanced and equanimous as it notes each object. This balanced state of mind (*tatramajjhattatā*) is called the enlightenment factor of equanimity (*upekkhāsaṃbojjhaṅga*). It is quite difficult to empirically understand this kind of equanimity or to explain it to somebody else. However, one can easily understand it through one's own experience with the knowledges beginning with insight knowledge of arising and passing away.

Balancing spiritual faculties

Faith and wisdom

When a meditator sees only the arising and passing away of mental and physical phenomena with each noting, he or she may repeatedly think and reflect (on this matter) based on his or her strong faith or confidence. For example, one may marvel that there is no person or being but only mental and physical phenomena that arise and immediately pass away without lasting for even the blink of an eye. One may think it so true that phenomena are impermanent, unsatisfactory, and conditioned that one believes that the Buddha knew everything. One may also think how true what the Buddha and teachers say is. However, as one ponders this with confidence and appreciation, one may forget to be aware of that very mental state of confidence, as well as other phenomena that are arising and passing away. This is excessive faith in the Dhamma that interferes with noting.

Those meditators whose wisdom is excessive may think and reflect quite often. For example, one may wonder whether one is noting a physical or a mental phenomenon, whether it is mental contact or feeling, whether one notes an object effectively, whether one is experiencing its characteristic, function, and so on, or whether one is seeing its arising, disappearing, or impermanence, and so on. Whenever such a meditator has a clear experience in practice, he or she is likely to compare it with familiar scriptures, his or her own opinions, or other people's accounts. However as a meditator thinks about these things, he or she forgets to be aware of those very mental states of thinking and reasoning, as well as other phenomena that are occurring from moment to moment. This is excessive analysis or reasoning that interferes with noting.

Due to the power of equanimity, which is by nature balancing, faith and wisdom become balanced such that neither faith nor analysis become excessive. One just notes all the arising objects without thinking and analyzing due to one's faith and wisdom. As a result one is able to note and clearly understand all mental and physical phenomena as they occur.

Energy and concentration

When energy is excessive one strives too much. One may end up searching for an object to note, be concerned that one cannot note objects effectively, or that one might miss objects to note. Sometimes one may end up thinking about how effectively one will note objects in the future, or how often one missed objects in the past. The mind cannot become well concentrated with all this excessive worry, and it will just be restless. Because of this restlessness one will not be able to be thoroughly aware of each arising mental and physical phenomena. Thus does excessive effort result in weak concentration and unclear experience when practicing. This is excessive effort that interferes with noting.

When concentration is excessive, however, the noting mind may remain on just one object for a long time. Because other objects do not appear to the mind, one does not strive to note other objects. As one continues to just note in a relaxed way without exerting effort, one's effort will weaken. This is like the weakening of effort that occurs when one repeats a chant that one has memorized by rote. As a result the object and the noting mind grow cloudy or vague, sloth and torpor begin to prevail, and one cannot be thoroughly aware of each arising mental and physical phenomena. This is excessive concentration that interferes with noting.

Due to the power of equanimity, which maintains balance between the faculties of effort and concentration, one will be able to note objects clearly from moment to moment. Even though many objects may occur, the mind will not grow restless. All the appearing mental and physical phenomena will be noted, as if by themselves, and the mind will remain steadfastly on the objects that one is aware of. Then one will think that no objects have been missed and that one is aware of all the objects occurring.

Balanced practice

Equanimity and balance between faith and wisdom and between energy and concentration, and balancing these mental faculties, is called the enlightenment factor of equanimity. When this equanimity matures, mental factors such as mindfulness are balanced, strong, and distinct. Then one does not have to look for an object; it will readily appear after the previous object has been noted. The object will be noted without exerting much effort, as if the noting process flows smoothly of its own accord. The mind will remain steadfastly on any object that occurs, and one will experience mental and physical phenomena in terms of their individual and universal characteristics.

At this stage you should maintain balance by refraining from analyzing your experiences or increasing or decreasing your effort. Allow the practice to proceed evenly without making any changes. Then you will be able to be aware of that balanced mental state itself, and you will experience the seven factors of enlightenment involved, as the instruction says:

> . . . there being the mindfulness enlightenment factor in him, a bhikkhu understands: "There is the mindfulness enlightenment factor in me"; . . .[390]

When one's practice does not go smoothly, and the enlightenment factors are no longer present due to excessive effort, failure to note objects, and so on, realize that the enlightenment factors are not present while noting "unsteady," "forgetting," "thinking," and so on. As the instruction says:

> . . . and there being no mindfulness enlightenment factor in him, he understands: "There is no mindfulness enlightenment factor in me"; . . .[391]

The proximate causes for the arising of the enlightenment factors are previous mindfulness and wise attention, such as the determination to arouse the enlightenment factors or reflecting on an object that arouses faith. One also understands what arouses the enlightenment factors, according to the Pāḷi passage:

> . . . and he also understands how there comes to be the arising of the unarisen mindfulness enlightenment factor, . . .[392]

Only when one realizes the arahant path and becomes fully enlightened do all of the enlightenment factors become fully developed. One understands the completion of their development with reviewing knowledge, immediately following full enlightenment. As the Pāḷi passage says:

> . . . and how the arisen mindfulness enlightenment factor comes to fulfillment by development.[393]

The seven types of suffering

There are Four Noble Truths, namely: (1) the noble truth of suffering (*dukkhāriyasacca*), the truth about unsatisfactoriness that noble ones understand; (2) the noble truth of the origin of suffering (*samudayāriyasacca*), the truth about the origin of unsatisfactoriness that noble ones understand; (3) the noble truth of the cessation of suffering (*dukkhanirodha-ariyasacca*), the truth about the cessation of unsatisfactoriness that noble ones understand; and (4) the noble truth of the path leading to the cessation of suffering (*dukkhanirodhagāminīpaṭipadā-ariyasacca*), the truth of the path leading to the cessation of unsatisfactoriness understood by noble ones.

These four truths are called "noble truths" because they are only experienced by noble beings. In brief, they are referred to as the truth of suffering (*dukkhasacca*), the truth of origin (*samudayasacca*), the truth of cessation (*nirodhasacca*), and the truth of the path (*maggasacca*).

The emergence of the first mental and physical phenomena in an existence is called "birth" (*jāti*), the continued occurrence and maturing of those phenomena is called "aging" (*jarā*), and the disappearance of the last mental and physical phenomena in an existence is called "death" (*maraṇa*). The dynamics of birth, aging, and death are suffering (*dukkha*),[394] since they cause us mental and physical distress in each existence. Suffering means that the phenomena are not good, are devoid of anything that could be enjoyed, and are repulsive. Thus it is said:

> Birth is suffering, aging is suffering, death is suffering; . . .[395]

Suffering of pain

The various kinds of physical pain, such as aches, pains, and so on, and different kinds of mental pain, such as sadness, sorrow, and so on, are all called "suffering of pain" (*dukkhadukkha*) or obvious suffering. These types of mental and physical phenomena are obviously distressing.

Suffering of change

Even though they are pleasant the moment they occur, pleasant mental and physical feelings—what we call comfort, happiness, and so on—are considered to be suffering of change (*vipariṇāmadukkha*), because we feel distressed when they vanish or something goes wrong with them. The more pleasant a feeling is while it exists, the more distressing it is when it disappears.

It's like taking a fall: the greater the height we fall from, the more painful the injury will be, even to the point of death. It's also like having to part from the people or things that we love: the more attached to a person we are, the more painful it is to leave them. The pleasant feeling that we had when we were with them turns to distress when it comes time to part. Such is the nature of all pleasant feelings. This kind of suffering is also like an evil demon appearing in the guise of a lovely angel: if we knew the true nature of the angel, we would fear and detest it. This is why pleasant feelings are called "suffering of change."

Suffering of conditioned phenomena

Because they are subject to impermanence, neither-unpleasant-nor-pleasant feeling and all worldly mental and physical phenomena, except attachment,[396] are called "suffering of conditioned phenomena" (*saṅkhāra-dukkha*). This kind of suffering permeates all the other kinds of suffering. Suffering of change includes pleasant and unpleasant feelings as well. The Pāḷi text says:

> And I have also said: "Whatever is felt is included in suffering." That has been stated by me with reference to the impermanence of formations.[397]

Pleasant feeling is distinctive, and we feel distressed when it disappears. So we can say that we are more afraid and distressed by suffering of change than we are by suffering of conditioned phenomena. Unpleasant feeling is also distinctive, in that it is more obviously painful and so we are more afraid and distressed by it than we are by other types of suffering—it is the worst of all suffering. This is why commentators deal with these two kinds of suffering separately, even though each can be included in the category of suffering of conditioned phenomena.

When regarding the truth of suffering in the context of insight practice, we must thoroughly understand what it is to suffer conditioned phenomena. We enjoy internal and external phenomena because we mistakenly believe them to be permanent. If we understand that they are conditioned and impermanent, we will no longer take them to be permanent and satisfactory; instead we will regard them as fearful and distressing.

Hidden and manifest suffering

Physical pain that is not externally apparent—such as headaches, earaches, toothaches—and mental distress—such as worry caused by want, or worry, frustration, or sadness caused by aversion—are called "hidden pain or distress" or "hidden suffering" (*paṭicchannadukkha*). Other people can only perceive this kind of suffering when its victims communicate it, and not otherwise. This is also referred to as "obscure pain or distress" or "obscure suffering" (*apākaṭadukkha*). Physical pain caused by external injuries or afflictions is called "manifest pain" or "manifest suffering" (*appaṭicchanna-dukkha*) or "plain pain" or "plain suffering" (*pākaṭadukkha*).

Explicit and implicit suffering

Unpleasant feelings are explicit suffering (*nippariyāyadukkha*) or apparent suffering. But other types of suffering—such as repeated rebirth, aging, and so on—are implicit suffering (*pariyāyadukkha*), because they are not painful in an apparent way yet lead to suffering nonetheless. It is for this reason that, among the seven kinds of suffering, birth, aging, and death are called "the truth of suffering."

The four noble truths

The truth of suffering

The scriptures say: "Birth (repeated rebirth) is suffering; aging is suffering; death is suffering." If we were to lose our relatives, friends, health, wealth, moral conduct, or moral beliefs, or if we were punished, tortured, or thrown into jail, we would suffer sorrow (*soka*). Out of strong sorrow, lamentation (*parideva*) arises. Unbearable and inconsolable despair is a form of aversion called "tribulation" (*upāyāsa*). All forms of physical pain are called "suffering." Ordinary mental pain is called "distress" (*domanassa*).

Sorrow, suffering, and mental distress are called true suffering because they cause us to suffer pain and produce future mental and physical suffering. Lamentation and inconsolable mental despair are only called true suffering because they result in mental and physical suffering due to the fact that they are inferred suffering. To have to associate with persons or things we dislike is also suffering, as is being separated from what we love or like. Craving what we cannot obtain is suffering too. These three forms of suffering are called true suffering because they produce various kinds of mental and physical pain.

If we fail to be aware of the five aggregates—materiality, feeling, perception, mental formations, and consciousness—that are involved in seeing, hearing, and so on, they become objects of clinging and wrong beliefs. This is why they are referred to as "aggregates subject to clinging" (*upādānakhandhā*). I explained this point in chapter 3, when I dealt with the *Bhaddekaratta Sutta*. If these aggregates subject to clinging exist, these seven forms of suffering, beginning with repeated birth, can arise; suffering cannot arise when they do not exist. Thus these five aggregates are true suffering since they are subject to impermanence and the other kinds of suffering mentioned here. This is why the Buddha said:

> . . . in brief, the five aggregates subject to clinging are suffering.[398]

The truth of origin

The phenomena that we can directly experience in a moment of seeing, hearing, and so on are called the five aggregates subject to clinging and are true suffering. Attachment to and enjoyment of them is craving. Because of craving, we long for a better life now and in the future, and to this end we perform wholesome and unwholesome actions of body, speech, and mind, which form wholesome and unwholesome kamma. We have performed countless kammas throughout our lives.

In the last moment of this life when we are on our deathbed, one of those kammas, or an image that was impressed in our memory when we performed a kamma (*kammanimitta*), or an image of the new life we will go to (*gatinimitta*) will arise in the mind. When our present life ends, rebirth—the first emergence of the five aggregates in the next life—will immediately follow, taking the same mental image as the one that appeared last to us on our deathbed.[399] It is like the fear that one experiences in a dream that lingers even after one wakes up. The relationship between death and relinking is similar to the relationship between actually seeing something and then thinking about what was seen: both take the same sense object in different ways. A yogi will be able to understand this.

From relinking until death the five aggregates subject to clinging constantly occur and will do so repeatedly throughout our next life, just as they do in this life. We see something, for example, and then think about what we have seen, then we hear something, and so on. In this way the five aggregates affected by clinging happen continuously. The first emergence of the five aggregates subject to clinging in a new life is the suffering of birth, their repeated occurrence and maturing is the suffering of aging, and their last disappearance is the suffering of death. Any sorrow, lamentation, and so on that we experience before death is, of course, also suffering. The five aggregates subject to clinging that continuously arise based on seeing, hearing, and so on are also suffering.

The truth of suffering is produced by kamma, which is in turn initiated by craving—attachment to and craving for the five aggregates subject to clinging. If one eliminates craving, new kamma cannot be formed, nor can the kamma that has already been formed give rise to a new life. So craving is the origin of all kinds of suffering, beginning with the arising of the five aggregates subject to clinging in each life. The moment we see something, for example, we become attached to the five aggregates subject to clinging that are involved in seeing, because we mistakenly believe them to be pleasurable. This craving is the truth of the origin of suffering (*samudayasaccā*). That is why it is said:

> It is craving, which brings renewal of being, is accompanied by delight and lust, . . .[400]

The truth of cessation

When we attain nibbāna by means of path knowledge, we will truly understand that all arising and disappearing mental and physical phenomena are utterly suffering. Therefore craving for these mental and physical aggregates will no longer arise, and we will thus no longer experience rebirth. In other words, mental and physical phenomena will cease. This is the cessation of all suffering or nibbāna without residue (*anupādisesanibbāna*). The term "cessation" here means that the aggregates no longer arise. Thus the commentaries call it nibbāna without residue. Nibbāna as the cessation of craving and the cessation of the mental and physical aggregates is called the truth of cessation (*nirodha*). Path knowledge takes nibbāna as its object. This is the truth of the cessation of all suffering (*nirodhasaccā*).

> ... it is the remainderless fading away and cessation of that same craving, ...[401]

The truth of the path

The Noble Eightfold Path—including right view and so on—that directly takes nibbāna as its object is the truth of the path.

In short, all of the mental and physical phenomena that arise and pass away in ordinary people are suffering and the causes of suffering: attachment, desire, or craving is the truth of the cause of suffering, and everything else is the truth of suffering. The cessation of both the objects of awareness and awareness of them is the truth of the cessation of suffering. The mental state of experiencing that cessation is the truth of the path.

Mindfulness of the Four Noble Truths

Truths in the round of existence and truths beyond it

Among the Four Noble Truths, one should observe only the two in the round of existence (*vaṭṭasacca*)—suffering and the cause of suffering—for the development of insight. One can only intellectually appreciate and know the two truths beyond the round of existence (*vivattasacca*)—cessation of suffering and the path to cessation of suffering—so one must simply aspire to them. By doing so, awareness of these two truths is fulfilled. According to the commentary:[402]

> Out of the four truths, the first two are in the round of existence (*vaṭṭa*), while the latter two are beyond the round of existence (*vivaṭṭa*). Among them, only the two truths in the round of existence become meditation subjects for a monk; he does not observe the two truths that are beyond the round of existence. Regarding the two truths in the round of existence, a monk should learn from a teacher, in brief, that the five aggregates subject to clinging are suffering and that craving is its origin; or he should learn in detail that the five aggregates subject to cling-

> ing are such and such. A meditator does the work of insight by repeatedly reflecting on this.
>
> Regarding the other two truths, a monk simply hears or learns that the truth of the cessation of suffering is a dhamma to be wished for since it is a good dhamma; it is a dhamma to be liked because it is a noble dhamma; it is a dhamma that nurtures the heart and it is a dhamma to be cherished. The truth of the path to the cessation of suffering is a dhamma to be wished for, to be liked, and to be nurtured. Thusly he also does the work of insight. Then when he finally penetrates the Four Noble Truths at the moment of path knowledge, he thoroughly realizes them once and for all.
>
> One penetrates the truth of suffering by fully understanding it, penetrates the truth of the cause of suffering by abandoning it, penetrates the truth of the cessation of suffering by experiencing it, and penetrates the truth of the path to the cessation of suffering by developing it. One realizes the truth of suffering by fully understanding it, realizes the truth of the cause of suffering by abandoning it, realizes the truth of the cessation of suffering by experiencing it, and realizes the truth of the path to the cessation of suffering by developing it.
>
> Thus one initially understands the first two mundane truths by learning, listening, discussing, memorizing, and observing them. The truth of the cessation of suffering and the truth of the path to the cessation of suffering are only understood by hearing about them. Later, at the moment of path knowledge, one functionally accomplishes the three truths of suffering, the cause of suffering, and the path, and penetrates the truth of the cessation of suffering by taking it as one's object.[403]

Cessation and path are not to be observed for the purpose of developing insight. Ordinary people cannot take supramundane phenomena as sense objects. They also cannot help noble ones, having realized any of the various knowledges of the path, to further eradicate mental defilements. The commentary uses the phrase "to be wished for, to be liked, and to be nurtured" merely to illustrate the enthusiasm and aspiration to realize the supramundane truths of cessation and the path to cessation. Just as one expresses one's intent with the resolve, "Through this practice may I be liberated from aging and death,"[404] so too, one need only aspire to realize these two truths. However, one needn't excessively wish for it or repeatedly think about it. Otherwise it may encourage craving and wrong views, and disturb one's practice. I explained this point in chapter 2 in regard to the first hindrance to liberation. As the subcommentary says:

> The two truths in the round of existence can become meditation subjects because one can experience them through their own characteristics. But this is not so of the two truths beyond the round of existence—cessation and the path to cessation—because ordinary people cannot take them as sense objects and they serve no purpose when taken as sense objects by noble ones. So the phrase "to be wished for, to be liked, and to be nurtured" is used to incline the mind toward the truth of cessation of suffering and the truth of the path to the cessation of suffering, and not to promote obsession with them on the basis of craving and wrong view. One must simply aspire to realize the two truths that are beyond the round of existence.[405]

How suffering is realized

Noting each mental and physical phenomenon that arises, one understands the unique characteristics of each respective phenomenon. One understands the changeable and oppressing characteristics of the body, as well as its characteristic of bending toward the objects of the mind. One understands the characteristics of torment (*bādhanalakkhaṇā*) as being tortured by arising and disappearance, unpleasant feelings, and mental distress and physical pain for the one they afflict.

When they realize the characteristic of arising and disappearing, even those who have no intellectual knowledge whine as their insight knowledge matures, saying: "All that exists are these continually arising and disappearing phenomena! They disappear and then they are gone. Whatever I note is not satisfactory. There is no peace so long as these phenomena continue. Because these phenomena exist there is suffering. When will they cease to exist?" This is consistent with the following passages:

> Here a bhikkhu understands as it actually is: "This is suffering"; . . .[406]

> Except for craving, all phenomena in the three worlds[407] are suffering. One understands them as they really are.[408]
>
> The phrase "as they really are" means that one understands them in an ultimate sense [—that is, as torment in the form of unpleasant feeling, mental and physical distress, and impermanence]—in other words, in terms of their individual natures of changeability, hardness, and so on.[409]

The phrase "all phenomena in the three worlds" used in the above commentary refers only to animate phenomena in the three worlds and not to inanimate ones. Inanimate physical material is not the noble truth of suffering. The reasons for this are: inanimate phenomena do arise and pass away, and although they can be called impermanent and suffering they are not caused by craving and path knowledge does not bring them to an end. One can still observe external objects, such as clothing and so on, so that mental defilements do not arise because of them, to evaluate the impermanence and impersonality of external objects, and so that they easily become internally distinct. Although external objects arise by themselves at the six sense doors and should be observed, we cannot say that these inanimate, external objects are "full understanding of the noble truth of suffering" (*pariññeyya-ariyadukkhasacca*).

Among the phenomena that occur in the lives of living beings, we need only understand the Four Noble Truths in ourselves. The reasons for this are: when the truth of suffering arises because of one's craving, it arises only in oneself; it cannot arise in another person. When suffering arises in somebody else due to his or her craving, it arises only in him or her; it cannot arise in oneself. Furthermore, one's truth of the path that leads to the cessation of suffering can only lead to the cessation of one's own suffering and craving; it cannot lead to the cessation of another person's suffering and craving. And another person's path can only lead to the cessation of his or her suffering and craving; it cannot lead to the cessation of one's own suffering and craving. Furthermore, noble ones experience their individual truths of the cessation of craving and suffering; they cannot experience another person's Four Noble Truths. After having experienced their own Four Noble Truths they can inferentially understand others' truths.

Therefore, although one can attain path and fruition by being aware of something external, the most important thing is to understand the four internal truths.

Pāḷi texts such as the *Satipaṭṭhāna Sutta* give priority to the awareness within oneself by mentioning it first. The following excerpts from the Pāḷi texts, commentaries, and subcommentaries illustrate this point:

> As to that end of the world, friend, where one is not born, does not age, does not die, does not pass away, and is not reborn—I say that it cannot be known, seen, or reached by travelling.
>
> However, friend, I say that without having reached the end of the world there is no making an end to suffering. It is, friend, in just this fathom-high carcass endowed with perception and mind that I make known the world, the origin of the world, the cessation of the world, and the way leading to the cessation of the world.[410]

> Here, "the world" refers to the truth of suffering, "the origin of the world" refers to the truth of the cause of suffering, "the cessation of the world" to the truth of the cessation of suffering, and "the way leading to the cessation of the world" refers to the truth of the path to the cessation of suffering. By saying "However, friend, I say that without . . ." and so on, [the Buddha indicates that he does not recognize] the Four Noble Truths in inanimate phenomena, such as a log or the trunk of a tree, but only in this very body constituted of the four primary material elements.[411]

> One's own suffering and craving are what cease, so cessation is regarded as internal and belonging to oneself. Thus the phrase "one's own four truths" is used. Understand the phrase "another's four truths" in the same way.[412]

Thus inanimate phenomena are not the noble truth of suffering, since according to the Pāḷi texts and commentaries the Four Noble Truths pertain only to animate phenomena. Also, even though the truth of the cessation of suffering is technically an external phenomenon, the subcommentary above clearly says that it should be regarded as part of one's own or someone else's Four Noble Truths. Although everyone possesses all Four

Noble Truths, one can only penetrate into and realize one's own craving by eradicating it; one can only penetrate into and realize the cessation of one's own suffering and craving by experiencing it; and one can only penetrate into and realize one's own path by developing it. No one can abandon anyone else's craving, experience anyone else's cessation, or develop anyone else's path. So the important thing is to be aware of one's own Four Noble Truths.

How the origin of suffering is realized

Noting each mental and physical phenomenon that arises, one understands craving and desire when one is mindful of them. This is an empirical understanding of craving in the present moment. However, present craving is not the origin of present suffering. It is the origin of suffering in a future life that will be produced by the kamma one does in this life. Similarly, the craving or sense desire that formed when one performed kamma in past lives is the origin of present suffering.

Due to attachment to oneself or to sense pleasure, one performed wholesome and unwholesome deeds in past lives just as one does in this life. That kamma has been generating one's mental and physical phenomena since one was born into this life. One cannot empirically know one's past craving; one can only know it inferentially by comparing it to one's present craving. The craving that one can empirically know in the present and past craving only differ in terms of being present or past, they do not differ in terms of their characteristic. One can even say that they are the same because they manifest in the continuum of the same individual. It is like saying that we see a mountain or the sea even though we actually only see a small part of either. If one is aware of one's present craving, one can understand the truth of craving as the cause of suffering. In any event one can also be inferentially aware of past craving, beginning when one's knowledge that discerns mental and physical phenomena matures.

A meditator can empirically observe the cause-and-effect relationship between mental and physical phenomena: only when there is an intention to bend does the bending movement occur; only when it is cold does cold manifest in the body; only when there is a visible form and functioning eye does eye-consciousness arise; only when there is a mental object does thought occur; only when there is a previous mind-moment does a following mind-moment occur.

This realization becomes more obvious at the higher levels of insight that lead to path knowledge. At that point one understands that the mental and physical phenomena that one observes are not devoid of causes and that these mental and physical phenomena that have been occurring since birth only happen due to causes. One easily understands that the cause of this life is the wholesome kamma one performed in a past life. This understanding is based on one's faith in kamma and its effects. Thus one gains right understanding regarding kamma.

Thus one uses analytical knowledge (*cintāmaya*) and theoretical knowledge (*sutamaya*) based on empirical knowledge (*bhāvanāmaya*) to realize that craving is the origin of this life. One realizes that—driven by craving and sense desire—one performed wholesome and unwholesome deeds in past lives, just as one does in the present life. That past kamma based on craving then generated this present life, as explained in the commentarial passage:

> It gives rise to this very suffering (mental and physical phenomena), and so "Craving in previous lives is the origin of this present suffering."[413]

This is an inferential understanding of the origin of this present life's suffering. Note that the long explanation given here is only for the sake of general knowledge. In practice, of course, it will not take a meditator very long to understand. Immediately after one understands, one can continue noting objects in the present moment as usual.

Obvious but difficult to see

The first two truths are quite obvious because they are always present in us. They are not very profound or obscure. However, it is extremely difficult to understand that they are simply distressing or unsatisfactory and that craving is their origin. This is not obvious at all. The difficulty in understanding obvious phenomena lies in the fact that we are not mindful of them or do not pay attention to them. As the Burmese saying goes: "We cannot see even a cave without attention." So if we are mindful and pay attention to phenomena, we are bound to understand them as they really are through insight knowledge. Later at the peak of insight, with path knowledge, this understanding will become firm and irreversible.

> The truth of suffering[414] is obvious once it appears. If a stump, stake, or thorn hurts one, one cries out, "It hurts!"[415] The truth of the origin of suffering [that is, craving] is also obvious when one experiences the desire to do something, to eat, and so on. But these two truths are profound when understood in terms of their specific characteristics. Thus these two truths are profound because they are difficult to observe and understand.[416]

> The expression "difficult to see" means that even though the truth of suffering and the truth of craving as the cause of suffering are quite obvious the moment they appear, they are so profound that it is impossible to use normal intelligence to see them in terms of their characteristics and functions. We can only see them with the profoundly developed wisdom that reaches its peak with realization of noble path knowledge.[417]

How cessation and path are realized

As the commentary says, the last two truths, cessation and path, are extremely profound since they never happen to ordinary people—we cannot empirically understand and see them. As mentioned before, all that a beginning meditator needs to do with respect to these two truths is to incline the mind toward them, having heard that they are noble. It is not necessary to contemplate and think about them.

However at the stage of insight knowledge of arising and passing away, a meditator may spontaneously start to reflect and understand that the five aggregates would not exist if there were no ignorance, craving, volition, nutriment, mental contact, or mental and physical phenomena. Beginning from the stage of insight knowledge of dissolution, a meditator may spontaneously start to reflect and understand that as long as mental and physical processes—such as seeing, hearing, touching, thinking, observing, and so on—exist, there will be no peace. Only when these processes no longer exist will there be peace. This is an intellectual understanding of cessation during insight practice. As the *Paṭisaṃbhidāmagga* says:

> Arising is torment; nonarising is peace.[418]

At the stage of insight knowledge of desire for deliverance (*muñcitu-kamyatāñāṇa*), we may not want to observe mental and physical phenomena, since we see only the negative aspects of the phenomena we note. Some meditators may even stop observing them. However, as the momentum of practice is still there, mental and physical phenomena appear as usual and meditators are aware of them without the need to exert much effort to observe them. Eventually meditators may understand that phenomena do not cease without observing them; peace only comes with the experience of the peace of nibbāna, and that only happens when we note as usual. This is an intellectual understanding of path during insight practice.

This is how all four truths are understood by observing them during the practice of insight meditation.

Cultivating mundane understanding

To understand the Four Noble Truths means to fully understand suffering, to abandon craving, to experience cessation, and to develop the path. Thus one really only understands these truths when one abandons craving, experiences cessation, and develops the path. The four functions of fully understanding, abandoning, experiencing, and developing are simultaneously fulfilled with each and every noting. So we can say that the Four Noble Truths are understood with each noting.

Suffering

The mental and physical phenomena that one is aware of when one notes are all suffering of conditioned phenomena. Their constant arising and passing away is oppressive and so they are the truth of suffering. When one's insight matures and one experiences them in terms of their unique characteristics and universal characteristics—impermanence and so on—one thoroughly understands them. This is why one also accomplishes the function of fully understanding (*pariññākicca*).

Craving and cessation

The more one is accurately aware of mental and physical phenomena, the weaker the illusions of permanence, satisfaction, and personality become for one. Thus one's craving for phenomena diminishes. When one's understanding prevents craving from arising, that craving is abandoned. This accomplishes the function of abandoning (*pahānakicca*) craving, which in turn prevents clinging or grasping (*upādāna*), kamma, and its effect of consequent rebirth. This is the truth of temporary cessation (*tadaṅga-nirodhasacca*) in the context of insight meditation practice. It amounts to the cessation of craving and suffering for that moment of noting. Thus one accomplishes the function of directly experiencing (*sacchikiriyākicca*) cessation with each noting. In the case of path knowledge, however, "directly experiencing" refers to taking nibbāna as one's object. In the case of insight practice, one does not experience cessation by taking it as one's object; one accomplishes only the function of cessation.

Path

Understanding mental and physical phenomena as they really are, in terms of their individual and universal characteristics, is right view. There are also right intention (*sammāsaṅkappa*), right effort (*sammāvāyāma*), right mindfulness (*sammāsati*), and right concentration (*sammāsamādhi*). The mental processes involved in noting are considered right speech (*sammāvācā*), right action (*sammākammanta*), and right livelihood (*sammāājīva*), since it is the opposite of wrong speech, wrong action, and wrong livelihood. I will explain this in detail later. This is the mundane Noble Eightfold Path.

Because one develops the truth of the path leading to the cessation of suffering with every noting, noting accomplishes the function of developing the path (*bhāvanākicca*). As the *Visuddhimagga* says:

> When one sees mental and physical phenomena arising and passing away [with fully developed knowledge of arising and passing away], that is the mundane Noble Eightfold Path. Thus the truth of the path leading to the cessation of suffering exists in one.[419]

Thus because the four functions are accomplished in every noting, one understands the four [mundane] truths while noting mental or physical phenomena when they arise. Since all four functions are simultaneously accomplished with one noting, a person who develops mindfulness will gradually attain the supramundane truth of the path leading to cessation of suffering when insight knowledge becomes penetrating and mature. At that point the Four Noble Truths will be simultaneously fully understood with path knowledge. The commentary explains the phrase "attainment of the true way" [from the *Satipaṭṭhāna Sutta*] as follows:

> The phrase "attainment of the true way" means realizing the Noble Eightfold Path. The mundane practice of mindfulness, developed before path, leads to the attainment of supramundane path knowledge.[420]

Cultivating supramundane understanding

Suffering: the first noble truth

We cannot take suffering as an object during path knowledge, but we fully understand it at the moment of path. The reason for this is that when the path is accomplished by experiencing nibbāna as the cessation of all conditioned phenomena, one realizes that both noted phenomena and the noting mind, like all phenomena, are suffering and not peace. One realizes that they are actually subject to impermanence, even though they appear permanent, satisfying, and personal. We can compare it to losing our sense of direction and getting lost: we may have no idea where to find a particular town, city, road, pond, or lake when we do not know which direction is east or west and so on, but once we regain our sense of direction, we will know how to find the town or city, and so on, without confusion.

Another simile is moving from a place that is extremely hot to a place that is less hot: in comparison we may think, "It's cool here!" If we then went to a third place that was even less hot, we would also think, "Now, this place is really cool!" But when we finally arrived at a place that was actually cool, we would know, "Oh, it really is cool here!" and realize that the prior places were actually hot. In the same way, a person who has never practiced insight meditation thinks that all mental and physical phenomena are good, except unpleasant feelings. He or she takes places that are not so hot to be cool places. An insight meditator understands that the mental and physical phenomena he or she observes are unsatisfactory but takes his or her awareness of that to be something good. This is like taking a less hot place to be a cool place. At the moment of path knowledge, he or she experiences nibbāna and so is able to understand that all conditioned mental and physical phenomena are not peaceful. This is like having finally arrived at the coolest place and fully realizing that all the other places were hot.

We can find many similar examples in ordinary life. For example, when we encounter an exceptionally wonderful view, fragrant scent, sweet voice, delicious flavor, pleasant touch, good friend, lovely town, and so on, we realize that those one has previously known were not really so wonderful. In the same way, even though suffering is not directly an object of path, the path knowledge penetrates into and realizes suffering with full understanding, since it accomplishes the function of understanding.

An ordinary person cannot definitively decide that all mental and physical phenomena are impermanent, unsatisfactory, and not-self using scriptural knowledge or the power of reasoning. They can only accomplish this with wisdom developed through direct, personal experience. So ordinary people who rely on scriptural knowledge or the power of reasoning cannot overcome skeptical doubt. Often the more they analyze phenomena, the more confused they become.

On the other hand noble ones who have attained full understanding by means of the path (*maggapariññā*) can definitively decide that all mental and physical phenomena are impermanent, unsatisfactory, and not-self. Unlike ordinary people they do not take mental and physical phenomena to be permanent, satisfactory, and personal, and so cannot become attached to these phenomena. The more they contemplate phenomena, the clearer their understanding of impermanence, unsatisfactoriness, and not-self becomes. So even though a person who has attained the first level of path knowledge is still attached to sense pleasures and strives to enjoy them, he or she no longer has any intentions toward unwholesome deeds that would lead to the lower realms of existence.

This is the supramundane understanding of suffering.

Craving: the second noble truth

As mentioned above, attachment and craving can no longer arise when one is clearly aware of mental and physical phenomena. Due to the first path, attachment or craving that generates kamma that would lead to the lower realms and more than seven rebirths in a blissful destination (*sugati*) can no longer arise. Due to the second path, attachment or craving that generates gross sense desire (*kāmarāga*) and more than two rebirths can no longer arise. Due to the third path, subtle sense desire and attachment to or craving for sensual pleasure can no longer arise. Due to the fourth path, attachment to or craving for existence in the fine-material realm or immaterial can no longer arise.

We can liken this to the situation of a poor person who has become a millionaire, king, or queen: such a person would be no longer attached to or crave for his or her life as a poor person. Another example is that of a person who had a wicked and blameworthy spouse but now has a respectful and blameless spouse: as soon as the person understands the virtues of his or her new spouse and the vices of his or her former spouse, he or she no longer loves the former spouse.

This nonarising of attachment and craving is called both "penetration by abandoning" (*pahānappaṭivedha*) and "realization by abandoning" (*pahānābhisamaya*) because of [the realization and penetration that occur with] path knowledge. The realization of the abandonment of craving means it is a straightforward and penetrating one, even though path knowledge does not take the craving as its object. This abandoning or nonarising is referred to as "penetration" (*paṭivedha*) and "realization" (*abhisamaya*) because it fulfills the function of understanding. The subcommentary explains:

> Having abandoned, one knows. That is why it is called "penetration by abandoning" (*pahānappaṭivedho*).[421]

Noble ones fully understand that attachment to mental and physical phenomena is the cause of suffering, while ordinary people mistake it for pleasure. We can compare this with the case of a person who used to be a heavy smoker but is no longer attached to smoking after coming to understand that smoking is an unhealthy and useless habit.

This is the supramundane understanding of craving, the origin or cause of suffering.

Cessation: the third noble truth

Both the mental and physical phenomena being noted and the noting mind are obvious in a moment of insight practice. The alteration and deformation of these mental and physical phenomena in accordance with their arising and passing away are also obvious. Further, their respective functions and unique characteristics are as obvious as material substance, the body, or a sign are.

But at the moment of path knowledge and fruition knowledge, those mental and physical phenomena are cut off and cease so that only their peaceful nature is obvious. There is no arising and passing away in this state of peace (or cessation), so it is devoid of alteration and deformation. It is also devoid of material substance, body, forms, shapes, and signs. Therefore, at the moment of path knowledge, one takes the truth of cessation called nibbāna as one's object and experiences it as the characteristic of peace (*santilakkhaṇā*), as the function of deathlessness (*accutirasa*), and as the manifestation of the signless (*animittapaccupaṭṭhāna*). This is "penetration through direct experience" (*sacchikiriyāpaṭivedha*) and "realization through direct experience" (*sacchikiriyābhisamaya*). Unlike intellectualization this experience of the cessation of phenomena is very clear, like seeing a precious jewel in one's hand.

Immediately after one realizes path knowledge, reviewing knowledge that sees nibbāna as devoid of conditioned phenomena and peaceful arises. Noble ones understand that nibbāna is devoid of arising and passing away, and thus it is free from alteration and deformation—is permanent—and devoid of material substance, form, shapes, and signs.

It is like knowing a cool place when one enters a cool and shady place after having been out in a hot place. Or it is like appreciating that one's disease has disappeared when one recovers from a chronic disease.

This is the supramundane understanding of the cessation of suffering.

Path: the fourth noble truth

When one practices insight in order to bring about the Noble Eightfold Path, which is the truth of the path leading to the cessation of suffering, one takes nibbāna as one's object, so the truth of the path leading to the cessation of suffering arises in oneself. This is "penetration of the path through development" (*bhāvanāpaṭivedha*) and "realization of the path through development" (*bhāvanābhisamaya*). It is impossible to understand the path through the path itself, just as it is impossible to touch one's finger using that same finger. As soon as a person finds the solution to a problem that he or she has been pondering, for example, he or she exclaims, "I've got it, I know!"

After understanding has come about, one recollects it, thinking, "Before I experienced the peace of nibbāna, the suffering of mental and physical phenomena had not yet ceased. Only with the occurrence of this understanding have the suffering of mental and physical phenomena ceased and been cut off. Thus this understanding is the right path leading to the cessation of suffering."

This is the supramundane awareness of the path leading to the cessation of suffering. Thus the Four Noble Truths are simultaneously understood by taking cessation as one's object and by accomplishing the function of understanding the other three. This point can be checked in the commentarial explanations.

How to develop the Noble Eightfold Path

If one wants to become a noble one and understand the Four Noble Truths, one must develop the truth of the path leading to the cessation of suffering. If one wants to bring about the supramundane path knowledge, one must develop, with insight practice, the mundane path that includes right view and so on, by noting all arising mental and physical phenomena as explained before. The reason for this is that the path of insight (*vipassanāmagga*) is the cause, the decisive supporting condition (*upanissayapaccaya*) for the resulting conditionally arisen state (*upanissayapaccayuppanna*), the supramundane path.

Thus when the mundane path of insight is not adequately developed, the supramundane path cannot arise. When the path of insight is adequately developed up to the stage of insight knowledge of adaptation, the supramundane path arises by itself without one deliberately exerting much effort. As the *Visuddhimagga* says:

> If one wants to accomplish the first path, there is nothing else to do. Practicing insight meditation [until adaptation] is all one need do.[422]

If one wants to realize path knowledge, one need only practice insight. Thus the mundane path of insight should also be included in the truth of the path that one must develop (*bhāvetabbāmaggasacca*). As the *Sammohavinodanī*[423] says:

> This is the supramundane Noble Eightfold Path, which together with the mundane path [i.e., insight] is called "the path that leads to the cessation of suffering" (*dukkhanirodhagāminīpaṭipadā*).[424]

The eight factors that are included in path consciousness are called "the supramundane path" (*lokuttaramagga*). However, it cannot lead to the cessation of suffering without insight. In other words, this path, which has nibbāna as its object, cannot occur in isolation from the development of insight. That is why the supramundane path and the mundane path together are considered the truth of the path, the truth of the path that leads to the cessation of suffering. The *Visuddhimagga-mahāṭīkā* says:

The mundane paths are implicitly included, since [the supramundane paths] cannot take place without developing [mundane] concentration and insight.[425]

How to develop the path factors seclusion, dispassion, and cessation

Here, Ānanda, a bhikkhu develops right view, which is based upon seclusion, dispassion, and cessation, maturing in release. He develops right intention . . . right speech . . . right action . . . right livelihood . . . right effort . . . right mindfulness . . . right concentration, which is based upon seclusion, dispassion, and cessation, maturing in release. It is in this way, Ānanda, that a bhikkhu who has a good friend, a good companion, a good comrade, develops and cultivates the Noble Eightfold Path.[426]

The term "seclusion [from defilements]" means that one develops right view based on temporary seclusion (*tadaṅgaviveka*), perpetual seclusion (*samucchedaviveka*), and liberation-related seclusion (*nissaraṇaviveka*). To elaborate: in a moment of insight practice, a meditator who is seeking the noble path develops right view based on temporary seclusion in the form of temporarily abandoning defilements and liberation-related seclusion in the form of the aspiration for nibbāna. At the moment of path knowledge, the meditator develops right view based on perpetual seclusion in the form of completely abandoning defilements and liberation-related seclusion in the form of taking nibbāna as an object. Understand the terms "dispassion" and "cessation [of defilements]" in the same way, as they have the same meaning.

However, there are two kinds of release (*vosagga*): release that abandons defilements (*pariccāgavosagga*) and release that rushes to nibbāna (*pakkhandanavosagga*). The first kind of release abandons defilements temporarily in a moment of mindful noting and permanently at the moment of path knowledge. The second kind of release rushes to nibbāna by aspiring to it in a moment of mindful noting and by taking it as an object at the moment of path knowledge. Here, both meanings of release serve to explain the mundane and supramundane together.

Thus right view both abandons defilement and rushes into

> nibbāna. The compound "maturing in release" (*vossagga-pariṇāmiṃ*) refers to both insight, which is maturing, and path, which is fully mature, as abandoning defilements and rushing into nibbāna. The point is that a bhikkhu who practices meditation develops the path in such a way that right view matures [in moments of practicing insight] and becomes fully mature [at the moment of path knowledge] to abandon defilements and to rush into nibbāna. The same is true of the other seven path factors.[427]

There are five kinds of seclusion (*viveka*), dispassion (*virāga*), and cessation (*nirodha*): temporary (*tadaṅga*), liberation-related (*nissaraṇa*), perpetual (*samuccheda*), stopping (*vikkhambhana*), and repeated (*paṭipassaddhi*).

Because there are no latent defilements connected with sense objects at the levels of insight knowledges beginning with knowledge of dissolution, defilements have no opportunity to become obsessive or transgressive. In the context of insight meditation, seclusion from defilements is called temporary seclusion (*tadaṅgaviveka*), dispassion toward the defilements is called temporary dispassion (*tadaṅgavirāga*), and cessation of the defilements is called temporary cessation (*tadaṅganirodha*).

Every time one notes, one understands mental and physical phenomena as they really are. This is insight right view, which is accompanied by insight right thinking or aiming at an object, insight right effort, insight right mindfulness, and insight right concentration. The remaining mental states led by volition constitute right speech, right action, and right livelihood. These eight insight path factors that arise with each noting are referred to as "seclusion-based" (*vivekanissita*), "dispassion-based" (*virāganissita*), and "cessation-based" (*nirodhanissita*), because they are based on the above-mentioned temporary seclusion, dispassion, and cessation. Here "based" means only that each noting leads to seclusion, dispassion, and cessation with regard to the three kinds of defilement; it does not mean that seclusion, dispassion, and cessation are taken as objects.

Nibbāna is called escape (*nissaraṇa*) because it is escape from the cycle of defilement, kamma, and resultant (*vipaka*) mental and physical phenomena. Because nibbāna is also seclusion, dispassion, and escape from defilements, it is called "escape by means of seclusion" (*nissaraṇaviveka*), "escape by means of dispassion" (*nissaraṇavirāga*), and "escape by means of cessation" (*nissaraṇanirodha*). The above mentioned insight path factors only arise for those who aspire to experience nibbāna and who note mental and physical phenomena every time they arise. Those who enjoy life and do not aspire to attain nibbāna do not practice and so the insight path factors do not arise for them. Thus these path factors are called "based on nibbāna" due to bearing the aspiration to attain it. For this reason, too, they are based upon the seclusion of nibbāna, based upon the dispassion of nibbāna, and based upon the cessation of nibbāna. In this case, at the time of noting, one does not take nibbāna as one's object. It's only referred to as "based on nibbāna" because of the aspiration to experience nibbāna.

This is like performing an act of generosity with the aim of attaining nibbāna. The intention that arises during the act of offering takes the offering as its object, not nibbāna. Yet because the action was done with the aim of attaining nibbāna it is called "a nibbāna-based wholesome action" or "a wholesome action based beyond the round of rebirth" (*vivaṭṭanissita*). In the same way, although one takes the presently arising mental and physical phenomena as one's object, insight is called "nibbāna-based" because one notes with the aspiration to attain nibbāna. Thus an insight meditator who notes every arising mental and physical phenomenon is said to develop the insight path factors that are based on temporary seclusion, temporary dispassion, and temporary cessation, as well as escape by means of seclusion, by means of dispassion, and by means of cessation. As I have said, this is the truth of temporary seclusion that one can experience with insight practice.

The seclusion, dispassion, and cessation through the four supramundane knowledges of the path (in connection with the complete eradication of the respective defilements at each path) are called "perpetual seclusion" (*samucchedaviveka*), "perpetual dispassion" (*samucchedavirāga*), and "perpetual cessation" (*samucchedanirodha*). Because the supramundane path factors accomplish the seclusion, dispassion, and cessation of the defilements by eradicating them completely they are called "nibbāna-based seclusion," "nibbāna-based dispassion," and "nibbāna-based cessation." Further, because they also take nibbāna (which is called "escape by means of seclusion," "escape by means of dispassion," and "escape by means of cessation") as their object, they are called "escape-based seclusion," "escape-based dispassion," and "escape-based cessation."

Maturing in release

The insight path factors are in the process of maturing in order to abandon the defilements. Because these path factors only arise for those who aspire to attain nibbāna, the process of maturing also includes release in nibbāna by way of aspiring to it. Therefore, it is called "maturing in release" (*vosaggapariṇāmī*).

When the meditator notes every arising mental and physical phenomenon he or she is said to develop the vipassanā path factors. The supramundane path factors are brought to full maturity in order to completely abandon their respective defilements. They are also brought to full maturity so that one will be released into nibbāna by taking it as one's object. This is why it is called "maturing in release."

Here "fully mature" means that at the moment of path knowledge, one need not exert effort in order to take nibbāna as one's object or to abandon the defilements. Taking nibbāna as one's object and eradicating the defilements happen by themselves, due to the momentum of the preliminary path (*pubbabhāgamagga*) gained through the development of the insight path factors [up to insight knowledge of adaptation]. A person who wants to jump over a wide ditch, for example, begins running toward it from some distance away and needn't make further efforts once they've leaped from the brink of the ditch; he or she will simply be carried to the other side due to their momentum. This is difficult to understand!

The morality path factors

Insight practice includes the morality path factors of right speech, right action, and right livelihood. The commentaries on Abhidhamma and Khuddaka Nikāya explain:

> The same is true of the other seven path factors.[428]

> The three factors of right speech and so on refer to abstinence and mental volition. In the case of path, however, they refer only to abstinence.[429]

Refraining from immoral conduct in speech, action, and livelihood is abstinence. This constitutes moral conduct, consisting of right speech, right action, and right livelihood. Actively engaging in wholesome speech, actions, and thoughts involves wholesome intention, and is accordingly also referred to as right speech and so on. However, at the time of path knowledge, only the mental factors connected with abstinence are called right speech and so on. Since insight meditation falls within the realm of wholesome thought, the intention involved in wholesome mental states constitutes right speech and so on. In the case of insight knowledge and the various knowledges of the path, however, the abstinence involved is not the same as that involved in ordinary moral conduct.

> In the Pāḷi text called *Sikkhāpadavibhaṅga*,[430] a moral precept is defined, in an ultimate sense, as abstinence, intention, and associated dhammas (*sampayuttadhammā*). Of these three, only abstinence and intention are mentioned here, as they are the dominant factors. In other words, refraining from telling a lie, and so on, is abstinence, while telling the truth, and so on, is intention.[431]

Contemplation of the four truths

According to the commentary, insight meditation is called "contemplation of the four truths" (*catusaccakammaṭṭhāna*) because it leads to attainment of the path knowledge that understands the Four Noble Truths by observing mental and physical phenomena [i.e., suffering and craving] with the aim of attaining the various knowledges of the path and nibbāna, and because it produces the special happiness of bliss of the knowledges of path and fruition that comes from meditation aimed at understanding the Four Noble Truths.

> Insight meditation that leads to the understanding of the Four Noble Truths, or insight meditation that is practiced with the aim of experiencing the Four Truths, is called "contemplation of the four truths" and becomes the cause for the meditator's special happiness of bliss of the knowledges of path and fruition.[432]

The example of mindfulness of in- and out-breath

The commentary says that any meditation that is practiced according to one of the twenty-one sections mentioned in the *Satipaṭṭhāna Sutta* leads to knowledge that is the fruit of arahantship (*arahattaphala*), and is considered to be contemplation of the Four Noble Truths. The practice of mindfulness of in- and out-breath (*ānāpānasati*) is considered here as an example:

> Mindfulness of the in- and out-breath is the truth of suffering. Previous craving is its origin. The cessation of both is nibbāna. The path knowledge that fully understands suffering, abandons craving, and takes nibbāna as its object is the truth of the path leading to the cessation of suffering. By means of contemplating the Four Noble Truths one gradually becomes more purified and reaches the cessation of defilements. Thus this in- and out-breath practice becomes the cause for a monk's liberation from the cycle of suffering through knowledge that is the fruit of arahantship (*arahattaphala*).[433]

If a meditator notes the in- and out-breath in harmony with this text, he or she will experience the air element or the sensation of touch every time he or she notes. This is the awareness or mindfulness that is considered the preliminary insight path. Because it is necessary for attainment of the supramundane path, it is included figuratively under development of the path. But since it is mundane, this mindfulness is not really part of the truth of the path to the cessation of suffering but is actually part of the truth of suffering. Contemplation of the Four Noble Truths is insight practice that is only aimed at the definite noble truths. Thus in the explanation of how contemplation of the Four Noble Truths occurs, the commentators say that mindfulness belongs only to the truth of suffering.

The passage above says: "Mindfulness of the in- and out-breath is the truth of suffering." Mindfulness is singled out as the truth of suffering, but this is only a figure of speech based on the fact that mindfulness is the dominant factor involved. Actually, all of the mental and physical phenomena associated with mindfulness are also the truth of suffering. This includes the consciousness and mental factors that accompany mindfulness, the physical body upon which mindfulness depends, and the air element or sensations of touch from the in- and out-breath that mindfulness takes as its object. Mindfulness, along with all of these mental and physical phenomena, is seen in a moment of insight and fully understood as the truth of suffering at the moment of path knowledge. This process that is mindful of previous mindfulness and its accompanying mental factors is called "counter insight."

> The craving that was the origin of the body is also the origin of mindfulness, since mindfulness arises dependent on that body. If there were no craving, the body could not come into existence, and neither could mindfulness. Thus it is said: "Previous craving is its origin." Just as "conditioned phenomena is the origin of consciousness" refers to all mundane states of consciousness that originated from those conditioned phenomena, in line with the discourses.[434]

All mental and physical phenomena, beginning with the moment of relinking consciousness, are results of one of the wholesome volitional deeds performed in previous lives. The cause of those wholesome volitional deeds was the craving for life and the results of actions. Thus craving is regarded as the origin of all mental and physical phenomena in one's present life.

In the Pāḷi passage above, this is compared to the use of the word "consciousness" in the expression "conditioned phenomena are the origin of consciousness." "Consciousness" refers only to "resultant" consciousness—consciousness that is the direct result of previous conditioned phenomena. However, by extension, it includes all other types of consciousness: wholesome, unwholesome, and functional (*kriyacitta*). This is so because these other types of consciousness all originate in turn from the resultant consciousness.

Likewise, the craving that we harbored in previous lives has been generating the cycle of mental and physical phenomena, including mindfulness, throughout our present life. This is why craving is said to be the origin of mindfulness. It is said that mindfulness is the truth of suffering and that its origin, craving in previous lives, is the truth of the cause of suffering. Although it is impossible to be empirically aware of craving from a past life, we can inferentially realize it when our insight practice matures enough to perceive craving in the present life. Every time we note craving in the present, we are said to see the truth of the cause of suffering, because both past and present craving have the same characteristics and belong to the same individual person.

Nibbāna, which is the cessation of the truth of suffering as well as the cessation of craving (the cause of suffering), is called "the truth of the cessation of suffering." The eight supramundane path factors that accomplish the function of fully understanding the truth of suffering and abandoning craving as its cause, while taking nibbāna as its object, are called the truth of the path to the cessation of suffering. As a meditator, all that one need do with regard to cessation and path is to appreciate their nobility and arouse the aspiration to attain them. Thus, according to the *Visuddhimagga*:

> It is certain that I will be liberated from the cycle of rebirth, aging, sickness, and death through this practice.[435]

When, based on the previous aspiration for cessation and the path, a person observes the presently arising in-breath and out-breath or any other mental and physical phenomena [that constitute the truth of suffering and the truth of the cause of suffering], they are said to practice the insight meditation called contemplation of the Four Noble Truths (*catusacca-kammaṭṭhāna*). This person attains the cessation of all defilements by gradually going through the levels of purification (*visuddhi*), beginning with purification of view, and the four kinds of purification of knowledge and vision (*ñāṇadassanavisuddhi*), beginning with the first path knowledge. This means that the person has become an arahant. The commentators in the above quotes have explained this.

The moment of path knowledge

At the moment of the four various knowledges of the path that are also called "the purification of knowledge and vision," one simultaneously understands the Four Noble Truths. I have already explained how they are realized, but I will offer some further explanation here.

How one understands suffering

Path knowledge experiences nibbāna, which is the cessation of all mental and physical phenomena (such as constantly arising and disappearing in-breath and out-breath or mindfulness). Due to this experience, one fully understands without confusion that all these phenomena (i.e., the in-breath and out-breath, mindfulness, dependent material phenomena, constantly arising and disappearing mental and physical phenomena, conditioned phenomena) are suffering and not peaceful.

How one understands craving

When one has fully understood that all conditioned phenomena are unsatisfactory, craving for these conditioned mental and physical phenomena no longer arises. This absence is penetration by abandoning (*pahānappaṭivedha*) and realization by abandoning (*pahānābhisamayā*).

How one understands cessation and path

By taking nibbāna—the cessation of all conditioned phenomena—as one's object, path factors such as right view arise distinctly in oneself. Experiencing nibbāna at that moment is penetrating or realizing the truth of cessation. The arising of the path factors, the truth of the path leading to the cessation of suffering while taking nibbāna as one's object, comes about by observing objects such as the in and out breath. This is called "penetration through development" and "realization through development."

For a detailed explanation, see above.

Other objects of meditation

So far, I have explained how, by observing the in- and out-breath as his or her basic object, an insight meditator becomes enlightened, up to the attainment of knowledge that is the fruit of arahantship (*arahattaphala*). The commentary gives similar explanations of how to develop the Four Noble Truths and become an arahant for the twenty other sections of the text that deal with alternate objects of meditation, such as the bodily postures and so on. The only difference among these various practices is the primary object of mindfulness. I will briefly mention the different objects here:

"Bodily postures" (*iriyāpatha*) refers to awareness of bodily postures, such as walking, standing, sitting, and lying down as the truth of suffering.

"Clear comprehension" (*sampajañña*) refers to awareness of moving forward or back, bending and stretching the limbs, and so on as the truth of suffering.

"Attention to repulsiveness" (*pāṭikūlamanasikāra*) refers to awareness of the thirty-two parts of the body—hair on the head, body hair, nails, teeth, skin, and so on—as the truth of suffering. However, this awareness is a form of tranquility meditation, not insight. Body parts, such as hair, are conceptual objects and not absolute realities. Therefore, the objects of the awareness cannot be included in the truth of suffering.

"Attention to the elements" (*dhātumanasikāra*) refers to awareness of the four primary material elements as the truth of suffering.

"Charnel ground contemplation" (*sivathika*) refers to awareness of a swollen corpse and so on as the truth of suffering.

"Contemplation of feeling" (*vedanānupassanā*) refers to awareness of feeling as the truth of suffering.

"Contemplation of mind" (*cittānupassanā*) refers to awareness of mind as the truth of suffering.

"Hindrances" (*nīvaraṇa*) refers to awareness of hindrances as the truth of suffering.

"Aggregates subject to clinging" (*upādānakkhandhā*) refers to awareness of the five aggregates as the truth of suffering.

"Sense bases" (*āyatana*) refers to awareness of the sense bases and fetters as the truth of suffering.

"Factors of enlightenment" (*bojjhaṅgā*) refers to awareness of the factors of enlightenment as the truth of suffering.

"Four Noble Truths" (*ariyasaccā*) refers to awareness of the truth of suffering and the truth of craving as the cause of suffering, and the awareness of the truth of the cessation of suffering and the truth of the path to the cessation of suffering, in the form of the aspiration to attain it, as the truth of suffering.

Among these twenty sections, only mindfulness is explicitly said to be the truth of suffering. However, as explained above, this is only a figurative way of speaking and refers to the fact that mindfulness is the dominant factor involved. Actually all of the accompanying mental factors, physical and mental objects, and the physical bases associated with mindfulness are also the truth of suffering that insight knowledge and path knowledge must realize. Thus, when one practices insight using these meditation subjects, in order to attain path knowledge and nibbāna one should be aware of: the meditation object itself, such as the body posture, and so on; one's awareness of the object; mental factors that accompany one's awareness; the physical basis of that awareness, if it is obvious; and the present craving that is similar to past craving, which was the origin of the present phenomena.

When one's insight knowledge matures, one will automatically become inferentially aware of the past origins of phenomena. So one need not exert effort or reflect on them. If one practices in this way, one will be practicing the form of insight meditation that is called contemplation of the Four

Noble Truths. Going through the different levels of purification, one will attain the defilement-free state of arahantship.

In accordance with the commentary, this is briefly how a person who practices any of the twenty-one sections mentioned in the *Satipaṭṭhāna Sutta* develops contemplation of the Four Truths and attains the knowledges of path and fruition up to the knowledge that is the fruit of arahantship (*arahattaphala*).

The Benefits of Mindfulness

After having attained all the four stages of path knowledge and fruition knowledge, a person who practices according to the *Satipaṭṭhāna Sutta*: becomes purified of all mental defilements such as lust, aversion, and delusion; overcomes all forms of worry and grief, as well as weeping and lamentation; overcomes all forms of physical suffering and mental suffering—there is no more physical suffering after having entered *parinibbāna* and there is no more mental suffering after having attained knowledge that is the fruit of arahantship (*arahattaphala*); attains the four various knowledges of the path, which are also called "right conduct" (*ñāya*); and understands nibbāna, which is the cessation of all kinds of suffering.

The only way

The Buddha praised the mindfulness practice of the foundations of mindfulness as follows:

> Bhikkhus, this is the [only way][436] for the purification of beings, for the surmounting of sorrow and lamentation, for the disappearance of pain and grief, for the attainment of the true way, for the realization of Nibbāna—namely, the four foundations of mindfulness."[437]

This passage explicitly states that mindfulness is the only way to purify the mind of mental defilements and realize nibbāna. So being mindful of the body, feelings, mind, and mind objects, which are all ultimate realities, is certainly contemplation of the Four Noble Truths, the development of insight, and the preliminary path. The development of the four efforts, five mental faculties, seven factors of enlightenment, eight path factors, and so on, are all included in this mindfulness practice. No practice can lead to nibbāna without mindfulness of the body, feelings, mind, and mind objects. This is the commentarial explanation of this point:

> The phrase "this is the only way" means that this path is the only path; it is not a divided path or two paths.[438]

> The term "only way" means the one-and-only path, as there is no other path besides mindfulness that leads to nibbāna. One may wonder: "Why does 'path' refer only to mindfulness practice, when there are many other paths?" It is true that there are many other paths, but all are embraced by mindfulness practice, which is indispensable. That is why wisdom, effort, and so forth are mentioned in the *Niddesa*, while only mindfulness is mentioned in the *Uddesa*, according to the inclination of the Dhamma audience (*veneyyajjhāsaya*). The phrase "not a divided path" indicates that there is not any other path and that it is impossible that this path does not lead to nibbāna.[439]

Furthermore, the commentaries say that it is only through path knowledge based on mindfulness that the countless buddhas, silent buddhas, and noble followers have been purified of mental defilements. It is impossible to arouse wisdom without noting the body, feelings, mind, and mind objects. It is also due to path knowledge based on mindfulness that some people in the Buddha's time attained the knowledges of path and fruition by listening to just a single verse of discourse.

So it should be clear in one's mind that the only practice that leads to knowledges of path and fruition is the mindfulness practice of contemplating the body, feelings, mind, and mind objects, which are ultimate realities.

The Buddha's acknowledgment

The Buddha acknowledged that a person of middling intelligence, wisdom, or understanding (*majjhimapaññāneyya*) who practiced in harmony with one of the twenty-one methods would become an arahant or a nonreturner within a maximum of seven years and after a minimum of seven days:

> If anyone should develop these four foundations of mindfulness in such a way for seven days, one of two fruits could be expected for him: either final knowledge here and now, or if there is a trace of clinging left, non-return.[440]

In the *Bodhirājakumāra Sutta*,[441] the Buddha acknowledged that a person of sharp intelligence, wisdom, or understanding (*tikkhapaññāneyya*) can even become fully enlightened within a night or a day:

> When a bhikkhu who possesses these five factors of striving finds a Tathāgata to discipline him, then being instructed in the evening, he might arrive at distinction in the morning; being instructed in the morning, he might arrive at distinction in the evening.[442]

These are the five factors of striving: (1) faith in the Buddha, Dhamma, Saṅgha, one's meditation teacher, and the meditation method, (2) sufficient health to digest the food one eats, (3) enough honesty to state the facts of one's experience to one's teacher and fellow meditators without boasting about virtues that one is not endowed with or trying to conceal one's shortcomings, (4) the determination to persist in one's efforts until one becomes fully enlightened, even if the result is that one's flesh and blood wither away, leaving only skin, sinew, and bones, and (5) arousing insight knowledge of the arising and passing away of mental and physical phenomena.

"May you be able to attain the knowledges of path and fruition and reach nibbāna within seven years, or seven days, or even within one night or day." These words are not the words of an ordinary person but of the Buddha, who understood by himself all phenomena as they really are. Because he only said what was true and beneficial they are the words of the *Sugata*, as the Buddha was called. Therefore, may you all be endowed with faith and the aspiration to become free from the cycle of suffering.

> The buddhas do not speak ambiguously [they only speak what is true]; the Victorious Ones do not speak fruitlessly [they only speak what is beneficial].[443]

If one has faith that the Buddha only speaks what is true and beneficial, and having faith in the two acknowledgments mentioned before, then one should aspire like this: "If I am a person with sharp intelligence, wisdom, and understanding, I will become fully enlightened even within one night or one day. If I am a person with middling intelligence, wisdom, and understanding, I will become fully enlightened within seven days, or within fifteen days, or within seven years."

With this aspiration may you be able to practice mindfulness meditation.

Suitable contemplations

The *Satipaṭṭhāna Sutta* and its commentary state that one can attain the final fruition knowledge by practicing in harmony with one of the twenty-one meditations (i.e., the contemplation of the in- and out-breath, and so on). However this does not mean that the knowledges of path and fruition can only be attained by practicing exclusively according to one particular section, without following the practices in any of the other sections. When asked about this, the Buddha taught bhikkhu Uttiya and others to develop all four foundations of mindfulness.[444] Practicing in that way, they attained arahantship.

When it is said that one is bound to attain the knowledge that is the fruit of arahantship (*arahattaphala*) by practicing in line with one of the twenty-one meditations, this refers to the contemplation of an object from one particular section as a primary object. It does not mean that one should only contemplate a particular object mentioned in a particular section and ignore any objects mentioned in other sections, however obvious they may be. If one did this, it would lead to a sense of permanence, satisfaction, personality, and beauty in regard to those mental and physical phenomena that are not noted.

These days it is quite difficult to accurately determine which particular meditation object is most suitable for a particular person. However, based on my own experience, the contemplation of the body as a primary object is suitable for most people. That is why, in the next chapter, I will explain how to practice the four foundations of mindfulness using contemplation of the body as the primary object. I will present the foundations in the order that they should be practiced, rather than the order in which they are taught. In conclusion, I offer this wish:

May you all be able to observe mental and physical phenomena as instructed, using one or more of the contemplations that are suitable for your own particular inclination and disposition, and quickly attain to the knowledges of path and fruition, nibbāna, by going through the stages of insight knowledge.

Here ends chapter 4 regarding the Development of Mindfulness.

Practical Instructions[445]

5

In this chapter, I will explain how to practice insight meditation and experience path knowledge and fruition knowledge from a practical perspective. So I will use everyday language rather than technical terminology. I will also not be including many textual references or quotations. If the readers have any doubts on a subject, they can refer to the supporting material and references included in the previous chapters.

Preparations for Practice

If a meditator aspires to attain path knowledge and fruition knowledge and nibbāna in this very life, he or she should cut any impediments during the time of meditation practice through the following preparations.

Purify moral conduct as explained in chapter 1, and cultivate the wish: "May my moral conduct be supportive of path knowledge." If you suspect that you may have ever committed some offense toward an enlightened person, you should apologize for the mistake. If you cannot go to see that person to apologize, you should offer the apology in front of a teacher.

Entrust yourself to the Buddha's wisdom, in order to be free from fear in the event that frightening objects appear during intensive practice. Also you should entrust yourself to a teacher's care, so that the teacher may guide you without any hesitation. This may not be necessary if you are already following a teacher's instructions respectfully.

Reflect on the merits of: nibbāna, which is completely free from any mental or physical suffering; path knowledge, which eradicates defilements and leads directly to nibbāna; and insight practice, which will surely lead to the attainment of path knowledge and nibbāna. You should find inspiration by remembering that the path of insight you are practicing is the same path that the Buddha, arahants, and all of the noble ones have followed.

You should then bow to the Buddha, reflecting on as many of his attributes as you know. After this, it is recommended that one cultivate loving-kindness toward all living beings, beginning with the devas that guard the monastery. If possible, you should then contemplate death and the impurity of your own body.

Finally, you should sit with legs crossed, or in any other sitting posture that is comfortable, and observe as explained below.

The Basic Practice

The primary object

A meditator should focus his or her mind on the abdomen. You will feel it rising and falling. If you don't feel this clearly, place a hand on the abdomen and its rise and fall will become obvious after a while. When breathing in, you will experience the rising movement of the abdomen. Note this as "rising." When breathing out, you will experience the falling movement. Note this as "falling."

While doing this you may reflect that observing the form or concept of the abdomen is not what you ought to be doing. This is not a cause for worry. Initially, of course, it is almost impossible to avoid a conceptual sense of solid form. So in the beginning, you must observe objects on a conceptual level. That is the only way that your concentration, awareness, and insight knowledge will mature. In due time, however, insight knowledge will break through to the absolute reality beyond concepts.

True insight practice is an awareness of all of the mental and physical phenomena that constantly arise at the six sense doors. However, because concentration and awareness are not strong enough in the beginning, it will be difficult to observe all of the phenomena that constantly arise. You will not be skillful enough to follow all of the objects, or may get caught up in searching for an object to note. For these reasons you should initially focus just on the rise and fall of the abdomen that occurs all the time and is noticeable enough to observe without much difficulty. Later, when your practice matures, you will be able to note objects as they arise.

So you should concurrently and continuously note the movements of the abdomen as "rising" and "falling" from moment to moment. A meditator should do this mentally, not audibly. Do not make the breath more vigorous than usual so as to make the rise and fall more distinct; neither slow down nor speed up the breath. If a meditator changes his or her natural pattern of breathing, he or she may get tired quickly and not be able to note properly. Just breathe in and out normally and regularly, and observe concurrently.

A textual note

The rise and fall of the abdomen is a manifestation of the air element, one of the types of tactile, physical phenomena. When observing the rise and fall, you will experience pressure and movement—characteristics of the air element—in accord with the following Pāḷi passages:

> Bhikkhus, attend carefully to form. Recognize the impermanence of form as it really is.[446]

> Bhikkhus, a bhikkhu sees as impermanent form which is actually impermanent: that is his right view.[447]

This is stated in discourses contained in Khandhasaṃyutta of the Saṃyutta Nikāya. And it is also in accordance with the contemplation of mind-objects (the five aggregates) in the *Mahāsatipaṭṭhāna Sutta*.

> Bhikkhus, attend carefully to tactile objects. Recognize the impermanence of tactile objects as it really is.[448]

> Bhikkhus, a bhikkhu sees as impermanent tactile objects which are actually impermanent: that is his right view.[449]

> . . . by directly knowing and fully understanding the eye . . . the mind, by developing dispassion towards it and abandoning it, one is capable of destroying suffering.[450]

> When one knows and sees [tactile objects] as impermanent, ignorance is abandoned and true knowledge arises.[451]

This is stated in discourses contained in Saḷāyatanasaṃyutta of the Saṃyutta Nikāya. It is also in accordance with the contemplation of mind-objects (the six bases) in the *Mahāsatipaṭṭhāna Sutta*.

> Now both the internal air element and the external air element are simply air element. And that should be seen as it actually is with proper wisdom thus: "This is not mine, this I am not, this is not my self."[452]

This is as stated in the discourses dealing with the elements. It is also in accordance with the contemplation of the body (elements) in the *Mahāsatipaṭṭhāna Sutta*.

Moreover the air element is part of the materiality aggregate subject to clinging (*rūpa upādānakkhandha*) and is therefore included in the truth of suffering. It should be seen as it really is, in accord with the Buddha's teaching:

> This noble truth of suffering is to be fully understood.[453]

This is in accordance with the discourses dealing with the noble truths. It is also included in the contemplation of mind-objects (the Four Noble Truths) in the *Mahāsatipaṭṭhāna Sutta*.

Therefore, observing the rise and fall of the abdomen is clearly consistent with the teaching of the Buddha, because one understands the pressure and movement of the air element as it really is. With regard to the observation of the in- and out-breath as explained in chapter 4, it is said:

> He understands accordingly however his body is disposed.[454]

Distracting thoughts

As you continually note the rise and fall of the abdomen, various kinds of thoughts will arise. When this happens, you note them using everyday language. For example when you find yourself thinking, note it as "thinking, thinking." If you daydream, note it as "daydreaming, daydreaming." If you imagine something, note it as "imagining, imagining." If you find yourself considering something, note it as "considering, considering." When the mind wanders off, note it as "wandering, wandering." If you imagine traveling to some other place, note it as "traveling, traveling." If you imagine meeting someone, note it as "meeting, meeting." If you imagine speaking with someone, note it as "speaking, speaking." Whenever you imagine seeing something or someone, repeatedly note it as "seeing, seeing," until the mental image disappears. Then immediately return to noting the rise and fall of the abdomen.

Physical discomfort

While noting the rise and fall of the abdomen, you may feel like you want to swallow or spit out the saliva in your mouth. This should be noted as "wanting to swallow," or "wanting to spit." If a meditator actually swallows or spits, he or she notes it as "swallowing, swallowing" or "spitting, spitting," and immediately returns to noting the rise and fall of the abdomen. If you want to lower your head, note it as "wanting to lower." If you bend the neck to lower the head, note it as "bending, bending," while continuing to focus on every movement involved. Do this slowly, not quickly. Follow the same procedure when bringing the head back up again. Afterward, go right back to the primary object of the rise and fall of the abdomen.

When an uncomfortable stiffness arises in any part of the body, focus only on the stiffness and continuously note it as "stiffness, stiffness." Keep your noting concurrent with the actual sensation. The stiffness may slowly fade away, or it may grow even more intense. If it becomes unbearable and you want to shift your posture, note that mental state as "wanting to shift, wanting to shift." If you actually shift your posture, continue to note each of the physical movements involved in that process. When you want to lift a limb, for example, note it as "wanting to lift." Then, when you actually lift it, note each movement as "lifting, lifting." When stretching it, note that as "stretching." When bending it, note that as "bending." When lowering it again, note that as "lowering." Do not make any of these movements quickly, but rather make them slowly and steadily. If you feel something touching any part of the body during the movement, note it as "touching." When you are done shifting your posture, or if the stiffness fades away without shifting your posture, immediately return to noting the rise and fall of the abdomen.

If you feel heat somewhere in your body, focus the mind on it and concurrently and continuously note it as "heat, heat." If it fades away, return to noting the rise and fall of the abdomen. If it becomes unbearable and you want to shift your posture, note it as "wanting to shift." If you actually shift your posture, concurrently and continuously note the entire process of lifting each limb as described above. Afterward, immediately return to noting the rise and fall of the abdomen. A meditator does not leave any gap in the flow of noting.

When a meditator feels a bodily itch, he or she focuses on it and steadily and continuously notes it as "itching, itching." While noting it in this way, the itch may fade away. If it does, return to noting the rise and fall of the abdomen. If the itch becomes unbearable and you either want it to disappear or want to scratch it, note it as "wanting to disappear," or "wanting to scratch." If a meditator wants to raise his or her hand to scratch, he or she notes it as "wanting to raise." As you actually raise your hand, note it as "raising." Do this slowly and steadily. When touching the itchy part of your body, note it as "touching." As you scratch, every time your hand or fingers move back and forth note it as "scratching." When you feel like you want to stop scratching, note it as "wanting to stop." When you want to put your hand back down, note it as "wanting to put down." A meditator then notes "lowering, lowering" as he or she actually lowers the hand. When you feel the touch of your hand coming to rest back in its place, note it as "touching." Immediately afterward, a meditator returns to noting their primary object, the rise and fall of the abdomen.

When any kind of unpleasant sensation arises and becomes distinct, a meditator focuses his or her mind on it and notes it accurately and steadily using everyday language such as "pain, pain," "numb, numb," "ache, ache," "tired, tired," or "dizzy, dizzy." When you note it in this way, it may fade away or increase. If noted with patience and perseverance, it often fades away. If it becomes unbearable, ignore it and take extra care to concurrently and continuously note the rise and fall of the abdomen.

Odd experiences

As concentration grows stronger, you may experience unbearable pain in your body. You may feel strong pressure, as if an airbag were being inflated inside your chest, a sharp pain, as if being stabbed with a dagger, a stinging pain, as if being pricked with many small needles, or an overall irritation, as if insects were crawling all over your body. You may feel fierce heat, severe itchiness, unbearable aching, extreme cold, or a variety of other unpleasant sensations.

If a meditator becomes frightened and stops noting when any of these kinds of extreme sensations occur, he or she will find that they immediately disappear. But they will generally reappear when his or her noting becomes strong again. A meditator should not be afraid of encountering any of these kinds of experiences. These are not signs of some serious disease; they are ordinary sensations that we often have in our bodies. We rarely notice them, however, because our attention is usually occupied with more obvious sensations. It is actually the strength of our concentration that makes them obvious in this way. So you needn't worry that something is wrong. Simply continue to note the sensation in order to overcome it. If a meditator stops noting, he or she may end up encountering the same kind of sensation every time concentration becomes strong. If you note it with patience and perseverance, though, at some point it will suddenly disappear for good.

If you feel like your body wants to sway, note it as "wanting to sway." If your body starts to actually sway, note it as "swaying, swaying." If a meditator finds him- or herself swaying unintentionally, he or she should not be afraid of it, nor should he or she encourage it. You simply continue noting it, steadily and gradually, as "swaying, swaying," confident that it will disappear if noted. If the swaying becomes very strong, you can practice while sitting against a wall or other firm support, or while lying down; the swaying will soon entirely cease. Follow the same procedure if you experience trembling in the body.

Sometimes you may get goose bumps or a chill may run up your back or through your whole body. You needn't be afraid of this; it's just rapture brought on by your meditation. Sometimes any sound you hear may cause fear to arise. You needn't fear this either; it's just that your sensitivity to mental contact has become very keen as a result of strong concentration. Any time you feel like rearranging your limbs or posture, first note the intention to do so, and then note every single successive movement involved as well. A meditator should not move quickly. He or she should move slowly and steadily.

Getting a drink

When you are thirsty, note it as "thirsty." If you intend to stand up to get a drink, note it as "intending to stand up." As a meditator prepares to stand up, he or she notes all of the physical movements involved using everyday language. When standing up, focus on the gradual rise of the body and note it as "standing up, standing up." Move slowly and steadily. When you have risen and are standing, note it as "standing, standing." If you happen to see or look at something or someone, note it as "seeing" or "looking." When you want to go get some water, note it as "wanting to go." While you are actually going, note every step as "stepping, stepping" or "right, left." Follow each step mindfully from the moment the foot is lifted until it is dropped back down again. When walking slowly, or during formal walking meditation, note two parts of each step: either "lifting, moving," "lifting, dropping," or "moving, dropping." Once you can easily note two parts of each step, switch to noting three parts: "lifting, moving, dropping."

When you look at and see the container of drinking water, note it as "looking, seeing." When standing still in front of it, note that as "standing, standing." When reaching for a cup, note that as "reaching, reaching." When touching the cup, note that as "touching, touching." When taking hold of the cup, note that as "holding, holding." When pouring water into the cup, note that as "pouring, pouring." When lifting the cup of water to the mouth, note that as "lifting, lifting." When the cup touches the lips, note that as "touching, touching." When feeling the coldness of the water, note that as "cold, cold." When drinking and swallowing the water, note that as "drinking, swallowing." When feeling the coldness of the water in your throat or stomach, note it as "cold, cold." When putting the cup down, note that as "putting down, putting down." When lowering the hand, note that as "lowering, lowering." When the hand touches the body, note that as "touching, touching."

When the intention arises to turn and go back to your seat, note it as "intending to turn," and as you actually turn, note it as "turning, turning." As you walk back to your seat, note each step in the same way described above. When you intend to come to a stop and stand still, note that as "intending to stand," and then note "standing, standing" as you stand. If you remain standing for some time, you can note the rise and fall of the abdomen along with the standing posture as "rising, falling, standing." When you intend to sit down, note that as "intending to sit." If you need to position yourself on your seat, note that in a similar manner. If you need to turn, note it as "turning."

As you actually lower yourself to sit, note it as "sitting down, sitting down," with awareness of the weight of the body gradually being lowered. Do everything slowly and steadily. Once you are seated, you will need to arrange your hands and legs again. Carefully note all of the movements involved, using everyday language. Then if there are no other obvious objects to note, return to noting the primary object, the rise and fall of the abdomen, as usual.

Going to bed

When you want to lie down, note it as "wanting to lie down." As you prepare the bed, note all of the movements of the arms and legs as "lifting," "stretching," "repositioning," and so on. As you actually lie down, focus on the whole body as it gradually lies down and note it as "lying down, lying down." When feeling the touch of the pillow and bedding, note it as "touching, touching." When finally lying, note the movements of the arms, legs, and body, and note any adjustment of your laying posture as well. Do this slowly and mindfully. Then if there is nothing else to note, focus on the rise and fall of the abdomen, continuously noting it.

As a meditator lies in bed noting the rise and fall of the abdomen, he or she may feel some unpleasant sensations, such as stiffness, heat, pain, itchiness, and so on. If you do, note these mindfully in the same way you do in sitting meditation. Carefully note any distractions, such as swallowing, thinking, imagining, and so on, as you would at other times. If you want to turn over, bend or stretch your limbs, or adjust your position in any other way, first note the intention and then note every single movement involved without missing any. When there is nothing else in particular to note, return to noting the primary object, the rise and fall of the abdomen.

If you feel sleepy, note it as "sleepy, sleepy." If your eyelids feel heavy, note that as "heavy, heavy." When your meditation matures, sleepiness disappears and the mind becomes clear again. If that happens, note it as "clear, clear," and return to noting the rise and fall of the abdomen. If sleepiness has not disappeared, do not stop noting; simply continue noting the rise and fall of the abdomen or any other object, without any intention of falling asleep. When your body gets really tired, you will eventually fall asleep in the middle of noting.

Sleep is a prolonged period of the "life-continuum" or "functional" consciousness. This is the same kind of consciousness that arises during the first and last moments of our lives. This type of consciousness is so subtle that its sense objects cannot be known. Life-continuum consciousness also occurs between successive moments of full consciousness while we are awake. It occurs between moments of seeing and thinking, hearing and thinking, and so on, for example. However, it does not last long enough for us to notice on such occasions. When we sleep, it lasts long enough that we notice it, but we still cannot detect its characteristics or its object. So it is not possible to note any objects when we are asleep.

Getting up

As soon as you wake up, note it as "waking up, waking up." At the beginning of your practice you will find it difficult to catch the first moments of waking. If a meditator is not yet able to note right from the moment of waking up, he or she should start noting whatever object arises from the time he or she remembers to note. If you find yourself thinking, note it as "thinking, thinking," and then continue to note the rise and fall of the abdomen. If a sound awakens a meditator, he or she notes it as "hearing, hearing." If there is nothing else to note, he or she continues noting the rise and fall of the abdomen.

Turn over, bend, and stretch slowly and mindfully, while noting each using everyday language. If you think about what time it is, note it as "thinking, thinking." If you feel that you want to get up, note it as "wanting to get up." Note without any gap all of the movements involved in the process of getting out of bed. Focus on the body getting up and note it as "getting up, getting up." If a meditator sits afterward, he or she notes it as "sitting, sitting." Then he or she returns to noting the primary object, the rise and fall of the abdomen.

If you wash your face or bathe, note every single action involved, without any gap. For example, note looking at and seeing the bathing bowl, reaching for it, picking it up, scooping up the water, pouring the water over the body, the coolness of the water, rubbing the body, and so on.[455] You should also note any other activities, such as putting on clothes, making the bed, opening or closing the door, arranging your things, and so on, without any gap.

Eating a meal

When having a meal and looking at the plate, note it as "looking" or "seeing." When gathering a morsel of rice, note that as "gathering, gathering." As the morsel is lifted to the mouth, note that as "lifting, lifting." If you lower your head, note it as "lowering, lowering." As your fingers touch your lips, note it as "touching, touching." As your mouth is opening, note it as "opening, opening." As you place the morsel of rice into your mouth, note it as "placing, placing." As you close your mouth, note it as "closing, closing." As you lower your hand, note it as "lowering, lowering." If you raise your head again, note it as "raising, raising." Each time you chew the food, note it as "chewing, chewing." As you taste the flavor of the food, note it as "tasting, tasting." When swallowing the food, note it as "swallowing, swallowing." If you feel the food passing through your throat and digestive tract, note it as "touching, touching."[456]

In this way a meditator meticulously notes during the entire process of eating. At the beginning of practice when you are not yet able to note things as they arise, there will be many gaps in your noting. There will also be many instances when you cannot be aware of nor note your intention to move the body. A meditator shouldn't feel frustrated by this! If a meditator has the attitude to note meticulously and carefully, he or she will be able to note and observe more and more. As your understanding matures, you will be able to easily note even more objects than I have explained here.

Increasing the number of objects

After about a day, you are likely to feel that simply noting the rise and fall of the abdomen is too easy. You may find that there is a gap or break between the movements of rising and falling. In that case, a meditator should switch to noting three objects, adding the sitting posture itself as a third object. You will then be noting: "rising, falling, sitting; rising, falling, sitting; . . ." In the same way that you note the rise and fall of the abdomen, you must now be aware of the sitting posture of the body and note it as "sitting." If lying down, note the three objects of "rising, falling, lying."

If a meditator still finds that there are gaps while noting these three objects, he or she can add a distinct sensation of touch in any part of the body as a fourth object and note "rising, falling, sitting, touching." If you are not comfortable with this approach, then you can note "rising, sitting, falling, sitting" instead. If lying down, the four objects to note are: "rising, falling, lying, touching" or "rising, lying, falling, lying." If the breath becomes so subtle that you cannot clearly feel the rise and fall of the abdomen, you can note the sitting or lying posture or "touch points." A meditator can note four, five, or six touch points, one after the other.

General objects

While you are carefully noting phenomena within the body, such as the rise and fall of the abdomen and so on, there is no need to note ordinary seeing or hearing. Careful noting of the rise and fall of the abdomen and so on, fulfills the aim of noting and understanding seeing or hearing; it is simply seeing or hearing. However, if you intentionally look at something or someone, note it as "looking, looking," and then continue to note the primary object. Even if you don't do it intentionally, if you happen to see an object like a woman or a man, note "seeing, seeing" two or three times and then continue to note the primary object. If you intentionally listen to a sound, note "listening, listening," and then continue to note the primary object. If you hear a distinct sound, such as people talking, a song, a loud noise, dogs barking, birds chirping, and chickens clucking, and so on, note "hearing, hearing" two or three times and then continue to note the primary object.

If you do not note these other distinct objects that capture your attention, you cannot be clearly aware of the primary object. You may also get caught up in thinking about them and mental defilements will be aroused. In that case, you should note "thinking, thinking," and then return to the primary object. If a meditator forgets to note bodily phenomena or thought, he or she should note "forgetting, forgetting" and then continue to note the primary object.

If the breath becomes very subtle and the movements of rising and falling are no longer distinct, note "sitting, touching" if practicing in the sitting posture or "lying, touching" if lying down. When noting "touching," direct the mind toward four, five, or six different sensations of touch.

Mental states

If a meditator has been practicing for a long time and is not making any progress, he or she may become lazy. Note that as "lazy, lazy." When mindfulness, concentration, and special insight knowledges have yet to arise, you may assume that noting gets you nowhere, and so doubt will arise. Note this as "doubting, doubting."

At times, a meditator may hope for smoother practice or some special experience. Note that as "hoping, hoping." If you reflect on previous practice, note it as "reflecting." If you wonder whether the object is mental or physical, note that as "wondering." Sometimes when practice doesn't go smoothly, you may feel frustrated. Note that as "frustrated, frustrated." Sometimes when you find that practice is going well, you may feel happy. Note that as "happy, happy."

A meditator should note all mental states in this way, whenever they arise, and then continue to note the primary object.

Diligence

You should note each and every thought, whether wholesome or unwholesome. You should note each and every physical movement, whether large or small. You should note each and every feeling that arises in the body or mind, whether pleasant or unpleasant. You should note each and every mental object, whether wholesome or unwholesome. If there is nothing else in particular to note, then note the primary object, the rise and fall of the abdomen when sitting, or the lifting, moving, and dropping of the foot when walking. Note these objects uninterruptedly and continuously.

In this way, you should continuously and uninterruptedly note all day and all night, except during the hours of sleep. Before long the meditator will be able to observe all mental and physical phenomena the moment they arise and disappear. Thus you will gradually come to experience insight knowledge of arising and passing away as well as higher stages of insight knowledge.

Insight

Mind and body

When a meditator practices noting as described above, and his or her mindfulness, concentration, and insight mature, he or she will find that the noting mind and the noted objects occur in pairs. You will observe, for example, both the physical phenomena (body) involved in the rise of the abdomen and the mental phenomenon (mind) that notes it; the physical phenomena involved in the fall of the abdomen, and the mental phenomenon that notes it; the physical phenomena involved in lifting the foot, and the mental phenomenon that notes it; the physical phenomena involved in moving the foot forward, and the mental phenomenon that notes it;

the physical phenomena involved in dropping the foot and the mental phenomenon that notes it; and so on.

When practice is going well, you will see the rise and fall of the abdomen and the mind that notes it separately in this way. Thus you will be able to distinguish between mental and physical phenomena, or mind and body. It will seem like the noting mind rushes toward noted objects. This is awareness of the mind's characteristic of inclining toward its objects (*namana-lakkhaṇā*). The clearer your observation of physical objects becomes, the more obvious the noting mind will become. The *Visuddhimagga* says:

> Whenever physical phenomena become clear, unambiguous, and obvious to a meditator, the mental phenomena associated with those physical sense objects will also become obvious to him or her of their own accord.[457]

When ordinary people experience this realization of mind and body in meditation, they are pleased and tend to have thoughts such as: "Nothing exists but mind and body. There is only the rising of the abdomen and the mind noting it; only the falling of the abdomen and the mind noting it; only the sitting posture and the mind noting it; only the bending movement and the mind noting it. What we call a human being is nothing but these two kinds of phenomena. Except for these two phenomena there is nothing else. Also what we call a woman or man is only these two phenomena. Except for these two phenomena there is no independent person or being."

When people with scriptural knowledge clearly experience physical sense objects, the sense bases, and the knowing mind, they are pleased and tend to reflect on it in this way: "It really is true that there are only mental and physical phenomena. In a moment of noting, what I really experience are the noted physical phenomena and the noting mind. The same is true at other times, too. There is no 'woman,' 'man,' or other living being that exists independent of these phenomena. The mental and physical phenomena of the present moment are all that really exists. These phenomena are commonly called a person, being, woman, or man, but those are just names. In reality, there is no independent 'person,' 'being,' 'woman,' or 'man,' only the mental and physical phenomena I experience while noting them."

When these kinds of reflections arise, note the mental state of reflection itself as "reflecting, reflecting," then return to the primary object and note it uninterruptedly.

Cause and effect

As practice matures further, the intention to move becomes obvious by itself when you intend to move your body. As soon as an intention arises, you will easily be able to be aware of it. At the beginning of practice, for example, even if he or she notes "intending to bend," a meditator is not able to be clearly aware of the intention to bend his or her arm. However when practice matures, you will be clearly aware of the intention to bend without confusing it with anything else. Any time you want to change your bodily posture, first note the intention and then note the actual movements involved.

When first beginning to practice, you change your bodily posture often without noticing it. Due to this, you tend to think, "The body is fast; the noting mind is slow." But as empirical knowledge matures, it will seem as if the noting mind welcomes objects in advance. You will be able to note the intentions to bend or stretch, sit, stand, or walk, and so on and notice the different movements involved in bending and so on, as well. Then you will realize: "The body is slow; the noting mind is quick." You will experience for yourself that only after the intention to move has arisen can the movement of bending, stretching, and so on take place.

When you feel hot or cold, note "hot, hot" or "cold, cold." As you note, you will be able to experience the heat or cold getting stronger. When you note while eating, you will be able to experience your strength being replenished. After you have noted an object, do not return to the primary object if another object arises. A meditator should stay with a newly arisen object and note it uninterruptedly. Moreover, while noting mental images (such as images of the Buddha or an arahant) or physical sensations (like itchiness, heat, aching, or pain), another object may arise even before the object being presently noted has disappeared. In this case, you should change to the new object and continue to note it uninterruptedly.

By noting every object that occurs, you will experience that the noting mind arises whenever there is an object. Moreover, at times the rise and fall of the abdomen will become so subtle that you cannot note them. Then, you will realize that the noting mind cannot arise if there is no object. In this case, you should switch to noting "sitting, touching" as the primary object if you are sitting, or "lying, touching" if you are lying down, rather than noting "rising, falling." You can also alternate between various touch points. For example, after noting "sitting" once, you can note the touch point of the right foot as "touching." Then note "sitting" again, followed by the touch point of the left foot. In this manner, you can alternate among four, five, or six touch points. Furthermore, when noting "seeing" or "hearing" you will clearly understand that when the eye and a visible form are present you experience seeing, and when the ear and a sound are present you experience hearing.

Thus as you note various objects, you will clearly understand the different causes that give rise to different effects. For example: the intention to bend or stretch results in the movement of bending or stretching; a cold or hot environment results in cold or hot physical sensations; eating nutritious food results in the survival of the physical body; the presence of objects to note, such as the rise and fall of the abdomen, results in the noting mind; attention to mental objects results in the mental states of thought or imagination; the presence of visible objects of form or audible objects of sound results in eye-consciousness or ear-consciousness; and the presence of the physical phenomenon of the eye or ear also results in eye-consciousness or ear-consciousness. A meditator also comes to clearly understand that the volitional actions that he or she has performed in past lives give rise to pleasant or unpleasant feeling in the present. Mental and physical phenomena have happened throughout this present life since birth because of past volitional actions. These phenomena have no creator. They arise in accord with the law of cause and effect.

When these realizations happen, you needn't stop noting in order to intellectualize or reflect on them. These realizations will occur suddenly and of their own accord as you note. Note these realizations as "realizing, realizing" or "comprehending, comprehending" or "reflecting, reflecting," and then return to continuously noting the primary object.

After realizing how the law of cause and effect or the interaction of mind and body operates in this life, you will comprehend how it operated in past lives and how it will operate in future lives as well. You may reflect: "The mental and physical phenomena of past and future lives had, or will have, the same causes as these present phenomena. There is neither an independent person, a being, nor a 'creator' that exists in relation to them, but only the law of cause and effect."

These kinds of reflections tend to occur more often for people of high intelligence and less often for those of average intelligence. The more intelligent the person, the broader his or her comprehension tends to be. However, a meditator should simply note these reflections and return to the primary object. If you make continuing to note a higher priority than engaging in reflection, you will spend less time reflecting, and your practice will develop faster. Just a few moments of reflection will suffice.

Effects of concentration

As concentration grows particularly strong, you may experience a variety of unpleasant feelings, such as itchiness, heat, aches and pains, a feeling of heaviness or tightness, and so on. These often disappear immediately if you stop noting and tend to reappear when noting is resumed. Such feelings are not a sign of any kind of disease. The practice itself is what causes them to appear. So a meditator shouldn't fear them but should focus exclusively on these feelings, noting them persistently, and they will gradually weaken and fade away.

A meditator may also see various kinds of images or visions. These can be as vivid as if you were actually seeing them with your eyes. You may see, for example, the radiant image of a graceful Buddha, a group of monks, or other noble people approaching you. You may feel as if you are actually in front of a Buddha statue, a pagoda, a panoramic vista of woods, hills, gardens, clouds, and so on. Or you may feel as if you are actually seeing a swollen corpse or skeleton lying nearby, or a huge building or giant person disintegrating. Or a meditator may see visions of his or her body swelling, bleeding, being torn into two or three pieces, or turning into a skeleton. You may see images of the internal parts of your body, such as the bones, flesh, sinews, intestines, liver, and so on. Or visions of the hell realms and its victims, the hungry ghosts, or the celestial world with its devas and devīs may appear. It is only concentration that gives rise to these unusual kinds of conceptual images and visions. So you shouldn't be elated or frightened by them. Such images are just like dreams.

However, the mind-consciousness that experiences these mental images is an ultimate reality, so you must note it. But you shouldn't note it if it is not very obvious. You should only note an object when it is obvious. Therefore, focus your mind on whatever image you are seeing and note it as "seeing, seeing" until it disappears. You will find that the image or vision will undergo some changes and fades away or disintegrates. Initially, you will have to note three, four, or more times before it disappears. However, when your insight matures, you will find that it disappears after you note it just once or twice.

On the other hand, if you are curious about, afraid of, or attached to these images, they will tend to last for a long time. So take extra care not to think about any of these unusual objects. If a meditator finds himself or herself thinking about them, he or she should immediately abandon that thought by closely noting it. Since some do not experience any of these unusual visions or feelings and only note the primary object, they grow lazy. Note this laziness as "lazy, lazy" until it disappears.

Seeing the three characteristics

Regardless of whether or not you have any unusual experiences at this level of insight, you will clearly see the beginning, middle, and end of an object each time you note it. Prior to this stage, you will have had to note new objects that arose before previous objects had disappeared, so you will not have been able to clearly see objects disappear. At this level, you will be able to see one object disappear before noting a new one, and you will thus clearly see the beginning, middle, and end of an object. Clearly seeing each object instantly arise and immediately disappear with each noting, you will understand the impermanence of objects as described in Pāḷi texts and commentaries:

> . . . impermanent in the sense of destruction . . . impermanent in the sense of nonexistence after having come to be.[458]

You may reflect: "These objects are just disappearing! They are just vanishing. It is true that they are impermanent."

> Anything that is impermanent is unsatisfying. Because it is frightening, it is unsatisfactory. It is suffering to be constantly tormented by arising and passing away.[459]

You may reflect: "We enjoy our lives because of delusion. In truth, there is nothing to enjoy in our lives. It is really frightening that everything arises and passes away. It is constant torment. Everything is miserable and unsatisfying because it arises and immediately passes away. We can die at any time." When you encounter unpleasant feelings, you will tend to comprehend the misery and suffering in things as described in the Pāḷi texts and commentaries:

> . . . as suffering, as a disease, as a boil, as a dart, . . .[460]

Or you may reflect: "All mental and physical phenomena are unsatisfying, and no one can make them otherwise. They do not obey anyone's will. They pass away immediately after arising, so they lack a solid core, are insubstantial and useless. There is no self that has control and can keep them from arising or passing away. In truth they arise and pass away of their own accord." This realization is in accordance with the Pāḷi texts and commentaries:

> What is suffering is [not-self[461]].[462]

> . . . is not-self in the sense of having no core . . .[463]

> . . . and does not obey anyone's will.[464]

Immediately after you note these reflections, return to noting the primary object.

After seeing for yourself that every object that you directly note is impermanent, unsatisfying, and impersonal, you will reflect that all other phenomena you experience must also be impermanent, unsatisfying, and impersonal. This is called inferential knowledge (*anumānañāṇa*). Those who are less analytical or knowledgeable and those who give priority to continuous noting rather than to analyzing will experience less reflection on this inferential knowledge. Those who give precedence to it will tend to reflect a lot. Some meditators, though, continue to analyze this realization, interspersed with their noting, and their practice stagnates. Even without such analysis, however, your understanding will become clearer at higher levels of insight, so prioritize noting rather than analyzing. If you do analyze, note it without fail.

After you inferentially realize the arising and passing away of all phenomena, you will simply be aware of whatever arises without any further analysis. The five mental faculties—faith, energy, mindfulness, concentration, and wisdom—will then fall into harmony, and the noting mind will become quicker than ever before. Your object—that is, mental and physical phenomena—will also appear extremely quickly. Each time you breathe in, for example, you will clearly see that the rising movement of the abdomen consists of many segments. The same is true for other movements, such as the falling of the abdomen, bending, stretching, and so on. You will clearly experience subtle vibrations or sensations all over your body, which arise very quickly one after another. Some experience fine sensations of itchiness or prickling that arise very quickly and instantly one after another. Unpleasant sensations are rarely experienced during this period of practice.[465]

You will be unable to keep up with objects by trying to label or name each of them when they arise so quickly. A meditator should simply be aware of them from moment to moment, without naming them, so that he or she can follow them. If a meditator wants to name them, he or she does not try to name them all. When one object is labeled, he or she may become aware of four, five, or ten other objects. This isn't a problem. You may tire if you attempt to name all the objects that occur. What matters most is being precisely and accurately aware of each object. In this case, note any objects that come in through the six sense doors, without following the normal procedure. Of course if noting in this way does not go smoothly, you can always revert to the normal procedure.

Mental and physical phenomena arise and pass away much faster than the twinkling of an eye or a flash of lightning. But when your insight knowledge matures, you will be able to clearly perceive each fleeting phenomena without missing a single one by simply being aware of them from moment to moment. Your mindfulness will become so strong it will seem as if it rushes into the object that arises; it will seem as if objects fall into the noting mind. The knowing mind, too, will clearly and distinctly know each and every single object that arises. You might even think: "Phenomena are arising and passing away instantaneously; their appearance and disappearance are very fast, like a machine running at full speed. Yet I am able to perceive them all from moment to moment. I don't think I am missing anything or that there's anything else that I should be aware of."

This is the personally experienced insight knowledge that we cannot even dream of.

Distractions from the path

Due to the momentum of this insight knowledge you are likely to see a bright light or experience rapture as a result of being greatly delighted with both the noting mind and the noted objects. You may get goose bumps, feel a tear roll down your cheek, or find your body shaking. A meditator may experience a "springy" feeling, often mistaken for dizziness, or a light, comfortable feeling, as if swaying back and forth in a hammock, that creeps over his or her whole body. You may experience a peaceful calm that makes you feel comfortable whether sitting, reclining, standing, or in any other posture. Both the mind and body will become so light, supple, and flexible due to this quality of lightness that you will feel comfortable even during long periods of sitting or reclining, without any pain, heat, or stiffness.

At this point, the noting mind and the noted objects flow along concurrently and harmoniously. Your mental attitude becomes straightforward. Your mind avoids unwholesome activities and becomes extremely clear due to your strong faith and confidence. At times this mental clarity may last for a long period, even when there is no object to be noted. As your faith grows stronger, you may reflect: "It really is true that the Buddha knew everything," or, "There really is nothing other than impermanent, unsatisfying, and impersonal mental and physical phenomena." While noting, you will often see, extremely clearly, the arising and passing away of mental and physical phenomena, as well as impermanence and unsatisfactoriness, and you will probably think about encouraging others to practice. Without too much strain and free from laziness, balanced effort will manifest. It will seem as if objects are known of their own accord and so insight equanimity (*vipassanupekkhā*) dawns. A meditator is likely to experience an unusual degree of very strong delight or happiness and will be excited to tell others about it.

A meditator may like any of the pleasant experiences that occur—the bright light, good mindfulness, insight, rapture, and so on. This liking will cause him or her to think: "This practice is exceedingly enjoyable!" He or she may really enjoy the practice. But do not waste time enjoying the bright light and other pleasant experiences. Instead, whenever they arise, note them as "brightness, comfort, knowing, reflecting, venerating, happiness, liking, delight," and so on, according to whatever you experience.

If you notice brightness, note it as "bright, bright." If you think that you see it, note it as "seeing, seeing" until it disappears. You may often forget to note bright light and other pleasant experiences because you are so happy to experience them. Although you are noting, the light may not disappear very quickly because you are delighting in it. Only after experiencing it many times will you be able to note it skillfully enough that it disappears quickly. For some meditators, light is so powerful that even if they note it for a long time, it doesn't disappear; it remains. In this case, ignore the light completely and divert your attention to some other mental or physical object. Do not think about whether the light is still bright. If you do, you will find that it is. Any thoughts about the light should be noted so precisely that your awareness of them is very clear and firm.

Since your concentration will have become very powerful, other unusual objects besides bright light can arise if you incline your mind toward them. Do not let the mind incline in this way. If you do, quickly note it until it disappears. Some meditators see various kinds of faint shapes and forms arise one after another, like the linked carriages of a train. If this happens, note it as "seeing, seeing." With each noting, an object will disappear. If your insight weakens, the shapes and forms will tend to become more pronounced. But if you note them closely, each object will disappear on the spot as it is noted. Eventually they will stop coming.

To delight in bright light and other pleasant experiences is to be on the wrong path. The correct path of insight is to just continue noting. If you keep this in mind and carry on noting mental and physical phenomena that actually arise, your awareness will grow clearer and clearer. You will clearly see the sudden appearance and disappearance of phenomena. Every time you note, you will see each object arising and passing away on the spot. A meditator clearly sees that successive occurrences are distinct from one another, break up bit by bit, and cease. Thus every object you note helps you to realize impermanence, unsatisfactoriness, and not-self.

After practicing for quite a while, a meditator may feel satisfied with his or her practice and take a break every now and again, thinking: "It can't get any better than this. There can't be anything else special to experience." But you should not just relax whenever you want. Instead, you should practice for longer and longer periods without taking a break.

Disappearance

When insight knowledge develops to the next stage, you will no longer see objects arising but only passing away. You will think that they are disappearing faster and faster. A meditator will also see that the noting minds disappear one after the other. When the rise of the abdomen is noted, for example, you will clearly see how the tiny movements of rising instantly disappear and how the noting mind, too, vanishes very quickly. So you see that moments of both the rising movement and your awareness of it disappear one after the other. You will clearly see this for all other objects, as well, such as the falling of the abdomen, sitting, bending, stretching, stiffness, and so on: each object and your awareness of them disappears moment by moment, one after the other. Some meditators even find that there are three things arising and passing away in sequence: a sense object, their awareness of it, and their knowledge of that very awareness. But it is sufficient to observe that objects and the mind that notes them disappear in pairs.

When noting becomes clear enough that you can see both sense objects and your awareness of them disappearing in pairs, you will lose the illusory sense of conceptual forms or shapes, such as the form of your body, head, arms, legs, and so on. You will only experience instantly disappearing phenomena. As a result, you may feel like your practice has become superficial, is not as good as it had been before, or that there are many gaps in your noting. But that is not actually the case. It's only that the mind naturally delights in concepts of solid form, and so it cannot feel comfortable when those concepts are absent.

In any case this condition is an indication of progress in practice. When your meditation practice is immature, you first perceive concepts of solid form or shape when you note seeing, hearing, touching, and so on. But at this level of insight meditation, you perceive the instant disappearance of phenomena first. In other words, you experience insight knowledge of dissolution first; the sense of solid form will only return when you deliberately evoke it. Otherwise, due simply to uninterruptedly noting, your awareness will remain attuned to the ultimate reality of the dissolution of phenomena. Thus you verify that the saying from sages of old is true:

> When conventional reality emerges, absolute reality submerges;
> When absolute reality emerges, conventional reality submerges.

Although your awareness will have become extremely clear at this point, it may seem like there are gaps between successive moments of awareness. This is because you are starting to become aware of the life-continuum that occurs between cognitive processes (*vīthi*). For example, when you note an intention to bend or stretch the arm, you may find that the movement of bending or stretching seems to be delayed for some time. This means that your awareness has become sharp and powerful. In this case, you should also note any distinct objects that arise at the six sense doors.

After your practice gains momentum due to noting the main objects, such as the rise and fall of the abdomen, sitting, and so on, you should note any obvious objects that arise, such as any sensations in other parts of the body, seeing, hearing, and so on. If your awareness becomes less precise or accurate while noting in this way, or if thoughts begin to interfere, or if you feel exhausted, return to just noting the primary objects of rising, falling, sitting, and so on. When, after a while, your practice again gains momentum, return to noting whatever arises. A meditator should let his or her practice proceed in this way some of the time.

Once you are able to extend, without strain, the range of objects that you note and observe, you will clearly see that whatever you see or hear instantly disappears and that two consecutive moments are not connected but are separate units. This is "understanding things as they really are." As a result of this, however, things may seem blurry or hazy when you look at them. A meditator is likely to worry: "I think something is wrong with my eyesight; it's getting dim." But nothing is actually wrong with your vision. It's just that your awareness is discerning each individual moment of seeing separately, which causes conceptual forms to blur.

At this point, as well, a meditator will continue to be aware of mental and physical phenomena even if he or she stops trying to practice. You may not even be able to fall asleep when trying to, but you will instead feel alert and awake day and night. There is no need to worry about this, as it will not harm your health in any way. A meditator should simply continue practicing energetically. When your insight becomes powerful enough, it will seem as if your awareness pierces objects.

Disillusionment

When you deeply understand that both objects and the mind that notes them instantly disappear, you will tend to reflect: "Nothing lasts for the twinkling of an eye or a flash of lightning. They are indeed impermanent. Previously I was simply ignorant of this fact. Everything that has happened in the past must have also disappeared in this way. Everything that happens in the future will disappear in this way, too." Note these reflections.

You may also occasionally reflect on how unstable and incessantly vanishing phenomena are, thinking: "Clearly, we are able to enjoy ourselves due to ignorance. To realize that phenomena instantly disappear is truly terrifying. Each time they disappear could be the moment of my death. To have come into existence and to have to continue existing endlessly is really horrible. How dreadful to make such great effort in order to be well off in a situation in which everything constantly vanishes. How appalling it is that these instantly disappearing phenomena continue to occur, now and in a new life. That we are all subject to aging, sickness, death, distress, worry, lamentation, and so on is truly frightening." Note this mental state of reflection without fail.

At this stage of practice, a meditator generally feels helpless, dejected, and languid, being frightened by mental and physical phenomena that disintegrate so quickly. You have no enthusiasm or joy, and you tend to feel sad. There is no need to worry. This indicates that your practice is improving according to the usual development of the meditation process. All you need do is remain equanimous by noting any reflections and other objects that arise. If you do so, you will soon overcome this stage. Otherwise, being long caught up in these reflections while feeling displeasure, a meditator might become so afraid that he or she cannot stand it. This kind of fear based on displeasure is not insight knowledge. Therefore note all these reflections without fail so that fear based on displeasure cannot arise.

In between instances of noting, you may have thoughts that find fault, such as: "These mental and physical phenomena are no good, because they constantly vanish and do not last. It is depressing to see how they have continuously arisen since the beginning of this life without ever coming to an end, and that they create all kinds of forms and shapes although they do not exist. Striving hard to gain happiness and well-being feels so miserable. A new existence is undesirable. It is depressing to be subject to aging, sickness, death, distress, worry, grief, and lamentation. This is all suffering and devoid of peace." You should not forget to note these kinds of reflections.

Sometimes, it will seem like every phenomenon that you note and the mind that notes them are terrible, harsh, useless, disgusting, rotten, decaying, and fragile. At such times, even though you note mental and physical phenomena as they arise, you will no longer feel pleased with them. You will clearly see them to be passing away every time they are noted, but you will not be as enthusiastic about this as before. Instead, you will feel weary of phenomena. As a result, you will become lazy about noting. But you will not be able to help being aware. It is like being forced to travel on a filthy road, wherein every step arouses disgust and disillusionment.

Thus when you consider human life, you will understand that you cannot exist without these incessantly vanishing mental and physical phenomena. So you won't see anything delightful in becoming a man, a woman, a king, a rich person, or a celestial being. These instead will inspire disenchantment and disillusionment.

Looking for relief

Because you feel so weary of phenomena every time they are noted, it will seem as if the mind is struggling to escape from them. With the desire to be liberated from the conditioned phenomena, a meditator may think: "It would be so nice if there were no such thing as seeing, hearing, touching, thinking, sitting down, standing up, bending, stretching, and so on. I wish I could escape from those things or go somewhere where they don't exist." Do not fail to note such thoughts.

At other times, a meditator may wonder: "What can I do to escape from these phenomena? Continuing to note them seems like deliberately contemplating vile things. Everything I notice is disgusting. It would be nice not to have to notice them at all." Of course, you should note these mental states of wondering and thinking.

Based on such reflections, some meditators even try to avoid noting at this point and put off practice. But mental and physical phenomena such as seeing, hearing, knowing, the rise and fall of the abdomen, sitting, bending, stretching, thinking, and so on will not stop arising; they will continue to appear as always. They continue to be apparent to meditators as a result of their intensive insight practice. Awareness of phenomena simply continues of its own accord. A meditator will be encouraged by this, considering: "Even though I'm not trying to note, I keep noticing phenomena that arise anyway; my awareness of them just keeps going. So just avoiding practice won't help me get away from them. It's only when I note these phenomena, as they are, and realize their three characteristics that I won't worry about them and will be able to note with equanimity. That's what will lead me to the experience of nibbāna, where none of these exist. Only then can I realize liberation." Once you are able to appreciate your own experience in this way, you will carry on with your practice. Some meditators do not come to this conclusion by themselves. However, once their teachers explain their experience to them, they can carry on with their practice.

Some meditators will experience unbearable pain when their practice gains this kind of momentum. Do not despair. The true characteristics of unpleasant sensation are actually becoming obvious to you as pain (*dukkhato*), disease (*rogato*), an ulcer (*gaṇḍato*), a thorn (*sallato*), unprofitable (*aghato*), afflictions (*ābādhato*), and so on. Note the pain until you can overcome it.

Those who do not encounter severe pain may experience one of the forty qualities of impermanence, unsatisfactoriness, or not-self whenever they note. Even though their practice is going well and their thoughts do not wander, they will tend to think that their practice is no good or feel that objects and the mind that notes them are not concurrent. Actually it is simply that you are so eager to realize the impermanent, unsatisfactory, and not-self nature of mental and physical phenomena that you cannot feel satisfied with your practice. As a result, you may often change your posture. For example, when you are sitting you feel like you want to walk; when you are walking, you want to sit down again. You feel agitated and want to rearrange your arms and legs, move to another place, or lie down. You cannot manage to stay in your place or posture for very long and keep changing. Do not feel frustrated!

A meditator lacks satisfaction because he or she rightly understands that there are no pleasurable conditioned mental and physical phenomena. At this point, you think that your noting is no good. You will not yet be able to note with equanimity, as you will be when you attain the next insight knowledge, knowledge of equanimity toward phenomena. Try your best to practice without constantly changing your posture and to remain in one posture for a long time. After a while, you will be able to practice calmly again. If you practice with patience and persistence, your mind will grow clearer and clearer, until all the agitation and dissatisfaction disappear.

Equanimity

Eventually, your insight meditation will strengthen enough that you will be effortlessly able to be equanimous with respect to conditioned mental and physical phenomena. The noting mind will become so clear and subtle that your awareness will seem to easily flow by itself. A meditator will even be able to perceive very subtle mental and physical activities without any effort, and will see their impermanence, unsatisfactoriness, and not-self natures without reflecting about it.

If a meditator notes touch points at different places on the body, he or she will be aware of just one sensation of touch after another, but not of any physical form or shape, and the sensations of touch will feel very subtle, like the touch of a cotton ball. Sometimes you may feel so many different sensations in the body that your awareness moves very quickly all around the body. Sometimes it will feel as if both the body and the mind are moving upward. At other times, only a few regular objects will be obvious, and you will be able to calmly and steadily note them.

Sometimes the rising, falling, touching, hearing, and so on, together with the whole body, may disappear, and you will only be aware of the mind arising and passing away. You may experience a rapture that feels like being bathed in a cool, soothing shower, a tranquility, or a crystal-clear light like a bright sky. Although a meditator may not take such extreme delight in such pleasant experiences as he or she would have before, he or she may still become attached to them. Note any attachment that arises, in addition to noting the rapture, tranquility, or clear light. If these experiences persist, ignore them and note other objects instead.

At this level of insight meditation, a meditator will clearly comprehend every object and the mind that notes them. You will know: "These phenomena are not me or mine, and they are also not anyone else or anyone else's. They are only conditioned mental and physical phenomena. Conditioned phenomena are noting conditioned phenomena." Observing objects becomes very pleasant at this point, like tasting a delicious flavor. No matter how long you practice, you will not be gratified and will not feel any unpleasant sensations, such as stiffness, numbness, pain, or itching. Thus your meditation postures will become very stable. You will be able to easily maintain the positions of your head, body, arms, and legs, and will be able to practice for two or three hours in a single posture, whether sitting or reclining, without getting tired or feeling stiff. Time will pass so quickly that two or three hours of practice will seem like just a few moments.

Sometimes the noting mind will become very swift and your noting will be especially good. If you begin to feel anxious about what is happening, note it as "anxious, anxious." If you begin to think that your practice is improving, note it as "evaluating, evaluating." And if you begin to anticipate further progress in insight knowledge, note it as "anticipating, anticipating." Afterward, return to steadily noting the usual objects.

You should neither increase nor decrease your energy at this stage. Because some meditators fail to note mental states such as anxiety, excitement, attachment, or anticipation, their awareness gets dispersed and decreases. Some meditators feel excited and increase their energy. Ironically, this leads to a decline in practice because the wandering minds of anxiety, excitement, attachment, or anticipation take them far away from insight. This is why, when your awareness becomes swift and your noting becomes especially good, you should keep your practice steady, without increasing or decreasing your energy. Using this approach, your practice will lead directly to nibbāna, where all conditioned phenomena cease.

Nonetheless, a meditator may experience many fluctuations in his or her practice at this level of insight meditation. Do not be disappointed; be persistent. Priority should be given to noting any objects that arise at the six sense doors as they present themselves and to widening your awareness to note whatever arises in any part of the body. But it is impossible to note this way once your practice becomes very subtle and continuous. So once your practice gains momentum, before it becomes too subtle, note objects without setting any limits. If a meditator notes objects carefully, whether it is "rising," "falling," "sitting," or other mental and physical activities, his or her practice will gain momentum before long. Then your awareness will flow smoothly, as if by itself, without much effort. A meditator clearly and calmly perceives conditioned phenomena that instantaneously disappear.

At this point your mind will no longer be vulnerable to any kind of temptation or disturbance. However alluring an object might be, it will not be able to captivate your mind. Likewise, however disgusting an object might be, it will not affect your mind either. A meditator simply perceives seeing as seeing, hearing as hearing, smelling as smelling, tasting as tasting, touching as touching, and knowing as knowing. Thus "sixfold equanimity" or equanimity regarding the six senses will appear every time you note. Even thoughts or reflections like, "How long have I been sitting? What time is it?" will no longer arise; these thoughts, let alone the previous kinds of reflections, will have ceased.

However, if your insight knowledge is not yet mature enough to produce noble path knowledge, after one, two, or three hours your concentration will weaken and the mind will begin to wander. Then your noting mind may slacken and have gaps in between. On the other hand, if your noting becomes swift and especially good, you may become excited and anticipate progress. This, too, can lead to slackening. If you note these mental states of evaluation, anticipation, or excitement without fail, then your practice will regain strength.

But if your insight knowledge is still not mature enough, your practice will eventually decline again. Thus there can be a great deal of fluctuation in practice at this time. Those who know or have heard about the stages of insight knowledge may encounter even more fluctuations. This is why it is better not to learn how the insight knowledges progress in advance. In any event, do not be disappointed. These fluctuations indicate that your insight is coming very close to path knowledge and fruition knowledge. You could realize path, fruition, and nibbāna at any time, once the mental faculties of faith, energy, mindfulness, concentration, and wisdom fall in harmony.

The Experience of Nibbāna

These fluctuations in insight knowledge are like the flights of a bird sent out from a ship at sea: in the old days when sailors didn't know where the nearest land was, they would send out a crow that they had brought along on the voyage. The bird would fly in every direction, looking for the nearest shore. As long as it couldn't find any nearby land, the bird would keep returning to the ship. But once it spied land, it would fly directly to it.

In the same way, as long as your insight is not strong enough to realize nibbāna by attaining path knowledge, it keeps drawing back—that is, there will be gaps in your noting. But once your insight knowledge is mature enough and the five mental faculties are in harmony, for at least three or four moments you will see mental and physical phenomena arising and passing away with increasing swiftness and clarity. Then, immediately after noting an obvious object from among the six kinds of conditioned mental and physical phenomena,[466] you will attain to path and fruition while experiencing nibbāna as the cessation of both noted objects and the mind that notes them.

Those who reach that spiritual state clearly experience their awareness accelerating prior to their attainment. They also clearly experience how all conditioned objects are abandoned after a final moment of noting and how the mind takes nibbāna, the cessation of all those conditioned phenomena, as its object. These are some of the ways meditators describe the experience:

"Both the objects and the noting mind were abruptly cut off and stopped."

"The objects and the noting mind were cut off, like a creeping vine being hewn down."

"I saw the objects and the noting mind drop away, like a heavy burden being dumped."

"Objects and the mind noting them seemed to fall away, as if I had lost my hold on them."

"I got away from objects and the mind that notes them, as if suddenly escaping from confinement in prison."

"Objects and the mind that notes them suddenly disappeared, like the light of a candle being blown out."

"I escaped from objects and the mind that notes them, as if suddenly emerging from darkness into light."

"I emerged from objects and the mind that notes them, as if suddenly emerging from a mess into a clear space."

"I found that both objects and the mind that notes them submerged, as if sinking into water."

"Both objects and the mind that notes them suddenly stopped, like a running person thwarted by a blocked passage."

The experience of the cessation of conditioned mental and physical phenomena does not last very long. It's as brief as a single moment of noting. Afterward one has a recollection of the event, such as: "The cessation of objects and the mind that notes them that I've just experienced must have been either something special, or path, fruition, and nibbāna." Those with scriptural knowledge might reflect: "The cessation of conditioned mental and physical phenomena is nibbāna. What I have realized while experiencing the cessation is path knowledge and fruition knowledge. I have realized nibbāna, and I have attained the path and fruition of the first stage of enlightenment." These kinds of reflections tend to arise in a systematic and thorough way for those who have heard how it is to experience the cessation of conditioned mental and physical phenomena. Such people also tend to reflect on which mental defilements have been eliminated and which have not.

After these recollections they return to noting mental and physical phenomena as usual. At that time the arising and disappearance of phenomena is quite coarse and so is obvious. They are clearly aware of the beginning and end, or of the arising and passing away, of phenomena. Thus they may think that there must be gaps in their noting again or that their practice must have declined. This is actually true. They have returned to insight knowledge of arising and passing away. Accordingly, they may again experience bright light and images, as is usual at this stage. Some meditators may find that their noting mind is suddenly not concurrent with the objects it notes, as it was in the beginning stages of practice, or they encounter moments of various kinds of unpleasant sensation.

For the most part, however, their minds remain very clear from moment to moment. At this stage they will feel very peaceful, as if their minds were floating alone in space. But they will not be able to note that mental state. Even if they try to note it, they will not be able to be effectively aware of it. They will not want to contemplate anything else and will not be able to note other objects. Their minds are simply clear and peaceful. Gradually this clear mental state will grow weaker and weaker. Then if they continue noting, they will be able to clearly see arising and passing away again. After some time they will return to a state of very subtle noting, and if their insight is strong enough, they may fall into the cessation of phenomena again, as they did before. They might experience this repeatedly, depending on the strength of their concentration and insight knowledge. Nowadays many repeatedly attain the first fruition knowledge that they have already experienced, because their main aim is only to attain the first path and fruition. This is how the fruition of the first stage of enlightenment is attained through successive insights.

The mental attitude of those who have achieved path and fruition is not the same as it was before; it is so special that they feel as if they have been reborn. Their faith becomes extremely strong and, as a result, they experience very powerful rapture and tranquility. Happiness also often spontaneously arises. Sometimes the mental factors of faith, rapture, tranquility, and happiness may be so strong that immediately after having attained path and fruition objects cannot be distinguished very well, even though meditators note them. However, after a few hours or days, those mental factors will weaken, and they will be able to distinguish objects again, so the practice will improve once more.

Some meditators feel relieved, reluctant to note, or satisfied immediately after attaining the path and fruition. Such contentment probably arises because their initial motivation was only to achieve that path knowledge and fruition knowledge. If they wish to realize and experience the peace of nibbāna again by means of the fruition that they have already attained, they should note present phenomena as usual.

Entering fruition

The first insight knowledge that ordinary meditators encounter in the course of insight meditation is the insight knowledge that discerns mental and physical phenomena. But for meditators with path knowledge and fruition knowledge it will be the insight knowledge of arising and passing away. So if the insight knowledge of arising and passing away is the first to occur while you are noting phenomena, it will soon be followed by successively higher insight knowledges, up through equanimity toward phenomena, which is the most subtle and best knowledge. When that knowledge is strong enough, the mind will shift its attention to nibbāna, the cessation of all conditioned phenomena, just as before, and the mental process of fruition will appear.

If you do not determine the period for this fruition absorption in advance, it may last for only a few moments or for quite a long time—five, ten, or fifteen minutes, half an hour, or an hour. The commentaries say that it can even last for a whole day and night, or for whatever period you have predetermined. These days, too, we can find meditators with strong concentration and sharp insight who are able to become absorbed in fruition for long periods of time, such as one, two, or three hours, or a period that they have predetermined, as described in the commentaries. Even when there is no need to do so, if you predetermine that the fruition absorption should end, you will easily emerge. In the case of such long periods of absorption, however, there may be intervals of reflection. If you note such reflection four or five times, you will become absorbed in fruition again. In this way, you may experience fruition absorption for hours.

During fruition absorption, the mind is fully absorbed in its object, nibbāna, the cessation of all conditioned phenomena. It does not perceive anything else. Nibbāna is completely different from the conditioned mental and physical phenomena and conceptual objects that belong to this world or any other. So you cannot perceive or remember this world (i.e., your own body) or any other during fruition absorption, and you are free from all thoughts. Even if there are obvious objects around to see, hear, smell, touch, and so on, you will not be aware of any of them. Your bodily posture will also be firm and stable while you are absorbed, even if for long periods. For example, if you are sitting when you become absorbed in fruition, you will maintain that sitting posture without swaying, slouching, or changing it in any way. As the Pāḷi passage says:

> . . . the [impulsions] of absorption also uphold the bodily postures.[467]

When the mental process of fruition ends, the first object that you experience might be the recollection of cessation or of absorption in that cessation, some kind of visual image, or simply a thought. Then the normal noting process, brightness, or reflections will accordingly appear. Initially you will only intermittently be able to be aware of obvious objects after you emerge from absorption in fruition. However, there may also be times when you will be continuously able to be aware of subtle objects immediately after the fruition process if your insight is strong. Remember that the determination to enter fruition quickly or to be absorbed for a long time should be made before beginning to note. While you are noting, you should not think about it.

When your insight is not yet strong enough for you to become absorbed in fruition, you may experience goose bumps, yawning, shaking, and deep breaths, followed by intermittent noting. At other times, when your noting is improving, you may become excited, thinking that nibbāna is near. But, as a result of this, your noting will then become discontinuous. So you should not entertain such thoughts. If they arise, note them precisely and accurately. Some meditators encounter these kinds of fluctuations many times before they are able to enter fruition absorption. Even then, if your concentration and insight knowledge are still weak, it may take some time to reach the state of fruition, or you may not be able to remain there for very long.

Clarifying the insight knowledges

Sometimes, the insight knowledges of fear, danger, disenchantment, and desire for deliverance are not clear because you have not experienced them for a long time. If you want to experience them clearly and distinctly, you should determine a time period for the experience of each insight knowledge. For example, if you set a time limit when you practice by resolving, "May the knowledge of arising and passing away last for half an hour," then that insight knowledge will occur within that time period but not beyond. Afterward, the subsequent insight knowledge of dissolution will occur spontaneously, since you only see phenomena passing away. But if that knowledge does not occur spontaneously, you should resolve that it will arise. Then it will be present for that period of time, and the next higher insight knowledge will spontaneously follow it. Proceed this way, in order, for all of the knowledges.

If your practice does not automatically move to the next higher insight knowledge after achieving mastery of the current level of knowledge, resolve that it will arise. So after attaining insight knowledge of dissolution, resolve: "May insight knowledge of fear arise." That knowledge will then occur. When you are satisfied with it, resolve: "May insight knowledge of danger arise." Then you will realize that knowledge by seeing the dangers of phenomena every time you note them. When you are satisfied with that knowledge, resolve to attain insight knowledge of disenchantment. That knowledge will then occur, causing you to become weary and disenchanted. When you are satisfied with that knowledge, resolve: "May insight knowledge of desire for deliverance arise." Then that knowledge will arise, causing you to wish to escape from phenomena every time you note them. Then resolve to attain insight knowledge of reobservation. That knowledge will then occur, accompanied by unpleasant sensations, discontentment, and the desire to change posture. Finally, resolve to attain insight knowledge of equanimity toward phenomena. Then that very subtle knowledge will arise, during which the momentum of noting will flow as if by itself.

Thus you will find that you can reach a particular level of insight knowledge within a specified time limit, according to your resolve. You will also find that your knowledge shifts, in due time, like the needle of a compass, to the next higher level of knowledge once you are satisfied with the current level. If you have not yet experienced all of the insight knowledges distinctly, repeatedly practice in this way. On the other hand, people with strong concentration and sharp insight may reach insight knowledge of equanimity within a short time, that is, within about four, five, or ten notings, when they note without resolve. They can often experience fruition, too. If you become very proficient at the practice, you can even experience fruition while walking, eating, and so on.

Practicing for higher paths and fruitions

When you are skilled enough in the practice that you can very quickly enter the fruition that you have attained and remain in it for a long time, you should practice with the purpose of attaining higher paths and fruitions. To do this, you should first determine how many days you are going to practice, and then resolve: "May the fruition that I have already attained no longer arise during this period of time; may the next higher path knowledge and fruition knowledge arise instead." After this, simply note present phenomena as usual.

The reason for making a resolution is so that your insight knowledge, if strong enough, can lead directly to a higher path and fruition within the specified time period, rather than returning to the previous one. Otherwise, you will often return to the fruition that you have already attained. The benefit of making a resolution in the form stated above is that if the higher path knowledge and fruition knowledge do not arise, the previous fruition knowledge may be realized again after your period of practice. Otherwise if you resolve, "From now on, may the next higher path knowledge and fruition knowledge arise," you may find it difficult to return to the previous fruition. Then the meditator may feel upset if he or she can neither gain a higher path knowledge and fruition knowledge nor return to one previously attained.

After determining a time period and wishing not to return to the previous fruition before the period ends, simply note phenomena as usual. Then the insight knowledges will arise in order, beginning with insight knowledge of arising and passing away, and insights will develop in a manner similar to that which led to the first path, rather than that which led to the first fruition. Before the insight knowledge of arising and passing away matures, you may experience bright lights, images, and unpleasant sensations. The arising and passing away of mental and physical phenomena tends to be not very refined or distinct. Even if when you practice to reach fruition it usually only takes a few moments to return to knowledge of equanimity toward phenomena and the absorption of fruition, you may now spend a long time at lower levels of insight knowledge. But you will not experience as much difficulty or delay in attaining knowledge of equanimity toward phenomena as you experienced in the immature stages of practice. You will be able to progress through the successive stages of insight knowledge to return to knowledge of equanimity toward phenomena within a single day.

Your awareness will be much better than it was during the first stages of practice. It will be more precise and accurate. Your understanding will be broader and clearer. Sensual, worldly objects and the cycle of suffering will be more frightening, dangerous, and wearying to the meditator, and the desire to escape will be stronger than before. Even if you were formerly able to enter fruition three or four times an hour, your insight knowledge may now stagnate at the level of equanimity toward phenomena, because it is not strong enough to progress to the next higher path knowledge. You may remain in that condition for a long time, anywhere from one or two days to months or years.

When your insight knowledge eventually grows strong enough, your noting mind will become extremely clear and swift. Following this acceleration, your mind will shift its focus and take nibbāna, the cessation of all conditioned phenomena, as its object. Thus will you attain the second stage of path knowledge and fruition knowledge, followed by recollection of this new path and fruition, and a review of remaining mental defilements. Afterward, as you note as usual, knowledge of arising and passing away will arise together with an extremely clear mind. This is how you should practice for and experience the second stage of path knowledge and fruition knowledge, and become a once returner.

If you want to attain the path knowledge and fruition knowledge of the third stage of enlightenment, you should determine a period of time to practice and stop wishing for the absorption of the fruition that you have already attained. Resolve: "May the fruition already realized no longer arise during this period of time." Then note mental and physical phenomena in the usual way. Beginning with insight knowledge of arising and passing away, the insight knowledges will progress in sequence until, before long, you reach knowledge of equanimity toward phenomena. If your insight knowledge is not yet mature, it will stagnate at that level for some time. As it did previously, when it is powerful enough, it will shift its focus and take nibbāna, the cessation of conditioned phenomena, as its object. Thus will the path knowledge and fruition knowledge of the third stage of enlightenment arise, followed by the usual process of recollection. This is how you should practice for and experience the third path knowledge and fruition knowledge and become a nonreturner.

To attain the path knowledge and fruition knowledge of the fourth and final stage of enlightenment, simply follow the same procedure: after determining a time period, setting aside your desire for the current fruition absorption, and resolving to experience the peak of enlightenment, note present mental and physical phenomena. There is no other way to practice. This is why the *Satipaṭṭhāna Sutta* uses the term "the only way." Beginning with insight knowledge of arising and passing away, the knowledges will progress in sequence until, before long, you will reach insight knowledge of equanimity toward phenomena. If this knowledge is not yet powerful enough, you will stop and remain at this stage. When it is powerful enough, it will shift its focus and take nibbāna, the cessation of conditioned phenomena, as its object, just as it did previously. Thus will the path knowledge and fruition knowledge of the fourth stage of enlightenment arise.

Immediately after you have attained the path and fruition knowledge of arahantship, you will recollect the path, fruition, and nibbāna that you have clearly comprehended. You might reflect: "All mental defilements have been eradicated; they will no longer arise. I have accomplished everything that needed to be done." This is how you should practice for and experience the attainment of arahantship.

A note on pāramī[468]

The phrase "Thus will such-and-such path knowledge and fruition knowledge arise" is only intended for those whose *pāramī* are mature. If your *pāramī* is not yet mature enough, your insight will not move beyond insight knowledge of equanimity toward phenomena.

In addition, it is relatively easy to attain the second path knowledge and fruition knowledge fairly soon after attaining the first, but it will probably take a long time to attain the third path knowledge and fruition knowledge after the second. The reason for this is that only training in morality need be completely fulfilled in order to attain both the first and second path knowledge and fruition knowledge, but you must also completely fulfill training in concentration (*samādhisikkhā*) in order to attain the third path knowledge and fruition knowledge. Therefore, someone who has already attained the first path knowledge and fruition knowledge can easily attain the second, but it is not so easy to then attain the third.

In any event, it is not possible to know in advance whether your *pāramī* are mature enough to reach a particular level of path knowledge and fruition knowledge. Moreover, different people may need days, months, or years to attain enlightenment. If you have just been practicing for a few days or months without attaining path knowledge and fruition knowledge, you cannot yet decide that your *pāramī* are not mature. Besides, your current practice itself naturally helps your *pāramī* to mature, so you should not evaluate whether or not your *pāramī* are mature.

One should never give up, but continue practicing with full energy, keeping this point in mind: "If I don't practice, then there is no way that my *pāramī* can develop. And even if my *pāramī* were mature, I cannot attain path and fruition in this life without practice. On the other hand, if my *pāramī* are mature and I also practice, then I can easily and quickly attain path and fruition. And if my *pāramī* are fairly mature, then my current practice will help it to mature enough to attain path and fruition in this very life. At the very least, my current practice certainly develops my *pāramī* and my potential to attain path and fruition in the life to come."

A Word of Advice

> During this, the era of Gotama Buddha, those who aspire to know the truly enjoyable taste of insight should practice mindfulness that penetrates the phenomena of the body, feelings, mind, and mental objects.[469]

The explanations of how to practice insight that I have given here in this book are perfectly sufficient for those of fair intelligence. If they read this book and properly and systematically practice, with strong faith, aspiration, and energy, they can surely attain the different insight knowledges as well as path knowledge and fruition knowledge. However, it is impossible to mention here all of the different experiences that meditators may have, and there are many that I have not included. A meditator will not experience everything that is mentioned here either. The experience particular to one may be quite different from another's, depending on the maturity of his or her *pāramī* and the accuracy, precision, and continuity of his or her awareness.

Moreover, it is impossible for a meditator's faith, aspiration, and energy to remain strong all the time. If a person practices by following teachings based on intellectual knowledge and without a teacher, he or she may have doubts and feel uncertain, just like a person traveling alone in an unfamiliar place. So it is not easy for an ordinary person to attain the insight knowledges, as well as path knowledge and fruition knowledge, if he or she practices without a teacher who can give careful guidance. That is why the Saṃyutta Nikāya says:

> One . . . should search for a teacher in order to know this as it really is.[470]

So I would like to advise you to practice under the close guidance of an experienced teacher who can clearly explain the stages of insight knowledge up through path knowledge and fruition knowledge, reviewing knowledge, and fruition absorptions. Please be humble. Remember the story of Venerable Potthila, and do not proudly think, "I am special and don't need anyone's guidance!" When you practice, do so sincerely and keep in mind the following advice given by the Buddha:

> Not by means of slack endeavor,
> Not by means of feeble effort,
> Is this Nibbāna to be achieved,
> Release from all suffering.[471]

This means that with great effort and a firm practice, you can attain nibbāna.

Here ends chapter 5 regarding Practical Instructions.

Stages of Insight Knowledge 6

In chapter 1, I explained the purification of morality, and in chapter 2 the purification of mind. The purification of wisdom (*paññāvisuddhi*), ranging from the purification of view through the purification of knowledge and vision (*ñāṇadassanavisuddhi*), I covered in chapters 3, 4, and 5. In this chapter, I will correlate the various stages of insight knowledge with the five types of purification of wisdom.

Insight Knowledge that Discerns Mental and Physical Phenomena: Purification of View

> Purification of view (*diṭṭhivisuddhi*) means to see mental and physical phenomena as they really are.[472]

Awareness of phenomena

As I explained in chapter 5, a meditator will rarely have wandering thoughts once his or her concentration becomes strong. Instead, most of the time his or her noting mind will flow uninterruptedly. If a wandering thought does enter the mind, the meditator will be able to note it immediately and, with this, the thought will pass away (that is, it will come to an end and be cut off).

At that point the meditator will realize that physical activities generated by the air element (such as the rise and fall of the abdomen, sitting, standing, walking, lying down, bending, stretching, and so on) and other bodily sensations generated by the other elements (such as hardness, softness, heat, coldness, tightness, looseness, and so on) are all subject to alteration. He or she will also realize that those physical phenomena are unable to know or experience anything; they are just like inanimate logs or stones.

The meditator will also see and understand derived material elements, such as visible forms and the eye-sensitivity that receives them, audible sounds and the ear-sensitivity that receives them, smellable odors and the nose-sensitivity that receives them, tasteable flavors and tongue-sensitivity that receives them, feelable physical sensations and body-sensitivity that receives them, and the thinking mind and the mind-sensitivity of the heart that is its physical basis.

This is what "seeing physical phenomena as they really are" (*rūpayāthāvadassana*) means: to see their characteristic of being subject to alteration and their manifestation of being insensate (*abyākata-paccupaṭṭhānā*). According to the subcommentaries, here the term *abyākata*[473] means "insensate." The *Mahāṭīkā* and *Mūlaṭīkā* define it in this way, which is in harmony with meditators' actual experience:

> *Abyākata* should mean "insensate," as in the phrase "lack of consciousness is *abyākata*."[474]

As the meditator notes, it will become obvious that the noting mind seems to be running to and sticking with the object that it notes, such as the rise and fall of the abdomen. Likewise, it becomes obvious that the six types of consciousness (seeing, hearing, smelling, tasting, touching, and thinking) seem to run to their respective sense objects. This is what "seeing mental phenomena as they really are" (*nāmayāthāvadassana*) means: to see their characteristic of inclining or being drawn toward sense objects.

Discerning mental and physical phenomena

It is obvious to meditators who see things as they really are that mental and physical phenomena are different. Such meditators no longer take them to be one and the same, as they seemed before they took up the practice of meditation, or at the beginning of their practice of meditation. When a meditator observes the rising movement of the abdomen, he or she can at least discern the difference between the rising movement and the mind that notes it. Similarly, a meditator can differentiate between the falling movement and the noting of it, the sitting posture and the noting of it, the intention to bend, the bending movement, and the noting of them, the intention to stretch, the stretching movement, and the noting of them, and between the visible form, the eye, the seeing, and the noting of them. As the *Visuddhimagga* says:

> The pentad based on contact comes not from the eye,
> Or from things seen, or from something that is in between;
> Due to a cause it comes to be, and formed as well.
> Just as the sound that issues from a beaten drum.[475]

Before a drum is beaten its sound does not exist in the drum itself, the drumstick, or anywhere in between. Even though a sound occurs when the drum is beaten, the sound does not originate from the drum or the drumstick. The physical phenomena of the drum and the drumstick are not transformed into a sound, which is also a physical phenomenon, nor does the sound originate from anywhere in between. The sound of the drum is a completely new phenomenon each time the drum is hit and depends on the drum, the drumstick, and the striking of the drum. Thus the drum and the stick are different from the sound.

In the same way, before we see something or someone, seeing does not exist in the eye, in the visible form, or anywhere in between. When we discern a visible form, the seeing that takes place originates neither in the eye nor in the visible form. The eye-consciousness originates neither in the eye nor in the visible forms, which are physical phenomena. Neither does seeing originate from anywhere in between. Seeing is actually a new phenomenon that arises due to the combination of the eye, the visible form, light, and one's attention. Thus the eye and the visible form are different from sight. The same is true for the other senses:

> The pentad based on contact comes not from the ear.
> Or yet from sound, or something that is in between;
> Due to a cause . . .
> The pentad based on contact comes not from the nose
> Or yet from smells, or something that is in between;
> Due to a cause . . .
> The pentad based on contact comes not from the tongue,
> Or yet from tastes, or something that is in between;
> Due to a cause . . .
> The pentad based on contact comes not from the body,
> Or yet from touch, or something that is in between;

> Due to a cause . . .
> Being formed, it does not come from the material basis.
> Nor does it issue from the mental-datum base;
> Due to a cause it comes to be, and formed as well.
> Just as the sound that issues from a beaten drum.[476]

Seeing things as they really are

When you understand the difference between mental and physical phenomena, you are likely to reflect that neither the mind nor the body alone can perform actions such as sitting, standing, walking, bending, stretching, seeing, hearing, and so on. Only the mind and body together can perform these activities, due to which the mind and body together are mistaken for "I." One thinks: "I am sitting; I am standing up; I am going; I am bending; I am stretching; I am seeing; I am hearing," and so on. In reality, there is no "I," or being that sits, stands up, and walks, and so on, but only mental and physical phenomena. That is why the *Visuddhimagga* says:

> In reality, mind conditions matter and matter conditions mind. When the mind wants to eat, drink, speak, or change posture, it is the body that actually eats, drinks, speaks, or changes posture.[477]

Expanding this formula more fully, we see that: the volition to eat is mental, but what actually eats is the body; the volition to drink is mental, but what actually drinks is the body; the volition to speak is mental, but what actually speaks is the body; the volition to sit down is mental, but what actually sits down is the body; the volition to stand up is mental, but what actually stands up is the body; the volition to walk is mental, but what actually walks is the body; and the volition to lie down is mental, but what actually lies down is the body.

Some meditators may use similes to describe their experience of mental and physical phenomena. The *Visuddhimagga* gives the following similes:

> A coach is so called because of the way that its components—the axles, wheels, body, and shafts—are assembled. However, if one examines each component separately, there is no coach to be found.

> A house is so called when its materials—posts, beams, and so on—are fit together. Other than these materials, however, there is no house that can be found.
>
> A tree is so called because it includes a trunk, branches, leaves, and so on. But apart from these parts no tree can be found.
>
> In the same way, a being is so called because he or she is composed of the five aggregates subject to clinging (i.e., mental and physical phenomena). However, if one pays attention to each of these phenomena separately, one will no longer have the conceit that "I am so and so," or the wrong view that "I am a person." One will realize that, in terms of ultimate reality, there is no being that exists. The mind (which is able to incline toward objects and know objects) and matter (which is unable to know objects and is subject to alteration) are all there is. This realization is called "seeing things as they really are."[478]

However, it doesn't matter if you are able to come up with a good simile. Without deliberate thought, as you simply note, you are able to discern between mental and physical phenomena, and to understand that there are only mental phenomena that are able to know objects and physical phenomena that are not able to know objects in this body. There is no being, "I," soul, or self aside from these two phenomena. This understanding comes naturally and is the peak of insight knowledge that discerns mental and physical phenomena (*nāmarūpaparicchedañāṇa*). This insight knowledge in turn is called "purification of view," since it helps to remove the wrong view that a self really exists (*attadiṭṭhi*). This is why the *Mahāṭīkā* says:

> The phrase "seeing mind and matter as they really are" means to see them as just phenomena and not as a being by observing their unique characteristics thus: "This is mind; this much is mind; there is nothing more than this (i.e., no being). This is matter; this much is matter; there is nothing more than this (i.e., no being)." This is purification of view since it eliminates the wrong view that a self really exists. Thus should it be understood.[479]

The unique characteristics of physical phenomena, such as alteration or roughness and hardness (*kakkhalatta*), and the unique characteristics of mental phenomena, such as inclining toward objects, mental contact with objects, feeling, perceiving (*sañjāyana*), or knowing (*vijānana*) objects, only really exist in the moment they occur, not before or after. This is why one can only be truly aware of the specific characteristics of mental and physical phenomena when one observes them from moment to moment. In this way one understands that there is no "I" or being but only mental and physical phenomena. This understanding is called "purification of view," meaning that this understanding can eliminate the wrong view of a person or being.

Insight Knowledge that Discerns Conditionality: Purification by Overcoming Doubt

> The insight that overcomes skeptical doubt about past, future, and present phenomena by realizing their causes is called "purification by overcoming doubt" (*kaṅkhāvitaraṇavisuddhi*).[480]

When a meditator understands the characteristics of mind and matter as they truly are by noting presently arising objects, he or she comes to see the causes of those phenomena in an adequate manner. Thereby will arise insight knowledge that discerns conditionality (*paccayapariggahañāṇa*): the realization that certain causes give rise to certain phenomena, whether in the past, present, or future. This knowledge can take various forms depending on a person's aspiration (*ajjhāsaya*), spiritual maturity, and intellectual ability. The *Visuddhimagga* identifies five forms that I will explain in the sections below.

Those meditators who have understood that there is no "I" that exists apart from mental and physical phenomena might reflect and analyze the causes of those phenomena of mind and matter even while they meditate. They can no longer accept that things happen without any causes, because they have personally experienced some of their causes. Furthermore, they can no longer accept that God, Brahmā, or other divine beings have created everything. They have seen, based on personal experience, that mind and matter arise because of certain causes, and further they have reflected that God, Brahmā, or other divine beings are likewise constituted only of mind and matter. Their minds and matter are unable to create other beings, just as a meditator's mind is not able to create other creatures. If they were able to do so, then we could ask, "Who created the creator?" We could ask the same question about the creator's creator, and so on *ad infinitum*.

The first way of seeing conditionality

Seeing the causes of matter

Some meditators see the causes of matter. They see that physical phenomena have continuously occurred, from birth up to the present moment, due to the four causes of past ignorance, craving, clinging, and volitional actions. They also see that nutrition received in the present preserves the body, that the desire to sit, bend, and so on results in the physical actions of sitting, bending, and so on, and that hot and cold environments give rise to the physical sensations of heat and coldness.

A meditator can empirically observe the present causes of physical phenomena, such as nutrition, consciousness, and weather, but he or she cannot directly observe past causes, such as ignorance, craving, clinging, and volitional actions. However, even before they begin practicing meditation, an insight meditator has already intellectually accepted that "wholesome actions lead to a good life and beneficial results, whereas unwholesome actions lead to a bad life and harmful results." So when he or she practices and empirically observes present ignorance, craving, clinging, and volitional actions, he or she will inferentially realize that they also operated in the past.

The mental and physical phenomena that make up our lives are all unsatisfying, and attachment to them is the cause of suffering. Not knowing this truth is called "ignorance of suffering and its cause" (*appaṭipatti-avijjā*). Believing that the phenomena of life are actually satisfying and the cause of happiness is called "ignorance of pleasure and its cause" (*micchāpaṭipatti-avijjā*). These two kinds of ignorance are so deeply rooted in the hearts of ordinary people that they cannot be overcome simply by study. This is why ordinary people devote themselves, day and night, to enjoying as much pleasure as possible. Day and night people do everything they can to get the most out of their present lives and to enjoy better lives in the future.

On the other hand, the cessation of the defilements and volitional actions leads to the complete cessation of all the mental and physical phenomena (*parinibbānacuti*) that they cause, and you will no longer be reborn as a human or deva, or as a man or woman. Not being reborn is called "the truth of cessation" or "nibbāna without residue" (*anupādisesan-*

ibbāna). Ignorance of the happiness and peace of nibbāna and ignorance of insight practice and path knowledge that are the causes of happiness and peace are also called "ignorance of suffering and its causes." On the other hand, believing that nibbāna must be awful and that insight practice and path knowledge are causes of suffering is called "ignorance of pleasure and its causes." In other words, this is a distorted and wrong understanding of the truths of the cessation of suffering and the path that leads to the cessation of suffering.

When these two kinds of ignorance are very strong, one may actually fear nibbāna, thinking that after complete cessation (*parinibbāna*) nothing will arise, nothing can be known or experienced, and one can no longer meet others. One may even make disparaging comments about liberation, saying, "Nibbāna is complete annihilation. It can't possibly be good. Practicing to attain it is simply going to a lot of trouble, mentally and physically, to attain annihilation!" This active form of ignorance and wrong understanding of the Four Noble Truths occurs only at certain times for ordinary people, but it accompanies every object that is not noted in latent form. However, if a meditator notes ignorance when it occurs, he or she can empirically see it. He or she can also see it by recollecting past experiences.

If one mistakenly believes that these mental and physical phenomena are satisfying, one will like and crave them. As a result, one will develop the desire to become more prosperous. This is clinging. One performs various activities due to clinging. These are volitional actions. One can see craving, clinging, and volitional actions by noting them when they occur in the present and by remembering when they have occurred in the past. When a meditator sees in practice how volitional actions have their origins in ignorance, craving, and clinging, he or she realizes that the continuity of physical phenomena in this life that has been ongoing since the moment of rebirth-linking happens due to wholesome volitional actions done in the past. At the same time, he or she understands that these physical phenomena also arise due to ignorance, craving, and clinging. This is to empirically and inferentially realize the causes of physical phenomena.

Seeing the causes of mind

When a meditator notes seeing, he or she understands and comprehends that seeing occurs when there is an eye and a visible form. Or he or she understands and comprehends that when the eye, the visible form, and seeing meet, there is contact between the object and the mind. The same is true for hearing. When a meditator notes hearing, he or she understands and comprehends that hearing occurs when there is an ear and a sound. Or he or she understands and comprehends that when the ear, the sound, and the hearing meet, there is contact between the object and the mind. When a meditator notes touching, he or she understands and comprehends that touching occurs when there is a body and a tangible object. Or he or she understands and comprehends that when the body, the tangible object, and touching meet, there is contact between the object and the mind. When a meditator notes thinking, knowing, or noting, he or she understands and comprehends that thinking, knowing, or noting occur when there is both a heart-base and a mental object. Or he or she understands and comprehends that when the heart-base, the mental object, and knowing meet, there is contact between the object and the mind.

Furthermore, when a meditator notes "seeing," or "hearing," or "touching," or "thinking," and so on, he or she can see that contact with the object arouses pleasure or displeasure in the body or the mind. Pleasure is enjoyed and produces desire for continuous enjoyment. The meditator wants to get rid of displeasure and wants pleasure instead. Clinging to pleasure causes actions of body, speech, and thought with the aim to gain enjoyment. In this way, the meditator empirically sees the causes of the mind in an adequate manner.

Inferential knowledge regarding the past and future

Once a meditator has empirically seen the causes of mental and physical phenomena in the present life, he or she concludes with inferential knowledge that they must have been the same in the past and must be the same in future: "In the past, there were only these mental and physical phenomena that occurred due to certain causes. In the future, there will only be these mental and physical phenomena that will occur due to certain causes."

> When a meditator sees that mental and physical phenomena come into existence due to causes, he or she considers that, just like the phenomena of this present life, those of past lives came into existence due to causes and those of future lives will also.[481]

Overcoming the sixteen skeptical doubts

A meditator who understands and comprehends that in the three periods of time, namely the past, future, and present, there are only mental and physical phenomena that give rise to other mental and physical phenomena will be able to abandon and overcome belief in a self and the sixteen kinds of skeptical doubt related to it.

There are five doubts about one's past existence: (1) "Did I exist in previous lives?" (wondering whether one has existed forever); (2) "Or did I not exist in previous lives? (wondering whether one only exists in this life); (3) "What was I in previous lives?" (wondering whether one was rich or poor, lay, ordained, Myanmar, Indian, brahmā, deva, human, animal, and so on); (4) "What did I look like in previous lives and who or what created me in previous lives?" (wondering whether one was tall, short, fat, thin, fair, dark, and so on, and whether God, Brahma, or another celestial being created one, or whether one spontaneously came into existence); and (5) "What type of person was I in previous lives?"

There are a further five doubts about one's existence in the future: (6) "Will I have another life after death?" (wondering whether one is indestructible and eternal); (7) "Will I not have another life after death?" (wondering whether one will disappear after death); (8) "What will I be in my next life?" (wondering whether one will be rich or poor, lay, ordained, Myanmar, Indian, brahmā, deva, human, animal, and so on); (9) "What will I look like in my next life, and who or what will create my next life?" (wondering whether one will be tall, short, fat, thin, fair, dark, and so on, and whether God, Brahma, or another celestial being will create one, or whether one will spontaneously come into existence); and (10) "What type of person will I be in my next life?"

And lastly there are six doubts about one's present existence: (11) "Is there a self in this body?"; (12) "Is there not self in this body?"; (13) "What is this self?" (wondering whether it is rich or poor, lay, ordained, Myanmar, Indian, brahmā, deva, human, or animal, and so on); (14) "What does this self look like and what has created it?" (wondering whether it is small, big, round, flat, square, six-sided, and so on, and whether it was created by some sort of creator or whether it spontaneously came into existence); (15) "What previous life did this self transmigrate from?"; and (16) "What future life will this self transmigrate to?"

> The sixteen kinds of doubt, such as whether one existed in past lives and so on, have their origin in a deep-seated belief in the existence of a "self."[482]

According to the subcommentary, these sixteen kinds of skeptical doubt only arise in those who believe in the existence of a "self." They do not arise in those who understand that there is only a succession of mental and physical phenomena based on cause and effect that are devoid of a "self" or an "I." There is a simile for this: One can only have doubts about whether or not a rabbit has horns if one doesn't really know what a rabbit looks like. But if one has actually seen a rabbit, it would not be possible to entertain such doubt. This is the first way of overcoming doubt through seeing the causes of mental and physical phenomena.

The second way of seeing conditionality

Some meditators see the conditionality of mental and physical phenomena in these ways:

> "It is due to the eye and visible forms that I see. It is due to the ear and sounds that I hear. It is due to the nose and odors that I smell. It is due to the tongue and flavors that I taste sweet, sour, and so forth. It is due to the body and tangible objects that I know the sensation of touch. It is due to the heart-base and various mental objects that I think, reflect, and note objects. It is due to wise attention, living in a suitable place, associating with virtuous people, listening to the Dhamma expounded by the wise, and having mature *pāramī*s, that both wholesomeness and the ability to practice insight meditation arise. It is due to unwise attention, living in an unsuitable place, associating with evil people, listening to the words of immoral people, and having poorly developed *pāramī*s that unwholesomeness arises."
>
> "Good kamma based on wholesome volitional actions, ignorance, craving, and clinging produces a fortunate rebirth, good and pleasant objects at all six sense doors, and many beneficial results. Bad kamma based on unwholesome volitional actions, ignorance, craving, and clinging produces an unfortunate rebirth, bad and unpleasant objects at all six sense doors, and many unbeneficial results."
>
> "The life-continuum leads to adverting consciousness."[483]

> "The physical phenomena that make up the heart-base, eye, ear, and so on have been arising continuously since the first moment of this life due to past volitional actions."
>
> "The physical activities of sitting, walking, bending, and so on are caused by the intention or desire to do them."
>
> "The temperature of the external environment causes physical sensations of heat or cold. The nutrition in the food one eats gives energy to the body, and so on . . ."

A meditator who sees and understands, with regard to the present, that there are only mental and physical phenomena that give rise to other mental and physical phenomena inferentially understands that the same is true with regard to the past and the future. Therefore, he or she can abandon and overcome the sixteen kinds of doubt. This is the second way of overcoming these doubts.

The third and fourth ways of seeing conditionality

Some meditators see the arising, presence, and disappearance of conditioned phenomena while observing presently arising objects. From this they understand that the first arising of the mind in this life is just another moment of arising of mind, that death is just another moment of disappearance of mind, and that aging is the successive presence of mental and physical phenomena. Thus they understand the causes for mental and physical phenomena.

We can understand it in this way: for aging and death to occur, there must first be arising or rebirth. Arising or rebirth must in turn have been generated by volitional actions. Volitional actions are generated by clinging; clinging is caused by craving mental and physical phenomena; pleasant and unpleasant feelings cause craving; feelings are brought about by contact between the mind and sense objects; contact originates from the sense bases, the sensitive matter of the eye, ear, nose, tongue, body, and mind (that is, seeing and such occur due to the eye-sensitivity and the mind); the sense bases come into existence based on the mental and physical phenomena on which they depend (that is, the sensitive matter of eye, ear, nose, tongue, and body are based on the physical organs, and the mind is based on its physical basis and other mental elements); mental and physical phenomena are generated by various types of consciousness, such as relinking consciousness, the life-continuum, and sense consciousness; consciousness has its origin in volitional deeds that one has performed in past lives for one's well-being; and volitional actions arise from ignorance.

Noble beings, such as bodhisattas, fully realize conditionality in this way by seeing dependent origination in reverse order. Ordinary meditators are also able to realize conditionality in this way and to overcome the sixteen kinds of doubt. This is the third way of seeing the conditionality of mental and physical phenomena.

Other meditators realize conditionality by seeing dependent origination in forward order. That is, they realize that ignorance generates volitional actions, that volitional actions generate consciousness, and so on. Noble beings, such as bodhisattas, fully realize conditionality in this way. Ordinary meditators are also able to realize conditionality this way and to overcome the sixteen kinds of doubt. This is the fourth way of seeing the conditionality of mental and physical phenomena.

The fifth way of seeing conditionality

Some meditators see the conditionality of mental and physical phenomena in terms of the relationship between volitional actions and their results. That is, a volitional action generates a result, and a new volitional action is generated based on this result. That new volitional action then generates a new result, and so on. This relationship between volitional action and its results is divided into the cycle of volitional actions (*kammavaṭṭa*) and the cycle of results (*vipākavaṭṭa*). The cycle of volitional actions includes ignorance, volitional action, craving, clinging, and existence based on intentional actions (*kammabhava*). The cycle of results includes consciousness, mental and physical phenomena, the sense bases, mental contact, and feeling.

If a meditator considers conditionality in detail, he or she will see each of the five causal factors and the five resultant factors. If one considers it in general, one does not differentiate each individual cause and result. Instead one simply sees volitional action as the cycle of volitional actions and kammic results of volitional actions as the cycle of results. In the following sections, I will describe how the *Paṭisambhidāmagga* of the Pāḷi canon explains the cycle of volitional actions and the cycle of results.

Causal factors from previous lives

> When volitional actions were performed in previous lives, these five factors were generated: ignorance or delusion, wholesome or unwholesome volition, craving, clinging, and volition that would result in new life. These five factors generated in previous lives were the causes of this life.[484]

The commentaries mention three differences between wholesome and unwholesome volition (*saṅkhāra*) and volition that results in new life. However, I will only explain it in terms of the first of these, since this is easiest to understand. Volition refers to the volition generated as one plans to perform a wholesome or unwholesome action. It is this volition that compels one to perform that action right away. But the volition generated while actually performing the wholesome or unwholesome action is intentional action (*kammabhava*).

Examples of intentional action include: with respect to the act of giving, letting go of a thing and handing it over to a recipient so that he or she can do with it what he or she pleases; or with respect to the act of killing, committing the action and another being dying as a result of it. Actions are completed in this way and must be understood in the same way with respect to other wholesome or unwholesome deeds.

The five causal factors are listed in the passage above in the order in which they are taught. But they actually occur in a slightly different order: Ignorance leads to craving, craving leads to clinging, clinging leads to volition involved in preparing to act, and preparing to act leads to volition involved in carrying out the action. After having carried out the action, one mistakenly thinks that the action is a cause of happiness and that one will experience happiness as a result of it. This again produces ignorance, followed by craving, clinging, and so on. In this way, volitional actions can lead to rebirth supported by ignorance and craving. This is why the *Paṭisambhidāmagga* says that the two roots of ignorance and craving condition rebirth at the moment of attachment,[i.e., immediately prior to death].[485]

Resultant factors in the present life

> Here, in the present life, there are relinking consciousness, mental and physical phenomena, the six sense bases, contact

> between the mind and sense objects, and feeling. These five resultant factors in the present existence are caused by volitional actions performed in previous lives.[486]

When a meditator notes mental and physical phenomena from moment to moment, it is obvious to them that successive moments of consciousness (seeing, hearing, and so on) are part of an ongoing mental process. In the same way, we can understand the moment of relinking consciousness of this life to be the successor to the last moment of consciousness (i.e., death) of the previous life. The *Visuddhimagga* says:

> For example, eye-consciousness occurs immediately after adverting consciousness. However, eye-consciousness does not come from adverting consciousness, it just immediately follows it.
>
> Similarly, the mental process begins with the moment of relinking consciousness. The preceding moment of consciousness ceases, and a new moment of consciousness replaces it. [That is, the last moment of consciousness of the previous life ends, and the first moment of consciousness of the present life immediately follows it.][487]

If a meditator continuously notes phenomena from moment to moment, he or she will see new phenomena coming into existence. He or she can then inferentially realize that the phenomena at the moment of rebirth arose in the same manner. The same is true for the six senses, contact, and feeling. These resultant phenomena eventually give rise to the five causal phenomena when the six sense bases mature.

Causal factors in the present life and resultant factors in future lives

> When the sense bases mature here [in this life], they produce the five causal factors: ignorance or delusion, wholesome or unwholesome volition, craving, clinging, and volitional actions that result in a new life. These five factors are produced when we perform volitional actions here [in this life] and are the causes of future rebirth.[488]

These present causal factors lead to the arising of the five resultant factors in the future.

> There will occur in the future relinking consciousness, mental and physical phenomena, the six sense bases, contact between the mind and sense objects, and feeling. These five resultant factors will arise in future existences caused by volitional actions performed in this life.[489]

Inferential knowledge

The five causal factors generated in past lives are the same as those generated in the present life. The five resultant factors that will be generated in future lives will also be the same as those generated in this life. Therefore, if one empirically perceives the causal and resultant factors in the present life, one will also inferentially realize causes produced in past lives and results that will be produced in future lives.

These five resultant factors are all contained within one moment of consciousness. So if you are aware of these resultant factors in a general way, you will see all of them together as a whole. When one notes a pleasant or unpleasant object, for example, one is aware that sight, sound, smell, taste, touch, or thought simply arise of their own accord as the result of past volitional actions. One is not separately aware of each resultant factor, noticing, "This is consciousness; these are the mental and physical phenomena," and so on. Likewise, one experiences all five of the causal factors together during a single moment of noting and sees that they are the past causes. One then realizes that all volitional activities performed for the sake of one's well-being, whether physical, verbal, or mental, whether in this life or the next, constitute volitional action that will lead to rebirth. But one does not see the causal factors separately as "This is ignorance; this is volitional action," and so on.

Because a meditator finds only causal and resultant factors when they note, he or she concludes: "In past lives too, there were only volitional actions and their results. In future lives too, there will only be volitional actions and their results. There is only volitional actions and their results; there is no individual or personality who produces volitional actions or who enjoys or suffers their results." In this way, a meditator abandons and overcomes the sixteen kinds of doubt.

> If one sees the conditionality of mental and physical phenomena in terms of the cycle of volitional actions and the cycle of results in this present life, one concludes: "Just as it is now, so in the past these [mental and physical] phenomena were produced by the cycle of volitional actions and the cycle of results, and they will also be so in the future. There exists only volitional action and its result, the cycle of volitional action and the cycle of its result, the flow of volitional action and the flow of its result, the unbroken process of volitional action and the unbroken process of its result, action and its result."
>
> Result proceeds from volitional action,
> Result has volitional action for its source,
> Future becoming springs from volitional action,
> And this is how the world (*sattaloka*) goes round.[490]
>
> There is no doer of a [wholesome or unwholesome] deed
> Or one who reaps the deed's [pleasant or unpleasant] result;
> Phenomena alone flow on—
> No other view than this is right.
> And so, while kamma and result
> Thus causally maintain their round,
> As seed and tree succeed in turn,
> No first beginning can be shown.[491]

When one performs an act of generosity, or kills a being, the intention to do so is generated. That intention is then followed by physical or verbal actions. Both the intention and the physical or verbal actions are called wholesome or unwholesome volitional actions. Thus volitional action includes both physical and mental phenomena. However, the Buddha said that intention is the leading factor for volitional action.[492] Only mental and physical phenomena are involved in the performance of a volitional action and not any individual or personality. These mental and physical phenomena are mistaken for a person with the thought: "So-and-so is offering a gift," or "So-and-so has killed a being."

Moreover in a moment of seeing, hearing, and so on, the phenomena of cognizing and feeling the good or bad object arise as results. Because these results depend on mental and physical phenomena, we say, "The person feels." But this is just a conventional expression. There is no independently existing person who feels. When volitional actions were performed in previous lives, there was no person doing it, only the wholesome or unwholesome volitional action itself. The relinking consciousness, life-continuum, seeing, hearing, and so on in this life are all results of volitional action. We produce more wholesome or unwholesome volitional actions in this life based on those results. This new volitional action, in turn, will produce results in the future. Thus the cycles of volitional actions and their results go on and on. There is no individual or personality who performs wholesome and unwholesome actions (*kāraka-atta*) and no individual or personality who experiences their results (*vedaka-atta*). This understanding is called "right seeing" (*sammādassana*), or "knowledge that discerns conditionality."

The tree and its seed

When there is a seed, there must have been a tree that bore it, a seed from which that tree had grown, and so on. Thus we cannot trace the origin of the seed and the tree. The same is true of the chicken and the egg. Likewise, given that resultant mental and physical phenomena occur in this life, causal volitional actions must have been produced in previous lives. That volitional action must in turn have been a result of volitional actions produced in an even earlier life, and so on. Therefore, we cannot find a beginning to the continuum of mental and physical phenomena.

Some people believe that God created everything. But if there were a God who created everything, that God must have been created at some point. But who could have created such a God? For what purpose, and when? And if God was created, how could God have created everything? These contradictions show that such a God can only be imaginary. Thus it is unreasonable to accept any so-called "God" as the creator of everything.

On the other hand some believe that nothing is created by anyone or anything. They believe that everything has happened of its own accord since the beginning of time. But if that were so, then everything should happen of its own accord right now as well. Yet we cannot find, either through empirical or inferential knowledge, any mental and physical phenomena that arise by themselves without any cause. So it is also unreasonable to accept that things have no origin, or that they happen without any cause.

The metaphors of the tree and seed and the chicken and egg are not completely apt in an ultimate sense, since we can in fact trace their origins back to the early days of life on earth. We use these metaphors in the same way that we use the metaphor "The Buddha's face is as graceful as a lotus flower." We do not actually mean that the Buddha's face looks exactly like a lotus flower. In reality, the origin of mental and physical phenomena or the cycle of volitional action and its results cannot be traced, unlike the examples given in these metaphors.

The future will unfold like this: the tree will produce a seed, the seed in turn will produce a tree that will again produce a seed, and so on. Thus we cannot find an end to the tree and seed. The same holds true of the chicken and egg. Likewise, volitional actions produced in this life will produce results in a future life, beginning with relinking consciousness. Based on this result, wholesome and unwholesome volitional actions will also be produced in that life, and these will in turn generate yet another life. Thus we cannot find an end to volitional action and its results or an end to mental and physical phenomena. If path knowledge cannot bring the cause or volitional action to an end, it will never end. When the last moment of consciousness ceases in any given life, the next moment of consciousness, relinking consciousness, will immediately arise. We can understand it thusly. The *Visuddhimagga* says:

> There is no [volitional action] in result,
> Nor does result exist in [volitional action];[493]
> Though they are void of one another,
> There is no fruit without the [volitional action].
> . . .
> [Volitional action] of its fruit is void;
> No fruit exists yet in [volitional action];
> And still the fruit is born from it,
> Wholly depending on [volitional action].
> For here there is no Brahmā God,
> Creator of the round of births,
> Phenomena alone flow on—
> Cause and component their condition.[494]

Death and relinking

If a meditator sees mental and physical phenomena in terms of volitional actions and their results, he or she understands the process of death and relinking. When a visible form strikes the eye, for example, adverting consciousness occurs, immediately followed by eye-consciousness. In the same way, there is no gap between death consciousness and relinking consciousness. When the last moment of consciousness in the previous life ceases, the first moment of consciousness in the new life arises due to previous volitional action. This is how a knowledgeable meditator understands "death and relinking."

A less knowledgeable meditator understands that death is a mind-moment, relinking is a mind-moment, and the death mind-moment is followed by the relinking mind-moment as a result of one's volitional action, just as a mental process of seeing, hearing, and so on is followed by one of observing and so on. If one understands how death and relinking happens to this extent, one is said to understand the conditionality of all phenomena—past, future, or present. As the *Visuddhimagga* says:

> All past, future, and present phenomena are understood in terms of death and relinking . . . Complete and powerful is the knowledge of conditionality obtained by those who know all phenomena in terms of death and relinking.[495]

In this commentary the phrase "those who know all phenomena" might seem to refer to some kind of omniscience. This is why the commentator adds the qualification "in terms of death and relinking," in order to show the limit of this knowledge.

Once a meditator understands how the process of death and relinking happens, he or she clearly understands that there are no phenomena that transfer from one life to another. They disappear without remainder in that very life. Only new mental and physical phenomena arise in the new life, due to past volitional action. A meditator reflects that these mental and physical phenomena cease to exist, whether in a past, present, or future life, and thereby realizes that they are impermanent. In this way, one begins to develop the insight knowledge by comprehension.

Thus while a meditator is noting presently arising mental and physical phenomena, he or she sees the conditionality of mental and physical phenomena in one of the five ways described above. He or she can then confirm that in the three periods of time (past, future, and present) there are only mental and physical phenomena that are interrelated on the basis of cause and result. This is the peak of the insight knowledge that discerns conditionality. This knowledge is also called the "purification by overcoming doubt," since it abandons and overcomes the aforementioned sixteen kinds of doubt, as well as eight other kinds of doubt. These are: doubt regarding the Buddha, the Dhamma, the Saṅgha, the three trainings, past mental and physical phenomena, future mental and physical phenomena, present mental and physical phenomena, and the law of cause and effect.

The lesser stream enterer

> An insight meditator who has attained this insight is considered a lesser stream enterer (*cūlasotāpanna*): one who has gained spiritual relief, a firm foothold, and a secure rebirth in the Buddha's teaching.[496]

The attainment of the noble fruition is what actually gives one genuine spiritual relief and the attainment of the noble path is what actually gives one a genuine foothold in the Buddha's teaching. However, meditators at this stage of insight are said to have gained relief and a foothold in the Buddha's teaching, even though they have yet to attain path and fruition. This is because they are making the proper effort in the practice that will eventually lead them to the path knowledge and fruition knowledge.

In other words, they are said to have gained relief because they derive gladness in relation to the Dhamma by understanding the true nature of mental and physical phenomena. Based on the insight knowledge that discerns conditionality one understands that there are only conditioned mental and physical phenomena. As a result, one understands that there is no "I" or person, that there is no God that creates living beings, or that the self does not arise by itself without any causes. Thus false view or wrong belief can no longer arise and one's faith grows strong, firm, and unshakable. Being endowed with this strong, firm, and unshakable faith, one is said to have gained a firm foothold in the Buddha's teaching.

The *Visuddhimagga-mahāṭīkā* explains why a meditator at this stage of insight is called a lesser stream enterer, with a "secure rebirth":

> "Secure rebirth" means that even if an insight meditator who is endowed with steadfast purification by overcoming doubt does not attain any further insight, he or she will be destined for a wholesome rebirth because he or she possesses mundane

> morality, concentration, and wisdom. Simply for this reason one is considered a lesser stream enterer.[497]

The phrase "steadfast purification by overcoming doubt" indicates that you are only destined for a wholesome rebirth when you are free from wrong view and skeptical doubt. This purification is only mundane, and not supramundane. So it can still become deficient due to unwholesome thoughts or others' immoral talk. Skeptical doubt and wrong view can also still arise, as a result of which this purification can become deficient and one's rebirth unsecure.

The phrase "because he or she possesses mundane morality, concentration, and wisdom" explicitly points out that one is destined for a wholesome rebirth due to the purified morality, concentration, and wisdom developed during practice. This implies that one's rebirth will no longer be secure if one's morality, concentration, and wisdom are deficient when one stops one's insight practice. Thus we can draw the conclusion that one will be destined for a wholesome rebirth only so long as one is able to keep wrong views and skeptical doubts at bay by practicing insight, or at the very least, by maintaining pure morality. For this reason, one should not rest on one's laurels, thinking, "I am a lesser stream enterer and destined for a wholesome rebirth," and give up practicing insight or moral conduct.

You may wonder: "Is every future rebirth of a lesser stream enterer secure, or only the one immediately following this life?" The answer is that only the very next rebirth is secure. As the above subcommentary mentions, only when one's purification by overcoming doubt, along with its morality, concentration, and wisdom, is unspoiled will one be destined for a wholesome rebirth. At this stage, these qualities are mundane and fragile. If you lose them during the present life, then your very next rebirth will not be secure at all, not to mention future rebirths beyond that.

One should keep in mind that even the Buddha-to-Be, who had matured his perfections, was sometimes reborn in the lower worlds prior to his enlightenment. The commentary on the *Buddhavaṃsa* says that our Buddha-to-Be became a monk under nine previous Buddhas, including the Kondañña Buddha, who lived over three eons and world cycles ago. According to the commentary on the *Ghatikāra Sutta*,[498] if a buddha-to-be is fortunate enough to become a monk under a buddha, one can assume that he will then realize the insight knowledges up through the insight knowledge of adaptation, the highest insight knowledge prior to attaining the first path knowledge. During the time of buddhas Sumana and Vipassī, he received prophecies as a nāga king; during the time of Buddha Paduma he received a prophecy as a lion king. According to the Jātaka tales, he was reborn as an animal several times during the current world cycle. And according to the *Temiya Jātaka*, he was even reborn in a hell realm.

We can conclude from these accounts that even the Buddha-to-Be, who had attained the insight knowledge of equanimity toward phenomena, which excels purification by overcoming doubt, was not assured of eternal fortunate rebirths and had to suffer in the lower worlds. If that is the case, then it must certainly be true as well for those at the level of purification by overcoming doubt, whose spiritual faculties [of faith, effort, and so on] and insight are far inferior to the faculties and insight knowledge of equanimity toward phenomena of the Buddha-to-Be. So if you really want to secure your future rebirths and escape any chance of rebirth in the lower worlds, you should make the utmost effort to uproot the wrong view of personality by means of the first path knowledge. You should not overestimate the security that comes with purification by overcoming doubt or be content to rest on your laurels. The Saṃyutta Nikāya gives this noble advice:

> As if smitten by a sword,
> As if his head were on fire,
> A bhikkhu should wander mindfully
> To abandon identity view.[499]

Insight Knowledge by Comprehension

> The understanding that comes from contemplating past, future, and present phenomena, as a whole, is called "knowledge by comprehension."[500]

When the insight knowledge that discerns conditionality reaches its peak, one clearly sees mental and physical phenomena arising and passing away. After an object has arisen, one sees that it immediately disappears. From this one understands that: all phenomena are impermanent, because they pass away right after arising; they are unsatisfactory, because one is constantly oppressed by arising and passing away; and they are not-self, because one cannot exercise control over them. One may also reflect in this way: "It is really true that phenomena are impermanent, unsatisfactory, and not-self."

After this understanding occurs a number of times with regard to directly experienced present phenomena, one inferentially understands that all past, future, and present phenomena, as a whole, are impermanent, unsatisfactory, and not-self. This is the insight knowledge by comprehension (*sammasanañāṇa*): insight that contemplates all past, future, and present phenomena as a whole, rather than perceiving the individual details and specific characteristics of each phenomenon in the present moment. That is why this insight knowledge is also called "knowledge that comprehends all phenomena as a whole" (*kalāpasammasanañāṇa*). And since the comprehension is based on mental and physical phenomena that have already been personally experienced, it is also called "inferential insight" (*nayavipassanā*). It can also be called "inferential attention" (*nayamanasikāra*) and "inferential observation" (*nayadassana*). According to the *Vibhaṅga Aṭṭhakathā*, a commentary of the Abhidhamma:

> If one empirically observes a single phenomenon to be impermanent, one can inferentially confirm that it is true for the rest. Thus: "all conditioned phenomena are impermanent."
>
> The stanzas beginning with "All conditioned phenomena are impermanent, all conditioned phenomena are unsatisfactory, all phenomena are not self . . ." are said to refer to inferential insight, rather than to the empirical experience of a single mental process.[501]

This commentary makes it clear that insight knowledge by comprehension is not a type of understanding that one need purposely develop from the start. Instead, this understanding arises by itself following empirical understanding of the impermanent, unsatisfactory, and impersonal characteristics of phenomena. If one is intelligent, knowledgeable, and prone to contemplate things, this insight knowledge can arise on a large scale. In this case, deliberate contemplation and reflection impede pure noting. So one may spend a long time at this stage of insight knowledge without progressing to higher stages. Therefore be careful!

In the *Paṭisambhidāmagga* the Buddha explained in detail the various ways that this insight knowledge arises according to individual inclinations. Some of these follow:

> Any kind of form whatsoever, bhikkhu, whether past, future, or present, internal or external, gross or subtle, inferior or superior, far or near—one sees all of them as impermanent. This is one contemplation. One determines all physical phenomena to be distressing. This is another contemplation. One determines all physical phenomena to be not-self. This is also another contemplation.[502]

> [Insight] knowledge by comprehension is the understanding that determines in a general way that all physical phenomena of the past, present, and future are impermanent since they vanish, are unsatisfying since they are oppressive, and are not self since they are insubstantial.[503]

> [Insight] knowledge by comprehension is the understanding that determines in a general way that all past, present, and future physical phenomena are impermanent, conditioned, causal, vanishing, decaying, disappearing, and ceasing.[504]

The Buddha goes on to describe this insight knowledge in a similar way with regard to the four mental aggregates, the six sense doors, the six sense objects, the six types of consciousness, six types of mental contact, six types of feeling, and so on. It would be too much to explain all of those here, so I will explain how these insight knowledges unfold only with regard to physical phenomena instead.

Comprehension of impermanence

When one is able to note presently arising objects, such as the physical phenomena involved in the rise and fall of the abdomen, sitting, bending, stretching, moving, and so on, one clearly will see that they instantaneously appear and disappear. Based on this one understands that all physical phenomena are impermanent and that physical phenomena in previous lives must have vanished in the same way as present physical phenomena do. No physical phenomena from previous lives were carried over into this life; they all vanished then and there. This understanding is a form of insight knowledge by comprehension. No previous physical phenomena last until the moment that one notes in the present; they are impermanent because they vanish the moment they arise. This understanding is another form of insight knowledge by comprehension. One also understands that all physical phenomena that will arise in future lives will immediately vanish, too, just as present phenomena do. None of them will carry over into future lives; they are impermanent because they will vanish then and there. This understanding is also a form of insight knowledge by comprehension. One also understands that any physical phenomena that arise in the future will disappear just as present phenomena do. None of them will last until the next moment; they are impermanent because they will vanish the moment they appear. This understanding is another form of insight knowledge by comprehension. Finally, one understands that none of the physical phenomena in this present life can carry over into the next life. They are impermanent because they will vanish in this very life just as all physical phenomena observed in this life do. This understanding is also a form of insight knowledge by comprehension.

When one notes the activities of exhaling air, exhaling cigarette smoke, spitting out saliva, passing urine or feces, and so on, as one does them, one will find that the physical phenomena involved vanish the moment they arise; whatever physical phenomena there are that are internal are not carried over to the outside. Therefore, they are impermanent. This realization is a form of insight knowledge by comprehension. Similarly, when one notes the physical phenomena involved in activities such as breathing in air, inhaling cigarette smoke, taking in food or drink, swallowing saliva, and so on, one will find that they disappear the moment they arise; whatever physical phenomena there are that are external are not carried over to the inside. Therefore, they are impermanent. This understanding is another form of insight knowledge by comprehension.

When observing a coarse visible form, audible sound, smellable odor, tasteable flavor, or feelable touch, one will see that it gradually becomes more subtle, and one will notice that the physical phenomenon vanishes the moment it arises; whatever physical phenomena there are that are coarse do not become subtle. They are impermanent because they vanish the moment they appear. This understanding is a form of insight knowledge by comprehension. Likewise, when observing a subtle visible form, audible sound, smellable odor, tasteable flavor, or feelable touch, one will see that it gradually becomes more distinct, and will notice that the physical phenomenon vanishes the moment it arises; whatever physical phenomena there are that are subtle do not become coarse. They are impermanent because they vanish in the moment they appear. This understanding is another form of insight knowledge by comprehension.

When one recovers from lethargy or an illness, one becomes active, alert, or healthy. If one notes the physical phenomena involved in this process, one will find that they disappear the moment they appear. Seeing this, one understands that they are impermanent because the physical phenomena associated with poor health do not become physical phenomena associated with good health, but rather they vanish then and there. This understanding is a form of insight knowledge by comprehension. When one's good health and alertness give way to illness or lethargy, and one notes the physical phenomena involved in that process, one will find that they disappear the moment they appear. Seeing this, one understands that they are impermanent because the physical phenomena associated with good health do not become physical phenomena associated with poor health, but rather they vanish then and there. This is another form of insight knowledge by comprehension.

When one notes the process of bending one's limbs, one can observe that the physical phenomena involved in bending do not go from one moment of movement to the next moment of movement. One understands that they are impermanent because the physical phenomena that are further away do not become the physical phenomena that are nearer, but rather they vanish then and there. This understanding is a form of insight knowledge by comprehension. Similarly when one notes the process of stretching one's limbs, one can observe that the physical phenomena involved in stretching do not go from one moment of movement to the next moment of movement. One understands that they are impermanent because the physical phenomena that are nearer do not become the physical phenomena that are further away, but rather they vanish then and there. This is another form of insight knowledge by comprehension.

Comprehension of suffering

It is very difficult to recognize that the mind and body are oppressive when you are young and healthy and only associate with others whose situation and condition are the same as yours. However, when you frequently encounter old people dying from various terminal diseases or when you become sick yourself, you will reflect that you too must die just as others do. Then you will also easily be able to understand that your body and mind are oppressive.

When one has yet to empirically observe that mental and physical phenomena incessantly arise and disappear, it will be difficult to recognize that mental and physical phenomena are oppressive. However, if you continuously observe arising and disappearing mental and physical phenomena, you will experience that they do not even last for the twinkling of an eye but incessantly arise and disappear. They are oppressive because of their constant arising and disappearance; they are impermanent and die or pass away all the time. They are oppressive because their constant arising and disappearing is torture. Then you will be easily able to understand that they are detestable, dreadful, and unsatisfactory. If new phenomena did not come into existence to replace old ones, there would be nothing but death. The fact that we can never be sure that we will not die within a certain period of time is also distressing. By experiencing various types of pain and distress, we are able to understand that the mind and body are nothing but a mass of suffering.

By noting the physical phenomena involved in the rise and fall of the abdomen, sitting, bending, stretching, moving, and so on, you can experience that they instantly vanish even as you observe them. Because this incessant arising and disappearing is frightening or dreadful, one understands that mental and physical phenomena are oppressive. They are frightening or dreadful because they vanish or die in one moment. They are dreadful because they are painful or unpleasant. They are all suffering and unsatisfactory. Having had this experience and understanding, one understands that past and future physical phenomena are the same as present ones. They are constantly oppressive, frightening, dreadful, and unsatisfactory. For more detail refer to the section above on the comprehension of impermanence.

Comprehension of not-self

Theories about the self

Ordinary people who have not yet come to a personal, empirical understanding of the true nature of mental and physical phenomena have a very deep-seated, deluded belief that there is a self within the body. Those who hold such beliefs describe the self in various ways in their scriptures.[505] According to these sources, the self is the owner of the body. It possesses the entire body, or certain parts of the body comprised of the five sensory faculties (*buddhindriya*: eye, ear, nose, tongue, and skin), the five functional faculties (*kammindriya*: mouth, hands, feet, sex organs, and anus), the faculty that is both sensory and functional consciousness (*ubhayindriya*), and so on.

In order to refute this belief in a self, the Buddha explained in discourses such as the *Anattalakkhaṇa Sutta*[506] that:

> Bhikkhus, form is [not-self]. For if, bhikkhus, form were self, this form would not lead to affliction, and it would be possible to have it of form: "Let my form be thus; let my form not be thus."[507]

In the Hindu text called the *Vīmaṃsā*, the so-called self is described as the agent or doer. The text provides the example of using a sword or saw to cut something as an illustration of this: Although one uses a tool such as a sword or a saw to cut something, the actual "cutter" is a person, oneself. In the same way, when one uses the "tools" of the eyes, ears, limbs, and so on to perform actions such as seeing, hearing, walking, standing, sitting, sleeping, bending, stretching, and so on, the self is the actual agent or doer. To remove this delusion, the *Abhidhammatthavibhāvinī* (a subcommentary on Abhidhamma) and the commentaries say:

> This indicates that there is no doer or agent other than the law of causality of phenomena.[508]

> When moving forward, ignorant people delude themselves that it is the self that moves, or that it is the self that accomplishes the movement, or that it is "I" who moves, or that it is "I" who accomplishes the movement.[509]

> There is no self inside that looks ahead or looks to the side . . . There is no self inside that bends or stretches.[510]

In Vīmaṃsā and Sankhyā texts, the soul is described as the agent that feels pleasure and pain. Thus they identify feeling itself with the self. To help eliminate this type of delusion, the commentary on the *Satipaṭṭhāna Sutta*[511] says:

> Who feels? There is not any individual, being, or person who feels. Thus one realizes that feeling itself is what feels the pleasure associated with pleasant sense objects and so on. We conventionally say with regard to the appearance of feeling, "I feel."[512]
>
> In order to point out that there is no doer apart from actual phenomena, the commentary says that feeling itself is what feels.[513]

They [the Vīmaṃsā and Sankhyā texts] also describe the self as: a permanent resident (*nivāsi*) that lasts forever, even after the body that is its home is destroyed; a commander (*sayamvasi*) that controls the entire body with its physical organs and faculties; or a superintendent (*adhiṭṭhāyaka*) that makes all arrangements. Thus they sometimes identify the self with just one of the five aggregates, sometimes with two, sometimes with three, sometimes with four, and sometimes with all five. Saccaka, a well-known wandering ascetic during the Buddha's time, identified the self with all of the five aggregates. As he once said to the Buddha:

> I assert thus, Master Gotama: "Material form is my self, feeling is my self, perception is my self, mental formations are my self, consciousness is my self."[514]

Overcoming the sense of self

Burmese people also have more or less the same deluded sense of self that one finds in these Hindu texts. They believe of the self that: it is what sees, hears, and so on; it is what walks, stands, sits, lies down, bends, stretches, speaks, and so on; it is what experiences pleasure and pain; it is what can see, go, and so on each time there is a desire; or that it is a truly existing soul, ego, or self that is permanent and indestructible. Even if they repeatedly reflect, "There is no self that can exercise complete control but only mental and physical phenomena that constantly arise and disappear," they are unable to completely eliminate their deep-seated belief in a self.

When one notes each arising mental and physical phenomenon, what one comes to experience within a short time is that there are only mental and physical phenomena that arise and disappear. There is no self or entity that exercises complete control. Thus one can clearly ascertain that there is no self but only mental and physical phenomena that constantly arise and pass away. When one clearly experiences the conditioned and instantaneous appearance and disappearance of the physical phenomena involved in rising, falling, sitting, bending, stretching, moving, and so on, one understands that: even if one doesn't want these physical phenomena to arise, one cannot prevent them from doing so—they will arise when all the necessary causes and conditions come together; even if one doesn't want these physical phenomena to disappear, one cannot prevent them from doing so—they will disappear when it is "their time;" there is no entity that possesses any control over these appearing and disappearing physical phenomena; there is no entity that is permanent and everlasting; there is no entity that carries out one's desires. These physical phenomena do not comprise a controlling entity called self, are not a permanent entity, and are not an entity that carries out one's desires. Thus one correctly understands that there is no control, that the self does not exist, that there is no self, and that there is only the nature of not-self.

This understanding might begin to arise when one observes a phenomenon arising against one's will or when one experiences a physical phenomenon disappearing although one wishes it to be lasting and stable. One can only clearly experience the appearance and disappearance of mental and physical phenomena when one observes them. Only then will one understand that there is no permanent self that has control or can carry out one's desires; there are only constantly arising and disappearing phenomena. This is a genuine experience of the characteristic of not-self, or a genuine contemplation of insight knowledge by comprehension. The *Visuddhimagga* explains it this way:

> [Phenomena] all are not-self because they are insubstantial. The phrase "they are insubstantial" means that they lack any substantial self that could be called their owner, the permanent resident, the agent, the feeler, or the commander. That which is impermanent and unsatisfying cannot possibly be the owner, the permanent resident, the agent, and so on, simply because it cannot prevent impermanence or the oppression of arising and passing away.[515]

Because they do not qualify as the owner, permanent resident,

> agent, feeler, or commander, [the five aggregates] are empty. Because they have no owner themselves, they are not-self.[516]

Note that in view of these commentaries it is not possible to develop a true understanding of not-self just by considering it in terms of lack of solid form. One only develops a true understanding of not-self when one realizes that there is no self that could be identified as owner, permanent resident, and so on. Keep in mind that even formless, immaterial deities can still be subject to wrong view of self.

Having understood present physical phenomena as explained above, one comes to understand past physical phenomena. One clearly understands: "Because they cannot exercise any control, are not everlasting, and cannot carry out one's desires, they are not-self. There are only natural phenomena." The other details are the same as for the contemplation of impermanence.

Contemplation of mental phenomena

The contemplations that I have described above with regard to physical phenomena apply also to feeling, perception, mental formations, and consciousness. I will briefly explain how awareness of mental phenomena leads to insight knowledge by comprehension.

Internal and External: The mind that observes internal sense objects is called "internally oriented mind" (*ajjhatta-citta*), while the mind that observes external sense objects is called "externally oriented mind" (*bahiddha-citta*). When one's awareness is free from mental hindrances, one will find that the mind that observes internal and external phenomena disappears at that very moment. One will understand that the mind observing internal phenomena does not become the mind that observes external ones; because the mind observing internal phenomena vanishes, it is impermanent. And the mind observing external phenomena does not become the mind that observes internal ones; because the mind observing external phenomena vanishes, it is impermanent.

Coarse and Subtle: When a coarse mental state turns into a subtle mental state, the coarse one does not itself actually turn into the subtle one, nor does a subtle one itself turn into a coarse one. Because they vanish in that very moment, they are impermanent. One understands it in this way.

Inferior and Superior: An inferior mental state that is unwholesome, unprofitable, or defiled does not turn into a superior mental state that is wholesome, profitable, or purified, or vice versa. Because these mental states vanish in that very moment, they are impermanent. One understands it in this way.

Far and Near: When one's attention shifts from an object that is far away to one that is near, or vice versa, one understands that the mind observing a distant object does not turn into the mind that observes a near one, and that the mind observing a near object does not turn into the mind that observes a distant one. Because these minds vanish in that very moment, they are impermanent. One understands it in this way.

Other types of contemplation

One may contemplate impermanence in the following ways mentioned in the *Visuddhimagga*:

> Whatever is impermanent, that is certainly classed as conditioned and so on. In order to enumerate its synonyms or to show several ways of contemplating this, the Pāḷi canon says: "Physical phenomena in the past, future, and present are impermanent, conditioned, causal, vanishing, decaying, disappearing, and ceasing."[517]

There are forty aspects to this contemplation, such as impermanence, distress, disease, and so on. The *Paṭisambhidāmagga* and *Visuddhimagga* divide these aspects among the contemplations of impermanence, unsatisfactoriness, and not-self. I will briefly explain these in the section on insight knowledge of reobservation.

The *Paṭisambhidāmagga* also mentions this kind of brief contemplation: "Birth conditions old age and death. Without birth there is no old age and death."[518] According to this, when observing presently arising mental and physical phenomena, one comes to see their arising, presence, and disappearance. Thus one understands that arising conditions presence and disappearance. Without arising there is no presence and disappearance.

The same is true for past lives: arising (birth) conditioned old age and death, so without arising there would not have been old age and death. Likewise for future lives: arising will condition old age and death, so without arising there will be no old age and death. In this way, one might contemplate the factors in pairs (cause and effect) connected with each of the three periods (past, present, and future) consistent with dependent origination. However, this contemplation is not considered knowledge derived from insight knowledge by comprehension. Instead it is considered part of the preceding insight knowledge that discerns conditionality. As the commentary to the *Paṭisambhidāmagga* explains:

> The passage "old age and death are conditioned by birth" and so on does not refer to knowledge by comprehension but to a brief contemplation of each factor of dependent origination. This is only called knowledge by comprehension in a figurative sense. Thus it is not a form of insight contemplation but only a form of knowledge that discerns conditionality (*dhammaṭṭhitiñāṇa*).[519]

The *Visuddhimagga* mentions other methods for contemplation: the contemplation of mental and physical phenomena, beginning with relinking-consciousness; seven ways of contemplating physical phenomena (*rūpasattaka*); and seven ways of contemplating mental phenomena (*nāmasattaka*).

The first of these is more or less in line with the contemplation described above based on the Pāḷi canon. But the others are based on Dhamma discourses that would be too extensive to cover here. Instead, I will briefly explain the main points that a meditator should learn: the nine factors that help strengthen mental faculties, the seven ways of contemplating physical phenomena, and the seven ways of contemplating mental phenomena.

Strengthening the mental faculties

> Nine factors strengthen the mental faculties: (1) observing the destruction of each and every phenomenon that occurs, (2) accomplishing insight by observing respectfully, (3) making constant effort, (4) creating suitable conditions, (5) recognizing the conditions for concentration, (6) cultivating the factors of enlightenment, (7) having no regard for life and limb, (8) overcoming pain and distress with the help of courageous effort, and (9) not relaxing until the attainment of path and fruition.[520]

I will elaborate briefly on each of these nine factors.

Observe the destruction of each and every phenomenon that occurs: Try to pay attention to the destruction of each and every phenomenon that occurs, even when your insight knowledge is not yet strong enough to do so. Do not consider them to be permanent. Once your noting becomes strong enough to observe destruction, continue to do so without contemplating phenomena in any other way. This will cause your mental faculties to grow stronger and stronger.

Accomplish insight by observing respectfully: In order to see the destruction of phenomena, you must observe respectfully.

Make constant effort: You must constantly note without any breaks.

Create suitable conditions: In order to gain new insight knowledges and strengthen old ones, ensure that these seven conditions are suitable for meditation—place, resort [for alms], conversation, companions, food, weather, and bodily posture. Live in a suitable place, go for alms in a suitable place, make suitable conversation, associate with suitable companions, eat suitable food, seek suitable weather, and assume a suitable bodily posture.

Recognize the conditions for concentration: Try to remember what conditions led to strong concentration in the past and arouse those conditions.

Cultivate the factors of enlightenment: Develop the factors of rapture, effort, and investigation when your mind is lax, and the factors of tranquility, concentration, and equanimity when overly excited.

Have no regard for life and limb: Make courageous effort without worrying about life and limb.

Overcome pain and distress with the help of courageous effort: Deal with any kind of pain or distress that arises as a result of intensive practice by noting it with steadfast diligence.

Do not relax until attaining path and fruition: Continue to practice, without giving up, until you attain those supramundane states of path knowledge and fruition knowledge you have yet to attain.

If your practice becomes stagnant, focus on trying to cultivate whichever of these nine factors is lacking.

Seven ways to contemplate physical phenomena

Taking up and putting down

Relinking consciousness is called "taking up" (*ādāna*), because it takes up the burden of the body in a new life. Death consciousness is called "putting down" (*nikkhepana*), because it puts down the burden of the body from the old life. Seeing the physical phenomena that occur between birth and death in this life as impermanent, unsatisfying, and not-self is a type of contemplation referred to as "taking up and putting down" (*ādānanikkhepana*), meaning that with it one clearly sees the three characteristics.

After experiencing the appearance and disappearance of physical phenomena that one directly observes, one reflects that all physical phenomena in this life from birth until death are impermanent because they appear and disappear in the same way that the phenomena one directly observes in the present moment do. They are impermanent because they do not stay the same; they change and deteriorate. They are impermanent because they do not last for even a moment. They are impermanent because they are the opposite of permanence and refute any claim to permanence. These are four ways of contemplating impermanence.

It is as if the phenomena, being correctly observed to be impermanent by the meditator, confess: "We are indeed impermanent, even though you thought that we were otherwise. It is true that we are impermanent." This is why we say that phenomena refute any claim to permanence (*niccapaṭikkhepa*). In the same way, we can understand that phenomena refute any claim to satisfactoriness or self.

The appearance of physical phenomena transforms into their presence or aging, and their presence or aging transforms into their disappearance or death. So one may contemplate that all physical phenomena in this life, up until death, are just like the ones that one has empirically observed. They are unsatisfactory because they are constantly oppressed by appearance and disappearance. They are unsatisfactory because they are not stable but are unbearable due to their appearance and disappearance. They are unsatisfactory because they are the basis of all mental and physical pain. They are unsatisfactory because they are the opposite of satisfaction and refute any claim to satisfactoriness.

To wish that physical phenomena that do arise will not arise is an impossible wish. To wish that physical phenomena that have arisen will not age is an impossible wish. To wish that physical phenomena that are aging will not disappear is an impossible wish. Thus one may reflect that all of the physical phenomena in this life are empty of self, just like the ones that one has empirically observed. They are empty of anything that can be identified as "I," anything that is everlasting, that performs all activities, that feels pleasure and pain, or that wills things to happen. Phenomena are like a deserted village where no one lives. They are not-self because they do not belong to anyone, there is no "I" who owns them, and they are no one's property. They are also not-self because they do not obey anyone's will and, not obeying anyone's will, they deny any claim to self.

This is the first way of contemplating physical phenomena.

The three universal characteristics

Some think that they should contemplate the three universal characteristics based on knowledge gained through reading or reflection, simply by reciting "impermanence, unsatisfactoriness, not-self," without any direct experience of the appearance and disappearance of mental and physical phenomena. They think that this is the only way to "put the three universal characteristics on mind and body." But this isn't true.

In reality, one understands that mental and physical phenomena are impermanent when one notes them the moment they occur and sees that they arise and pass away since they disappear once they have arisen. They are unsatisfactory because they are constantly oppressed by appearance and disappearance. They are not-self because they do not obey anyone's will. This is how to use empirical knowledge to "put the three universal characteristics on mind and body." Based on this empirical knowledge one inferentially understands that other mental and physical phenomena are exactly the same. This is how to use inferential knowledge to "put the three universal characteristics on mind and body."

The phrase "put the three universal characteristics on mind and body" has this meaning: The characteristic of impermanence is the mode of change or the nonexistence of something that has arisen (*hutvā abhāva*); the characteristic of unsatisfactoriness is the mode of being constantly oppressed by appearance and disappearance (*udayabbhayappaṭipīḷana*); the characteristic of not-self is the mode of being insusceptible to the exercise of mastery (*avasavattana*).

The three universal characteristics are always present in mental and physical phenomena but cannot be experienced until observed. They also cannot be experienced when one first begins to observe phenomena but only when knowledge gained through meditation matures. So it seems as if one "puts the characteristics on mind and body" by observing them with the help of empirical knowledge. That is why the scriptures say that one practices "putting the three characteristics on the mind and body." This is explained in the *Visuddhimagga-mahāṭīkā*:

> The three characteristics are always present, but have gone previously unnoticed. By observing and contemplating them, one seems to put them on the physical phenomena (or on the mind, as the case may be).[521]

The unique characteristics of mental and physical phenomena exist for the three moments of appearance, presence, and disappearance. These characteristics include such qualities as hardness, being felt, perceiving, touching, knowing, or cognizing. We can experience these individually even at the beginning of practice. Thus the scriptures do not say that one has to "put the unique characteristic on mind and body."

On the other hand, universal characteristics are not apparent for the three moments, do not manifest individually, and are not experienced at the beginning of practice, even though they are shared among all mental and physical phenomena. Only when one's insight knowledge matures will one be able to experience them. At that point the experience of universal characteristics is added to the experience of unique characteristics that one is already familiar with. This is why scriptures say that one "puts the universal characteristics on mind and body." The *Visuddhimagga-mahāṭīkā* explains further:

> Unique characteristics, such as the hardness of the earth element, the touch of mental contact and so on, manifest for three moments and are individually apparent, and can thus be well known. In contrast, when one clearly sees the universal characteristics of impermanence and so on (manifesting as passing away, oppression by appearance and disappearance, and not following anyone's will), they appear to be superimposed onto unique characteristics. Therefore, the commentary uses the phrase, "puts the universal characteristics on . . ."[522]

It is unreasonable, based on these references, to advise someone to become familiar with the universal characteristics by reciting or visualizing them before actually observing mental and physical phenomena arise and pass away. By observing mental and physical phenomena as they occur, one sees their actual arising and passing away. Only then does one empirically understand [regarding the mental and physical phenomena that one has directly experienced] and inferentially understand [regarding other phenomena] that, "All mental and physical phenomena are truly impermanent, unsatisfactory, and unamenable to the exercise of control."

Aging and decay in stages

The term "aging and decay in stages" (*vayovuḍḍhatthaṅgama*) refers to the gradual decay of physical phenomena. By dividing the lifecycle of physical phenomena into several stages, we can observe them in terms of impermanence, unsatisfactoriness, and not-self. That is, in the wake of having experienced physical phenomena that one noted arising and passing away, one tends to reflect that the body that existed in one's youth disappeared at that age, without continuing on into middle age, and thus it was impermanent, unsatisfactory, and not-self. Likewise, the body that exists during middle age cannot continue to exist into one's old age, and the body that exists during old age cannot continue to exist into one's next life.

These days few people live to be one hundred years old. According to the commentaries, however, we are supposed to have a life span of one hundred years. So if we divide a hundred year life into ten stages of ten years each, we can reflect that the body that existed during the first ten years of life did not continue into the second ten years but rather disappeared within that first stage, just like the physical phenomena that one notes now do. Thus that body was impermanent, unsatisfactory, and not-self. The same applies to the body in the second stage of ten years, and so on.

We can further divide the lifespan of one hundred years into twenty stages of five years each, twenty-five stages of four years each, fifty stages of two years each, or one hundred stages of one year each. We can then divide each year into three seasons of four months each or six stages of two months each. We can divide each month into two stages: the waxing and the waning of the moon. We can divide each day into two stages (day and night) or six stages (three periods of daytime and three periods of night). In this way, we may reflect that the body in each and every stage does not continue into the next stage. Therefore it is impermanent, unsatisfactory, and not-self.

This type of reflection is an inferential contemplation of the body based on empirical contemplation. However, the *Visuddhimagga* explains how the contemplation can be both inferential and empirical at the same time:[523]

> The physical phenomena involved in moving forward disappear in that very moment and do not continue into moving backward. Those involved in moving backward do not continue into looking ahead; they disappear. Those involved in looking ahead do not continue into looking to the side; they disappear. Those involved in looking to the side do not continue into bending one's limbs; they disappear. Those involved in bending one's limbs do not continue into stretching; they disappear. Thus the three universal characteristics of impermanence, unsatisfactoriness, and not-self are "put on (the body)."[524]

The commentarial explanation is given in this order for the purpose of illustration only, and not for practice. It is not necessary to memorize and follow the exact order mentioned above, since the sequence of successive activities cannot be controlled. The activity of moving backward, for example, is not necessarily followed by the activity of looking ahead. Any other activity, such as moving forward, swaying, looking to the side, bending, stretching, and so on, can follow it. Looking ahead is not necessarily followed by looking to the side. Walking forward and so on can follow it. Looking to the side is not necessarily followed by bending and bending is not necessarily followed by stretching. Going forward, swaying, and so on can follow them.

An insight meditator should note physical activities in the order that they actually occur. When one empirically observes the disappearance of these movements, understanding of their impermanent, unsatisfactory, and not-self nature will arise clearly and without deliberation.

When walking one can observe that the physical phenomena involved in taking a step with the right foot do not continue into taking a step with the left foot, and the physical phenomena involved in taking a step with the left foot do not continue into taking a step with the right foot. Because they disappear, one after the other, within one step, they are impermanent, unsatisfactory, and not-self. One will clearly understand this without deliberately pondering it, even while noting.

The physical phenomena involved in the lifting movement of even a single step do not continue into the pushing forward movement, the physical phenomena involved in the pushing forward movement do not continue into the dropping movement, and the physical phenomena involved in the dropping movement do not continue into the lifting movement of the other foot that follows. Because they disappear while being lifted, pushed forward, or dropped, they are impermanent, unsatisfactory, and not-self. One will clearly understand this without deliberately pondering it, even while noting.

At the peak of insight knowledge by comprehension, six segments in each step may become obvious: lifting the foot (*uddharaṇa*), pulling it even with the other foot (*atiharaṇa*), pushing it forward in front of the other foot (*vītiharaṇa*), dropping the foot (*sajjana*), touching the ground (*sannikkhepana*), and pressing (*sannirumbhana*). Within these six parts of the step, the physical phenomena involved in the lifting movement do not continue into the pulling movement, the physical phenomena involved in the pulling movement do not continue into the pushing forward movement, the physical phenomena involved in the pushing forward movement do not continue into the dropping movement, the physical phenomena involved in the dropping movement do not continue into the touching, the physical phenomena involved in the touching do not continue into the pressing, and the physical phenomena involved in the pressing do not continue into the next lifting movement of the other foot. Because they disappear one after the other or one segment after another in that very moment, they are impermanent, unsatisfactory, and not-self. One will clearly understand this without deliberately pondering it, even while noting. The Pāli passage relevant to this has been explained in chapter 4.[525]

When one is able to clearly observe and understand each activity that arises in this way, insight knowledge by comprehension has reached its peak and is leading into the next stage of knowledge, insight knowledge of arising and passing away. As the *Visuddhimagga* says:

> When a meditator sees conditioned phenomena in this way, segment by segment, his or her contemplation of the body is subtle and refined.[526]

This means that insight knowledge by comprehension regarding physical phenomena becomes refined and reaches its peak when one can clearly see and understand that the physical phenomena of going forward do not continue into going backward, or that they do not continue from one of the six parts of the step into the next. This is the subtlest form of this insight, the culmination of insight knowledge by comprehension.

One might think: "The other types of contemplation that will be described in the sections that follow this one, such as comprehension of nutrition (*āhārasammasana*), must certainly be subtler and more refined than this one." But this assumption is incorrect. Just because one type of contemplation is mentioned later than another does not mean it is any more refined. They are only described in different sections because they cannot be described together. In practice, if one sees phenomena in one of these ways, one also sees them in the other ways. So it isn't necessary to practice them separately, one after another, in the order in which they are described. Thus it is correct to say that this contemplation is subtle and refined.

Moreover, insight knowledge by comprehension reaches its peak for people of average abilities when they observe the process of one action following another, as a whole. This can happen, for example, when they realize that the physical phenomena involved in moving forward do not continue into moving backward, and so on. For those whose abilities are above average, insight knowledge by comprehension reaches its peak when they see the process involved in a single action occurring stage by stage, such as observing the six parts of a single step.

The commentary explains the seven ways of contemplating mental phenomena separately from physical phenomena only for the sake of giving a clear theoretical presentation. In practice, one should observe whatever phenomena become obvious, whether mental or physical, in whatever order they happen to occur. Thus it is possible to observe mental phenomena as well as physical phenomena. This is why one is advised, in the description of contemplating mental phenomena, to note the mental phenomena that are themselves aware of physical phenomena. This does not mean that one stops contemplating physical phenomena in order to contemplate mental phenomena. In reality, both types of contemplation are accomplished simultaneously.

This is the second way of contemplating physical phenomena.

Materiality arising from nutriment

> Materiality arising from nutriment (*āhāramaya rūpa*) can be known through the effects of being hungry or feeling full.

> When hungry, the body becomes worn out and fatigued. It looks ugly like a burnt tree stump or a crow crouched in a basket full of charcoal. On the other hand, when the body is well fed, it appears bright, soft, smooth, and pleasing to the touch. When a meditator observes these physical phenomena associated with being hungry or being full, he or she understands that the physical phenomena associated with being hungry do not continue into the stage of being full; they disappear while being hungry. The physical phenomena associated with being full do not continue into the stage of being hungry again; they disappear while being full. Therefore, a meditator understands that the physical phenomena generated by nutrition are impermanent, unsatisfactory, and not-self.[527]

This is how to contemplate physical phenomena in terms of nutrition. It is the third way of contemplating physical phenomena.

Materiality arising from temperature

> Materiality arising from temperature (*utumaya rūpa*) can be known through the effects of heat and cold. When it is hot, the body becomes worn out, fatigued, and unattractive. When it is cool, the body appears bright, soft, smooth, and pleasing to the touch. [When a meditator observes these physical phenomena associated with heat or cold, she or he] understands that the physical phenomena associated with heat do not continue into those associated with cold; they disappear while feeling hot. The physical phenomena associated with cold do not continue into those associated with heat; they disappear while feeling cold. Therefore, the meditator understands that the physical phenomena generated by temperature are impermanent, unsatisfactory, and not-self.[528]

This is the fourth way of contemplating physical phenomena.

Kamma-generated materiality[529]

> Kamma-generated materiality (*kammaja rūpa*) can be known as the sense doors that lead to mental contact: the eye door, ear door, nose door, tongue door, body door, and mind door. The body door consists of forty-four constituent physical phenomena: a set of ten kamma-generated phenomena related to the body, a set of ten kamma-generated phenomena related to gender, and twenty-four supportive phenomena resulting from temperature, consciousness, and nutrition. The other sense doors consist of fifty-four constituent physical phenomena: the forty-four included in the body door, plus a set of ten additional kamma-generated phenomena related to the particular sensitivity of the eye, ear, nose, tongue, or mind, respectively.[530]

If during a moment of seeing one is aware of the sensitive eye as a whole, we can say that one experiences the eye door with all of its fifty-four constituent physical phenomena. But it is impossible to be aware of each and every individual constituent. The commentary itself does not intend this. That is why it says that kamma-generated materiality should be known in the form of the sense doors that lead to mental contact. Some people may think that the only way to fully know the constituent phenomena of the sense doors is to analyze them all in detail according to the enumeration above. This is not true. No one but an omniscient buddha would be able to do this.

Moreover, even if it were possible to identify and enumerate each and every phenomenon involved in a moment of seeing, it would not be necessary. This is because the purpose of insight is to eliminate the field of latent defilements. When one truly experiences the impermanent, unsatisfactory, and not-self nature of the sensitive eye, with all of its constituent phenomena, no attachment arises with respect to them, taking them to be permanent, satisfactory, and self. This automatically removes all of the fifty-four physical phenomena associated with the eye from the field of latent defilements. This is why discourses on insight meditation in the Pāḷi scriptures never say that one should observe the constituents enumerated in the various sets of physical phenomena. Instead, the Buddha instructs us to be aware of the eye that includes its fifty-four physical constituents, in this way:

> He understands the eye . . .[531]

> He understands as it really is: "The eye is impermanent."[532]

The *Visuddhimagga* also instructs us to be aware of physical phenomena as a whole and not of the different sets of physical constituents generated by nutrition, temperature, and consciousness that it enumerates. So with regard to kamma-generated physical phenomena, it should be clear that when one experiences the sensitive eye, one automatically experiences all fifty-four of its constituents as well.

> Contemplating physical phenomena as a whole, one realizes: "The physical phenomena of the eye door disappear then and there and do not continue into those of hearing. The same is true for those of the ear door, nose door, tongue door, body door, and mind door. Thus the three universal characteristics of impermanence, unsatisfactoriness, and not-self are 'put on [the kamma-generated physical phenomena].'"[533]

Again, this commentarial passage describes phenomena in this particular order only for the purpose of illustration, and not for practice. So it is not necessary to practice observing phenomena in this order, since seeing is not necessarily followed by hearing but may also be followed by smelling and so on.

If seeing is followed by smelling, for example, an ordinary person will have the delusion that the body that exists during the moment of seeing continues to exist during the following moment of smelling. Or such a one may think that the seeing itself turns into smelling, that the person who sees is also the one who smells, that it is "I" who see and smell, that it is the same person who sees and smells and so on. These same kinds of delusions arise when seeing is followed by tasting, touching, or thinking. The purpose of insight meditation is to observe mental and physical phenomena as they truly are, from moment to moment, and to uproot the attachment that lies dormant in them. Therefore one should be aware of them in the order that they actually occur, even though they are described here in a particular order for the purpose of illustration.

When one uninterruptedly observes seeing, hearing, and so on, in the order that they occur, one understands that the physical phenomena associated with one moment of one sensory experience do not continue into a subsequent moment of a different sensory experience; they disappear in that moment. Furthermore, when one sensory experience, such as seeing, occurs repeatedly, one understands that the physical phenomena in the first moment of seeing do not continue into the second moment of seeing, those in the second moment of seeing do not last until the third moment of seeing; they disappear in that very moment. One also understands this with regard to hearing and so on. Since one understands that the physical phenomena that arise in a given moment do not continue into the next moment; they disappear in that very moment, one will see physical phenomena, as a whole, to be impermanent, unsatisfactory, and not-self. One will clearly understand this without deliberately pondering it, even while noting.

This is the fifth way of contemplating physical phenomena.

Consciousness-generated materiality

> The consciousness-generated [materiality] manifests during mental states of happiness and unhappiness.[534]

Physical phenomena that are generated by consciousness (*citta-samuṭṭhāna rūpa*) manifest when one feels happy or unhappy. Although the text does not explicitly mention having a neutral feeling, it can also cause physical phenomena to manifest at times when one is not particularly happy or unhappy. When one intends to sit, stand up, bend, stretch, and so on, for example, the physical phenomena will become obvious. In order to illustrate the most obvious cases, I will explain here only the two very distinct states of happiness and unhappiness.

When one observes happiness giving way to unhappiness, one notes and understands the mental state of happiness and the physical comfort that accompanies it, as well as the mental state of unhappiness and the physical discomfort that accompanies it. By noting these phenomena the moment they occur, one understands that the physical phenomena associated with happiness do not continue into unhappiness; they disappear while one is happy. The physical phenomena associated with unhappiness do not continue into happiness; they disappear while one is unhappy. Also when one is aware of mental phenomena, such as the intention to sit, stand up, bend, stretch, and so on, and the physical actions that they give rise to—sitting, standing, bending, stretching, and so on—the moment they occur, one sees that they disappear in that very moment. Thus one understands that consciousness-generated materiality or physical activities are impermanent, unsatisfactory, and not-self. One will clearly understand this without deliberately pondering it, even while noting.

This is the sixth way of contemplating physical phenomena.

The *Visuddhimagga* illustrates for meditators who observe and understand the three universal characteristics of consciousness-generated materiality in the aforementioned way the shortness of conditioned phenomena:

> Life, person, pleasure, pain—just these alone
> Join in one conscious moment that flicks by.[535]

All phenomena, such as life, happiness, unhappiness, and the body, are not the self, have nothing to do with a self, and are not permanent. They are merely separate phenomena that appear and disappear accordingly. Because they only last for one mind-moment or because they can only live for a mind-moment, their lives are incredibly fast and short.

> Gods, though they live for four-and-eighty thousand
> Eons, are not the same for two such moments.
> Ceased aggregates of those dead or alive
> Are all alike, gone never to return;[536]

We can observe the phenomena that constitute the experiences of seeing, hearing, bending, stretching, and so on disappearing in each moment and never returning again. Once they vanish, they are gone forever, just like the last mental and physical phenomena at the moment of death.

> And those that break up meanwhile, and in future,
> Have traits no different from those ceased before.[537]

The way mental and physical phenomena have disappeared in the past and the way they will disappear in the future is no different from the way they disappear in the present—it is exactly the same. Therefore a meditator who empirically experiences the disappearance of mental and physical phenomena while meditating can conclude that these phenomena also disappeared in the past and they will also disappear in the future, just as they do in the present.

> No [world is] born if [consciousness is] not
> Produced; when that is present, then it lives;
> When consciousness dissolves, the world is dead:
> The highest sense this concept will allow.[538]

There is no consciousness that exists before it has actually arisen. Therefore a being cannot live when consciousness has yet to arise but only when a moment of consciousness is actually present. So we only live in each present moment of consciousness. Past moments no longer exist anywhere. They never return. They are gone forever, just like the dead consciousness of one who has died. This is why the cessation of each moment of consciousness is said to be a being's death. But it appears that the being conceptually referred to as Mr. or Mrs. So-and-So is really alive in an ultimate sense. This is because he or she is alive in each individual moment of consciousness, moment after moment. If no new consciousness arose when the last one disappeared, the being would be dead in a conceptual sense. So a meditator understands that the disappearance of each moment of consciousness is like death, and he or she can conclude that death is no different from the observable momentary disappearance of consciousness.

> No store of broken states, no future stock;
> Those born balance like seeds on needle points.[539]

Extinct phenomena have vanished completely, leaving behind no trace. Future phenomena do not gather, hidden in someplace, nor are they already there before they appear. Only momentarily arising phenomena exist and even these phenomena do not last long. If a mustard seed is put on the tip of a needle, it will fall off within a moment. Likewise phenomena disappear the very moment after they have arisen.

> Breakup of states is foredoomed at their birth;
> Those present decay, unmingled with those past.
> They come from nowhere, break up, nowhere go;
> Flash in and out, as lightning in the sky.[540]

Generally, not until the mature level of insight knowledge of arising and passing away does one begin to clearly see the fleeting nature of conditioned phenomena as described in this last quote. Those of average ability will only be able to observe this at the higher stages of insight knowledge. On the other hand, those with above average abilities may begin to see phenomena this way during insight knowledge by comprehension. However, it is not expected that everyone will see phenomena this way at this stage.

This is the sixth way of contemplating physical phenomena.

Inanimate objects

The term "inanimate objects" (*dhammatārūpa*) refers to objects, such as clothing, mats, pots, dishes, soil, water, air, fire, posts, trees, rocks, gold, silver, and so on. In Pāḷi these things are called "lifeless" (*anindriyabaddha*), because they lack the life-controlling faculty (*jīvitindriya*). If one observes them when one sees, hears, smells, or touches them, one sees that they momentarily arise and pass. Then one understands that they are impermanent, unsatisfactory, and not-self.

Moreover, by comparing them with the internal or external physical phenomena that one has experienced, one inferentially understands that those external physical phenomena that one cannot directly experience are also all impermanent, unsatisfactory, and not-self. This is how one should observe inanimate objects.

This is the seventh way of contemplating physical phenomena.

Seven ways to contemplate the mind

The mind as a whole

As mentioned above in the section on seven ways of contemplating physical phenomena, one first observes a physical phenomenon and then becomes aware of that very act of observing by labeling it, "observing, observing" or "noting, noting" or "knowing, knowing." Then one understands its universal characteristics of being impermanent, unsatisfactory, and not-self. In this way one observes the mind as a whole (*kalāpa*).

Pairs of phenomena

Every time one observes a physical phenomenon, one also notes the mental phenomenon of observing itself. Thus one will alternate between noting a physical phenomenon and noting a mental phenomenon. As one observes phenomena in pairs (*yamaka*), one will understand that they are impermanent, unsatisfactory, and not-self.

There is some distinction between observation of the mind as a whole and observation of pairs of phenomena. When observing the mind as a whole one observes the mind as a whole, without distinguishing any of the individual mental constituents involved, such as consciousness, mindfulness, insight, concentration, energy, mental contact, volition, feeling, and so on. This is called "contemplation of the mind as a whole" (*kalāpasammasana*). When observing pairs of phenomena one mainly observes one of the particular mental constituents involved in observing the body, such that as one is observing the mind, one is aware of one of its constituents, such as mental contact, feeling, volition, perception, mindfulness, insight, concentration, effort, and so on. Comprehending mental phenomena by distinguishing specific mental constituents is called "contemplation of pairs of phenomena" (*yamakasammasana*).

Regarding the contemplation of the mind: "observing the mind" refers to the mind that is the leader of mental phenomena. But one must also observe mental factors that accompany the mind as well, such as mental contact, feeling, volition, perception, mindfulness, insight, concentration, energy, and so on. This is why the subcommentary says, ". . . explained under the heading 'mind'" (*cittasīsena hi niddeso*).

Momentary nature

Every time that one observes a physical phenomenon, one observes one's noting mind with a second noting. One then observes the second noting with a third noting, the third noting with a fourth noting, and finally, the fourth noting with a fifth noting. Thus each observation of a physical phenomenon is followed by four observations of the noting mind that follow in sequence. In this way, one will understand them to be impermanent, unsatisfactory, and not-self. By observing four successive occurrences of the noting mind, one comes to comprehend its momentary nature (*khaṇika*), thus this way of noting is called "contemplation of momentary nature" (*khaṇikasammasana*).

Successive mental objects

Every time one observes a physical phenomenon, one observes the mind that notes it with a second noting. One then observes the second noting with a third noting, the third noting with a fourth noting, the fourth noting with a fifth noting, the fifth noting with a sixth noting, the sixth noting with a seventh noting, the seventh noting with an eighth noting, the eighth noting with a ninth noting, the ninth noting with a tenth noting, and, finally, the tenth noting with an eleventh noting. Thus each noting of a physical phenomenon will be followed by ten successive notings of subsequent noting minds. In this way one will understand them to be impermanent, unsatisfactory, and not-self. Thus this way of noting is called "successive" (*paṭipāṭi*). [The *Ariyāvaṃsakathā* says]:

> It is possible to successively observe for a whole day. However, it is sufficient to note just ten [successive] noting minds in order to comprehend the material meditation subject and the immaterial meditation subject. Therefore, observation should be stopped at the tenth noting mind.[541]

After observing the tenth noting mind, one should once again observe a physical object and then the ten subsequent noting minds that follow. One should continue in this way, following every observation of a physical object with the observation of ten noting minds. One need not observe the eleventh noting mind or beyond.

Practical Advice

At this point I would like to offer some practical advice, in the same way that the authors of the commentaries do. None of the methods of observation described in this section are meant to serve as instructions for one's practice. Instead they are meant to serve as criteria by which one may evaluate insights gained by practicing according to the guidelines given in chapter 5.

Therefore a meditator should practice only by observing distinctly arising mental and physical phenomena, and clearly see them as they are. You should not try to practice according to the methods described as part of these sections on the seven ways to contemplate physical phenomena and the seven ways to contemplate the mind. If a meditator were to do this, he or she would become unnecessarily preoccupied about whether the way he or she is practicing is correct and in harmony with such-and-such a method, and his or her mind would wander. You would then fail to observe that your wandering mind interferes with your practice, and thus your observation would no longer be continuous. This in turn would prolong your development of mindfulness, concentration, and insight knowledge.

Moreover, if a beginner were to try to observe a succession of noting minds in this way, his or her object may gradually grow faint and unclear. Then he or she would have to search for a new object, which would be like establishing his or her meditation all over again. The practice would stagnate. This point is confirmed by the *Visuddhimagga-mahāṭīkā*, which says:

> Thus one may have to begin one's practice of mindfulness over again and again.[542]

So just follow the practice guidelines given in chapter 5. In due time your observation of physical phenomena followed by observation of successive minds that note them will gradually increase to two, three, or more notings by itself. But the Pāḷi canon and its commentaries only mention observation of one physical phenomenon and one subsequent mental phenomenon when they explain the development of insight knowledge of dissolution. Therefore we can conclude that simply observing one physical phenomenon and one subsequent noting mind is sufficient for the attainment of path knowledge and fruition knowledge.

If you eventually master the practice and gain fruition absorption as a result of path knowledge and fruition knowledge, you can then try to observe successive noting minds according to the methods described in this section. At that point you may be able to note hundreds or thousands of successive noting minds without them fading away. But, for beginning meditators who have yet to attain path knowledge and fruition knowledge, it is best not to attempt to practice this way.

Removing wrong view

If you think that you are practicing, or that the practice is yours, then the practice is not free from personal identification and cannot be considered to be removing erroneous view of personality. Of course, even if your view has been purified to some extent by the first two stages of purification, this wrong view may still return as long as the fetter of wrong view has not yet been uprooted with path knowledge.

> It is true that one is purified of wrong view because one has

> attained purification of view and purification by overcoming doubt. However, the commentary says [that meditators are deluded that they are the ones who are practicing, or that they practice] with reference to the subtle wrong view that has yet to be uprooted with path knowledge.[543]

So even after attaining insight knowledge by comprehension, you can still experience subtle forms of wrong view and doubt. But if you practice in such a way that you are able to understand that both the observed object and the observing subject are conditioned phenomena devoid of self, your practice is considered to be removing wrong view (*diṭṭhi-ugghāṭana*). This is a very profound way of contemplating not-self. As the *Visuddhimagga* and the *Visuddhimagga-mahāṭīkā* say:

> One practices in such a way that one sees conditioned phenomena [both subject and object] to be not-self. Such practice is called removing wrong view.[544]

> When the contemplation of not-self grows sharp, powerful, and clear, the other two [contemplations of impermanence and unsatisfactoriness] follow it. This removes wrong view.[545]

Removing conceit

If you are proud of your practice, thinking, "I am able to practice well, I have learned to practice properly," then your practice cannot be considered removing conceit (*māna-samugghātana*). On the other hand, if your practice causes you to understand that both the observed object and observing subject are impermanent conditioned phenomena, then your practice is considered to be removing conceit. This is a very profound way of contemplating impermanence.

> Seeing impermanence leads to the removal of conceit.[546]

> When contemplation of impermanence grows sharp, powerful, and clear, the other two [contemplations of unsatisfactoriness and not-self] follow it. This removes conceit.[547]

Removing attachment

If you are attached to your practice, thinking that you observe well, that your practice is going well, or that your noting is good, then your practice is not yet considered to be removing attachment (*nikantipariyādāna*), because it cannot remove attachment. On the other hand, if you practice in such a way that you are able to understand that both the observed object and observing subject conditioned phenomena that constantly arise and disappear, then your practice is considered to be removing attachment. This is a very profound way of contemplating unsatisfactoriness. As the *Visuddhimagga* and the *Visuddhimagga-mahāṭīkā* say:

> Seeing unsatisfactoriness leads to the removal of attachment.[548]

> When contemplation of unsatisfactoriness grows sharp, powerful, and clear, the other two [contemplations of impermanence and not-self] follow it. This removes attachment.[549]

Insight Knowledge of Arising and Passing Away

> What exists is conditioned. Remove [attachment to it] and gain equanimity. This [passage from the Uparipaṇṇāsa of the Majjhima Nikāya] refers to equanimity that arises from contemplation [of impermanence, unsatisfactoriness, and not-self]. This is the equanimity associated with insight. It is wisdom in an ultimate sense, and it has two functions.
>
> "Suppose a man sees something that appears to be a snake lying inside his house at twilight. Not sure whether it really is a snake or not, the man goes to check. Once he sees that there are three marks on its neck, he becomes equanimous [because he is not concerned anymore about whether it is a snake or not because he has come to know]. In the same way, once a meditator sees the three universal characteristics of conditioned phenomena using knowledge by comprehension, he or she becomes equanimous regarding the three characteristics of conditioned phenomena. This is insight equanimity (*vipassanupekkhā*).[550]

> "I abandon [the presently existing five aggregates]." Thus does a meditator attain equanimity.[551]

Eliminating attachment

At the beginning of practice, when one's knowledge is still weak, one cannot yet see that mental and physical phenomena are impermanent, unsatisfactory, and not-self. Therefore one takes them to be permanent, satisfactory, and self. As a result of this, attachment[552] can still arise. However, once one realizes their three universal characteristics with mature insight knowledge by comprehension, one will no longer take them to be permanent, satisfactory, and self. Thus desire, attachment, or lust will no longer be able to arise. It is said that this understanding due to which attachment and lust can no longer arise also removes the attachment and lust that could have arisen with regard to mental and physical phenomena.

Once one has contemplated the impermanent, unsatisfactory, and not-self nature of the mental and physical phenomena that one has observed and those that one has not observed, one can ascertain beyond any doubt that these phenomena are impermanent, unsatisfactory, and not-self. Thus one will no longer be concerned about the way things happen. While one observes mental and physical phenomena as they occur, by seeing their beginning and end, one develops an equanimity associated with insight knowledge that clearly understands arising and passing away. At this point one begins to develop insight knowledge of arising and passing away (*udayabbayañāṇa*). As the *Paṭisambhidhāmagga* explains:

> Seeing how present phenomena change is knowledge of arising and passing away.[553]

Whenever one practices, one will see the beginning of each phenomenon, appearing as if emerging from somewhere or sticking its head in somewhere. One also will see phenomenon ending, disappearing suddenly like the flame of a candle when it is blown out. Seeing the arising and passing away of phenomena in this way is called "insight knowledge of arising and passing away."

> Currently arising physical phenomena are called "present physical phenomena." Their initial arising is called "arising" (*udaya*), and their changing into something else is called "passing away" (*vaya*). The knowledge that penetrates arising and passing away is called "knowledge of arising and passing away."[554]

> To gain insight into arising and passing away, one should contemplate the present phenomena, process-by-process or moment-by-moment, rather than past or future phenomena. This is why the Buddha said, "See changes in present phenomena, and so on."
>
> The term "arising" refers to phenomena that have come into existence and can be experienced. The term "present physical phenomena" refers to the physical phenomena that are currently arising and observed in the three stages of arising, presence, and passing away. However, it is difficult to contemplate such present physical phenomena at the beginning of insight knowledge of arising and passing away. Therefore, begin your insight practice by observing the apparent continuity or duration of present phenomena (*santatipaccuppanna*).[555]

According to the subcommentary, the phrase "currently arising physical phenomena" used in the above passage from the *Paṭisambhidāmagga* refers to present physical phenomena (*khaṇapaccuppanna*). These are present, momentary phenomena that can be observed to have three stages: arising, presence, and passing away. The phrase does not refer to the present in a conventional sense (*addhāpaccuppanna*) or to the continuity of mental and physical processes happening in the present (*santatipaccuppanna*). During the immature stages of insight knowledge of arising and passing away, it is only possible to observe the arising and passing away of present phenomena as a continuity or process. However, when that insight knowledge matures, one will also be able to observe the arising and passing away of present momentary phenomena.

Continuity of processes vs. momentary phenomena

All of the physical phenomena involved in bodily activities, such as the rise and fall of the abdomen, standing up, sitting down, walking, bending, stretching, and so on, are present the moment they occur or are performed. Their initial appearance is called "arising" and their disappearance is called "passing away." During the immature stages of insight knowledge of arising and passing away, one will be able to observe the beginning and end of the overall process of each action, such as the rising, falling, standing up, sitting down, walking, bending, or stretching. That observation is called "seeing present physical phenomena as continuity" (*santatipaccuppannarūpa*). Insight knowledge of arising and passing away of phenomena begins to develop when one begins to see arising and passing away. At that point one will clearly understand, without confusion, that each action is separate from the other, that each action instantaneously arises and disappears without spilling over into the next. One sees, for example, the rising of the abdomen as separate from the falling, the bending of a limb as separate from its stretching, a step taken with the left foot as separate from the next taken with the right, and so on.

In contrast, during the mature stages of insight knowledge of arising and passing away, one observes phenomena as they momentarily happen. As one breathes in, for example, one finds that the rising movement of the abdomen consists of many little movements that happen in stages. In addition one sees that each of these little movements instantaneously and individually disappear, without blending into the next, like the continuous disappearance of individual bubbles formed on the surface of a pond when it rains. One also sees other bodily activities, such as the motion of falling, sitting, walking, bending, stretching, moving, or adjusting the posture, occurring in the same way. At that time, by seeing their beginning and end, one will clearly understand, without confusion, that such movements are constantly arising and passing away. According to the Pāḷi texts, this is the powerful (*balava*) insight knowledge of arising and passing away, which sees the arising and disappearance of momentarily present physical phenomena (*khaṇapaccuppannarūpa*).

In the same way, when one sees, hears, and so on, one will come to see the instantaneous arising and disappearance of visible forms, sounds, and so on, or of the eye-sensitivity, the ear-sensitivity, and so on. When one's insight becomes sharp and swift and is able to see arising and passing away in this momentary manner, one may be unable to label each separate physical phenomenon. In that case, just be mindful of all these phenomena as they are happening, in a relaxed way.

> Feeling that is currently arising is present feeling. Perception that is currently arising is present perception. Mental formations that are currently arising are present mental formations. Consciousness that is currently arising is present consciousness. Their initial appearance is called arising and their changing into

> something else is called passing away. This is called knowledge of arising and passing away.[556]

The feeling involved in seeing, hearing, smelling, tasting, touching, or thinking is present feeling (*paccuppannavedanā*). Likewise, the perception involved in these is present perception (*paccuppannasaññā*), the consciousness involved in these is present consciousness (*paccuppannaviññāṇa*), and the remaining mental factors involved in these are present mental formations (*paccuppannasaṅkhāra*).

Mental formations are factors that assist in the whole process of seeing, hearing, and so on. Among them are: contact (*phassa*) between the mind and sense objects, as if the mind were going toward its objects, or its objects were coming toward the mind; volition (*cetanā*), which seems to rush toward sense objects and arranges the acts of seeing, hearing, and so on; initial application (*vitakka*); sustained application (*vicāra*); rapture or zest (*pīti*); tranquility (*passaddhi*); faith (*saddhā*); mindfulness (*sati*); effort (*vīriya*); concentration (*samādhi*); wisdom (*paññā*); greed or attachment (*lobha*); aversion (*dosa*); delusion (*moha*); conceit (*māna*); restlessness (*uddhacca*); wrong view of self (*diṭṭhi*); doubt (*vicikicchā*); and so on.[557]

The initial appearance of these mental phenomena is arising, and their disappearance is passing away. Understanding, when one sees, hears, and so on, their arising and passing away regarded either as a continuity of processes or as momentary phenomena, is called "insight knowledge of arising and passing away."

Observing the continuity of processes

Suppose one feels stiffness and then finds some relief from it, and then feels pain or itching. In this example, the initial feeling of stiffness, from the time that it begins until it is relieved, is actually a process made up of many distinct moments of stiffness. During the immature stages of insight knowledge of arising and passing away, one will only be able to see the process of that stiffness as a continuous whole. One will not be able to observe the separate, momentary phenomena of stiffness, because they are very similar to each other. To be mindful of the feeling of stiffness as a unitary whole throughout its duration is called "continuity of present feeling" (*santatipaccuppannavedanā*).

The same is true of the second process given in this example, finding relief from stiffness, and of the third process, feeling pain or itching. Thus one will be able to see these three successive processes separately and distinctly. One will also be able to observe the process of perceiving these sense objects as a whole, i.e., the continuity of present perceptions. The consciousness that cognizes these objects is called "the continuity of present consciousness," and the mental formations that manage the actions is called "the continuity of present mental formations." One will also be able to see all of these processes arising and passing away separately and distinctly.

Observing momentary phenomena

At the mature stages of insight knowledge of arising and passing away, one will be able to experience a succession or series of separately arising and disappearing moments of stiffness. One will see, for example, that the stiffness one experiences in one moment arises and passes away separately from that of the next moment that, in turn, is separate from the moment after that, and so on. One will also see relief from the stiffness, and any other processes that follow, such as the processes of perception, seeing consciousness, or mental formations, in the same way.

When one perceives an object, for example, one experiences that perception momentarily happening. That is, one finds that the first moment of perception of the object arises and passes away separately from the second, and so on. In the case of seeing consciousness, one experiences seeing momentarily happening. That is, one finds that the first moment of seeing arises and passes away separately from the second, and so on. In the case of the mental formations, one experiences mental formations momentarily happening. That is, one finds that the first moment of mental formations arises and passes away separately from the second, and so on.

When one's insight becomes sharp and swift and is able to see mental phenomena in this momentary manner, one may be unable to label each separate mental phenomenon. In such cases, just be mindful of all of these mental phenomena that are instantaneously arising and disappearing like a smoothly running machine. The *Paṭisambhidāmagga* mentions many processes that one can observe in this way, such as the six sense doors, the six types of consciousness, the six types of mental contact, the six types of feeling, and so on. But it would be too much to enumerate them all here.

When one experiences mental and physical phenomena that are momentarily arising and disappearing, one can also come to understand them in the following way: "The mental and physical phenomena that are arising and disappearing as one observes them do not exist anywhere before they arise. They do not come from anywhere when they arise, and they do not go anywhere when they disappear. They are not stored anywhere now that they are gone. The truth is that they arise and disappear, right in this place, based on the conditions at this time."

Before one reaches this stage of insight knowledge, one will be deluded with regard to these points. For example when one goes to raise one's arm, one believes that the arm one means to raise already exists. Then, while one is actually raising one's arm, one thinks that it is the same arm that existed before one started raising it. Then, when one lowers one's arm again, one thinks that it is the same arm that one raised before, the same arm that has always existed, unchanged. However, at this stage of insight knowledge, one will no longer fall under these kinds of delusion. This is because one will be able to see all of the momentary phenomena involved in activities such as the rise and fall of the abdomen, sitting, walking, seeing, hearing, and so on. This is the most important aspect of insight knowledge of arising and passing away.

The characteristics of arising and passing away

The explanations above give the criteria by which one can evaluate one's experience of insight knowledge of arising and passing away. Below are a number of textual passages and explanations that are not intended for use in that way but are instead intended to describe the abilities that accompany insight knowledge of arising and passing away.

> If one sees the appearance of the five aggregates, one sees twenty-five characteristics with respect to them. If one sees the disappearance of the five aggregates, one sees twenty-five characteristics with respect to them. If one sees both the appearance and the disappearance of the five aggregates, one sees fifty characteristics with respect to them.[558]

The five characteristics of arising

> With the arising of ignorance, physical phenomena arise. In this way, one sees the causal aspect of the arising of the aggregate of physicality. Similarly, with the arising of craving, volitional

> actions, and nutrition, physical phenomena arise. In these ways, one sees the causal aspect of the arising of the aggregate of physicality. By seeing the characteristic of arising, one sees the arising of the aggregate of physicality. Therefore, if one sees the arising of the aggregate of physicality, one sees these five characteristics.[559]

From this passage, we see that the five characteristics of the arising of physical phenomena are: the ignorance involved in volitional actions performed in past lives (*avijjā*), craving (*taṇhā*), volitional actions that one has performed (*kamma*), nutrition from the food one consumes in this life (*āhāra*), and the arising of present physical phenomena (*nibbatti*).

The five characteristics of disappearance

> With the cessation of ignorance, there is the cessation of physical phenomena. In this way, one sees the causal aspect of the cessation of the aggregate of physicality. Similarly, with the cessation of craving, volitional actions, or nutrition, there is the cessation of physical phenomena. In these ways, one sees the causal aspect of the disappearance of the aggregate of physicality. By seeing the characteristic of change, one sees the disappearance of the aggregate of physicality. Therefore, if one sees the disappearance of the aggregate of physicality, one sees these five characteristics.[560]

From this passage, we see that the five characteristics of the disappearance of physical phenomena are: the disappearance of ignorance because it is uprooted through the path knowledge of arahantship, the disappearance of craving, the disappearance of volitional actions, the absence of nutrition, and the disappearance of present physical phenomena.

The Buddha gave a similar analysis of the five characteristics of appearance and disappearance for the four mental aggregates of feeling, perception, mental formations, and consciousness. The only difference is in regard to the fourth aspect, which is food in the case of the physical aggregate. For the first three mental aggregates—feeling, perception, mental formations—food is replaced by mental contact, and for the last aggregate—consciousness—it is replaced by mental and physical phenomena.

Observing true arising and passing away

Thus ten characteristics of each aggregate have been described: five associated with arising and five with disappearance, giving a total of fifty characteristics for the five aggregates as a group. However, out of these fifty characteristics, only the present arising of the five aggregates can be called "true arising," and only their present disappearance can be called "true passing away." This is because one only develops empirical knowledge by observing the present arising and passing away of phenomena. Realization of the other aspects is only inferential knowledge, which was explained in chapter 4. Inferentially perceived phenomena do not really exist in the moment. One simply reflects about them and realizes that when ignorance, craving, and so on are present, the aggregates of body, feeling, and so forth are also, and when ignorance and so on vanish, the aggregates vanish also. That is why the *Visuddhimagga-mahāṭīkā* says:

> Some teachers say that the arising and passing away of mental aggregates can only be experienced in the conventional present (*addhā*) or as a whole process, but not momentarily. According to them it may even be impossible to see the momentary arising and passing away of mental aggregates.
>
> However, many other teachers say that if one sees the causes of arising and passing away in a general way, regardless of their duration, one does not really see true arising and passing away. One may see arising in the sense that potential for the mental aggregates to come into existence exists due to causes such as ignorance and so on, but that is not really seeing true arising. One may see passing away in the sense that the potential for the mental aggregates to come into existence ceases to exist due to the absence of causes such as ignorance and so on, but that is not really seeing true passing away. In reality, one sees the true arising and passing away of present mental aggregates when one sees them momentarily arising and passing away.
>
> This is reasonable. Insight gradually becomes powerful, sharp, and clear enough to experience momentary arising and passing away by first observing mental and physical phenomena as an entire process.[561]

Here, "to see the present mental aggregates momentarily arising and passing away" refers to the insight consciousness that currently observes objects moment by moment. Technically, we can only really say that one observes present mental phenomena momentarily if the phenomena observe themselves in each moment: in other words, if a single mental phenomenon would have to serve as both subject and object of observation at the same time. Of course, this is impossible, just as it is impossible for the tip of a finger to touch itself. This is why some teachers say that it is impossible to see present mental aggregates momentarily arising and passing away, and it is nearly impossible to refute this argument.

However, the Pāḷi texts explicitly describe how to experience present mental phenomena momentarily as follows:

> Seeing the characteristic of arising, seeing the characteristic of change.[562]

> Known to him these states arose, known they were present, known they disappeared.[563]

The commentaries on the Majjhima and Dīgha Nikāyas explain these passages as follows: the three stages—appearance, presence, and disappearance—of the mental phenomena that have just occurred remain as vivid for the meditator as if they were actually present phenomena. This is because meditators have just observed their sense objects and sense bases. This is why the Buddha says, "the appearance of phenomena is obvious," and so on.

So the argument that a few teachers put forward regarding the impossibility of observing momentary mental phenomena is not actually in harmony with either meditators' experience, nor with the Pāḷi texts and commentaries. This is why the *Visuddhimagga-mahāṭīkā* says that according to these teachers, it might be impossible even to see momentary arising and passing away. So the argument of these few teachers is rejected. The *Visuddhimagga-mahāṭīkā* supports "many teachers," and their view should be considered the generally accepted one (*samānavāda*).

Inferential knowledge

Once one experiences the arising and passing away of present phenomena, one inferentially realizes that past and future phenomena must behave in the same way. One may reflect: "Phenomena in the past, or in past lives, must also have appeared and disappeared. Those in the future, or in future lives, will also appear and disappear in the same way as the present phenomena."

> First, one experiences the arising and passing away of present phenomena. Then, one inferentially realizes the arising and passing away of past and future phenomena.[564]

An insight beginner

Once one is able to observe the arising and passing away of momentarily present mental or physical phenomena, one will understand that phenomena that arise never existed before and that they disappear completely, leaving nothing behind. One will see how they freshly arise and immediately disappear, like bubbles caused by raindrops falling on the surface of a pond, like flashes of lightning in the sky, or like the rhythmic sound of a machine. One will also understand the insubstantiality of phenomena, like gold that magically appears in a conjurer's trick, like a dream that seems real as one dreams it, like the circle of fire that appears when a torch is spun in the dark, like towns and villages created by the *gandhabba*s (celestial musicians) that appear in space, like foam in turbulent water, or like the trunk of a banana tree. It will become obvious to one's awareness that conditioned phenomena are not only devoid of a solid substance but also devoid of anything that could be useful. In this way, one develops immature insight knowledge of arising and passing away. A meditator at this level of vipassanā is called "an insight beginner" (*āraddhavipassaka*).

> Thus one develops insight into arising and passing away, realizing that all phenomena that come into existence are fragile and come to an end. In this way, one gains an immature knowledge of arising and passing away from exactly fifty aspects. Such a person is considered an insight beginner.[565]

Note that according to the *Visuddhimagga-mahāṭīkā*, simply seeing the arising and passing away of phenomena can constitute seeing all fifty aspects.

> The analyses of contemplation of the mind as a whole and so on

are not really true insight. Only the contemplation of arising and passing away is true insight.[566]

The ten corruptions of insight

One's mind wavers due to light, knowledge, and rapture.
The mind is moved by tranquility and happiness.
It shakes due to resolution, energy, and mindfulness,
equanimity along with equilibrium and delight.[567]

During the immature stages of insight knowledge of arising and passing away, one may encounter these ten corruptions of insight (*vipassanupakkilesā*). The *Visuddhimagga* explains which types of meditators tend to experience and which tend not experience these obstacles:

> The obstacles to insight do not arise for noble disciples who have accomplished path knowledge and fruition knowledge, for meditators who are practicing incorrectly, for meditators who stop practicing, or for those who are too lazy to practice. These obstacles arise for meditators who practice properly and continuously, and for those energetic meditators who have reached knowledge of arising and passing away.[568]

Note that the *Mahāṭīkā* says that this passage mentions noble disciples as the "upper limit" of those who would not experience the corruptions of insight. These corruptions would also not arise for those at the higher stages of insight knowledge, such as insight knowledge of disenchantment (*nibbidāñāṇa*) and so on.

Light

Light (*obhāsa*) may arise simply as a result of concentration or, at times, as a result of insight knowledge. It may occur, for example, as a result of concentration when one practices a form of tranquility meditation, such as contemplation of the attributes of the Buddha and so on. It may also occur when an insight meditator is not yet able to be mindful of and distinguish the very swift arising and passing away of mental and physical phenomena. An illustration of the first case can be found in the experience of Anāthapiṇḍika.

The Story of Anāthapiṇḍika

The rich merchant Anāthapiṇḍika first heard about the Buddha at the house of another merchant in Rājagaha. He was so excited that he immediately wanted to go and see the Buddha. But it was already dark and too late to visit, so he decided to stay overnight and go early the next morning. Even so, he could not stop thinking about the Buddha. He woke up three times during the night, and each time he found himself surrounded by light as a result of his contemplation of the Buddha. The light was so bright that he thought that it was dawn and got up. The first two times, he eventually realized that it was not yet daybreak and went back to bed again. But the third time he thought that it really was day and set out alone to see the Buddha. Along the way he passed through a cemetery and happened to step on a corpse. This gave him a fright, which caused his contemplation of the Buddha to weaken, and the light disappeared. Finding himself alone in the dark, he was about to turn back when the celestial being that guarded the cemetery spoke up to encourage him onward:

A hundred [thousand] elephants,
A hundred [thousand] horses,
A hundred [thousand] mule-drawn chariots,
A hundred thousand maidens
Adorned with jewelry and earrings,
Are not worth a sixteenth part
Of a single step forward.[569]

This encouraged him to go on since he felt that he had companions with him and so was not alone. He then resumed his contemplation of the attributes of the Buddha and found himself surrounded by light again. This happened to him three times before he finally reached his destination without further incident.

This story from the commentary to the Saṃyutta Nikāya shows that concentration alone can give rise to light.

As an insight meditator, one may also begin to see sparkling light once insight knowledge that discerns mental and physical phenomena becomes strong. Once one attains insight knowledge that discerns conditionality, one may sometimes see colored lights (green, red, blue, yellow, and so on). But it is only concentration that causes these kinds of lights. One may not only see lights but also inspiring images, such as images of the Buddha, fully enlightened beings, and so on. Since these are generated by concentration, they tend to begin to arise in one's mind at the mature levels of insight knowledge that discerns mental and physical phenomena. One may also encounter them frequently with insight knowledge by comprehension and less frequently at the immature stages of insight knowledge of arising and passing away.

People experience these lights and images in different ways at the different stages of insight knowledge. At the stage of discerning mental and physical phenomena, one cannot yet clearly see light or images arising and passing away. At the stage of discerning conditionality, one can see them arise, but their passing away is not yet clear. One will often lose old objects as new ones arise. With insight knowledge by comprehension, the beginning, middle, and end will all be distinct. After they have arisen, they are clearly present, and then they disappear by changing location, becoming smaller, or fading away. At the stage of insight knowledge of arising and passing away, the object disappears with each noting or by just being aware of it (without labeling it). One will see it suddenly arise and immediately disappear, without changing location, shrinking, or fading away. While one is clearly seeing it arise, one will not see the middle part of being present. This is a distinctive feature of this stage. Moreover, at these three stages of insight knowledge concentration is able to make the factors of rapture, tranquility, happiness, and faith unusually apparent.

When one is able to observe the very swift arising and passing away of mental and physical phenomena, the bright light that arises will be a light caused by insight knowledge. For some meditators it will be a small, brief light, like using a flashlight for a short moment. Or else it may be a round bright light like an alms bowl or like a big tray spinning in a circle. For others it will be very large, filling the whole room or beyond. It may also last for a long time and not disappear despite observation or other thoughts. It may seem like the light from a headlight, a torch, the moon or the sun, and so on. It may seem to be emanating from one's body or from in front, behind, above, or below one. One may be able to see things around one at night as clearly as in daylight, and in the daylight things may appear strangely clear. Things that are far away may appear as clear as if they were right in front of one.

One might wonder: "Am I seeing this light with the physical eye or with the 'mind's eye?'" According to the *Mahāṭīkā*, one sees this kind of light with the mind's eye, as one sees things with the supernormal power of the divine eye. But I think it might be possible to see it with the physical eye as well. You should answer this question for yourself, based on your own experience in meditation.

When one experiences these kinds of lights, one may think that it is a sign of path knowledge and fruition knowledge, or even of nibbāna itself. Or even if one doesn't take it to be a sign of some special attainment, one may still enjoy it and grow attached to it. By doing so one's noting is disturbed and, even though one still observes them, objects become less clear than they were before. It is for these reasons that light is considered to be a corruption of insight. Actually, the unwholesome defilements of delight and pride that one takes in light, along with wrong view, are the real obstacles or enemies to insight.

Knowledge

In this context knowledge refers to the clear, lucid, and distinct understanding of the swift arising and passing away of mental and physical phenomena while observing them as they arise at the six sense doors. Whatever mental and physical phenomena arise and are noted, due to this knowledge one comes to clearly see them arising and passing away as distinct processes, like cutting gourds or eggplants into separate pieces with a sharp knife. One also comes to clearly understand the nature of impermanence, unsatisfactoriness, and not-self while reflecting about them. However, one doesn't think that one has come to this understanding due to reflection but assumes that it arose by itself while one was observing.

One may mistake this knowledge for path knowledge and fruition knowledge or may think that one's attainment of path knowledge and fruition knowledge has been very swift and, therefore, one delights in it, which in turn disturbs one's practice. This is why this knowledge is also considered to be a corruption of insight. Actually, the delight and pride that one takes in knowledge, along with wrong view, are the real obstacles to insight. This is also true of the next seven obstacles, from rapture through equanimity.

Rapture

There are five types of rapture,[570] which are listed below. With this insight knowledge [of arising and passing away] they are present to some degree in every noting. They progress gradually, beginning at the immature level of insight knowledge of arising and passing away. According to the *Mahāṭīkā*, rapture refers only to the fifth type, pervasive rapture (*pharaṇāpīti*), which arises at the mature level of insight knowledge of arising and passing away.

The five types of rapture are:

Minor rapture (*khuddikāpīti*): This type of rapture manifests suddenly as goose bumps, abrupt movement in the skin or flesh, tearing up of the eyes, sudden jerks in the chest or heart, or rapturous pleasure. It is called minor rapture because it usually occurs suddenly and only lasts for a moment.

Momentary rapture (*khaṇikāpīti*): This type of rapture manifests in the form of sudden and repeated gooseflesh, or the other manifestations as mentioned under minor rapture, and so on, like a series of flashes of lightning in the sky. It is called momentary rapture because it typically occurs repeatedly.

Showering rapture (*okkantikāpīti*): This is a feeling of pleasure and excitement that spreads through the whole body. It seems to undulate in the body like the waves of the sea as they roll in to the shore and disappear.

Uplifting rapture (*ubbegāpīti*): This indescribably pleasant feeling is very powerful and spreads all over the body. Due to its strength, the whole body or parts of it may be caused to lift up, to move, or to be flung about. The commentary mentions two meditators in Sri Lanka, a monk and a laywoman, who experienced this. Directing their attention to a pagoda they were filled with reverence. Due to the uplifting rapture that they experienced, they were lifted up and carried through the air and in just one moment found themselves on the platform of that very pagoda. These days, too, some meditators find that their limbs, or other parts of the body, rise, vibrate, or suddenly shake of their own accord. One insight meditator once found his body jumping up about a foot into the air several times, without changing his sitting posture.

Pervasive rapture (*pharaṇāpīti*): This is an extremely pleasant feeling that permeates the whole body. One feels that the entire body is completely suffused with comfort, like a ball that is completely filled with air.

This type of rapture is so pleasant that one will not want to move at all, even to simply blink or open one's eyes.

> Rapture may occur in a person who is speaking about, listening to, or teaching the Dhamma, giving rise to excitement, triggering tears, or raising gooseflesh. This rapture helps put an end to the cycle of suffering and leads toward the destination of arahantship. Therefore, rapture arising from the Dhamma is superior to any other kind.[571]

> Q: Venerable Nāgasena, someone may shed tears when his or her mother dies, or someone may shed tears from enjoyment of the Dhamma. Which of these two kinds of tears is healing and which is not?

> A: The first kind of tears, oh king, is defiled and burning with passion and aversion, the other is pure and cool from rapture and happiness. The cool one is healing, and the burning one is not.[572]

Given that the five types of rapture are included among oblivion and its causes, so I will briefly mention them here. Oblivion and its causes are as follows:

The Five Types of Rapture: When the five kinds of rapture grow strong, one may fall into a state that is like oblivion, a blackout or unconsciousness, for a few moments. This kind of rapture was presumably what occurred to the hermit Sumedhā, the merchant Anāthapiṇḍika, and King Mahākappina when they heard about the Buddha's enlightenment for the first time.

Higher Stages of Insight Knowledge: One may fall into oblivion for a few moments when one's practice is going smoothly not only at this level of insight knowledge but also at higher levels, such as insight knowledge of dissolution and so on. These intervals of oblivion are followed by similar or superior moments of practice. Presumably, the power of one's insight is so strong that the rapture associated with it also becomes very strong and leads to oblivion.

Tranquility: At times one's practice may go so smoothly and the factor of tranquility may become so strong that one does not observe or think about anything. It will feel as if one is simply gazing. Then one may fall into a state of oblivion for some time. Immediately afterward, however, one finds that one's practice continues as smoothly as before.

Equanimity: At times one's practice may go so smoothly and the factor of equanimity may become so strong that one does not need to exert any energy. One may then suddenly fall into a state of oblivion for just a moment, after which one's practice continues as smoothly as before. In this case, we can presume that equanimity as a balanced state of mind (*tatramajjhattatā*) caused the moment of oblivion.

Sloth and Torpor: Sometimes one's practice may go so smoothly and comfortably that objects and awareness gradually become faint and one eventually drifts off into a state of oblivion. One may even fall asleep for quite a long time. When one wakes up and resumes practice, one will find that it goes as smoothly as before, without any sloth and torpor. Sloth and torpor can lead to oblivion because the energy that enables one to observe objects energetically and attentively becomes weak, while one's concentration remains strong.

One can overcome the intervals of oblivion caused by tranquility, equanimity, and sloth and torpor by observing more objects or by paying closer attention to objects.

Tranquility[573]

Mental and physical tranquility is freedom from any agitation or worry. It manifests as a soothing feeling, like when one finds a cool place to escape the heat of summer or gets a good rest when exhausted. This is the kind of tranquility that tends to lead to the third kind of oblivion mentioned above. It is always accompanied by the mental factors of lightness, pliancy, adaptability, proficiency, and rectitude, which are experienced as follows:

With lightness and agility of mind and body comes the subsiding of heaviness, and one's awareness becomes very alert and swift. One's thoughts will be very fast when one thinks about anything. One will feel so light that it will seem as if one has no legs when one walks. One will feel so light that it will seem as if one has no body, arms, or legs when sitting down, lying, or bending. One may feel as if one could walk somewhere in no time, even to places quite far away. One may even feel the urge to run. Be careful not to yield to that impulse.

Pliancy is the subsiding of rigidity; it is softness and flexibility of mind and body. The mind and body become gentle and soft and lose any roughness or rigidity. One's mind becomes flexible and adaptable enough to observe any object one wishes. One becomes respectful of others and prefers to practice quietly and calmly rather than engaging with coarse objects or people.

Adaptability is wieldiness of mind and body. The mind and body become steady and strong enough to sit comfortably in meditation for one or two hours at a time without stiffness, burning, pain, or fatigue. One's practice proceeds smoothly for a long time without being disturbed by wandering thoughts.

Proficiency is dexterity of mind and body. Just as with the body, the mind becomes proficient and powerful enough to observe one object after another, moment after moment, without hesitation, procrastination, or stagnation. This observation becomes as easy and automatic as reciting a prayer that has been memorized.

Rectitude is mental straightforwardness and honesty. Hypocrisy and deceit no longer arise in one's mind. One may even resolve to be truthful for the rest of one's life.

When these six factors are strong, one feels happy and comfortable all of the time, whether one is sitting, standing, walking, lying down, bending, stretching, or meditating. As the *Visuddhimagga-mahāṭīkā* says:

> Tranquility and so on apply not only to the mental constituents but also to the physical body, because mental tranquility also eliminates physical fatigue.[574]

Happiness and comfort

The noting mind is accompanied by a very powerful feeling of happiness and joy. Due to this happiness and joy in one's mind, a feeling of happiness and pleasure also arises in the body. Symptoms of physical disease may even disappear. Every thought will lead to so much happiness that one can barely keep from sharing one's experience with fellow meditators. When this kind of happiness and comfort is present, along with rapture and tranquility, a meditator enjoys a type of happiness that is far superior to ordinary human happiness, or even that of the celestial realms. Thus the Buddha says:

> For a *bhikkhu* with a peaceful mind,
> Who enters an empty dwelling,

And clearly sees the true Dhamma,
There is superhuman joy.

Fully knowing
The arising and passing of the *khandha*s
One attains joy and delight.
For those who know, this is the deathless.[575]

Note that the verses in the commentary on the Majjhima Nikāya describe genuine happiness (*nirāmisasukha*), which I have included above under the topic of unworldly pleasure.

Faith and confidence

A very obvious degree of faith and confidence (*adhimokkha*) accompany the noting mind. Due to this strong faith, the noting mind is very clear and without any defilement. It even remains clear when one takes a break from observation. One's faith in insight practice, as well as light, knowledge, and so on, strengthen one's faith in kamma, its results, and the virtues of the Triple Gem. As a result one may make plans to do more practice and encourage others to do so. One may also greatly respect and venerate one's fellow meditators and teachers.

Balanced energy

Balanced energy (*paggaha*) refers to a quality of energy or effort balanced between too much exertion and too little exertion in observing presently arising mental and physical phenomena. The practice proceeds very smoothly with this kind of balanced energy. It seems as if one's awareness of whatever should be noted goes well of its own accord, without any effort on one's part.

Effortless mindfulness

Effortless mindfulness (*upaṭṭhāna*) is mindfulness that manifests in such a way that the presently arising mental and physical phenomena seem to appear in the noting mind, as if by themselves, or the noting mind seems to sink into the phenomena, as if by itself. When one's mindfulness is that strong, even very subtle phenomena become obvious. The next object to be noted simultaneously appears with the vanishing of the previous noting.

At this point any past memories that may arise will be very vivid, as if they were actually happening. But do not engage in such thoughts.

Equanimity

Balance of mind in insight knowledge, and in the adverting consciousness that precedes it, is called "equanimity." Adverting consciousness is the mental event that turns or adverts the mind to an object. It precedes every mental process, including seeing, hearing, observing, and so forth. Depending on how adverting consciousness turns to an object, the mental process that follows will be either wholesome or unwholesome. A meditator's mind is already committed to observing every phenomenon that occurs, and that practice is already very familiar. Thus the adverting consciousness first turns to each phenomenon as the meditator resolved to do and insight that understands the arising and passing away of that phenomenon then follows.

During the immature stages of practice, one requires a great deal of exertion to find a continuous series of objects and observe them concurrently, as they actually happen. One finds that one's mind often wanders off or is hesitant or tardy in observing objects. However at the stage of insight knowledge of arising and passing away, one is able to observe objects directly and concurrently without much effort, as though the mind rushes toward them by itself. This is "equanimity of adverting" (*āvajjanupekkhā*). It is followed by "insight equanimity" *(vipassanupekkhā)*,[576] which easily perceives arising and disappearing mental and physical phenomena. These two types of balanced mind are present in every observation and are considered potential obstacles to insight.

Delight

Taking pleasure in and enjoying extraordinary insight or in lights and other corruptions of insight is a form of craving called "delight" (*nikanti*). Delight is so soft and subtle that it is often mistaken for the bliss of meditation (*bhāvanārati*), enlightenment, or a sign of enlightenment. Actually, delight is a real corruption of insight. Delight can spoil one's insight practice by itself, and even more so if accompanied by craving, conceit, and wrong view.

Any moment of observation can be accompanied by any of the corruptions or by a combination of any of the ten of them. In the worst case, the first nine corruptions (excluding delight) may all occur simultaneously.

However, the assessment of and clinging to each forms separately, rather than as a whole group. So note well that the ten corruptions are described here, in this particular order, only for the purpose of exposition. They do not necessarily occur in this order in practice or experience.

> All nine corruptions can occur together at the same moment, but the assessment of them is formed individually.[577]

If one mistakes any unusual experiences that occur (lights, knowledge, rapture, and so on) for path knowledge and fruition knowledge or its signs, one will fall away from the path of insight. One will end up wasting one's time enjoying these experiences, without making an effort to attain the higher stages of insight knowledge or path knowledge and fruition knowledge. If one takes delight in these experiences, one is obsessed by craving. If one takes pride in them, thinking, "I must be the only one experiencing such unusual things" or "I must be superior to others," one is obsessed by conceit. If one regards them as pertaining to oneself, thinking, "I am emitting the light" or "Light is radiating from me" or "This light is mine," one is obsessed by wrong view. These three obsessions (*gāha*) of craving, conceit, and wrong view can be associated with any of the ten corruptions, giving a total of thirty possible combinations.

> Light and so on are only said to be corruptions in the sense that they become the objects of the real defilements [craving, conceit, and wrong view]. They themselves are not actually defilements. Delight, however, is both defilement and an object of defilements. Thus there are ten kinds of corruptions, but they have thirty hooks.[578]

According to the *Visuddhimagga*, the first nine corruptions are only considered defilements when they are accompanied by craving, conceit, or wrong view, and not otherwise. For this reason one should not mistake happiness, faith, the factors of enlightenment, and so on for obstacles at the higher stages of insight, such as insight knowledge of dissolution and equanimity toward phenomena. Lights that those who have already attained path knowledge and fruition knowledge experience at the stage of insight knowledge of arising and passing away should also not be mistaken for corruption.[579]

If one receives proper guidance from a teacher, one can effectively deal with any obstacles that arise by reflecting: "This must be one of the obstacles to insight that the teacher mentioned. It is not enlightenment or its sign. Dwelling on this is not the method of insight. Without having existed before, this experience has now arisen; therefore, it is impermanent, unsatisfactory, and not-self. It is just another object to observe. To observe it the moment it occurs is the correct method and will lead to attainment of higher stages of insight knowledge and to path knowledge and fruition knowledge." With this attitude, one will be able to spend one's time properly, observing every mental and physical phenomenon that arises without being preoccupied with any light, rapture, and so on. Then one will be able to very clearly see mental and physical phenomena arising and passing away, and the three universal characteristics will become very obvious. One will see that all phenomena are impermanent, immediately vanishing after they arise, are unsatisfactory, oppressed by constant arising and passing away, and are not-self, not obeying one's wishes. In this way, one frees one's insight knowledge of arising and passing away from obstacles to insight.

Purification by knowledge and vision of what is path and not path

Purification by knowledge and vision of what is path and not path (*maggāmaggañāṇadassanavisuddhi*) means being able to distinguish between correct and incorrect paths in practice. For example, one may reflect: "Neither these lights and so forth nor thinking about them are the noble path. Only constant mindfulness of these mental and physical phenomena as they arise is the correct path of insight."

Purification by knowledge and vision of the way, beginning with mature insight knowledge of arising and passing away

As one is no longer attached to lights and so on that may arise while observing the arising and passing away of mental and physical phenomena, one is freed from the corruptions of insight. This is also called "insight knowledge of arising and passing away that discerns the correct path," because one understands the appearance and disappearance of phenomena. This is the first of nine insight knowledges, culminating with insight knowledge of adaptation, that together are called "purification by knowledge and vision of the way" (*paṭipadāñāṇadassanavisuddhi*). In other words, these constitute the purified knowledge and vision of the way that lead to attainment of the noble path.

This purification arises when one begins to clearly understand the three universal characteristics of impermanence, unsatisfactoriness, and not-self while very clearly seeing the arising and passing away of mental and physical phenomena. Or, in other words, if one observes mental and physical phenomena arising and passing away, the three universal characteristics appear by themselves. I will explain this further in chapter 7 and provide some examples. According to the *Visuddimagga* subcommentary:

> If one realizes arising and passing away, then impermanence is clear to one. Then, one will also realize: "Whatever is impermanent is unsatisfactory; whatever is unsatisfactory is not-self." In other words, due to the observation of arising and passing away, one clearly realizes that phenomena are impermanent, because they cease to exist immediately after they occur; that they are unsatisfactory, because they are constantly oppressed by arising and passing away; and that they are not-self, because they do not arise or pass away according to anyone's will.[580]

For the meditator who clearly sees the three general characteristics by observing the arising and passing away of mental and physical phenomena in the mature phase of insight knowledge of arising and passing away, the noting mind becomes very quick and sharp. It will seem as if the awareness is happening by itself. Because the awareness is so swift, objects being observed will also appear very swiftly.

Insight Knowledge of Dissolution

At this point one will no longer be able to observe the arising and the middle part (presence) of phenomena, and one will no longer see them as a continuous process of phenomena that flow like a stream of water. This means that mental and physical phenomena no longer appear as a constant and coherent process. Mental images of solid forms and shapes no longer arise. If one bends or stretches the limbs, for example, one no longer has mental images of the form and shape of an arm or a leg as was previously the case. Instead, each time an object is observed, one only sees its constant disappearance or dissolution. This is how insight knowledge of dissolution (*bhaṅgañāṇa*) begins to develop.

The following passage explains how insight knowledge of arising and passing away matures into the insight knowledge of dissolution:

> With insight into arising and passing away, which is free from obstacles and constitutes the correct path of insight practice, a meditator becomes aware of the true characteristics of all phenomena. By repeatedly discerning mental and physical phenomena and confirming impermanence, unsatisfactoriness, and not-self, his or her insight becomes sharp. The appearance of phenomena is very swift. Eventually, a meditator will no longer notice their arising, their presence, the continuity of processes, or the appearance of solid forms in stages. Instead, mindfulness will only register their passing away, vanishing, disappearance, and cessation.[581] In this way, contemplation of dissolution (*bhaṅgānupassanā*) arises out of the meditator's realization of the arising and passing away of phenomena.[582]

The *Paṭisambhidāmagga* explains in detail how insight knowledge of dissolution develops. I will just mention a few key points here.

Insight and counter-insight

> Observing an object and seeing its dissolution constitutes the insight called "knowledge of dissolution."[583]

> The phrase "observing an object" refers to seeing an object vanish or pass away. The phrase "seeing its dissolution" refers to seeing the dissolution of the first insight that observed the object vanishing or passing away. This is knowledge.[584]

According to these quotes, one sees the dissolution of phenomena when one observes the present moment phenomena involved in the rise and fall of the abdomen, sitting, standing, walking, bending, stretching, seeing, hearing, thinking, and so on. Then one also sees the dissolution of that very observation. Thus, anytime one is aware of an object, one sees both the object itself and the mental observation of it dissolving in turn. This is insight knowledge of dissolution.

> The mind, taking a physical phenomenon as its object, arises and passes away. One sees the disappearance of both the physical phenomenon and the mind that observes it. The same is true when the mind takes a feeling, perception, mental formation, or consciousness as its object. After seeing the dissolution of the object, the dissolution of the noting mind is contemplated in turn.[585]

When one observes the physical phenomena involved in the rise and fall of the abdomen, sitting, bending, stretching, eye-sensitivity, visible form, and so on, the moment they occur, one sees that they vanish, disappear, or pass away. This understanding of the disappearance of the observed object is called "the first insight knowledge of dissolution" (*paṭhamabhaṅgañāṇa*). Afterward, one sees that the first insight knowledge of dissolution itself also vanishes. This is called "the second insight knowledge of dissolution" (*dutiyabhaṅgañāṇa*) or "counter-insight" (*paṭivipassanā*), since it in turn observes the dissolution of the observing mind. Insight knowledge of dissolution includes these two levels of observation.

Similarly, when observing the other aggregates, one sees both the observed object and the mind that observes it very swiftly vanish or pass away. This is the criterion for insight knowledge of dissolution. The phrase "vanish or pass away" refers to the normal dissolution or disappearance of phenomena, and not to some kind of chaotic destruction.

Take note that the commentary says, ". . . mindfulness will only register their passing away, vanishing, disappearance, and cessation" (*khayavayabhedanirodheyeva sati*),[586] and also says ". . . seeing an object vanish or pass away . . ." (*khayato vayato disvā*).[587] These statements are worthy of serious consideration. The Pāḷi texts explain in detail the six sense doors, the six sense objects, the six consciousnesses, and so on in a similar way. The phrase "contemplate in turn" (*anupassati*) is defined in seven ways, which I will explain later in chapter 7.

> Transfer to another object, transformation of insight, and powerful adverting—these are counter-insight into knowledge of dissolution.[588]

In this line, "transfer to another object" refers to a shifting of awareness from the disappearance of the observed object to the disappearance of the mind that observes it. The phrase "transformation of insight" means that a meditator's insight changes so that he or she only sees the disappearance of phenomena. The meditator no longer sees the arising of phenomena, as he or she did during the previous insight knowledge of arising and passing away. The term "powerful adverting" means that the mind-moment that adverts to each phenomenon is powerful enough to detect the disappearance of the observing mind immediately after the disappearance of the observed object. When a meditator's insight is characterized by these three factors, it can be taken to be insight knowledge of dissolution.

Note that the first and third of these three factors are successive mind-moments in a single mental process of observation. If the first mind-moment properly adverts to an object, then the following mind-moments can properly observe it.

> "Transfer to another object" means that one sees the disappearance of an object, such as a physical phenomenon and so on, and then sees the disappearance of the very mind that observed the disappearance of the object. Thus one's attention transfers from the first object to the second one. "Transformation of insight" means that one's insight stops perceiving the arising of phenomena and becomes focused only on their disappearance. "Powerful adverting" means that one's power of observation is so strong that one can see the disappearance of an object and immediately afterward see the disappearance of the mind that just observed the disappearance of the object.[589]

Note that here the term "immediately afterward" means immediately after the first mental process. The second moment of adverting can only actually occur after an interval of the life-continuum consciousness. The phrases "transfer to another object" and "immediately afterward" should be understood to mean that a single object should only be observed once, and not several times in succession. It is also not necessary to observe each and every phenomenon involved in a single action in order to enumerate or classify them all. Instead, one should focus on observing those phenomena that are most obvious. It is not necessary to individually observe each successive mind-moment of a single mental process.[590] One should just observe the process as a whole.

Inferential knowledge

One should not try to observe past or future phenomena, or phenomena that are not distinct. One should just be aware of obvious phenomena that are arising and passing away in the present moment. Meditators should remember these points very well.

> Observing the present, one is certain that both [past and future] are the same. Deeply focused on disappearance, thus is knowledge of dissolution.[591]
>
> The first line of this verse means that based on those objects that one empirically experiences one can be sure that conditioned phenomena in the past and future also vanish. One may reflect: "Conditioned phenomena of the past have vanished, and in the future they will vanish, too, just as these phenomena that I am currently experiencing do. All of these phenomena have the same nature." Thus the ancient sages have said:
>
> > With a purified vision of the present,
> > One infers those past and future to be alike.
> > One infers that conditioned phenomena disappear
> > Like dew-drops when the morning sun comes up.[592]

Thus one should begin one's insight practice by observing the phenomena that are arising and passing away in the present moment and not those of the past or future. Once one empirically observes the present phenomena clearly, inferential understanding of past and future phenomena will arise naturally by itself. This is all that is required with regard to past and future phenomena. So do not deliberately attempt to observe past or future phenomena.

Mature knowledge

At the mature level of insight knowledge of dissolution, one can see observed objects and the mind that observes them continuously disappearing, like the continuous popping of sesame seeds in a skillet, the patter of bursting bubbles from raindrops striking a pond, or a constantly shifting mirage. The *Visuddhimagga* says[593] that the Buddha aimed the following verse from the *Dhammapada* at meditators whose experience is like this.

> If one sees the world as a bubble,
> If one sees it as a mirage,
> One won't be seen
> By the King of Death.[594]

When with insight knowledge of dissolution one sees each object disappearing, one won't be subject to ignorance, craving, clinging, kamma, rebirth, or the aggregates. Since there are no aggregates for a new life, there is no death. By gradually passing through the stages of insight knowledge, beginning with insight knowledge of dissolution and culminating in knowledge that is the fruit of arahantship, one will absolutely experience no more rebirth and consequently no more death. The line "one won't be seen by the King of Death" refers to this fact.

The Three Aspects of Disillusionment: Insight Knowledges of Fear, of Danger, and of Disenchantment

Insight knowledge of fear

At the peak of insight knowledge of dissolution one clearly realizes that mental and physical phenomena vanished in the past, are vanishing in the present, and will also vanish in the future. As a result, conditioned phenomena begin to appear fearful. At this point insight knowledge of fear (*bhayañāṇa*) arises.

> By realizing that conditioned phenomena have vanished in the past, are vanishing in the present, and will also vanish in the future, one attains knowledge of fear [of phenomena].[595]

At that time the mind will see the frightening or fearful aspect of conditioned phenomena that vanish with each noting. Also those objects that one reflects upon will be seen as frightening or fearful. Thus the noting mind will not be as willing, joyful, and enthusiastic as it was during the stages of insight knowledge of arising and passing away and insight knowledge of dissolution. Instead one will feel unhappy or dismayed. This fear doesn't feel like the kind of fear that frightening ghosts or enemies arouse. It is merely feeling disheartened or distressed due to truly understanding how frightening things really are.

> Is knowledge of fear really frightening? Of course not. Actually, it is simply feeling sure that past conditioned phenomena have vanished, present phenomena are vanishing, and future phenomena will vanish.[596]

Insight knowledge of danger

When insight knowledge of fear matures, it is followed by insight knowledge of danger (*ādīnavañāṇa*). At this point one will not see any of the conditioned phenomena that one observes or reflects upon as pleasant, good, or substantial. Instead whatever one observes or reflects upon will be experienced as unpleasant, detestable, and harsh.

The *Paṭisambhidāmagga* describes the insight knowledges of fear and danger in four sections. The first sentence of the first section is as follows:

> The arising [of phenomena in this life] is fearful and, based on that, is seen to be dangerous. This understanding is called knowledge of danger.

The second sentence of the section replaces "arising" (*uppādo*) with "occurrence" (*pavattaṃ*) in the same formula. "The occurrence of phenomena" refers to the constant vanishing of previous phenomena and arising of subsequent phenomena. With each noting this process of mental and physical phenomena is seen as fearful due to its constant appearance. Thus the second sentence says:

> The occurrence [of phenomena] is fearful and, based on that, is seen to be dangerous. This understanding is called knowledge of danger.

The remainder of the first section continues in this way, repeating the same observation with regard to other aspects of phenomena. The other aspects that it identifies as fearful are: sign as having a solid form, shape, or substance, accumulation of wholesome actions (*āyūhanā*), relinking, destination (*gati*), first arising or generating (*nibbatti*), reappearance (*upapatti*), birth (*jāti*), old age (*jarā*), sickness (*byādhi*), death (*maraṇa*), grief or lamentation (*soka*), and anxiety (*upāyāsa*). Note that the term "sign" refers to the belief that phenomena such as the rise and fall of the abdomen, sitting, bending, stretching, seeing, hearing, and so on possess a solid form, shape, or substance.

The second, third, and fourth sections of the Pāḷi passage have a parallel structure to that of the first section. The same fifteen aspects of phenomena are mentioned, but rather than being identified as fearful, the second section identifies them as unsatisfactory (*dukkha*), the third section as worldly (*sāmisa*), and the fourth section as conditioned (*saṅkhāra*).

Whenever one experiences only the disappearance of observed objects and the mind that notes them, one sees them as fearful. When one reflects on the first arising of these mental and physical phenomena in this life, one sees it as fearful. Seeing and understanding it in this way is called "insight knowledge of fear" and "insight knowledge of danger." This is how these insight knowledges arise. Even without deliberately reflecting on occurrence, sign, and so on, one can still see phenomena as fearful by simply observing or noting them.

The first five of these fifteen aspects—arising, occurrence, sign, accumulation of wholesome actions, and relinking—are key meditation subjects for insight knowledge of danger. The other ten aspects are simply synonyms for the first five, but the Buddha mentions them here because some people use these synonyms to describe their experience. Initial arising and birth are included in arising and relinking; destination and reappearance are similar in an ultimate sense to occurrence; and the six aspects from old age through anxiety are included in sign. So it is enough to simply observe the first five aspects of phenomena from this list.

According to the commentary, the first section of the passage refers to the development of insight knowledge of fear, while the other three refer to the insight knowledge of danger:

> Seeing the fifteen aspects as something to be feared is knowledge

> of fear, while seeing them to be unsatisfying, worldly, and conditioned is knowledge of danger. It should be regarded thusly.[597]

Once one sees the existence of these fifteen aspects as fearful, unsatisfying, worldly, and conditioned, one may consider the opposite possibility: "A state of nonarising, nonoccurrence, as well as the absence of conditioned phenomena, illusory impressions, volitional actions, and relinking is free from danger and misery. This is happiness and peace, free from the cords of sensual desire and defilements." This is why the *Paṭisambhidāmagga* says:

> One understands peace thus: "Nonarising is peaceful."
> One understands peace thus: "Nonarising is pleasant."
> One understands peace thus: "Nonarising is free from sense desire."
> One understands peace thus: "Nonarising is nibbāna."[598]

Insight knowledge of disenchantment

When one's knowledge of danger matures, it will be followed by insight knowledge of disenchantment (*nibbidāñāṇa*). At this point one has understood the flaws of phenomena, so one feels weary whenever one observes or reflects on them. Even thinking or fantasizing about them one merely feels weary of and fed up with them. The *Dhammapada* describes how this insight knowledge develops as follows:

> "All created things are impermanent"
> Seeing this with insight,
> One becomes disenchanted with suffering.
> This is the path to purity.
>
> "All created things are suffering"
> Seeing this with insight,
> One becomes disenchanted with suffering.
> This is the path to purity.
>
> "All things are not-self"
> Seeing this with insight,

> One becomes disenchanted with suffering.
> This is the path to purity.[599]

We can understand these verses as follows: with the inferential insight (*anvayavipassanā*) that occurs spontaneously as a result of mature, empirical insight knowledge of dissolution, a meditator sees that all conditioned phenomena are impermanent, unsatisfactory, and not-self. Then seeing the danger and defects with his or her insight knowledge of fear and insight knowledge of danger, the meditator grows weary of and fed up with the unsatisfactory nature of conditioned phenomena. This is the path to purification.

However, according to the *Mahāṭīkā*, the verses should be explained in this way: with his or her preliminary knowledge by comprehension and later insight knowledges of arising and passing away and so on, and higher insight, a meditator sees that all conditioned phenomena are impermanent, unsatisfactory, and not-self. Then seeing the danger and defects with his or her insight knowledge of fear and insight knowledge of danger, the meditator grows weary of and fed up with the unsatisfactory nature of conditioned phenomena. This is the path to purification.

The three insight knowledges of fear, danger, and disenchantment actually only differ in degree. They are the immature, intermediate, and mature forms of the same understanding of the imperfection of conditioned phenomena. Due to this, for some meditators who experience insight knowledge of fear, the insight knowledges of danger and disenchantment follow immediately or within a short time. For those meditators who proceed to higher stages of insight knowledge very quickly, only one or two of these three insight knowledges will be distinct.

> The sages of old said that knowledge of fear has three names. Insight is called "knowledge of fear" when all conditioned phenomena are seen as fearful, "knowledge of danger" when fearful phenomena are seen as flawed, and "knowledge of disenchantment" when flawed phenomena are seen as wearisome. Also, [the *Paṭisambhidāmagga*] says that these three knowledges are the same in an ultimate sense and only differ in name.[600]

Insight Knowledge of Desire for Deliverance

> As a result of knowledge of disenchantment, a person becomes weary, tired, and sick of [all conditioned phenomena] and does not attach, stick, or fasten his mind to any of the three existences, four modes of birth, five destinations, seven stations of consciousness, or nine spheres of beings. Instead, one wishes to get free or get away from all conditioned phenomena . . . Knowledge that desires deliverance (*muñcitukamyatāñāṇa*) then arises in one who has no more attachment to any conditioned phenomena and wishes to escape from them all.[601]

The various forms of life referred to in this passage are as follows:

The three existences (*bhava*) are sensuous existence (*kāmabhava*), fine-material existence (*rūpabhava*), and immaterial existence (*arūpabhava*). *The four modes of birth* (*yoni*) are birth from an egg (*aṇḍaja*), birth from a womb (*jalābuja*), birth from moisture (*saṃsedaja*), and spontaneous birth (*papātika*). *The five destinations* (*gati*) are the hell realms, the animal realm, the realm of hungry ghosts, the human realm, and the celestial realms.

The seven stations of consciousness (*viññāṇaṭṭhiti*)[602] are: beings that differ in body (*nānattakāya*) and in perception (*nānattasaññī*)—that is, humans and sense-sphere celestial beings; beings that differ in body but are alike in perception (*ekattasaññī*)—that is, first-jhānic Brahmā and beings in the hell realms; beings alike in body and different in perception (*ekattakāya*)—that is, second-jhānic Brahmā; beings alike in body and in perception—that is, third-jhānic Brahmā, Vehapphala Brahmā, and Suddhāvāsa Brahmā; beings of the realm of infinite space (*ākāsānañcāyatanasaññī*); beings of the realm of infinite consciousness (*viññāṇāyatanasaññī*); and beings of the realm of nothingness (*ākiñcaññāyatanasaññī*).

The nine spheres of beings (*sattāvāsā*) are nonpercipient beings (*asaññasatta*), beings of the realm of neither perception nor non-perception (*nevasaññānāsaññāyatana*), and beings of the seven stations of consciousness listed above.

One's knowledge is limited to those realms of existence that one has experienced, so those realms that one is not familiar with cannot arouse either mental defilement or insight in one. However, if one at least develops insight knowledge of disenchantment regarding the three kinds of existence, one accomplishes insight knowledge. The other forms of life given in the above lists are all included in these three types of existence.

It is natural to wish to leave a place where one cannot enjoy oneself. In the same way, when one has seen conditioned phenomena, which include observed objects as well as the mind that notes them, to be fearful and flawed, it is natural to wish to leave or escape them. Insight knowledge of disenchantment arises very strongly due to this and before long one develops the wish to leave or escape not only from observed objects and the mind that notes them but also from the different existences, modes of birth, destinations, and so on that one reflects upon. This desire for deliverance is called insight knowledge that desires deliverance.

At this point, one wants to give up or get away from all of the phenomena involved in bodily actions (such as walking, sitting, sleeping, bending, stretching, and so on), mental activities (such as seeing, hearing, thinking, noting, and so on), and all forms of existence (human, celestial, female, male, Brahmā, and so on). All one wants is to be free from these phenomena. As a result, some meditators may think that it would be better not to observe or be mindful, as a result of which they may stop noting and observing.

Insight Knowledge of Reobservation

> Wishing to escape from the fragile, conditioned phenomena that constitute the existences, births, destinations, stations, and spheres, and with the purpose of escaping all those phenomena, the meditator contemplates those very phenomena yet again in terms of the three universal characteristics through the knowledge of reobservation (*paṭisaṅkhāñāṇa*).[603]

When one is completely free from the illusion that conditioned phenomena are permanent, satisfying, or self, then one experiences nibbāna, the cessation of all conditioned phenomena. At that point no phenomena are able to cause one any more worry or distress. This applies even before complete cessation, let alone after complete cessation.

Therefore if one wants to be free from conditioned phenomena, there is nothing else to be done but to deeply understand the three general characteristics of these conditioned phenomena and to continue with the observation as usual in order to reach an equanimous noting mind. Therefore at the insight knowledge of the desire for deliverance, one must observe the arising and passing away of conditioned phenomena once again as one did before. Then one is able to see forty aspects of the universal characteristics: ten aspects of impermanence, twenty-five aspects of unsatisfactoriness, and five aspects of not-self. Every time one observes a phenomenon, one sees one of the three characteristics from one of these forty aspects. This understanding is the insight knowledge of reobservation because this observation happens once again.

The ten aspects of insight into impermanence

The ten aspects of insight into impermanence given in the *Paṭisambhidāmagga* are as follows:

1. One sees that conditioned phenomena are impermanent (*aniccato*).
2. One sees that conditioned phenomena deteriorate (*palokato*). Seeing the deterioration of observed objects, like a collapsing or eroding sand bank, or a sheet of paper being torn into pieces, or a fire being doused with water, or smoke being dispersed by the wind, falls under contemplation of deterioration (*palokānupassanā*).
3. One sees that conditioned phenomena are unstable, quivering, or transient (*calato*). When one experiences arising and passing away with each noting, one understands that nothing whatsoever is firm and stable; everything is unstable. This is contemplation of instability (*calānupassanā*).
4. One sees that conditioned phenomena are frail and easily destroyed (*pabhaṅguto*). Sometimes, phenomena appear to be so frail that they seem to vanish even before one can observe them.
5. One sees that conditioned phenomena are not everlasting (*addhuvato*).
6. One sees that conditioned phenomena change (*vipariṇāmato*). This is observing that conditioned phenomena change from their initial state through the process of aging and so on.
7. One sees that conditioned phenomena have no solid core or substance (*asārakato*).
8. One sees that conditioned phenomena do not endure (*vibhavato*). If one is not able to see through the illusion of solidity of

phenomenal processes, then one is bound to believe that mental and physical phenomena have remained the same from childhood up to the present moment. This is like thinking that a tree is the same as the seed that it grew from or that the sprouts and leaves are the same as the trunk of the tree. But if one is able to see through the illusion of solidity, one will no longer suffer from that illusion but will be able to distinguish between different successive phenomena. One will realize that previous phenomena disappear before new ones arise and that new phenomena do not arise out of previous phenomena, because one phenomenon does not transform into another but is rather linked to it by causes and conditions.

9. One sees that conditioned phenomena arise depending on causes (*saṅkhatato*). One understands that phenomena are conditioned by such causes as kamma, consciousness, weather, and nutrition.
10. One sees that conditioned phenomena are subject to death (*maraṇadhammato*).

The *Visuddhimagga* mentions three additional aspects of insight into impermanence: (1) one sees that conditioned phenomena are limited by disappearance (*aniccantikā*); (2) one sees that conditioned phenomena are momentary (*tāvakālika*); and one sees that conditioned phenomena are limited by arising and passing away (*uppādavayaparicchinna*).

The twenty-five aspects of insight into unsatisfactoriness

The twenty-five aspects of insight into unsatisfactoriness given in the *Paṭisambhidāmagga* are:

1. One sees conditioned phenomena as suffering, unsatisfactory, or painful (*dukkhato*).
2. One sees conditioned phenomena as a chronic disease (*rogato*).
3. One sees conditioned phenomena as abcesses or ulcers (*gaṇḍato*). Mental and physical phenomena that are the objects of mindfulness arise, are present for a moment, and then disappear again. This is like an abscess from which pus trickles out upon ripening. Phenomena are like an abscess in that the defilements ooze from them just as pus and serum ooze from an abscess.

4. One sees conditioned phenomena as thorns or arrows in the flesh (*sallato*), because they cause intolerable pain, bring mental and physical distress, and are difficult to remove.
5. One sees conditioned phenomena as unprofitable (*aghato*),[604] because they are like censuring a noble person, they do not yield to profit and prosperity, and are the base of a great array of unwholesomeness.
6. One sees that conditioned phenomena are the source of a great array of unwholesomeness (*aghamūlato*).
7. One sees conditioned phenomena as afflictions (*ādhato*), because they are an immediate cause for affliction and prevent one from living a carefree life.
8. One sees conditioned phenomena as calamities (*ītito*), because they cause one to suffer due to the loss of relatives (*ñātivyasana*) and so on.
9. One sees conditioned phenomena as accidents (*upaddavato*), because they allow one to encounter unpredictable misfortunes and leave one at the mercy of rulers and governments.
10. One sees conditioned phenomena as fearful (*bhayato*), because they are the source of many types of fear, danger, and are the opposite of the cessation of suffering.
11. One sees conditioned phenomena as dangerous (*upasaggato*), because they are associated with external misfortunes, such as the loss of loved ones and so on, and internal misfortunes, such as physical diseases or mental defilements such as lust and so on, and because they can torment one deeply, like the black magic practiced by sorcerers or evil spirits.
12. One sees that conditioned phenomena are not good hideouts (*atāṇato*), because they cannot hide one from suffering and danger.
13. One sees that conditioned phenomena are not shelters (*aleṇato*), because they cannot provide a shelter from suffering and danger.
14. One sees that conditioned phenomena are not refuges (*asaraṇato*), because one cannot find a refuge from suffering and danger in them; no matter how sublime one's mental and physical phenomena may be, they cannot free one from suffering and danger. Therefore, whatever mental and physical phenomena there are, they are neither a hide-out, a shelter, nor a refuge, nor

are they able to help a person to become free from suffering and danger.

15. One sees conditioned phenomena as disadvantages (*ādīnavato*). Due to the constant arising of suffering, all they are is a heap of defects. Because they are impermanent, unsatisfactory, and changing for the worse, they are defective and incredibly wretched.
16. One sees conditioned phenomena as murderous (*vadhakato*), because one could die any time they go awry.
17. One sees conditioned phenomena as intoxicating (*sāsavato*), because they support the taints (*āsava*).
18. One sees conditioned phenomena as subject to death and mental defilements (*mārāmisato*).
19. One sees conditioned phenomena as subject to birth (*jātidhammato*).
20. One sees conditioned phenomena as subject to aging and decay (*jarādhammato*).
21. One sees conditioned phenomena as subject to sickness (*byādhidhammato*).
22. One sees conditioned phenomena as subject to and a source of grief (*sokadhammato*).
23. One sees conditioned phenomena as subject to and a source of lamentation (*paridevadhammato*).
24. One sees conditioned phenomena as subject to and a source of trouble (*upāyāsadhammato*).
25. One sees conditioned phenomena as an affliction or impurity (*dukkhavatthu*).

The *Visuddhimagga* mentions three additional aspects of insight into unsatisfactoriness: one sees conditioned phenomena as constant torment (*abhiṇhasampaṭipīlana*); one sees conditioned phenomena as painful (*dukkhama*); and one sees conditioned phenomena as the base of suffering (*dukkhavatthu*).

A special note: Meditators experience many forms of strong and obvious unpleasant sensation at the stages of insight knowledge by comprehension and the immature stages of insight knowledge of reobservation, and so they may see and experience many of the aspects of unsatisfactoriness mentioned above. Thus the *Visuddhimagga* mentions these various aspects of unsatisfactoriness with regard to both of these stages of insight knowledge. The difference between the two insight knowledges is that during the earlier stage one sees unsatisfactoriness in a general way, while at this higher stages of insight one sees unsatisfactoriness moment by moment whenever one observes phenomena.

The five aspects of insight into not-self

The five aspects of insight into not-self (*anattā*) given in the *Paṭisambhidāmagga* are:

1. One sees conditioned phenomena as mere dhammas that are devoid of self (*anattato*). There is no self that is able to control, to own, to feel, to give orders, to behave according to one's will, no self that is everlasting, or that is the agent of going, seeing, and so on.
2. One sees conditioned phenomena as strangers or outsiders (*parato*), because phenomena do not happen according to one's will and because one is unable to order them not to age and die.
3. One sees conditioned phenomena as mere dhammas devoid of (*rittato*) a personal identity that is enduring, satisfying, or beautiful.
4. One sees conditioned phenomena as mere dhammas that are insubstantial, useless, and empty (*tucchato*).
5. One sees conditioned phenomena as mere dhammas that are empty of self (*suññato*). Here "self" (*atta*) means an entity that is the owner of the body, permanently residing in the body, the agent of going, seeing, and so on, the agent who feels pleasant and unpleasant feelings, able to give any orders, and able to exercise mastery. Such an entity, which is [a product of one's] speculation, belief, or obsession, may be called being, soul, ego, or self.

The Visuddhimagga mentions three additional aspects of insight into not-self: one sees that conditioned phenomena are merely dhammas that have no owner (*assāmikato*); one sees that conditioned phenomena are merely dhammas that are not under anyone's control (*anissarato*); and one sees that conditioned phenomena are merely dhammas that are not able to exercise mastery (*avasavattīto*).

Mature reobservation

The forty aspects of the three universal characteristics listed above are referred to as the forty "*-tos*," because the Pāḷi terms for each of them end with the syllable *to—aniccato*, *dukkhato*, and so on. They are also called the "forty insights" in regard to the forty aspects of insight. The more innate wisdom or acquired learning one has, the more apparent and distinct these aspects will become. They grow even more clearly apparent with the insights that lead to higher stages of path knowledge. However, according to the *Paṭisambhidāmagga*, if one can clearly see just one of these forty aspects, one's insight is good enough to attain path knowledge. This is because path knowledge occurs immediately after seeing a single aspect of the universal characteristics at the highest stage of insight called insight leading to emergence (*vutthānagāminīvipassanā*), which leads directly to path knowledge.

For some meditators it will take only a few moments for insight knowledge of reobservation to mature; for others it may take a day, a night, or up to three days to mature. Before this insight knowledge matures, meditators will be dissatisfied, thinking that his or her meditation is not going well, even though it is. This is because they very clearly experience the unpleasant aspects of phenomena mentioned earlier, and because they are not yet able to be equanimous with regard to these phenomena, not yet having attained insight knowledge of equanimity toward phenomena. When this insight knowledge matures, one will think that one's practice is going especially well. Recall that one must pass through two phases during insight knowledge of arising and passing away, one that occurs before one overcomes the corruptions of insight and one after. In the same way, one must pass through two phases with respect to insight knowledge of reobservation and insight knowledge of dissolution, an early one that feels unsatisfactory and a mature one that feels satisfactory.

Insight Knowledge of Equanimity toward Phenomena

When one's insight knowledge of reobservation becomes fully mature, one will be able to experience the three universal characteristics of present phenomena as they arise and pass away, without much effort. At that point one's practice gains momentum and proceeds smoothly for long periods, and it will seem as if phenomena are observing themselves (*saṅkhārāva saṅkhāre vipassanti*).[605] One will also be able to clearly experience any of the various aspects of impermanence, unsatisfactoriness, or not-self. One will no longer be fearful, weary, disillusioned with conditioned phenomena, or preoccupied with desire for deliverance. There will be absolutely no more dissatisfaction or thoughts that one's practice is not going well. One will have no worry or anxiety regarding the destruction or loss of material things. One no longer has the fear one had during insight knowledge of fear. The mind will be extremely clear and one will think that one is having the most peaceful experience one has ever known.

But one will not take extreme delight in one's experience, as was the case during the immature stages of insight knowledge of arising and passing away. Instead one's practice will proceed smoothly and steadily for long periods. Knowledge that is aware of phenomena without exerting much effort and proceeds smoothly and uninterruptedly becomes, as if by itself, insight knowledge of equanimity toward phenomena.

> Just as [a person who has lost all interest in a former spouse who acted unfaithfully], a meditator wishes to be free from all conditioned phenomena and so observes them again. Because he or she does not take them to be "I" or "mine," he or she abandons fear and delight with respect to these phenomena. The meditator's mind is balanced and he or she feels equanimity toward all conditioned phenomena.
>
> Seeing it in this way, the meditator's mind retreats, departs, withdraws from, and no longer expands into the three existences, four births, five destinations, seven stations of consciousness, and nine spheres. Either equanimity or repulsion (*pāṭikūlyatā*) become well established in the mind. This insight is called knowledge of equanimity toward phenomena.[606]

Note that the expression "no longer expands" means that the process of observing cannot be directed or spread to many objects according to one's will but simply becomes spontaneously aware of objects. At this point one's mind does not delight in any object, however pleasant it may be, even if one deliberately tries to enjoy it. One is uninterested in relishing or enjoying anything. One's mind is unable to wander off for long periods and, when it does wander, it returns to being mindful of its own accord.

For the benefit of your general knowledge, I will explain how phenomena are observed from two aspects (*dvikoṭika*), and so on, in the following sections.

How phenomena are observed from two aspects

In accord with the *Āneñjasappāya Sutta* of the Majjhima Nikāya, and other texts, the *Visuddhimagga* explains how emptiness is observed in two aspects:

> Again, bhikkhus, a noble disciple . . . considers thus: "This is void of [the existence of] a self or [the existence] of what belongs to a self."[607]

Note that, in accord with the commentary to the *Ratana Sutta* of the Kuddakapātha,[608] I have translated *attena vā, attaniyena vā* as "the existence of a self or the existence of what belongs to self," rather than using the usual translation of "self and belonging to a self."

By observing or reflecting on mental and physical phenomena, one sees that they are empty of the existence of a self or empty of a self that accomplishes things according to its will. One also understands that they are empty of the existence of what belongs to a self or empty of what belongs to a self. This is contemplation of phenomena from two aspects.

If one only believes in a self, one can also believe in what belongs to a self. If one only sees that there is no self, however, one can no longer believe in what belongs to a self. Therefore, if one understands well that there is no self, one also accomplishes observation of the second aspect, seeing that there is nothing that belongs to a self.

How phenomena are observed from four aspects

In accord with the *Āneñjasappāya Sutta* of the Majjhima Nikāya, and other texts, the *Visuddhimagga* explains how emptiness is observed in four aspects:

> Again, bhikkhus, a noble disciple considers thus: "I am not anything belonging to anyone anywhere, nor is there anything belonging to me in anyone anywhere."[609]

Whenever one observes phenomena, one sees that they vanish. But one does not see any "self" that is able to accomplish anything according to its will. Due to this, one thoroughly understands that there is no self that exists either internally or externally, at any place or at any time in the past, present, or future. One thoroughly understands that there is no self involved in one's physical or mental phenomena, in any physical activities (such as walking, standing, sitting, sleeping, bending, stretching, and so on), or in any mental activities (such as seeing, hearing, touching, thinking, and so on, as well as feeling, perception, or other mental formations). There is no self in anything whatsoever. Observing that phenomena are empty of self produces this understanding; this is the first aspect.

Whenever one observes phenomena, or reflects on them based on that observation, one understands that there are only vanishing phenomena, and no self or any being. Not understanding this, others take one to be "my father," "my mother," "my son," "my daughter," and so on. One realizes that, in fact, there is no self that can belong to one in these ways. There is no self that can be identified as something that belongs to another, such as father or mother, son or daughter, and so on. Thus self does not belong to anyone else. Observing that phenomena are empty of self produces this understanding; this is the second aspect.

Whenever, based on that observation, one sees, hears, or reflects on an observed visible form or a sound, one thoroughly understands that a self with respect to others neither exists inside nor outside their body nor in any place whatsoever. It does not exist at any time, not in the past, present, or future, nor does it exist in mental or physical phenomena, nor in the form that is seen or the sound that is heard. There is no self in anything whatsoever. Observing that phenomena are empty of self produces this understanding; this is the third aspect.

One used to think that there really existed a self with respect to others, such as one's mother, father, brothers, sisters, sons, daughters, and so on, because one did not understand that there are only vanishing phenomena and no self or any being. As a matter of fact, one understands that there is no self with respect to others; there is only vanishing phenomena. One sees that they are not something that can belong to him or her. Observing that phenomena are empty of self produces this understanding; this is the fourth aspect.

In sum, understanding that phenomena are empty of self involves seeing their emptiness from these four aspects: there is no self [that accomplishes things according to its will], there is no self that belongs to another, there is no self of another, and there is no self of another that belongs to oneself.

If one only thoroughly understands the first of these four aspects, namely that the self does not exist, that is enough. This is the main point. Seeing clearly that the self does not exist, one can easily conclude that there is no self in other beings and that one does not belong to another being nor do other beings belong to one.

How phenomena are observed from six aspects

The *Visuddhimagga* mentions that not-self can be observed from the following six aspects according to the Pāḷi text called the *Niddesa*:

> One sees thus: the eye is empty of the existence of a self, what belongs to a self, permanence, durability, eternity, and stability.[610]

The same is true for the other sense doors and other phenomena, such as sense objects, sense consciousness, mental contact, feeling, and so on. One should also note that the last four of these six aspects are simply synonyms.

To elaborate, while one notes "seeing," one understands: "The eye-sensitivity that is the basis of eye-consciousness is empty of [the existence of] a self that willfully arises. It is also not a self. It is empty of [the existence of] a part of the self. It does not belong to me. It is not permanent and is empty of permanence. It is also neither durable, eternal, nor stable." This is observing that phenomena are empty of self from six aspects.

How phenomena are observed from eight aspects

> One sees physical phenomena as being without essence: empty of any permanent and substantial (*niccasāra*), durable and substantial (*dhuvasāra*), pleasurable and substantial (*sukhasāra*), substantial self (*attasāra*), permanent, durable (*dhuva*), eternal (*sassata*), or stable core.[611]

This is observing that phenomena are empty of self from eight aspects with regard to physical phenomena or the aggregate of materiality. The same is true for the four aggregates of mentality, the sense doors, sense objects, sense consciousnesses, contact, feeling, and so on. Moreover, six of these eight aspects (permanent and substantial, durable and substantial, permanent, durable, eternal, and stable) are synonyms.

How phenomena are observed from ten aspects

> One sees physical phenomena as: empty [of permanence, pleasure, beauty, and the ability to control] (*ritta*), insubstantial [and therefore vain, empty of the above qualities] (*tuccha*), empty of a substantial self [that accomplishes things according to its will] (*suñña*), having no self [that accomplishes things according to its will] (*anattā*), not having control (*anissariya*), not subject to creation by will (*akāmakāriya*), not subject to control [by desire] (*alabbhanīya*), not subject to anyone's wishes (*avasavattana*), strangers or outsiders (*para*), and secluded [because there is neither the effect within the cause nor the cause within the effect, cause and effect are empty of each other] (*vivitta*).[612]

In order to understand the aspect of not being subject to creation by will, consider the example of a bubble. There is no way that a bubble can be fashioned into a [durable] cup [that will hold liquid]. In the same way, it is impossible to command physical phenomena to become permanent, pleasurable, beautiful, and identified with a self. In other words, only when the necessary conditions exist do physical activities occur (such as walking, standing, sitting, lying down, bending, stretching, feeling hot or cold, seeing clearly, and so on). It is impossible to cause a physical activity to occur simply by will.

The term "secluded" (*vivittato*) means "secluded from cause and effect":

> Kamma does not exist in its result, and the kammic result does not exist in kamma, either. They are secluded from each other, although there is no result without kamma.[613]

The subcommentary, consistent with this passage, explains:

> Causal phenomena are not pregnant with resultant phenomena, nor vice versa.[614]

For a more detailed explanation, see the section on insight knowledge that discerns conditionality earlier in this chapter.

It is interesting that only the first four of the ten aspects mentioned above are the same as those found in the *Niddesa*, which says:

> Then one sees the world in terms of emptiness. One sees physical phenomena as: empty [of permanence, pleasure, beauty, and the ability to control] (*ritta*), insubstantial [and therefore vain, empty of the above qualities] (*tuccha*), empty of a substantial self [that accomplishes things according to its will] (*suñña*), having no self [that accomplishes things according to its will] (*anattā*), without core or essence (*asāraka*), a murderer (*vadhaka*), non-enduring (*vibhāva*), the root of [a great array] of unwholesomeness (*aghamūla*), intoxicating, being associated with mental defilements (*sāsava*), and conditioned (*saṅkhatā*).[615]

Thus the commentary on this Pāḷi text lists ten aspects that are not all the same as those found in the original source material. Given this inconsistency, one should not consider it necessary to memorize these ten aspects or to follow them in exact order when one practices. If one is able to experience only one or a few of these aspects of impermanence, unsatisfactoriness, and not-self, it will serve the purpose. However, one may experience all the aspects mentioned here, depending on one's perfections and disposition. So understand that these are possible manifestations of practice, rather than a procedure to follow.

How phenomena are observed from twelve aspects

> One sees that physical phenomena are not a being, not a soul, not a human, not a child, not a female, not a male, not a self, not "I," not belonging to a self, not "mine," not belonging to another, and not belonging to anyone.[616]

This is how physical phenomena are observed. The same applies for feeling, perception, and so on.

The first eight of these twelve aspects reject the existence of an everlasting self in the body with the ability to perform actions according to its will; the last four show that physical phenomena do not belong to a self. But these are not meant to reject the conventional understanding that people apply in their daily lives, such as saying "a person," "his property," "my property," "his limbs," "my limbs," "her children," "my children," and so on.

Some are critical of this commentary because it mentions different aspects than the original Pāḷi text, and they claim that the commentary written by Venerable Buddhaghosa rejects not only the notion of a self, as did the Buddha, but rejects also the conventional truth that is applied in everyday life. This is just a misinterpretation. There are many commentarial descriptions of not-self, as was the case with insight knowledge by comprehension, wherein some of the aspects mentioned in the commentary differ from those found in the original text. But their purpose is certainly not to refute the validity of conventional truth, but rather to refute the validity of an everlasting self.[617] This is why the *Visuddhimagga-mahāṭīkā* says:

> In statements such as, "The body is not a being," and so on, the word "being" is not used in the everyday sense because it is already implicitly understood that the body is not a "being" in that conventional sense. No one would ever call the body alone a "being." Instead, it refers to the "self" that others imagine to be a being. They consider the self to be an entity that is attached [to the body] or attaches [the body] to itself. However, the body is not [associated with] such a self. Thus, seeing that the body is not a being refers to knowing that the body is empty of any self. The same applies for the statements, "The body is not a soul," and so on.[618]

The three stages of equanimity

> Initially, there is the desire for deliverance; in the middle, there is renewed observation; finally, there is balanced awareness. How? Initially, there is the desire for deliverance; in the middle, there is renewed observation; finally, there is balanced awareness of arising [. . . of occurrence, . . . of sign, . . . of accumulation, . . . of relinking, . . . of despair.] This is called knowledge of equanimity toward phenomena. Arising is unsatisfactory. Thus it is seen with desire for deliverance, renewed observation, and balanced awareness. This is called knowledge of equanimity toward phenomena. Arising is fearful . . . Arising is worldly . . . Arising is

> conditioned . . . This is called knowledge of equanimity toward phenomena.[619]

Note that in subsequent repetitions of this verse, initial arising is replaced in turn by occurrence, sign as having a solid form, shape, or substance, accumulation of wholesome actions, relinking, destination, first arising, reappearance, birth, old age, sickness, death, worry, lamentation, and despair. The second paragraph is repeated four times for each of these, replacing unsatisfactory with fearful, worldly, and conditioned.

> Desire for deliverance, renewed observation, and a balanced awareness constitute this knowledge. In early stages, when one feels weary of the initial arising and so on [of phenomena] due to the knowledge of disenchantment and is eager to escape from them, it is knowledge that desires deliverance. In the intermediate stages, when one observes phenomena once more with the purpose of getting free from them, it is knowledge of reobservation. In the last stage, after one has been freed [from attachment and concern regarding phenomena], balanced awareness becomes well established.[620]

Note that here the phrase "after one has been freed" means that one has eliminated any attachment to, or concern about, conditioned phenomena. The statement "balanced awareness becomes well established" means that from the mature stages of insight knowledge of reobservation through peak knowledges that lead to it, the awareness that contemplates conditioned phenomena continues very smoothly, balanced, and steadily for long periods without much effort.

These three insight knowledges are actually the immature, intermediate, and mature phases of the same insight knowledge. They all involve the same understanding that both observed objects and the mind that observes them are constituted of nothing but conditioned phenomena with the same characteristics. Thus the *Paṭisambhidāmagga* says:

> The insights called desire for deliverance, reobservation, and equanimity are the same in terms of their characteristics. They are different in expression only.[621]

For this reason, one may experience insight knowledge of equanimity toward phenomena very soon after insight knowledge that desires deliverance and insight knowledge of reobservation.

Peak insight knowledge of equanimity toward phenomena

For some meditators, insight knowledge of adaptation, knowledge of change-of-lineage, and path knowledge and fruition knowledge quickly follow insight knowledge of equanimity toward phenomena. But others at this stage may experience many fluctuations over a long period, moving between an insight of strong and moderate quality. The *Visuddhimagga* describes the dynamic in this way:

> [In days of old, sailors at sea would release a land-finding crow to find the nearest land. If it sighted land, the crow would immediately fly to the coast, otherwise it would return to the ship.] In the same way, if a meditator's knowledge of equanimity toward phenomena recognizes the peace of nibbāna as peaceful, it leaves the ongoing process of phenomena behind and rushes to nibbāna. If not, it returns again to take conditioned phenomena as its objects. Like sifted rice or carded cotton that becomes increasingly refined with repeated processing, this insight becomes well established by repeatedly observing conditioned phenomena in a variety of ways, abandoning fear and delight in them, maintaining a balanced contemplation of them [without too much or too little effort] and resting [awareness] on the three universal characteristics.[622]

The *Visuddhimagga-mahāṭīkā* says that when knowledge of equanimity toward phenomena is at its peak, objects become apparent without much effort and awareness of them happens by itself. It will seem as if observed objects and the mind that observes them happen by themselves. Therefore, it is said that one is able to observe conditioned phenomena and the three general characteristics without much effort and with a balanced mind, free from fear or delight.

The passage above says that insight knowledge of equanimity toward phenomena sees and rushes to nibbāna. This means that this insight has developed into an insight that leads to emergence, which leads directly to insight knowledge of adaptation that occurs just prior to the knowledge of change-of-lineage that actually takes nibbāna as its object. In other words, when one repeatedly develops insight knowledge of equanimity toward phenomena, it becomes sharp, clear, and powerful enough to produce insight knowledge of adaptation, which in turn leads to knowledge of change-of-lineage with which one actually sees nibbāna. Thus the mind rushes into nibbāna, taking it as its object. As the *Mahāṭīkā* describes it:

> Being sharp, clear, and powerful, equanimity toward delightful and fearful phenomena is well established. Such equanimity toward phenomena, when repeatedly developed until mature enough to produce knowledge of adaptation, is said to see nibbāna as ultimate peace. Then, abandoning the ongoing process of conditioned phenomena, this knowledge is said to rush straight to nibbāna. Thus it can be said that knowledge of equanimity toward phenomena is one with knowledge of adaptation and knowledge of change-of-lineage.[623]

Insight Knowledge Leading to Emergence

When insight knowledge of equanimity toward phenomena matures enough to produce insight knowledge of adaptation, one's confidence will become very strong. Due to the power of one's confidence, the observing mind will become very clear and its energy very steady, being neither too strong nor too weak. Mindfulness will become very obvious and the mind well focused on objects to be noted. Thus does insight knowledge of equanimity toward phenomena become remarkably sharp and powerful, and one clearly notices that the observing mind has improved and become better, being especially swift and distinct.

Eventually, two or three mental processes of insight occur (called *sadisānupassanāvīthi*) that see conditioned phenomena in one of their three aspects, as either impermanent, unsatisfactory, or not-self. For example, if with the first of these mental processes one sees impermanence, then one will also see impermanence with the second and third. Or if with the first process one sees unsatisfactoriness or not-self, then that is what one will see with the second and third processes as well. In addition, if one sees impermanence, one will see it from one of its ten aspects. If one sees unsatisfactoriness, one will see it from one of its twenty-five aspects, and if one sees not-self, one will see it from one of its five aspects.

These two or three final mental processes of insight knowledge of equanimity toward phenomena are called "peak-reaching equanimity" (*sikhāpattasaṅkhārupekkhā*) and "insight that leads to emergence" (*vuṭṭhānagāminīvipassanā*). The term "emergence" refers to path knowledge in two ways: It "emerges" from phenomena, in that it does not take any signs of phenomena (*saṅkhāranimitta*) as its object; or it "emerges" from the mental defilements, kamma and its result, in that it prevents them from occurring (*pavatta*).

The three knowledges that include peak-reaching knowledge of equanimity toward phenomena, insight knowledge of adaptation, and knowledge of change-of-lineage are referred to as "insight that leads to emergence," because they lead directly to the path known as "emergence." That is why the *Abhidhammattha-saṅgaha* says:

> Peak-reaching equanimity, along with adaptation, is called insight that leads to emergence.[624]

> If insight that leads to emergence arises by seeing [phenomena] to be not-self, then the path that follows is called "liberation through emptiness" (*suññatovimokkho*); if it arises by seeing them to be impermanent, it is called "liberation through signlessness" (*animittovimokkho*); if it arises by seeing them to be unsatisfactory, it is called "liberation through desirelessness" (*appaṇihitovimokkho*).[625]

Understand that here knowledge of adaptation, by inference, sees the same aspect of phenomena (either not-self, impermanence, or unsatisfactoriness) as equanimity that reaches its peak.

> "Reaches its peak" and "leads to emergence" are both synonyms for these three knowledges, beginning with equanimity toward phenomena. They are said to "reach their peak" because they lead to the peak [of insight] and are said to "lead to emergence" because they go toward emergence. "Emergence" is used to refer to the path because it emerges from phenomena to be observed externally and from [defilements and] resultant phenomena

> that are possible internally. Thus the insight that goes toward that emergence associated with the path is called "[insight that] leads to emergence."[626]

Note that the phrase "phenomena to be observed externally" used in this passage does not refer to phenomena associated with other beings or inanimate objects. It refers to all phenomena that arise in oneself but that may seem strange or foreign.

Adaptation

We can describe the peak-reaching equanimity that is part of insight knowledge that leads to emergence in terms of the mental processes (*vīthicitta*) that it involves.[627] First the vibration of the life-continuum (*bhavaṅgacalana*) occurs for two mind-moments. This is followed by one mind-moment of adverting consciousness that adverts to sense objects [at the mind door] and seven mind-moments of impulsion consciousness. According to the commentary on the *Vibhaṅga*, the impulsion consciousness associated with insight is not followed by any registration of the sense object. Thus immediately after the impulsion consciousness, the life-continuum occurs several more times, concluding the mental process. Two or three of these mental processes occur in a row.

Immediately afterward the mental process associated with the path occurs. It begins with a mind-moment of adverting consciousness that adverts to the mental or physical phenomenon that is currently arising and passing away. The quality of this adverting is the same as that of the preceding two or three mental processes—that is, it considers the same aspect of impermanence, unsatisfactoriness, or not-self.

This adverting consciousness is followed by three mind-moments of insight impulsion consciousness, which contemplate the same object from the same aspect. The first of these three mind-moments of impulsion consciousness is called "preparation" (*parikamma*), the second is called "access" (*upacāra*), and the third is called "adaptation." The first is called preparation because it is the impulsion consciousness of preparation. The second is called access because it is the impulsion consciousness that serves as the access to the absorption of the path (*magga-appāna*). The third mind-moment is called adaptation because it is consistent with, or adapts to, both the preceding insights starting from the insight knowledge of arising and passing away and the thirty-seven requisites of enlightenment (*bodhipakkhiyādhammā*) that are part of path consciousness (*magga-cittuppāda*). These are the specific names given to each of these three individual mind-moments of impulsion consciousness. They may each also be referred to as a "repetition impulsion consciousness" (*āsevanajavana*), a "preparation impulsion consciousness," an "access impulsion consciousness," or an "adaptation impulsion consciousness."

Insight knowledge of adaptation includes these three mind-moments of adaptation impulsion consciousness. A meditator cannot individually notice either the preceding adverting consciousness or these three adaptation impulsion consciousnesses. Instead, the meditator notices them as a whole, in the same way that one would notice an ordinary mental process of seeing and so on, along with the adverting consciousness and the seven mind-moments of impulsion consciousness, as a whole.

This portion of the mental process [of realizing the unconditioned] is described as follows in the texts:

> When the path is about to occur, [knowledge of] equanimity toward phenomena sees conditioned phenomena as impermanent, unsatisfactory, or not-self, and descends into the life-continuum. Immediately after the life-continuum, mind-door-adverting consciousness arises and takes formations as its object, seeing them as either impermanent, unsatisfactory, or not-self in the same way that [knowledge of] equanimity toward phenomena did. This adverting consciousness replaces the preceding life-continuum and is immediately followed by the first impulsion consciousness, without any gap in between. This first impulsion consciousness, called "preparation," takes formations as its object in the same way.[628]
>
> The phrase "sees conditioned phenomena as either impermanent, unsatisfactory, or not-self, and descends into the life-continuum" means that the impulsion consciousness associated with [knowledge of] equanimity toward phenomena occurs seven times, contemplates one of the three universal characteristics of the phenomena, and ends with a return to the life-continuum. That is, the life-continuum arises immediately afterward.
>
> The phrase "in the same way that [knowledge of] equanimity toward phenomena did" means [that the adverting consciousness sees the phenomena] in the same way that insight

> with equanimity toward phenomena that was involved in the last two or three preceding mental processes did—that is, it contemplates [the same aspect of] impermanence, unsatisfactoriness, or not-self with respect to conditioned phenomena.[629]

A misleading mistake

Recently I found that in the Burmese edition of the *Visuddhimagga-mahāṭīkā*, the phrase "two or three" (*dvatti*) in the above passage has been replaced by the number "thirty-two" (*dvattiṃsa*). Mistakenly thinking this typographical error to be correct, some scholars have gone so far as to explain the number "thirty-two" by multiplying the eight attainments (*samāpatti*) by the four styles of meditation.[630]

Grammatically, however, it is clear that the phrase "two or three" refers to the number of impulsion consciousness mental processes, and not to an enumeration of equanimity toward phenomena. In fact, it is clear, based on the subcommentary, that this number obviously refers to the number of preceding impulsion consciousness mental processes and not to the so-called "thirty-two types of equanimity toward phenomena."

Some other scholars say that the number "thirty-two" itself refers to the number of impulsion consciousness mental processes. But this claim is not supported by any other commentary or subcommentary and is directly contradicted by this passage from the *Mahāṭīkā*:

> Because such repetition is required, two or three impulsion consciousness processes accompanied by neutral feeling must necessarily occur before attaining the fourth jhāna, just as two or three impulsion consciousness processes with the same insight contemplation must occur before the path mental process.[631]

This passage supports the fact that two or three impulsion consciousness processes occur before the fourth jhāna by comparing it to the fact that two or three impulsion consciousness processes occur before path consciousness. This implies that the latter fact would have been universally accepted (*samāṇavāda*) and well enough established to support the former assertion.

This confusion cannot be attributed to a simple spelling mistake, since *dvatti* is very different from *dvattiṃsa*. However, two or three impulsion consciousness processes will provide adequate repetition to lead to the path, and the Sinhalese edition of the *Visuddhimagga-mahāṭīkā* also says "two or three" in this passage, rather than "thirty-two." Based on this evidence, we must conclude that "two or three" is the correct reading, and "thirty-two" has only come into use through some kind of typographical error.

Knowledge of change-of-lineage

Immediately after insight knowledge of adaptation, the impulsion consciousness called "change-of-lineage" (*gotrabhū javana*) occurs. This mind-moment abandons conditioned objects and takes the unconditioned, nibbāna, as its object. The insight associated with this moment of impulsion consciousness is called knowledge of change-of-lineage (*gotrabhūñāṇa*). When the mind takes nibbāna as its object at this point, it is different from taking any other sense object as its object. Unlike previous mental states, which experienced objects as if seeing them "from outside," one experiences this change-of-lineage as "rushing into" the unconditioned state, which is the opposite of what is conditioned. The *Paṭisambhidāmagga* defines change-of-lineage as follows:

> It is called "change-of-lineage" because it abandons arising and rushes into non arising. It is called "change-of-lineage" because it overcomes conditioned phenomena, which [should be seen as] external [like strangers or outsiders], and rushes into nibbāna, which is the cessation of conditioned phenomena.[632]

Path knowledge and fruition knowledge

Knowledge of change-of-lineage is immediately followed by one mind-moment of the impulsion consciousness associated with the [attainment of the supramundane] path (*maggajavana*), which takes nibbāna as its object. The insight or wisdom that accompanies this path consciousness is called "path knowledge." It is also referred to as the "purification by knowledge and vision."

Immediately after path consciousness, the fruition consciousness (*phala*) arises. It occurs for two mind-moments in an average person, but it will occur for three in a person with sharp insight or wisdom. This is because such people only required two mind-moments of adaptation impulsion consciousness [to accomplish the knowledge of adaptation], rather than three.[633] Later on, when absorbed in fruition (*phalasamāpatti*), countless mind-moments of fruition consciousness may occur in a row. The insight or wisdom that accompanies this fruition consciousness is called "fruition knowledge."

The object of path and fruition consciousness is not taken as if it stands outside and one is focusing on it. Instead, it is as if the mind enters or is absorbed into the cessation of conditioned phenomena. This is why these types of consciousness are referred to as "absorption" (*appanā*); that is, they enter into or get absorbed in nibbāna.

The two or three mind-moments of fruition are followed by several mind-moments of the life-continuum, which are in turn followed by mind-moments of reviewing (*paccavekkhaṇā*).

The experience of cessation

The consciousness of change-of-lineage, path consciousness, and fruition consciousness that take nibbāna as their object only last for a few mind-moments. Therefore, these three kinds of consciousness will usually not be distinct as separate [entities] for the meditator. They are normally only distinct as a whole.

This is how one can experience them: one can clearly see how the mind initially enters into the state of the cessation of conditioned phenomena by escaping from observed objects and the mind that notes them, which constitute conditioned phenomena. One can also obviously see how the consciousness stays for a short moment in the cessation of conditioned phenomena. Reflecting about the state where conditioned phenomena have ceased can be distinct, too. This is like waking up from sleep or suddenly emerging from water. If one has scriptural knowledge, one can discern that the initial entry into cessation is change-of-lineage, the short moment of cessation is path consciousness, and the final stage of the cessation that is immediately followed by reflection is fruition consciousness.

The simile of crossing a canal

The *Visuddhimagga* gives the following simile for the experience of path and fruition:

> Wishing to get to the other bank of a canal, one rushes toward it, takes hold of a rope or vine attached to an overhanging branch, and jumps over the canal with one's body bent toward the other bank. Once one is over the other bank, one releases the rope and lands there. Initially, one is unsteady on one's feet, but one gradually regains one's balance.
>
> In the same way, a meditator who wishes to reach nibbāna, the other bank of existences, births, destinations, stations, and spheres, rushes toward it with the help of the eight knowledges beginning with knowledge of arising and passing away, and so on. One takes hold of the rope of one physical phenomenon or the vine of one mental phenomenon that are attached to the branch of the body by adverting to its impermanence, unsatisfactoriness, or not-selfness through the adverting consciousness that constitutes the immature stage of adaptation knowledge.
>
> Then, without releasing the object, one jumps toward the other bank through the first adaptation mind-moment, which is actually the preparation impulsion consciousness. One bends one's mind toward nibbāna, just as one would bend one's body toward the other bank of the canal, with the second adaptation mind-moment, which is actually the access impulsion consciousness. One comes within range of nibbāna with the third adaptation mind-moment, like one who has swung far enough that one is over the other bank.
>
> Once the third mind-moment of adaptation disappears, one releases the conditioned phenomenon that was its object and lands in nibbāna, the other bank that is the cessation of conditioned phenomena, with change-of-lineage. One is initially unsteady, because one is unfamiliar with the experience of nibbāna, but later one regains one's balance with the help of path knowledge.[634]

This simile is very consistent with a meditator's actual experience. So one should repeatedly reflect on it and try to understand it through practice!

Contemplation of jhāna

Here is another explanation of how one can experience path knowledge from the *Mahāmālunkya Sutta*[635] or the *Pañcama Sutta*[636]:

> Here, with seclusion from [objects of attachment],[637] with the abandoning of unwholesome states, with the complete tranquillization of bodily inertia, quite secluded from sensual pleasures, secluded from unwholesome states, a bhikkhu enters upon and abides in the first jhāna, which is accompanied by applied and sustained thought, with rapture and pleasure born of seclusion.
>
> Whatever exists therein of material form, feeling, perception, formations, and consciousness, he sees those states as impermanent, as suffering, as a disease, as a tumor, as a barb, as a calamity, as an affliction, as alien, as disintegrating, as void, as not self. He turns his mind away from those states and directs it towards the deathless element thus: "This is the peaceful, this is the sublime, that is, the stilling of all formations, the relinquishing of all attachments, the destruction of craving, dispassion, cessation, Nibbāna."[638]

At the moment of path consciousness, of course, a meditator does not think or reflect that it is "peaceful, sublime," and so on. He or she simply experiences directly that quality of peacefulness and sublime contentment. It is only afterward, during the mental process, that one reviews one's attainment and may have such thoughts and reflections. As the commentary on the Majjhimapaṇṇāsa[639] explains:

> Taking nibbāna as its object, path consciousness is directed toward it. One does not verbally reflect, "This is the peaceful, this is the sublime." Rather, one realizes that nibbāna has those qualities and directs the mind toward it.[640]

The forty aspects of phenomena

The *Paṭisambhidāmagga* explains the process of path knowledge in this way: path knowledge occurs due to the insight knowledge of adaptation that is developed by contemplating phenomena from one of their forty aspects, called the forty "*-to*s," and one sees nibbāna as the opposite of any of the forty "*-tos*." I will mention just six of these forty aspects of phenomena here.

> Seeing that the five aggregates are impermanent, one attains knowledge of adaptation. Seeing that the cessation of the five aggregates is timeless peace, permanent nibbāna, one falls into the noble path.[641]

The phrase "seeing that the five aggregates are impermanent" is said to apply to all meditators in general. It does not mean that a particular meditator sees all five aggregates at once. In fact, one arrives at insight knowledge of adaptation by contemplating only one of the aggregates or, to be precise, only a single phenomenon from among one of them. That is why the simile from the *Visuddhimagga* says, "One takes hold of the rope of one physical phenomenon, or the vine of one mental phenomenon, attached to the branch of the body, by adverting to its impermanence, unsatisfactoriness, or not-self."

In addition many other commentaries use the expression "emerging from physical phenomena, emerging from immaterial phenomena" (*rūpā vutthāti . . . arūpe vutthāti*)[642] when explaining how insight knowledge of adaptation is immediately followed by knowledge of change-of-lineage and path knowledge. This is because the wisdom of some is so outstanding that the insight knowledges and path knowledge arise within a single sitting or within a moment. It is with reference to this that it is figuratively said that one "emerges from the five aggregates once and for all."

Thus the correct interpretation of the above verse is that insight knowledge of adaptation results from seeing one mental or physical phenomenon to be impermanent, and it is immediately followed by knowledge of change-of-lineage and path knowledge that experience the state that is empty of impermanent phenomena.

To explain further, a meditator directly experiences the arising and passing away of conditioned phenomena, and so their impermanence is obvious during the moments of insight. But during the moments of change-of-lineage and path and fruition consciousness that take nibbāna as their object, one does not experience arising and passing away and only the cessation of conditioned phenomena is obvious. Therefore, the nature of nibbāna can be understood as permanent, free from arising and passing away.

You should understand the following verses from the *Paṭisambhidāmagga* in the same way.

> Seeing that the five aggregates are broken, one attains knowledge of adaptation. Seeing that the cessation of the five aggregates is nibbāna as an unbroken peace, one enters the noble path.
>
> Seeing that the five aggregates are unsatisfactory, one attains knowledge of adaptation. Seeing that the cessation of the five aggregates is nibbāna as happiness, one enters the noble path.
>
> Seeing that the five aggregates are fearful, one attains knowledge of adaptation. Seeing that the cessation of the five aggregates is nibbāna free from fear, one enters the noble path.
>
> Seeing that the five aggregates are not-self, one attains knowledge of adaptation. Seeing that the cessation of the five aggregates is nibbāna as an ultimate state, one enters the noble path.[643]

Note that, in this verse, nibbāna is described in an ultimate sense, rather than as the opposite of one of the forty "*-tos*." Elsewhere nibbāna is described with terms like "lacking in causes" (*aparappaccaya*) and "ultimate emptiness" (*paramasuñña*), which are not direct opposites of any of the forty "*-tos*." So the above statement that "nibbāna is the opposite of any of the forty '*-tos*'" is only meant in a general sense.

> Seeing that the five aggregates are useless, one attains knowledge of adaptation. Seeing that the cessation of the five aggregates is nibbāna, is useful and noble, one enters the noble path.[644]

Out of these six verses, the first two show how the path known as "signless (*animitta*) emancipation" arises by using insight knowledge of adaptation to contemplate impermanence. The second two show how the path known as "desireless (*appaṇihita*) emancipation" arises by using insight knowledge of adaptation to contemplate unsatisfactoriness. The third two show how the path known as "empty (*suññata*) emancipation" arises by using insight knowledge of adaptation to contemplate not-self.

For details about the other thirty-four "*-tos*," refer to the *Paṭisambhidāmagga*. If you want to know them in a general way, see the section in this book that deals with knowledge of reobservation, where the forty "*-tos*" are explicitly mentioned. These forty "*-tos*" are aspects that insight knowledge of adaptation should see.

An explanation for King Milinda

The *Milindapañha* explains the process of attaining the path and fruition as follows:

> By repeatedly contemplating phenomena, the noting mind itself attains to a state of nonoccurrence that is beyond the occurrence of phenomena. O Great King, one who arrives at such a state by practicing properly is said to experience nibbāna.[645]

While experiencing insight, a meditator observes the continuous flow of mental and physical phenomena, just as one might watch the continuous flow of a current of water. As one is observing in this way, one's insight grows increasingly swift and eventually turns into insight that leads to emergence. This insight then carries the meditator to that state that is opposite to the phenomena being observed, that is, to the state of cessation of phenomena. The types of consciousness that enter this state are change-of-lineage and path and fruition consciousnesses. This means that a person who arrives at that state experiences nibbāna.

Vision of the Dhamma

Many discourses describe the arising of path knowledge in this way:

> . . . the spotless immaculate vision of the Dhamma arose: "All that is subject to arising is subject to cessation."[646]

But this contemplation is not occurring at the moment of path. At that moment, one only experiences nibbāna in the form of the cessation of all conditioned phenomena.

However, one is able to understand that one has entered the cessation of all conditioned phenomena, which is the cessation of objects and the mind that notes them, at the moment of reviewing knowledge, which reviews the path, the fruit, and nibbāna. One can also understand that with the attainment of "the element of nibbāna without the residue remaining" (*anupādisesanibbānadhātu*), all conditioned phenomena cease [to arise].[647]

Moreover, one is able to understand that any phenomena that come into existence are bound to vanish. This is why, if one continues practicing after path and fruition and reviewing knowledge, one's insight resumes at the stage of seeing the arising and passing away of phenomena. The commentary to the *Ambaṭṭha Sutta* of the Dīgha Nikāya explains the vision of the Dhamma as follows:

> "The vision of the Dhamma" refers to path knowledge of stream entry. In order to demonstrate what the path involves, it is said [that one realizes]: "All that is subject to arising is subject to cessation." This is because path consciousness, when taking the cessation of all conditioned phenomena, nibbāna, as its object, accomplishes the function of giving rise to this clear and penetrating understanding regarding all conditioned phenomena.[648]

This commentary addresses the question of why path consciousness is said to realize "All that is subject to arising is subject to cessation," even though it only takes unconditioned phenomena (*asaṅkhata*) as its object and not conditioned phenomena (*saṅkhata*). It is interesting to note that the expression "the vision of the Dhamma" is also used to refer to the first three path knowledges in the *Brahmāyu Sutta*,[649] and to all four path knowledges in the *Cūḷarahulovāda Sutta*.[650]

A word of caution

One should be aware that the commentaries and this book only explain the details of the process of the path in order to provide some theoretical understanding. In practice, it is impossible to distinguish every individual mind-moment involved in a single mental process with a single object. Therefore, a meditator should not try to analyze which moments of his or her experience are impulsion consciousness and so on. The only aspects of the practice that are appropriate to be checked against the texts are: the sequence of the insight knowledges up to insight knowledge of adaptation; the extraordinary occurrence of insight that leads to emergence; the last awareness of phenomena during adaptation that immediately and by itself falls into nibbāna; the occurrence of reviewing knowledge; and the return to insight knowledge of arising and passing away.

Reviewing Knowledge

Five subjects to consider

After a person has experienced nibbāna with path knowledge and fruition knowledge, first he or she reviews the path, fruition, and nibbāna that have been attained. Meditators with theoretical knowledge may further review which of the defilements have been abandoned and which have yet to be abandoned. This knowledge is called "reviewing knowledge" (*paccavekkhaṇañāṇa*). According to the *Abhidhammatthasaṅgaha*:

> The wise person reviews the path, fruit, nibbāna, and he either reviews or does not review the defilements destroyed and the remaining defilements.[651]

The following three kinds of reviewing certainly always occur: reviewing the path, reviewing the fruit, and reviewing nibbāna. These two kinds of reviewing, however, may or may not occur: reviewing which defilements have been destroyed and reviewing which defilements still remain. It is not certain that these always occur. In other words they may occur only for those persons who have learned which path abandons which defilements. They may not occur for those who have no theoretical knowledge [about this matter]. In most of the important commentaries, it is also explained in this way. The fact that some of the reviewing knowledges may not occur is shown below with quotes from the Pāḷi text and the commentaries:

> "I have wondered, venerable sir, what state is still unabandoned by me internally, owing to which at times these states of greed, hate, and delusion invade my mind and remain."
>
> "Mahānāma, there is still a state unabandoned by you internally, owing to which at times states of greed, hate, and delusion invade your mind and remain."[652]

According to the following commentary on this text, some noble persons only consider one or two of the five reflections:

> It is said that Mahānāma, who had reached the second path knowledge, thought that attachment, aversion, and delusion

> could be eradicated by the second path. However, he knew that they had not yet been abandoned from his mind. Therefore, he suspected that what had not been abandoned could recur later.
>
> Is it possible for a noble disciple to have this kind of uncertainty? Yes, it is. Why? Because he was not well versed in the teachings about which paths abandon which defilements.
>
> Does this mean that he did not experience the reviewing knowledge that reviews path, fruition, and so on? Of course not. However, the complete set of reviewing does not occur for all noble disciples. Some review only the mental defilements that have been abandoned. Some consider only the remaining defilements. Some consider only path, some only fruition, and others only nibbāna. Among the five possible subjects of reviewing one or two of them are reviewed for sure.[653]

It is interesting that, while most other commentaries unanimously agree that all noble beings review at least the three subjects of path, fruition, and nibbāna, this commentary says that a noble disciple might only review just one of the five subjects. It is impossible for an ordinary person to be sure whether or not some noble person only reviews one of the five subjects during reviewing knowledge. Only a very extraordinary person, who knew the ways of reflection of all noble persons in the Buddha's dispensation, can be sure about this point. So the claim of this commentary is noteworthy.

Abandonment of defilements[654]

I will now briefly explain the defilements that are abandoned by the four paths, so that you can become well versed in the teachings about them.

The ten fetters

> Out of the ten mental fetters, five are abandoned by the first path: wrong view, doubt, adherence to rites and ceremonies (*sīlabbatāparāmāsa*), and sensual desire and aversion (*paṭigha*) that are strong enough to result in lower rebirths. The gross forms of sensual desire and aversion are abandoned by the second path, and the subtle forms of sensual desire and aversion are abandoned by the third path. The remaining five fetters are

abandoned by the fourth path: desire for fine-material existence (*rūparāga*), desire for immaterial existence (*arūparāga*), conceit, restlessness, and ignorance.[655]

The ten defilements

> Out of the ten defilements (*kilesā*), wrong view and doubt are abandoned by the first path, hatred is abandoned by the third path, and greed, delusion, conceit, sloth, restlessness, moral shamelessness, and moral fearlessness are abandoned by the fourth path.[656]

Note that in the Pāḷi, the modifier "only" (*eva*) does not appear in the above passage. Therefore it does not contradict the understanding that the forms of hatred that lead to lower rebirth and the gross forms of hatred are abandoned by the first and second stages of the path, respectively. Regarding the seven defilements abandoned by the fourth path, the forms of them that lead to lower rebirth are abandoned by the first path, their gross forms are abandoned by the second path, and their subtle forms are abandoned by the third path.

The ten "wrongs"

> Out of the ten "wrongs," wrong view, false speech (*musāvāda*), wrong action (*micchākammanta*), and wrong livelihood (*micchā-ājīva*) are abandoned by the first path. Wrong thought (*micchāsaṅkappa*), slanderous speech, and harsh speech are abandoned by the third path. Here, speech refers to the volition to engage in such talk. Frivolous speech,[657] wrong effort (*micchāvāyāma*), wrong mindfulness (*micchāsati*), wrong concentration (*micchāsamādhi*), wrong deliverance (*micchāvimutti*), and wrong knowledge (*micchāñāṇa*) are abandoned by the fourth path.[658]

The Pāḷi word *vācā* used in this passage literally means "speech." However, this does not mean that the physical voice is something to be eliminated with the stages of the path. In reality it is the volition that gives rise to these forms of unwholesome speech that are abandoned by the paths.

Thus here only the unwholesome volition are referred to as wrong speech, slanderous speech, and harsh speech. Without volition these types of wrong speech rarely happen. This only occurs in a very few cases, such as that of the Venerable Pilindavaccha,[659] a senior monk and arahant who was a fully enlightened being who often used harsh language without unwholesome volition. So it is the volition that gives rise to unwholesome speech that is called "wrong speech."

Similarly the volition that gives rise to unwholesome action is called "wrong action," and the volition that leads to unwholesome speech and action related to one's livelihood is called "wrong livelihood." The memory of worldly things, such as one's family, previous sense pleasures, past quarrels, and so on, is called "wrong mindfulness." And the delusion that leads one to plan, to engage in, and to think about retrospectively unwholesome actions is called "wrong knowledge."

Thinking that one is free from defilements although one is not yet liberated from them, and assuming certain states to be enlightenment although these states are not free from defilement, is called "wrong deliverance." In an ultimate sense, it is a type of desire. Thus its forms that can lead to lower rebirth are abandoned by the first path, while its gross and subtle forms are abandoned by the second and third paths, respectively. The wrong notion of deliverance that is due to desire for existence (*bhavarāga*) is only abandoned by the fourth path.

The nature of the remaining "wrongs" is obvious.

The eight vicissitudes of life

> Out of the eight vicissitudes of life (*lokadhamma*), aversion [to the four disagreeable conditions] is abandoned by the third path, while delight [in the four agreeable conditions] is abandoned by the fourth. However, some scholars assert that fame and praise are also abandoned by the third path.[660]

Some scholars also say that fame and praise are "abandoned by the fourth path" (*catuttañāṇavajjho*). But since this doesn't differ in meaning from what had already been stated at the beginning of the passage, I consider "abandoned by the third path" (*tatiyañāṇavajjho*) to be the original and correct reading of the Pāḷi here.[661]

The five types of stinginess

> Stinginess is abandoned by the first path.[662]

There are five types of stinginess (*macchariya*): stinginess regarding lodgings, supporters, friends, or relatives, gain, beauty, and knowledge. The first path abandons these:

"Stinginess regarding lodgings" (*āvāsamacchariya*) is to not want to share one's lodgings, such as one's monastery campus, building, or room, with somebody else. Wanting someone else to leave the place where one lives or is staying is also stinginess regarding lodging. But it is not stinginess to wish to protect one's lodgings from a person who is unscrupulous.

"Stinginess regarding friends" (*kulamacchariya*) is to not want one's supporters, friends, or relatives to be friendly with others. It is not stinginess regarding friends, however, to wish them to avoid associating with unscrupulous people.

"Stinginess with regard to gain" (*lābhamacchariya*) is to be jealous of another person's gain. It is also stinginess regarding gain to be unwilling to share one's belongings with worthy people, such as respectable fellow monks and so on. It may not be stinginess, however, if one is too fond of something to give it away; it could also be attachment. Note that the characteristic of stinginess is to be unable to bear that others possess or use one's belongings, whereas the characteristic of greed is to be attached to one's belongings without being able give them away. It is also not considered stinginess to not want somebody to obtain things if one believes that he or she will destroy them or misuse them in some way, such as to bully or intimidate others. Sometimes thoughtful reconsideration (*paṭisaṅkhāna*) prevents one from giving something away, if one realizes that one really cannot do without it. See the section that deals with "the ten fetters" in chapter 4.

"Stinginess with regard to beauty" (*vaṇṇamacchariya*) is to be jealous of another's beauty, virtuous conduct, or reputation. This kind of jealousy happens when one does not want to hear about someone else's good reputation, or if one does not want someone else to be as popular as one is. It is not stinginess, however, if one does not want to hear praises of virtue that someone is actually not endowed with.

"Stinginess with regard to knowledge" (*dhammamacchariya*) is to be unwilling to share one's knowledge or learning of the Dhamma and the scriptures with others. It is not stinginess, however, to withhold one's knowledge from someone who one believes to be dishonest or unscrupulous.

The twelve perversions

> Out of the twelve perversions (*vipallāsā*), the perversions of perception, consciousness, and view that take [mental and physical phenomena that are] impermanent to be permanent, and that take [mental and physical phenomena that are] not-self to be self, are abandoned by the first path. The perversion of view that takes [mental and physical phenomena that are] painful to be pleasurable, and that takes [physical phenomena that are] ugly to be beautiful, is also abandoned by it. The perversion of perception and consciousness that take [physical phenomena that are] ugly to be beautiful are abandoned by the third path. The perversions of perception and consciousness that take [mental and physical phenomena that are] painful to be pleasurable are abandoned by the fourth path.[663]

Those who have reached the first and second paths still enjoy sensual pleasures because they have not yet abandoned the perversions of perception and consciousness that take their own bodies and the bodies of others to be beautiful and pleasurable. However, they no longer have the perversion of view that phenomena are beautiful and pleasurable. Therefore, when they think and reflect about them, they do not find anything beautiful or pleasurable. A person who has attained the third path is not yet free from the perversions of perception and consciousness that take what is painful to be pleasurable. As a result, while still being attached to their own bodies, they can enjoy fine-material and immaterial existence.

The wrong ways of behaving

> The wrong ways of behaving (*agati*) are abandoned by the first path.[664]

When one judges a case or divides property amongst people, or when praising, punishing, admonishing, or supporting, and so on, one may act wrongly due to desire (*chandāgati*), act wrongly due to hatred (*dosāgati*), act wrongly due to delusion (*mohāgati*), or act wrongly due to fear (*bhayāgati*). These unjust biases or wrong ways of behaving are abandoned by the first path.

The four taints

> Out of the four taints, the taint of wrong view is abandoned by the first path, the taint of sensual desire is abandoned by the third path, and the taint of existence and the taint of delusion are abandoned by the fourth path.[665]

There are two different views of the distinction between the taint of sensual desire (*kāmāsava*) and the taint of existence (*bhavāsava*):

According to the discourses, the desire for the pleasures of the five senses is called the taint of sensual desire. The desire for fine-material and immaterial existence, for fine-material and immaterial absorption, the desire connected with eternity view (*sassatadiṭṭhi*), and the desire for sensual existence (*kāmabhava*) such as a human, celestial being, nagā, garuda, woman, man, and so on[666] is called the taint of existence.

However, according to the Abhidhamma, only the desires for fine-material and immaterial existence, and for fine-material and immaterial absorption, are called taints of existence. In an ultimate sense, these are forms of desire dissociated from wrong view. Such desires are still present even at the third path and are only abandoned with the fourth path. The taint of sensual desire, on the other hand, includes all of the other desires mentioned in the previous paragraph.

The five hindrances

> Out of the five hindrances (*nīvaraṇā*), doubt is abandoned by the first path; sensual desire, aversion, and regret are abandoned by the third path; and sloth and torpor and restlessness are abandoned by the fourth path.[667]

Note that, according to the Abhidhamma:

> . . . it is said that desire for the sense-sphere is abandoned by the third path; all desire [for fine-material and immaterial spheres]

> that is considered sensual desire[—that is, all greed and the hindrance of sense desire—] is abandoned by the fourth path.[668]

The four types of clinging

> Out of the four types of clinging, clinging to sense pleasures because all worldly phenomena are considered potential objects of desire is abandoned by the fourth path. The other three types of clinging are eradicated by the first path.[669]

The other three types of clinging not explicitly named here in this text are: Clinging to the belief that rites and rituals—such as the ancient practices of imitating bulls or dogs—lead to eternal bliss and liberation from the cycle of suffering (*sīlabbatupādāna*). This also includes the belief that moral conduct alone, without realization of the Four Noble Truths, can lead to liberation from the cycle of suffering; clinging to any of the twenty types of personality view that are based on the view of self (*attavādupādāna*); and clinging to any other type of wrong view (*diṭṭhi-upādāna*).

The seven latent defilements

> Out of the seven latent defilements (*anusaya*), wrong view and doubt are abandoned by the first path; sensual lust and aversion are abandoned by the third path; and conceit, desire for existence, and ignorance are abandoned by the fourth path.[670]

Note that one can confirm whether or not these latent defilements have been abandoned based on whether or not they become active in the mind.

The ten unwholesome courses of action

> Out of the ten types of unwholesome courses of action, these five are abandoned by the first path: killing, taking what is not given, sexual misconduct, lying, and wrong view. These three are abandoned by the third path: slander, harsh language, and ill will. Frivolous speech and covetousness are eradicated by the fourth path.[671]

Note that the unwholesome action of lying is only consummated when it affects another's welfare, that of slander only when it damages the relationship between two parties, and that of frivolous speech only when others take it seriously.

Here again the modifier "only" is not used to limit the abandoning of some of these unwholesome actions to the third and fourth paths alone. Note that the forms of slander, harsh language, ill will, frivolous speech, and covetousness that lead to lower rebirths are abandoned by the first path, their gross forms related to sensual desire and ill will are abandoned by the second path, and their subtle forms related to sensual desire and ill will are abandoned by the third path. Frivolous speech and covetousness that are related to desire for existence are abandoned by the fourth path.

The twelve unwholesome states of consciousness

> Out of the twelve unwholesome states of consciousness, doubt and the four associated with wrong view are abandoned by the first path, the two associated with aversion are abandoned by the third path, and the others are abandoned by the fourth path.[672]

The "others" refer to the four dissociated from wrong view and one accompanied by restlessness.

Here, also, there is no qualification of "only" that would limit the abandoning of some of these unwholesome states of consciousness entirely to the third and fourth paths. In fact, the four states of consciousness dissociated from wrong view rooted in greed and the two states of consciousness rooted in aversion that lead to lower rebirth are abandoned by the first path. Those same six states of consciousness in their gross forms related to sensual desire and aversion, and the state of consciousness accompanied by restlessness that is eliminated together with the gross forms of sensual desire and aversion, are abandoned by the second path.

The subtle forms of these six states of consciousness related to sensual desire and aversion, and the state of consciousness accompanied by restlessness that is eliminated together with the subtle forms of sensual desire and aversion, are abandoned by the third path. The four states of consciousness dissociated from wrong view related to desire for existence and the remaining states of consciousness accompanied with restlessness are abandoned by the fourth path.

Simultaneous elimination

If through the power of path a defilement is eliminated in a person, then other defilements that are equal in degree will also be eliminated. "Simultaneous elimination" (*pahānekaṭṭha*) refers to the fact that all these defilements are eliminated together at a single time. In other words, it means "dhammas are eliminated together from a person's mind."

Other defilements

> The first path abandons the four states of consciousness associated with wrong view and accompanied by greed as well as the two states of consciousness rooted in hatred that lead to a lower rebirth.
>
> The state of consciousness accompanied by restlessness, however, is only abandoned by the three higher paths that are called "meditation."[673]

We should understand, based on this Pāḷi quote, that it is only abandoned by the fourth path. Logically the state of consciousness accompanied by restlessness that is present in those who have attained the second and third paths is not as gross as in ordinary people and those who have attained the first path. Thus it is shown that the state of consciousness accompanied by restlessness is only abandoned by the three higher paths that are called "meditation" (*bhāvanā*).

There are many more unwholesome states to be abandoned (*pahātabba akusula dhamma*)[674] that neither the *Visuddhimagga* nor this book explicitly mention. Among these unwholesome states, the ones that are directly mentioned by name [in the *Abhidhammattha Saṅgaha*] should be understood as shown above in the section that deals with abandonment of defilements. The unwholesome states that are not directly mentioned by name should be included in the relevant unwholesome state of consciousness, so that you may know which path abandons them. This is explained in the *Visuddhimagga-mahāṭīkā* as follows:

> It should be noted that these mind states, such as contempt (*makkha*), domineering attitude (*paḷāsa*), deceit (*māyā*), hypocrisy (*sāṭheyya*), heedlessness (*pamāda*), obstinacy (*thambha*), and disdain (*sārambha*) should be included.[675]

The *Vatthūpama Sutta*[676] and others list sixteen imperfections that defile the mind that are to be abandoned: covetousness and unrighteous greed (*abhijjāvisamalobha*), ill will (*byāpāda*), anger (*kodha*), revenge (*upanāha*), contempt (*makkha*), a domineering attitude (*paḷāsa*), envy (*issā*), avarice (*macchariya*), deceit (*māyā*), fraud (*sāṭheyya*), obstinacy (*thambha*), disdain (*sārambha*), conceit (*māna*), arrogance (*atimāna*), vanity (*mada*), and negligence (*pamāda*).

Further, more than one thousand unwholesome states to be abandoned are mentioned in other discourses and in the *Khuddakavatthuvibhaṅga* of the Abhidhamma. Among these the ones that cannot be known in an ultimate sense (such as contempt, a domineering attitude, and so on) should be inferred to their relevant unwholesome state of consciousness and so one can know which paths abandon them.

Here "contempt" is disrespect toward a person to whom one should feel grateful for previous assistance or kindness. One obliterates the previously performed good deeds when talking to this person. In an ultimate sense, this is a state of consciousness accompanied by displeasure.

Having "a domineering attitude" is to consider oneself on equal footing with a highly noble and virtuous person and speak in a way that belittles this person's virtue. In an ultimate sense, the wish to turn against someone is a state of consciousness rooted in hatred.

"Deceit" is to cover one's faults or shortcomings. In an ultimate sense, it is a state of consciousness rooted in greed.

"Fraud" is to make others believe that one is endowed with virtuous qualities although one is not. In an ultimate sense, it is a state of consciousness rooted in greed.

"Obstinacy" is not to respect those who are worthy of respect, to treat them in an impolite and harsh manner. In an ultimate sense, it is a state of consciousness associated with conceit.

"Disdain" means the desire to outdo others, to triumph over them, to oppress them. In an ultimate sense, it is conceit that is a state of consciousness dissociated from wrong view.

"Negligence" means to engage in sensual pleasures and unwholesome actions based on negligence. In an ultimate sense, it is a state of consciousness rooted in greed.

> Six defilements are abandoned by the first path: contempt, a domineering attitude, envy, stinginess, deceit, and fraud. Four are eradicated by the third path: ill will, anger, revenge, and

> negligence. Six defilements are eradicated by the fourth path: covetousness, selfishness, obstinacy, disdain, conceit, arrogance, and vanity.[677]

Here it is said that certain defilements are abandoned by the third or fourth path. This is only said with reference to their complete abandonment. Of the ten defilements that are completely abandoned by the third and fourth path, the forms of those defilements leading to rebirth in the lower realms are abandoned by the first path, their gross forms are abandoned by the second path, and their subtle forms are abandoned by the third path.

Confirming stream entry

The mirror of the Dhamma

> Therefore, Ānanda, I will teach you a Dhamma exposition called the mirror of the Dhamma, equipped with which a noble disciple, if he wishes, could by himself declare of himself: "I am one finished with hell, finished with the animal realm, finished with the domain of ghosts, finished with the plane of misery, the bad destinations, the nether world. I am a stream enterer, no longer bound to the nether world, fixed in destiny, with enlightenment as my destination."
>
> And what, Ānanda, is that Dhamma exposition, the mirror of the Dhamma, equipped with which a noble disciple, if he wishes, could by himself declare thus of himself? Here, Ānanda, a noble disciple possesses confirmed confidence in the Buddha thus: "The Blessed One is an arahant, perfectly enlightened, accomplished in true knowledge and conduct, fortunate, knower of the world, unsurpassed leader of persons to be tamed, teacher of devas and humans, the Enlightened One, the Blessed One." He possesses confirmed confidence in the Dhamma thus: "The Dhamma is well expounded by the Blessed One, directly visible, immediate, inviting one to come and see, applicable, to be personally experienced by the wise." He possesses confirmed confidence in the Saṅgha thus: "The Saṅgha of the Blessed One's disciples is practicing the good way, practicing the straight way,

> practicing the true way, practicing the proper way; that is, four pairs of persons, the eight types of individuals—this Saṅgha of the Blessed One's disciples is worthy of gifts, worthy of hospitality, worthy of offerings, worthy of reverential salutation, the unsurpassed field of merit for the world."
>
> He possesses the virtues dear to the noble ones—unbroken, untorn, unblemished, unmotted, freeing, praised by the wise, ungrasped, leading to concentration.
>
> This, Ānanda, is that Dhamma exposition, the mirror of the Dhamma, equipped with which a noble disciple, if he wishes, could by himself declare of himself: "I am one finished with hell . . . I am a stream enterer, no longer bound to the nether world, fixed in destiny, with enlightenment as my destination."[678]

According to this discourse, after a layperson has repeatedly reflected that he or she is fulfilled with the four qualities, he or she can decide [that the attainment of stream entry has been accomplished] and mention the attainment to another person of the same level, if necessary. There is no need for anyone else to confirm the attainment, because no one other than the Buddha could do that. Nonetheless it is the responsibility of a meditation teacher to explain the progression of the insight knowledges, the path knowledge and fruition knowledge, the reviewing knowledge, and this Dhamma exposition called the mirror of Dhamma. This is because it is impossible for most noble persons[679] to enumerate all of the insight knowledges and their attributes that they have experienced during the course of their practice, or the defilements that they have or have not yet abandoned. In this respect noble persons can be compared to travelers visiting an unfamiliar place. There is no way for them to know the names of all of the places that they see along the way if no one tells them, even though they have passed by them.

For this reason the Buddha gave talks on the qualities of a stream enterer to noble disciples, such as the merchant Anāthapiṇḍika, to provide them with the necessary information. Only after hearing such a talk could they properly claim their realization and be congratulated on their achievement by senior monks such as Venerable Sāriputta. Those at the three lower paths of enlightenment could only know that they were no longer vulnerable to rebirth in the lower realms by hearing the Buddha's explanation. (I will clarify this later.)

Therefore, understand that most noble persons are not able to comprehensively understand the attributes of an ariya. Also, as explained earlier, they cannot necessarily discern which defilements they have and have not yet abandoned. So a meditation teacher should explain the insight knowledges and their progress to his or her students. However a monk who is an ariya can only reveal his spiritual attainment, if he wishes, in such a way that he would not violate the monastic rule that allows a monk to reveal his spiritual achievement to his fellow monks and nuns for only two purposes (*bhūtārocana*): to help them appreciate the virtues of the Dhamma and to arouse their interest in practice.

Unshakable faith

A noble one's faith is so unshakable that no one will be able to persuade, threaten, or mislead them into abandoning their faith. These three qualities are illustrated by the stories of Suppabuddha, Dhanañjānī, and Sūrambaṭṭha respectively.

> *The Story of Suppabuddha*
>
> In the time of the Buddha, there lived a leper named Suppabuddha who was always complaining about his painful disease. He was very poor and had nobody to care for him and had begged for his food since he was a child. One day he happened to listen to a Dhamma talk given by the Buddha, standing at the fringes of the audience. As he listened he became a stream enterer. He was then very eager to report his attainment to the Buddha, but he was embarrassed to do so in front of the crowd. So he moved off some distance as the audience dispersed and then started walking back toward the Buddha.
>
> As he did so Sakka, the king of the devas, appeared in front of him in the sky and wanting to test him, said: "O Suppabuddha, you are so poor, helpless, and miserable! I will grant you boundless wealth. In exchange for my aid, all you must do is say, 'The Buddha is not the genuine Buddha. The Dhamma is not the genuine Dhamma. The Saṅgha is not the genuine Saṅgha. I renounce the Buddha, Dhamma, and Saṅgha.'"
>
> "Who are you?" asked Suppabuddha.
>
> "I am Sakka, King of the Devas," was the answer.
>
> "How dare you! Shame on you!" scolded Suppabuddha.

"You are not even worthy of speaking with me, yet you insult me by saying that I am poor, helpless, and miserable. That is not true at all. Am I not a true son of the Buddha? I am a rich man, possessing the greatest wealth." Then he recited this verse:

The wealth of faith, the wealth of virtuous behavior,
the wealth of moral shame and moral dread,
the wealth of learning and generosity,
with wisdom, the seventh kind of wealth:
when one has these seven kinds of wealth,
whether a woman or a man,
they say that one is not poor,
that one's life is not lived in vain.[680]

Sakka then departed, went to the Buddha, and reported this exchange. The Buddha replied, "Neither you alone, nor thousands like you, would be able to persuade him to deny his faith in the Buddha, Dhamma, and Saṅgha."

Suppabuddha also made his way back to the Buddha. After he had spoken with the Buddha and was departing, he was gored to death by a cow. But due to the virtues that he had started to develop while hearing the Dhamma—such as faith, moral conduct, knowledge, generosity, and wisdom—he was reborn as a powerful celestial being in the heaven realm of the thirty-three gods. While living in the human realm, he had belonged to a very low class, but as a result of the power of the noble path, he was so much more powerful than many of the other celestial beings that many of them were excessively jealous of his virtues. Eventually Sakka himself had to intervene and explain why Suppabuddha possessed such power. The power of the noble path is indeed incredibly strong.

This story is found in the commentaries to the *Udāna* and *Dhammapada* of the Khuddaka Nikāya and commentaries to the Saṃyutta Nikāya. It illustrates how promises of wealth or fame cannot induce a person who is indeed a noble one to reject the Buddha, Dhamma, and Saṅgha. A noble person is never able to abandon the Triple Gem for any reason. This same kind of unshakable faith is found in anyone, if he or she is a noble one.

The Story of Dhanañjānī

"My dear, I have invited five hundred brahmins to come for dinner tomorrow," said the brahmin Bhāradvāja to his wife, Dhanañjānī. "Lately, you have been paying homage to that bald-headed bhikkhu, reciting 'homage to the Buddha' any time you stand, sit, sneeze, or cough. I implore you not to do this tomorrow in the presence of my honorable guests while they are dining. If they overhear you, they will not be pleased with me at all."

"I don't care whether your brahmins or the celestial beings are pleased with you or not," Dhanañjānī replied frankly. "I can't help paying homage to the Buddha."

"My dear," chided the brahmin, "even the great city gate can be kept closed. It shouldn't be a problem to keep your mouth that is only two fingers wide closed for just that short moment while the brahmins are dining, should it?"

But his pleas were in vain.

Then, grabbing his double-edged sword, he threatened, "Look here! I will slice you into pieces like a bamboo shoot from head to toe if you pay homage to the bald-headed bhikkhu tomorrow."

But Dhanañjānī simply replied: "You may slice my limbs however you wish, brahmin, I will not deviate from the exalted Buddha's teaching."[681]

"Very well," said the brahmin in resignation, "do as you please."

The next day, while the brahmins were dining, Dhanañjānī accidentally fell and hit her head. Feeling the pain, she remembered the Buddha and paid homage to him by holding her hands in *añjali* and turning in the direction of the Veḷuvana monastery where the Buddha was residing, reciting three times: "Homage to the Blessed One, the Arahant, the Perfectly Enlightened One."

The brahmins overheard her and were so angry that they left, saying they did not want a meal served by those who held to a different doctrine. The brahmin Bhāradvāja was also very angry, and after reviling his wife in many ways he went to see the Buddha in order to question him. However he was so inspired by the Buddha's responses that he ended up becoming a monk in the Buddha's holy order and eventually became an arahant.

This story is found in the Brāhmaṇa Saṃyutta of the Saṃyutta Nikāya. Nobody can intimidate a noble person into rejecting the Triple Gem. If one is really a noble one, one's faith is as firm as Dhanañjānī's.

The Story of Sūrambaṭṭha

One hundred thousand world-cycles ago, during the time of the Padumuttara Buddha, Sūrambaṭṭha made a wish to be honored as being foremost among those who had firm faith in the Triple Gem. Later, during the time of our Gotama Buddha, he was reborn into a rich family in the city of Sāvatthi and one day invited the Buddha for a meal. Afterward, as he listened to the talk given by the Buddha, Sūrambaṭṭha became a stream enterer.

After the Buddha had left, Māra came to Sūrambaṭṭha's house disguised as the Buddha and stood in front of the door. Sūrambaṭṭha thought that there must be a special reason for the Buddha to return within such a short time. He rushed to the Buddha, paid homage to him, and asked for the reason.

Māra replied, "Sūrambaṭṭha, I'm sorry that I spoke so carelessly before by saying that all the five aggregates are impermanent, unsatisfactory, and not-self. Actually only some of them are, some others are permanent, everlasting, and eternal."

"This is a very suspicious statement," Sūrambaṭṭha thought. "A buddha's words are never ambiguous or uncertain. This must be Māra who opposes the Buddha." Then Sūrambaṭṭha asked him frankly, "You are Māra, aren't you?"

"Yes. It's true," admitted Māra.

"My faith is so unshakable," declared Sūrambaṭṭha, "that neither you alone nor a thousand māras like you are able to mislead me into abandoning it. Gotama Buddha has just given a talk saying that all conditioned phenomena are impermanent. Don't stay under my door!" Clapping his hands he drove Māra away. Thus Sūrambaṭṭha was honored as the foremost of the laymen who rightly understood the attributes of the Triple Gem with unshakable faith.

This story is found in the commentary to the Aṅguttara Nikāya. Although a truly noble person's faith may not be strong enough to receive the title of being foremost (*etadagga*) in faith like Sūrambaṭṭha, it is strong enough to prevent any deviation from the Buddha's teaching. However skilled someone else may be in deceiving or lying, the noble person's faith in the Triple Gem would not be broken or destroyed. If somebody says that the Buddha taught that conditioned phenomena are permanent, satisfactory, and self, a noble person is able to conclude that this is not the Buddha's teaching. Furthermore, if anyone makes any of the following statements, a noble person is able to conclude that these are contradictory and false: there is no omniscient buddha existing in this world; the Buddha is not able to know some phenomena; path knowledge and fruition knowledge and nibbāna do not exist; it is not possible to lessen or abandon defilements through practice; based on a concentrated mind, there is no such supramundane understanding that personally sees conditioned phenomena as impermanent, unsatisfactory, and not-self; or there are no noble persons who have practiced in order to abandon defilements or who are currently practicing to do so.

Noble conduct

> Noble ones are endowed with this desirable, loveable, and agreeable moral conduct. These five precepts are not given up in the course of a lifetime and are desired by the noble ones. [So referring to this form of the five precepts] it is said [that one is endowed with conduct that satisfies noble ones.][682]
>
> If in a given life, one did not know that one was a noble one, even if somebody were to say to one, "Kill this insect and you can rule the universe," since one is a noble disciple one would be unable to kill the insect. Or if someone said, "If you do not kill this insect, I will chop off your head," since one is a noble disciple one would be unable to kill the insect, even though one would lose one's head.[683]

Similarly, a noble one is incapable of engaging in stealing, sexual misconduct, telling lies that affect another being's welfare, or abusing intoxicants. He or she cherishes these five precepts more than wealth or power, more than his or her own life and limbs.

Thus when reflecting or being confronted with a situation that could give rise to defilements, a stream enterer finds that his or her faith is unshakable and his or her moral conduct is pure as was shown earlier in the *Mahāparinibbāna Sutta*.[684] Furthermore, it is also obvious that the defilements abandoned by the first path never arise again, even if one is confronted with a situation that could give rise to them.

Freedom from rebirth in lower realms

The noble ones, although still subject to the aggregates, are completely free from rebirth in the lower realms. Stream enterers and once returners are reborn in the realms of sensual pleasures (*kāmasugatibhūmi*), the fine-material realms (*rūpabhūmi*), or the immaterial realms (*arūpabhūmi*). And if they are reborn in the human realm, they are only reborn into upper class families. Nonreturners are only reborn in the fine-material and immaterial realms.

One may wonder whether these noble ones realize that they are completely free from rebirth in the lower realms. The answer can be inferred from a dialogue between the Buddha and Venerable Sāriputta found in the Aṅguttara Nikāya:

> Now on that occasion those wanderers had assembled and were sitting together when this conversation arose among them: "Friends, anyone who passes away with a residue remaining is not freed from hell, the animal realm, or the sphere of afflicted spirits; he is not freed from the plane of misery, the bad destination, the lower world."
>
> Then the Venerable Sāriputta neither delighted in nor rejected the statement of those wanderers, but rose from his seat and left, [thinking]: "I shall find out what the Blessed One has to say about this statement."
>
> . . .
>
> "Who, Sāriputta, are those foolish and incompetent wanderers of other sects and who are those that know one with a residue remaining as 'one with a residue remaining' and one without residue remaining as 'one without residue remaining'?
>
> "These nine persons, Sāriputta, passing away with a residue

remaining, are freed from hell, the animal realm, and the sphere of afflicted spirits; freed from the plane of misery, the bad destination, the lower world."[685]

The Buddha then goes on to enumerate the nine types of person:

1. An attainer of nibbāna in the interval (*antarāparinibbāyī*): perfect in moral conduct, perfect in concentration, but with only medium development of wisdom. After abandoning the five lower fetters, this one, having been reborn spontaneously in a higher world, generates the final path before he or she has reached the midpoint of the lifespan.
2. An attainer of nibbāna upon landing (*pahaccaparinibbāyī*): perfect in moral conduct, perfect in concentration, but with only medium development of wisdom. After abandoning the five lower fetters, this one generates the final path after passing the midpoint of the life-span, even when on the verge of death.
3. An attainer of nibbāna without exertion (*asaṅkhāraparinibbāyī*): perfect in moral conduct, perfect in concentration, but with only medium development of wisdom. After abandoning the five lower fetters, this one attains the final path without exertion.
4. An attainer of nibbāna with exertion (*sasaṅkhāraparinibbāyī*): perfect in moral conduct, perfect in concentration, but with only medium development of wisdom. After abandoning the five lower fetters, this one attains the final path with exertion.
5. One bound upstream, heading toward the Akaniṭṭha realm (*uddhaṃsotakaniṭṭhagāmī*): perfect in moral conduct, perfect in concentration, but with only medium development of wisdom. After abandoning the five lower fetters, this one passes from one higher realm to another until he or she reaches the Akaniṭṭha realm, the highest pure abode, and there attains the final path.
6. A once returner (*sakadāgāmī*): perfect in moral conduct, with medium development of concentration and wisdom. After abandoning the three fetters and weakening greed, hatred, and delusion, this one returns once to this world.
7. A one seed attainer (*ekabījīsotāpanna*): perfect in moral conduct, with medium development of concentration and wisdom. After abandoning the three fetters, this one becomes "one who sprouts

up once more," coming back only once more to the human realm.

8. A family-to-family attainer (*kolaṃkolasotāpanna*): perfect in moral conduct, with medium development of concentration and wisdom. After abandoning the three fetters, this one becomes "one who rushes from house to house," coming back two or three times to good families.
9. A seven-times-at-most attainer (*sattakkhattusotāpanna*): perfect in moral conduct, with medium development of concentration and wisdom. After abandoning the three fetters, this one is reborn at the most seven times, coming back to the celestial or human realms.[686]

The Buddha concluded this talk with a statement that demonstrates that noble ones do not automatically know that they are no longer subject to rebirth in the lower realms. He said:

> "Sāriputta, I had not been disposed to give this Dhamma exposition to the bhikkhus, bhikkhunīs, male lay followers, and female lay followers. For what reason? I was concerned that on hearing this Dhamma exposition, they might take to the ways of heedlessness. However, I have spoken this Dhamma exposition for the purpose of answering your question."[687]

It is clear, based on this statement, that those of the Buddha's disciples who had attained the three lower stages of path knowledge and fruition knowledge did not know by themselves that they were no longer vulnerable to lower rebirths, but they instead had to learn this from the Buddha. The Buddha realized that they would be negligent and make no further effort to attain the fourth path if they, who had attained the first, second, or third paths, still being subject to clinging, knew that they were completely free from rebirth in the lower realms. As a result, he did not previously answer this question. Only after hearing the Buddha's discourse were those who had attained the first, second, or third paths able to know and conclude that they were destined for a good rebirth. So it is obvious that they were not able to know and decide it for themselves.

That is why Mahānāma once had doubts about his future destination, even though he had attained the second path knowledge. This is the dialogue that took place between the Buddha and Mahānāma, which can be found in the Saṃyutta Nikāya:

> ". . . In the evening, when I am entering Kapilavatthu after visiting the Blessed One or the bhikkhus worthy of esteem, I come across a stray elephant, a stray horse, a stray chariot, a stray cart, a stray man. On that occasion, venerable sir, my mindfulness regarding the Blessed One becomes muddled, my mindfulness regarding the Dhamma becomes muddled, my mindfulness regarding the Saṅgha becomes muddled. The thought then occurs to me: 'If at this moment I should die, what would be my destination, what would be my future bourn?'"
>
> "Don't be afraid, Mahānāma! Don't be afraid, Mahānāma! Your death will not be a bad one, your demise will not be a bad one. When a person's mind has been fortified over a long time by faith, virtue, learning, generosity, and wisdom, right here crows, vultures, hawks, dogs, jackals, or various creatures eat his body, consisting of form, composed of the four great elements, originating from mother and father, built up out of rice and gruel, subject to impermanence, to being worn and rubbed away, to breaking apart and dispersal. But his mind, which has been fortified over a long time by faith, virtue, learning, generosity, and wisdom—that goes upwards, goes to distinction."[688]

> ". . . A noble disciple who possesses four things slants, slopes, and inclines towards Nibbāna. What four? Here, Mahānāma, a noble disciple possesses confirmed confidence in the Buddha . . . in the Dhamma . . . in the Saṅgha . . . He possesses the virtues dear to the noble ones, unbroken . . . leading to concentration."[689]

The Buddha went on to give these two similes:

> "Suppose, Mahānāma, a man submerges a pot of ghee or a pot of oil in a deep pool of water and breaks it. All of its shards and fragments would sink downwards, but the ghee or oil there would rise upwards. So too, Mahānāma, when a person's mind has been fortified over a long time by faith, virtue, learning, gen-

> erosity, and wisdom, right here crows . . . or various creatures eat his body . . . But his mind, which has been fortified over a long time by faith, virtue, learning, generosity, and wisdom—that goes upwards, goes to distinction."[690]
>
> "Suppose, Mahānāma, a tree was slanting, sloping, and inclining towards the east. If it was cut down at its foot, in what direction would it fall?"
>
> "In whatever direction it was slanting, sloping, and inclining, venerable sir."
>
> "So too, Mahānāma, a noble disciple who possesses these four things slants, slopes, and inclines towards Nibbāna."[691]

Based on these dialogues, it is clear that a stream enterer or a once returner may not be sure about his or her prospects for future destination, nor of which defilements have and have not been abandoned. However, this type of uncertainty should not be confused with the doubt that is uprooted by the first path. It can be classified into eight or sixteen particular types of doubt, as described earlier [in the section on insight knowledge that discerns conditionality: purification by overcoming doubt.].

The great reviewing knowledges (Mahāpaccavekkhaṇañāṇa)

I will now translate the Pāḷi text that explains seven ways in which a stream enterer reviews his or her attainment.

> And how does this view that is noble and emancipating lead the one who practices in accordance with it to the complete destruction of suffering?
>
> Here a bhikkhu, gone to the forest or to the root of a tree or to an empty hut, considers thus: "Is there any obsession unabandoned in myself that might so obsess my mind that I cannot know or see things as they actually are?" If a bhikkhu is obsessed by sensual lust, then his mind is obsessed. If he is obsessed by ill will, then his mind is obsessed. If he is obsessed by sloth and torpor, then his mind is obsessed. If he is obsessed by restlessness and remorse, then his mind is obsessed. If he is obsessed by doubt, then his mind is obsessed. If a bhikkhu is absorbed

> in speculation about this world, then his mind is obsessed. If a bhikkhu is absorbed in speculation about the other world, then his mind is obsessed. If a bhikkhu takes to quarrelling and brawling and is deep in disputes, stabbing others with verbal daggers, then his mind is obsessed.
>
> He understands thus: "There is no obsession unabandoned in myself that might so obsess my mind that I cannot know and see things as they actually are. My mind is well disposed for awakening to the truths." This is the first knowledge attained by him that is noble, supramundane, not shared by ordinary people.[692]

When a noble person is engaged in insight meditation, although at times obsessive defilements arise, they are not able to hinder his or her understanding of arising and passing away of mental and physical phenomena as they really are. And when obsessive defilements do arise, they can be abandoned by him or her by immediately noting them. Noting proceeds smoothly and there are no long periods of wandering thought that cannot be noted. Sometimes, when the momentum of the practice is very good, obsessive defilements no longer arise. While practicing insight meditation, a noble one investigates and reflects that he or she does not experience any obsessive defilements that hinder the understanding of the arising and passing away of mental and physical phenomena as they really are. As a result he or she can know and conclude thus:

> Again a noble disciple considers thus: "When I pursue, develop, and cultivate this view [knowledge], do I personally obtain serenity [i.e., without wandering thoughts], do I personally obtain quenching [peacefulness, i.e., without defilements aroused by the objects that are observed]?"
>
> He understands thus: "When I pursue, develop, and cultivate this view, I personally obtain serenity, I personally obtain quenching." This is the second knowledge attained by him that is noble, supramundane, not shared by ordinary people."[693]

A noble one who has attained this noble view while repeatedly arousing knowledge pursues, develops, and cultivates this noble view. Because of doing this, he or she can personally experience that obsessive hindrances or defilements are abandoned. One can also experience that defilements are unable to arise when one's noting is continuous. Therefore, when reflecting on this, the third and fourth knowledges arise:

> Again a noble disciple considers thus: "Is there any other recluse or brahmin outside [the Buddha's dispensation] possessed of a view such as I possess [by observing mental and physical phenomena the moment they arise through the six sense doors]?"
>
> He understands thus: "There is no other recluse or brahmin outside [the Buddha's dispensation] possessed of a view such as I possess [by observing mental and physical phenomena the moment they arise through the six sense doors]." This is the third knowledge attained by him that is noble, supramundane, not shared by ordinary people.
>
> Again a noble disciple considers thus: "Do I possess the character of a person who possesses right view [an enlightened being]?" What is the character of a person who possesses right view? This is the character of a person who possesses right view: although he may commit some kind of offense for which a means of rehabilitation has been laid down, still he at once confesses, reveals, and discloses it to the Teacher or to wise companions in the holy life, and having done that, he enters upon restraint for the future. Just as a young tender infant lying prone at once draws back when he puts his hand or foot on a live coal, so too, that is the character of a person who possesses right view.
>
> He understands thus: "I possess the character of a person who possesses right view." This is the fourth knowledge attained by him that is noble, supramundane, and not shared by ordinary people."[694]

A noble monk would only break a major precept such as building a clay hut, or a minor precept such as unintentionally sleeping under the same roof as laypeople. These types of activities are actually only considered offenses because of the rules laid down by the Buddha [i.e., there is no inherent moral wrongdoing involved]. In any event he would never try to hide an offense he had committed; he would readily confess it to his fellow monks. He would go right away to do this, regardless of whether it was day or night, or how dark the night might be. A layperson who is a noble one would behave in the same way, not trying to hide any offense, but rather willingly admitting it if asked.

> Again, a noble disciple considers this: "Do I possess the character of a person who possesses right view?" What is the character of a person who possesses right view? This is the character of a person who possesses right view: although he may be active in various matters for his companions in the holy life, yet he has a keen regard for [pays very careful attention to] training in the higher virtue, training in the higher mind, and training in the higher wisdom. Just as a cow with a new calf, while she grazes, watches [pays very careful attention to] her calf, so too, that is the character of a person who possesses right view.
>
> He understands thus: "I possess the character of a person who possesses right view." This is the fifth knowledge attained by him that is noble, supramundane, not shared by ordinary people.
>
> Again, a noble disciple considers this: "Do I possess the strength of a person who possesses right view?" What is the strength of a person who possesses right view? This is the strength of a person who possesses right view: when the Dhamma and discipline proclaimed by the Tathāgatha is being taught, he heeds it [cherishes it as if it were a great treasure]; gives it attention, engages it with all his mind, hears the Dhamma as with eager ears.
>
> He understands thus: "I possess the strength of a person who possesses right view." This is the sixth knowledge attained by him that is noble, supramundane, not shared by ordinary people.
>
> Again, a noble disciple considers this: "Do I have the strength of a person who possesses right view?" What is the strength of a person who possesses right view? This is the strength of a person who possesses right view: when the Dhamma and discipline proclaimed by the Tathāgatha is being taught, he gains inspiration in the meaning, gains inspiration in the Dhamma [appreciates its essence, comprehends its consistency], and gains gladness connected with the Dhamma.
>
> He understands thus: "I possess the strength of a person who

> possesses right view." This is the seventh knowledge attained by him that is noble, supramundane, and not shared by ordinary people.
>
> When a noble disciple is thus possessed of seven factors, he has well sought the character for realization of the fruit of stream-entry. When a noble disciple is thus possessed of seven factors, he possesses the fruit of stream-entry.[695]

Attainment of Fruition

What is attainment of fruition? It is the mind absorbed in the cessation of all mental and physical phenomena (i.e., nibbāna). Ordinary people cannot enter attainment of fruition because they have never attained fruition consciousness. On the other hand, all those who have attained fruition consciousness can enter attainment of fruition, but only for the highest level of fruition that they have attained. They cannot enter a previous level of fruition [that has since been superseded] or a higher level of fruition that they have not yet attained.

Some scholars have said that only nonreturners and arahants can enter fruition because they have fully developed the training of concentration, while stream enterers and once returners cannot because they have not yet fully developed the training of concentration. However, the *Visuddhimagga* states that there is no reason why any noble one should not be able to enter the attainment at whatever level of fruition she or he has attained, since even ordinary people can enter absorption in the [mundane] jhānas that they have attained. Moreover, the *Paṭisambhidāmagga* explicitly uses the terms "attainment of the fruition of stream entry" (*sotāpattiphalasamāpatti*) and "attainment of the fruition of once returning" (*sakadāgāmiphalasamāpatti*). So it should be clearly understood that any noble one can enter the fruition he or she has attained.

If a noble one is not able to enter the fruition he or she has attained, this is only due to a weakness in concentration and the other remaining mental faculties [rather than any inherent limitation]. In order to fully develop concentration and the other faculties, all one need do is to continue practicing insight meditation. When these faculties are fully developed, one will attain fruition. Only when one can repeatedly enter attainment of fruition should one be satisfied.

Three types of insight

> There are three types of insight: path-oriented, fruition-oriented, and cessation-oriented. Path-oriented insight will lead to path regardless of whether it is strong or weak. Fruition-oriented insight is effective only when it is strong, because it is similar to the development of path. Cessation-oriented insight is effective only when it is neither too strong nor too weak.[696]

The only difference between the strong and weak forms of path-oriented insight mentioned here is that strong insight quickly leads to path (*khippābhiññā*), while weak insight slowly leads to path (*dandhābhiññā*).

According to the subcommentary, even though fruition-oriented insight takes conditioned phenomena as its objects, its function is to withdraw from them and incline toward the fruition consciousness that takes their cessation as its object. In these respects, it is similar to the path consciousness and thus it is said to be "similar to the development of path." The statement "Fruition-oriented insight is effective only when it is strong" refers to the insight of a person who is just learning to master the attainment of fruition, as the commentary to the *Paṭisambhidāmagga* states:

> If insight knowledge of equanimity toward phenomena is sharp, it brings about a path which is able to abandon the defilements. To emphasize how sharp this insight is, the original words are precisely repeated and supplemented with synonyms. However, because the attainment of fruition occurs without any effort, it is naturally tranquil and is related to the path [that one has already attained], and even a weak degree of insight knowledge of equanimity toward phenomena may bring it about. To emphasize this point, only the original words are used here.[697]

Thus when one becomes skilled at entering the attainment of fruition, one will find that even weak insight knowledge of equanimity toward phenomena can lead to it.

The benefit of attaining fruition

What is the benefit of attaining fruition? Just as monarchs and celestial beings enjoy the types of worldly bliss that are unique to their circumstances in life, so too the noble ones enjoy the supramundane bliss associated with their own attainment of fruition and nibbāna.

During the period that they are absorbed in fruition, they are at peace, enjoying the cessation of all conditioned phenomena that are subject to arising and passing away. They remain absorbed in this state for a period of time that they have previously determined by deciding, "I will only allow the fruition consciousness to continue for this long." Furthermore, by frequently entering the attainment of fruition for long periods, they can assure their teachers and fellow meditators of their realization of path and fruition.

Entering the attainment of fruition

> Friend, there are two conditions for the attainment of the signless deliverance of mind[698]: non-attention to all signs and attention to the signless element. These are the two conditions for the attainment of the signless deliverance of mind.[699]

The procedure for entering the state of attainment of fruition is as follows:

> A noble disciple who seeks to attain fruition retreats to a solitary place and observes conditioned phenomena. Beginning from knowledge of arising and passing away, one should develop the various insights until the change-of-lineage that takes a conditioned phenomenon as its object arises. Immediately afterward, one's mind will enter the state of cessation [of conditioned phenomena] in the form of the attainment of fruition. In this case, only the fruition consciousness arises, rather than a new path consciousness, even if one is still a trainee, [that is, one who has attained one of the first three stages of enlightenment]. This is because the mind has previously determined to enter the attainment of fruition.[700]

Note that the *Visuddhimagga* here refers to the [peak] insight that takes a conditioned phenomenon as its object as "change-of-lineage." This is based on the description given in the *Paṭisambhidāmagga*. However, this insight is called "insight knowledge of adaptation" in the *Paṭṭhāna* [and is referred to by that name in this book].

Based on the above passage, understand that a noble person begins his or her insight practice from insight knowledge of arising and passing away. That is, if a noble disciple practices insight, he or she is immediately able to see phenomena arising and passing away. Thus in order to enter the attainment of fruition, one is able to develop the sequence of insight knowledges quite rapidly, quickly moving from insight knowledge of arising and passing away to insight knowledge of equanimity toward phenomena in due course. If the noble one has previously made the determination to become absorbed in fruition, and his or her insight knowledge of equanimity toward phenomena is mature, it is then followed by the insight knowledge of adaptation that leads directly to the cessation of the conditioned phenomena that she or he has been observing.

Path-oriented insight and fruition-oriented insight

This procedure for reaching the attainment of fruition is similar to that for reaching a path consciousness that one has already attained. This is because the fruition consciousness is simply the result of that very attainment of the path. Since, in this case, insight has been practiced expressly for the purpose of entering the fruition, only the fruition consciousness arises, rather than a new path consciousness.

If, on the other hand, one practices insight with the goal of attaining a higher path [i.e., path-oriented insight], then the course of one's insight knowledge will be different from this fruition-oriented insight. This is because the path-oriented insight must fulfill the four functions of right effort.[701] So it may not be as easy to develop higher insight knowledges during path-oriented insight as it was during fruition-oriented insight. That is why the *Mahāṭīkā* states, "The course of fruition-oriented insight is different from that of path-oriented insight."

When practicing path-oriented insight, the different stages of insight knowledge develop in sequence. When one's insight knowledge of equanimity toward phenomena is mature, the higher path that one has aspired to arises. It is not possible that a fruition consciousness that one has not aspired to will arise. However, if insight knowledge of equanimity toward phenomena is not yet mature enough to attain a higher path, one will just continue to experience equanimity toward phenomena over and over again. In this case, it may be that one's mind is actually inclined to experience the fruition that one has already attained [rather than the next path]. Therefore, if one is practicing insight in order to attain a higher path and fruition, one should make a firm resolution not to become absorbed for a specified number of days in the fruition that one has already attained and be careful not to allow one's mind to incline in that direction.

Determining the duration of the attainment

> Friend, there are three conditions for the persistence of the signless deliverance of mind: non-attention to all signs and attention to the signless element, and the prior determination [of its duration].[702]

If a noble one wishes to become absorbed in the attainment of fruition, he or she should determine a time limit for the attainment in advance by resolving, "May the fruition attainment persist for such and such a period of time." This period of time may be five minutes, ten minutes, fifteen minutes, half an hour, one hour, two hours, or longer. While practicing, however, one should just continue observing phenomena without exerting too much effort or giving further thought to this resolve. When the insight knowledge of equanimity toward phenomena matures, the mind then becomes absorbed in the cessation of conditioned phenomena for the time period that was previously determined. Thus the duration of the attainment of fruition persists for the time period that has been determined. However, it is only likely that the duration [of the attainment of fruition] will persist for the whole period of time that has been determined for those whose knowledge is sharp and penetrating. It is likely that it will not persist for the whole period of time that has been determined for those whose knowledge is not sharp and penetrating. And it very often does not persist for long if one enters it without making a prior determination.

The experience of the attainment of fruition

In the Aṅguttara Nikāya, the attainment of fruition is described in this way:

> Here, Ānanda, a bhikkhu is percipient thus: "This is peaceful, this is sublime, that is, the stilling of all activities, the relinquishing of all acquisitions, the destruction of craving, dispassion, cessation, nibbāna."[703] It is in this way, Ānanda, that a bhikkhu could obtain such a state of concentration that he would not be percipient of earth in relation to earth; of water in relation to water; of fire in relation to fire; of air in relation to air; of the basis of the infinity of space in relation to the basis of the infinity of space; of the basis of the infinity of consciousness in relation to the basis of the infinity of consciousness; of the base of nothingness in relation to the base of nothingness; of the base of neither perception-nor-non-perception in relation to the base of neither-perception-nor-non-perception; of this world in relation to this world; of the other world in relation to the other world; of anything seen, heard, sensed, cognized, reached, sought after, and examined by the mind, but he would still be percipient.[704]

The first four points in this last paragraph illustrate how the minds of those who have attained the fine-material jhānas do not go to any of the fine-material jhānas, such as the earth-kasina, water-kasina, and so on, during the attainment of fruition. Similarly, the next four points illustrate how the minds of those who have attained the immaterial jhānas will also cease to give attention to, or go to any objects of, the immaterial jhānas during the attainment of fruition. The two statements about "this world" and "the other world" mean that neither natural nor supernatural thought processes will interfere with the fruition attainment. The phrase "but he would still be percipient" shows that one perceives nibbāna, the cessation of conditioned phenomena.

According to the commentary to the Aṅguttara:

> The string of epithets "the stilling of all activities, the relinquishing of all acquisitions, the destruction of craving, dispassion, cessation, nibbāna" in the first paragraph are all synonymous.
>
> The exclamatory sentence "This is peaceful, this is sublime!" means that if one's entire attention is absorbed in how peaceful nibbāna is, the fruition consciousness (*phalacittuppāda*) may be absorbed in that peace for an entire day. If one's entire attention

> is absorbed in how sublime nibbāna is, the fruition consciousness may be absorbed in that sublime state for an entire day. The expressions "where all suffering ends" and so on all refer to the fruition attainment.[705]

Note that it is mentally, not verbally, that one makes such exclamations as, "This is peaceful, this is sublime!" These expressions are meant to demonstrate how, in fruition consciousness, one's entire attention is absorbed in nibbāna.

Emerging from the attainment of fruition

> Friend, there are two conditions for emergence from the signless deliverance of mind: attention to all signs and non-attention to the signless element.[706]

One emerges from the attainment of fruition when one abandons the cessation of conditioned phenomena as one's object and takes one of the signs among the five signs of conditioned phenomena.[707] The *Visuddhimagga* explains the above Pāḷi quote:

> The phrase "all signs" means the sign of materiality, sign of feeling, sign of perception, sign of formations, and sign of consciousness. Of course, it is not possible to take all the five signs simultaneously as one's object. Therefore, emergence from attainment means that the object is any of these possible signs.[708] Because one can only take one of these signs as one's object, it is the object of the life-continuum. This marks the emergence from the attainment of fruition.[709]

The arising of the life-continuum consciousness is called "emergence from the attainment of fruition." However, it is difficult for ordinary noble ones to clearly know the life-continuum consciousness. Immediately after the life-continuum consciousness arises, either reviewing knowledge that reviews the fruition and nibbāna, reflection about something else, or the noting mind will arise. Only the reviewing, reflecting, and noting minds are obvious and easy to know. Thus when any of these kinds of consciousness arise, this is considered to be emergence from the attainment of fruition.[710]

Unstable attainment

When some meditators practice fruition-oriented insight in order to enter fruition, they may go in and out of the attainment very quickly. In this case his or her consciousness repeatedly alternates between fruition consciousness and ordinary mental states. If they have no mastery regarding entering [the attainment] or no theoretical knowledge [about the attainment], they may think that they are able to observe those ordinary mental states even after having entered the fruition.

In fact, Venerable Moggallāna once had an experience like this, and he told his fellow monks: "My brothers, while I was absorbed in imperturbable absorption (*āneñja jhāna*) on the bank of the Sippinikā River, I heard the cries of elephants that were going to and from the river to drink." According to the commentary on the *Udāna* of the Khuddaka Nikāya, "imperturbable absorption is either the five aspects of absorption in the fourth jhāna or one of these five kinds of concentration that serve as a basis on which the attainment of fruition is entered for an arahant. This concentration is said to be so strong and steady that one who is absorbed in it does not even hear the roar of thunder overhead. Thus Venerable Moggallāna's fellow monks were skeptical about what he said, and they asked the Buddha about it. The Buddha replied:

> Bhikkhus, it is that concentration (i.e., imperturbable absorption), but it has not been fully purified yet.[711]

This means that Venerable Moggallāna's absorption was not yet fully stable, and he was alternating between imperturbable absorption and ordinary mental states. Therefore, he heard the cries of the elephants on this occasion.

The Vinaya commentary explains that Venerable Moggallāna became an arahant just seven days after his ordination. As a newly enlightened monk, he had not yet mastered the five aspects of absorption[712] in the fourth jhāna. Thus during a moment when he had inadvertently emerged from the absorption, he heard the elephants' cries and mistakenly thought that he had heard them during the absorption.

Note that, although only the fourth jhāna is mentioned here, it should be understood to refer to the jhāna associated with the attainment of fruit of arahantship, since Venerable Moggallāna was absorbed in it shortly after becoming an arahant. Also note that, since Venerable Moggallāna mistakenly thought he had heard the elephants during his absorption, it is safe to assume that the attainment of fruition is not always followed by reviewing that reviews the fruition or nibbāna, but it may also be followed by awareness of other objects.

Varying degrees of mastery

From this story we may conclude that even though two noble persons have attained the same stage of path knowledge and fruition knowledge, their degree of mastery in entering fruition may differ. According to the commentary on the Uparipaṇṇāsa of the Majjhima Nikāya:

> There are two types of arahants, one is constantly engaged in tranquility and insight meditation (*satatavihārī*), and the other is not constantly engaged in tranquility and insight meditation (*nosatatavihārī*). The first has the ability to enter the attainment of fruition even after performing a major task. The second does not have the ability to enter the attainment of fruition even after performing a minor task.[713]

The commentary tells the following story to illustrate this point: Once, a senior monk and his novice disciple spent the rains retreat at a forest monastery. Unfortunately there were only enough accommodations at the monastery to provide lodging for the senior monk but not for the novice. The senior monk was so concerned about his novice's lack of shelter that he could not enter the attainment of fruition during the entire three months of the rains retreat. The novice, on the other hand, was able to enjoy his attainment of fruition during those three months.

After the rains retreat, the novice inquired, "Venerable sir, was this forest monastery a suitable place to stay?"

The senior monk replied, "This forest monastery was not suitable for me."

The novice in this story was an arahant constantly engaged in tranquility and insight meditation, and so he could enter the fruition whenever he wished, even though he did not have any accommodation. The senior monk was an arahant, but he was not constantly engaged in tranquility and insight meditation. Because of his concern for the novice he could not enter fruition. Those noble ones who want to enter the attainment of fruition whenever they wish must live their lives constantly engaged in insight meditation.

Nibbāna

I will now briefly explain something about nibbāna, which path and fruition take as their object.

Definitions of nibbāna

Nibbāna is not like a splendid palace, city, or country. It is not like a bright light or some kind of clear, calm element. All of these things are not unconditioned ultimate realities but are concepts or conditioned realities.

In fact nibbāna, as an unconditioned reality, has simply the nature of cessation called "the characteristic of peacefulness" (*santilakkhaṇā*). It is the cessation of the defilements and the rounds of suffering. Or, it is the nonexistence of conditioned phenomena (*visaṅkhāra*), the cessation of conditioned phenomena, and the opposite of what is conditioned. Thus the *Paṭisambhidāmagga* defines it by contrasting it with conditioned phenomena in these ways:

> [Mental and physical] arising is conditioned phenomena. Nonarising is nibbāna.
> [Mental and physical] occurrence is conditioned phenomena. Nonoccurrence is nibbāna.
> [Mental and physical] sign is conditioned phenomena. Nonsign is nibbāna.
> [Mental and physical] accumulation [of kamma] is conditioned phenomena. Nonaccumulation [of kamma] is nibbāna.
> [Mental and physical] rebirth is conditioned phenomena. Nonrebirth is nibbāna.[714]

This Pāḷi quote shows that the nature of nibbāna[715] is the complete cessation of conditioned phenomena, expressed in terms of the cessation of arising, occurrence, sign, accumulation, and rebirth.

Grammatically the word nibbāna can be considered a "verbal noun" and could be interpreted as having any of the following three senses:

> Nibbāna: where the cycle of suffering ceases. (loc., act.)
> Nibbāna: through which the cycle of suffering ceases. (instr., act.)
> Nibbāna: the cessation of the cycle of suffering. (med.)[716]

This definition of nibbāna does not mean that it is simply some kind of empty state that can be understood through everyday ideas. Nibbāna is described as being beyond logic (*atakkāvacaro*), too profound (*gambhīro*), and difficult to be understood (*duddaso*) through common knowledge, and experienced only by the wise (*paṇḍitavedanīyo*) with empirical knowledge. Moreover, since it is beyond the reach of craving, it is also beyond entanglement (*vāna*), which is another term for craving. When nibbāna is experienced by a meditator through path knowledge, that person's mind is freed from craving. Thus the commentaries also define it as follows:

> Nibbāna: liberation from entanglement. (med.)
> Nibbāna: where there is no entanglement. (loc., act.)
> Nibbāna: through which entanglement is eradicated. (instr., act.)[717]

Nibbāna is simply the cessation of mental and physical phenomena that becomes manifest as the signless (*animittapaccupaṭṭhānaṃ*) to a noble one. So although one has experienced it, one cannot describe it in terms of color or form or say what it is like. It can only be experienced or described as the cessation or end of all conditioned mental and physical phenomena. In the *Milindapañha* of the Kuddhaka Nikāya it is shown in this way:

> O Great King [Milinda], nibbāna is incomparable. It cannot be described in its color, shape, size, dimension, likeness, remote cause, immediate cause, or any other logical way of thinking.[718]

Nibbāna is said to be the cessation, liberation, nonarising, or nonexistence of conditioned phenomena. It is also said that nibbāna has no color, form, or size. It cannot be described by using a simile. Because of these points one might believe that nibbāna is nothing and think that it is the same as the concept of nonexistence (*abhāvapaññatti*). But it is absolutely not like the concept of nonexistence. It is obvious that it has the nature of cessation, liberation, nonarising, or nonexistence of conditioned phenomena. And because this nature is obvious, the phenomena of path and fruition can arise while directly experiencing the cessation of conditioned phenomena. The mental and physical processes of an arahant do not arise anymore after they have entered parinibbāna; they have completely ceased. The following texts from the Khuddaka Nikāya show how the nature of nibbāna is obvious when directly experienced.

> There is, bhikkhus, a not-born, a not-brought-to-being, a not-made, a not-conditioned. If, bhikkhus, there were no not-born, not-brought-to-being, not-made, not-conditioned, no escape would be discerned from what is born, brought-to-being, made, conditioned. But since there is a not-born, a not-brought-to-being, a not-made, a not-conditioned, therefore an escape is discerned from what is born, brought-to-being, made, conditioned.[719]

Because there is no arising in the nibbāna element [which is the cessation of conditioned phenomena through their nonarising], it is called not-born (*ajāta*) and not-brought-to-being (*abhūta*). Because it is not made by a cause it is called not-made (*akata*). Because it is not made dependent on causes and conditions, it is called not-conditioned. If the nibbāna element does not exist, then the cessation of the mental and physical processes or the aggregates could not happen. Thus it is not true that the nibbāna element is nothing, like the concept of nonexistence. Being the object of path and fruition, it is obvious in an ultimate sense. And because it is so obvious, the constantly arising mental and physical processes or aggregates in a person who practices correctly do not arise anymore after that person's parinibbāna. Then, they are able to cease forever. It means that the cessation is something that can be obvious. May you believe this!

> There is, bhikkhus, that base where there is no earth, no water, no fire, no air; no base consisting of the infinity of space, no base consisting of the infinity of consciousness, no base consisting of nothingness, no base consisting of neither-perception-nor-non-

> perception; neither this world nor another world nor both; neither sun nor moon. Here, bhikkhus, I say there is no coming, no going, no staying, no deceasing, no uprising. Not fixed, not movable, it has no support. Just this is the end of suffering.[720]

The nonexistence of the four elements shows the nonexistence of the derived material phenomena (*upādārūpa*) and the nonexistence of the mental phenomena that arise in the sense desire and fine-material existences based on physical phenomena.

There are no sense objects connected with the immaterial existence.

"Neither this world nor another world" refers to the nonexistence of any phenomena concerning these worlds. Therefore, at the moment of path and fruition that take nibbāna as its object, one knows no objects concerning this or another world.

"Neither sun nor moon" means that because there are no material phenomena there is no darkness. Thus no light is needed to dispel darkness. Thus it is shown that the sun, moon, other planets, and stars do not exist.

"There is no coming, no going, no staying, no deceasing, and no uprising" means that while one can come and go to another realm from the human or the celestial realm, one cannot come to nibbāna, and from nibbāna one cannot go somewhere else. Unlike the human and celestial realms, there are no persons or beings in nibbāna.

"Nothing new arises in nibbāna" means that it can only be known and taken as an object by path, fruition, and reviewing knowledges.

"It has no support" means that because it is not a material phenomenon, it is not located anywhere and it is not based on any other phenomena. Even though it is a mental phenomenon, it is not a result or an effect. This means that it is not based on any conditions.

"Just this is the end of suffering" means that there is no occurrence in nibbāna. Nibbāna is the opposite of the constantly arising process of mental and physical phenomena. Although it is a mental phenomenon, it does not have the characteristic of being aware of an object as consciousness and the mental factors do. Because it is the object of path and fruition, when one experiences nibbāna there is no suffering at all and so it is the end of suffering.

> Because nibbāna is the opposite of all conditioned phenomena [such as fire and water, heat and cold, light and dark], there is no nibbāna in conditioned phenomena, and there are also no

> conditioned phenomena in nibbāna. The conditioned and the unconditioned never co-exist.[721]

In accordance with this commentary from the *Udāna*, as long as there are still conditioned phenomena, nibbāna cannot yet be reached. While experiencing nibbāna, no conditioned phenomena arise. When entering parinibbāna, conditioned phenomena no longer arise; they cease to exist.

When nibbāna is realized by means of the four path knowledges, there is no room left for any form of craving, either those that lead to lower rebirths, gross forms of sense desire, subtle forms of sense desire, or fine-material and immaterial forms; all these forms of craving are totally destroyed. All these forms of craving have been discarded, destroyed, their bondage has been severed, and the tangle has been untangled. That is why the Buddha also spoke with these words about nibbāna:

> And what, bhikkhus, is the noble truth of the cessation of suffering? It is the remainderless fading away and cessation of that same craving, the giving up and relinquishing of it, freedom from it, nonreliance on it. This is called the noble truth of the cessation of suffering.[722]

> And it is hard to see this truth, namely, the stilling of all formations, the relinquishing of all acquisitions, the destruction of craving, dispassion, cessation, Nibbāna.[723]

Two types of nibbāna

There is only one kind of nibbāna in terms of being the cessation of all mental and physical suffering that has the characteristic of peacefulness. However, in another sense, nibbāna may be further divided into two types as follows: with residue remaining (*sa-upādisesa*)—this is the nibbāna of an arahant, one who has completely extinguished all mental defilements but still experiences the "residue" of the aggregates as a result of past craving, clinging, and volitional actions; and without residue remaining (*anupādisesa*)—this is the nibbāna of an arahant who has passed away, that is, after entering parinibbāna, and refers to the complete cessation of all conditioned phenomena.

The Buddha explained these two types of nibbāna as follows:

> Bhikkhus, there are these two Nibbāna-elements. What are the two? The Nibbāna-element with residue left and the Nibbāna-element with no residue left.
>
> What, bhikkhus, is the Nibbāna-element with residue left? Here a bhikkhu is an arahant, one whose taints are destroyed, the holy life fulfilled, who has done what had to be done, laid down the burden, attained the goal, destroyed the fetters of being, completely released through final knowledge. However, his five sense faculties remain unimpaired, by which he still experiences what is agreeable and disagreeable and feels pleasure and pain. It is the extinction of attachment, hate, and delusion in him that is called the Nibbāna-element with residue left.
>
> Now what, bhikkhus, is the Nibbāna-element with no residue left? Here a bhikkhu is an arahant . . . completely released through final knowledge. For him, here in this very life, all that is experienced, not being delighted in, will be extinguished. That, bhikkhus, is called the Nibbāna-element with no residue left.[724]

Note that in the first section of this passage that describes nibbāna with residue left, a living arahant is said to have "laid down the burden" of the five aggregates, even though one still possesses a mind and body. This is because they are one's last aggregates, and no more will arise, so we can say that they have effectively set down the burden of the five aggregates.

Note that in the second section of this passage that describes nibbāna with no residue left, the feeling that is mentioned refers to the particular type of feeling that is experienced only by arahants. This is kammically indeterminate (*abyākata*) feeling, that cannot be said to be wholesome or unwholesome and produces no kammic results. Also, although only feeling is mentioned explicitly, it should be taken to include all five aggregates. The arahant has no involvement with any of the aggregates that might lead to rebirth. None of the phenomena that one experiences while still alive are associated with desire, pride, or wrong view. Thus they all arise and pass away completely, without leaving any kammic residue that might create the potential for another life.

A fire that does not get any more fuel cannot continue to burn but simply dies down and becomes extinguished. Likewise, an arahant's aggregates that have been caused through previous kamma do not arise as a new life or new aggregates but, after having arisen, simply cease and become extinguished. After the cessation of the aggregates the aggregates no longer arise. As a result, the aggregates that constantly arise in an arahant due to the momentum of previous kamma do not continue to arise in a new life but are extinguished in this very life.

Nibbāna without residue remaining is synonymous with the cessation of the aggregates (*khandhaparinibbāna*). Once the path has been attained and after having entered parinibbāna, there is no longer any opportunity for the arising of mental and physical phenomena that would come into existence if the path were not attained. In addition, cessation of the five aggregates is accomplished with the realization of the path knowledge of arahantship.

However, this cessation is not something that actually arises, so it cannot be described in terms of time. Prior to the development of the path, the defilements and their resultant phenomena (new life, aggregates) may arise at any time when the conditions are favorable. However, such potential defilements and phenomena cannot be said to actually exist in the past, present, or future. Thus they are considered to be "independent of time" (*kālavimutta*). Thus both kinds of nibbāna, nibbāna with residue (*sa-upādisesanibbāna = kilesaparinibbāna*) and nibbāna without residue (*anupādisesanibbāna = khandhaparinibbāna*), are independent of time. Thus they cannot be said to exist in the past, present, or future.

Therefore, one should not ask questions such as, "Did the nibbāna that was experienced at the moment of knowledge of change-of-lineage occur in the past, present, or future?"

> These two Nibbāna-elements were made known
> By the Seeing One,[725] stable[726] and unattached:
> One is the element seen here and now
> With residue, but with the cord of being[727] destroyed;
> The other, having no residue for the future,
> Is that wherein all modes of being utterly cease.
> Having understood the unconditioned state,
> Released in mind with the cord of being destroyed,
> They have attained to the Dhamma-essence.
> Delighting in the destruction (of craving),
> Those stable ones have abandoned all being.[728]

In these verses, the cessation of the defilements or the aggregates, that is nibbāna either with or without residue remaining, is called the unconditioned. Just as the opposites of fire and water, heat and cold, dark and light, or jungle and open space, so is it the opposite of conditioned phenomena and therefore called the unconditioned. Nibbāna is also called a "state" (*pada*) because it can be attained and experienced through the path knowledge and fruition knowledge. Based on this, it can be concluded that the nibbāna that is experienced through path and fruition is the same as the two types of nibbāna with and without residue remaining. If this were not the case, then the Abhidhamma would be incorrect in saying:

> Though nibbāna is onefold according to its intrinsic nature, by reference to a basis (for distiction), it is twofold, namely, the element of nibbāna with the residue remaining, and the element of nibbāna without the residue remaining.[729]

The unique characteristic of nibbāna is the peacefulness associated with the cessation [of conditioned phenomena]. Or, in other words, this unique characteristic must necessarily belong to any type of nibbāna. In this sense there is only one type of nibbāna, even though it may be divided into two types, one with and one without residue remaining.

Even though it is clearly stated that nibbāna is twofold, if nibbāna either with or without residue remaining and nibbāna that is experienced through path and fruition were divided, it would also contradict the *Abhidhammattha Saṅgaha*. If nibbāna were divided in such a way, then we would have to say that the nibbāna that is experienced through path and fruition is real, being an ultimate reality, while the nibbāna that is with or without residue remaining is imaginary, being simply a concept. But if this were the case, then nibbāna would have to be classified into three types, rather than two: one real nibbāna, having its unique characteristic of peace, and two [other conceptual types of nibbāna], one with and one without residue remaining.

Some even claim that nibbāna is conceptual nonexistence (*abhāvapaññatti*) and that in an ultimate sense it does not exist. Then one would also have to say that cessation of the defilements and aggregates is just a concept like the concept of a self [based on wrong view]. This would mean that there is no cessation of potential defilements and aggregates. In that case the defilements would continue to arise in an arahant's mind continuum, and after having entered parinibbāna the aggregates would also continue to arise. There would be no possibility of escape from the round of suffering.

Therefore we must conclude that the nibbāna that is experienced by means of path and fruition is general nibbāna (*sāmaññanibbāna*). The two types of nibbāna—with and without residue remaining—that are specific nibbāna (*visesanibbāna*) are included within general nibbāna. This is why the nibbāna that is experienced by means of path and fruition is not identified as being with or without residue remaining, or as the cessation of desire, aversion, delusion, material phenomena, or feeling, or as present, past, or future, or as the cessation of defilements or phenomena. In reality nibbāna is simply experienced and known as the cessation of conditioned phenomena that perceive or are perceived. Because all mental and physical phenomena are extinguished in nibbāna, it also includes nibbāna with residue remaining and nibbāna without residue remaining.

Experiencing nibbāna

Because you do not yet rightly understand the cessation of the defilements and aggregates, you may think that it is just the concept of nonexistence, that it is not profound, or that it is so profound that you will be unable to rightly understand it. So if you are not yet satisfied, you should resolve to practice in order to forever extinguish not only the defilements but also the arising of the aggregates in a new life. Only then will you be able to comprehend that the cessation of the defilements and aggregates is not a concept of nonexistence but an ultimately and obviously existing unconditioned phenomenon, profound, difficult to see, and beyond the reach of logical thought.

Before you have realized nibbāna by means of the four paths, you must develop diligence and mindfulness in order to protect your mind from yielding to temptation.

> Therefore, bhikkhus, that base should be understood, where the eye ceases and perception of forms fades away. That base should be understood, where the ear ceases and perception of sounds fades away. That base should be understood, where the nose ceases and perception of smells fades away. That base should be understood, where the tongue ceases and perception of tastes fades away. That base should be understood, where the body

> ceases and perception of touch fades away. That base should be understood, where the mind ceases and perception of mental phenomena fades away. That base should be understood.[730]

A meditator may arrive at the realization of nibbāna by primarily observing the eye and perception of forms, or any of the other pairs of phenomena mentioned above. If cessation of the eye and perception of forms is obvious, then cessation and awareness of their physical and mental constituents will also be obvious. The same applies to the other pairs of phenomena. In fact, the cessation of all conditioned phenomena is obvious when one experiences nibbāna. This is why the perception of conditioned phenomena completely ceases the moment one experiences nibbāna.

Thus nibbāna is described as the cessation of any of these pairs of phenomena. Taken as a whole, nibbāna is the cessation of all twelve of these sense bases. Venerable Ānanda once explained this, saying:

> This was stated by the Blessed One, friends, with reference to the cessation of the six [internal and external] sense bases.[731]

The commentary to the *Udāna* of the Khuddaka Nikāya also describes nibbāna as the cessation of all twelve sense bases and refers to an explanation that the Buddha gave to Bāhiya, which other scholars cite. According to those scholars, the passage "Then, Bāhiya, you will neither be here nor beyond nor in between the two"[732] can be explained as follows:

> [If one is no longer involved with defilements in what is seen, heard, experienced, or perceived, then, Bāhiya,] one will no longer exist here in the internal [sense bases of the eye, ear, nose, tongue, body, and mind], nor there in the external [sense bases of visible form, sound, odor, flavor, touch and mental objects], nor anywhere else in the sense consciousnesses [of seeing, hearing, smelling, tasting, touching, and perceiving. This is the end of suffering].[733]

A meditator proceeds by observing the most obvious object from among these twelve sense bases, consciousnesses, and mental factors. But at the moment of path and fruition, the meditator stops perceiving the object and instead experiences the total cessation of all of these objects. This experience of cessation is nibbāna. It is very important to understand this.

The sense bases actually represent all conditioned phenomena. So the cessation of the sense bases refers to the cessation of all conditioned phenomena. In the following discourse, nibbāna is said to be that state that is the opposite of conditioned phenomena. According to the texts:

> Where water, earth, fire, and air do not gain a footing:
> It is from here, that the streams [of phenomena] turn back,
> Here that the round [of the defilements, kamma, and its
> result] no longer revolves.
> There, name-and-form ceases.[734]

> Where consciousness is signless, boundless, all-luminous,
> That's where earth, water, fire, and air find no footing,
> There both long and short, small and great, fair and foul—
> There "name-and-form" [mental and physical phenomena] are
> wholly destroyed.
> With the cessation of consciousness this is all destroyed.[735]

The statement that nibbāna is "all-luminous" in this passage means that it is completely cleansed of all defilements. Similar metaphors are used in such expressions as "the light of wisdom" (*paññā-āloka*), "the luster of wisdom" (*paññā-obhāsa*), and "the torch of wisdom" (*paññāpajjota*). It is in this same sense that the Buddha said, "Bhikkhus, the mind is luminous." The sense here is that nibbāna is always luminous. The mind and wisdom, which possess an innate luminosity, can be soiled by defiling phenomena. Nibbāna, however, which is the cessation of defilements or conditioned phenomena, can never be connected with defiling phenomena. Therefore there is no way that any of these phenomena can soil or defile nibbāna, just as the sky can never be painted. As a result it is said that "nibbāna is all-luminous." To be straightforward, the meaning of the commentary and subcommentary is only that nibbāna is absolutely not connected to the defilements, or is completely cleansed of them.

So one should not misinterpret this statement to mean that nibbāna is literally shining like the sun, moon, or stars, and that one sees this luminosity by means of path knowledge and fruition knowledge. This kind of interpretation would negate previous statement that nibbāna is signless, would be inconsistent with its unique "signless" manifestation (*animitta-paccupaṭṭhāna*), and would contradict Venerable Nāgasena's answer to King Milinda's question about the nature of nibbāna. In fact this kind of literal interpretation would be in opposition to all the Pāḷi texts and commentaries that say that there is no materiality in nibbāna. In any event the cessation of potential defilements and aggregates is not something that is luminous and bright. If it were, the Pāḷi texts and commentaries could easily have said that "nibbāna is luminous and bright." Otherwise they would not explain it with difficult names such as "destruction of lust" (*rāgakkhayo*), "the peaceful ending of all conditioned phenomena" (*sabbasaṅkhārasamatho*), "nonarising" (*anuppādo*), and so on, which are taken to be opposites of conditioned phenomena. One should reflect deeply about this!

> That's where earth, water, fire, and air find no footing,
> *There* both long and short, small and great, fair and foul—
> There "name-and-form" [mental and physical phenomena] are
> wholly destroyed.
> With the cessation of consciousness this is all destroyed.[736]

These lines point out nibbāna, or cessation. The last line points out the cause of this cessation. "Consciousness" here refers to both the death consciousness (*cuticitta*) and the volitional mind (*abhisaṅkhāraviññāṇa*) at the time of parinibbāna. All presently existing conditioned phenomena come to an end due to the destruction of death consciousness at the time of parinibbāna, and because there is no volitional mind that can produce results, new phenomena do not arise but cease to exist. Thus, with the cessation of these two kinds of consciousness, all conditioned phenomena cease. This is like the cessation of the emission of light from an oil lamp whose oil and wick have been completely consumed.

In summary:

> *Nissesa saṅkhāra vivekalakkhaṇaṃ*
> *sabhala saṅkhata vidhura sabhāvaṃ*
> *nibbāna metaṃ sugatana desitaṃ*
> *jhāneyya saṅkhāranirodha mattakaṃ.*

The Buddha described nibbāna as having the characteristic of being secluded from conditioned phenomena and as being their complete opposite. To the wise, nibbāna is simply known as the utter cessation of conditioned phenomena.

Here ends chapter 6 regarding the Stages of Insight Knowledge.

7 The Eighteen Great Insight Knowledges

The eighteen great insight knowledges (*aṭṭhārasa mahāvipassanā*) are:

1. One abandons the perception of permanence by developing contemplation of impermanence.
2. One abandons the perception of satisfaction by developing contemplation of unsatisfactoriness.
3. One abandons the perception of self by developing the contemplation of not-self.
4. One abandons delight by developing the contemplation of disenchantment.
5. One abandons passion by developing the contemplation of dispassion.
6. One abandons origination by developing contemplation of cessation.
7. One abandons grasping by developing contemplation of relinquishment.
8. One abandons the perception of solidity by developing contemplation of destruction.
9. One abandons the accumulation of kamma by developing contemplation of fall.
10. One abandons the perception of stability by developing contemplation of change.
11. One abandons the sign by developing contemplation of the signless.
12. One abandons desire by developing contemplation of the desireless.
13. One abandons adherence by developing contemplation of emptiness.

14. One abandons adherence to the grasping after substance by developing contemplation of "insight into phenomena that is higher wisdom."
15. One abandons adherence to delusion by developing knowledge and vision of things as they really are.
16. One abandons adherence due to reliance by developing contemplation of danger.
17. One abandons nonreflection by developing contemplation of reflection.
18. One abandons adherence due to bondage by developing contemplation of turning away.[737]

The Seven Main Contemplations

Contemplation of impermanence

Contemplation of impermanence (*aniccānupassanā*) refers to seeing conditioned phenomena arise and pass away while observing their unique characteristics. According to the *Visuddhimagga*, one should understand three aspects of this contemplation: impermanence, the characteristic of impermanence, and contemplation of impermanence.

> The five aggregates are impermanent. Why? Because they arise, pass away, and change, or because of their immediate disappearance after having arisen. Arising, passing away, and change are the characteristics of impermanence or the mode of change—that is, nonexistence after having arisen.[738]
>
> The characteristic of impermanence is arising, passing away, and change, or nonexistence after having arisen. Phenomena that have arisen do not remain in their initial state due to change; they disappear that very moment. Contemplation of impermanence is seeing phenomena to be impermanent.[739]

For the characteristic of impermanence, two kinds of definitions are given [in the quotes above]. The second one of these (nonexistence after having arisen) becomes especially apparent at the higher stages of knowledge, such as knowledge of dissolution, and so becomes an outstanding characteristic. When one clearly sees that characteristic, one's knowledge derived from contemplation of impermanence becomes sharp and keen. This is why the subcommentary to the Abhidhamma says:

> Because four kinds of definitions are included in this phrase and can be taken as a whole, the commentary mentions this phrase separately.[740]

The *Sammohavinodanī Aṭṭhakathā,* a commentary on Abhidhamma, mentions four ways that one can see the characteristic of impermanence, all of which can be included in "impermanence—that is, nonexistence after having arisen."[741] The four definitions from this commentary are arising and passing away (*uppādavayavantata*), change (*vipariṇāma*), momentariness (*tāvakālika*), and denying permanence (*niccapaṭikkhepa*).

According to the *Visuddhimagga-mahāṭīkā*:

> Appearance, presence, and disappearance characterize the impermanence of all conditioned phenomena. However, the first two are not as obviously characteristics of impermanence as is the last. Therefore, the commentary says that "disappearance is the outstanding portion of impermanence."[742]

Phenomena that arise depending on many causes and conditions are called conditioned phenomena. All these conditioned phenomena are marked by appearance, presence, and disappearance. These three phases can also be called birth, aging, and death, since they are noted as conditioned phenomena, they are called "conditioned characteristics" (*saṅkhatalakkhaṇā*). Impermanent phenomena are also conditioned. And because the conditioned characteristics of arising, presence, and disappearance are impermanent as well, they are also called "impermanent characteristics" (*aniccalakkhaṇā*).

However, one cannot yet clearly know impermanence by just knowing the appearance and presence of conditioned phenomena. Where there is appearance and presence, there must always be disappearance too. Due to this, we can know their impermanent nature by reflecting about it. The impermanent nature of phenomena is not very obvious while they are appearing and being present. But when one knows the disappearance or end of phenomena, one can clearly know their impermanent nature. Thus at the moment of disappearance their impermanent nature becomes easily apparent. Among the three phases of appearance, presence, and disappearance, the characteristic of impermanence is particularly obvious at the moment of disappearance. This is why the commentary says that disappearance is the outstanding portion of impermanence.

The five aggregates that are called "impermanent" are actually different from impermanence itself, which is called "the characteristic of impermanence." However, if one is only aware of impermanence itself, without observing the unique characteristics of the aggregates, then genuine knowledge derived from contemplation of impermanence cannot develop. This is because the impermanence that one is aware of is merely conceptual. In fact, one can only directly see the impermanence of the mental and physical aggregates (characterized by appearance, presence, and disappearance) while one is observing their unique characteristics. So only then can genuine contemplation of impermanence develop. This is why the commentary on the Abhidhamma says:

> What is the object of the insight called "knowledge that leads to emergence"? It is the three universal characteristics [of impermanence, unsatisfactoriness, and not-self].
>
> However, by themselves, these characteristics are merely concepts and cannot be described [as something that exists in the sensual, fine-material, or immaterial realms]. But if a person sees these three universal characteristics, the five aggregates will seem like a rotten carcass hung about his or her neck. Thus [by simultaneously seeing phenomena and their three universal characteristics] by means of knowledge that takes conditioned phenomena as its object, one emerges from those very phenomena.
>
> Suppose a bhikkhu wishes to buy an alms bowl. He will be initially pleased when he sees a bowl-seller bringing him a bowl. However, if he examines the bowl and finds that there are three holes in it, he will lose interest, not in the three holes, but in the bowl itself. In the same way, when one sees the three characteristics, one will lose interest in conditioned phenomena. Thus one emerges from conditioned phenomena by means of the insight that takes those very phenomena as its object.[743]

This passage addresses the question of whether the objects that knowledge that leads to emergence takes are themselves conditioned phenomena, or the three universal characteristics of impermanence, unsatisfactoriness, and not-self. If the meditation only took the phenomena themselves as its objects, then it would not be able to see impermanence and so on. On the other hand, if it only took impermanence and so on as its objects, then we could not say that knowledge of change-of-lineage, and the path knowledge and fruition knowledge that follow it, are an escape from conditioned phenomena.

Thus, the meaning of this passage is that knowledge that leads to emergence sees phenomena in terms of their unique characteristics (such as hardness, mental contact, or knowing an object) and, by simultaneously seeing their disappearance, sees one of their three universal characteristics (impermanence, unsatisfactoriness, and not-self). This causes the meditator to feel thoroughly repulsed by phenomena connected with the observed characteristic, just as he or she would be disgusted by a rotten carcass hung about his or her neck. It is obvious that just as that person wants to get rid of the carcass, so will meditators look at phenomena as something to be gotten rid of by means of their knowledge.

Not only does one observe characteristics, one also observes conditioned phenomena as a whole. This is why knowledge of change-of-lineage and path knowledge emerge from conditioned phenomena while knowledge of adaptation sees their impermanent nature, and so on. "To emerge" means that conditioned phenomena are no longer the mind's object and that the mind takes nibbāna, the cessation of conditioned phenomena, as its object.

This is the example of how one wants to abandon conditioned phenomena that are connected with the characteristics by experiencing these very characteristics. The monk who decided to buy an alms bowl found out, after inspecting it, that it had three holes. So he no longer had any desire for the alms bowl. The monk still wanted the alms bowl before he saw the three holes. When he saw the holes, it wasn't that he didn't want the holes, he did not want the bowl itself. Why? Because his previous desire was only for the bowl, and not for the holes.

Likewise, meditators are attached to conditioned phenomena before they see the three universal characteristics, but they have never been attached to the characteristics of impermanence, unsatisfactoriness, and not-self. So when they see the three characteristics, their desire to abandon them or to be freed from attachment is connected only with the conditioned phenomena that are bound up with these characteristics. One wants only to abandon conditioned phenomena. Because one had no attachment to the characteristics, one has no desire to abandon them.

Conditioned phenomena along with their characteristics are something to be abandoned. So the knowledge of change-of-lineage and path knowledge that take nibbāna as their object [which arise based on the highest knowledges] do not emerge only from conditioned phenomena. A subcommentary to the Abhidhamma further explains the commentary's meaning as follows:

> One knows the three universal characteristics by realizing that conditioned phenomena are impermanent and so on. When one sees phenomena in this way, it is said that knowledge that leads to emergence takes the three characteristics as its object. In this sense, insight is said to take the three characteristics as its object, even though it actually takes phenomena as its object.
>
> Thus [the commentary says], "by themselves, these characteristics are merely concepts," and so on. If these characteristics are perceived independent [of phenomena] as impermanent, unsatisfactory, and not-self, they should be considered to be concepts and not something that truly exists in an ultimate sense. For this reason, they cannot be described [as anything belonging to the sensual, fine-material, or immaterial worlds]. In an ultimate sense, it is impossible to find any characteristics that are separate from the actual phenomena.
>
> So it is only when one sees phenomena in terms of their unique characteristics [such as hardness and so on], that one can see their universal characteristics [impermanence, unsatisfactoriness, and not-self]. Thus [the commentary says], "if a person sees these three universal characteristics," and so on. Because one sees conditioned phenomena themselves to be impermanent and so on, they are what should be discarded, as if they were a rotten carcass hung about one's neck.[744]

According to these texts contemplation of impermanence is insight into impermanence brought about by observing the unique characteristics of mental and physical phenomena. So we cannot say that knowledge that discerns mental and physical phenomena and knowledge that discerns conditionality are contemplations of impermanence, because these insights only consider unique characteristics. It is the higher insight knowledges, beginning from insight knowledge by comprehension that one should consider contemplations of impermanence, because these insight knowledges see universal characteristics as well.

Moreover, if one sees impermanence, one is considered to be contemplating impermanence but not unsatisfactoriness or not-self. Similarly if one sees unsatisfactoriness, one is considered to be contemplating unsatisfactoriness but not the other two contemplations. And if one sees not-self, one is considered to be contemplating not-self but not the other two. The *Mūlaṭīkā* refers to this point:

> The universal characteristics of impermanence and so on are mentioned separately from the phenomena that are impermanent and so on, because understanding impermanence and so on is different from knowledge that discerns the unique characteristics of the phenomena. Therefore, knowledge that discerns mental and physical phenomena cannot, by itself, bring about insight. Rather, one must see impermanence, unsatisfactoriness, and not-self by means of further insight. We cannot say that seeing impermanence is [the same as] seeing unsatisfactoriness or not-self. The same applies for the other two.[745]

Developing contemplation of impermanence

We begin to develop contemplation of impermanence from the moment that insight becomes clear enough to break up the continuity of phenomena. To explain further, unless one notes the mental and physical phenomena involved in mental and physical movements or actions the moment they occur, it is impossible to see them as they really are, let alone to see them arising and passing away. Because of this one mistakes a series of successive phenomena for a single phenomenon. When one sees something repeatedly or over a prolonged period, for example, one thinks that what one is currently seeing is the same as what one saw before. This kind of delusion also occurs when one hears something and so on. The term "continuity" (*santati*) refers to the continuity of phenomena that causes one to think that the thing one is currently seeing is the same thing one saw before, and so on. Because this continuity obscures it, one is not able to see the impermanence of phenomena and thinks that they exist forever.

Thus continuity can only hide phenomena when one fails to observe their arising and passing away. But if one uninterruptedly observes phenomena, he or she will be able to see them occurring one by one and to distinguish between successive phenomena. One will even be able to distinguish between the initial arising and final disappearance of a single object. As a result of seeing phenomena as separate entities that are not joined to the previous or following one, the continuity of phenomena is destroyed, and the characteristic of impermanence—including appearance, presence, and disappearance, or nonexistence after having arisen—becomes obvious of its own accord. In this way one begins to develop contemplation of impermanence.

When one clearly sees the characteristic of impermanence, one may begin to note phenomena in a different way, as simply "impermanent, impermanent." Similarly, if one sees phenomena as unsatisfactory or not-self, one may note, "unsatisfactory, unsatisfactory," or "not-self, not-self," respectively. However, simply reciting "impermanent," "unsatisfactory," or "not-self," does not accomplish anything at all. What is important is to accurately understand these characteristics. We can develop the contemplations of impermanence, unsatisfactoriness, and not-self without using this kind of labeling at all, if we understand the true characteristics of impermanence, unsatisfactoriness, and not-self by observing phenomena the moment they occur.

Such labeling may give rise to assumed knowledge, without any actual understanding of impermanence and so on. So (as shown in chapter 5) I advise meditators to observe the actual mental and physical phenomena involved in actions or movements the moment they occur, rather than reciting "impermanence," "unsatisfactoriness," and "not-self." I mention this other way of labeling only for general information.

> Impermanence does not appear because continuity hides it, because one has not contemplated arising and passing away. If one sees arising and passing away and continuity is broken, the characteristic of impermanence appears in its true nature.[746]

> For one [who does not pay attention] the characteristic of impermanence does not appear because continuity hides it. Continuity is able to hide it because one does not pay attention to arising and passing away. [This means that the characteristic

> of impermanence does not appear while continuity is concealing it.] For one who sees arising and passing away, arising does not go into passing away, and passing away does not go into the next arising: the moment of arising is one thing, and the moment of passing away is another thing. Separate moments [of arising and passing away] appear even for a single phenomenon, not to mention for past phenomena. [This means that past and present phenomena, as well as present and future phenomena, are separate things.] This is why the commentary says, "If one sees arising and passing away," and so on. Here, "continuity is broken," means that observation that phenomena happen one after the other and in succession reveals that the continuity of mental and physical phenomena is false. Phenomena do not appear to be joined together to one who correctly observes arising and passing away. Actually, they appear to be separate, like iron bars [that are not joined together]. In this way, the characteristic of impermanence is exceedingly obvious.[747]

In accordance with this text, the initial arising and the final passing away of a single phenomenon becomes apparent to a meditator who uninterruptedly observes phenomena at the moment they occur; so it becomes obvious that the previous phenomenon is one thing and the following phenomenon is another. They are seen as separate [things] and not as one thing or two things joined together. This reveals and destroys the previously held concept of continuity. For one who has destroyed the concept of continuity, the characteristic of impermanence arises in its true nature and becomes obvious of its own accord. We can see the characteristic of impermanence in one of these two ways: as arising, presence, and passing away, or as nonexistence after having arisen. When we experience this genuine and real characteristic of impermanence, we call the knowledge that understands phenomena to be impermanent "contemplation of impermanence." Whenever this genuine knowledge occurs, the perception of permanence (*niccasaññā*) and resulting unsatisfactoriness are abandoned. The *Paṭisambhidāmagga* says:

> One who sees impermanence abandons the perception of permanence.[748]

Here "one abandons the perception of permanence" refers explicitly to perversion of perception and implicitly to perversion of consciousness and perversion of view. This method of implying the full meaning [of a statement] is called "figurative usage" (*padhānanaya*). The most important or obvious aspect is mentioned explicitly when using it, and the other aspects are implied. In the statement "The king is coming," for example, it is implied that not only the king but also his retinue of many attendants is coming. In the same way, this sentence explicitly mentions perversion of perception, which implicitly includes perversion of view and perversion of consciousness, and all of their mental constituents. According to the *Mahāṭīkā*:

> The perception of permanence believes in permanence and is taken as the leader of [the various kinds of] perception for the purpose of this description. The same is true for the perception of pleasure (*sukhasaññā*) and the perception of self (*attasaññā*).[749]

Abandoning latent defilements

Which perception of permanence must be abandoned—past, present, or future? Past defilements have already disappeared and no longer exist, so one does not need to abandon previous defilements. Future defilements will come into existence at some point, but they have not yet arisen at the moment of observation, so one does not need to abandon future defilements either. Whenever one is observing impermanence in the present moment, only wholesome insight awareness exists and there are no defilements to be abandoned, so one doesn't need to abandon present defilements, either. When the mental and physical phenomena that arise at the six sense doors are not rightly observed and understood to be impermanent, while these mental and physical phenomena are being perceived to be permanent, conditions are actually right for defilements to be able to arise. So you should understand that defilements that could arise when conditions are right are the defilements that must be abandoned. These defilements, which cannot be described as actually existing in the past, present, or future, are called "latent defilements."

There are two types of latent defilements: those that dwell in a continuum (*santānānusaya*) and those that dwell in objects (*ārammaṇānusaya*). "Defilements that dwell in a continuum" are defilements that dwell in the [mental] continuum of ordinary people (*puthujjana*) and trainees, those noble ones who have not yet attained the fourth fruition knowledge, the fruit of arahantship (*arahattaphala*). These may arise any time that conditions become favorable. "Defilements that dwell in objects" are defilements that dwell in objects when they are not observed. Whenever an object is not rightly understood to be impermanent, unsatisfactory, and not-self, defilements may arise in ordinary people and trainees because they take it to be permanent, satisfactory, and self and in accordance with conditions. This kind of defilement is also called "defilements that arise when sense objects are not observed" (*ārammaṇādhiggatuppanna*). It is only this defilement that dwells in the objects that is abandoned by means of insight.

> Latent defilements are of seven kinds, namely: desire for sensual objects (*kāmarāgānusaya*), aversion (*paṭighānusaya*), conceit (*mānānusaya*), wrong view (*diṭṭhānusaya*), doubt (*vicikicchānusaya*), desire for existence (*bhavarāgānusaya*), and ignorance (*avijjānusaya*). In this world, attachment to sensual objects and to existence lies dormant in everything that is lovable and pleasant, while aversion lies dormant in everything that is unlovable and unpleasant. Delusion lies dormant in both of these. Also conceit, wrong view, and doubt, which go hand in hand with delusion, should be regarded to exist in that mind.[750]

The "lovable and pleasant" sense objects (*iṭṭhārammaṇa*) mentioned here are of two types: those that are inherently pleasing (*sabhāva iṭṭhārammaṇa*) and those that deceptively appear to be pleasing (*parikappa iṭṭhārammaṇa*). For example those objects, beings, sounds, and so on that are truly beautiful are regarded as inherently pleasing. While human waste, rotting corpses, and so on may be pleasing to a dog, pig, or vulture, that appearance is deceptive. But both are considered to be pleasing objects (*piyarūpa, sātarūpa*) in which desire for sensual objects and existence lies dormant.

Likewise, there are two types of disagreeable objects: those that are inherently unpleasant (*sabhāva aniṭṭhārammaṇa*) and those that deceptively appear to be unpleasant (*parikappa aniṭṭhārammaṇa*). Both of these, the inherently unpleasant one and the deceptively unpleasant one, are considered unpleasant objects (*appiyarūpa, asātarūpa*). Aversion lies latent in all of these unpleasant worldly phenomena. Whenever desire or aversion lies latent in these pleasant-pleasing and unpleasant-displeasing objects, delusion also lies latent in them. And, if delusion lies latent in them, it also means that conceit, wrong view, and doubt, which go hand in hand with delusion, lie latent in that mind. "To lie dormant" does not mean that they exist hiding somewhere but that they provide an opportunity for the mental defilements to arise when conditions are right, because either insight knowledge or path knowledge has yet to abandon the defilements. According to the texts:

> Here, "desire lies latent" means that it lies latent in pleasing objects, because it has not yet been abandoned.[751]

> Of [the two types of] potential defilements, attachment lies latent in pleasant objects by means of the defilements latent in objects.[752]

> Of the two types of potential defilement, desire, having not yet been completely abandoned by the paths, lies latent in one's mental continuum in such a way that it may arise when conditions are favorable. The same is true when it lies latent in pleasing and agreeable sense objects.[753]

There exists the possibility that defilements will arise with respect to every object that insight knowledge or path knowledge has not yet rightly understood. This is obvious in the phrase "defilements lie latent in these objects" mentioned above in the commentary and subcommentary. Therefore, the Buddha said:

> The underlying tendency to lust should be abandoned in regard to pleasant feeling. The underlying tendency to aversion should be abandoned in regard to painful feeling. The underlying tendency to ignorance should be abandoned in regard to neither-painful-nor-pleasant feeling.[754]

Defilements that lie dormant in sense objects

The type of defilement that lies dormant in sense objects is also called "defilements that arise when sense objects are not observed" (*ārammaṇādhiggahituppanna*). This term is defined by the commentaries as follows:

> When with the arising of a visible form [and so on, at the eye door and so on] one apprehends the object first, defilements do not yet arise. Only after the object has been firmly grasped and in accordance with the conditions do they arise. That is why they are called "defilements that lie dormant in sense objects."[755]

If one clearly experiences a pleasing or displeasing object [such as visible form, sound, smell, taste, touch, or mental object], then defilements [like greed, aversion, and so on] can arise either in that very moment or later. If they arise at that very moment, it is obvious that they are able to recur later on. Due to wise attention and other factors, the defilements may not yet arise at that very moment. However for a person who has a distinct impression and keeps the object firmly in mind, the defilements can certainly arise later when one reflects on the object, when similar or dissimilar objects are encountered, or when somebody else gives a reminder.

The defilements arise because the object has left a lasting impression and is kept firmly in the mind. Thus this kind of defilement that is ready to arise because the object has left a lasting impression and is kept firmly in the mind is called "a defilement that lies dormant in sense objects." Regarding this matter, one should pay special attention to the passage "Only after the object has been firmly grasped." It is only because the object has left a lasting impression and is kept firmly in the mind that the defilements connected with that object arise at a later time. One should understand that if this were not the case, the defilements would not be able to arise.

There is no doubt that a noble one is free from this kind of latent defilement, having completely abandoned them by means of path knowledge. How can one abandon it by means of insight? If one observes objects [such as visible form, seeing consciousness, sound, hearing consciousness, and so on] the moment they arise at the six sense doors, and sees them to be impermanent, unsatisfactory, and not-self, then one does not perceive them as permanent, satisfactory, and self, either in that moment or later when one thinks about those objects. Thus defilements do not arise, are not able to arise, or do not have an opportunity to arise based on an object that one has observed. "Having no opportunity to arise" means that whenever an object is observed, defilements do not lie dormant in it, and that such firmly grasped objects are free from latent defilements. Being free from defilements that lie dormant in objects, one is also free from obsessive and transgressive defilements, as well as from wholesome and unwholesome kamma and their resultant mental and physical phenomena. Because right understanding emerges from insight, it becomes impossible for defilements, kamma, and its results to arise, since all of these are based on wrong perception. They are abandoned by means of knowledge. The subcommentary says:

> First, contemplation of impermanence temporarily abandons the perception of permanence [by means of substitution of opposites]. Without this contemplation, defilements based on the perception of permanence and the volitional deeds resulting from these defilements will give rise to resultant phenomena later on. All of these are abandoned by not giving them an opportunity to arise. They are likewise abandoned by means of contemplation of unsatisfactoriness and so on. This is why the commentary says that insight temporarily abandons defilements together with their resultant phenomena.[756]

If one fails to understand the characteristic of impermanence with respect to an object that occurs at the six sense doors, the defilements associated with the perception of permanence will have the opportunity to arise. These defilements are said to "lie dormant" in objects that are not understood to be impermanent, because due to this lack of understanding one will again think about these objects later when the necessary conditions are present. Such thought is actually an obsessive defilement. And again, after one has thought about this object, when the necessary conditions are present, because one still sees it to be permanent, one may act on it, either to obtain or enjoy it or to destroy it. So these defilements amount to the real volitional actions (*abhisaṅkhārā*). Resultant phenomena arise in a new existence due to these wholesome and unwholesome volitional actions, in accordance with conditions.

In a new existence mental and physical phenomena can only arise when there is kamma. They cannot arise without kamma. Kamma cannot arise without the defilement that perceives things as permanent. Defilement cannot arise without the opportunity to perceive things as permanent. When an object is rightly understood to be impermanent the moment it arises at the six sense doors, there is also no longer any opportunity to perceive it to be permanent. Therefore, when we rightly understand an object that arises at the six sense doors to be impermanent and contemplation of impermanence arises, then the object is completely freed from the latent defilement that perceives it to be permanent. The object will also be completely freed from the obsessive defilement that thinks about it as being permanent, as well as from the transgressive defilement that commits [unwholesome acts] connected with that object.

When there are no volitional actions, a new existence that is the result of kamma can no longer arise; one has been completely freed from it. Because contemplation of impermanence is able to completely free one from even a new existence, it is said that it abandons the defilements, beginning with the latent defilements, kamma, and their resultant phenomena. "Abandon" means to cause to disappear, to not arise, or to give no opportunity to arise. The same is true with respect to contemplations of unsatisfactoriness and not-self: the defilements that will arise when perceiving things to be satisfactory or self are abandoned in the same way. This is why the commentary says that insight temporarily abandons the defilements together with their resultant phenomena.

Defilements latent in the mind-continuum

Some defilements lie dormant in the mind-continuum of ordinary people and noble ones at the three lower stages of enlightenment. Such defilements can arise any time, when conditions are right, because they have not yet been abandoned by means of the four paths. This is similar to the situation of a person with malaria: one is considered sick so long as one has not been completely cured of the disease, even though one may not currently be experiencing any of its symptoms. Likewise, if a person who has not given up eating meat is asked, "Do you eat meat?" then, although this person isn't eating meat at that very moment, he or she would have to answer, "I eat meat," because he or she has previously eaten meat and will eat it again in the future.

In the same way, the seven types of potential defilements lie dormant in the continuum of ordinary people. Five of these are also dormant in noble ones at the first and second stages of enlightenment, where wrong view and doubt have been abandoned. Three—desire for existence, conceit, and delusion—are dormant in noble ones at the third stage of enlightenment. Although these defilements may not be arising with the three phases of appearance, presence, and disappearance at this moment, they have arisen in the past and will arise in the future according to conditions. Because the possibility that they will arise has not yet been eliminated, they are ready to arise or lie dormant in each and every person's continuum. This is why the Abhidhamma says:

> The latent defilement of delusion, the latent defilement of conceit, and the latent defilement of desire for existence lie dormant in the continuum of a nonreturner (*anāgāmi*). The latent defilement of delusion, the latent defilement of desire for sensual objects, the latent defilement of aversion, the latent defilement of conceit, and the latent defilement of desire for existence lie dormant in the continuum of noble beings [at the first and second stages of enlightenment (stream enterer and once returner)]. But the latent defilement of wrong view and the latent defilement of doubt do not lie dormant in their continuum. The latent defilement of delusion, the latent defilement of desire for sensual objects, the latent defilement of aversion, the latent defilement of conceit, the latent defilement of wrong view, the latent defilement of doubt, and the latent defilement of desire for existence lie dormant in the continuum of an ordinary person.[757]

However, all seven of these latent defilements cannot occur together at once. For example, desire for sensual objects cannot arise at the same time as desire for existence; desire cannot arise along with aversion and doubt; aversion cannot occur at the same time as conceit, wrong view, doubt, and desire; conceit cannot accompany wrong view, doubt, and aversion; wrong view cannot coexist with doubt, desire for existence, and conceit. However they can all lie dormant together.

We also cannot say that latent defilements arise, exist, and pass away like the obsessive and transgressive defilements. Actually, because path knowledge has not yet abandoned them, they lie dormant in the continuum of beings and have the potential to arise in accordance with their conditions. The following passages from the Abhidhamma show how these latent defilements of desire for sensual objects and aversion lie dormant together, and how they arise.

> The latent defilement of desire for sensual objects lies dormant in a person's continuum. Can the latent defilement of aversion lie dormant in that person's continuum as well? Yes.
>
> The latent defilement of desire for sensual objects is arising

in a person's continuum. Can the latent defilement of aversion arise in that person's continuum as well? Yes.[758]

> The latent defilements have not yet been abandoned in a person's continuum, nor are they prevented from arising when conditions are favorable. They arose in his or her continuum before and will do so again later, even though they are not arising at the moment. It is with reference to this that it was said, "The latent defilement of desire for sensual objects arises in a person's continuum, and the latent defilement of aversion arises in a person's continuum as well."[759]

Based on the phrase "nor are they prevented from arising," the *Mūlaṭīkā*, a subcommentary on the Abhidhamma, says that only seven types of defilement, and not others, are strong enough to lie dormant in one's continuum. The commentary also explains that these are called "latent defilements" because if conditions are favorable they will arise, not only because the paths have not yet abandoned them, but because tranquility and insight are not preventing them from arising.

According to the Pāḷi texts and commentaries, seven, five, or three types of latent defilement always lie dormant in the continuum of ordinary people and trainees. These latent defilements also lie dormant when wholesome states, resultant states, relinking consciousness, life-continuum, and death consciousness are occurring. They even lie dormant in nonpercipient beings, not to mention when unwholesome states are occurring. These latent defilements lie dormant in the continuum of ordinary people and trainees because they have yet to be abandoned and can arise when the necessary conditions are present. Only path knowledge can completely abandon these kinds of latent defilements. Insight, however, cannot completely abandon them, but it can only temporarily abandon them by means of suppression. This is in accordance with this passage from the *Visuddhimagga*:

> Even when suppressed by serenity or insight, they are still called "arisen through nonabolition."[760]

Thus, as the phrase "contemplation of impermanence abandons the perception of permanence" illustrated before, we should understand that the latent defilements lying dormant in objects and the states that are connected to them (obsessive and transgressive defilements, kamma, resultant phenomena) are only temporarily abandoned. The *Visuddhimagga* says with this aim: "Contemplation of impermanence abandons the perception of permanence."

Impermanence reveals unsatisfactoriness and not-self

In this case it is obvious that if one has understood the object to be impermanent the perception of it as permanent can no longer arise. But one may wonder: "Although one has understood objects to be impermanent, can the defilements that perceive them to be satisfactory and self still arise?" We can conclude that they cannot.

If one has clearly experienced the characteristic of impermanence by seeing objects disappearing after they have arisen, then one cannot see these impermanent objects to be satisfactory, to be a self, or to be a being.

In fact, if one reflects on phenomena that disappear as soon as they have arisen [according to one's empirical knowledge of impermanence], one can determine that because they constantly arise and pass away, these phenomena are unsatisfactory, unpleasant, not to be accepted, and undesirable. And because these phenomena do not obey one's wishes, they do not belong to anyone but arise and pass away of their own accord. The following text from the Aṅguttara Nikāya provides an irrefutable example:

> The perception of impermanence should be developed to eradicate the conceit "I am." When one perceives impermanence, the perception of [not-self] is stabilized. One who perceives non-self eradicates the conceit "I am," [which is] nibbāna in this very life.[761]

This passage makes the point that perception of impermanence establishes perception of not-self. In other words, perception of not-self develops of its own accord when one sees things to be impermanent. The phrase "the conceit 'I am'" (*asmimāna*) refers to the type of conceit that believes "I am." This type of conceit of self-existence arises even in the continuum of life of a noble being of the first three stages. When they do something admirable, for example, they may think, "It is I who has done this thing." This is also called "pride in what is worthy" (*yāthāvamāna*). Noble ones, of course, know that there is no such thing as what ordinary people identify in a conventional sense as a self, a being, or life. However, when they do something praiseworthy, they may still act or speak with conceit, thinking, "It is I who thinks, speaks, or acts this way."

This type of conceit that occurs in noble ones should be called "conceit of view" (*diṭṭhimāna*), because it is uprooted in a similar way to the way that the wrong view of personality is uprooted. When we say that right view abandons wrong view in the case of the higher paths, the wrong view being referred to is actually this kind of conceit rather than the wrong view of personality that the first path abandons. Only the fourth and final path knowledge of arahantship can completely abandon this kind of conceit. When one clearly sees impermanence, one can also see not-self. When one clearly sees not-self, one can completely abandon the conceit "I am" by means of the path knowledge of arahantship. Therefore, in order to abandon the conceit "I am" the Buddha said, "The perception of impermanence should be developed." The commentary gives this explanation:

> The line "When one perceives impermanence, the perception of non-self is stabilized" means that if one sees the characteristic of impermanence, one also sees the characteristic of not-self. If one sees one of the three universal characteristics, one also sees the other two. This is why [the Buddha] says, "When one perceives impermanence, bhikkhus, the perception of non-self is stabilized."[762]

If one understands one among the three characteristics of impermanence, unsatisfactoriness, and not-self, then one also understands the remaining two. According to the two texts mentioned above, when one reflects on an object that one has seen to be impermanent, one only sees it as unsatisfactory and not-self by nature all the time; one does not see it as satisfactory and self by nature. So understand that when one understands an object to be impermanent, one eliminates not only the defilements that would arise based on the perception of permanence, but the defilements that would arise based on the perception of satisfaction and self are also eliminated because one can also see that the object is by nature unsatisfactory and not-self.

Conceptual and absolute characteristics

I will now discuss the following passage from a commentary on the Abhidhamma:

> People tend to say, "It's impermanent," when, for example, a pot or a cup breaks. The characteristic of impermanence appears to them in this way. They tend to say, "It's suffering," when they experience [pain, such as from] a boil or a thorn. The characteristic of unsatisfactoriness appears to them in this way. The characteristic of impersonality, however, does not appear; it is like darkness. It is not evident and is difficult to know. It is difficult to talk about and explain. Whether or not a buddha has arisen, the characteristics of impermanence and unsatisfactoriness appear. But the characteristic of not-self does not appear when a buddha has not arisen, only when a buddha has arisen.
>
> Even the most powerful masters, the Bodhisatta Sarabhanga and other hermits and ascetics, could only teach the characteristics of impermanence and unsatisfactoriness, but not not-self. If they could have taught [about the third characteristic], their disciples might have attained path knowledge and fruition knowledge. However, the characteristic of not-self is the domain of only an omniscient buddha, and no one else. Thus it is said that the Buddha had to teach about the characteristic of not-self from the basis of either the characteristic of impermanence, the characteristic of unsatisfactoriness, or both of them.[763]

Actually the characteristics of impermanence and unsatisfactoriness that non-Buddhist teachers are able to teach are not the real characteristics of impermanence and unsatisfactoriness that are objects of insight; they are only conventional ideas connected with the characteristics of impermanence and unsatisfactoriness. To elaborate, a pot or a cup is a conventional idea that does not really exist in the ultimate sense. So the breaking of a cup does not reflect the real characteristic of impermanence that one must experience with insight. The understanding of impermanence upon the death of a person is only a fake understanding of the characteristic of impermanence. For ordinary people, the characteristic of unsatisfactoriness that appears as unpleasantness resulting from a boil or a thorn is not the characteristic of unsatisfactoriness in its ultimate sense. This is because they identify it as something that belongs to a person, who doesn't really exist in the ultimate sense. They think, "I am suffering; I am in pain," and so on. Thus it has nothing to do with the ultimate mental and physical phenomena that one must understand with knowledge.

The three characteristics that are referred to in the passage from the commentary on the Aṅguttara Nikāya explained above are the real ones that can only be understood by means of knowledge. If one understands one among those three characteristics, then one understands the other two. So, as the commentary to the *Sammohavinodanī* says, in order to cause people to understand the characteristic of not-self, the Buddha taught it on the basis of the characteristics of impermanence and unsatisfactoriness.

Having said this, the characteristics of impermanence and unsatisfactoriness by means of which one can understand the characteristic of not-self are the real characteristics that one must understand by means of insight. Like the characteristic of not-self, they are also difficult to understand, and persons other than the Buddha cannot teach them. That is why the *Mūlaṭīkā* says:

> Teaching the characteristic of not-self is not the domain of any one other than the Buddha. The teaching of the characteristics of impermanence and unsatisfactoriness that reveal the characteristic of not-self is not the domain of any one other than the Buddha. [It is difficult to teach these because they are not obvious.][764]

The commentary states that no one other than the Buddha can teach the characteristic of not-self, and that he had to teach it on the basis of the characteristics of impermanence and unsatisfactoriness. In light of this, it is shown that when one has not understood the real characteristics of impermanence and unsatisfactoriness, one has not understood the characteristic of not-self. Or in other words, if one understands the real characteristics of impermanence and unsatisfactoriness, one also understands the characteristic of not-self. Other than the Buddha, no other person can understand the characteristic of not-self, nor can they understand the characteristics of impermanence and unsatisfactoriness. Therefore, other than the Buddha, no other person can teach the characteristics of impermanence and unsatisfactoriness that reveal the characteristic of not-self; only the Buddha can do it. This means that it is difficult to teach the real characteristics of impermanence, unsatisfactoriness, and not-self, because they are not obvious.

The characteristics of impermanence and unsatisfactoriness that reveal the characteristic of not-self that are mentioned in this subcommentary are the real characteristics of impermanence and unsatisfactoriness that one must understand with insight. They are not the fake characteristics of impermanence and unsatisfactoriness connected with a broken pot or a piercing thorn. The *Anuṭīkā*, a subcommentary, distinguishes between these two types of knowledge as follows:

> The understanding of the characteristics of impermanence and unsatisfactoriness gained from seeing a broken pot or from feeling a piercing thorn is not a way that can lead beings to a definite understanding of the characteristic of not-self. The characteristic of not-self is only definitely understood when one understands the conditioned and oppressive [nature of phenomena].[765]
>
> To elaborate, one who has developed insight or cultivated insight pāramī and observes mental and physical phenomena is able to see: "The mental and physical phenomena that constitute the eye and so on are conditioned by kamma, the primary elements, and so on. Thus they are impermanent, since they arise without having existed before and vanish after they have arisen; they are unsatisfactory, being constantly oppressed by arising and passing away; and they are not-self, occurring of their own accord without obeying anyone's will."[766]

Summary

Contemplation of impermanence is to understand impermanence by observing the unique characteristics of mental and physical phenomena that arise at the six sense doors and to see both their arising and passing away or only their disappearance. Knowledge that understands a presently observed object to be impermanent is called "empirical contemplation of impermanence" (*paccakkha aniccānupassanā*).

After thoroughly empirically understanding this, one also understands that the mental and physical phenomena from the past, which one cannot directly know, were likewise impermanent. One also understands that whatever mental and physical phenomena there are in this world are also impermanent in the same way. This understanding that comes by way of reflection is called "inferential contemplation of impermanence" (*anumāna aniccānupassanā*).

The contemplation of impermanence, either empirically or inferentially, begins to arise with insight knowledge of comprehension. It is fully developed with regard to its function of abandoning the defilements beginning with insight knowledge of dissolution. This is why in the *Paṭisambhidāmagga* of the Khuddaka Nikāya the Buddha said:

> One who sees impermanence abandons the perception of permanence.[767]

I will now briefly explain contemplations of unsatisfactoriness and not-self. One can understand them in detail in the same way that contemplation of impermanence has been explained above.

Contemplation of unsatisfactoriness

Contemplation of unsatisfactoriness (*dukkhānupassanā*) is to understand unsatisfactoriness by observing the unique characteristics of mental and physical phenomena and seeing that arising and passing away continuously oppress them.

The mental and physical phenomena that arise at the six sense doors are called "that which is unsatisfying" because continuous arising and passing away oppresses them. The condition of being oppressed by continuous arising and passing away is called "the characteristic of unsatisfactoriness" (*dukkhalakkhaṇā*). While observing mental and physical phenomena as they arise and pass away, one can also see the characteristic of unsatisfactoriness; the insight that understands them to be unsatisfactory is called "contemplation of unsatisfactoriness." It sees phenomena as fearful, dangerous, disenchanting, bad, or detestable.

> In accord with [the statement that] "what is impermanent is unsatisfactory," the five aggregates [of mental and physical phenomena] themselves are called unsatisfactory. Why? Because they are constantly oppressed [by arising and passing away]. The condition of being constantly oppressed [in this way] is the characteristic of unsatisfactoriness.[768]

There are three aspects of unsatisfactoriness: the occurrence of mental or physical pain (*dukkhadukkha*), the impermanence of mental or physical pleasure (*vipariṇāmadukkha*), and the condition of being subject to arising and passing away (*saṅkhāradukkha*).

Of these three aspects, we use the last one here because it is common to all conditioned phenomena. As the *Mahāṭīkā* says:

> Of the three types of unsatisfactoriness, being subject to arising and passing away is common to all conditioned phenomena.[769]

If one does not observe the mental and physical phenomena that constantly arise and pass away at the six sense doors, one cannot understand that arising and passing away oppresses them. If one adjusts the posture as soon as one experiences any kind of unpleasant feeling due to remaining in one position for a long time, then even the occurrence of mental and physical pain doesn't appear, let alone the impermanence of mental or physical pleasure or the condition of being subject to arising and passing away, because they are concealed by changing the posture. In the case of not even seeing the roughest form of unsatisfactoriness, contemplation of unsatisfactoriness cannot arise.

On the other hand if one observes mental and physical phenomena that arise and pass away at the six sense doors, one can see how arising and passing away continuously oppress them. Because one is aware of the continuous oppression by arising and passing away, one can also know the disappearance of a pleasant feeling that had appeared earlier while sitting in the same posture. Then one observes the unpleasant feelings such as stiffness or heat that have arisen. Because they are unpleasant, one wants to change the posture, or one actually changes the posture. After changing the posture the unpleasant feeling disappears and is replaced by a pleasant feeling. One will see all of this while noting. Thus one uncovers how changing postures obscures the characteristic of unsatisfactoriness when one sees continuous oppression through arising and passing away and observes the unpleasant feeling that comes from prolonged sitting, the desire to change the posture, and the act of actually changing it. Then real contemplation of unsatisfactoriness arises because the subtle characteristic of being subject to arising and passing away appears.

> The characteristic of unsatisfactoriness does not appear when continuous oppression is not given attention, because it is concealed by the postures . . . When one exposes the postures by

> paying attention to continuous oppression, the characteristic of unsatisfactoriness appears in its true nature.[770]

The phrase "When one exposes the postures, the characteristic of unsatisfactoriness appears" makes it seem that this passage only applies to the characteristic of the occurrence of mental or physical pain. But it also applies to the characteristics of "being subject to arising and passing away" and "the impermanence of mental or physical pleasure," which are referred to with the phrase "by paying attention to continuous oppression." So this is how all the three types of characteristic of unsatisfactoriness appear.

Whenever real contemplation of unsatisfactoriness arises due to seeing the characteristic of unsatisfactoriness, the perception of satisfaction and so on is abandoned. To explain further, if one does not rightly understand the object (mental and physical phenomena) to be unsatisfactory, then a perversion of perception that perceives the object to be satisfactory can arise. The perversions of view and consciousness can also arise. Based on that, defilements can also arise, and this in turn leads to wholesome and unwholesome volitional actions, the effects of which are resultant phenomena. However, if one rightly understands phenomena to be unsatisfactory, then the perversion of perception and so on can no longer arise. Thus all the phenomena beginning with perversion of perception and ending with resultant phenomena cannot arise because they are abandoned and cut off by contemplation of unsatisfactoriness. Thus the *Visuddhimagga* says:

> One who develops contemplation of unsatisfactoriness abandons the perception of satisfaction.[771]

In the *Paṭisambhidāmagga*, the Buddha says:

> One who sees unsatisfactoriness abandons the perception of satisfaction.[772]

Summary

Contemplation of unsatisfactoriness is to understand unsatisfactoriness by observing the unique characteristics of mental and physical phenomena that arise at the six sense doors and seeing either oppression by arising and passing away, change and destruction, or unbearable torture. The knowledge that understands presently observed objects to be unsatisfactory is called "empirical contemplation of unsatisfactoriness" (*paccakkha dukkhānupassanā*).

After thoroughly empirically understanding unsatisfactoriness, one also understands that mental and physical phenomena from the past and future as well as all mental and physical phenomena there are in this world are also unsatisfactory in the same way. The understanding that comes by means of reflection is called "inferential contemplation of unsatisfactoriness" (*anumāna dukkhānupassanā*).

Contemplation of unsatisfactoriness, whether empirical or inferential, begins to arise with insight knowledge of comprehension. Beginning from insight knowledge of dissolution it is fully developed with regard to its function of abandoning the defilements.

Contemplation of not-self

Contemplation of not-self (*anattānupassanā*) is to understand not-self by observing the unique characteristics of mental and physical phenomena and to see that they are unamenable to the exercise of control and that they are phenomena that happen of their own accord.

The term self, which is the opposite of not-self, does not refer to groups of physical or mental phenomena, the body, or any visible forms. Actually it only refers to what ordinary people think of as the soul or self. They mistakenly think that this "self" is a master, an eternal resident, a doer, a feeler, a director, or a controller. But this so-called self is neither the five aggregates of mental and physical phenomena, nor is it inside the five aggregates of mental and physical phenomena, or anywhere else. It is merely a concept held by ordinary people who are not yet free from wrong view.

Therefore the five aggregates of mental and physical phenomena are called not-self. This means that they do not possess a self. Why? If there was a self, it could exercise control. But as there is no exercising of control over the five aggregates, they are not-self. Being unamenable to the exercise of control is called "the characteristic of not-self" (*anattālakkhaṇa*). If one observes all mental and physical phenomena when they arise, one can only see phenomena that arise and pass away of their own accord. One cannot find anything in them that might be called a "self" that could be identified as the master or the controller [of the phenomena]. Thus one understands that the phenomena one observes are not a self that has mastery or control, but only natural phenomena. This understanding is the contemplation of not-self.

> In accord with [the statement that] "what is unsatisfying is not-self," these five aggregates are called not-self. Why? Because there is no exercising of control over them. Being unamenable to the exercise of control is the characteristic of not-self.[773]

If one does not observe the phenomena that arise at the six sense doors, one will not see that they are of different types, characteristics, functions, and objects. Instead, one will see them appear as one single and solid entity. The moment one sees, for example, eye-consciousness does not appear as a separate entity. Rather all the phenomena such as the intention to see, eye-consciousness, and thoughts about what one sees appear as one single and solid entity. The concept of solidity conceals the characteristic of not-self. When the characteristic of not-self doesn't appear, real understanding regarding contemplation of not-self cannot arise.

On the other hand, when one's mindfulness, concentration, and insight are mature, and one observes phenomena at the six sense doors, each of these phenomena appear as separate entities in various ways: as objects, or in terms of their momentariness, characteristics, or functions. They do not appear as a single and solid entity. The moment we see, for example, eye-consciousness alone appears as a single and separate entity. Then the concept of solidity is broken and the characteristic of not-self appears in its true nature, of its own accord. Therefore only when the characteristic of not-self appears can real understanding regarding contemplation of not-self arise.

> The characteristic of not-self does not appear because when one does not pay attention to resolution into the various elements it is concealed by solidity . . . When the breaking up of the solid is effected by resolution into elements, the characteristic of not-self appears in its true nature.[774]

There are four types of concept of solidity that conceal the characteristic of not-self: those associated with the continuity of phenomena, called "solidity of continuity" (*santatighana*), those associated with the mass of phenomena, called "solidity of mass" (*samūhaghana*), those associated with the functions of phenomena, called "solidity of function" (*kiccaghana*), and those associated with the objects of phenomena, called "solidity of object" (*ārammaṇaghana*).

The first of these has also been explained elsewhere in this book (see chapter 3).

The solidity of continuity

Solidity of continuity refers to all concepts of solidity that are based on the continuity of phenomena.

If one does not know that the visual process consists of separate phenomena such as the intention to see, the initial eye-consciousness, the recurring eye-consciousness, and thoughts about what has been seen, then all these phenomena are perceived as one single entity. Because of taking these phenomena to be continuous, one thinks that there is a self that exercises control and that it is this self that can look, see, or think whenever it wants.

Understand this likewise with respect to a moment of hearing. This also applies to moments of bending, stretching, walking, standing, sitting, or lying down. If one does not understand the separate processes involved in these activities, such as the desire and the actual activity [as well as the separate segments within one movement or activity], one thinks that there is a self that can do these activities whenever it wants. Solidity of continuity prevents us from distinguishing separate phenomena by means of their momentariness and so conceals the characteristic of not-self. Not being able to differentiate between successive mental and physical phenomena, one takes them to be a self.

How can one break down the concept of solidity of continuity and make the characteristic of not-self appear? When one practices insight meditation, one understands that the desire to look and the actual act of looking are different or separate. One understands other phenomena likewise; one does not perceive any of them to be continuous or a self, and so the solidity of continuity is broken. When the solidity of continuity is broken, one understands: "The desire to look cannot accomplish looking or seeing. Looking cannot accomplish the desire to look or seeing. Seeing cannot accomplish the desire to look or looking." Therefore there is no self that can do whatever it wants, but only natural phenomena that arise according to conditions. Understand the characteristic of not-self in this way.

Understand this, too, with regard to a moment of hearing. This also applies to moments of bending, stretching, walking, standing, sitting, or lying down. If one understands the separate processes involved in these activities [such as the desire and the actual activity as well as the separate segments within one movement or activity], one can understand that the desire to bend cannot accomplish bending. Bending cannot accomplish the desire to bend. Likewise, the desire to stretch cannot accomplish stretching, and stretching cannot accomplish the desire to stretch. Therefore there is no self that can bend or stretch whenever it wants but only natural phenomena that arise according to conditions. Understand the characteristic of not-self in this way. Understand walking and so on in the same way as well.

The solidity of mass

Solidity of mass refers to all concepts of solidity that are based on the apparent mass of phenomena.

If one has not already observed and distinguished between the mental and physical phenomena that arise at the six sense doors by means of insight, one will perceive mentality and physicality as a single entity. One cannot differentiate that mentality is one thing and that physicality is another. While bending the arm, for example, one will perceive the intention to bend (i.e., mentality) and the arm that is bending (i.e., physicality) as a single thing.

Further, one will also perceive the eye, the ear, and so on within the continuum of one's person as a single thing, and one will also perceive visible form, audible sound, and so on as a single thing. So when one sees the hand touching something, one will perceive the visible form (that is touched) and the sensation of touch as one thing. Moreover one will perceive the physical basis of seeing and the physical basis of touch as one thing. This is just one example. There are too many cases to explain them all in detail. Perceiving the totality of mental and physical phenomena as one mass is the concept of solidity of mass. Because one cannot differentiate the phenomena by means of their different natures through insight meditation practice, their characteristic of not-self is concealed by the concept of solidity of mass.

How can one break down the concept of solidity of mass? When one continuously observes the mental and physical phenomena that arise at the six sense doors, at the very least mind and matter will appear as separate. While bending, for example, it will be obvious that the intention to bend is one thing and the actual bending movement is another. Likewise, while stretching it will be obvious that the intention to stretch is one thing and the actual stretching movement is another. Or when observing the rising movement of the abdomen, it will be obvious that the rising movement is one thing and that the mind that notes it is another. Or else when one observes any other object, it will be obvious in the same way that they are separate. If this much is apparent, the concept of mental and physical phenomena being one mass will be broken.

Then one can understand: "The intention to bend or to stretch cannot carry out the movement of bending or stretching, and also the movement of bending or stretching cannot happen by itself without the intention to bend or to stretch. Moreover the noting mind cannot arise by itself without something to note, such as the rise or fall of the abdomen." Thus the characteristic of not-self appears in its true nature.

Furthermore, when one continuously observes seeing, hearing, touching, and so on, it becomes apparent that visible form is one thing, audible sound is another thing, and the sensation of touch is yet another. It also becomes apparent that the eye that is the base of seeing is one thing, the ear that is the base of hearing is another thing, and the body that is the basis of the touch is yet another. And moreover, it becomes apparent that eye-consciousness is one thing, the contact between the visible form and eye-consciousness is another thing, and pleasant or unpleasant feeling is yet another. When each and every phenomenon appears as separate, one has thoroughly broken the concept of solidity of mass.

Thus one understands that none of the bodily, verbal, and mental actions can happen due to the exercise of control; they can only be accomplished in accordance with conditions. Then the true nature of the characteristic of not-self, namely the inability to exercise control, clearly appears.

The solidity of function

Solidity of function refers to all concepts of solidity that are related to the functions of phenomena.

Mental and physical phenomena are different from each other with regard to their functions. However, without having distinguished them by means of insight, one perceives these phenomena to be one single entity. At a moment of seeing, the eye is able to see the visible form, eye-consciousness is able to see, and visible form is able to be seen. Although these functions are distinct, one perceives the eye, the visible form, and eye-consciousness that happen in a single continuum to be one entity. It is the same with hearing.

Eye-consciousness is able to see, ear-consciousness is able to hear, nose-consciousness is able to smell, tongue-consciousness is able to taste, body-consciousness is able to know touch, and mind-consciousness is able to think. Although these functions are different, one perceives these mental phenomena that happen in a single continuum to be one entity. One thinks that it is "I" who sees and likewise that it is "I" who hears, smells, tastes, touches, and thinks.

A pleasant feeling makes the mind happy, an unpleasant feeling withers the mind, and a neither-unpleasant-nor-pleasant feeling, while neither making the mind happy nor withering it, puts it in a peaceful state. Although these functions are different, one perceives these three kinds of feeling that happen in a single continuum to be one entity. One thinks that it is "I" who is happy and glad, it is "I" who is unhappy and depressed, it is "I" who is neither happy nor unhappy but peaceful.

It is the intention to bend that is able to cause movement to happen. Although these functions are different, one perceives the mind (intention) and the movements (matter) to be one entity. One thinks that it is "I" who have the intention to bend and it is "I" who am bending; or that "I" am the intention to bend and that "I" am the bending. It is the same for stretching and walking. Because one does not understand by means of insight that the mental and physical phenomena that are distinct according to their functions are separate, one perceives them to be one entity. This is the concept of solidity of function.

How can one break down the concept of solidity of function? While observing mental and physical phenomena at the time of their occurrence by means of insight, one can differentiate them as separate phenomena. It becomes apparent that these mental and physical phenomena have different functions and do not mix with each other, but happen separately. Thus the previously held perception that saw them as one entity will be broken, and one will understand that phenomena that have one specific function cannot perform another. Then the true nature of the characteristic of not-self, namely the inability to exercise control, clearly appears.

The solidity of objects

Solidity of object refers to all concepts of solidity related to objects taken by mental phenomena.

Mental phenomena are distinct with regard to their objects. However without having distinguished them by means of insight, one perceives these different mental phenomena as a single entity. In reality, eye-consciousness takes visible forms as its object, ear-consciousness takes sounds as its objects, nose-consciousness takes odors as its objects, tongue-consciousness takes flavors as its objects, body-consciousness takes bodily sensations as its objects, and mind-consciousness takes the various kinds of mental phenomena as its objects. The consciousness that sees visible forms is distinct from the consciousness that hears sounds or experiences any of the other objects; the consciousness that hears is distinct from the consciousness that sees or experiences any of the other objects. Eye-consciousness is distinct with respect to each different color it sees as well. The consciousness that sees white, for example, is distinct from the consciousness that sees black, blue, or yellow, and the consciousness that sees black, blue, or yellow is distinct from the consciousness that sees white. The same is true of the ear-consciousness that hears each different sound. Furthermore, when one sees the same color for some period of time, each successive moment of eye-consciousness is distinct from those before and after it. The same is true when one hears the same sound for some time.

Each different object is experienced by a different consciousness. But one perceives all these mental objects that happen in a single continuum to be one entity. One thinks: "It is I myself who is seeing and hearing"; or "I am the one who wants to look at something and then sees it"; or "I see white, black, blue, and yellow"; or "I have been seeing this same color for some time," and so on. In this way, one perceives these mental phenomena that are distinct with regard to their objects as one single entity. This is the concept of solidity of object. This concept is another reason why the characteristic of not-self does not appear to ordinary persons but remains concealed.

How can the solidity of object be broken? If one's concentration, mindfulness, and insight knowledge are strong and one observes seeing, hearing, and so on the moment they occur, one will thoroughly break through the concept of solidity of objects. At the time of seeing it will become apparent that the intention to see is one thing and the noting mind that notes the intention is another; the seeing mind is one thing and the noting mind that notes the seeing mind is another, and likewise at the time of hearing. It also becomes apparent that the seeing mind is different from the hearing mind, the touching mind, or the thinking mind. Or when seeing colors, it will become apparent that the mind that sees white is different from the mind that notes it, and the mind that sees black is different from the mind that notes it. When hearing various sounds it will become apparent that the first mind that hears is different from the first mind that notes it, and the second mind that hears is different from the second mind that notes it. When one hears a sound for a long time, it is the same.

If one can distinguish between these mental phenomena that take different objects, then the true nature of the characteristic of not-self, the inability to exercise control, clearly appears.

The *Visuddhimagga-mahāṭīkā* gives this summary of the different perceptions of solidity:

> When mental and physical phenomena have arisen and are mutually steadying each other, then, owing to misinterpreting that as a unity, solidity of mass is assumed through failure to subject formations to examination by means of insight. And likewise solidity of function is assumed when, although definite differences exist in the functions of such and such states, they are taken as one. And likewise solidity of object is assumed when, although differences exist in the ways in which states that take objects make them their objects, those objects are taken as one. But when they are seen after resolving them by means of knowledge into these elements, they disintegrate like froth subjected to compression by the hand. They are mere states (*dhamma*) occurring due to conditions and are void. In this way the characteristic of not-self becomes more evident.[775]

According to the commentary and subcommentary, when the concept of solidity is broken and the object is observed in its true nature of having the characteristic of not-self, then the concept of self is abandoned whenever real contemplation of not-self arises. If objects (mental and physical phenomena) are not rightly understood to be not-self, then based on these objects that are not rightly understood perversion of perception that takes them for an "I" or a self can arise. The perversions of view and consciousness can also arise. Based on these perversions, defilements and volitional actions are able to arise as well. These, in turn, can turn into resultant phenomena.

However, if one rightly understands these phenomena to be not-self, then the perversions of perception, view, and consciousness that arose in connection with the objects cannot arise anymore. Thus all the suffering that starts with the perversion of perception and ends with the resultant phenomena cannot arise anymore because it has been abandoned by the contemplation of not-self. That is why the *Visuddhimagga* says:

> One who sees not-self abandons the perception of self.[776]

Summary

The contemplation of not-self is to understand not-self by observing the unique characteristics of mental and physical phenomena that arise at the six sense doors, and to see either that they do not happen according to one's wishes, are unable to exercise control, or are impermanent and unsatisfactory. Insight knowledge that understands presently observed objects to be not-self is called "empirical contemplation of not-self" (*paccakkha anattānupassanā*).

After thoroughly empirically understanding not-self, one also understands in the same way that the mental and physical phenomena from the past and future, as well as all mental and physical phenomena that are in this world, are also not-self and not a being but just natural phenomena. The understanding that comes by means of reflection is called "inferential contemplation of not-self" (*anumāna anattānupassanā*).

The contemplation of not-self, whether empirical or inferential, begins to arise with insight knowledge of comprehension. Beginning from insight knowledge of dissolution it is fully developed with regard to its function of abandoning the defilements.

Seeing three characteristics through disappearance

> The momentary cessation of mental and physical phenomena, in particular, is impermanence. Thus the commentary mentions the phrase "nonexistence after having arisen," and so on.[777]

> Disappearance is the culminating point for one who under-

> stands impermanence. Thus contemplation of impermanence is suitable for one who observes disappearance.[778]

According to these passages, the second of the two characteristics of impermanence—that is, "nonexistence after having arisen"—is the outstanding one. This refers to the momentary disappearance of present phenomena. Thus one should understand that contemplation of impermanence is accomplished by just observing the disappearance, vanishing, or dissolution of mental and physical phenomena that are arising and passing away. This happens at the mature stage of insight knowledge of dissolution. When one sees their disappearance, one no longer regards these phenomena as satisfactory or pleasant. Actually because of their continuous oppression by disappearance, one understands them to be phenomena that are unsatisfactory, bad, and devoid of pleasure. Then contemplation of unsatisfactoriness arises.

When one understands that one is not able to prevent these mental and physical phenomena from disappearing or that one cannot make them pleasurable or last forever, then the contemplation of not-self arises. This is how each of the three contemplations arises by paying attention to observing the disappearance of present mental and physical phenomena. The *Visuddhimagga* says:

> Dissolution is the peak of impermanence. The meditator who observes it contemplates that all conditioned phenomena are impermanent and not permanent. Then because what is impermanent is unsatisfactory, and unsatisfactoriness is not-self, the meditator can also see that these very phenomena are unsatisfactory—not satisfactory—and not-self—not related to a self.[779]

Thus one can accomplish these three contemplations at the peak of insight knowledge of dissolution by seeing disappearance alone. This point will become clearer in the following sections.

Contemplation of disenchantment

Contemplation of disenchantment (*nibbidānupassanā*) refers to insight knowledge of disenchantment that follows insight knowledge of danger as described in chapter 6. With the momentum gained from insight knowledge of dissolution, one only sees disappearance whenever one notes. After seeing conditioned phenomena to be fearful and full of flaws, one becomes weary of and fed up with them, either by seeing their disappearance and dissolution while noting them, or by reflecting about conditioned phenomena. This is how contemplation of disenchantment arises.

Without this contemplation, one perceives conditioned phenomena as something to delight in, and so "attachment accompanied by joy" (*sappītikataṇhā*) can arise. Based on this kind of delight, defilements and volitional actions can arise, and they in turn can lead to resultant phenomena. But due to this contemplation, such delight and attachment cannot arise with regard to conditioned phenomena that one usually perceives to be something to delight in. Thus contemplation of disenchantment abandons delight and attachment. This is why the *Visuddhimagga* says:

> One who develops contemplation of disenchantment abandons delight.[780]

This is further explained by the *Visuddhimagga-mahāṭīkā*, which says:

> Contemplation of disenchantment refers to contemplation that manifests as a sense of feeling weary of conditioned phenomena. Delight refers to attachment accompanied by joy.[781]

Contemplation of dispassion

> The contemplation of dispassion (*virāgānupassanā*) is contemplation that manifests as detachment from conditioned phenomena.[782]

According to this subcommentary passage, one becomes weary of conditioned phenomena by means of insight knowledge of disenchantment. Because one only sees the disappearance of conditioned phenomena whenever one observes them, one becomes detached from phenomena and inclines toward nibbāna, the cessation of conditioned phenomena. This contemplation is contemplation of dispassion. According to the *Visuddhimagga*:

> Destructional dispassion (*khayavirāga*)[783] refers to the momentary disappearance of conditioned phenomena. Complete dispassion (*accantavirāga*) refers to nibbāna. Seeing these two kinds of dispassion when insight or path knowledge occurs is contemplation of dispassion.[784]

Destructional dispassion is insight knowledge that arises due to insight practice by understanding disappearance while taking conditioned phenomena as one's object. Complete dispassion is being free and cut off from all conditioned phenomena, that is, it is nibbāna. Insight cannot see nibbāna, complete dispassion, as nibbāna is not an object of insight. However, insight knowledge of desire for deliverance, which follows insight knowledge of disenchantment, wishes to become free from conditioned phenomena. The desire for deliverance is the inclination of the mind toward nibbāna, freedom from conditioned phenomena. So insight in the form of the desire for deliverance sees nibbāna by inclining the mind toward it. Thus, because it observes these two kinds of dispassion, insight knowledge of desire for deliverance is contemplation of dispassion.

The phrase from the *Mahāṭīkā* "one becomes detached from the conditioned phenomena" is synonymous with the phrase "sees nibbāna by inclining the mind toward it." The noble paths see nibbāna (or the complete dispassion) since nibbāna is taken as their object. They also see destructional dispassion because the function of seeing is also accomplished. Therefore it is the contemplation of dispassion. One should know that here we analyze the mundane knowledges, and so only knowledge that results from insight is contemplation of dispassion.

Contemplation of disenchantment and contemplation of dispassion only arise in a meditator whose insight knowledge of dissolution is sharp and mature. This is why the *Paṭisambhidāmagga* of the Khuddaka Nikāya says regarding the insight knowledge of dissolution:

> One becomes weary rather than taking delight; one becomes detached rather than attached.[785]

The *Visuddhimagga* says:

> But what is impermanent, unsatisfactory, not-self, is not something to delight in; and what is not something to delight in is

> not something to become attached to; consequently when that field of formations is seen as impermanent, unsatisfactory, not-self, in accordance with contemplation of dissolution, then one becomes weary, one does not delight; one becomes detached, one does not become attached.[786]

As mentioned in the case of contemplations of impermanence and so on, it is suitable to note "impermanence, impermanence" in order to pay attention. However, in the case of contemplations of disenchantment and dispassion, it is obvious that it is not suitable to label "disenchantment, disenchantment" or "dispassion, dispassion." As shown above in the *Visuddhimagga*, after one understands that conditioned phenomena are impermanent, unsatisfactory, and not-self by means of insight knowledge of dissolution, one progresses to understanding that these conditioned phenomena are not delightful but wearisome. This insight knowledge is contemplation of disenchantment. Then one becomes detached. This insight knowledge is contemplation of dispassion.

As was the case with contemplation of impermanence and so on, to label "impermanence, impermanence" is not the main point. One should bear in mind that the main point is to understand whatever mental and physical phenomena one happens to note or think about to be impermanent.

Contemplation of cessation

> Contemplation of cessation (*nirodhānupassanā*) is contemplation of the cessation of conditioned phenomena, or contemplation that causes the cessation of conditioned phenomena so that they cannot arise again later. Contemplating in this way is contemplation of cessation. It is insight knowledge of desire for deliverance that has reached its full strength.[787]

According to this passage, contemplation of cessation can be defined in two ways: as either "contemplation of cessation" or "contemplation for cessation." In the ultimate sense, however, these two are not different. Insight knowledge of desire for deliverance sees conditioned phenomena disappearing and also wants to become free of them. This insight knowledge of desire for deliverance, when it is sharp and keen, is "empirical contemplation of cessation" (*paccakkhanirodhānupassanā*). The conditioned phenomena, from which one wants to become free (but whose cessation one has not seen), will lead to the arising of new existences and conditioned phenomena in the future. Conditioned phenomena that are observed with this contemplation of cessation cannot lead to the arising of new existences and conditioned phenomena. Thus this contemplation that is undertaken in order that new existences and conditioned phenomena cannot arise anymore causes them to cease. Therefore the *Mahāṭīkā* defines the first way as contemplation that contemplates the cessation of conditioned phenomena and the second way as contemplation that contemplates in order to cause new existences and conditioned phenomena to cease.

The commentaries on in- and out-breath define contemplation of cessation in the same way. While empirically experiencing the [momentary] cessation and destruction (*khayanirodha*) of conditioned phenomena that are observed in the present, the mind inclines toward the complete cessation (*accantanirodha*) of conditioned phenomena, nibbāna. Thus insight knowledge of desire for deliverance, when sharp and keen, is contemplation of cessation. And the inclination to complete cessation is desire for deliverance from these conditioned phenomena.

The following line from the *Paṭisambhidāmagga* explains contemplation of cessation as follows:

> He causes cessation, not origination. Having caused cessation, origination is abandoned.[788]

According to the *Visuddhimagga*, we can interpret this in these two ways: "Thus one who is not attached causes the cessation of lust (*rāga*), not its origination. This happens firstly by means of mundane knowledge. The meaning is that one does not cause origination"; or alternatively, "One who has become detached and has caused the cessation of the seen (the presently experienced) field of conditioned phenomena also causes the cessation of the unseen (the past and the future) by means of inferential knowledge; one does not originate it. The meaning is that one gives attention only to its cessation. One sees only its cessation, not its origin."[789] But although the phrase "causes cessation" (*nirodheti*) can be formed and interpreted in these two ways, they mean the same thing. Both refer to insight knowledge of the desire for deliverance that has reached its full strength. Contemplation of cessation is not differentiated into two ways of contemplation.

The first definition says, "one causes cessation of lust." But it does not say which phenomena have to be observed in which way and which lust is caused to cease. However as said in the second definition, it is the cessation of the presently experienced conditioned phenomena and of those in the past and future. So one should adequately understand that one causes cessation of greed while perceiving those phenomena to exist.

The second definition shows which defilements have been caused to cease. But since the first definition says, "one causes cessation of lust," one should adequately understand this statement. How? If one contemplates the cessation of conditioned phenomena, one does not perceive them to exist forever, and so lust does not arise. Thus the meaning of these two definitions is the same.

One should understand that the phrase "one causes cessation of lust" also refers to the cessation of other defilements, the volitional actions for which lust is the fundamental cause, and the resultant phenomena of these volitional actions. Thus one should understand that the two explanations from the *Mahāṭīkā* and this passage from the *Visuddhimagga* are actually the same.

The contemplation of cessation that observes the cessation of the present conditioned phenomena is called "empirical knowledge." When this empirical knowledge matures, there arises the contemplation of cessation that reflects that past and future conditioned phenomena are subject to cessation, just as the present ones are. This is called "inferential knowledge." According to the *Visuddhimagga-mahāṭīkā*:

> One is aware of the cessation of conditioned phenomena that have presently arisen and are seen. Likewise, one reflects by the power of inferential knowledge on past and future conditioned phenomena that are not seen: "Like these present conditioned phenomena, others cease in the same way." Thus one is also aware of the cessation of those phenomena one has reflected on.[790]

The subcommentary says that this contemplation of cessation refers to insight knowledge of desire for deliverance that has reached its full strength. Thus it should be understood that contemplation of dispassion refers to the tender stage of that same insight knowledge.

One is aware of conditioned phenomena that are able to give rise to greed and other defilements by means of inferential knowledge. The abandonment of these defilements is only temporary. Therefore the *Mahāṭīkā* says:

> It is said: "He causes the temporary cessation of greed." He abandons the defilements, and so the temporary cessation of greed is accomplished. This is what is meant by "to abandon."[791]

This is because the latent defilements lying dormant in conditioned phenomena from the past and future cannot be completely uprooted by mundane knowledge but only by supramundane path knowledge.

Contemplation of relinquishment

> Contemplation of relinquishment (*paṭinissaggānupassanā*)[792] is the contemplation that occurs as a way of relinquishing conditioned phenomena [or the defilements that perceive conditioned phenomena to be permanent, satisfactory, and self.] It is [insight knowledge of] reobservation [and insight knowledge of equanimity toward phenomena].[793]

The phrase "that occurs as a way of relinquishing conditioned phenomena" is used here in a figurative sense, since it is not actually phenomena themselves that should be relinquished but the defilements associated with them. Therefore I have translated this phrase more explicitly to include "the defilements that perceive conditioned phenomena as permanent, satisfactory, and self." This is similar to the Buddha's teaching:

> Bhikkhus . . . Material form is not yours. Abandon it.[794]

The commentary explains that the term "abandon" in this case does not mean to abandon one's body but to give up one's attachment to the body.

Suppose, for example, that one has a disobedient and very wicked child who frequently gives one much trouble and causes one to suffer. In that case one would want to disown this child and would repeatedly reflect on the heavy and deplorable flaws he or she has. If one completely abandons the perception of him or her as one's son or daughter, then one not only abandons the mental and physical suffering connected with the wicked child but also the child him- or herself. In this case when one is able to completely abandon the perception of the child as one's son or daughter, then one has truly abandoned one's child. Likewise when one reobserves conditioned phenomena and sees them to be impermanent, unsatisfactory, and not-self, then one's relinquishment of the defilements (that take conditioned phenomena to be permanent, satisfactory, and self) is also the relinquishment of conditioned phenomena. Therefore, the subcommentary says that contemplation that is able to relinquish the defilements "occurs as a way of relinquishing conditioned phenomena." The *Visuddhimagga* says:

> This contemplation of impermanence and so on is also called both "relinquishment as giving up" and "relinquishment as entering into" because it temporarily abandons defilements along with volitional actions and resultant phenomena and because, by seeing the unsatisfactoriness of conditioned phenomena, it inclines toward and enters into nibbāna, which is the opposite of conditioned phenomena. Therefore the bhikkhu who possesses this [contemplation] gives up defilements and enters into nibbāna in the way stated; he does not grasp defilements by causing arising, nor does he grasp a conditioned object by failing to see its danger. Hence it was said, "He relinquishes, he does not grasp."[795]

As explained in this passage, the term "relinquishment" can have the sense of either "giving up" (*pariccāgapaṭinissagga*) something one does not need any more or "entering into," that is, "launching out into" (*pakkhandanapaṭinissagga*) the place to which one aspires. Being included in insight knowledges of reobservation and equanimity toward phenomena, it is able to temporarily relinquish the defilements that arise based on the perception of permanence, satisfactoriness, and self, the volitional actions caused by these defilements, and the resultant phenomena. Thus it is relinquishment.

Just as somebody, when seeing a place full of danger, wants to go to another place that is free of danger, so does insight knowledge, when seeing the danger of conditioned phenomena, incline toward nibbāna, the opposite of conditioned phenomena. "To incline" only means to desire to become free of conditioned phenomena; it does not mean to take nibbāna as one's object. By so inclining one is able to enter into nibbāna and relinquish one's body. Thus it is relinquishment. It is contemplation of relinquishment because it is able to observe giving up of the defilements by means of insight knowledge of reobservation and insight knowledge of equanimity toward phenomena, and because it is able to observe entering into nibbāna by inclining toward it.

If one does not contemplate phenomena as impermanent, unsatisfactory, and not-self, then defilements get an opportunity to arise depending on those objects that go unobserved. When we say that they get an opportunity, we actually mean "they are caused to arise" or "grasping." However, by clearly observing phenomena to be impermanent, unsatisfactory, and not-self, defilements do not get an opportunity to arise in dependence on objects that go unobserved. When we say that they do not get an opportunity, we mean "they are not caused to arise" or "not grasping." Therefore it is said, "he does not grasp defilements by causing arising."

Failing to see the danger of impermanence and so on, whenever one is aware of or reflects on these conditioned phenomena, one grasps conditioned objects with defilements. However, if one sees the danger of impermanence and so on through awareness, then although one takes conditioned phenomena as one's object, one does not grasp them. And since defilements do not arise when one observes a conditioned object, one relinquishes it, not having grasped it. Therefore it is said, "one does not grasp a conditioned object by failing to see its danger."

As the passage from the *Mahāṭīkā* [at the beginning of this section] mentioned, contemplation of relinquishment is insight knowledge of reobservation and insight knowledge of equanimity toward phenomena.

Summary

If one has fully established these first seven contemplations, from contemplation of impermanence through to contemplation of relinquishment, one also establishes the following eleven contemplations, which are included in them. For this reason there are many places in the commentaries that say that meditators should practice these seven contemplations. The Buddha also spoke many times about these seven contemplations in the *Paṭisambhidāmagga*.

Furthermore if one fully establishes the three contemplations of impermanence, unsatisfactoriness, and not-self, the four contemplations of disenchantment, dispassion, cessation, and relinquishment, which are included in them, will also be established. For this reason the three baskets of the Pāḷi canon mostly mention only the contemplations of impermanence, unsatisfactoriness, and not-self. The following example from the *Visuddhimagga-mahāṭīkā* is given in order to make the reader firmly believe this:

> Although there are seven different kinds of contemplation and eighteen different kinds of insight [that should be contemplated], they are all included in the three contemplations of impermanence, unsatisfactoriness, and not-self. Thus, due to their power, [these three contemplations] are the culminating point of insight.[796]

Although these contemplations and insight knowledges are divided into seven contemplations, eighteen great insight knowledges, forty insight knowledges, and so on, they are all included in the three contemplations of impermanence, unsatisfactoriness, and not-self. If the three contemplations are fully established, all the remaining insight knowledges, which are included in them, are also established. Therefore when insight knowledge is sharp and fully developed and reaches its peak, it is well established even with only the three contemplations of impermanence, unsatisfactoriness, and not-self.

> Contemplation of impermanence and contemplation of the signless are one in meaning and different only in the letter; as are contemplation of unsatisfactoriness and contemplation of the desireless; as are contemplation of not-self and contemplation of emptiness.[797]

Thus if one establishes contemplation of impermanence, contemplation of the signless is also established. If one establishes contemplation of unsatisfactoriness, contemplation of the desireless is also established. If one establishes contemplation of not-self, contemplation of emptiness is also established.

> But insight into states that are higher understanding is all kinds of insight, and knowledge and vision of things as they really are is included in the purification by overcoming doubt.[798]

Therefore, if one establishes the three contemplations of impermanence, unsatisfactoriness, and not-self, the states that are higher understanding are also established. Because of these three contemplations, insight knowledge and vision of things as they really are is established first of all. The *Mahāṭīkā* illustrates how the remaining eleven contemplations are included and established:

> When contemplation of impermanence is established, then the contemplations of cessation, destruction, fall, and change are partly established. When contemplation of unsatisfactoriness is established, then the contemplations of disenchantment, dispassion, and danger are partly established. When contemplation of not-self is established, then the other contemplations are partly established.[799]

This text says "are partly established" in reference to the stage of insight knowledge of comprehension. One should bear in mind that contemplations of impermanence and so on, together with their corresponding insights, are established at the higher stages of insight knowledge, beginning with insight knowledge of dissolution.

The subcommentaries do not mention contemplation of dispassion being included in contemplation of unsatisfactoriness. Why? The *Paṭisambhidāmagga* of the Khuddaka Nikāya says that contemplation of dispassion abandons attachment to sensual desire, but it does not say that contemplation of dispassion abandons attachment to view, rites and rituals, and self, as contemplation of not-self does. Therefore, contemplation of dispassion should not be included in contemplation of not-self, since contemplation of not-self has a different function of abandoning. It should only be included in contemplation of unsatisfactoriness, since contemplation of unsatisfactoriness has the same function of abandoning. However, one should understand that this phrase has been dropped since one does not find it in those texts.

According to the text of the *Visuddhimagga-mahāṭīkā*, when one establishes contemplation of impermanence, the four contemplations of cessation, destruction, fall, and change are also established. When one establishes contemplation of unsatisfactoriness, the three contemplations of disenchantment, dispassion, and danger are also established. When one establishes contemplation of not-self, the three contemplations of relinquishment, reflection, and turning away are also established. So this is how all the insight knowledges are included and established within the three contemplations of impermanence, unsatisfactoriness, and not-self.

The three contemplations of impermanence, unsatisfactoriness, and not-self are only established when one's insight knowledge into the dissolution of conditioned phenomena becomes sharp. According to the *Mahāṭīkā*:

> Some scholars say that at this stage of insight knowledge of dissolution, there is no need to see impermanence in various ways. Rather, by seeing just the disappearance of phenomena, one sees all of the characteristics of impermanence. But this is only true when contemplation of dissolution reaches its peak. Before that it is necessary to see impermanence in a variety of ways.[800]

What "some scholars" say in this passage from the *Mahāṭīkā* refers only to the tender stage of insight knowledge of dissolution. The subcommentator supports the view that [the three contemplations are only established] when insight knowledge of dissolution reaches its peak. This is why, in the *Paṭisambhidāmagga* of the Khuddaka Nikāya, the Buddha said:

> The identity of the characteristic of fall is the single cause of the arising of the mind of insight [a meditator's mind, free of defilements].[801]

The Remaining Contemplations

Contemplation of destruction

According to the *Visuddhimagga-mahāṭīkā*, contemplation of destruction (*khayānupassanā*) is insight knowledge that sees the momentary dissolution of conditioned phenomena while observing their unique characteristics, or insight knowledge that sees the momentary dissolution of the noting mind itself. This contemplation is an insight knowledge of dissolution that understands the dissolution of both the object and the noting mind. Thus this contemplation becomes fully developed when one breaks the concept of things as solid forms and sees conditioned phenomena are merely dissolving processes.

> Contemplation of destruction is to see the dissolution of present aggregates immediately followed by seeing the dissolution of the very mind and mental factors that observed those aggregates.[802]

> Contemplation of destruction, however, is the insight knowledge in one who breaks through the concept of solidity and so sees destruction as "impermanent in the sense of destruction."[803]

I have explained above how to break through the four types of concept of solidity. If one's insight knowledge of dissolution becomes sharp and keen so that the solidity is broken, then, while one is bending one's arm, only the little movements happening one after the other appear, and so these little movements are seen as dissolving or disappearing. One also sees the noting mind, which is different from the object, and successively follows it, as immediately dissolving or disappearing. Thus the material form that is called "bending" does not appear as a solid form such as an "arm" or a "hand," as it does for ordinary people. Even the arm no longer appears to permanently exist. Furthermore the noting mind no longer appears as somebody who is aware, as it usually does for ordinary people. With awareness it becomes apparent that the noting mind simply disappears moment by moment. One knows these mental and physical phenomena exactly the way they are, as "disappearing, disappearing." The same applies to stretching, seeing, and so on. Due to this understanding, the perversions of perception and so on can no longer arise. This is why it is said, "One who develops this contemplation abandons the perception of solidity."

> Contemplation of destruction is fully established beginning with insight knowledge of dissolution. Thus the perception of solidity is abandoned. Before that, the perception of solidity is not yet abandoned. The same is true for [all] the other contemplations. Thus whether or not one's insight is fully established should be regarded in terms of full understanding by abandoning (*pahānapariññā*) and full understanding by investigating (*tīraṇapariññā*).[804]

Based on the first sentence of this passage, one should clearly understand that one cannot abandon the concept of solidity before insight knowledge of dissolution has been attained. "Full understanding by investigating" refers to insight knowledge of comprehension and insight knowledge of arising and passing away. At that time insight knowledge is not yet powerful enough, so contemplations of impermanence and so on cannot yet completely abandon the perception of permanence and so on. "Full understanding by abandoning" refers to the insight knowledges beginning with insight knowledge of dissolution. At that time insight knowledge is fully established, so the contemplations of impermanence and so on can completely abandon the perceptions of permanence and so on.

Contemplation of fall

Contemplation of fall (*vayānupassanā*) is stated thus:

> Defining both to be alike
> by interference from that same object.
> Inclination on cessation—these
> are insight in the mark of fall.

> It is inclination toward cessation, in other words, toward that same dissolution, after seeing dissolution of [seen] formations by means of personal experience and [unseen] formations by means of inference. The abandoning of accumulation occurs due to these contemplations. When one sees with insight that "I might accumulate [kamma] for the sake of things that are thus subject to fall," one's mind no longer inclines to accumulation.[805]

After seeing the momentary dissolution of present mental and physical phenomena, one sees by means of inference that past and future phenomena also momentarily disappear. At that time one understands: "All conditioned phenomena are momentarily and relentlessly disappearing. There are no states that last forever without ceasing." With this there arises insight knowledge that is inclined toward cessation. This insight knowledge is called "contemplation of fall." This contemplation causes accumulation of sense pleasures to completely cease. When one does not yet fully understand that mental and physical phenomena are momentarily and relentlessly disappearing, one will think that one's body and the bodies of others are stable and firm. Because one wants to enjoy the conditioned phenomena that one perceives to be stable and firm (such as one's own or another person's body) one accumulates actions for both the present and future life.

When one thoroughly understands that all conditioned phenomena are momentarily and relentlessly disappearing by means of this contemplation of fall, one will see no need to expend any energy enjoying phenomena that one previously thought to be permanent. One has no further interest in accumulating actions. Suppose, for example, that there is a person who makes a huge effort and works hard to provide his beloved sons and daughters with beautiful and nice clothes. Upon hearing that his sons and daughters have passed away, that person would lose interest in making such efforts. Contemplation of fall abandons the accumulation of actions for the sake of enjoying sense pleasures; one simply has no more interest in it.

Contemplation of change

> Contemplation of change (*vipariṇāmānupassanā*) is the act of seeing, according to the material septad (*rūpasattaka*), etc., how [momentary] occurrences [in continuity] take place differently by [gradually] diverging from any definition; or, it is the act of seeing change in the two aspects of the aging and the death of what has arisen.[806]

The first way of seeing change by way of both observation and reflection is as follows: One sees that all the physical phenomena (i.e., one's body) that arise from the moment of relinking consciousness until the moment of death consciousness finally disappear and are destroyed at the time of death. One sees that the physical phenomena of the first phase of one's life have changed in the second phase of life and that they are not the same anymore; one sees that the physical phenomena of the second phase of life have likewise changed in the third phase of life and that they are not the same anymore; and finally one sees that the physical phenomena at the time of death have changed and that they are not the same anymore. One sees that the physical phenomena from the first ten years of one's life have changed in one's teens and that they are not the same anymore; and one sees that the physical phenomena from one's teens have changed when one is over twenty and that they are not the same anymore. One sees that the physical phenomena from the night have changed by day and that they are not the same anymore; and one sees that the physical phenomena from the day have changed by night and that they are not the same anymore. One sees that the physical phenomena from the morning have changed by midday and that they are not the same anymore; and one sees that they have changed by the afternoon, evening, first watch of the night, midnight, dawn, and morning, and that they are not the same anymore. This is the coarse way of seeing change.

This is how one can see change in more detail: One sees that the physical phenomena of going forward have changed when going backward, or one sees that they are not the same anymore. One sees that the physical phenomena of going backward, seeing, or bending have changed when going forward and that they are not the same anymore. One sees that the physical phenomena while being still have changed when being active and that they are not the same anymore; and vice versa. One sees that the physical phenomena of rising of the abdomen have changed when the abdomen is falling and that they are not the same anymore; and vice versa. One sees that the physical phenomena of lifting, pushing, dropping, pressing, and the next lifting have changed in the next phase and that they are not the same anymore. One sees that the physical phenomena while feeling cold have changed when feeling hot and that they are not the same anymore; and vice versa. One sees that the physical phenomena while feeling hungry have changed when feeling full and that they are not the same anymore; and vice versa. One sees that the physical phenomena while feeling glad have changed when feeling sad and that they are not the same anymore; and vice versa.

Whenever one sees the physical phenomena in a different activity or state, one sees their change. Furthermore, whenever one sees successive mind-moments, one sees that the preceding and following mind-moments are not the same—that they have changed. This is how contemplation of change comes about by means of the first way of seeing change.

The second way of seeing change mentioned above in the quote from the *Visuddhimagga* is to see the way that aging and death change mental and physical phenomena. Using these two aspects one sees that phenomena do not remain in their original state but change and deteriorate. This is the coarse way of seeing change.

This is how one can see change in more detail: When one constantly observes mental and physical phenomena when they occur and one's insight knowledge matures, then one sees that the middle phase of these phenomena, which we can also call aging, is not the same as the initial phase, since it has changed. One also sees that the final phase, which we can also call death, disappears or is destroyed. Thus whenever one observes mental and physical phenomena, one personally sees that the middle phase and the final phase are not the same as the initial phase and that they have changed. When one thoroughly understands that present mental and physical phenomena do not remain in their original state but change, by means of inferential knowledge one understands that past and future mental and physical phenomena, as well as all mental and physical phenomena in the entire world, are the same: they, too, do not remain in their original state but change. They change from the middle phase to the final phase, from presence to disappearance, or from aging to death. This is how the contemplation of change comes about by means of the second way of seeing change.

Both empirical and inferential insight knowledges that see that phenomena do not remain in their original state but change are called "contemplation of change." This contemplation removes the perception of stability that sees phenomena as unchanging and stable.

In reference to contemplation of destruction and "insight into phenomena that is higher wisdom" (*adhipaññādhammavipassanā*), the commentary to the *Paṭisambhidāmagga* says that inferential insight knowledge of dissolution is contemplation of fall and that the knowledge that sees "all states are changing" due to the power of this contemplation of fall is called "contemplation of change." The commentary to the *Paṭisambhidāmagga* in the Khuddaka Nikāya says the following:

> Contemplation of fall is the inferential insight that sees the dissolution of past and future aggregates and immediately follows the empirical experience of seeing the dissolution of present aggregates. Contemplation of change is the insight that sees, due to inclination toward cessation, that all past, future, and present aggregates are changing and thereby sees change in all states (*dhammā*).[807]

Understand, based on this passage, that contemplation of change only arises with peak insight knowledge of dissolution.

Contemplation of the signless

Contemplation of the signless (*animittānupassanā*) is actually the same as contemplation of impermanence, as I explained in the summary above. Nevertheless, this different term should be defined, so I will explain it in brief.

> "Sign" (*nimitta*) means the sign of conditioned phenomena or formations.[808]

> "The sign of conditioned phenomena" (*saṅkhāranimitta*) refers to phenomena that seem to be solid [to a nonmeditator] due to the concepts of solidity of mass and so on. But the sign of conditioned phenomena appears [to a meditator] due to the discernment and separation of their individual functions and so on.[809]

Bodily activities and movements that are conditioned physical phenomena—such as walking, standing, sitting, lying, bending, stretching, and so on—conditioned mental phenomena—such as seeing, hearing, smelling, tasting, touching, thinking, and so on—and the objects that appear at the six sense doors—such as visible form, sound, smell, taste, touch, and mental objects—do not appear to be mere activities and phenomena, or to be distinct from each other, or to only exist momentarily. Actually, they appear to have solid forms, to be one single entity, and to be permanent. This concept of solidity is also referred to as "the sign of permanence," "the sign of stability" (*dhuvanimitta*), or "the sign of eternity" (*sassatanimitta*).

Contemplation of impermanence, which sees conditioned phenomena as impermanent, is called "the signless" because it is opposite to the sign of permanence, the sign of stability, and the sign of eternity. It is called "contemplation" because it observes impermanence. When we compound the two terms we have "contemplation of the signless," which means to observe the opposite of the signs of solidity in conditioned phenomena.

When one constantly observes mental and physical phenomena at the time of their occurrence, the conditioned phenomena that arise at the six sense doors do not appear to have solid forms, to be one single entity, to be permanent, or to be enduring and stable. Actually they appear to be mere activities and phenomena, to be different from each other, to only exist momentarily, and to disappear a moment after they have arisen. Because they appear in this way when one attains insight knowledge of dissolution, one sees conditioned phenomena as disappearing, ending, being destroyed, vanishing, or impermanent. When one sees conditioned phenomena this way, they cannot appear as permanent and solid entities, and the defilements that develop based on seeing things to be permanent and solid can no longer arise. Because one can abandon the sign of solidity in conditioned phenomena, the *Visuddhimagga* says:

> Thus it is called the signless, because the sign of permanence, the sign of stability, and the sign of eternity are abandoned after breaking through the concept of solidity by means of contemplation of impermanence.[810]

If one uninterruptedly observes the signs of conditioned phenomena, each of the different functions of these conditioned phenomena will become apparent. Not only this, but their unique characteristics, their momentariness, and their objects (in the case of mental conditioned phenomena), will become apparent. For a detailed description of how they appear see the section dealing with the four types of concept of solidity under the heading "Contemplation of not-self."

The way conditioned phenomena appear when one is distinguishing between their function, characteristic, momentariness, and object is the sign of conditioned phenomena. When one can distinguish them by means of their function, characteristic, momentariness, and object, one sees these signs of conditioned phenomena and takes them as one's object at the same time. Thus contemplation of impermanence is neither the opposite of the signs of conditioned phenomena nor is it able to be free of them. This is why this contemplation is called contemplation of the signless: because it is the opposite of the signs of solidity (permanence, stability, and eternity) in conditioned phenomena and because its object is free from these signs of solidity in conditioned phenomena.

When contemplation of the signless, which is contemplation of impermanence, is well established, conditioned phenomena only appear by means of the nature of their dissolution. As a result, one will rightly understand the signs of conditioned phenomena that previously appeared to be solid and lasting entities.

How does this understanding happen? It is similar to finding that an unsophisticated and uncultured person that one imagined to be cultured and refined is not. Or it is similar to being unable to find any heartwood or core when one removes the different layers of a plantain tree. In the same way, with contemplation of impermanence one sees the conditioned phenomena that one previously perceived to be stable and permanent entities dissolving into separate entities, not lasting for even the duration of a flash of lightning. Thus one rightly understands the signs of conditioned phenomena by seeing that there is no permanent entity but only momentarily and unceasingly disappearing phenomena. As a result, one abandons the sign of solidity and the sign of permanence in conditioned phenomena, along with the defilements, volitional actions, and resultant phenomena that spring from them.

> The destruction of conditioned phenomena appears to one who pays attention to impermanence.[811]

> One who pays attention to impermanence knows and sees the signs as they really are.[812]

Contemplation of the desireless

People perceive the mental and physical phenomena that are involved in walking, standing, sitting, bending, stretching, seeing, hearing, touching, thinking, and so on to be something pleasing, good, and delightful. This is called desire (*paṇidhi*) or craving (*paṇihita*).

Contemplation of unsatisfactoriness understands that conditioned phenomena are constantly oppressed by arising and passing away and sees that they are unsatisfactory, not good, and nothing to delight in. This understanding, being the opposite of desire and craving, is called "contemplation of the desireless" (*appaṇihitānupassanā*). Therefore it is said, "One who develops this contemplation abandons desire."

Contemplation of emptiness

When one has not sufficiently developed one's contemplation of not-self, one thinks that there is a self or a being who is able to exercise complete control over mental and physical phenomena such as sitting, standing up, bending, stretching, seeing, hearing, and so on. However the power of one's insight knowledge of dissolution, which breaks up the four types of concept of solidity, causes contemplation of not-self to become well established, and thus one only sees objects swiftly arising and passing away whenever one observes them. When this happens, one cannot find any so-called "self" or "being" that is able to exercise complete control. Instead, one finds that when the necessary conditions are present, not only do states arise that one does not wish to arise, but also states disappear that one does not wish to disappear. One cannot find a self or being that has complete mastery [over phenomena]. Thus one understands that objects and the mind that notes them are merely natural phenomena that rapidly disappear, and that there is no self or being who is either able to perform such activities as sitting, standing up, bending, stretching, seeing, hearing, and so on or who is able to observe or to be aware. One understands that there are merely natural phenomena that disappear and are empty of a self. Since contemplation of not-self understands that phenomena are empty of a self, it is called "contemplation of emptiness" (*suññatānupassanā*). This contemplation is able to abandon defilements and so on that develop based on adherence to the perception of self.

Insight into phenomena that is higher wisdom

> "Insight into phenomena that is higher wisdom" is insight into emptiness by means of dissolution. It occurs thusly: "Only conditioned phenomena disintegrate; it is the death of conditioned phenomena that takes place; there is nothing else." This insight occurs after knowing physical phenomena and so on as objects by seeing the dissolution of both the object and the mind that noted that object. This insight is higher wisdom and insight into phenomena and it should be called "insight into phenomena that is higher wisdom." With it one abandons adherence to grasping at a core, because one clearly sees that there is no core of permanence and no core of self.[813]

When insight knowledge of dissolution grows sharp and keen and one is just aware of a given object occurring at the six sense doors, one knows its disappearance, and in turn one also knows the disappearance of the noting mind. In this way one sees that the object and the mind that notes it very swiftly and unceasingly disappear one after the other in succession and that the object and the mind that notes it are merely conditioned phenomena. Also all the things that disappear one after another are merely conditioned phenomena; it is these conditioned phenomena that are disappearing and dying. Apart from these conditioned phenomena there is nothing else, no self, no "I," and no being. One thoroughly understands that these conditioned phenomena are empty of a permanent entity, empty of a self or a being. This insight knowledge is "insight into phenomena that is higher wisdom" (*adhipaññādhammavipassanā*).

Knowledge and vision of things as they really are

> Knowledge and vision of things as they really are is the discernment of mental and physical phenomena, along with the discernment of their causes and conditions. With it one abandons adherence through confusion that occurs thusly: "Was I in the past?" and "Did God create living beings?"[814]

The insight knowledge that discerns conditionality is "knowledge and vision of things as they really are" (*yathābhūtañāṇadassana*). When this insight knowledge is sufficiently established, one sees that in the present there are only mental and physical phenomena related through cause and effect. Thus one is able to conclude that the totality of mental and physical phenomena in this life has arisen due to ignorance, craving, clinging, and kamma from past lives. And there were also ignorance, craving, clinging, and kamma based on mental and physical phenomena in past lives. Due to ignorance, craving, clinging, and kamma in this life, mental and physical phenomena will arise in a new life. In this way one can conclude that in all the three periods, past, present, and future, merely the mental and physical phenomena of cause and effect exist. As a result, one no longer doubts that one has existed in the past and is no longer confused about whether God or another divine being has created living beings. This means that one has abandoned this doubt and confusion. The *Mahāṭīkā* says:

> Delusion (*sammoha*) is deep confusion by means of doubt and misinterpretation.[815]

Contemplation of danger

> Contemplation of danger (*ādīnavānupassanā*) is knowledge that sees danger in all kinds of becoming and so on. It arises due to the appearance [of phenomena] as frightening. With it one abandons adherence based on reliance, because one does not see anything reliable.[816]

As shown in chapter 6, when insight knowledge of fear becomes sharp and keen, as one sees conditioned phenomena to be dangerous insight knowledge of danger arises. This is also contemplation of danger. When this insight knowledge arises, one does not see even a single conditioned phenomenon to be something reliable: neither objects nor the mind that notes them; neither objects that are reflected upon nor the mind that reflects upon them. One used to think: "If only I were a human being in every life, that would be good. If only I were a millionaire, that would be good. If only I were a king, that would be good. If only I were a devā, that would be good. If only I were a brahmā, that would be good." Before insight knowledge of danger arises, the meditator thought that there was something reliable, a reliable existence, or some reliable conditioned phenomena. But now he or she has not found anything reliable. Thus this insight knowledge abandons adherence to the thought that there is anything reliable in conditioned phenomena connected with sense realm existence, fine-material realm existence, or immaterial realm existence. Here in an ultimate sense, adherence to conditioned phenomena as something reliable (*ālayābhinivesa*) is attachment to existence.

> Adherence to conditioned phenomena as something reliable or as something that gives protection is, in the ultimate sense, attachment to existence.[817]

When one's insight knowledge of danger has not yet been well established, one is not able to relinquish existence along with conditioned phenomena, however miserable one may feel. One thinks that there must be something in existence that can make one happy, and so one only wishes to escape from present misery. If one feels sick or has a fever, for example, one wishes only for good health. If one is poor, one only wishes to be rich and affluent. If one's present life seems hopeless, one longs for a better life in the next existence. If one thinks that human life is miserable, one wishes for existence as devā or brahmā. But one does not desire to be completely free from all existences or conditioned phenomena. This attachment to, delight or entanglement in, existence and conditioned phenomena is adherence due to reliance. Contemplation of danger abandons adherence due to reliance. Thus when this insight knowledge is mature, insight knowledge of disenchantment and so on arises.

Contemplation of reflection

> Contemplation of reflection (*paṭisaṅkhānupassanā*) is knowledge of reflection that effects the means to gain liberation. With it one abandons nonreflection.[818]

> Insight knowledge of reobservation is the correct means for liberation from conditioned phenomena. It is contemplation of reflection. With it one abandons the ignorance that is the nonreflection on impermanence and so on, which is the opposite of the reflection of impermanence and so on.[819]

Insight knowledge of desire for deliverance arises so that one is able to relinquish conditioned phenomena or to escape from conditioned phenomena. When this insight knowledge is well established, insight knowledge of reobservation, which is contemplation of reflection, arises. In this case, one should note that the two expressions "so that one is able to relinquish conditioned phenomena" and "so that one is able to escape from conditioned phenomena" have the same meaning. Thus is it said that the commentary uses these two expressions interchangeably with reference to insight knowledge of desire for deliverance.

This is how one can relinquish conditioned phenomena: If one does not yet thoroughly understand conditioned phenomena to be impermanent, unsatisfactory, and not-self whenever they arise, then desire and delight may arise regarding such conditioned phenomena. When unpleasant feelings arise or pleasant feelings change one sees the arising and passing away of all conditioned phenomena, and so distress, fear, or disenchantment may arise. Due to adherence to conditioned phenomena when this happens, one cannot yet relinquish conditioned phenomena nor escape from them.

If one thoroughly understands conditioned phenomena to be impermanent, unsatisfactory, and not-self whenever they arise, one does not take any of these conditioned phenomena to be pleasurable or likeable, nor does one take them to be a self or something related to a self. Thus one does not hope or wish for the pleasure of these conditioned phenomena, nor does one hope or wish for their disappearance, should one not want them. One doesn't worry if they are not pleasant; one is not concerned about the arising of phenomena one does not want. It is like not having any hopes, wishes, worries, or concerns about things one does not care about, such as stones, sand, grass, leaves, or rubbish. Being free from such want and worry, one is able to simply be aware of each conditioned phenomena as they arise. Since there are no obstacles with regard to these conditioned phenomena, one has already relinquished them. One has also escaped from these conditioned phenomena. One should also understand the meaning of the example of the disobedient and wicked child in the section on contemplation of relinquishment in the same way.

An arahant, a fully enlightened being, completely accomplishes this escape from conditioned phenomena. In the case of insight meditation, at the stage of equanimity toward formations, which is endowed with the six-limbed equanimity, one has well escaped from conditioned phenomena. However the function of escaping from conditioned phenomena is not yet accomplished by merely having the desire for deliverance, or by merely spending one's time without observing or being aware of these phenomena. It can only be accomplished when one thoroughly understands by means of insight that conditioned phenomena are impermanent, unsatisfactory, and not-self. This understanding can only be established when conditioned phenomena are again observed as usual and without any gaps. Thus insight knowledge of reobservation becomes the means to relinquish conditioned phenomena with respect to insight knowledge of desire for deliverance, since one wants to relinquish conditioned phenomena on its account. If one wants to relinquish them, one must actually reobserve each arising conditioned phenomenon. When one observes in this way, but is not yet able to be equanimous regarding conditioned phenomena, one's insight knowledge is considered to be contemplation of reflection.

At the beginning of their insight knowledge of reobservation, some meditators want to give up conditioned phenomena because they are afraid of or disenchanted with them. They think that they could become free of them without observing them any further, assuming that they will have to continuously face these dreadful states if they continue to note. So they may stop meditating and no longer think of being mindful. But then the latent defilement of delusion will creep in with regard to unobserved conditioned phenomena. This delusion only has the opportunity to arise because the meditator's noting was not continued as usual. But if noting continues uninterruptedly, delusion will not have an opportunity to arise. So this delusion that does not understand phenomena to be impermanent, unsatisfactory, and not-self is called "nonreobservation" (*appaṭisaṅkhāna*), the opposite of insight knowledge of reobservation. What this means is that insight knowledge of reobservation abandons nonreobservation or delusion, or does not allow it an opportunity to arise.

Contemplation of turning away

> Contemplation of turning away (*vivattānupassanā*) includes both insight knowledge of equanimity toward formations and insight knowledge of adaptation. At this point, one's mind is said to turn away, shrink back, and withdraw from all conditioned phenomena, just as a water drop rolls off a slightly sloping lotus leaf. With it one abandons adherence due to bondage.[820]
>
> With change-of-lineage, path, and fruition the mind relinquishes conditioned phenomena and rushes into nibbāna, which is the cessation of the round [of conditioned phenomena]. Considering this, it should be said that insight knowledge of equanimity toward formations and insight knowledge of adaptation are contemplation of turning away. The fetters and other defilements that are engrossed in and derived from [conditioned phenomena] are adherence due to defilements (*kilesābhinivesa*).[821]

The two insight knowledges of equanimity toward formations and adaptation are contemplation of turning away. When these two insight knowledges arise, although one observes the disappearance of conditioned phenomena [the objects and the noting mind], on one hand, one has neither attachment nor liking as one has at the lower stages of knowledge, and on the other hand, one has no fear, disenchantment, weariness, or a desire to escape, as one does with insight knowledges starting with insight knowledge of fear.

One needs no effort to make objects appear, and one does not worry or fear that unpleasant objects will appear. Actually, having an extremely clear and purified mind, one is just aware of the dissolution of conditioned phenomena while uninterruptedly being aware of them. At this point, it is as if the mind is turning away from these conditioned phenomena. In the same way that a water drop runs down a lotus leaf that slopes a little, so the mind turns away from any conditioned phenomenon that it observes. Whether it is an extremely good object or a terribly distressing one, the mind does not engage in thinking about it but is simply aware of it. Due to this turning away from conditioned phenomena (and after the insight knowledge of adaptation has arisen), the mind at the moment of change-of-lineage and path relinquishes all these conditioned phenomena and is able to rush into nibbāna, which is free from conditioned phenomena. This way of observing is done in order that the mind at the time of change-of-lineage and path can rush into the object of nibbāna (or the cessation of the round). These two insight knowledges are called "contemplation of turning away."

This contemplation of turning away abandons all of the fetters, such as the fetter of lust for sensual desires that is fed by interest in pleasant sensual objects, the fetter of aversion that is fed by interest in unpleasant sensual objects, and so on. So if one has reached the stage of equanimity toward formations, the mind neither relishes worldly objects nor becomes engrossed in them if thoughts arise about them. The mind shows no interest in such things, and there are long periods where the wish to think does not occur. Only when one stops practicing insight for some time is one able to think about or imagine worldly objects.

The commentary on the *Paṭisambhidāmagga* gives a different definition for contemplation of turning away. It says that it is the insight knowledge of change-of-lineage that arises due to the power of insight knowledge of adaptation. It also says that the definition given in the *Visuddhimagga* seems to contradict the *Paṭisambhidāmagga*. When the Buddha explained contemplation of turning away, he did not mention adverting consciousness, the first mind-moment that adverts to a new object. Given this fact, the commentary states that insight knowledge of change-of-lineage, which does not require adverting consciousness, is the most appropriate function for contemplation of turning away. One can take whichever view one finds most suitable on this issue.

Mahāsi Sayadaw's Closing Words

Bhāvetabbā yogībiyā databbā ca paccakkhato. Vaṇṇitātā aṭṭhārāsa, mahāvipassanā māya. Dubbodhaṃ subodhetuna, yogīnaṃ sutavuddhiyā.

As an insight meditator, one should develop and experience these eighteen great insight knowledges. This topic may be difficult to understand. However, in order to increase the knowledge of insight meditators, I have tried to explain these contemplations in such a way that they may be easily understood.

Here ends chapter 7 regarding the great insight knowledges.

List of Abbreviations

Visuddhimagga-mahāṭīkā	Vism-mhṭ
Abhidhamma-mūlaṭīkā	Abhidh-mlṭ
Atthasālini	As
Vinaya Piṭaka	Vin
Visuddhimagga	Vism
Cullaniddesa	Nidd II
Mahāniddesa	Nidd I
Sumaṅgalavilāsinī (Dhīga-nikāya-aṭṭhakathā)	Sv
Papañcasūdanī (Majjhima-nikāya-aṭṭhakathā)	Ps
Dhammapada	Dhp
Puggalapaññatti	Pp
Nettipakaraṇa	Nett
Manorathapūraṇi (Aṅguttara-nikāya-aṭṭhakathā)	Mp
Nettipakaraṇa-aṭṭhakathā	Nett-a
Dhammapada-aṭṭhakathā	Dhp-a
Pañcapakaraṇaṭṭhakathā	Ppk-a
Abhidhammatthavibhāvinī-ṭīkā	Abhidh-vibh-ṭ
Abhidhammatthasaṅgaha	Abhidh-s
Abhidhammatthasaṅgaha-aṭṭhakathā	Abhidh-s-a
Itivuttaka-aṭṭakathā	It-a
Majjhima-nikāya-ṭīkā	MN-ṭ
Dhammasaṅgaṇi-aṭṭhakathā	Dhs-a
Dhīga-nikāya-ṭīkā	DN-ṭ
Udāna-aṭṭhakathā	Ud-a
Vibhaṅga-aṭṭhakathā (Sammohavinodanī)	Vibh-a
Sāratthappakāsinī (Saṃyutta-nikāya-aṭṭhakathā)	Spk
Milindapañha	Mil
Dhammasaṅgaṇi-mūlaṭīkā	Dhs-mlṭ

Dhammasaṅgaṇi . . . . Dhs
Paṭṭhāna (Mahāpakaraṇa) . . . . Paṭṭh
Vibhaṅga . . . . Vibh
Yamaka . . . . Yam

Notes

1. Homage to the Blessed One, the Perfect One, the Fully Enlightened One!
2. The Blessed One (*bhagavā*) is (1) accomplished (*arahaṃ*), (2) fully enlightened (*sammāsambuddho*), (3) perfect in true knowledge and conduct (*vijjācaraṇasampanno*), (4) sublime (*sugato*), (5) knower of worlds (*lokavidū*), (6) incomparable leader of persons to be tamed (*anuttaro purisadammasārathi*), (7) teacher of gods and humans (*satthā devamanussānaṃ*), (8) enlightened (*buddho*), and (9) blessed (*bhagavā*).
3. The Dhamma is (1) well proclaimed by the Blessed One (*svākkhātobhagavatā dhammo*), (2) visible here and now (*sandiṭṭhiko*), (3) immediately effective (*akāliko*), (4) inviting inspection (*ehipassiko*), (5) onward leading (*opanayyiko*), and (6) to be experienced by the wise for themselves (*paccattaṃ veditabbo viññūhī*).
4. The Saṅgha of the Blessed One's disciples (1) practices the good way (*supaṭipannobhagavato sāvakasaṅgho*), (2) practices the straight way (*ujupaṭipanno*), (3) practices the true way (*ñāyapaṭipanno*), (4) practices the proper way (*sāmīcipaṭipanno*), are the four pairs of persons (*cattāri purisayugāni*) and eight types of individuals (*aṭṭha purisapuggalā*) who are (5) worthy of gifts (*āhuṇeyyo*), (6) worthy of hospitality (*pāhuṇeyyo*), (7) worthy of offerings (*dakkhiṇeyyo*), (8) worthy of reverential salutation (*añjalikaraṇīyo*), and are (9) the unsurpassed field of merit for the world (*anuttaraṃ puññakkhettaṃ lokassā*).
5. *The Dhammapada: A New Translation of the Buddhist Classic with Annotations*, trans. Gil Fronsdal (Boston: Shambhala, 2005), 43.
   Yo sāsanaṃ arahataṃ, ariyānaṃ dhammajīvinaṃ;
   paṭikkosati dummedho, diṭṭhiṃ nissāya pāpikaṃ;
   phalāni kaṭṭhakasseva, atthaghātāya phallati. (Dhp 164)
6. *The Middle Length Discourses of the Buddha: A New Translation of the Majjhima Nikāya*, trans. Bhikkhu Bodhi (Boston: Wisdom, 1995), 1039.
   Ajjeva kiccamātappaṃ, ko jaññā maraṇaṃ suve. (MN 131.3)
7. Ibid., 210.
   Jhāyatha, bhikkhave mā pamādattha; mā pacchā vippaṭisārino ahuvattha.
   Ayaṃ vo amhākaṃ anusāsanī. (MN 19.27)
8. See fn. 3 above regarding the nine attributes of the Dhamma.
9. A meditation manual written in the sixth century CE by Bhadantācariya Buddhaghosa.
10. See also *The Path of Purification: Visuddhimagga*, trans. Bhikkhu Ñāṇamoli, (Onalaska: BPS Pariyatti Editions, 1991), 605.
    Sīlavisuddhi nāma suparisuddhaṃ pātimokkhsaṃvarādicatubbidhaṃ sīlaṃ. (Vism 18.1)

11. *The Long Discourses of the Buddha: A Translation of the Dhīgha Nikāya*, trans. Maurice Walshe (Boston: Wisdom, 1987), 99.
    ... anumattesu vajjesu bhayadassāvī, samādāya sikkhati sikkhāpadesu ... (DN 2)
12. *Vinaya*: the monastic code of 227 rules and regulations for bhikkhus.
13. The four requisites are food, clothing, shelter, and medicine.
14. These are the four grave offenses that immediately disqualify a person from remaining a bhikkhu or nun or becoming a bhikkhu or nun again in this life: taking a human life, stealing, engaging in sexual intercourse, and misrepresenting one's spiritual attainments.
15. The *Visuddhimagga-Mahāṭīkā* attributed to Dhammapāla.
16. *Iṇavasena paribhogo iṇaparibhogo, paṭiggāhakato dakkhināvisuddhiyā abhāvato inam gahetvā paribhogo viyāti attho.*
17. *Yathā iṇāyiko attano ruciyā iccitadesaṃ gantuṃ na labhati. Evaṃ iṇaparibhogayutto lokato nissarituṃ na labhati.*
18. For an overview of Theravāda Buddhist cosmology, see "Appendix 6: Planes of Existence."
19. *The Dhammapada*, 63.
    Ayasāva malaṃ samuṭṭhitaṃ, tatuṭṭhāya tameva khādati.
    Evaṃ atidhonacārinaṃ, sāni kammāni nayanti duggatiṃ. (Dhp 240)
20. I.e., *Aggikkhandhopama Sutta*, AN 7.72. See *The Numerical Discourses*, 1090–94.
21. One who has attained the first stage (path and fruition) of enlightenment.
22. One who has attained the second stage (path and fruition) of enlightenment.
23. One who has attained the third stage (path and frutition) of enlightenment.
24. *Imaṃ pana desanaṃ sutvā jātasaṃvegā ṭhānaṃ jahitvā sāmaṇerabhūmiyaṃ ṭhitā dasa sīlāni pūretvā yoniso manasikāre yuttappayuttā keci sotāpannā keci sakadāgāmino keci anāgāmino ahesuṃ, keci devaloke nibbattiṃsu, evaṃ pārājikāpannānampi saphalā ahosi.* (Mp)
25. *Yāmakālikaṃ sattāhakālikaṃ yāvajīvikaṃ āhāratthāya paṭiggaṇhāti, āpatti dukkaṭassa. Ajjohāre ajjhohāre āpatti dukkaṭassa.* (Vin)
26. A *Thera* is one who has been an ordained bhikkhu for at least ten years.
27. These are comprised of *suttas* (discourses), *vinaya* (monastic rules and regulations), and *abhidhamma* (higher teaching).
28. *Tipiṭakacūḷanāgatthero panāha—"pātimokkhasaṃvarova sīlam, itarāni tīṇi sīlanti vuttaṭṭhānaṃ nāma natthī"ti. Vatvā taṃ anujānanto āha—"indriyasaṃvaro nāma chadvārarakkhaṇamattameva, ājīvapārisuddhi dhammeneva samena paccayuppattimattakaṃ, paccayasannissitaṃ paṭiladdhapaccaye idamatthanti paccavekkhitvā paribhuñjanamattakaṃ. Nippariyānyena pātimokkhasaṃvarova sīlam. Yassa so bhinno, ayaṃ chinnasīso viya puriso hatthapāde, sesāni rakkhissatīti na vattabbo. Yassa pana so arogo, ayaṃ acchinnasīso viya puriso jīvitaṃ, sesāni puna pākatikāni katvā rakkhitumpi sakkoti"ti.* (Spk)
29. MN 2. See *The Middle Length Discourses*, 91–96.
30. AN 6.58. See *The Numerical Discourses of the Buddha: A Translation of the Aṅguttara Nikāya*, trans. Bhikkhu Bodhi (Boston: Wisdom, 2012), 942–44.
31. *Paṭilābhakālepi hi dhātuvasena vā paṭikūlavasenā vā paccavekkhitvā ṭhapitāni cīvarādīni tato uttari paribhuñjantassa anavajjova paribhogo, paribhogakālepi.*
32. *The Middle Length Discourses*, 274.

33. *The Path of Purification*, 23.
Yaṃ tattha bhūtaṃ, tadeva gaṇhāti. (Vism 1.54)
34. See "Appendix 5: Materiality" for a full description of the primary and secondary elements.
35. These five states constitute the quality of lacking restraint (*asaṃvaradhammā*).
36. Specifically the *Mūlaṭīkā* and *Mahāṭīkā*.
37. There are three grades of defilements: transgressive defilements that are acted out by body or speech (*vītikkama kilesā*), defilements that arise as obsessive thought (*pariyuṭṭhāna kilesā*), and defilements that are latent within us (*anusaya kilesā*).
38. *The Long Discourses of the Buddha*, 100.
Cakkhundriyaṃ asaṃvutaṃ viharantaṃ abhijjhā domanassā pāpakā akusalā dhammā anvāssaveyyuṃ. (DN 2)
39. *Sotānaṃ saṃvaraṃ brūmi paññāyete pidhīyareti ayaṃ ñāṇasaṃvaro.*
40. *Path of Purification*, 10 (Vism 1.18).
41. *"Sabbe saṅkhārā aniccā" ti jānato passato paññāyete sotā pidhīyyanti* . . . (Nidd II)
42. *The Middle Length Discourses*, 636.
Anuppannānaṃ pāpakānaṃ akusalānaṃ dhammānaṃ anuppādāya chandaṃ janeti, vāyamati . . . (MN 77.16)
43. *Tassa iminā niyamitavasena, pariṇāmitavasena, samudācāravasena, ābhujitavasena ca kusalaṃ nāma jātaṃ hoti.* (As)
44. The eight worldly vicissitudes are pleasure and pain, gain and loss, fame and disrepute, and praise and blame.
45. The five aggregates (*khandhā*) are: material form, feelings, perceptions, mental formations, and consciousness.
46. *The Path of Purification*, 23.
Tassa dantaṭṭhikaṃ disvā, pubbasaññaṃ anussari; tattheva so ṭhito thero, arahattaṃ apāpuṇī"ti. (Vism 1.55)
47. There are ten perfections or forces of purity in Theravāda Buddhism: (1) generosity, (2) morality, (3) renunciation, (4) wisdom, (5) energy, (6) patience, (7) truthfulness, (8) resolution, (9) loving-kindness, and (10) equanimity.
48. A noble one (*ariya*) is someone who has attained any stage of enlightenment.
49. A fully enlightened being enters *parinibbāna* when the body passes away.
50. *Yaṃ pubbe taṃ visosehi, pacchā te māhu kiñcanaṃ majjhe ce no gahessasi, upasanto carissasi.* (Nidd II)
51. That is, he passed through the stages of becoming a stream enterer, a once returner, a nonreturner, and an *arahant* as he sat listening.
52. I.e., immoral laypeople such as Minister Santati, the woman called Patācārī, etc.
53. *Yasmā pana kāyavedanācittadhammesu kañci dhammaṃ anāmasitvā bhāvanā nāma natthi,tasmā tepi imināva maggena sokaparideve samatikkantāti veditabbā.* (Ps; Sv)
54. Observing the monastic precepts.
55. A correct view of kamma.
56. *The Connected Discourses of the Buddha: A Translation of the Saṃyutta Nikāya*, trans. Bhikkhu Bodhi (Boston: Wisdom, 2000), 1645. Text modified to match translation of terms herein.
Tasmātiha tvaṃ, uttiya ādimeva visodhehi kusalesu dhammesu. Ko cādi kusalānaṃ dhammānaṃ? Sīlañca suvisuddhaṃ diṭṭhi ca ujukā. Yato ca kho te, uttiya sīlañca suvisuddhaṃ bhavissati diṭṭhi ca ujukā, tato tvam, uttiya sīlam nissāya sīle patiṭṭhāya cattāro satipaṭṭhāne bhāveyyāsi. (SN 5.47)

57. *The Dhammapada*, 70.
    Na tena ariyo hoti, yena pāṇāni hiṃsati;
    ahiṃsā sabbapāṇāṃ, "ariyo"ti pavuccati. (Dhp 270)
58. *The Dhammapada*, 17.
    Yo bālo maññati bālyaṃ, paṇḍito vāpi tena so;
    bālo ca paṇḍitamānī, sa ve "bālo"ti vuccati. (Dhp 63)
59. *The Connected Discourses*, 1811.
    Acchariyaṃ vata bho, abbhutaṃ vata bho, ettha'dāni kho na sotāpanno bhavissati. Yatra hi nāma sarakāni sakko kālakato, so bhagavatā vyākato: 'sotāpanno avinipātadhammo niyato sambodhiparāyaṇo'ti, sarakāni sakko sikkhāya aparipūrakārī ahosīti. (SN 5.55)
60. The Buddha's explanation can be found in the *Sarakāni Vagga* of the Sotāpattisaṃyutta in the Saṃyutta Nikāya, pages 1808–21 of *The Connected Discourses.*
61. Ibid., 1813.
    Kimaṅgaṃ pana saraṇāniṃ sakkaṃ! Saraṇāni, mahānāma, sakko maraṇakāle sikkhāya paripūrakārī ahosī"ti.
62. For an examination of the Pali terms *ugghaṭitaññū, vipañcitaññū*, and *neyya*, see *The Numerical Discourses*, 1702, fn. 831.
63. Specifically the Four Noble Truths.
64. *Katamo ca puggalo neyyo? Yassa puggalassa uddesato paripucchato yonisomanasikaroto, kalyāṇamitte sevato bhajato payirupāsato, evam anupubbena dhammābhisamayo hoti: ayaṃ vuccati puggalo"neyyo."* (Pp)
65. *Ugghaṭitaññussa samathapubbaṅgamā vipassanā sappāyā. Neyyassa vipassanāpubbaṅgamo samatho, vipañcitaññussa samathavipassanā yuganaddhā, ugghatitaññussa mudukā desanā [adhipaññāsikkhā*[MS]*] neyyassa tikkhā desanā [adhisīlasikkhā ca adhicittasikkhā ca adhipaññāsikkhā ca*[MS]*], vipañcitaññussa tikkhamudukā desanā [adhicittasikkhā ca adhipaññāsikkhā ca*[MS]]. (Nett)
66. *Yassa hi samādhipi taruṇo vipassanāpi. Tassa vipassanaṃ paṭṭhapetvā aticiraṃ nisinnassa kāyo kilamati, anto aggi viya uṭṭhahati, kacchehi sedā muccanti, matthakato usumavaṭṭi viya uṭṭhahati, cittaṃ haññati vihaññati vipphandati. So puna samāpattiṃ samāpajjitvā taṃ paridametvā mudukam katvā, samassāsetvā puna vipassanaṃ paṭṭhapeti. Tassa puna aticiraṭṃ nisinnassa tatheva hoti. So puna samāpattiṃ samāpajjitvā tatheva karoti. Vipassanāya hi bahūpakārā samāpatti.* (Ps)
67. *The Dhammapada*, 27.
    Sahassampi ce vācā, anatthapadasaṃ hitā;
    ekaṃ atthapadaṃ seyyo, yaṃ sutvā upasammati. (Dhp 100)
68. MN 51. See *The Middle Length Discourses*, 443–53.
69. Knowledge that discerns mental and physical phenomena and knowledge that discerns conditionality.
70. Nonrestlessness.
71. Insight knowledge.
72. See also *The Path of Discrimination*, trans. Bhikkhu Ñāṇamoli (Oxford: Pali Text Society, 2009), 43–48.
    Ñāṇena avijjāya . . . Aniccānupassanāya niccasaññāya . . . pahānaṃ sīlaṃ, veramaṇī sīlaṃ, cetanā sīlaṃ, saṃvaro sīlaṃ, avītakkamo sīlam. evarūpāni sīlāni cittassa avippaṭisārāya saṃvattanti . . . Pāmojjāya saṃvattanti, pītiyā saṃvattanti, passaddhiyā saṃvattanti , somanassāya saṃvattanti . . . ekantanibbidāya virāgāya nirodhāya upasamāya abhiññāya sambodhāya nibbānāya saṃvattanti . . . Yo tattha saṃvaraṭṭho, ayaṃ adhisīlasikkhā. Yo

tattha avikkhepaṭṭho, ayaṃ adhicittasikkhā. Yo tattha dassanaṭṭho, ayam adhipaññāsikkhā. (Paṭis 251–66)

73. *The Connected Discourses*, 101. Text modified to match translation of terms herein.
    Sīle patiṭṭhāya naro sapañño, cittaṃ paññañca bhāvayaṃ . . . (DN 1.23)
74. *Visuddhimagga-mahāṭīkā*, VRI 1.12.
75. *The Numerical Discourses*, 125.
    Accharāsaṅghātamattampi ce bhikkhave bhikkhu mettācittaṃ āsevati, bhāveti, maniskaroti. Ayaṃ vuccati bhikkhave bhikkhu arittajjhāno viharati satthusāsanakaro ovādapatikaro amoghaṃ raṭṭhapiṇḍaṃ bhuñjati, ko pana vādo, ye naṃ bahulīkaronti.
    Accharāsaṅghātamattampi ce, bhikkhave, bhikkhu . . . Kāye kāyānupassī viharati . . . vedanāsu vedanānupassī viharati . . . pe . . . citte cittānupassī viharati . . . pe . . . dhammesu dhammā-nupassī viharati ātāpī sampajāno satimā vineyya loke abhijjhādomanassaṃ . . .. Ayaṃ vuccati, bhikkhave—'bhikkhu arittajjhāno viharati satthusāsanakaro ovādapatikaro, amoghaṃ raṭṭhapiṇḍaṃ bhuñjati.' Ko pana vādo, ye naṃ bahulīkaronti"ti. (AN 1.18)
76. *Mettāya sabbapubbabhāgo nāma neva appanā, na upacāro, sattānaṃ hitapharaṇamattamevā"ti.* (Mp)
77. Having already attained the path of a stream enterer (*sotāpattimagga*).
78. *Paribhuñjatī'ti cattāro paribhogā theyyaparibhogo iṇaparibhogo, dāyajjaparibhogo sāmiparibhogoti . . . Tattha imassa bhikkhuno ayaṃ raṭṭhapiṇḍaparibhogo dvīhi kāraṇehi amogho hoti. Accharāsaṅghātamattampi mettācittaṃ āsevanto bhikkhu raṭṭhapiṇḍassa sāmiko hutvā, aṇaṇo hutvā, dāyado hutvā paribhuñjatītipissa amogho raṭṭhapiṇḍaparibhogo. Accharāsaṅghātamattampi mettaṃ āsevantassa bhikkhuno dinnadānaṃ mahaṭṭhiyaṃ hoti, mahapphalaṃ, mahānisaṃsaṃ, mahājutikaṃ mahāvipphārantipissa amogho raṭṭhapiṇḍaparibhogo . . . ye pana imaṃ mettācittaṃ bahulaṃ āsevanti bhāventi punappunaṃ karonti, te amoghaṃ raṭṭhapiṇḍaṃ paribhuñjantīti ettha vattabbameva kim? Evarūpā hi bhikkhū raṭṭhapiṇḍassa sāmino aṇaṇā dāyādā hutvā paribhuñjantīti.* (Mp)
79. These are the attitudes of loving-kindness (*mettā*), compassion (*karuṇā*), sympathetic joy (*muditā*), and equanimity (*upekkhā*).
80. *The Path of Purification*, 605.
    Cittavisuddhi nāma sa-upacārā aṭṭha samāpattiyo. (Vism 18.1)
81. The *Sumaṅgalavilāsinī* and *Papañcasūdanī*, commentaries on the Dīgha and Majjhima Nikāyas, respectively, describe fourteen types of mindfulness of the body. Two of these—contemplation of the in- and out-breath and contemplation of the loathsomeness of the body—are accomplished via momentary concentration. The remaining twelve—contemplation of the four postures, contemplation of the four clear comprehensions (*sampajaññā*), contemplation of the elements, and the nine charnel-ground contemplations—are accomplished via access concentration. It is this last group that constitutes "the other twelve" mentioned in this Pāḷi passage.
82. *Samathova yānaṃ samathayānaṃ, taṃ etassa atthīti samathayāniko. jhāne, jhānūpacāre vā patiṭṭhāya vipassanaṃ anuyuñjantassetaṃ nāmaṃ . . . samathayānikassa samathamukhena vipassanābhiniveso, vipassanāyānikassa pana samathaṃ anissāyāti āha "suddhavipassanāyāniko"ti. Samathabhāvanāya amissitavipassanāyānavāti attho.* (Vism-mhṭ)
83. The "gateway to liberation" is comprised of the threefold knowledge of impermanence, unsatisfactoriness, and not-self.

84. *Samathayānikassa hi upacārappanāppabhedam samādhim, itarassa khaṇikasamādhiṃ, ubhayesampi vimokkhamukhattayaṃ vinā na kadācipi lokuttarādhigamo sambhavati. Tenāha "samādhiñceva vipassanañca bhāvayamāno"ti.* (Vism-mhṭ)
85. *The Connected Discourses*, 101. Text modified to match translation of terms herein.
    Sīle patiṭṭhāya naro sapañño, cittaṃ paññañca bhāvayaṃ; ātāpī nipako bhikkhu, so imaṃ vijaṭaye jaṭaṃ. (DN 1.23)
86. *Ariyamagga*. The path (*magga*) of noble ones (*ariyā*).
87. *Bhāvanānayoti koci samathapubbaṅgamaṃ vipassanaṃ bhāveti, koci vipassanāpubbaṅgamaṃ samathaṃ. Kathaṃ? Idhekacco paṭhamaṃ upacārasamadhiṃ vā appanāsamādhiṃ vā uppādeti, ayaṃ samatho; so tañca taṃsampayutte ca dhamme aniccādīhi vipassati, ayaṃ vipassanā. Iti paṭhamaṃ samatho, pacchā vipassanā. Tena vuccati "samathapubbaṅgamaṃ vipassanaṃ bhāvetiti. Tassa samatha-pubbangamam vipassanam bhavayato maggo sanjayatī"ti.* (Ps)
88. *Idha panekacco vuttappakāraṃ samathaṃ anuppādetvāva pañcupadānākkhandhe aniccādīhi vipassati . . . Tassa vipassanāpāripūriyā tattha jātānaṃ dhammanaṃ vosaggārammaṇato uppajjati cittassa ekaggatā, ayaṃ samatho. Iti paṭhamaṃ vipassanā, pacchā samatho. Tena vuccati "vipassanāpubbaṅgamaṃ samathaṃ bhāvetī"ti. Tassa vipassanāpubbaṅgamaṃ samathaṃ bhāvayato maggo sañjāyati, so taṃ maggaṃ asevati bhāveti bahulīkaroti, tassa taṃ maggaṃ āsevato bhāvayato bahulīkaroto saṃyojanāni pahīyanti, anusayā byantīhonti.* (Ps)
89. *Vasena vutto, dutiyo vipassanāyānikassa.* (Ps)
90. *Maggo sañjāyatīti paṭhamo lokuttaramaggo nibbattati.* (Mp)
91. *The Numerical Discourses*, 535.
    So taṃ maggaṃ āsevati, bhāveti, bahulīkaroti. (AN 4.170)
92. *So taṃ magganti ekacittakkhaṇikamaggassa āsevanādīni nāma natthi, dutiyamaggādayo pana uppādento tameva āsevati bhāveti bahulīkarotīti vuccati.* (Mp)
93. See also *The Path of Discrimination*, 287.
    Tassa taṃ maggaṃ āsevato, bhāvayato, bahulīkaroto saññyojanāni pahīyanti, anusayā byantī honti. (Paṭis 11.1)
94. Ibid., 47.
    Yo tattha avikkhepaṭṭho, ayaṃ adhicittasikkhā. (Paṭis 1.265)
95. The Pāḷi terms for these types of knowledge (*ñāṇa*) do not explicitly state that they are insight knowledges (*vippasanāñāṇa*). But when he taught, Mahāsi Sayadaw often appended the term "insight" to the various types of knowledge attained as a result of the practice of insight meditation in order to distinguish them from similar forms of knowledge that are not forms of insight, or that do not lead to insight. Technically speaking, knowledge that discerns mental and physical phenomena and knowledge that discerns conditionality are knowledges developed on the basis of mindfulness rather than insight. However, as Mahāsi Sayadaw explains here, these knowledges can be considered insight because they dispel hindrances associated with them. This is why, in many places throughout this book, Mahāsi Sayadaw refers to these types of knowledge as insight knowledges.
96. The unit of mind that immediately precedes path knowledge.
97. *Yaṃ nāmarūpaparicchedādīsu vipassanāñāṇesu paṭipakkhabhāvato dīpālokeneva tamassa, tena tena vipassanāñāṇena tassa tassa anatthassa pahānaṃ. Seyyathidaṃ, nāmarūpavavatthānena sakkāyadiṭṭhiyā, paccayapariggahena ahetuvisamahetudiṭṭhīnaṃ . . . gotrabhunā saṅkhāranimittaggāhassa pahānaṃ. Etaṃ tadaṅgappahānaṃ nāma.* (Ps)

98. *Khaṇikacittekaggatāti khaṇamattaṭṭhitiko samādhi. Sopi hi ārammaṇe nirantaraṃ* [. . .[Vism]] *ekākārena pavattamāno paṭipakkhena anabhibhūto appito viya cittaṃ niccalaṃ ṭhapeti.* (Vism-mhṭ)
99. A commentary on the Vinaya.
100. The passage from the Majjhima Nikāya commentary under the heading "The method of those who take the vehicle of insight to enlightenment."
101. See *The Connected Discourses*, 1638.
102. Ibid., 1639.
103. See also *The Path of Discrimination*, 289.

    Rūpaṃ aniccato anūpassanāṭṭhena vipassanā, rūpaṃ dukkhato anupassanaṭṭhena vipassanā, rūpaṃ anattato anupassanaṭṭhena vipassanā. Tattha jātānaṃ dhammānañca vosaggārammaṇatā cittassa ekaggatā avikkhepo samādhi. Iti paṭhamaṃ vipassanā, pacchā samatho. Tena vuccati—"vipassanāpubbaṅgamaṃ samathaṃ bhāveti" ti. (Paṭis II.73)

104. *Tatthajātānanti tasmiṃ ariyamaggakkhaṇe* [*uppannānaṃ*[VRI]][*jātānaṃ*[MS]] *sammādiṭṭhiādīnaṃ dhammānaṃ. Niddhāraṇe cetaṃ sāmivacanaṃ.* [*Vavassaggārammaṇatoti vavassaggassa*[VRI]] *ārammaṇatāya* [*Vossaggārammaṇatāti vossaggassa*[MS]] *ārammaṇatāya . . . . nibbānassa ārammaṇakaraṇenāti attho. Citta ekaggatāti* [*maggasammāsamādhimāha*[VRI]] [*maggasamādhimāha*[MS]].
105. The ten obstacles to—or corruptions of—insight include bright lights, rapture, tranquility, resolution, exertion, happiness, knowledge, mindfulness, equanimity, and delight. See "Appendix 1: The Progress of Insight."
106. "The internal field" refers to that aspect of mental and physical objects.
107. See also *The Path of Discrimination*, 165.

    Nekkhammaṃ ariyānaṃ niyyānaṃ. Tena ca nekkhammena ariyā niyyanti. Kamācchando niyyānāvaraṇaṃ. Tena ca kamācchandena nivutatta nekkhammaṃ ariyānaṃ niyyānaṃ nappajānātīti— kamacchando niyyānāvaraṇaṃ. (Paṭis 3.5)

108. *Pabbajjā paṭhamaṃ jhānaṃ, nibbānañca vipassanā; sabbepi kusalā dhammā, nekkhammanti pavuccare.*
109. *The Middle Length Discourses*, 1069.

    Anuttaresu vimokkhesu pihaṃ upaṭṭhāpeti. (MN 137.13)

110. The passage reads: *Anussavūpaladdhe pana anuttaravimokkhe uddissa pihaṃ upaṭṭhapento "tattha pihaṃ upaṭṭhapeti" ti vutto.* (DN 21)
111. Or "nonfrustration."
112. See also *The Path of Discrimination*, 165.

    Abyāpādo ariyānaṃ niyyānaṃ. Tena ca abyāpādena ariyā niyyanti. Byāpādo niyyānāvaraṇaṃ. Tena ca byāpādena nivutattā abyāpādam ariyānaṃ niyyānaṃ nappajānātīti byāpādo niyyānāvaraṇaṃ. (Paṭis 3.5)

113. Ibid.

    Ālokasaññā ariyānaṃ niyyānaṃ. Tāya ca ālokasaññāya ariyā niyyanti. Thinamiddhaṃ niyyānāvaraṇaṃ. Tena ca thinamiddhena nivutattā ālokasaññaṃ ariyānaṃ niyyānaṃ nappajānātīti—thinamiddhaṃ niyyanāvāranaṃ. (Paṭis 3.5)

114. Or mental restlessness.
115. Ibid.

    Avikkhepo ariyānaṃ niyyānaṃ. Tena ca avikkhepena ariyā niyyanti.

Uddhaccaṃ niyyānāvaraṇaṃ. Tena ca uddhaccena nivutattā avikkhepaṃ ariyānaṃ niyyānaṃ nappajānātīti—uddhaccaṃ niyyānāvaranaṃ. (Paṭis 3.5)

116. "Phenomena" refers to the wholesomeness (*kusala*) and unwholesomeness (*akusala*) of phenomena.
117. Ibid.

 Dhammavavatthānaṃ ariyānaṃ niyyānaṃ. Tena ca dhammavavatthānena ariyā niyyanti. Vicikicchā niyyānāvaraṇaṃ. Taya ca vicikicchāya nivutattā dhammavavatthānaṃ ariyānaṃ niyyānaṃ nappajānātīti—vicikicchā niyyanavaraṇaṃ. (Paṭis 3.5)
118. Chapter 3, p. 138–42, and chapter 4, p. 201-204.
119. *Ubhayapakkhasantīraṇamukhena vicikicchā vañceti.* (Nett-a)
120. MN 23. See *The Middle Length Discourses*, 237–39.
121. The threefold training on the Noble Eightfold Path is training in morality, concentration, and wisdom.
122. Chapter 3, p. 126–31.
123. Chapter 4, p. 158–59.
124. See also *The Path of Discrimination*, 165.

 Ñāṇaṃ ariyānaṃ niyyānaṃ. Tena ca ñāṇena ariyā niyyanti. Avijjā niyyānāvaraṇaṃ. Tāya ca avijjāya nivutattā ñāṇaṃ ariyānaṃ niyyānaṃ nappajānātīti—avijjā niyyānāvaraṇaṃ. (Paṭis 3.5)
125. Sakka is the ruler of the Tāvatiṃsa celestial realm. Brahma is the highest ruler of the first three planes of the fine-material celestial realm (*rūpaloka*) and is sometimes called "Great Brahma."
126. Or nondelight.
127. Ibid.

 Pāmojjaṃ ariyānaṃ niyyānaṃ. Tena ca pāmojjena ariyā niyyanti. Arati niyyānāvaranaṃ. Tāya ca aratiyā nivutattā pāmojjaṃ ariyānaṃ niyyānaṃ nappajānātīti—arati niyyānāvaraṇaṃ. (Paṭis 3.5)
128. *The Dhammapada*, 96.

 Yato yato sammasati, khandhānaṃ udayabbayaṃ,
 labhati pītipāmojjaṃ, amataṃ taṃ vijānataṃ. (Dhp 374)
129. Chapter 5, p. 281.
130. *The Dhammapada*, 46.

 Andhabhūto ayaṃ loko, tanukettha vipassati,
 sakuṇo jālamuttova, appo saggāya gacchati. (Dhp 174)
131. The eight sources of spiritual urgency as described in the Visuddhimagga are: birth (*jāti*), old age (*jāra*), sickness (*byadhi*), death (*maraṇa*), the suffering of the lower realms (*apāyadukkhaṃ*), the suffering of presently being rooted in the round of rebirths (*atite vaṭṭamūlakaṃ dukkhaṃ*), past suffering of being rooted in the round of rebirths (*anāgate vaṭṭamūlakaṃ dukkhaṃ*), and future suffering of being rooted in the round of rebirths (*paccuppanne vaṭṭamūlakaṃ dukkhaṃ*).
132. *Kusala*: virtuous, skillful, or wholesome.
133. *Akusala*: nonvirtuous, unskillful, or unwholesome actions.
134. See also *The Path of Discrimination*, 165.

 Sabbepi kusalā dhammā ariyāna niyyānaṃ. Tehi ca kusalehi dhammehi ariyā niyyanti. Sabbepi akusalā dhammā niyyānāvaraṇaṃ tehi ca akusalehi dhammehi nivutattā kusale dhamme ariyānaṃ niyyānaṃ nappajānātīti—sabbepi akusalā dhammā niyyānāvaraṇā. (Paṭis 3.5)

135. *Sammā paṇihitaṃ cittaṃ . . . sammā paṇihitāya diṭṭhiyā . . .*

136. *Satthā tassa sādhukāraṃ datvā, "Bhikkhave, yassa mayi sineho atthi, tena attadatthena [therena*[MS]*] viya bhavituṃ vaṭṭati. Na hi [bhikkhave*[MS]*], gandhādīhi pūjentā maṃ pūjenti. Dhammānudhammapaṭipattiyā pana maṃ pūjenti. Tasmā aññenapi attadatthasadiseneva bhavitabban"ti.* (Dhp-a)

137. *The Dhammapada*, 44.

   Attadatthaṃ paratthena, bahunāpi na hāpaye;
   Attadatthamabhiññāya, sadatthapasuto siyā. (Dhp 166)

138. *"Attadattham na hāpemi"ti bhikkhunā nāma saṅghassa uppanna▸ cetiyapatisaṅkharaṇādikiccam vā, upajjhāyādivattaṃ vā, na hāpetabbam. Ābhisamācārikavattañhi pūrentoyeva ariyaphalādīni sacchikaroti, tasmā ayampi attadatthova. Yo pana accāraddhavipassako "ajja vā, suve vā"ti paṭivedhaṃ patthayamāno vicarati, tena upajjhāyavattādīnipi hāpetvā attano kiccameva kātabbaṃ.* (Dhp-a)

139. See also *The Long Discourses*, 262.

   Na kho, ānanda, ettāvatā tathāgato sakkato vā hoti garukato vā mānito vā pūjito vā apacito vā, yo kho, ānanda, bhikkhu vā bhikkhunī vā upasako vā upasika vā dhammānudhammappaṭipanno viharati sāmīcippaṭipanno anudhammacāri, so tathāgataṃ sakkaroti garuṃ karoti māneti pūjeti apaciyati paramāya pūjāya. Tasmātihānanda, dhammānudhammappaṭipannā viharissāma sāmīcippatipannā anudhammacārinoti. Evañhi vo, nanda sikkhitabbaṃ. (DN 16)

140. *The Middle Length Discourses*, 97.

   Dhammadāyādā me, bhikkhave, bhavatha, mā āmisadāyādā. Atthi me tumhesu anukampā—"kinti me sāvakā dhammadāyādā bhaveyyuṃ, no āmisadāyādā" ti. (MN 3.2)

141. It is an "imitation Dhamma inheritance" rather than the true Dhamma inheritance of the realization itself.

142. Chapter 4, pp. 161ff.

143. *The Dhammapada*, 70.

   Na silabbatamattena, bāhusaccena vā pana;
   atha vā samādhilābhena, vivittasayanena vā.
   Phusāmi nekkhammasukhaṃ, aputhujjanasevitaṃ;
   bhikkhu vissāsamāpādi, appatto āsavakkhayaṃ. (Dhp 271–72)

144. See chapter 1, p. 14.

145. See chapter 1, p. 33.

146. *Nāhaṃ dāso bhato tuyhaṃ. Nāhaṃ posemi dani taṃ. Tvaṃeva posento dukkhaṃ, pattovaṭṭe anappakaṃ.* This verse is based on the Majjhima Nikāya commentary: *Nahaṃ daso na kammakaro anamagge saṃsāre taṃ yeva upaṭṭhanto vicariṃ.*

147. *The Middle Length Discourses*, 212.

   Asati amanasikāro āpajjitabbo. (MN 20.5)

148. *The Middle Length Discourses*, 213.

   Evameva kho, bhikkhave, tassa ce bhikkhuno tesampi vitakkānaṃ vitakkasaṅkhārasaṇṭhānaṃ manasikaroto uppajjanteva pāpakā akusalā vitakkā chandūpasaṃhitāpi dosūpasaṃhitāpi mohūpasaṃhitāpi. Tena, bhikkhave, bhikkhunā dantebhidantamādhāya jivhāya tāluṃ āhacca cetasā cittaṃ abhiniggaṇhitabbaṃ. (MN 20.7)

149. SN 47:10 (10). See *The Connected Discourses*, 1638–40.

150. See also *The Path of Discrimination*, 169.

Atītānudhāvanaṃ cittaṃ vikkhepānupatitaṃ; taṃ vivajjayitvā ekaṭṭhāne samādahati—evampi cittaṃ na vikkhepaṃ gacchati. Anāgatapaṭikaṅkhanaṃ cittaṃ vikampitaṃ; taṃ vivajjayitvā tattheva adhimoceti—evampi cittam na vekkhepaṃ gacchati. (Paṭis 3.16)

151. Ibid.

Līnaṃ cittaṃ kosajjānupatitaṃ; taṃ paggaṇhitvā kosajjaṃ pajahati—evampi cittaṃ na vikkhepaṃ gacchati. Atipaggahitaṃ cittaṃ uddhaccānupatitaṃ. Taṃ viniggaṇhitvā uddhaccaṃ pajahati—evampi cittaṃ na vikkhepaṃ gacchati. (Paṭis 3.16)

152. Mahāvagga Aṭṭhakathā, PTS 3.789.
153. The full list is as follows:
    1. Reflecting on the dangers of the lower realms
    2. Reflecting on the benefits of practice
    3. Reflecting on the right path
    4. Respect and appreciation for requisites received
    5. Reflecting on the nobility of one's inheritance
    6. Reflecting on the nobility of the Buddha
    7. Reflecting on the nobility of the lineage
    8. Reflecting on the nobility of the companions in the holy life
    9. Avoiding companionship with lazy people
    10. Associating with energetic people
    11. Inclining the mind to strive continuously
154. About 5.12 kilometers or 3.18 miles!
155. 2,048 kilometers or 1,272 miles.
156. MN 129. See *The Middle Length Discourses*, 1016–28.
157. MN 130. See *The Middle Length Discourses*, 1029–36.
158. *The Dhammapada*, 96.

Jhāya [tuvam[MS]] bhikkhu mā pamādo, mā te kāmaguṇe ramessu cittaṃ.
mā lohaguḷaṃ gilī pamatto. mā kandi "dukkha-midan" ti ḍayhamāno. (Dhp 371)

159. *The Middle Length Discourses*, 115.

Ākaṅkheyyace, bhikkhave bhikkhu—"yesāhaṃ cīvarapiṇḍapātasenāsana gilānappaccayabhesajjaparikkhāraṃ paribhuñjāmi tesaṃ te kārā mahapphalā assu mahānisaṃsā"ti, sīlesvevassa paripūrakārī, ajjhattaṃ cetosamathamanuyutto anirākatajjhāno, vipassanāya samannāgato, brūhetā suññāgārānaṃ. (MN 6.5)

160. Mahāmitta was a monk to whom a very poor woman gave almsfood; after this, he practiced with great effort and became an arahant. (Ps; Sv); Piṇḍapātika Tissa was a Thera who became an arahant by developing mindfulness of in- and out-breaths (Vism 1.284).
161. *The Connected Discourses*, 553.

. . .alameva [. . . [SNCom'y]] saddhāpabbajitena [. . . [SNCom'y]] kulaputtena [. . . [SNCom'y]] vīriyaṃ ārabhituṃ . . . alameva appamādena sampādetuṃ (SN 12.22)

162. These four types of extreme resolve represent the four factors of great effort.
163. *The Connected Discourses*, 553.

Alameva saddhāpabhajjitena kulaputtena vīriyaṃ ārabhataṃ: "kāmaṃ taco ca, naharu ca aṭṭhi ca avasissatu, sarīre upasussatu maṃsalohitaṃ. Yaṃ taṃ purisathāmena purisavīriyena purisaparikkamena pattabbaṃ, na taṃ apāpuṇitvā vīriyassa saṇṭhānaṃ bhāvissatī"ti . . . . Na bhikkhave, hīnena aggassa patti hoti. Aggena ca [kho[VRI]*], bhikkhave, agassa patti hoti . . . tasmātiha, bhikkhave, viriyaṃ ārabata appatassa pattiyā, anadhigatassa adhigamāya, asaccikatassa saccikiriyāya. "Evaṃ no ayaṃ pabbajjā avañjhā bhavissati saphalā sa-udrayā. Yesañca mayhaṃ paribhuñjāma cīvara-piṇḍapātasenasana gilānapaccayabhesajjaparikkhāraṃ tesaṃ te kārā amhesu mahapphalā bhavissanti mahānisamsā" ti. Evañhi vo, bhikkhave, sikkhitabbaṃ. Attattaṃ vā hi, bhikkhave, sampassamānena alameva appamādena sampādetuṃ; paratthaṃ vā hi, bhikkave, sampassamānena [alameva appamādena sampādetuṃ*[VRI]*]; ubhayattaṃ vā hi bhikkhave, sampassamānena alameva appamādena sampadetuṃ.* (SN 12.22)

164. See also *The Path of Discrimination*, 169.
Abhinataṃ cittaṃ rāgānupatitaṃ; taṃ sampajāno hutvā rāgaṃ pajahati—evampi cittaṃ na vikkhepaṃ gacchati. Apanataṃ cittaṃ byāpādānupatitaṃ; taṃ sampajāno hutvā byāpādam pajahati—evampi cittaṃ na vikkhepaṃ gacchati. (Paṭis 3.15)

165. Chapter 4, p. 158–59; 195–96.

166. The Pāḷi word that underlies "one-pointedness" here is *ekatta*. This word is sometimes translated as "oneness," "unification," or "unity." In this case, *ekatta* refers quite specifically to mind-states associated with concentration, and it should not be interpreted to mean unity in the sense of nonduality.

167. The six remedies to the six obstacles to concentration are: countering distracting thoughts of the past by not thinking of the past, countering fantasies about the future by not thinking of the future, encouraging oneself when lazy, relaxing oneself when overzealous, recognizing lust when gratified, and recognizing aversion when frustrated.

168. See also *The Path of Discrimination*, 169.
Imehi chahi ṭhānehi parisuddhaṃ cittaṃ pariyodātaṃ ekattagataṃ hoti. Katame te ekattā? Dānavosaggupaṭṭhānekattaṃ, samathanimittupaṭṭhānekattaṃ, vayalakkhaṇupaṭṭhānekattaṃ, nirodhupaṭṭhānekattaṃ. Dānavosaggupaṭṭhānekattaṃ cāgādhimuttānaṃ, samathanimittupaṭṭhānekattañca adhicittamanuyuttānaṃ, vayalakkhaṇupaṭṭhānekattañca vipassakānaṃ, nirodhupaṭṭhānekattañca ariyapuggalānaṃ. (Paṭis 1.3)

169. There is one reality that can be viewed from different perspectives: the conventional, consensual view that we know from our everyday lives; and the "absolute" or "ultimate" view that is empirically experienced with awareness, without thought. These two views are both true perspectives on one reality.

170. *Paramo uttamo aviparīto attho paramassa.* (Abhidh-vibh-ṭ)

171. *Paramo uttamo [attapaccakkho*[MS]*] attho paramattho.* (Abhidh-s-a)

172. *Saccikaṭṭhoti māyāmarīci-ādayo viya abhūtākārena aggahetabbo bhūtaṭṭho. Paramatthoti anussavādivasena aggahetabbo . . . attano pana bhūtatāya eva saccikaṭṭho, attapaccakkhatāya . . . paramattho. Taṃ sandhāyāha.* (Ppk-a)

173. *Cakkhuviññāṇassa hi rūpe abhinipātamattaṃ kiccaṃ, na adhippāyasahabhuno calanavikārassa gahaṇaṃ. Cittassa pana lahuparivattitāya cakkhuviññāṇavithiyā anantaraṃ manovinnāṇena viññātampi calanaṃ cakkhunā diṭṭhaṃ viya maññanti avisesaviduno.* (Abhidh-Mūlaṭīkā)

174. AN 3.65. See *The Numerical Discourses*, 279–83.

175. *Anussavādivasena gayhamāno tathāpi hoti aññathāpīti tādiso ñeyyo na paramattho, attapaccakkho pana paramatthoti dassento āha: 'anussavādā . . . pe . . . uttamattho' ti.* (Abhidh-Mūlaṭīkā)

176. *Aviparītabhāvato eva paramo . . . atthoti paramattho, ñāṇassa paccakkhabhūto dhammānaṃ aniddisitabbasabhāvo. Tena vuttaṃ 'uttamattho'ti.* (Abhidh-Anuṭīkā)
177. *Dhammānam aniddisitabbasabhāvo.*
178. The *Abhidhammatthavibhāvinī Ṭīkā* is a commentary on the *Abhidhammatthasaṅgaha* written by Ācariya Sumangalasāmi of Sri Lanka in the twelth century CE. In Burma, this subcommentary is known as *ṭīkā-gyaw* or "The Famous Commentary."
179. I.e., the *Abhidhammatthavibhāvinī Ṭīkā.*
180. Consult the *Paramatthavibhāvinī* for explanations of other sometimes confusing terms—such as *saññavipallāsā, sammādiṭṭhi,* and *viparīta.*
181. Sumedha, upon seeing the former Buddha Dīpaṅkarā, vowed to become a buddha in a future lifetime. In his last lifetime, he was born as Prince Siddhattha and indeed became the Buddha of these times, Gotama Buddha.
182. "There is also no death of a person" means that there is only the last phenomenon of the current life: a person's last moment of consciousness along with the physical phenomena produced by kamma and the mind. The corpse is all that is left of materiality produced by temperature and nutrition.
183. See "Appendix 3: Stream of Consciousness." The first mental process simply sees a present visible form, the second mental process perceives the immediately preceding form, and the third mental process interprets the form as a person or thing.
184. *The Path of Purification*, 97. (Vism 3.56)
185. *Avisayattāvisayatte[pi*[MS]*] ca payojanābhāvato.*
186. Mentioned in the *Anupada Sutta* (MN 111). See *The Middle Length Discourses*, 901, fn. 1051.
187. *Lābhino eva Ken Knabb. . . mahaggatacittāni supākaṭāni honti.* (Vism-mhṭ)
188. *The Path of Purification*, 630.

    Yepi ca [sammasanūpagā[KNC]*][sammasanupagā*[MS,Vism]*], tesu ye yassa pākaṭā honti. Sukhena pariggahaṃ gacchanti, tesu tena sammasanaṃ ārabhitabbaṃ.* (Vism 20.12)
189. See "Appendix 5: Materiality."
190. *Rūpārūpaneva hi idha pariggayhanti, na rūpaparicchedavikāralakkhaṇāni.*
191. See "Appendix 2: Mental Factors Present in Each Consciousness."
192. See "Appendix 7: Mental Process Functions."
193. See "Appendix 7: Mental Process Functions."
194. See "Appendix 7: Mental Process Functions."
195. *Bhāventopi tesaṃyeva aññatarena bhāveti.* (As)
196. *Sammasantassa kadāci paricayabalena ñāṇavippayuttacittehipi sammasananti.* (From Ledi Sayadaw's *Paramaṭṭhadīpani Ṭīkā*)
197. *Paguṇaṃ samathavipassanābhāvanaṃ anuyuñjantassa antarantarā ñaṇavippayuttacittenāpi manasikāro pavattati . . .* (It-a)
198. MN 111. See *The Middle Length Discourses*, 899–902.
199. *Ekadesamevāti saka-attabhāve saṅkhāre anavasesato pariggahetuñca sammasituñca asakkontaṃ attano abhinīhārasamudāgatañāṇabalānurūpaṃ ekadesameva pariggahetvā sammasanto . . . . Tasmā sasantānagate sabbadhamme, parasantānagate ca tesaṃ santānavibhāge akatvā bahiddhābhāvasāmaññato sammasati. Ayaṃ sāvakānaṃ sammasanacāro.* (MN-ṭ)
200. *Ajjhattaṃ vā hi vipassanābhiniveso hotu bahiddhā vā. Ajjhattasiddhiyaṃ pana lakkhaṇato sabbampi nāmarūpaṃ anavasesato pariggahitameva hoti.* (Vism-mhṭ)
201. Chapter 7, pp. 466ff.

202. *The Middle Length Discourses*, 1039. (MN 131)
203. The present can be defined in three ways: as "the present life," a period of time that spans from birth to death (*addhāpaccuppanna*), as "the serial present," a period of time that covers a single mental process (*santatipaccuppanna*), or as "the momentary present," a period of time limited to a single mind moment (*khaṇapaccuppanna*).
204. These seven are:
    1. Contemplation of impermanence (*aniccānupassanā*)
    2. Contemplation of unsatisfactoriness (*dukkhānupassanā*)
    3. Contemplation of not-self (*anattānupassanā*)
    4. Contemplation of disenchantment (*nibbidānupassanā*)
    5. Contemplation of dispassion (*virāgānupassanā*)
    6. Contemplation of cessation (*nirodhānupassanā*)
    7. Contemplation of relinquishment (*paṭinissaggānupassanā*)

    All seven contemplations are explained in full in chapter 7.
205. *Tattha tatthāti paccuppannampi dhammaṃ yattha yatthāve so uppanno, tattha tattheva aniccānupassanādīhi sattahi anupassanāhi vipassati, . . .* (Nett)
206. *The Path of Purification*, 428.

    Addhāpaccuppannaṃ pana javanavārena dīpetabbanti saṃyuttaṭṭhakathāyaṃ vuttaṃ. Taṃ suṭṭhuvuttaṃ. (Vism 13.117)
207. *Addhāpaccuppannaṃ javanavārena dīpetabbam, na sakalena paccuppannaddhunātiadhippāyo.* (Vism-mhṭ)
208. *The Middle Length Discourses*, 146.

    Gacchanto vā "gacchāmī"ti pajānāti. (MN 10.6)
211. Ibid., 149.

    Sukhaṃ vedanaṃ vedayamāno sukhaṃ vedanaṃ vedayāmī'ti pajānāti. (MN 10.32)
210. Ibid., 151.

    Santaṃ vā ajjhattaṃ kāmacchandaṃ atthi me ajjhattaṃ kāmacchando'ti pajānāti. (MN 10.36)
211. Ibid., 150.

    Sarāgaṃ vā cittaṃ "sarāgaṃ cittan"ti pajānāti. (MN 10.34)
212. *Yasmiṃ yasmiṃ khaṇe yaṃ yaṃ cittaṃ pavattati, taṃ taṃ sallakkhento attano vā citte, parassa vā citte, kālena vā attano, kālena vā parassa citte cittānupassasī viharati.* (Sv and Ps)
213. *The Middle Length Discourses*, 165.

    Sarāgaṃ vā cittaṃ "sarāgaṃ cittan"ti pajānāti. (MN 12.8)
214. See also *The Path of Discrimination*, 53.

    Yaṃ kiñci rūpaṃ atītānāgatapaccuppānnaṃ ajjhattaṃ vā bahiddhā vā, oḷārikaṃ vā sukhumaṃ vā, hīnaṃ vā paṇītaṃ vā, yaṃ dūre santike vā, sabbaṃ rūpaṃ aniccato vavattheti. Ekaṃ sammasanaṃ. (Paṭis 1.278)
215. *Bahiddhā abhinivisitvā ajjhattaṃ vuṭṭhāti.* (Dhs-a)
216. *Ekasaṅkhārassāpi aniccatāya diṭṭhāya sabbe saṅkhārā aniccāti avasesesu nayato manasikāro hoti . . . sabbe saṅkhārā aniccāti ādivacanaṃ . . . nayato dassanaṃ sandhāya vuttaṃ, na ekakkhaṇe ārammaṇato, . . .* (Ppk-a)
217. *The Numerical Discourses*, 363–64.

    Sabbe saṅkhārā aniccā'ti . . . sabbe saṅkhārā dukkhā'ti . . . sabbe dhammā anattā'ti yada paññāya passati. (AN 3.136)
218. This section of the *Visuddhimagga* accords with the method used in the pāḷimuttaka

commentary. *Pāḷimuttaka* refers to words of the Buddha that were not included in the main body of the Tipiṭaka but were included in the commentaries.

219. *The Middle Length Discourses*, 539–40.

Idha bhikkhave bhikkhu vivicceva kāmehi vivicca akusalehi dhammehi savitakkaṃ savicāraṃ vivekajaṃ pītisukhaṃ paṭhamaṃ jhānaṃ upasampajja viharati. So yadeva tattha hoti rūpagataṃ vedanāgataṃ saññāgataṃ sankhāragataṃ viññānagataṃ te dhamme aniccato, dukkhato, rogato, gaṇḍato, sallato, aghato, ābādhato, parato, palokato, suññato, anattato, samanupassati. (MN 64.9)

220. See also *The Path of Purification*, 605.

Nāmarūpānaṃ yāthāvadassanaṃ diṭṭhivisuddhi nāma. Taṃ sampādetukāmena samathayānikena tāva ṭhapetvā nevasaññānāsaññāyatanaṃ avasesarūpārūpāvacarajjhānānaṃ aññatarato vuṭṭhāya vitakkādīni jhānaṅgāni, taṃsampayutta ca dhammā lakkhaṇarasādivasena pariggahetabbā. (Vism 18.3)

221. This implicitly excludes seeing them by means of visualization, enumeration, itemization, etc.

222. *Rūpārūpānadhammaṃ accantavidhuratāya ekajjham asammasitabbathā.* (Vism-mhṭ)

223. *Rūpe vipassanābhiniveso yebhuyyena vipassanayānikassa,* [*evaṃ*[VRI]] *arūpe vipassanābhiniveso yebhuyyena samathayānikassa hoti.* (Vism-mhṭ)

224. *Assāsapassāse pariggaṇhāti rūpamukhena vipassanaṃ abhinivisanto . . . jhānaṅgāni pariggaṇhāti arūpamukhena vipassanaṃ abhinivisanto.* (DN-ṭ)

225. For sensual phenomena, see "the sense-sphere" in "Appendix 6: Planes of Existence."

226. *The Middle Length Discourses*, 945.

Kāyesu kāyaññatarāham bhikkhave evam vadāmi, yadidam assāsapassāsa. (MN 118)

227. MN 33. See *The Middle Length Discourses*, 313–18.

228. Specifically, the Aṅguttara Nikāya and *Visuddhimagga*.

229. *Sāvakā hi catunnaṃ dhātūnaṃ ekadesameva sammasitvā nibbānaṃ pāpunanti.* (Sv)

230. SN 35.245. See *The Connected Discourses*, 1251–53.

231. The translation here is made according to Mahāsi Sayadaw's interpretation. For a more literal translation, consider Bodhi (*The Connected Discourses*, 1251): "In what way, friend, is a bhikkhu's vision well purified?"

Kittāvata, nukho ,āvuso, bhikkhunodassanaṃ suvisuddhaṃhotī"ti? . . . (SN 35.245)

232. *The Connected Discourses*, 1251.

. . .yato kho, āvuso, [*bhikkhu*[MS]] *channaṃ phassāyatanānaṃ samudayañca atthangamañca yathābhūtaṃ pajānāti. Ettāvatā kho āvuso bhikkhuno dassanaṃ suvisuddhaṃ hotī.* (SN 35.245)

233. Ibid.

Yato kho, āvuso, bhikkhu pañcannaṃ upādānakkhandhānaṃ samudayañca atthangamañca yathābhūtaṃ pajānāti, ettāvatā kho āvuso bhikkhuno dassanaṃ suvisuddhaṃ hotī. (SN 35.245)

234. Ibid.

Yato kho āvuso catunnaṃ mahābhūtānaṃ samudayañcaṃ atthaṅgamañca yathābhūtaṃ pajānāti, ettāvatā, kho āvuso, bhikkhuno dassanaṃ suvisuddhaṃ hotī. (SN 35.245)

235. Ibid.

Yaṃ kiñci samudayadhammaṃ sabbaṃ taṃ nirodhadhammanti yathābhūtaṃ pajānāti . . . (SN 35.245)

236. Ibid., 1252.

Yathā yathā adhimuttānaṃ tesaṃ sappurisānaṃ dassanaṃ suvisuddhaṃ hoti, tathā tathā kho tehi sappurisehi byākataṃ . . . (SN 35.245)

237. See "Appendix 2: Mental Factors Present in Each Consciousness" for a list of mental states that arise in the first jhāna.

238. *The Middle Length Discourses*, 899.

Sāriputto, bhikkhave, addhamāsaṃ anupadadhammavipassanaṃ vipassati. Tatridaṃ, bhikkhave sāriputtassa anupadadhammavipassanāya hoti. Idha bhikkhave sāriputto vivicceva kāmehi vivicca akusalehi dhammehi savitakkaṃ savicāraṃ vivekajaṃ pītisukham pathamaṃ jhānaṃ upasampajja viharati. Ye ca pathame jhāne dhammā, vitakko ca vicāro ca pīti ca sukhañca cittekaggatā ca, phasso vedanā saññā cetanā cittaṃ chando adhimokkho vīriyaṃ sati upekkhā manasikāro—tyāssa dhammā anupadavavatthitā honti. Tyāssa dhammā viditā uppajjanti, viditā upaṭṭhananti, viditā abbhatthaṃ gacchanti. So evam pajānāti—"evaṃ kirame dhammā ahutvā sambhonti, hutvā pativenti"ti. (MN 111.2–4)

239. See pp. 135–36.

240. *Samāpatti* is long-lasting meditative attainment in an object.

241. *Samāpattivasena vā jhānangavasena vā anupatipātiya dhammavipassanaṃ* . . . (Ps)

242. See *The Path of Discrimination*, 58–9.

243. See *The Path of Purification*, 648–51.

244. *Yathā hi teneva aṅgulena taṃ aṅgulaggaṃ na sakkā phusituṃ, evameva teneva cittena tassa [citassa*[VRI]*] uppādo vā ṭhiti vā bhaṅgo vā na sakkā jānitunti evam tāva taṃñāṇatā mocetabbā. Yadi pana dve cittāni ekato uppajjeyyuṃ, ekena cittena ekassa uppādo vā ṭhiti vā bhaṅgo vā sakkā bhāveyya jānitum. Dve pana phassā vā vedanā vā saññā vā cetanā vā cittāni vā ekato uppajjanakāni nāma natthi, ekamekameva uppajjati. Evaṃ ñāṇabahutā mocetabbā.* (Ps)

245. *Mahāmoggalānatthero hi sāvakānaṃ sammasanacāraṃ yaṭṭhikoṭiya uppīlento viya ekadesameva sammsanto sattadivase vāyamitvā arahattam patto. Sāriputtatthero thapetvā buddhānaṃ paccekabuddhānañca sammasanacāram sāvakānaṃ sammasanacāraṃ nippadesaṃ sammasi. Evaṃ sammasanto addhamāsaṃ vāyami, arahattañca kira [patvā*[VRI]*] aññāsi . . ." añño sāvako nāma paññāya mayā pattabbaṃ pattuṃ samattho nāma na bhavissatī"ti.* (Ps)

246. *Sammasanaṃ carati etthā'ti sammasanacāro, vipassanāya bhūmi.* (MN-ṭ)

247. These two views are the views of Buddhagosa's teacher and other teachers contemporary to him, respectively.

248. *The Middle Length Discourses*, 901.

Puna ca paraṃ bhikkhave, sāriputto sabbaso ākiñcaññāyatanaṃ samatikkamma nevasaññānāsaññāyatanaṃ upasampajja viharati. So tāya samāpattiyā sato vuṭṭhāhati. So tāya samāpattiyā sato vuṭṭhahitvā ye dhammā atītā niruddhā vipariṇatā, te dhamme samanupassati—"evam kirame dhammā ahutvā sambhonti, hutvā paṭiventī"ti .(MN 111.17–18)

249. *Te dhamme samanupassati.*

250. *Te dhamme samanupassatīti yasmānevasaññānāsaññāyatane buddhānaṃyeva*

anupadadhammavipassanā hoti, na sāvakānaṃ, tasmā ettha kalāpa vipassanaṃ dassento evamāha. (Ps)

251. *The Middle Length Discourses*, 127.

    Pare sandiṭṭhparāmāsī ādhānaggāhī duppatinissaggī bhvassanti. Mayamettha asandiṭṭhiparāmāsī anādhānaggāhī suppatinissaggī bhavissāmāti sallekho karaṇīyo . . . cittaṃ uppādetabbaṃ. (MN 8.44)

252. That is, "Should one observe ultimately real phenomena by using accurate names?"
253. *Nanu ca tajjā paññattivasena sabhāvadhammo gayhatīti? Saccaṃ gayhati pubbabhāge, bhāvanāya pana vaddhamānāya paññattiṃ samatikkamitvā sabhāveyeva cittaṃ tiṭṭhāti.* (Vism-mhṭ)
254. E.g., knowledge that discerns mental and physical phenomena (*nāmarūpaparicchedañāṇa*).
255. *Visuddhimagga-mahāṭīkā.*
256. Specifically, the *Mahāṭīkā* and *Abhidhammatthavibhāvinī.*
257. *Kasmā panettha ubhayaggahaṇaṃ? Puggalajjhāsayato. Ekaccassa hi dhātuyo manasi karontassa tā sabhāvato gahetabbataṃ gacchanti, ekaccassa sakiccakaraṇato. Yo rasoti vuccati.* (Vism-mhṭ)
258. This line refers to passages in the *Satipaṭṭhāna* (MN 10.40) and *Mahāsatipaṭṭhāna Suttas* (DN 22.15). The line has been translated here following Bodhi's *Middle Length Discourses*, 153.
259. *Cakkhupasādaṃ . . . rūpañca yathāvasarasalakkhanavasena.* (Sv)
260. *Upekkhā pana akusalavipākabhūtā aniṭṭhattā dukkhe avarodetabbā, itarā iṭṭhattā sukheti.* (Abhidhamma-mlṭ)
261. The exact passage as quoted by Mahāsi Sayadaw occurs only in the *Paṭisambhidāmagga* and the *Visuddhimagga*. A series of suttas in the Saṃyutta Nikāya, however, convey the same meaning, each with a slightly different emphasis. See *The Connected Discourses*, 1141–43 (SN 35:25–27).
262. [*Cakkhuṃ*[MS]][*Cakkhu*[VRI]] *bhikkhave abhiññeyyaṃ. Rūpā abhiññeyyā, cakkhuviññāṇaṃ abhiññeyyaṃ, cakkhusamphasso abhiññeyyo, yampidaṃ cakkhusamphassapaccayā upajjati vedayitaṃ sukhaṃ vā dukkhaṃ vā adukkhamasukhaṃ vā. Tampi abhiññeyyaṃ.* (Paṭis; Vism)
263. *Sabhāvadhammānaṃ lakkhanasallakkhaṇato ñeyya-abhimukhā paññā abhiññāpaññā.* (Vism-mhṭ)
264. *Apica sutamayāya, cintāmayāya, ekaccabhāvanāmayāya ca abhivisitthāyapaññāya ñātā abhiññātā.* (Vism-mhṭ)
265. SN 35:46. See *The Connected Discourses*, 1147.
266. SN 56:29. See *The Connected Discourses*, 1856–57.
267. *The Connected Discourses*, 1175.

    "*Taṃ kiṃ maññasi mālukyaputta, ye te cakkhuviññeyyā rūpā adiṭṭhā adiṭṭhapubbā, na ca passati, na ca te hoti passeyyanti? Atthi te tattha chando vā rāgo vā pemaṃ vā"ti? No hetaṃ bhante.* (SN 35:95)

268. Ibid., 1175–76.

    "*Ettha ca te Mālukyaputta diṭṭhasutamutaviññātesu dhammesu diṭṭhe diṭṭhamattaṃ bhavissati, sute sutamattaṃ bhavissati, mute mutamattaṃ bhavissati, viññāte viññānamattaṃ bhavissati. Yato kho te Mālukyaputta diṭṭhasutamutaviññātabesu dhammesu diṭṭhe diṭṭhamattaṃ bhavissati, sute sutamattaṃ bhavissati, mute mutamattaṃ bhavissati, viññāte viññānamattaṃ bhavissati; tato tvaṃ Mālukyaputta, na tena. Yato tvaṃ Mālukyaputta, na tena; tato tvaṃ mālukyaputta, na tattha; yato tvaṃ Mālukyaputta na tattha; tato tvaṃ*

Mālukyaputta, nevidha, na huraṃ, na ubhayamantarena. Esevanto dukkhassa"ti. (SN 35:95)

269. Udana-aṭṭhākathā: Bāhiyasuttavaṇṇanā.
270. "*Vipassanāya visayaṃ diṭṭhādīhi catūhi koṭṭhāsehi vibhajitvā tatthassa ñātatīraṇapariññaṃ dasseti.*" (Ud-a)
"*Heṭṭhimāhi visuddhīhi saddhiṃ saṅkhepeneva vipassanā kathitā.*" (Ud-a)
271. Attachment, pride, and wrong view constitute the three proliferating tendencies of mind (*papañca*).
272. *The Connected Discourses*, 1176.
Rūpaṃ disvā sati muṭṭhā, piyaṃ nimittam manasikaroto;
Sārattacitto vedeti, tañca ajjhosa tiṭṭhati.
Tassa vuḍḍhanti vedanā, anekā rūpasambhavā.
Abhijjhā ca vihesā ca, cittamassupahaññati;
Evaṃ ācinato dukkhaṃ, ārā nibbānavuccati. (SN 35:95)
273. Ibid., 1176–77.
Na so rajjati rūpesu, rūpaṃ disvā paṭissato;
Virattacitto vedeti, tañca najjhosa tiṭṭhati.
Yathāssa passato rūpaṃ, sevato cāpi vedanaṃ;
Khīyati nopacīyati, evaṃ so carati sato;
Evaṃ apacinato dukkhaṃ, santike nibbāna vuccati. (SN 35:95)
274. See *The Connected Discourses*, 1175–78, or Saḷāyatanavaggapāḷi, PTS 4.74.
275. See *The Connected Discourses*, 959–61 (SN 22.101).
276. See *The Connected Discourses*, 1250 (SN 35.244).
277. See "Appendix 3: Stream of Consciousness," Line H10-12/12A. Line H12A ending at investigation or determining without any impulsion is seen by the subsequent insight knowledge stream.
278. *Dandho bhikkhave satuppādoti satiyā uppādoyeva dandho uppannamattāya pana tāya kāci kilesā niggahitāva honti, na saṇṭhātuṃ sakkonti. Cakkhudvārasmiñhi rāgādīsu uppannesu dutiya . . . javanaṃyeva javati. Anacchariyañcetaṃ, yaṃ vipassako tatiyajavanavāre kilese nigganheyya. Cakkhudvāre pana iṭṭhārammaṇe āpāthagate bhavaṅgaṃ āveṭṭetvā āvajjanādīsu uppannesu voṭṭhabbanānantaraṃ sampattakilesajavanavāraṃ nivattetvā kusalameva uppādeti. Āraddhavipassakānañhi ayamānisaṃso bhāvanāpaṭisaṅkhāne patiṭṭhitabhāvassa.* (Spk)
279. *Balavavipassakassa sacepi cakkhudvārādīsu ārammaṇe āpāthagate ayoniso āvajjanaṃ upajjati, voṭṭhabbanaṃ patvā ekaṃ dve vāre āsevanaṃ labhitvā cittaṃ bhavaṅgameva otarati, na rāgādivasena uppajjati, ayaṃ koṭipatto tikkhavipassako. Aparassa rāgādivasena ekaṃ vāraṃ javanaṃ javati, javanapariyosāne panarāgādivasena evaṃ me javanaṃ javitanti āvajjato ārammaṇaṃ pariggahitameva hoti, puna vāraṃ tathā na javati. Aparassa ekavāraṃ evaṃ āvajjato puna dutiyavāraṃ rāgādivasena javanaṃ javatiyeva, dutiyavāravasane pana evaṃ me javanaṃ javitanti āvajjato ārammaṇaṃ pariggahitameva hoti, tatiyavāre tathā na uppajjati.* (Ps)
280. *The Numerical Discourses*, 761.
Sādhu bhikkhave bhikkhu kālena kālaṃ patikūlañca appaṭikūlañca tadubhayaṃ abhinivejjetvā upekkhako vihareyya sato sampajāno. (AN 5:144)
281. *Chaḷaṅgupekkhāvasena pañcamo. Chaḷaṅgupekkhā cesā khīṇāsavassa upekkhāsadisā, na pana khīṇāsavupekkhā . . . imasmim sutte pañcasu ṭhānesu vipassanāva kathitā. Taṃ āraddhavipassako . . . kātum sakkoti . . .* (Mp)
282. MN 28. See *The Middle Length Discourses*, 278–85.

283. *Upekkhā kusalanissitā santhātīti idha chaḷaṅgupekkhā, sā panesā kiñcāpi khīnāsavassa iṭṭhāniṭṭhesu . . . arajjanādivasena pavattati, ayaṃ pana bhikkhu vīriyabalena bhāvanāsiddhiyā attano vipassanaṃ khīṇāsavassa chaḷaṅgupekkhāthāne thapetīti vipassanāva chaḷaṅgupekkhā nāma jātā.* (Ps)

284. Mahāsi Sayadaw suggested "Good-for-nothing Potthila," "Useless Potthila," "Futile Potthila" as other renderings.

285. 1 *yojana* = approx. 8 miles.

286. *The Middle Length Discourses*, 1147.

   Evaṃ sante kho, Uttara, andho bhāvitindriyo bhavissati, badhiro bhāvitindriyo bhavissati, yathā pārāsiviyassa brāhmanassa vacanaṃ. Andho hi, Uttara, cakkhunā rūpaṃ na passati, badhiro sotena saddaṃ na sunāti. (MN 152.2)

287. *The Numerical Discourses*, 857.

   Cakkhunā rūpaṃ disvā neva sumano hoti na dummano, upekkhako viharati sato sampajāno. (AN 6:1)

288. *The Dhammapada*, 73.

   Yogā ve jāyatī bhūrī, ayogā bhūrisaṅkhayo;
   etaṃ dvedhāpathaṃ ñatvā, bhavāya vibhavāya ca;
   tathāttānaṃ niveseyya, yathā bhūrī pavaḍḍhati. (Dhp 282)

289. See also *The Path of Purification*, 610.

   Evaṃ suvisuddharūpapariggahassa panassa arūpadhammā tīhākārehi upaṭṭhahanti phassavasena vā, vedanāvasena vā, viññāṇavasena vā. (Vism 18.18)

290. *Tenassa phusanākārena supākaṭabhāvena upaṭṭhānaṃ dasseti. Phasse pana upaṭṭite yasmiṃ ārammaṇe so phasso, tassa anubhavanalakkhaṇā vedanā, sañjānanalakkhaṇā saññā, āyūhanalakkhaṇā cetanā, paṭivijānanalakkhaṇaṃ viññāṇanti imepi pākaṭā honti.* (Vism-mhṭ)

291. DN 21. See *The Long Discourses*, 321–34.

292. MN 10. See *The Middle Length Discourses*, 145–55.

293. *Yassa phasso pākaṭo hoti, sopi "na kevalaṃ phassova uppajjati, tena saddhiṃ tadeva ārammaṇaṃ anubhavanāmānā vedanāpi uppajjati, sañjānamānā saññāpi, cetayamānā cetanāpi, vijānanamānaṃ viññāṇampi uppajjatī"ti phassapañcamakeyeva parigganhāti.* (Vibh-a)

294. . . . *idha pana cakkhuviññāṇasampayuttā tayo khandhā. Te hi cakkhuviññāṇena saha viññātabbattā "cakkhuviññāṇaviññātabbā"ti vuttā.* (Spk)

295. *Phassāhāre tīhi pariññāhi pariññāte tisso vedanā pariññātāva honti tammūlakattā tamsampayuttattā ca.* (Spk)

296. That is, seeing phenomena as they really are.

297. That is, seeing phenomena in terms of impermanence and so on.

298. That is, seeing phenomena without attachment.

299. *Viññāṇasmiñhi pariññāte taṃ pariññātameva hoti tammūlakattā, sahuppannattā ca.* (Spk)

300. MN 115. See *The Middle Length Discourses*, 925–30.

301. *The Middle Length Discourses*, 926.

   Chayimā, Ānanda dhātuyo—pathavīdhātu, āpodhātu, tejodhātu, vāyodhātu, akāsadhātu, viññānadhātu. Imā kho ānanda cha dhātuyo yato jānāti passati—ettāvatāpi kho, Ānanda "dhātukusalo bhikkhūti alaṃ vacanāyā"ti. (MN 115.5)

302. This does not refer to theoretical knowledge (*sutamayañāṇa*) or analytical knowledge (*cintāmayañāṇa*) but to empirical knowledge (*bhāvanāmayañāṇa*), the understanding gained through insight and path.

303. *Jānāti passatīti saha vipassanāya maggo vutto. Pathvīdhātu-ādayo saviññāṇakakāyaṃ*

suññato nissattato dassetuṃ vuttā. Tāpi purimāhi aṭṭharasahi dhātūhi pūretabbā. Pūrentena viññāṇadhātuto nīharitvā pūretabbā. Viññāṇadhātu hesā cakkhuviññāṇādivasena chabbidhā hoti. Tattha cakkhuviññāṇadhātuyā pariggahitāya tassā vatthu cakkhudhātu, ārammaṇaṃ rūpadhātūti dve dhātuyo pariggahitāva honti. Esa nayo sabbattha. Manoviññāṇadhātuyā pana pariggahitāya tassā purimapacchimavasena manodhātu, ārammaṇavasena dhammadhātūti dve dhātuyo pariggahitāva honti. Iti [. . .[MS]] *idampi ekassa bhikkhuno niggamanaṃ matthakaṃ pāpetvā kathitaṃ hoti.* (Ps)

304. MN 10. See *The Middle Length Discourses*, 145–55.
305. *Ettha ca "kakkhaḷaṃ mudukaṃ saṇhaṃ pharusaṃ garukaṃ lahukan"ti padehi pathvīdhātu eva bhājitā.* [. . .[MS]] *"Sukhasamphassaṃ dukkhasamphassan"ti padadvayena pana tīnīpi mahābhūtāni bhājitāni.* (As)
306. See *The Path of Purification*, 463.
    Aniṭṭhaphoṭṭhabbānubhavanalakkhaṇaṃ dukkhaṃ. (Vism 14.127)
307. Ibid.
    Sampayuttānaṃ milāpanarasaṃ. (Vism 14.127)
308. Ibid.
    Kāyikābādhapaccupaṭṭhānaṃ. (Vism 14.127)
309. Ibid.
    Kāyindriyapadaṭṭhanaṃ;" . . . "Phassapadaṭṭhāna vedanā. (Vism 14.127)
310. *The Middle Length Discourses*, 145–46.
    . . . satova assasati, satova passasati (MN 10.4; DN 22.2)
311. Ibid., 146.
    . . . samudayadhammānupassī vā kāyasmiṃ viharati . . . (MN 10; DN 22)
312. Ibid.
    . . .vayadhammānupassī vā [kayasmi[VRI]*] viharati . . .* (MN 10; DN 22)
313. Ibid.
    Atthi kāyo"ti vā panassa sati paccupatthitāhoti . . . (MN 10; DN 22)
314. Ibid.
    . . . Yathā yathā vā panassa kāyo panihito hoti, tathā tathā naṃ pajānāti. (MN 10; DN 22)
315. The twenty parts that are dominated by earth element are: (1) head hair, (2) body hair, (3) nails, (4) teeth, (5) skin, (6) flesh, (7) sinews, (8) bones, (9) bone marrow, (10) kidneys, (11) heart, (12) liver, (13) diaphragm, (14) spleen, (15) lungs, (16) large intestines, (17) small intestines, (18) contents of the somach, (19) feces, and (20) brain.
316. The twelve dominated by water element are: (1) bile, (2) phlegm, (3) pus, (4) blood, (5) sweat, (6) fat, (7) tears, (8) grease, (9) spittle, (10) snot, (11) oil of the joints, and (12) urine.
317. The four dominated by fire element are: that by which one is warmed, ages, and is consumed, and that by which what is eaten, drunk, consumed, and tasted gets completely digested.
318. The six dominated by air element are: (1) up-going winds, (2) down-going winds, (3) winds in the belly, (4) winds in the bowels, (5) winds that course through the limbs, and (6) the in-breath and out-breath.
319. *The Middle Length Discourses*, 148.
    Imameva kāyaṃ yathāṭhitaṃ yathāpaṇihitaṃ dhātuso paccavekkhati "atthi imasmiṃ kāye pathavīdhātu āpodhātu, tejodhātu vāyodhātu"ti. (MN 10; DN 22)
320. See "Appendix 2: Mental Factors Present in Each Consciousness" for a list of the 52 mental factors.

321. *The Middle Length Discourses*, 146.
Gacchanto vā "gacchāmī"ti pajānāti. (MN 10; DN 22)

322. *Esa evaṃ pajānāti—"gacchāmī"ti cittaṃ uppajjati, taṃ vāyaṃ janeti, vāyo viññattiṃ janeti, cittakiriyavāyodhātuvipphārena sakalakāyassa purato abhinīhāro gamananti vuccati.* (Sv)

323. *Imassa pana bhikkhuno jānanaṃ sattūpaladdhiṃ pajahati. Attasaññaṃ ugghāṭeti kammaṭṭhānañceva satipaṭṭhānabhāvanā ca hoti.*

324. *The Middle Length Discourses*, 147.
. . . abhikkante paṭikkante sampajānakārī hoti. (MN 10; DN 22)

325. Referring to a Pāḷi word that means "a collection (or mass) of bones," Mahāsi Sayadaw inserted the following comment at this point into the original Pāḷi quote: "*rūpasanghāṭo* is preferred to *aṭṭhisaṅghāto*"; we have applied his preferred usage in the English translation.

326. *Abhikkamādīsu pana asammuyhanaṃ asammohasampajaññaṃ. Taṃ evaṃ veditabbaṃ—idha bikkhu abhikkamanto vā paṭikkamanto vā yathā andhbalāputhujjanāabhikkamādīsu "attā abhikkamati, attanā abhikkamo nibbattito"ti vā, "ahaṃ abhikkamāmi, mayā abhikkamo nibbattito"ti vā sammuyhanti tathā asammuyhanto "abhikkamāmī"ti citte uppajjamāne teneva cittena saddhiṃ cittasamuṭṭhānā vāyodhātu viññattiṃ janatamānā uppajjati. Iti cittakiriyavāyodhātuvipphāravasena ayaṃ kāyasammato aṭṭhisaṅghāto abhikkamati. Tassevaṃ abhikkamato ekekapāduddharaṇe pathvīdhātu āpodhātūti dve dhātuyo omattā honti mandā, itarā dve adhimattā honti balavatiyo; tathā atiharaṇavītiharaṇesu.* [*Vosajjane tejovāyodhātuyo omattā honti mandā, itarā dve adhimattā* [*honti*[MS]] *balavtiyo; tathā sannikkhepanasannirumbhanesu*[MS,MNCom'y]]. [*Vosajjane tejodhātu vāyodhātuti dve dhātuyo omattā honti mandā, itarā dve adhimattā balavtiyo; tathā sannikkhepanasannirujjhanesu*[DNCom'y]]. (Ps; Sv)

327. Literally: "The old mind vanishes and the new mind appears."

328. *Tattha uddharaṇe pavattā rūpārūpadhammā atiharaṇaṃ na pāpuṇanti, tathā atiharaṇe pavattā vītiharaṇaṃ vītiharaṇe pavattā vosajjanaṃ, vosajjane pavattā sannikkhepanaṃ, sannikkhepane pavattā sannirujjhanaṃ* [*sannirumbhanaṃ*] *na pāpuṇanti. Tattha tattheva pabbaṃ pabbaṃ sandhi sandhi odhi odhi hutvā tattakapāle pakkhittatilāni viya paṭapaṭāyantā bhijjanti. Tattha ko eko abhikkamati, kassa vā ekassa abhikkamanaṃ? Paramatthato hi dhātūnaṃyeva gamanaṃ, dhātūnaṃ ṭhānaṃ, dhātūnaṃ nisajjānaṃ, dhātūnaṃ sayanaṃ. Tasmiṃ tasmiṃ* [*hi*[MS]][*kaṭṭhāse MS*][*koṭṭhāseVRI*] *saddhiṃ rūpena.*

Aññaṃ upajjate cittaṃ, aññaṃ cittaṃ nirujjhati;
avīcimanusambandho, nadīsotova vattatīti.

Evaṃ abhikkamādīsu asammuyhaṃ asammohasampajaññaṃ nāmati. (Ps; Sv)

329. Mahāsi Sayadaw cites as an example: ". . . when standing, he understands: 'I am standing'" (*Ṭhitovāṭhitomhī'ti pajānāti*). (MN 10; DN 22)

330. *Eko hi bhikkhu gacchanto aññaṃ cintento aññaṃ vitakkento gacchati, eko kammaṭṭhānaṃ avisajjetvāva gacchati, tathā eko tiṭṭhanto, nisīdanto, sayanto, aññaṃ cintento aññaṃ vittakkento sayati, eko kammaṭṭhānaṃ avisajjetvāva sayati.* (Vibh-a)

331. *The Middle Length Discourses*, 147.
Ālokite vilokite sampajānakārī hoti. (MN 10; DN 22)

332. *Kammaṭṭhānassa pana avijahanameva gocarasampajaññaṃ. Tasmā* [*ettha*[DNCom'y]] *khandhadhātuāyatanakammaṭṭhānikehi attano kammaṭṭhānavaseneva, kasiṇādikammaṭṭhānikehi vā pana kammaṭṭhānasīseneva ālokanavilokanaṃ*[MNCom'y, SNCom'y,A-Com'y]][*ālokanaṃ vilokanaṃ*[DNCom'y]] *kātabbaṃ.* (Ps; Sv)

333. *The Middle Length Discourses*, 147.
   Samiñjite pasārite sampajānakārī . . . (MN 10; DN 22)
334. Ibid.
   Saṅghāṭipattacīvaradhāraṇe sampajānakārī . . .
335. Ibid.
   Asite pīte khāyite sāyite sampajānakārī . . .
336. Ibid.
   Uccārapassāvakamme sampajānakārī . . .
337. Ibid.
   Gate ṭhite nisinne sutte jāgarite bhāsite tuṇhībhāve sampajānakārī hoti.
338. In Burma strangers are addressed depending on their age. A woman who is about the same age as one's mother is addressed as "auntie," a man who is about the same age as one's grandfather is addressed as "grandfather," a child who is about the same age as one's child is addressed as "niece," a person who is about the same age as oneself is addressed as "sister" or "brother," and so on.
339. Ibid.
   Bahiddhā vā kāye kāyānupassī viharati . . .
340. Ibid.
   Ajjhattabahiddhā vā kāye kāyānupassī viharati . . .
341. Ibid.,
   Samudayadhammānupassī vā . . . *vayadhammānupassī vā kāyasmiṃ viharati* . . .
342. Ibid.
   . . . *Yathā yathā vā panassa kāyo panihito hoti, tathā tathā naṃ pajānāti.*
343. Ibid., 149.
   Sukhaṃ vā vedanaṃ vedayamāno "sukhaṃ vedanaṃ vedayāmī"ti pajānāti . . .
344. *Vatthuṃ ārammaṇaṃ katvā vedanāva vedayatīti sallakkhento esa "sukhaṃ vedanaṃ vedayāmīti pajānātī"ti veditabbo* . . . (Sv)
345. MN 44. See *The Middle Length Discourses*, 396–403.
346. DN 33. See *The Long Discourses*, 479–510.
347. MN 115. See *The Middle Length Discourses*, 925–30.
348. DN 21. See *The Long Discourses*, 321–34.
349. MN 10. See *The Middle Length Discourses*, 145–55.
350. *Adukkhamasukhā pana duddīpanā* [*andhakārāva* [MNCom'y]][*andhakarena viya* [DNCom'y]] [*andhakārā* [KN, ACom'ys]] *avibhūtā. Sā sukhadukkhānaṃ apagame sātāsātapaṭipakkhepavasena majjhattākārabhūtā adukkhamasukhā vedanāti nayato ganhantassa pākaṭā hoti.* (Ps; Sv)
351. *Duddīpanāti ñānena dīpetum asakkuneyyā, dubbiññeyyāti attho. Tenāha andhakārāva avibhūtāti.* (DN-ṭ)
352. *Sāmisaṃ vā sukhaṃ vedanaṃ vedayamāno sāmisaṃ sukhaṃ vedanaṃ vedayāmīti pajānāti* . . . (Ps; Sv)
353. *The Middle Length Discourses*, 1068.
   Rūpānaṃ tveva aniccataṃ viditvā viparināmavirāganirodhaṃ, "pubbe ceva rūpā tarahi ca sabbe te rūpā aniccā dukkhā vipariṇāmadhammā"ti evamevaṃ yathābhūtaṃ ammappaññāya passato uppajjati somanassaṃ. Yaṃ evarūpaṃ somanassaṃ idaṃ vuccati nekkhammasitaṃ somanassaṃ. (MN 137.11)
354. Ibid., 149.

Nirāmisaṃ vā sukhaṃ vedanaṃ vedayamāno "nirāmisaṃ sukhaṃ vedanaṃ vedayāmī"ti pajānāti. (MN 10; DN 22)

355. Ibid., 150.
Sāmisaṃ vā dukhaṃ vedanaṃ vedayamāno "sāmisaṃ sukhaṃ vedanaṃ vedayāmī"ti pajānāti.

356. Ibid.
Nirāmisaṃ vā dukkhaṃ vedanaṃ vedayamāno" nirāmisaṃ dukkhaṃ vedanaṃ vedayāmī"ti pajānāti.

357. Pavāraṇā is a ceremony at the end of the annual rains retreat wherein monks invite one another to make a kind remark concerning their moral conduct if they did something wrong during the annual rains retreat.

358. Ibid.
Sāmisaṃ vā adukkhamasukhaṃ vedanaṃ vedayamāno "sāmisaṃ adukkhamasukhaṃ vedanaṃ vedayāmī"ti pajānāti.

359. Ibid.
Nirāmisaṃ vā adukkhamasukhaṃ vedanaṃ vedayamāno "nirāmisaṃ dukkhamasukhaṃ vedanaṃ vedayāmī"ti pajānāti.

360. Ibid.
Samudayadhammānupassī vā . . . vayadhammānupassī vā vedanāsu viharati. . .

361. Ibid.
"Atthi vedanā"ti vā panassa sati paccupaṭṭhitā hoti.

362. Ibid.
Sarāgaṃ vā cittaṃ "sarāgaṃ cittan"ti pajānāti. Vītarāgaṃ vā cittaṃ "vītarāgaṃ cittan"ti pajānāti.

363. Ibid.
Sadosaṃ vā cittaṃ sadosaṃ cittanti pajānāti. Vītadosaṃ vā cittaṃ vītadosaṃ cittanti pajānāti.

364. Ibid.
Samohaṃ vā cittaṃ samohaṃ cittanti pajānāti, vītamohaṃ vā cittaṃ vītamohaṃ cittanti pajānāti.

365. *Yasmiṃ yasmiṃ khaṇe yaṃ yaṃ cittaṃ pavattati, taṃ taṃ sallakkhento attano vā citte, parassa vā citte, kālena vā attano, kālena vā parassa citte cittānupassasī viharati.* (Sv; Ps)

366. *The Middle Length Discourses*, 151.
Samudayadhammānupassī vā . . . vayadhammānupassī vā cittasmiṃ viharati (MN 10.35)

367. Ibid.
"Atthi cittan"ti vā panassa sati paccupaṭṭhitā hoti.

368. Ibid.
. . . . "Atthi me ajjhattaṃ kāmacchando"ti pajānāti.

369. Ibid.
. . . Santaṃ vā ajjhattaṃ byāpādaṃ . . . thinamiddhaṃ . . . uddhaccakukkuccaṃ . . . pajānāti.

370. For example, doubt about whether delusions result in formations and so on.

371. Ibid.
. . . Santaṃ vā ajjhattaṃ vicikicchaṃ "atthi me ajjhattaṃ vicikicchā"ti pajānāti.

372. Ibid.
. . . Santaṃ vā ajjhattaṃ vicikicchaṃ "atthi me ajjhattaṃ vicikicchā"ti pajānāti.

373. *Yoniso manasikāro nāma upāyamanasikāro pathamanasikāro. Anicce aniccanti vā, dukkhe dukkhanti vā, anattani anattāti vā asubhe asubhanti vā manasikāro.* (Ps; Sv)
374. *Yonisomanasikāro[nāma*[MS]*][. . .*[VRI]*]kusalādīnaṃ taṃtaṃsabhāvarasalakkhaṇa-ādikassa yāthāvato avabujjhanavasena uppanno ñāṇasampayuttacittuppādo. So hi aviparītamanasikāratāya "yonisomanasikāro"ti vutto, tadābhogatāya āvajjanāpi taggahikā eva.* (DN-ṭ)
375. *Ayonisomanasikāro nāma anupāyamanasikāro uppathamanasikāro. Anicce niccanti vā, dukkhe sukkhanti vā, anattani attāti vā, asubhe subhanti vā manasikāro.* (Ps; Sv)
376. See "Appendix 3: Stream of Consciousness."
377. *The Middle Length Discourses*, 151.

 Yathā ca anuppannassa kāmacchandassa uppādo hoti tañca pajānāti, yathā ca uppannassa kāmacchandassa pahānaṃ hoti tañca pajānāti, yathā ca pahīnassa kāmacchandassa āyatiṃ anuppādo hoti tañca pajānāti. (MN 10; DN 22)
378. Ibid.

 Iti rūpaṃ . . . ;iti vedanā . . . ;iti saññā . . . ;iti sankhārā . . . ;iti viññānaṃ . . .
379. *Iti rūpanti idaṃ rūpaṃ, ettakaṃ rūpaṃ, na ito paraṃ rūpaṃ atthīti sabhāvato rūpaṃ pajānāti. Vedanādīsupi eseva nayo.* (Sv)
380. *The Middle Length Discourses*, 151.

 Iti rūpassa samudayo, iti rūpassa atthaṅgamo.
381. Ibid.

 Iti vedanāya samudayo, iti vedanāya atthaṅgamo.
382. Ibid.

 Iti viññāṇassa samudayo, iti viññāṇassa atthaṅgamo.
383. Referring to the four reflections above; these reveal that the four causes of disappearance are: there is no craving, no kamma, and no individual causes such as nourishment, object, contact, and so on without ignorance.
384. See "Appendix 3: Stream of Consciousness," H2.
385. This etymology plays on the idea that the Pāḷi noun *nāma* has its origin in the verbal root √*nam*, which means "to bend or bow."
386. This etymology plays on the idea that the Pāḷi noun *rūpa* has its origin in the verbal root √*rup*, which means "to molest or violate."
387. *The Middle Length Discourses*, 153.

 Yañca tadubhayaṃ paticca uppajjati saṃyojanaṃ tañca pajānāti, yathā ca anuppannassa saṃyojanassa uppādo hoti tañca pajānāti, yathā ca uppannassa saṃyojanassa pahānaṃ hoti tañca pajānāti . . . (MN 10; DN 22)
388. Ibid.

 Yathā ca pahīnassa saṃyojanassa āyatiṃ anuppādo hoti, tañca pajānāti. . .
389. *The Dhammapada*, 91.

 Sabbaratiṃ dhammarati jināti. (Dhp 354)
390. *The Middle Length Discourses*, 153.

 Santaṃ vā ajjhattaṃ satisambojjhaṅgaṃ "atthi me ajjhattaṃ satisambojjhango"ti pajānāti . . . (MN 10; DN 22)
391. Ibid.

 Asantaṃ vā ajjhattaṃ satisambojjhangaṃ "natthi me ajjhattaṃ satisambojjhango"ti pajānāti . . .
392. Ibid.

 Yathā ca anuppannassa satisambojjhaṅgassa uppādo hoti, tañca pajānāti.
393. Ibid.

Yathā ca uppannassa satisambojaṅgassa bhāvanāya pāripūrī hoti, tañca pajānati.

394. The word *dukkha* is generally translated with the English words suffering, unsatisfactoriness, distress, or affliction. The Pāḷi word, however, also connotes impermanence, insubstantiality, unsatisfactoriness, emptiness, imperfection, and insecurity.

395. Ibid., 278.
Jātipi dukkhā, jarāpi dukkhā, maranampi dukkhaṃ (MN 28, 141; DN 22; AN 6.63; etc.)

396. Attachment (*taṇhā*) is technically not considered suffering because it is regarded as the origin of suffering.

397. *The Connected Discourses*, 1271.
Taṃ kho panetaṃ bhikkhu mayā saṅkhārānaṃyeva aniccataṃ sandhāya bhāsitaṃ—"yaṃ kiñci vedayitaṃ, taṃ dukkhasmin"ti... (SN 36.11)

398. *The Numerical Discourses*, 964.
Saṃkhittena pañcupādānakkhandhā dukkhā. (AN 6.63)

399. See "Appendix 3: Stream of Consciousness," at death of an ordinary unenlightened being.

400. *The Middle Length Discourses*, 135.
Yāyaṃ tanhā ponobbhavikā nandīrāgasahagatā... (MN 9, 44, 141; etc.)

401. *The Connected Discourses*, 1844.
Yo tassāyeva taṇhāya asesavirāganirodho... (SN 56.11)

402. This passage is not a literal translation but includes explanations by Mahāsi Sayadaw.

403. *Tattha purimāni dve saccāni vaṭṭaṃ pacchimāni vivaṭṭaṃ. Tesu bhikkhuno vaṭṭe kammaṭṭhānābhiniveso hoti, vivaṭṭe natthi abhiniveso. Purimāni hi dve saccāni "pañcakkhandhā dukkhaṃ, tanhā samudayo"ti evaṃ saṅkhepena ca, "katame pañcakkhandhā, rūpakkhandho"ti-ādinā nayena vitthārena ca ācariyassa santike uggaṇhitvā vācāya punappunaṃ parivattento yogāvacaro kammaṃ karoti. Itaresu pana dvīsu saccesu—"nirodhasaccaṃ iṭṭhaṃ kantaṃ manāpaṃ, maggasaccaṃ iṭṭhaṃ kantaṃ manāpan"ti evaṃ savanena kammaṃ karoti. So evaṃ karonto cattāri saccāni ekapaṭivedhena paṭivijjhati ekābhisamayena abhisameti. Dukkhaṃpariññāpativedena pativijjhati, samudayaṃ pahānapaṭivedhena pativijjhati, nirodhaṃ achikiriyāpaṭivedhena, [pativijjhati*[MS]*], maggaṃ bhāvanāpaṭivedena pativijjhati. Dukkhaṃ pariññābhisamayena [abhisameti. Samudayaṃ phānābhisamayena. Nirodhaṃ sacchikiriyābhisạmayena.*[MS]] [... *pe*...[VRI]] *Maggaṃ bhāvanābhisamayena abhisameti. Evamassa pubbabhāge dvīsu saccesu uggahaparipucchāsavanadhāraṇasammasanapaṭivedho hoti, dvīsu panasavannapaṭivedhoyeva. Aparabhāge tīsu kiccato paṭivedho hoti, nirodhe ārammanappaṭivedho.* (Sv)

404. *Addhā imāya paṭipadāya jarāmaraṇamhā parimuccissāmī.* (Dhs-a)

405. *Vaṭṭe kammaṭṭhānābhiniveso sarūpato pariggahasabbhāvato. Vivaṭṭe natthi avisayattā, visayatte ca payojanābhāvato*[...[MS]] *Iṭṭhaṃ kantanti nirodhamaggesu ninnabhāvaṃ dasseti, na abhinandanaṃ, tanninnabhāvoyeva ca tattha kammakaraṇaṃ daṭṭhabbaṃ.* (DN-ṭ)

406. *The Middle Length Discourses*, 154.
Idaṃ dukkhanti yathābhūtaṃ pajānāti. (MN 10; DN 22)

407. The three worlds are the sense sphere (*kāma*), the fine material sphere (*rūpa*), and the immaterial sphere (*arūpa*).

408. *Ṭhapetvā taṇhaṃ tebhūmakadhamme idaṃ dukkhan"ti yathāsabhāvato pajānāti.* (Ps; Sv)

409. *Yathāsabhāvatoti aviparītasabhāvato. Bādhanasakkhaṇato yo yo vā sabhāvo yathāsabhāvo, tato, ruppanādi kakkhaḷādisabhāvato.* (DN-ṭ)

410. *The Connected Discourses*, 158.

"Yattha [nu[AN]*] kho āvuso na jāyati na jiyyati na mīyati na cavati na upapajjati, nā'haṃ taṃ gamanena lokassa antaṃ ñāteyyaṃ diṭṭheyyaṃ patteyyanti vadāmi'"ti . . . a kho panāhaṃ āvuso appatvā lokassa antaṃ dukkhassa antakiriyaṃ vadāmi. Api ca khvāhaṃ āvuso, imasmimyeva byāmamatte kalevare sasaññimhi samānake lokañca paññapemi, lokasamudayañca, lokanirodhañca, lokanirodhagāminiñca patipadaṃ . . ."* (SN:2.26)

411. *Lokanti dukkhasaccaṃ. Lokasamudayanti samudayasaccaṃ. Lokanirodhanti nirodhasaccaṃ. Paṭipadanti maggasaccaṃ. Iti "nāhaṃ āvuso, imāni cattāri saccāni tinakaṭṭhādīsu paññapemi, imasmiṃ pana cātumahābhūtike kāyasmiṃyeva paññapemī"ti dasseti.* (Spk)

412. *Sasantatipariyāpannānaṃ dukkhasamudayānaṃ appavattibhāvena pariggayhamāno nirodhopi sasantatipariyāpanno viya hotīti katvā vuttaṃ "attano vā cattāri saccānī"ti. Parassa vāti etthāpi eseva nayo.* (DN-ṭ)

413. *Tasseva kho pana dukkhassa janikaṃ samuṭṭhāpikaṃ purimataṇhaṃ "ayaṃ dukkhasamudayo"ti.* (Sv)

414. This includes experiences such as seeing, bending, and so on.

415. This shows that unpleasant feeling is the type of truth of suffering that is especially easy to understand.

416. *Dukkhasaccañhi uppattito pākaṭaṃ. Khānukaṇṭakapahārādīsu "aho dukkhan"ti vattabbatampi āpajjati. Samudaympi khāditukāmatābhuñjitu-kāmatādivasena uppattito pākataṃ. Lakkhanapaṭivedato pana ubhayampi [taṃ*[SNCom'y]*] gambhīraṃ. Iti tāni duddasattā gambhīrāni.* (Sv and Spk)

417. *'Duddasattā'ti attano pavattikkhaṇavasena pākaṭānipi pakatiñāṇena sabhāvarasato daṭṭhuṃ asakkuṇeyyattā. Gambhīreneva ca bhāvanāñāṇena, tathāpi matthakapattena ariyamaggañāṇeneva yāthāvato passitabbattā gambhīrāni.* (Sv)

418. See also *The Path of Discrimination*, 60.

. . . *"Uppādo bhayaṃ, anuppādo kheman"ti* . . . (Paṭis 1.300)

419. See also *The Path of Purification*, 654–55.

Yañcassa udayabbayadassanaṃ, maggovāyaṃ lokikoti maggasaccaṃ pākaṭaṃ hoti. . . (Vism 20.100)

420. *Ñāyo vuccati ariyo aṭṭhaṅgiko maggo, tassa adhigamāya, pattiyāti vuttaṃ hoti. Ayañhi pubbabhāge lokiyo satipaṭṭhānamaggo bhāvito lokuttaramaggassa adhigamāya samvattati.* (Ps and Sv)

421. *Pahānameva vuttanayena paṭivedhoti pahānappaṭivedho.* (MN-ṭ and DN-ṭ)

422. See also *The Path of Purification*, 696.

Tattha paṭhamamaggañāṇaṃ tāva sampādetukāmena aññaṃ kiñci kātabbaṃ nāma natthi. Yañhi anena kātabbaṃ siyā, taṃ anulomāvasānaṃ vipassanaṃ uppādentena katameva. (Vism 12.3)

423. An Abhidhamma commentary.

424. *Esa lokuttaro ariyo atthaṅgiko maggo. Yo saha lokiyena maggena dukkhanirodhagāminīpatipadāti saṅkhyaṃ gato,* . . . (Vibh-a)

425. *Nānāntariyabhāvena panettha lokiyāpi gahitāva honti lokiyasamathavipassanāya vinā tadabhāvato.* (Vism-mhṭ)

426. *The Connected Discourses*, 180–81.

Idhānanda bhikkhu sammādiṭṭhiṃ bhāveti vivekanissitaṃ virāganissitaṃ nirodhanissitaṃ vosaggapariṇāmiṃ, sammāsaṅkappaṃ bhāveti . . . pe . . . sammāvācaṃ bhāveti . . . pe . . . sammākammantaṃ bhāveti . . . pe . . . sammā-ājīvam bhāveti . . .pe. . . sammāvāyāmaṃ bhāveti. . .pe. . . sammāsatiṃ bhāveti . . .pe. . . sammāsamādhiṃ bhāveti vivekanissitaṃ virāganissitaṃ nirodhanissitaṃ vosaggaparināmiṃ. Evaṃ kho Ānanda bhikkhu kalyāṇamitto kalyānasahāyo kalyānasampavaṅko ariyaṃ atthaṅgikaṃ maggaṃ bhāveti, ariyaṃ atthangikaṃ maggaṃ bahulīkaroti. (SN:3.18)

427. *Vivekanissitanti tadaṅgavivekanissitaṃ, samucchedavivekanissitaṃ, nissaranavivekanissitañca sammādiṭṭhiṃ bhāvetīti ayamattho veditabbo. Tathā hi ayaṃ ariyamaggabhāvanānuyutto yogī vipassanākkhaṇe kiccato tadangavivekanissitaṃ, ajjhāsayato nissaranavivekanissitaṃ, maggakāle pana kiccato samucchedavivekanissitaṃ, ārammaṇato nissaranavivekanissitaṃ, sammādiṭṭhiṃ bhāveti. Esa nayo virāganissitādīsu.*

Vivekatthā eva hi virāgādayo. Kevalañhettha vosaggo duvidho pariccāgavosaggo ca pakkhandanavosaggo cāti. Tattha pariccāgavosaggoti vipassanakkhane ca tadaṅgavasena, maggakkhaṇe ca samucchedavasena kilesappahānaṃ. Pakkhandanavosaggoti vipassanakkhaṇe tanninnabhāvena, maggakkhane pana ārammaṇakaraṇena nibbānapakkhandanaṃ, tadubhayampi imasmiṃ lokiyalokuttaramissake atthasamvaṇṇanānaye vattati.

Tathā hi ayaṃ sammādiṭṭhi yathāvuttena pakārena kilese ca pariccajati, nibbānaca pakkhandati. Vosaggapariṇāmin'ti iminā pana sakala vacanena vosaggatthaṃ pariṇamantaṃ parinatañca, paripaccantaṃ paripakkañcāti idaṃ vuttaṃ hoti. Ayañhi ariyamaggabhāvanānuyutto bhikkhu yathā sammādiṭṭhi kilesapariccāgavossaggatthaṃ nibbānapakkhandanavosaggatthañca paripaccati, yathā ca paripakkā hoti. Tathā naṃ bhāvetīti. Esa nayo sesamaggaṅgesu. (Spk)

428. *Esa nayo sesamaggaṅgesu . . .* (Vibh-a)

429. *Sammāvācādayo tayo [pubbabhāge*[AN Com'y, Psm Com'y]] [*musāvādāveramaṇītiādivibhāgā*[UdCom'y]] [*pubbabhāge nānākkhaṇā nānārammaṇā*[Abhi. Com'y]] *viratiyopi honti cetanādayopi maggakkhaṇe pana viratiyova.*

430. A commentary on the Abhidhamma.

431. *Sikkhāpadavibhaṅge "viraticetanā, sabbe sampayuttadhammā ca sikkhāpadānī"ti vuttāti [vuccantīti*[DNÁi]] *tattha padhānānaṃ viraticetanānaṃ vasena "viratiyopi honti cetanāyopī"ti āha. Musāvādādībhi viramanakāle vā viratiyo, subhāsitādivācābhāsanādikāle ca cetanāyo yojetabbā.* (DN-ṭ)

432. *Sammāvācādayo tayo [pubbabhāge*[AN Com'y,] *Psm Com'y*] [*musāvādāveramaṇītiādivibhāgā*[UdCom'y]] [*pubbabhāge nānākkhaṇā nānārammaṇā*[Abhi. Com'y]] *viratiyopi honti cetanādayopi maggakkhaṇe pana viratiyova.* (DN-ṭ)

433. *Tattha assāsapassāsapariggāhikā sati dukkhasaccaṃ, tassā samuṭṭhāpikā purimataṇhā samudayasaccaṃ ubhinnaṃ appavatti nirodhasaccaṃ, dukkhaparijānano, samudayappajahāno, nirodhārammaṇo ariyamaggo maggasaccaṃ. Evaṃ catusaccavasena ussakkitvā nibbutiṃ pāpunātīti idamekassa assāsapassāsavasena abhiniviṭṭhassa bhikkhuno yāva arahattā niyyānamukhanti.* (Sv)

434. *Sā pana sati yasmiṃ attabhāve, tassa samutthāpikā tanhā, tassāpi samutthāpikā nāma hoti tadabhāve abhāvatoti āha "tassā samutthāpikā purimataṇhā"ti, yathā "saṅkhārapaccayā [viññāṇan*[MS]]*"ti. Tamviññāṇavījataṃsantatisambhūto sabbopi lokiyo viññāṇappabandho "sankhārapaccayā viññāṇaṃ" teva vuccati suttantanayena.* (DN-ṭ)

435. See *The Path of Purification*, 176.

Addhā imāya paṭipadāya jarāmaraṇamhā parimuccissāmi . . . (Vism 6.22)

436. *Ekayāna*. Ven. Bhikkhu Bodhi translates this word as "direct path," but it can also be read as Mahāsi Sayadaw has read it, "the only way" or "the only path."

437. *The Middle Length Discourses*, 155. (Translation modified according to Mahāsi Sayadaw's reading.)

    Ekāyano ayaṃ bhikkhave maggo sattānaṃ visuddhiya, sokaparidevānaṃ samtikkamāya, dukkhadomanassānaṃ atthaṅgamāya, ñāyassa adhigamāya, nibbānassa sacchikiriyāya, yadidaṃ cattāro satipaṭṭhānā. (MN 10; DN 22)

438. *Ekāyano ayaṃ bhikkhave maggoti ettha ekamaggo ayaṃ, bhikkhave, maggo na dvidhā pathabhūtoti evamattho daṭṭhabbo.* (Ps and Sv)

439. *Ekamaggoti eko eva maggo. Na hi nibbānagāmimaggo añño atthīti. Nanu satipaṭṭhānaṃ idha maggoti adhippetaṃ, tadaññe ca bahū maggadhammā atthīti? Saccaṃ atthi, te pana satipaṭṭhānaggahaneneva gahitā, uddese pana satiyā eva gahaṇaṃ veneyajjhāsayavasenāti daṭṭhabbaṃ. "Na dvidhāpathabhūto"ti iminā imassa maggassa anekamaggabhāvābhāvaṃ viya anibbānagāmibhāvābhavañca dasseti.* (DN-ṭ)

440. *The Middle Length Discourses*, 155.

    Yo hi koci bhikkhave ime cattāro satipaṭṭhāne evaṃ bhāveyya sattāhaṃ, tassa dvinnaṃ phalānaṃ aññataraṃ phalaṃ pātikaṅkhaṃ diṭṭheva dhamme aññā; sati vā upādisese anāgāmitāti. (MN 10; DN 22)

441. MN 85. See *The Middle Length Discourses*, 704–9.

442. Ibid., 708.

    Imehi pañcahi padhāniyaṅgehi samannāgato bhikkhu tathāgataṃ vināyakaṃ labhamāno sāyamanusiṭṭho pāto visesaṃ adhigamissati, pātamanusiṭṭho sāyaṃ visesaṃ adhigamissati. (MN 85)

443. *Advejjhavacanā buddhā, amoghavacanā jinā* . . . (Buddhavamsa)

444. SN 47.16. See *The Connected Discourses*, 1646.

445. U Pe Thin and Myanaung U Tin have produced a fine translation of this chapter under the title *Practical Insight Meditation* (Kandy: Buddhist Publication Society, 1971). Readers familiar with that work will notice some differences in language and substance in our translation. We have tried as much as possible in this book to retain Mahāsi Sayadaw's original wording and style and have corrected a number of translation errors or omissions that appear in the earlier translation.

446. *The Connected Discourses*, 890.

    Rūpaṃ bhikkhave, yoniso manasi karotha, rūpāniccatañca yathābhūtaṃ samanupassatha. (SN 22.52)

447. Ibid., 889.

    [*Aniccaññeva*[Kvg]][*Aniccaññeva* Svg], *bhikkhave bhikkhu* [*Rūpaṃ*[Kvg]][*Rūpe*[Kvg]] *aniccanti passati. Sāssa hoti sammādiṭṭhi.* (SN 22.51)

448. Ibid., 1218.

    Phoṭṭhabbe, bhikkhave, bhikkhu yoniso manasikaronto. Phoṭṭhabbāniccatañca yathābhūtaṃ samanupassanto. (SN 35.159)

449. Ibid., 1217.

    Anicceyeva, bhikkhave, bhikkhu phoṭṭhabbe aniccāti passati, sāssa hoti sammāditthi. (SN 35.157)

450. Ibid., 1187.

    Phoṭṭhabbe . . . abhijānaṃ parijānaṃ virājayaṃ pajahaṃ bhabbo dukkhakkhayāyā. (SN 35.112)

    Mahāsi Sayadaw's reading of this passage is as follows: "Directly knowing, realizing, disowning, and abandoning tangible objects leads to the end of suffering, *arahatta* fruition knowledge, and *nibbāna*."

451. Ibid., 1148.
[Phoṭṭhabbe[MS]*] aniccato jānato passato avijjā pahīyati, vijjā uppajjati.* (SN 35.53)

452. *The Middle Length Discourses*, 282.
Yā ceva kho pana ajjhattikā vāyodhātu, yā ca bāhirā vāyodhātu vāyodhāturevesā. Taṃ "netaṃ mama; nesohamasmi, na meso attā"ti- evametaṃ yathābhūtaṃ sammappaññāya daṭṭhabbaṃ. (MN 28, 62, and 140)

453. *The Connected Discourses*, 1847.
Dukkhaṃ, bhikkhave, ariyasaccaṃ pariññeyyaṃ (SN 56.12)

454. *The Middle Length Discourses*, 146.
. . . *Yathā yathā vā panassa kāyo paṇihito hoti, tathā tathā naṃ pajānāti.* (MN 10; DN 22)
Mahāsi Sayadaw reads this passage to mean: "Whatever posture the body is in, be aware of it as it really is."

455. This describes the outdoor bathing commonly done in Burma where no hot and cold running water is piped into an interior shower stall. Use similar noting of all actions involved in bathing if using modern indoor plumbing.

456. This describes the traditional way of eating with one's fingers that is common in Burma, particularly in monasteries. When eating with utensils, the same meticulous noting of every moment of seeing, smelling, intention to lift a utensil of food, lifting, opening the mouth, placing food in the mouth, closing the mouth, withdrawing the utensil, lowering the utensil, beginning to chew, chewing, tasting, swallowing, and so on should be noted throughout the entire meal.

457. See also *The Path of Purification*, 609.
Yathā yathā hissa rūpaṃ suvikkhālitaṃ hoti nijjaṭaṃ suparisuddhaṃ, tathā tathā tadārammaṇā arūpadhammā sayameva pākaṭā honti. (Vism 18.15)

458. *The Path of Purification*, 631 and 650.
Aniccaṃ khayaṭṭhena . . . hutvā abhāvato aniccā (Vism 20.14 and 20.84)

459. Y*adaniccaṃ taṃ dukkhaṃ . . . dukkhaṃ bhayaṭṭhena . . . udayabbayappīḷanato dukkha* (Ps and Sv)

460. *The Numerical Discourses*, 507.
dukkhavatthutāya . . . rogato . . . gaṇḍato . . . sallato . . . (AN 4.124)

461. *Anattā*. Bhikkhu Bodhi here translates this term as "nonself." We have altered it to maintain consistency with Mahāsi Sayadaw's usage of the term in this translation.

462. *The Connected Discourses*, 869.
Yaṃ dukkhaṃ tadanattā (SN 22.15)

463. *The Path of Purification*, 631.
. . . *Anattā asārakaṭṭhena* . . . (Vism 20.16)

464. . . . *Avasavattanato anattā.* (Mp)

465. *Practical Insight Meditation* at this point says: "By and large, these are feelings hard to bear." However, the correct translation of Mahāsi Sayadaw's original Burmese is as written here.

466. The six kinds of conditioned mental and physical phenomena are, in order of frequency: touching, knowing, hearing, seeing, tasting, and smelling.

467. *A Comprehensive Manual of Abhidhamma*, 248. (Translation modified.)
appanājavanaṃ iriyāpathampi sannāmeti. (Abhid-s 6.11)

468. The Pāḷi word *pāramī* is usually translated as "perfection." However, its literal meaning is "deeds of a noble person" (*paramānaṃ uttamapurisanaṃ bhāvo kammaṃ*). The word specifically refers to the qualities of generosity, morality, renunciation, wisdom, effort, patience, honesty, determination, loving-kindness, and equanimity. The potential for these qualities lies dormant in one's mental processes throughout the life cycle.

469. This is Mahāsi Sayadaw's own Pāḷi composition:
Bhāvetabbā satacevaṃ, satipaṭṭhānabhāvanā,vipassanā rasassādaṃ, patthentenīdha.

470. *The Connected Discourses*, 620.
Yathābhūtam ñāṇāya satthā pariyesitabbo. (SN 12.82)

471. Ibid., 717.
Nayidaṃ sithilamārabbha nayidam appena thāmasā;
Nibbānaṃ adhigantabbaṃ sabbadukkhappamocanaṃ. (SN 21.4)

472. See also *The Path of Purification*, 605.
Nāmarūpānaṃ yāthāvadassanaṃ diṭṭhivisuddhi nāma. (Vism 18.3)

473. The Pāḷi term *abyākata* (or *avyākata*) literally means "indeterminate" or "neutral" as in *avyākatakamma*, "neutral or indeterminate kamma."

474. "*Acetano abyākato*"*ti ettha viya anārammaṇatā vā abyākatatā daṭṭhabbā.* (Vism-subcommentary)

475. *The Path of Purification*, 614.
Na cakkhāto jāyare phassapañcamā, na rūpato no ca ubhinnamantarā; hetuṃ paṭiccappabhavanti saṅkhatā, yathāpi saddho pahaṭāya bheriyā. (Vism 18.33)

476. Ibid.
Na sotato jāyare phassapañcamā, na saddato no ca ubhinnamantarā;
hetuṃ paṭiccappabhavanti saṅkhatā, yathāpi saddho pahaṭāya bheriyā.
Na ghānato jāyare phassapañcamā, na gandhato no ca ubhinnamantarā
hetuṃ paṭiccappabhavanti saṅkhatā, yathāpi saddho pahaṭāya bheriyā.
Na jivhato jāyare phassapañcamā, na rasato no ca ubhinnamantarā;
hetuṃ paṭiccappabhavanti saṅkhatā, yathāpi saddho pahaṭāya bheriyā.
Na kāyato jāyare phassapañcamā, na phassato no ca ubhinnamantarā;
hetuṃ paṭiccappabhavanti saṅkhatā, yathāpi saddho pahaṭāya bheriyā.
Na vatthurūpā pabhavanti saṅkhatā, na cāpi dhammāyatanehi niggahitā;
hetuṃ paṭiccapabhavanti saṅkhatā, yathāpi saddo pahaṭāya bheriyā. (Vism 18.33)

477. See also ibid.
Atha kho nāmaṃ nissāya rūpaṃ pavattati, rūpaṃ nissāya nāmaṃ pavattati, nāmassa khāditukāmatāya pivitukāmatāya, byāharitukāmatāya, iriyāpathaṃ kappetukāmatāya sati rūpaṃ khādati, pivati, byāharati, iriyāpathaṃ kappeti. (Vism 18.34)

478. See also ibid., 612–13.
Tasmā yathā akkhacakkapañjara-īsādīsu aṅgasambhāresu ekenākārena saṇṭhitesu rathoti vohāramattaṃ hoti, paramatthato ekekeasmiṃ aṅge upaparekkhiyamāne ratho nāma natthi. Yathā ca kaṭṭhādīsu gehasambhāresu ekenākārena ākāsaṃ parivāretvā ṭhitesu gehanti vohāranaṃ hoti, paramatthato gehaṃ nāma natthi. Yathā ca aṅguli-aṅguṭṭhādīsu ekenākārena ṭhitesu muṭṭhīti vohāramattaṃ hoti. Doṇitanti-ādīsu vīṇāti. Hatthi-assādīsu senāti. Pākāragehagopurādīsu nagaranti. kahandasākhāpalāsādīsu ekenākāreana

ṭhitesu rukkhoti vohāranaṃ hoti, paramatthato ekekasmiṃ avayave upaparikkhiyamāne rukkho nāma natthi. Evamevaṃ pañcasu upādanakkhandesu sati "sato puggalo"ti vohāramattaṃ hoti, paramatthato ekekasmiṃ dhamme upaparikkhiyamāne "asmīti vā ahanti vā"ti gāhassa vattthubhūto satto nāma natthi. Paramatthato pana nāmarūpamattameva atthīti. Evaṃ passato hi dassanaṃ yathābhūtadassanaṃ nāma hoti. (Vism 18.28)

479. *Nāmarūpānaṃ yāthāvadassananti "idaṃ nāmaṃ, ettakaṃ nāmaṃ, na ito bhiyyo. Idaṃ rūpaṃ, ettakaṃ rūpaṃ, na ito bhiyyo"ti ca tesaṃ lakkhaṇasallakkhaṇamukhena dhammamattabhāvadassanaṃ attadiṭṭhimalavisodhanato diṭṭhivisuddhīti veditabbaṃ.* (Vism-mhṭ)

480. See also *The Path of Purification*, 617.

    Etasseva pana nāmarūpassa paccayapariggahaṇena tīsu addhāsu kaṅkhaṃ vitaritvā ṭhitaṃ ñāṇaṃ kaṅkhāvitaraṇavisuddhināma. (Vism 19.1)

481. Ibid.

    So evaṃ paccayato nāmarūpassa pavattiṃ disvā, yathā edaṃ etarahi, evaṃ atītepi addhāne paccayato pavattittha, anāgatepi paccayato pavattissatīti samanupassati. (Vism 19.3)

482. Ibid., 622.

    Attābhinivesūpanissayā hi "ahosiṃ nu kho ahan"ti-ādi nayappavattā soḷasavutthukā kaṅkhā. (Vism 19.19)

483. See "Appendix 3: Stream of Consciousness."

484. See also *The Path of Discrimination*, 52.

    Purimakammabhavasmiṃ moho avijjā, āyūhanā saṅkhārā nikanti taṇhā, upagamanaṃ upādānaṃ, cetanā bhavoti ime pañca dhammā purimakammabhavasmiṃ idha paṭisandhiyā paccayā. (Paṭis 1.275)

485. The term attachment (*nikanti*) as used here specifically refers to attachment to new life that is a specific mental process preceding the relinking mental process. See "Appendix 3: Stream of Consciousness," H22.

486. See *The Path of Discrimination*, 52.

    Idha paṭisandhi viññāṇaṃ, okkanti nāmarūpaṃ, pasādo āyatanaṃ, phuṭṭho phasso, vedayitaṃvedanā, [iti [ma. ni. aṭṭha.,abhi. ṭī, Vism2.213–14]*] ime pañca dhammā idhupapatthibhavasmiṃ pure katassa kammassa paccayā.* (Paṭis 1.275)

487. *Yatheva cakkhuviññāṇaṃ, manodhātu-anantaraṃ; na ceva āgataṃ nāpi, na nibbattaṃ anantaraṃ.*

    Thateva paṭisandhimhi, vattate cittasantati; purimaṃ bhijjate cittaṃ, pacchimaṃ jāyate tato. (Sammohavinodaniyā)

488. See *The Path of Purification*, 52.

    Idha paripakkattā āyatanānaṃ moho avijjā, āyūhanā saṅkhārā, nikanti tanhā, upagamanaṃ upādānam, cetanā bhavoti, ime pañca dhammā idha kammabhavasmiṃ āyatiṃ patisandhiyā paccayā. (Paṭis 1.275)

489. See also ibid.

    Āyatiṃ paṭisandhi viññāṇaṃ, okkanti nāmarūpaṃ, pasādo āyatanaṃ, phuttho phasso, vedayitaṃ vedanā, [iti [ma. ni. aṭṭha.,abhi. ṭī, Vism 2.214]*] ime pañca dhammā āyatiṃ upapaṭṭhibhavasmiṃ idha katassa kammassa paccayā.* (Paṭis 1.275)

490. *The Path of Purification*, 621. (Translation modified.)

    So evaṃ kammavaṭṭavipākavaṭṭavasena paccayato nāmarūpassa pavattiṃ disvā, "yathā idaṃ etarahi, evaṃ atītepi addhāne kammavaṭṭavipākavaṭṭavasena paccayato pavattittha, anāgatepi kammavaṭṭavipākavaṭṭavaseneva paccayato pavattissatī"ti. Iti kammañceva kammavipāko ca, kammavaṭṭañca

vipākavaṭṭañca, kammapavattañca vipākapavattañca, kammasantati ca vipākasantati ca, kiriyā ca kiriyaphalañca.
Kammā vipākā vattanti, vipāko kammasambhavo;
kammā punabbhavo hoti, evaṃ loko pavattatī'ti.—samanupassati. (Vism 19.18)

491. Ibid., 622. (Translation modified.)
Kammassa kārako natthi, vipākassa ca vedako;
suddhadhammā pavattanti, evetaṃ sammadassanaṃ.
Evaṃ kamme vipāke ca, vattamāne sahetuke;
bījarukkhādikānaṃva, pubbā koṭī na nāyati;
anāgatepi saṃsāre, [appavatti[MS, Abhi. ṭī.]*][appavattaṃ*[VRI]*] na dissati.* (Vism 19.20)

492. See for example *The Numerical Discourses*, 963: "It is volition, bhikkhus, that I call kamma."
Cetanāhaṃ bhikkhave kammaṃ vadāmi. (AN 6.63)

493. That is, volitional action is not transformed into its results, like yarn that is transformed into a sweater.

494. *The Path of Purification*, 622–23. (Translation modified.)
Kammaṃ natthi vipākamhi, pāko kamme na vijjati.
Aññamaññaṃ ubho suññā, na ca kammaṃ vinā phalaṃ . . .
. . . kammañca kho upādāya, tato nibbatate phalaṃ . . .
. . . Na hettha devo brahmā vā, saṃsārassatthikārako;
suddhadhammā pavattanti, hetusambhārapaccayā. (Vism 19.20)

495. See also ibid., 623.
Sabbe atītānāgatapaccuppannādhammā cutipaṭisandhivasena viditā honti. . . .Evaṃcutipaṭisandhivasena viditasabbadhammassa sabbākārena nāmarūpassa paccayapariggahañāṇaṃ thāmagataṃ hoti. (Vism 19.21)

496. See also ibid., 625.
Iminā pana ñāṇena samannāgato vipassako buddhasāsane laddhassāso laddhapatiṭṭho niyatagatiko cūlasotāpanno nāma hoti. (Vism 19.27)

497. *Aparihīnakaṅkhāvitaraṇavisuddhiko vipassako lokiyāhi sīlasamādhipaññāsampadāhi samannāgatattā uttari appaṭivijjhanto sugatiparāyaṇo hotīti vuttaṃ "niyatagatiko"ti. Tato eva cūlasotāpanno nāma hoti.* (Vism-mhṭ)

498. MN 81. See *The Middle Length Discourses*, 669–76.

499. *The Connected Discourses*, 100.
Sattiyā viya omaṭṭho, ḍayhamānova matthake;
sakkāyadiṭṭhipahānāya, sato bhikkhu paribbaje. (SN 1.21)

500. See also *The Path of Discrimination*, 3.
Atītānāgatapaccuppannānaṃ dhammānaṃ saṅkhipitvā vavatthāne paññā sammane ñāṇaṃ. (Paṭis 1.0)

501. *Ekasaṅkhārassāpi aniccatāya diṭṭhāya sabbe saṅkhārā aniccāti avasesesu nayato manasikāro hoti . . . "sabbe sankhārā aniccā"ti ādivacanaṃ . . .nayato dassanaṃ sandhāya vuttaṃ. Na ekakkhaṇe ārammaṇato.* (Vibhaṅga Aṭṭhakathā)

502. See also *The Path of Discrimination*, 53.
Yaṃ kiñci rūpaṃ atītānāgatapaccuppannaṃ, ajjhattaṃ vā, bahiddhā vā, olārikam vā, sukhumaṃ vā, nīnaṃ vā, panītaṃ vā, yaṃ dūre vā, santike vā, sabbaṃ rūpaṃ aniccato vavattheti ekaṃ sammasanaṃ, dukkhato vavattheti, ekaṃ sammasanaṃ, anattato vavattheti, ekaṃ sammasanaṃ. (Paṭis 1.278)

503. Ibid.

Rūpaṃatītānāgatapaccuppannaṃ aniccaṃ khayatthena, dukkhaṃ bhayatthena, anattā asārakaṭṭhenāti saṅkhipitvā vavatthāne paññā sammasane ñāṇam. (Paṭis 1.278)

504. Ibid.

Rūpamatītānāgatapaccuppannaṃ aniccaṃ saṅkhataṃ paticcasamuppannaṃ khayadhammaṃ vayadhammaṃ virāgadhammaṃ nirodhadhammanti sankhippitvā vavatthāne paññā sammasane ñāṇaṃ. (Paṭis 1.280)

505. Such as in the non-Buddhist texts like the *Visesikadassana* of the Hindu Vaiśeṣika school, the *Nyāyadassana* of the Hindu Nyāya school, and so on.
506. SN 22:59. See *The Connected Discourses*, 901–3.
507. *The Connected Discourses*, 901.

Rūpaṃ, bhikkhave, anattā. Rūpañca hidaṃ, bhikkhave, attā abhavissa, nayidaṃ rūpaṃ ābādhāya saṃvatteyya, labbhetha ca rūpe—"evaṃ me rūpaṃ hotu, evaṃ me rūpaṃ mā ahosī"ti. (SN 22.59)

508. *Tathānidassanaṃ pana [dhammasabhāvavinimuttassa*[MS, Áikā-co-pāḷi]*][dhammasabhāvato aññassa*[Abhi. pu. abhi. ṭī.]*] kattādino abhāvadīpanatthanti veditabbaṃ.* (Abhidhammatthavibhāvinī)
509. *Yathā andha[bāla*[dī. ni. aṭṭha., Abhi. aṭṭha.]*] puthujjanā abhikkamādīsu—"attā abhikkamati, attanā abhikkamo nibbatto"ti vā, "ahaṃ abhikkamāmi, mayā abhikkamo nibbattito"ti vā sammuyhanti, tathā asammuyhanto. . . .* (Abhidhammatthavibhāvinī)
510. *Abbhantare attā nāma āloketā vā, viloketā vā natthi . . . Abbhantare attā nāma koci [samiñjanto*[MS]*][samiñjento*[VRI]*] vā pasārento vā natthi.* (Abhidhammatthavibhāvinī)
511. Note that this subcommentary also rejects the idea of a self who is the "doer."
512. *Ko vedayatīti? Na koci satto vā, puggalo vā vedayati . . . tasmā esa evaṃ pajānāti "taṃ taṃ sukhādīnaṃ vatthuṃ ārammanaṃ katvā vedanāva vedayati taṃ pana vedanāpavattiṃ [vedanāya pavattiṃ*[dī. ni. aṭṭha.]*] upādāya'aham vedayāmī'ti vohāramattaṃ hotī"ti* (Ps)
513. *Dhammavinimuttassa aññassa kattu abhāvato dhammasseva kattubhāvaṃ dassento "vedanāva vedayatī"ti āha.* (MN-ṭ)
514. *The Middle Length Discourses*, 325.

Ahañhi bho, Gotama, evaṃ vadāmi—"Rūpaṃ me attā, vedanā me attā, saññā me attā, saṅkhārā me attā, viññāṇaṃ me attā"ti. (MN 35.11)

515. See also *The Path of Purification*, 631.

Sabbampi taṃ anattā asārakaṭṭhena [sammasati[Psm aṭṭhā.]*]. Asārakaṭṭhenāti "[sāmī*[MS]*][attā*[VRI]*] nivāsī kārako vedako sayaṃvasī"ti evaṃ parikappitassa attasārassa abhāvena. Yañhi aniccaṃ, [dukkhaṃ*[VRI]*][taṃ*[MS, Vism]*] attanopi aniccataṃ vā, udayabbayapīḷanaṃ vā vāretuṃ na sakkoti, kuto tassa kārakādibhāvo.* (Vism 20.16)

516. Ibid., 632.

Sāmī-nivāsī-kāraka-vedakā-dhiṭṭhāyakavirahitatāya suññato. Sayañca assāmikabhāvāditāya anattato. (Vism 20.19)

517. Ibid., 631.

Yaṃ pana aniccaṃ, taṃ yasmā niyamato sankhatādibhedaṃ hoti. Tenassa pariyāyadassanatthaṃ, nānākārehi vā manasikārapavattidassanatthaṃ "rūpaṃ atītānāgatapaccuppannaṃ, aniccaṃ, saṅkhataṃ, paticcasamuppannaṃ, khayadhammaṃ, vayadhammaṃ, virāgadhammaṃ, nirodhadhamman"ti puna pāḷi vuttā. (Vism 20.16)

518. See *The Path of Discrimination*, 51.

519. *Jātipaccayā jarāmarananti-ādi na vipassanāvasena vuttaṃ. Kevalaṃ paticcasamuppādassa ekeka-aṅgavasena saṅkhipitvā vavatthānato sammasanañāṇaṃ nāma hotīti pariyāyena vuttaṃ. Na panetaṃ kalāpasammasanañāṇaṃ.* [*Dhammaṭṭhitiñāṇamev'etaṃ*MS][*Dhammaṭṭhitiñāṇameva taṃ*VRI] *hotīti.*

520. See also *The Path of Purification*, 634.

   Navāhā'kārehi indriyāni tikkhāni bhavanti—uppannuppannānam saṅkhārānaṃ khayameva passati, tattha ca sakkaccakiriyāya sampādeti, sātaccakiriyāya sampādeti, sappāyakiriyāya sampādeti, samādhissa ca nimittaggāhena, bojjhaṅgāṇaña anupavattanatāya, kāye ca jīvite ca anapekkhataṃ upaṭṭhāpeti, tattha ca abhibhuyya nekkhammena, antarā ca abyosānenā"ti. (Vism 20.21)

521. Ibid., 641.

   Rūpadhamme niruḷhaṃ lakkhaṇattayaṃ pubbe attanā asallakkhitaṃ sallakkhetvā sammasanto taṃ tattha āropetīti vuccati. (Vism 20.48)

522. *Yathā pathaviphassādīnaṃ kakkhaḷaphusanādilakkhaṇāni tīsupi khaṇesu sallakkhitabbāni paṭiniyatarūpatāya sabhāvasiddhāneva hutvā gayhanti, na evaṃaniccādilakkhaṇāni. Tāni pana bhaṅgudayabbayapīḷāvasavattanākāramukhena gahetabbato samāropitarūpāni viya gayhantīti vuttaṃ "sāmaññalakkhaṇaṃ āropetvā"ti.* (Vism-mhṭ)

523. This is Mahāsi Sayadaw's explanation; Bhikkhu Ñanamoli's translation of the final sentence of this passage reads "Therefore, it is impermanent, unsatisfactory, and not self."

524. See also *The Path of Purification*, 643–44.

   Abhikkame pavattarūpaṃ paṭikkamaṃ appatvā tattheva nirujjhati. Paṭikkame pavattarūpaṃ ālokanaṃ. Ālokane pavattarūpaṃ vilokanaṃ. Vilokane pavattarūpaṃ samiñjanaṃ. Samiñjane pavattarūpaṃ pasāraṇaṃ appatvā tattheva nirujjhati. Tasmā aniccaṃ dukkhaṃ anattā"ti tilakkhaṇaṃ āropeti. (Vism 20.61)

525. Chapter 4, p. 185–88.

526. See also *The Path of Purification*, 644.

   Evaṃ pabbapabbagate saṅkhāre vipassato rūpasammasanaṃ sukhumaṃ hoti. (Vism 20.66)

527. Ibid., 645.

   Āhāramayaṃ rūpaṃ chātasuhitavasena pākaṭaṃ hoti. Chātakāle samuṭṭhitaṃ rūpaṃ hi jhattaṃ hoti kilantaṃ, jhāmakhāṇuko viya, aṅgārapacchiyam nilīnakāko viya ca dubbaṇṇaṃ dussaṇṭhitam. Suhitakāle samuṭṭhitaṃ dhātaṃ pīnitaṃ mudu siniddhaṃ phassavantaṃ hoti. So taṃ pariggahetvā "chātakāle pavattarūpaṃ suhitakālaṃ appatvā ettheva nirujjhati. (Vism 20.68)

528. Ibid., 645–56.

   Utumayaṃ [*rūpaṃ*MS] *sītuṇhavasena pākaṭaṃ hoti. Uṇhakāle samuṭṭhitaṃ rūpaṃ hi jhattaṃ hoti kilantaṃ, dubbaṇṇaṃ. Sīta-utunā samuṭṭhitaṃ rūpaṃ dhātaṃ pīṇitaṃ siniddham hoti. So taṃ pariggahetvā "unha-kāle pavattarūpam sītakālam appatvā ettheva nirujjhati. . . ."* (Vism 20.69)

529. See "Appendix 5: Materiality."

530. See also *The Path of Purification*, 646.

   Kammajaṃ āyatanadvāravasena pākaṭaṃ hoti. Cakkhudvārasmiṃ hi cakkhukāyabhāvadasakavasena tiṃsa kammajarūpāni, upatthambhakāni pana tesaṃ utucittāhārasamuṭṭhānāni catuvīsatīti catupaṇṇāsa honti. Tathā sotaghānajivhādvāresu. Kāyadvāre kāyabhāvadasakavasena ceva utusamuṭṭhānādivasena ca catucattālisa. Manodvāre hadayavatthukāyabhāvadasakavaseva ceva utusamuṭṭhānādivasena ca catupaṇṇāsameva. (Vism 20.70)

531. *The Middle Length Discourses*, 153.
cakkhuñca pajānāti (MN 10; DN 22)

532. *The Connected Discourses*, 1181.
. . . [*Cakkhuṃ*MS][*Cakkhu*VRI] *aniccanti yathābhūtaṃ pajānāti* . . . (SN 35.99)

533. See also *The Path of Purification*, 646.
So sabbampi taṃ rūpaṃ pariggahetvā "cakkhudvāre pavattarūpaṃ sotadvāraṃ appatvā ettheva nirujjhati. Sotadvāre pavattarūpaṃ ghānadvāraṃ. Ghānadvāre pavattarūpaṃ jivhādvāraṃ. Jivhādvāre pavattarūpaṃ kāyadvāraṃ. Kāyadvāre pavattarūpaṃ manodvāraṃ appatvā ettheva nirujjhati, tasmā aniccaṃ dukkhamanattā"ti evaṃ tattha tilakkhaṇaṃ āropeti. (Vism 20.70)

534. Ibid., 646.
Cittasamuṭṭhānaṃ somanassitadomanassitavasena pākataṃ hoti. (Vism 20.71)

535. *The Path of Purification*, 646–47.
Jīvitaṃ attabhāvo ca, sukhadukkhā ca kevalā;
ekacittasamāyuttā, lahuso vattate khaṇo. (Vism 20.72)

536. Ibid., 647.
Cullāsītisahassāni, kappaṃ tiṭṭhanti ye marū.
Na tveva tepi tiṭṭhanti, dvihi cittehi samohitā.
Ye niruddhā marana, tiṭṭhamānassa vā idha;
[*Sabbepi*MS][*Sabbeva*VRI] *sadisā khandhā, gatā appatisandhikā.* (Vism 20.72)

537. Ibid.
Anantarā ca ye bhaggā, ye ca bhaggā anāgate;
Tadantarā niruddhānaṃ, vesamaṃ natthi lakkhaṇe. (Vism 20.72)

538. Ibid.
Anibbattena na jāto, paccuppannena jīvati;
Cittabhaṅgā mato loko, paññatti paramatthiyā.
Anidhānagatā bhaggā, puñjo natthi anāgate;
Nibbattā yepi tiṭṭhanti, āragge sāsapūpamā. (Vism 20.72)

539. Ibid.
Anidhānagatā bhaggā, puñjo natthi anāgate;
Nibbattā yepi tiṭṭhanti, āragge sāsapūpamā. (Vism 20.72)

540. See also ibid.
Nibbattānañca dhammānaṃ, bhaṅgo nesaṃ purakkhato;
Palokadhammā tiṭṭhanti, purāṇehi amissitā.
*Adassanato āyanti, bhaggā [gacchantyadassanaṃ*MS*][gacchantudassanaṃ*VRI*];*
Vijjuppādova ākāse, uppajjanti vayanti ca. (Vism 20.72)

541. See also ibid., 649.
Evaṃ vipassanā paṭipāṭiyā sakalampi divasabhāgaṃ sammasituṃ vaṭṭeyya. Yāva dasamacittasammasanā pana rūpakammaṭhānampi arūpakammaṭṭhānampi paguṇaṃ hoti. Tasmā dasameyeva ṭhapetabbanti vuttaṃ. (Vism 20.81)

542. *Tathā sati kammaṭṭhānaṃ navaṃ navameva siyā.* (Vism-mhṭ)

543. *Kāmañcāyaṃ diṭṭhivisuddhikaṅkhāvitaraṇavisuddhisamadhigamena visuddhad-*

iṭṭhiko, maggena pana asamugghāṭitattā anoḷārikāya diṭṭhiyā vasenevaṃ vuttaṃ. (Vism-mhṭ)

544. See also *The Path of Purification*, 649–50.
Evaṃ saṅkhāre anattato passana diṭṭhisamugghātanaṃ nāma hoti (Vism 20.82)

545. *Yadā anattānupassanā tikkhā sūrā visadā pavattati, itarā dvepi tadanugatikā. Tadānena diṭṭhi-ugghāṭanaṃ kataṃ hoti.* (Vism-mhṭ)

546. See also *The Path of Purification*, 649–50.
Aniccato passana mānasamugghātanaṃ nāma hoti. (Vism 20.82)

547. *Yadā pana aniccānupassanā takkhā sūrā visadā pavattati, itarā dvepi tadanugatikā. Tadānena mānasamugghātanaṃ kataṃ hoti.* (Vism-mhṭ)

548. See also *The Path of Purification*, 649–50.
Dukkhato passana nikantipariyādānaṃ nāma hoti. (Vism 20.82)

549. *Yadā pana dukkhānupassanā tikkhā sūrā visadā pavattati, itarā dvepi tadanugatikā. Tadānene nikantipariyādānaṃ kataṃ hoti.* (Vism-mhṭ)

550. See also *The Path of Purification*, 157–58.
Yā "yadatthi yaṃ bhūtaṃ, taṃ pajahati. Upekkhaṃ paṭilabhatī"ti evamāgatā vicinane majjhattabhūtā upekkhā, ayaṃ vipassanupekkhā nāma . . . . Paññā eva hi sā, kiccavasena dvidhā bhinnā. Yathā hi purisassa sāyaṃ gehaṃ paviṭṭhaṃ sappaṃ ajapadadaṇḍaṃ gahetvā pariyesamānassa taṃ thusakoṭṭhake nipannaṃ disvā "sappo nu kho, no"ti avalokena sovattikattayaṃ disvā nibbematikassa "sappo, na sappo"ti vicinane majjhattatā uppajjati. Evameva yā āraddhavipassakassa vipassanāñāṇena lakkhaṇattaye diṭṭhe saṅkhārānaṃ aniccabhāvādivicinane majjhattatā upajjati, ayaṃ vipassanupekkhā. (Vism 4.168–69)

551. *Taṃ pajahāmīti upekkhaṃ paṭilabhatīti taṃ tattha chandarāgappahānena pajahāmīti vipassanupekkhaṃ paṭilabhati.* (Mp)

552. *Chandarāga* in the form of attachment, greed, desire, or lust.

553. See also *The Path of Discrimination*, 4.
Paccuppannānaṃ dhammānaṃ vipariṇāmānupassane paññā udayabbayānupassane ñāṇaṃ. (Paṭis 1.0)

554. See also *The Path of Purification*, 652.
Jātaṃ rūpaṃ paccuppannaṃ, tassa nibbattilakkhaṇaṃ udayo, viparināmalakkhanaṃ vayo anupassanā ñāṇaṃ. (Paṭis 20.94)

555. *Santatipaccuppanne khaṇapaccuppanne vā dhamme udayabbayadassanābhiniveso kātabbo, na atītānāgateti vuttaṃ "paccuppannānaṃ dhammāna"ti . . .*
. . . Jātanti nibbattaṃ [paṭiladdhabhāvaṃ[MS]] [paṭiladdhattabhāvaṃ[VRI]] . . . paccuppannarūpaṃ nāma jātaṃ khaṇattayapariyāpannanti attho. Taṃ pana ādito duppariggahanti sanatipaccuppannavasena vipassanābhiniveso kātabbo. (Vism-mhṭ)

556. See also *The Path of Purification*, 652.
Jātā vedanā [paccuppannā[MS]][paccuppannaṃ[VRI]] . . . Jātā saññā [paccuppannā[MS]] [paccuppannaṃ[VRI]] . . . Jātā saṅkhārā [paccuppannā[MS]] [paccuppannaṃ[VRI]] . . . Jātaṃ viññāṇaṃ [paccuppannā[MS]][paccuppannaṃ[VRI]] . . . tassa nibbattilakkhaṇaṃ udayo. Vipariṇāmalakkhaṇaṃ vayo. Anupassanā ñāṇaṃ. (Vism 20.94)

557. This is a partial list of the fifty-two mental factors (*cetasikā*) described in the Abhidhamma. See "Appendix 2: Mental Factors Present in Each Consciousness" for complete list.

558. See also *The Path of Discrimination*, 55.

Pañcannaṃ khandhānaṃ udayaṃ passanto pañcavīsati lakkhaṇāni passati, vayaṃ passanto pañcavīsati lakkhaṇāni passati; udayabbayaṃ passanto paññāsa lakkhaṇāni passati. (Paṭis 1.285)

559. See also *The Path of Purification*, 653–54.

Avijjāsamudayā rūpasamudayoti paccayasamudayaṭṭhena rūpakkhandhassa udayaṃ passati. Taṇhāsamudayā... kammasamudayā... Āhārasamudayā rūpasamudayoti paccayasamudayaṭṭhena rūpakkhandhassa udayaṃ passati. Nibbattilakkhaṇaṃ passantopi rūpakkhandhassa udayaṃ passati. Rūpakkhandhassa udayaṃ[passanto MS][*passantopi* VRI] *imāni pañca lakkhaṇāni passati.* (Vism 20.97)

560. Ibid., 653–54.

Avijjānirodhā rūpanirodhoti paccayanirodhaṭṭhena rūpakkhandhassa vayaṃ passati. Taṇhānirodhā... kammanirodhā... āhāranirodhā... paccayanirodhaṭṭhena rūpakkhandhassa vayaṃ passati. Vipariṇāmalakkhaṇaṃ passantopi rūpakkhandhassa vayaṃ passati. Rūpakkhandhassa vayaṃ [*passanto* MS][*passantopi* VRI] *imāni pañca lakkhaṇāni passati.* (Vism 20.97)

561. *Ettha ca keci tāva āhu "arūpakkhandhānaṃ udayabbayadassanaṃ addhāsantativaseneva, na khaṇavasenā"ti tesaṃ matena khaṇato udayabbayadassanameva na siyā. Apare panāhu " paccayato udayabbayadassane atītādivibhāgaṃ anāmasitvā sabbasādhāraṇato* [*avijjādipaccayā vedanādīnaṃ sambhavaṃ* MS][*avijjādipaccayāvedanānasambhavaṃ* VRI] *labbhamānataṃ passati, na uppādaṃ. Avijjādi abhāve ca* [*tesaṃ* MS][*tassa* VRI] *asambhavaṃ alabbhamānataṃ passati, na bhaṅgaṃ. Khaṇato udayabbayadassane paccuppannānaṃ uppādaṃ, bhaṅgañca passatī"ti, taṃ*[... Abhi. Ṭī.] *yuttaṃ. Santativasena hi rūpārūpadhamme udayato, vayato ca manasi karontassa anukkamena bhāvanāya balapattakāle ñāṇassa tikkhavisadabhāvapattiyā khaṇato udayabbayāupaṭṭhahantīti.* (Vism-mhṭ)

562. See also *The Path of Purification*, 653–54.

Nibbattilakkhaṇaṃ passantopi... vipariṇāmalakkhaṇaṃ passantopi (Vism 20.97)

563. *The Middle Length Discourses*, 899.

Tyāssa dhammā viditā uppajjanti. Viditā upaṭṭhahanti. Viditā abbhattaṃ gacchanti. (MN 111.4)

564. *Paṭhamañhi paccuppannadhammānaṃ udayabbayaṃ disvā atha atītānāgate nayaṃ neti.* (Vism-mhṭ)

565. See also *The Path of Purification*, 655–56.

[*Ettāvatānena* MS, Vism][*Ettāvatācanena* Vi. ṭī.][*Ettāvatā tena* Khu. ni. aṭṭha.] *"vayadhammameva uppajjati, uppannañca vayaṃ upetī"ti iminā ākārena samapaññāsa lakkhaṇāni paṭivijjhitvā ṭhitaṃ udayabbayānupassanā nāma paṭhamaṃ taruṇavipassanāñāṇaṃ adhigataṃ hoti, yassādhigamā "āraddhavipassako"ti saṅkhaṃ gacchati.* (Vism 20.104)

566. *Kalāpasammasanādivasena pavattaṃ sammasanaṃ na nippariyāyena vipassanāsamaññaṃ labhati, udayabbayānupassanādivasena pavattameva labhati.* (Vism-mhṭ)

567. See also *The Path of Purification*, 660.

Obhāse ceva ñāṇe ca, pītiyā ca vikampati;
passaddhiyā sukhe ceva, yehi cittaṃ pavedhati.
Adhimokkhe ca paggāhe, upaṭṭhāne ca kampati;
upekkhāvajjanāya[*ca* MS][*ceva* VRI], *upekkhāya nikantiyā.* (Vism 20.125)

568. Ibid., 656.

Vipassanupakkilesā hi paṭvedhapattassa ariyasāvakassa ceva vippaṭipannakassa ca nikkhittakammaṭṭhānassa kusītapuggalassa nuppajjanti. Sammāpaṭipannakassa pana yuttapayuttassa āraddhavipassakassa kulaputtassa uppajjantiyeva. (Vism 20.105)

569. *The Connected Discourses*, 312.
Sataṃ hatthī sataṃ assā, sataṃ assatarīrathā,
sataṃ kaññāsahassāni, [*āmuttamanikundalā*[MS]][*āmukkamanikundalā*[VRI]],
ekassa padavītihārassa, kalaṃ nāgghanti soḷasiṃ . . . (SN 1.837)

570. For the occurrence of rapture as a mental state, see "Appendix 2: Mental Factors Present in Each Consciousness," column number 12 (Joy).

571. *Yā panesā dhammaṃ kathentassa vā suṇantassa vā vācentassa vā anto uppajjamānā pīti udaggabhāvaṃ janeti, assūni pavatteti, lomahaṃsaṃ janeti, sāyam saṃsāravaṭṭassa antaṃ katvā arahattapariyosanā hoti. Tasmā sabbaratīnaṃ evarūpā dhammaratiyeva seṭṭhā.* (Dhp commentary)

572. "*Bhante Nāgasena, yo ca mātari matāya rodati, yo ca dhammapemena rodati, ubhinnaṃ tesaṃ rodantānaṃ kassa assu bhesajjaṃ, kassa assu na bhesajjan*"*ti?* "*Kassa kho Mahārāja, assu* [*rāgadosehi*[MS]][*rāgadosamohehi*[VRI]] *samalaṃ unhaṃ, ekassa pītisomanassena vimalaṃ sītalaṃ . . . taṃ bhesajjaṃ, yaṃ uṇhaṃ, taṃ na bhesajjan*"*ti.* (Mil)

573. See "Appendix 2a: Mental Factors Present in Each Consciousness," numbers 35–46 for an enumeration of the following.

574. *Tattha kāyaggahaṇena rūpakāyassāpi gahaṇaṃ veditabbaṃ, na vedanādikkhandhattayasseva. Kāyapassaddhiādayo hi rūpakāyassāpi darathadinimmaddikāti.* (Vism-mhṭ)

575. *The Dhammapada*, 96.
Suññāgāraṃ paviṭṭhassa, santacittassa bhikkhuno;
Amānusī rati hoti, sammā dhammaṃ vipassato.
Yato yato sammasati, khandhānaṃ udayabbayaṃ,
[*Labhate*[MS]][*Labhati*[VRI]] *pītipāmojjaṃ, amataṃ taṃ vijānataṃ.* (Dhp 373–74)

576. The *Visuddhimagga-mahāṭīkā* says that in an ultimate sense, *vipassanupekkhā* is a balanced state of mind (*tatramajjhattatā*). It may give this definition in order to differentiate it from knowledge that is considered an obstacle to practice. However, the Paṭisambhidāmagga commentary refers to this view as a teachers' opinion, and describes it as concentration instead. Still another view is given in the "index of knotty points" (Gaṇṭhipada) for both the Paṭisambhidāmagga and Visuddhimagga, where it is identified with insight. The Gaṇṭhipada says that the function of *vipassanupekkhā* is equilibrium in examining or inspecting conditioned phenomena. So it cannot be confused with knowledge. The view expressed in the Gaṇṭhipada seems most acceptable to me, so I have given my explanation from that point of view.

577. *Na vāpi hi upakkilesā ekakkhaṇepi upajjanti, paccavekkhaṇā pana visuṃ hoti.* (Vism-mhṭ)

578. See also *The Path of Purification*, 659.
Ettha ca obhāsādayo upakkilesavatthutāya upakkilesāti vuttā, na akusalattā. Nikanti pana upakkileso ceva upakkilesavatthu ca. Vatthuvaseneva cete dasa. Gāhavasena pana samatiṃsa honti. (Vism 20.124)

579. When meditators (who have already attained any of the path knowledges) want to gain absorption in their respective fruitions, they have to practice *vipassanā* again starting from this level of *vipassanā* knowledge of arising and passing away. –Tr.

580. [*Udayavaye*[MS]][*Udayabbaye*[VRI]] *pana paṭividdhe aniccalakkhaṇaṃ pākataṃ hutvā*

upaṭṭhāti. Tato "yadaniccaṃ taṃ dukkhaṃ. Yaṃ dukkhaṃ tadanattā"ti itaralakkhaṇampi. Atha vā udayabbayaggahaṇena hutvā abhāvākāro, abhiṇhasampaṭipīḷanākāro, avasavattanākāro ca vibhūtataro hoti. (Vism-mhṭ)

581. The many synonyms for "passing away" in this sentence are given in order to avoid confusion between cessation (*nirodha*) and cessation of arising (*anuppādanirodha*).

582. See also *The Path of Purification*, 663.

Tayidaṃ sabbampi ayaṃ yogāvacaro [upakkilesavimuttena[VRI]*][upakkilesavinimuttena*[MS]*] vīthipaṭipannavipassanāsaṅkhātena udayabbayānupassanāñāṇena yāthāvasarasato sallakkheti. Tassevaṃ sallakkhetvā punapunaṃ "aniccaṃ dukkhaṃ anattā"ti rūpārūpadhamme tulayato tīrayato taṃ ñāṇaṃ hutvā vahati, saṅkhārā lahuṃ upaṭṭhahanti, ñāṇe tikkhe vahante saṅkhāresu lahuṃ upaṭṭhahantesu uppādaṃ vā ṭhitiṃ vā pavattaṃ vā nimittaṃ vā na sampāpunāti. Khayavayabhedanirodheyeva sati santiṭṭhati. [Tassa "evaṃ*[VRI]*] [evaṃ*[MS]*] uppajjitvā evaṃ nāma saṅkhāragataṃ nirujjhatī"ti passato etasmiṃ ṭhāne [bhaṅgānupassanaṃ*[MS]*][bhaṅgānupassanā*[MS]*] nāma vipassanāñāṇaṃ uppajjati.* (Vism 21.10)

583. See also *The Path of Discrimination*, 4.

[Ārammaṇaṃ paṭisankhā[VRI]*][Ārammaṇappaṭisankhā*[MS]*] bhangānupassane paññā vipassane ñāṇaṃ.* (Paṭis 1.0)

584. See also *The Path of Purification*, 664–65.

Arammaṇapaṭisaṅkhāti yaṃkiñci ārammaṇaṃ paṭisaṅkhāya jānitvā, khayato vayato disvāti attho. Bhaṅgānupassane paññāti tassa, ārammaṇaṃ khayato vayato paṭisaṅkhāya uppannassa ñāṇassa bhaṅgaṃ anupassane yā paññā, idaṃ vipassane [ñāṇaṃ[MS]*][ñāṇanti vuttaṃ*[VRI]*].* (Vism 21.12)

585. See also *The Path of Discrimination*, 55.

Rūpārammaṇatā cittaṃ uppajjitvā bhijjati . . . Taṃ ārammaṇaṃ paṭisaṅkhā . . . tassa cittassa bhaṅgaṃ anupassati . . . Vedanārammaṇatā (and so on. as for *rūpārammaṇatā*) . . . *saññārammanatā . . . saṅkhārārammaṇatā . . . viññāṇārammaṇatā cittaṃ uppajjitvā bhijjati. Taṃ ārammaṇaṃ paṭisaṅkhā tassa cittassa bhaṅgaṃ anupassati.* (Paṭis 1.284)

586. See *The Path of Purification*, 663. (Vism 21.10)

587. Ibid., 664. (Vism 21.12)

588. See also *The Path of Discrimination*, 59.

vatthusaṅkamanā ceva, paññāya ca vivaṭṭanā, āvajjanā balañceva, paṭisaṅkhā vipassanā. (Paṭis 1.297)

589. *Vatthusaṅkamanāti rūpādīsu ekekassa bhaṅgaṃ disvā, puna yena cittena bhaṅgo diṭṭho, tassāpi bhaṅgadassanavasena purimavatthuto aññavatthusaṅkamanā. Paññāya ca vivaṭṭanāti udayaṃ pahāya vaye santiṭṭhanā. Āvajjana balañcevāti rūpādīsu ekekassa bhaṅgaṃ disvā, puna bhaṅgārammaṇassa cittassa bhaṅgadassanatthaṃ anantarameva āvajjanasamatthatā.* (Paṭis subcommentary)

590. See "Appendix 3: Stream of Consciousness."

591. See also *The Path of Discrimination*, 59.

Ārammaṇa-anvayena, ubho ekavavattanā.
Nirodhe adhimuttatā, vayalakkhaṇāvipassanā. (Paṭis 1.297)

592. See also *The Path of Purification*, 666.

Ārammaṇa-anvayena ubho ekavavatthanāti paccakkhato diṭṭhassa ārammaṇassa anvayena anugamanena yathā idaṃ, tathā atītepi saṅkhāragataṃ bhijjittha, anāgatepi bhijjissatīti evaṃ ubhinnaṃ ekasabhāveneva vavatthāpananti attho. Vuttampi cetaṃ porāṇehi:

"Saṃvijjamānamhi visuddhadassano, tadanvayaṃ neti atītānāgate, sabbepi saṅkhāragatā palokino, ussāvabindū sūriyeva uggate"ti. (Vism 21.21)

593. *The Path of Purification*, 667. (Vism 21.27)

594. *The Dhammapada*, 46.
Yathā [pupphuḷakaṃ[MS]*][pubbuḷakaṃ*[Dhp, KNCom'y]*][bubbuḷakkam*[Vism]*] passe,*
Yathā passe marīcikaṃ,
Evaṃ lokaṃ avekkhantaṃ,
Maccurājā na passati. (Dhp 170)

595. See also *The Path of Purification*, 668.
Tassa "atītā saṅkhārā niruddhā, paccuppannā nirujjhanti, anāgate nibbattanakasaṅkhārāpi evameva nirujjhissantī"ti passato etasmiṃ ṭhāne bhayatupaṭṭhānañāṇaṃ nāma uppajjati. (Vism 21.29)

596. Ibid., 669.
Bhayatupaṭṭhānañāṇaṃ pana bhāyati na bhāyatī'ti? Na bhāyati. Tañhi atītā sankhārā niruddhā, paccuppannā nirujjhanti, anāgatā nirujjhissantī'ti tīranamattameva hoti. (Vism 21.32)

597. *Tattha bhayākārena pavattaṃ ñāṇaṃ bhayatupaṭṭhānañāṇaṃ. Itarākārena pavattaṃ ādīnavañāṇanti daṭṭhabbaṃ.* (Vism-mhṭ)

598. See also *The Path of Discrimination*, 59.
Anuppādo khemanti santipade ñāṇaṃ . . . anuppādo sukhanti santipade ñāṇaṃ . . . anuppādo nirāmisanti santipade ñāṇaṃ . . . anuppādo nibbānan"ti santipade ñāṇaṃ (Paṭis 1.300)

599. *The Dhammapada*, 72.
Sabbe sankhārā aniccā"ti, yadā paññāya passati;
atha nibbindati dukkhe, esa maggo visuddhiyā.
"Sabbe sankhārā dukkhā"ti, yadā paññāya passati;
Atha nibbindati dukkhe, esa maggo visuddhiyā.
"Sabbe dhammā anattā"ti, yadā paññāya passati;
Atha nibbindati dukkhe, esa maggo visuddhiyā. (Dhp 277–79)

600. See also *The Path of Purification*, 674.
Tenāhu porānā: "Bhayatupaṭṭhānaṃ ekameva tīṇi nāmāni labhati, sabbasaṅkhāre bhayato addasāti bhayatupaṭṭhānaṃ nāma jātaṃ. Tesuyeva saṅkhāresu ādīnavaṃ uppādetīti ādīnavānupassanā nāma jātaṃ. Tesuyeva saṅkhāresu nibbindamānaṃ uppannanti nibbidā [nibbidānupassanā[MS]*] nāma jātan"ti. Pāḷiyampi vuttaṃ:, "yā ca bhayatupaṭṭhāne paññā, yañca ādīnave ñānaṃ, yā ca nibbidā, ime dhammā ekattā, byañjanameva nānan"ti.* (Vism 21.44)

601. Ibid.
Iminā pana nibbidāññāṇena imassa kulaputtassa nibbindantassa ukkaṇṭhantassa nabhiramantassa sabbabhavayonigativiññāṇaṭṭhitisattāvāsagatesu sabhedakesu saṅkhāresu ekasaṅkhārepi cittaṃ na sajjati, na laggati, na bajjhati, sabbasmā saṅkhāragatā [muñcitukāmaṃ[MS]*][muccitukāmaṃ nissaritukāmaṃ*[VRI,sic]*] hoti . . . Athassa evaṃ sabbasaṅkhāresu vigatālayassa [sabba*[MS]*][sabbasmā*[VRI]*] saṅkhāragatā muñcitukāmassa uppajjati muñcitukamyatā ñāṇaṃ.* (Vism 21.45)

602. See "Appendix 6: Planes of Existence."

603. See also *The Path of Purification*, 674.
So evaṃ sabbabhavayonigatiṭṭhitinivāsagatehi [sabhedakehi[MS]*][sabhedakehi*

saṅkhārehi[VRI]] *muñcitukāmo sabbasmā saṅkhāragatā muccituṃ puna te evaṃ saṅkhāre paṭisaṅkhānupassanāñāṇena tilakkhanaṃ āropetvā pariggaṇhāti.* (Vism 21.45)

604. I.e., grief, pain, suffering, and misfortune.

605. *The Path of Purification*, 650. (Vism 20.83)

606. See also Ibid., 678–79.
Evamevāyaṃ sabbasaṅkhārehi [*muñcitukāmo*[MS]][*muccitukāmo*[VRI, sic]] *hutvā patisaṅkhānupassanāya saṅkhāre pariggaṇhanto "ahaṃ mamā"ti gahetabbaṃ adisvā bhayañca nandiñca vippahāya sabbasaṅkhāresu udāsīno hoti majjhatto. Tassa evaṃ jānato evaṃ passato tīsu bhavesu, castūsu yonīsu, pañcasu gatīsu, sattasu viññāṇaṭṭhitīsu navasu sattavāsesu cittaṃ patilīyati, patikutati, pativattati, na sampasāriyati, upekkhā vā pāṭikūlyatā vā saṇṭhati . . . Iccassa saṅkhārupekkhāñāṇaṃ nāma uppannaṃ hoti.* (Vism 21.61–62)

607. *The Middle Length Discourses*, 871.
Puna caparaṃ bhikkhave, ariyāsāvako . . . iti paṭisañcikkhati—"suññam'idaṃ attena vā, attaniyena vā."ti. (MN 106.7)

608. Paramatthajotikā I.

609. *The Middle Length Discourses*, 871.
Puna caparaṃ bhikkhave, ariyāsāvako iti paṭisañcikkhati—"nāhaṃ kvacani, kassaci, kiñcanatasmiṃ, na ca mama kvacani, kismiñci [*kiñcanatatthī"ti*[MS, VRI MN]][*kiñcanaṃ natthī"ti*[VRI, ANSCom'y]] (MN 106.8)

610. See also *The Path of Purification*, 677.
Cakkhu suññaṃ attena vā attaniyana vā niccena vā dhuvena vā sassatena vā avipariṇāmadhammena vā. (Vism 21.55)

611. Ibid., 677–78.
Rūpaṃ asāraṃ nissāraṃ sārāpagataṃ niccasārasārena vā dhuvasārasārena vā sukhasārasārena vā attasārasārena vā niccena vā dhuvena vā sassatena vā avipariṇāmadhammena vā. (Vism 21.56)

612. Ibid., 678.
rūpaṃ rittato passati. Tucchato . . . suññato . . . anattato . . . anissariyato . . . akāmakāriyato . . . alabbhanīyato . . . avasavattakato . . . parato . . . vivittato passati. (Vism 21.57)

613. Ibid., 622–23.
Kammaṃ natthi vipākamhi, pāko kamme vijjati;
Aññamaññaṃ ubosuññā, na ca kammaṃ vinā phalaṃ. (Vism 19.20)

614. [*Kammādi*[MS]][*Kārakādi*[VRI]] *viya, kāraṇehi phalena ca vivittato. Na hi kāraṇena phalaṃ, phalena vā kāraṇaṃ sagabbhaṃ tiṭṭhati.* (Vism-mhṭ)

615. *Api ca, dasahākārehi suññato lokaṃ avekkhati. Rūpaṃ rittato, tucchato, suññato, anattato, asārakato, vadhkato, vibhāvato, aghamūlato, sāsavato, saṅkhatato.* (Nidd II)

616. See also *The Path of Purification*, 678.
Rūpaṃ na satto na jīvo na naro na māṇavo na itthī na puriso [*na attā na aham na attaniyaṃ*[MS]][*na attā na attaniyaṃ nāhaṃ*[VRI]] *na mama na koci na kassaci* . . . (Vism 21.58)

617. Therefore it is explained as follows in the Visuddhimagga in the chapter on the *vipassanā* knowledge by comprehension: "All that [materiality] is '*not self in the sense of having no core*.' In the sense of having no core because of the absence of any core of self conceived as a self, an abider, a doer, an experiencer, one who is his own master . . . as *void* because devoid of the state of being an owner, abider, doer, experiencer, director." See *The Path of Purification*, 665. (Vism 21.16)

618. *Rūpaṃ na sattoti-ādīsu yo lokavohārena satto, rūpaṃ so na hotīti ayamattho idha nādhippeto, tassā'vutta-siddhattā. Na hi loko rūpamattaṃ "satto"ti voharati, -[bāhirakaparikappeto*[MS]*][bāhirakaparikappito*[VRI]*] pana attā "satto"ti adhippeto. So hi tehi rūpādīsu sattavisattatāya [pare ca*[MS]*][paresaṃ*[VRI]*] sañjāpanaṭṭhena "satto"ti vuccati, rūpaṃ so na hotīti attho. Suññatāpariggaṇhanañhetanti. Esa nayo na jīvoti-ādīsupi.* (Vism-mhṭ)

619. See also *The Path of Discrimination*, 61.
Kathaṃ muñcitukamyatāpaṭisaṅkhāsantiṭṭhanā paññā saṅkhārupekkhāsu ñāṇaṃ? Uppādaṃ muñcitukamyatāpaṭisaṅkhāsantiṭṭhanā paññā saṅkhārupekkhāsu ñāṇaṃ, pavattaṃ . . . nimittaṃ . . . āyūhanaṃ . . . paṭisandhiṃ . . . upāyāsaṃ muñcitukamyatāpaṭisaṅkhāsantiṭṭhanā paññā saṅkhārupekkhāsu ñāṇaṃ . . .Uppādo dukkhanti . . . bhayanti . . . sāmisanti . . . saṅkhārāti . . . upāyāso saṅkhārāti muñcitukamyatāpaṭisaṅkhāsantiṭṭhanā paññā saṅkhārupekkhāsu ñāṇaṃ. (Paṭis 1.306–7)

620. See also *The Path of Purification*, 683.
Tattha muñcitukamyatā ca sā paṭisaṅkhā ca santiṭṭhanā cāti muñcitukamyatā-paṭisaṅkhā-santiṭṭhanā. Iti pubbabhāge nibbidāñāṇena [nibbindantassa[MS]*][nibbinnassa*[VRI]*] uppādādīni pariccajitukāmatā . . . Muñcanassa upāya-karaṇattaṃ majjhe paṭisaṅkhānaṃ paṭisaṅkhā. Muñcitvā avasāne [ajjhupekkhanā*[MS]*][ajjhupekkhanaṃ*[VRI]*] santiṭṭhanā.* (Vism 21.81)

621. See also *The Path of Discrimination*, 263.
Yā ca muñcitukamyatā yā ca paṭisaṅkhānupassanā yā ca saṅkhārupekkhā, ime dhammā ekatthā, byañjanameva nāṇaṃ. (Paṭis 5.84)

622. See also *The Path of Purification*, 679.
Evameva sace saṅkhārupekkhāñāṇaṃ santipadaṃ nibbānaṃ santato passati, sabbaṃ saṅkhārapavattaṃ visajjetvā nibbānameva pakkhanadati. No ce passati, punappunaṃ saṅkhārārammaṇameva hutvā pavattati. Tadidaṃ suppagge piṭṭhaṃ vaṭṭiyamānaṃ viya. [Nippaṭṭitakappāsaṃ vihaṭiyamānaṃ[MS]*] [Nibbaṭṭitakappāsaṃ vihanamānaṃ*[VRI]*] viya [nānāpakārato*[MS]*][nānapakārato*[VRI]*] saṅkhāre pariggahetvā bhayañca nandiñca pahāya saṅkhāravicinane majjhattaṃ hutvā tividhānupassanāvasena tiṭṭhati.* (Vism 21.65)

623. *Tikkhavisadasūrabhāvena saṅkhāresu ajjhupekkhane sijjhamāne taṃ saṅkhārupekkhāñāṇaṃ anekavāraṃ pavattamānaṃ paripākagamanena anulomañāṇassa paccayabhāvaṃ gacchantaṃ nibbānaṃ santato passati nāma. Tathābhūtañca saṅkhārapavattaṃ vissajjetvā nibbānameva pakkhandati nāma. Tayidaṃ idha ñāṇaṃanulomagotrabhūñāṇehi saddhiṃ ekattaṃ netvā vuttaṃ ekattanayavasena.* (Vism-mhṭ)

624. *A Comprehensive Manual of Abhidhamma: The Abhidhammattha Sangaha of Ācariya Anuruddha*, trans. Bhikkhu Bodhi, (Onalaska: BPS Pariyatti Editions), p. 354: "That knowledge of equanimity toward formations together with knowledge that conforms (to the truths), when perfected, is also termed 'insight leading to emergence.'"

625. *Yā sikhāppattā, sā sānulomā saṅkhārupekkhā vuṭṭhānagāminīvipassanāti ca pavuccati . . . yadi vuṭṭhānagāminīvipassanā anattato vipassati, suññato vimokkho nāma hoti maggo. Yadi aniccato vipassati, animitto vimokkho nāma. Yadi dukkhato vipassati, appaṇihito vimokkho nāma.* (Abhid-s)

626. See also *The Path of Purification*, 684.
Sikhāpattavipassanāti vuṭṭhānagāminīti vā saṅkhārupekkhādiñāṇattayasseva etaṃ nāmaṃ. Sā hi sikhaṃ uttamabhāvaṃ pattattā sikhāpattā. Vuṭṭhānaṃ

gacchatīti vuṭṭhānagāminī. Vuṭṭhānaṃ vuccati bahiddhānimittabhūtato abhiniviṭṭṭhavatthuto ceva, ajjhattapavattato ca [vuṭṭhāhanato[MS]*][vuṭṭhahanato*[VRI]*] maggo, taṃ gacchatīti vuṭṭhānagāminī, maggena saddhiṃ ghaṭīyatīti attho.* (Vism 21.83)

627. Refer to "Appendix 3: Stream of Consciousness," H15–17: peak-reaching equanimity of *vipassanā* knowledge that leads to emergence; H18: mental process associated with path and fruition.

628. See also *The Path of Purification*, 691.

Tassa "dāni maggo uppajjissatī"ti saṅkhārupekkhā saṅkhāre aniccāti vā dukkhāti vā anattāti vā sammasitvā bhavaṅgaṃ otarati. [Bhangānantaraṃ[MS]*] [Bhavaṅgānantaraṃ*[VRI]*] saṅkhārupekkhāya katanayeneva saṅkhāre aniccāti vā, dukkhāti vā anattāti vā ārammaṇaṃ kurumānaṃ uppajjati manodvārāvajjanaṃ. Tato bhavaṅgaṃ āveṭṭetvā uppannassa tassa kriyācittassānantaraṃ avīcikaṃ [santatim anubandhamānaṃ*[MS]*][cittasantatim anuppabandhamānaṃ*[VRI]*] anubandhamānaṃ tatheva sankhāre ārammanaṃ katvā uppajjati paṭhamajavanacittaṃ, yaṃ [parikammaṃ*[MS]*] [parikammanti*[VRI]*] vuccati.* (Vism 21.129)

629. *Aniccāti vā dukkhāti vā anattāti vā sammasitvā bhavaṅgaṃ otaratīti aniccādīsu ekenākārena sammasantī sattakkhattuṃ pavattitvā bhijjantī bhavaṅgaṃ otiṇṇā nāma hoti tato paraṃ bhavaṅgassa vāroti katvā . . .*

. . . Tathevāti yathā atītāsu [dvattijavanāvīthisu[MS]*] [dvattiṃsajavanāvīthisu*[VRI]*] saṅkhārupekkhā "aniccā"ti vā, "dukkhā"ti vā "anattā"ti vā saṅkhāre ārammaṇamakāsi, tatheva.* (Vism-mhṭ)

630. The eight attainments refer to the eight *jhānas*: four material *jhānas* and the four immaterial *jhānas*. The four styles of meditation refer to whether the practice is either pleasant or unpleasant and whether it leads to enlightenment either quickly or slowly.

631. *Tādisāya āsevanāya icchitabbattā yathā maggavīthito pubbe dve tayo javanavārā sadisānupassanāva pavattanti, evamidhāpi appanāvārato pubbe dve tayo javanavārā upekkhāsahagatāva pavattantīti vadanti.* (Vism-mhṭ)

632. See also *The Path of Discrimination*, 67.

Uppādaṃ abhibhuyyitvā anuppādaṃ pakkhandatīti gotrabhū . . . bahiddhā saṅkhāranimittaṃ abhibhuyyitvā . . . nirodhaṃ nibbānaṃ pakkhandatīti gotrabhū. (Paṭis 1.332)

633. In either event there must be a total of seven impulsion moments.

634. See also *The Path of Purification*, 697.

Yathā hi mahāmātikaṃ laṅghitvā paratīre patiṭṭātukāmo puriso vegena dhāvitvā mātikāya orimatīre rukkhassakhāya bandhitvā olambitaṃ rajjuṃ vā yaṭṭiṃ vā gahetvā ullaṅghitvā paratīraninnapoṇapabbhārakāyo hutvā paratīrassa uparibhāgaṃ patto taṃ muñcitvā vedhamāno paratīre patitvā saṇikaṃ patiṭṭāti, evamevāyaṃ yogāvacaropi bhavayonigatiṭṭhitinivāsānaṃ paratīrabhūte nibbāne patiṭṭhātukāmo udayabbayānupassanādinā vegena dhāvitvā attabhāvarukkhasākhāya bandhitvā olambhitaṃ rūparajjuṃ vā vedanādīsu aññataradaṇḍaṃ vā aniccanti vā dukkhanti vā anattāti vā anulomavajjanena gahetvā taṃ amuñcamanova paṭhamena anulomacittena ullaṅgitva dutiyena paratīraninnapoṇapabbhārakāyo viya nibbananinnapoṇapabbhāramānaso hutvā tatiyena paratīrassa uparibhāgaṃ patto viya idāni pattabbassa nibbanassa āsanno hutvā tassa cittassa nirodhena taṃ saṅkārārammaṇaṃ muñcitvā gotrabucittena visaṅkhare paratīrabhute nibbāne patati. Ekarammaṇe pana aladdhāsevanatāya vedhamāno so puriso viya na tāva suppatiṭṭhito hoti, tato maggañaṇena patiṭṭhāti. (Vism 22.6)

635. MN 64. See *The Middle Length Discourses*, 537–41.

636. AN 9.36. See *The Numerical Discourses*, 1298–1301.

637. We prefer here Bhikkhu Bodhi's translation as it appeared in an older edition of his text. In the later edition cited throughout this book, Venerable Bodhi supplies the following information in a footnote to this passage:

 Upadhivivekā. MA glosses *upadhi* here as the five cords of sensual pleasure. Though the first three clauses of this statement seem to express the same ideas as the two more usual clauses that follow, MṬ indicates that they are intended to show the means for becoming "quite secluded from sensual pleasures, secluded from unwholesome states." *The Middle Length Discourses*, 539, fn. 654.

638. *The Middle Length Discourses*, 539–40.

 [*Idhānanda bhikkhu upadhivivekā akusalanaṃ dhammanaṃ pahānā sabbaso kāyaduṭṭhullānaṃ paṭippassaddhiyā*[MN] only] *vivicceva kāmehi vivicca akusalehi dhammehi savitakkaṃ savicāraṃ viviekajaṃ pītisukhaṃ paṭhamaṃ jhānaṃ upasampajja viharati. So yadeva tattha hoti rūpagataṃ vedanāgataṃ saññāgataṃ saṅkhāragataṃ viññāṇagataṃ te dhamme aniccato dukkhato rogato ghaṇḍato sallato aghato ābādhato parato palokato suññato anattato samanupassati. So tehi dhammehi cittaṃ paṭivāpehi. So tehi dhammehi cittaṃ paṭivāpetvā amatāya dhātuyā cittaṃ upasaṃharati: "etaṃ santaṃ etaṃ panītaṃ yadidaṃ sabbasaṇkhārasamatho sabbūpadhipaṭinissaggo taṇhākkhayo virāgo nirodo nibbānan"ti.* (MN 64.9)

639. The second section of fifty suttas in the Majjhima Nikāya.

640. *Maggacittaṃ nibbānaṃ ārammaṇakaranavaseneva "evaṃ santaṃ, etaṃ paṇītaṃ"ti na evaṃ vadati. Iminā* [*pana ākārena*[MNCom'y]][*panākārena*[ANCom'y]] *taṃ paṭivijjhanto tattha cittaṃ upasaṃharati.* (Ps)

641. See also *The Path of Discrimination*, 402.

 Pañcakkhandhe aniccato passanto anulomikaṃ khantiṃ paṭilabhati. Pañcānnaṃ khandhānaṃ nirodho niccaṃ nibbānanti passanto sammattaniyāmaṃ okkamati. (Paṭis 29.8)

642. See *The Path of Purification*, 684. (Vism 21.84)

 "*Ekappahārena pañcāhi khandhehi vuṭṭhā*"*ti.*

643. See also *The Path of Discrimination*, 402–3.

 Pañcakkhandhe palokato passanto anulomikaṃ khantiṃ paṭilabhati. Pañcānaṃ khandhānaṃ nirodho apalokadhammo nibbānanti passanto sammattaniyāmaṃ okkamati . . . Pañcakkhandhe dukkhato passanto anulomikaṃ khantiṃ paṭilabhati. Pañcānaṃ khandhānaṃ nirodho sukhaṃ nibbānanti passanto sammattaniyāmaṃ okkamati . . . Pañcakkhandhe bhayato passanto anulomikaṃ khantiṃ paṭilabhati. Pañcānaṃ khandhānaṃ nirodho abhayaṃ nibbānanti passanto sammattaniyāmaṃ okkamati . . . Pañcakkhandhe anattato passanto anulomikaṃ khantiŋ paṭilabhati. Pañcānaṃ khandhānaṃ nirodho paramatthaṃ nibbānanti passanto sammattaniyāmaṃ okkamati. (Paṭis 29.8)

644. Ibid., 403.

 Pañcakkhandhe tucchato passanto anulomikaṃ khantiṃ paṭilabhati.

Pañcānaṃ khandhānaṃ nirodho atucchaṃ nibbānanti passanto sammattaniyāmaṃ okkamati. (Vism 29.8)

645. *Taṃ cittaṃ aparāparaṃ manasikaroto pavattaṃ samatikkamitvā appavattaṃ okkamati, apavattamanupatto, Mahārāja, sammāpaṭipanno "nibbānaṃ sacchikarotī"ti vuccati.* (Mil)

646. *The Middle Length Discourses*, 485.

Dhammacakkhuṃ udapādi "yaṃ kiñci samudayadhammaṃ, sabbantaṃ nirodhadhamman"ti. (MN 56.18, 74.15, 91.36, and 147.10)

647. Note: "the element of *nibbāna* without the residue remaining" means the passing away of an *arahant*, because the five aggregates are discarded and are never acquired again.

648. *Dhammacakkhunti ettha sotāpattimaggo adhippeto. Tassa uppatti-ākāradassanatthaṃ "yaṃ kiñci samudayadhammaṃ sabbaṃ taṃ nirodhadhamman"ti āha. Tañhi nirodhaṃ ārammaṇaṃ katvā kiccavasena evaṃ sabbasaṅkhataṃ paṭivijjhantaṃ uppajjati.* (Sv)

649. MN 91. See *The Middle Length Discourses*, 743–54.

650. MN 147. See *The Middle Length Discourses*, 1126–28.

651. *Maggaṃ phalañca nibbānaṃ, peccavekkhati pandito. Hīne kilese sese ca, paccavekkhati vāna vā.* (Abidh-s)

652. *The Middle Length Discourses*, 186.

Tassa mayhaṃ, bhante, evaṃ hoti: "kosu nāma me dhammo ajjhattaṃ appahīno yena me ekadā lobhadhammāpi cittaṃ pariyādāya tiṭṭhanti, dosadhammāpi cittaṃ pariyādāya tiṭṭhanti, mohadhammāpi cittaṃ pariyādāya tiṭṭhantī"ti.

So eva kho te, mahānāma, dhammo ajjhattaṃ appahīno . . . (MN 14.2–3)

653. *Ayaṃ kira rājā "sakadāgāmimaggena lobhadosamohā niravasesā pahīyantī"ti saññī ahosi, "ayaṃ appahīnam me atthī"tipi jānāti, appahīnakam upādāya pahīnakam[pi*[VRI]*] puna pacchatovāvatatīti saññī hoti. Ariyasāvakassa evaṃ sandeho uppajjatīti? Āma uppajjati. Kasmā? Paṇṇattiyā akovidattā, "Ayaṃ kileso asukamaggavajjho"ti imissā paṇṇittiyā akovidassa hi ariyasāvakassapi evaṃ hoti. Kiṃ tassa paccavekkhaṇā natthīti? Atthi. Sā pana na sabbesaṃ paripuṇṇa hoti. Eko hi pahīnakilesameva paccavekkha[ti*[VRI]*]. Eko avasiṭṭhakilesameva, eko maggameva, eko phalameva, eko nibbānameva. Imāsu [pana pañcasu* [VRI]*] paccavekkhaṇāsu ekaṃ vā dve vā no laddhuṃ na vaṭṭati.* (Ps)

654. See "Appendix 4: Uprooting Defilements" for a presentation of the information contained in the section given in tabular form.

655. See also *The Path of Purification*, 710.

Saṃyojanesu tāva sakkāyadiṭṭhi vicikicchā sīlabbataparāmāso apāyagamanīyā ca kāmarāgapaṭighāti ete pañca dhammā paṭhamañāṇavajjhā, sesā kāmarāgapaṭighā oḷārikā dutiyañāṇavajjhā, sukhumā tatiyañāṇavajjhā, rūparāgādayo pañcapi catutthañāṇavajjhā eva. (Vism 22.64)

656. Ibid.

Kilesesu ditthivicikicchā paṭhamañāṇavajjhā, doso tatiyañāṇavajjho, lobhamohamānathina-uddhacca-ahirika-anottappāni catutthañāṇavajjhāni. (Vism 22.65)

657. The four kinds of unwholesome speech count as only one of the ten wrongs.

658. Ibid.

Micchattesu micchādiṭṭhi musāvādo micchākammanto micchā-ājīvoti ime paṭhamañāṇavajjhā, micchāsaṅkappo pisuṇavācā pharusavācāti ime tatiyañāṇavajjhā, cetanāyeva cettha vācāti veditabbā, Samhappalāpamicchāvāyāmasatisamādhivimuttiñāṇāni catutthañāṇavajjhā. (Vism 22.66)

659. Pilinda had a habit of addressing everyone as Vasala (outcaste). When this was reported to the Buddha he explained that this was because Pilinda had, for one hundred lives, been born among Vasalavādī-Brahmins (Udāna, PTS 3.6; Dhammapāda commentary PTS 4.181f). One day, on entering Rājagaha, Pilinda met a man carrying a bowl of *pipphalī* (long pepper). "What's in thy bowl, Vasala?" he asked, and the man, in anger, said, "The dung of mice." "So be it," said Pilinda, and the pepper turned into dung. The man was horrified and, seeking Pilinda, persuaded him to right the matter. (Aṅguttara Nikāya commentary PTS 1.154f)

660. See also *The Path of Purification*, 710.

Lokadhammesu paṭigho tatiyañāṇavajjho, anunayo catutthañāṇavajjho, yase ca pasaṃsāya ca anunayo [tatiyañāṇavajjho'ti[MS]*] [catutthañāṇavajjho'ti*[VRI]*] eke. Samhappalāpamicchāvāyāmasatisamādhivimuttiñāṇāni catutthañāṇavajjhā.* (Vism 22.67)

661. The different interpretations of this Visuddhimagga passage are reflected in the Pāḷi (see P438), with Mahāsi Sayadaw's gloss being *tatiyañāṇavajjho* and the VRI 6th Council's version being *catutthañāṇavajjho.*

662. See also *The Path of Purification*, 710.

Macchariyāni paṭhamañāṇavajjhāni. (Vism 22.67)

663. Ibid.

Vipallāsesu anicce [niccanti[MS]*] [niccaṃ*[VRI]*] anattani attāti ca saññācittadiṭṭhivipallāsā, dukkhe [sukhanti*[MS]*] [sukhaṃ*[VRI]*], asubhe subhanti diṭṭhivipallāso cāti ime paṭhamañāṇavajjhā, asubhe subhanti saññācittavipallāsā tatiyañāṇavajjhā, dukkhe sukhanti saññācittavipallāsā catutthañāṇavajjhā.* (Vism 22.68)

664. Ibid., 710–11.

Agati paṭhamañāṇavajjhā. (Vism 22.69)

665. Ibid., 711.

Āsavesu diṭṭhāsavo paṭhamañāṇavajjho. Kāmāsavo tatiyañāṇavajjho, itare dve catutthaññāṇavajjho (Vism 22.70)

666. See "Appendix 6: Planes of Existence."

667. See also *The Path of Purification*, 711.

Nīvaraṇesu vicikicchānīvaraṇaṃ paṭhamañāṇavajjhaṃ, kāmacchando byāpādo kukkuccanti tīṇi tatiyañāṇavajjhāni, thinamiddha-uddhaccāni catutthañāṇavajjhāni. (Vism 22.71)

668. *Kāmacchandassa anāgāmimaggena pahānaṃ ukkaṭṭhanīvaraṇavasena vuttanti veditabbaṃ . . . Tasmā sabbo lobho kāmacchandanīvaraṇanti arahattamaggenassa pahānavacanaṃ yuttaṃ.* (Dhs-mlṭ)

669. See also *The Path of Purification*, 711.

Upādānesu sabbesampi lokiyadhammānaṃ vatthukāmavasena kāmāti āgatattā rūpārūparāgopi kāmupādāne patati, tasmā taṃ catutthañāṇavajjhaṃ, sesāni paṭhamañāṇavajjhāni. (Vism 22.72)

670. Ibid.

Ausayesu diṭṭhivicikicchānusayā paṭhamañāṇavajjhāva, kāmarāgapaṭighānusayā tatiyañāṇavajjhā, mānabhavarāgāvijjānusayā catutthañāṇavajjhā. (Vism 22.73)

671. Ibid.

Akusalakammapathesu pāṇātipāto adinnādānaṃ micchācaro musāvādo micchādiṭṭhīti ime paṭhamañāṇavajjhā, pisuṇavācā pharūsavācā byāpādoti tayo tatiyañāṇavajjhā, samphappalāpābhijjhā catutthañāṇavajjhā. (Vism 22.75)

672. Ibid.

Akusalacittuppādesu cattāro diṭṭhisampayuttā vicikicchā sampayutto cāti pañca paṭhama-ñāṇavajjhāva, dve paṭighasampayuttā tatiyañāṇavajjhā sesā catutthañāṇavajjhā. (Vism 22.76)

See "Appendix 2: Mental Factors Present in Each Consciousness": first path, numbers 1, 2, 5, 6, and 11; third path, numbers 9 and 10; fourth path, numbers 3, 4, 7, 8, and 12.

673. *Cattāro diṭṭhigatavippayuttā lobhasahagatacittuppādā, dve dosamanassasahagatacittuppādā: ime dhammā siyā dassanena pahātabbā.*

Katame dhammā na dassanena pahātabbā? Uddhaccasahagato cittuppādo . . . Katame dhammā bhāvanāya pahātabbā? Uddhaccasahagato cittuppādo . . . (Dhs)

674. Eg., see the Abhidhamma (Paṭṭh).

675. *Cittuppādaggahaṇena cettha makkhapalāsamāyasāṭheyyapamādathambhasārambhādhīnaṃ saṅgaho katoti daṭṭhabbaṃ.* (Vism-mhṭ)

676. MN 7. See *The Middle Length Discourses*, 118–22.

677. *Sotāpattimaggena makkho paḷāso issā macchariyaṃ māyā sāṭheyyanti ime cha pahīyanti. Anāgāmimaggena byāpādo kodho upanāho pamādoti ime cattāro. Arahattamaggena abhijjhā visamalobho thambho sārambho māno atimāno madoti ime cha pahīyanti.* (Ps)

678. *The Connected Discourses*, 1800.

Tasmā tihānanda dhammādāsaṃ nāma dhammapariyāyaṃ desessāmi, yena samannāgato ariyasāvako ākaṇkhamāno attanāvo attānaṃ byākareyya: "khīṇaniryomhi khīṇatiracchānayoni khīṇapettivisayo khīṇapāyuduggativinipāto, sotāpannohamasmi avinipātadhammo niyato [sambodhiparāyano"ti[MS]*] [sambodhiparāyaṇo"ti*[VRI]*].*

Katamo ca so, Ānanda, dhammādāso dhammapariyāyo . . . [sambodhiparāyano"ti[MS]*] [sambodhiparāyaṇo"ti*[VRI]*]? Idhānanda, ariyasāvako Buddhe aveccappasādena samannāgato hoti: " itipi so bhagavā arahaṃ sammāsambuddho vijjācaranasampanno sugato lokavidū anuttaro purisadhammasārathi satthādevamanussanaṃ buddho bhagavā"ti. Dhamme aveccappasādena samannāgato hoti: "svākāto bhagavatā dhammo sandiṭṭhiko akāliko ehipassiko opaneyyiko paccattaṃ vedittabbo viññūhī'ti" Saṅghe aveccappasādena samannāgato hoti: "suppaṭipanno bhagavato sāvakasaṅgho, ujupaṭipanno bhagavato sāvakasaṅgho, ñāyapaṭipanno bhagavato sāvakasaṅgho, sāmīcipaṭipanno bhagavato sāvakasaṅgho, yadidaṃ cattāri purisayugāni aṭṭha purisapuggalā, esa bhagavato sāvakasaṅgho āhuneyyo pāhuneyyo dakkhiṇeyyo añjalikaraṇiyo anuttaraṃ puññaketaṃ lokassā"ti.*

Ariyakantehi sīlehi samannāgato hoti akhaṇḍehi acchiddehi asabalehi akammāsehi bhujissehi viññūpasatthehi aparāmaṭṭhehi samādhisaṃvattanikehi. Ayaṃ kho so, Ānanda, dhammādāso dhammapariyāyo, yena samannāgato ariyasāvako ākaṅkhamāno attanāva attānaṃ byākareyya: "khīṇaniryomhi . . . (pe) . . . [sambodhiparāyano"ti[MS]*] [sambodhiparāyaṇo"ti*[VRI]*].* (SN 55.8)

679. Any being who has attained any of the four paths is known as a noble person, noble disciple, or noble one (*ariya*).

680. *The Numerical Discourses*, 1000.

Saddhādhanaṃ sīladhanaṃ hirī ottappiyaṃ dhanaṃ.
sutadhanañca cāgo ca, paññā ve sattanaṃ dhanaṃ.
Yassa ete dhanā atthi, itthiyā purisassa vā;
adaliddo'ti taṃ āhu, amoghaṃ tassa jīvitaṃ. (AN 7.5)

681. *Sace me [aṇgamaṇgāni*[MS]*][aṅgamaṅgāni*[VRI]*] kāmaṃ chejjasi brāhmana; nevāhaṃ viramissāmi, buddhaseṭṭhassa sāsanā.* (Spk)

682. *Ariyakantehīti ariyānaṃ kantehi piyehi manāpehi. [Pañcasīlāni hi*[MS]*][Pañca hi sīlāni*[VRI]*] ariyāsāvakānaṃ kantāni honti bhavantarepi avijahitabbato. Tāni sandhāyetaṃ vuttaṃ.* (Sv)

683. *Sacepi [hi*[VRI]*] bhavantaragataṃ ariyasāvakaṃ attano ariyabhāvaṃ ajānantampi koci evaṃ vadeyya "imaṃ kunthakipillikaṃ jīvitā voroepetvā sakalacakkavāḷagabbhe cakkavattirajjaṃ paṭipajjāhī"ti, neva so taṃ jātita voropeyya. Atāpi naṃ evaṃ [vadeyyaṃ*[MS]*][vadeyya*[VRI]*] "sace imaṃ ne [ghātessati*[MS]*][ghātessasi*[VRI]*] sīsaṃ te chindissāmā"ti. Sīsamevassa [chindeyyaṃ*[MS]*][chindeyya*[VRI]*][neva*[MS]*][na ca*[VRI]*] so taṃ ghāteyya.* (Ps)

684. DN 16. See *The Long Discourses of the Buddha*, 231–78.

685. *The Numerical Discourses*, 1264–65.

Tena kho pana samayena tesaṃ aññatitthiyānaṃ paribbājakānaṃ sannisinnānnānaṃ sannipatitānaṃ [ayamantarakathā[MS]*] [ayamantarākathā*[VRI]*] udapādi: "yo hi koci, āvuso, sa-upādiseso kālaṃ karoti, sabbo so aparimutto nirāya aparimutto tiracchānayoniyā aparimutto pettivisayā aparimutto apāyaduggativinipātā"ti. Atha kho ahaṃ, bhante tesaṃ aññatitthiyānaṃ paribbājakānaṃ bhāsitaṃ neva abhinandiṃ nappaṭikkosiṃ. Anabhinanditvā appaṭikkositvā uṭṭhāyāsana pakkamiṃ; "bhagavato santike etassa bhāsitassa atthaṃ ājānissāmī"ti . . . Ke ca, Sāriputta, aññatitthiyā paribbājakā bālā abyattā, ke ca sa-upādisesaṃ vā "sa-upādiseso"ti jānissanti, sa-upādisesaṃ vā anupādisesaṃ vā "anupādiseso"ti jānissanti! Navayime Sāriputta puggalā sa-upādisesā kālaṃ kurumānā parimuttā nirayā, parimuttā tiracchānayoniyā, parimuttā pettivisayā, parimuttā apāyaduggatinipātā.* (AN 9.12)

686. Numbers 1 through 5 denote those who have reached the third path, number 6 denotes those who have reached the second path, and numbers 7 through 9 denote those who have reached the first path.

687. Ibid., 1266–67.

Na tāvāyaṃ Sāriputta dhmmapariyāyo paṭibhāsi bhikkhūnaṃ bhikkhūninaṃ upāsakānaṃ upāsikānaṃ. Taṃ kissa hetu? Māyimaṃ dhammapariyāyaṃ sutvā pamādaṃ āhiriṃsūti. Api cā [yaṃ[MS]*] mayā Sāriputta dhammapariyāyo pañhādhippāyena bhāsito'ti.* (AN 9.12)

688. *The Connected Discourses*, 1808.

Tassa mayhaṃ bhante tasmiṃ samaye mussateva bhagavantaṃ ārabhta sati, mussati dhammaṃ ārabhta sati, mussati [saṃghaṃ[MS]*][saṅghaṃ*[VRI]*] ārabhta sati. Tassa mayhaṃ bhante, evaṃ hoti: "imamhi cāhaṃ samaye kālaṃ kareyyaṃ, kā mayhaṃ gati, ko abhisamparāyo"ti?*

Mā bhāyi, Mahānāma, mā bhāyi, Mahānāma! Apāpakaṃ te maraṇaṃ bhavissati, apāpikā kālaṃkiriyā. Yassa kassaci Mahānāma dīgharattaṃ saddhāparibhāvitaṃ cittaṃ [sīla, suta, cāga, paññāparibhāvitaṃ cittaṃ[MS]*] [sīlaparibhāvitaṃ cittaṃ, sutaparibhāvitaṃ cittaṃ, cāgaparibhāvitaṃ cittaṃ, paññāparibhāvitaṃ cittaṃ*[VRI]*], tassa yo hi kvāyaṃ kāyo rūpī . . . [pe*[MS]*] . . . taṃ idheva kākā vā, khādanti gijjhā vā, [khādanti*[VRI]*]kulala vā, [khādanti*[VRI]*]* *sunakhā vā, [khādanti*[VRI]*]sigālā vā, [khādanti*[VRI]*]vividhā vā pāṇakajātā kādanti; yañca kvassa cittaṃ dīgharattaṃ saddhāparibhāvitaṃ, [sīla, suta, cāga*[MS]*][pe*[VRI]*] paññāparibhāvitaṃ taṃ uddhaṃgāmi hoti visesagāmi . . . Catūhi kho Mahānāma dhammehi samannāgato ariyasāvako nibbānaninno hoti nibbānapoṇo nibbānapabbhāro.* (SN 5.21)

689. Ibid., 1809.

Yassa kassaci Mahānāma dīgharattaṃ saddhāparibhāvitaṃ cittaṃ [sīla, suta, cāga, paññāparibhāvitaṃ cittaṃ[MS]*][sīlaparibhāvitaṃ cittaṃ, sutaparibhāvitaṃ cittaṃ, cāgaparibhāvitaṃ cittaṃ, paññāparibhāvitaṃ cittaṃ*[VRI]*], tassa yo hi kvāyaṃ kāyo rūpī . . .[pe*[MS]*] . . .taṃ idheva kākā vā, khādanti gijjhā vā, [khādanti*[VRI]*]kulala vā, [khādanti*[VRI]*]sunakhā vā, [khādanti*[VRI]*]sigālā vā, [khādanti*[VRI]*]vividhā vā pāṇakajātā kādanti; yañca kvassa cittaṃ dīgharattaṃ saddhāparibhāvitaṃ, [sīla, suta, cāga*[MS]*][pe*[VRI]*] paññāparibhāvitaṃ taṃ uddhaṃgāmi hoti visesagāmi . . . Catūhi kho Mahānāma dhammehi samannāgato ariyasāvako nibbānaninno hoti nibbānapoṇo nibbānapabbhāro.* (SN 5.22)

690. Ibid.

Seyyathāpi, Mahānāma, puriso sappikumbhaṃ vā telakhumbhaṃ vā gambhīraṃ udakarahadaṃ ogāhitvā bhindeyya, tatra yā assa sakkharā vā kaṭhalā vā sā adhogāmi assa, yañcakhvassa tatra sappi vā telaṃ vā taṃ uddhagamī assa visesagamī. Evameva kho, Mahānāma, yassa kassaci dīgharattaṃ saddhāparibhāvitaṃ cittaṃ . . . pe . . . paññāparibhāvitaṃ cittaṃ tassa yo hi khvāyaṃ kāyo rūpī . . . dīgharattaṃ saddhāparibhāvitaṃ . . . pe . . . paññāparibhāvitaṃ cittaṃ . . . Apāpakaṃ te maraṇaṃ bhavissati, apāpika kalaṃkiriyā'ti. (SN 5.21)

691. Ibid., 1809.

Seyyathāpi, Mahānāma, rukkho pācīnaninno pācīnapoṇo pācīnapabbhāro, so mūlacchinno katamena papateyyā'ti? Yena, bhante, ninno yena poṇo yena pabbhāro'ti. Evameva kho, Mahānāma, catūhi dhammehi samannāgato ariyasāvako nibbānaninno hoti nibbānapoṇo nibbānapabbhāro'ti. (SN 5.22)

692. *The Middle Length Discourses*, 421–22.

Kathañca bhikkhave yāyaṃ diṭṭhi ariyā niyyānikā niyyati takkarassa sammā dukkhakkhayāya?

Idha, bhikkhave, bhikkhu araññagato vā rukkhamūlagatro vā suññāgāragato vā iti paṭisañcikkhati: "atthi no kho me taṃ pariyyuṭṭhānaṃ ajjhattaṃ appahīnaṃ, yenāhaṃ pariyuṭṭānena pariyuṭṭhitacitto yathābhūtaṃ nappajāneyyaṃ na passeyyan"ti? Sace, bhikkhave, bhikkhu kāmarāgapariyuṭṭhito hoti, pariyuṭṭhitacittova hoti. Sace, bhikkhave, bhikkhu byāpādapariyuṭṭhito [hoti, pariyuṭṭhitacittova hoti. Sace, bhikkhave, bhikkhu[VRI]*] thīnamiddhapariyuṭṭhito [hoti, pariyuṭṭhitacittova hoti. Sace, bhikkhave, bhikkhu*[VRI]*] uddhaccakukkuccapariyuṭṭhito [hoti, pariyuṭṭhitacittova hoti. Sace, bhikkhave, bhikkhu*[VRI]*] vicikicchāpariyuṭṭhito [hoti, pariyuṭṭhitacittova hoti. Sace, bhikkhave, bhikkhu*[VRI]*]. idhalokacintāya pasuto[hoti, pariyuṭṭhitacittova hoti. Sace, bhikkhave, bhikkhu*[VRI]*] paralokacintāya pasuto hoti pariyuṭṭhitacittova hoti. Sace, bhikkhave, bhikkhu. Bhaṇḍanajāto kalajāto vivādāpanno aññamaññanaṃ mukhasattī'ti vitudanto viharati, pariyuṭṭhitacittova hoti. So evaṃ pajānāti: "natthi no kho me taṃ pariyyuṭṭhānaṃ ajjhattaṃ appahīnaṃ, yenāhaṃ pariyuṭṭānena pariyuṭṭhitacitto yathābhūtaṃ nappajāneyyaṃ na passeyyaṃ. Suppaṇihitaṃ me* *mānasaṃ saccānaṃ bodhāyā'ti. Idamassa paṭhamaṃ ñāṇaṃ adhigantaṃ hoti ariyaṃ lokuttaraṃ asādhāraṇaṃ puthujjanehi.* (MN 48.8)

693. Ibid., 422 (Mahāsi Sayadaw's glosses in brackets).

Puna ca paraṃ, bhikkhave, ariyasāvako iti paṭicañcikkhati: "imaṃ nu kho ahaṃ diṭṭhiṃ āsevanto bhāvento bahulīkaronto labhāmi paccattaṃ samathaṃ, labhāmi paccattaṃ nibbutin'ti? So evaṃ pajānāti: "imaṃ kho ahaṃ diṭṭiṃ āsevanto bhāvento bahulīkaronto labhāmi paccattaṃ samathaṃ, labhāmi paccataṃ nibbutin'ti. Idamassa dutiyaṃ ñāṇaṃ adhigantaṃ hoti ariyaṃ lokuttaraṃ asādhāraṇaṃ puthujjanehi. (MN 48.9)

694. Ibid.

Puna ca paraṃ, bhikkhave, ariyasāvako iti paṭicañcikkhati: "yathārūpāyāhaṃ diṭṭiyā samannāgato, atthi nu kho ito bhahiddhā añño samaṇo vā brāhmaṇo vā tathārūpāya diṭṭhiyā samannāgato"ti? So evaṃ pajānāti: "yathārūpāyāhaṃ diṭṭiyā samannāgato, natthi ito bhahiddhā añño samaṇo vā brāhmaṇo vā tathārūpāya diṭṭhiyā samannāgato"ti. Idamassa tatiyaṃ ñāṇaṃ adhigantaṃ hoti ariyaṃ lokuttaraṃ asādhāraṇaṃ puthujjanehi.

Puna ca paraṃ, bhikkhave, ariyasāvako iti paṭicañcikkhati: "yathārūpāyā dhammatāya diṭṭhisampanno pugalo samannāgato, ahampi tathārūpāya dhammatāya samannāgato"'ti. Kathaṃrūpāyā ca, bhikkhave dhammatāya diṭṭhisampanno pugalo samannāgato? Dammatā esā, bhikkhave, diṭṭhisampannassa pugalassa "kiñcāpi tathārūpiṃ apattiṃ āpajjati, yathārūpāya apattiyā vuṭṭhānaṃ paññāyati, atha kho naṃ khippameva satthari vā viññūsu vā sabrahmacārīsu deseti vivarati uttānīkaroti; desetvā vivaritvā uttānīkatvā āyatiṃ saṃvaraṃ āpajjati." Seyyathāpi, bhikkhave daharo kumāro mando uttānaseyyako hatthena vā pādena vā aṅgāraṃakkamitvā khippameva paṭisaṃharati; evameva kho, bhikkhave, dammatā esā diṭṭhisampannassa pugalassa: "kiñcāpi . . . (pe) . . . saṃvaraṃ āpajjati." So evaṃ pajānāti: "yathārūpāyā dhammatāya diṭṭhisampanno pugalo samannāgato, ahampi tathārūpāya dhammatāya samannāgato"'ti. Idamassa catuttaṃ ñāṇaṃ adhigantaṃ hoti ariyaṃ lokuttaraṃ asādhāraṇaṃ puthujjanehi. (MN 48.10–11)

695. Ibid., 422–23 (Mahāsi Sayadaw's glosses in brackets).

Puna ca paraṃ, bhikkhave, ariyasāvako iti paṭicañcikkhati: "yathārūpāyā dhammatāya diṭṭhisampanno pugalo samannāgato, ahampi tathārūpāya dhammatāya samannāgato"'ti. Kathaṃrūpāyā ca, bhikkhave dhammatāya diṭṭhisampanno pugalo samannāgato? Dammatā esā, bhikkhave, diṭṭhisampannassa pugalassa "kiñcāpi yāni tāni sabrahmacārīnaṃ uccāvacāni kiṃkaraṇīyāni tattha [ussukkamāpanno[MS]*] [ussukkaṃ āpanno*[VRI]*] hoti, atha khvāssa [tibbāpekkho*[MS]*][tibbāpekkhā*[VRI]*] hoti. adhisīlasikkhāya, adhicittasikkhāya, adhipaññāsikāya." Seyyathāpi, bhikkhave, gāvī taruṇavacchā [thambaṃ ca*[MS]*][thambañca*[VRI]*] āllumpati [vacchakaṃ ca*[MS]*][vacchakañca*[VRI]*] apacinati; evameva kho, bhikkhave, dhammatā esā, bhikkhave, diṭṭhisampannassa pugalassa "kiñcāpi . . .(pe) . . . adhipaññāsikāya."*

So evaṃ pajānāti: "yathārūpāyā dhammatāya diṭṭhisampanno pugalo samannāgato, ahampi tathārūpāya dhammatāya samannāgato"'ti. Idamassa pañcanaṃ ñāṇaṃ adhigantaṃ hoti ariyaṃ lokuttaraṃ asādhāraṇaṃ puthujjanehi.

Puna ca paraṃ bhikkhave ariyasāvako iti paṭisañcikkhati: "yathārūpāya balatāya diṭṭhisampanno puggalo samannāgato ahampi balatāya samannāgato"ti. Kathaṃrūpāya ca, bhikkhave, balatāya diṭṭhisampanno puggalo sammagāto? Balatā esā, bhikkhave, diṭṭhisampannassa puggalassa yaṃ tathāgatappavedite dhammavinaye desiyamāne aṭṭhiṃkatvā manasikatvā sabbacetasā samannāharitvā ohitasoto dhammaṃ suṇāti.

So evaṃ pajānāti: "yathārūpāya balatāya diṭṭhisampanno puggalo sammagāto, ahampi tathārūpāya balatāya samannāgato"ti. Idamassa chaṭṭhaṃ ñāṇaṃ adhigataṃ hoti ariyaṃ lokuttaraṃ asādhāraṇaṃ puthujjanehi.

Puna ca paraṃ bhikkhave ariyasāvako iti paṭisañcikkhati: "yathārūpāya balatāya diṭṭhisampanno puggalo samannāgato ahampi balatāya samannāgato"ti. Kathaṃrūpāya ca, bhikkhave, balatāya diṭṭhisampanno puggalo sammagāto? Balatā esā, bhikkhave, diṭṭhisampannassa puggalassa yaṃ tathāgatappavedite dhammavinaye desiyamāne labhati atthavedaṃ, labhati dhammavedhaṃ, labhati dhammūpasaṃhitaṃ pāmojjaṃ.

So evaṃ pajānāti: "yathārūpāya balatāya diṭṭhisampanno puggalo sammagāto, ahampi tathārūpāya balatāya samannāgato"ti Idamassa sattamaṃ ñāṇaṃ adhigataṃ hoti ariyaṃ lokuttaraṃ asādhāraṇaṃ puthujjanehi.

Evaṃ sattaṅgasamannāgaa kho bhikkhave ariyasāvakassa dhammatā susamaniṭṭhā hoti sotāpattiphalasacchikiriyāya. Evaṃ sattaṅgasamannāgato kho bhikkhave ariyasāvako sotāpattiphalasamannāgato hoti. (MN 48.12–15)

696. See also *The Path of Purification*, 734.

Vipassanā [paneso[KN, ViTi]*][panesā*[Vism]*] tividhā hoti: saṅkhārapariggaṇhanakavipassanā phalasamapattivipassanā nirodhasamāpattivipassanāti. Tattha saṅkhārapariggaṇhanakavipassanā mandā vā hotu tikkhā vā, maggassa padaṭṭhānaṃ hotiyeva. Phalasamāpattivipassanā tikkhāva vaṭṭati maggabhāvanāsadisā. Nirodhasamāpattivipassanā pana nātimanda nātitikkhā vaṭṭati* . . . (Paṭis 23.33)

697. *Saṅkhārupekkhāya tikkhabhāve sati kilesappahāne samatthassa maggassa sambhavato ā tikkhabhāvadassanatthaṃ vevacanapadehi saha daḷhaṃ katvā mūlapadāni vuttāni. Phalassa nirussāhabhāvena santasabhāvattā maggāyattattā ca mandabhūtāpi saṅkhārypekkhā phalassa paccayo hotīti dassanatthaṃ mūlapadāneva vuttānīti veditabbāni.* (Paṭis commentary)

698. *The Middle Length Discourses*, 393, fn. 449: "MA: The 'signless deliverance of mind' (*animittā cetovimutti*) is the attainment of fruition; the 'signs' are objects such as forms, etc.; the 'signless element' is Nibbāna, in which all signs of conditioned things are absent."

699. *The Middle Length Discourses*, 393.

Dve kho, āvuso paccayā animittāya cetovimuttiyā samāpattiyā sabbanimittānañca amanasikāro, animittāya ca dhātuyā manasikāro. (MN 43.27)

700. See also *The Path of Purification*, 728.

Phalasamāpattitthikena hi ariyasāvakena rahogatena paṭisallīnena udayabbayādivasena saṅkhārā [passitabbā[MS]*][vipassitabbā*[VRI]*]. Tassa pavattānnupubbavipassanassa saṅkhārārammaṇagotrabhuñāṇānantarā phalasamāpattivasena nirodhe cittaṃ appeti. Phalasamāpattininnatāya cettha sekkhassāpi phalameva uppajjati, na maggo.* (Vism 23.10)

701. These are: preventing the arising of unwholesome mental states, eliminating unwholesome mental states when they do arise, promoting the arising of wholesome mental states, and sustaining wholesome mental states when they do arise. – Tr.

702. *The Middle Length Discourses*, 393.

Tayo kho, āvuso paccayā animittāya cetovimuttiyā ṭhitiyā sabbanimittānañca amanasikāro, animittāya ca dhātuyā manasikāro, pubbe ca abhisaṅkhāro. (MN 43.28)

703. With this is shown how the object is experienced during the absorption in fruition.

704. *The Numerical Discourses*, 1558.

[*Idha, āvuso, Ānanda*[AN XI]][*Idhānanda*[AN X, XI]], *bhikkhu evaṃsaññī hoti: "etaṃ santaṃ etaṃ paṇītaṃ, yadidaṃ sabbasaṅkhārasamatho sabbūpadhipaṭinissaggo taṇhākkhayo virāgo nirodho nibbānan"ti. Evaṃ kho Ānanda siyā bhikkhuno tathārūpo samādhipaṭilābho yathā neva pathaviyaṃ pathavisaññī assa, na āpasmiṃ āposaññī assa, na tejasmiṃ tejosaññī assa, na vāyasmiṃ vāyosaññī assa, na ākāsānañcāyatane ākāsānañcāyatanasaññī assa, na viññāṇañcāyatane viññāṇañcāyatanasaññī assa, na ākiñcaññāyatane ākiñcaññāyatanesaññī assa, na nevasaññānāsaññāyatane nevasaññānāsaññāyatanasaññī assa, na idhaloke idhalokasaññī assa, na paraloke, paralokasaññī assa. Yampi diṭṭhaṃ sutaṃ mutaṃ viññātaṃ pattaṃ pariyesitaṃ anuvicaritaṃ manassā, tatrāpi na saññī assa ca pana assā'ti.* (AN 11.7)

705. *Etaṃ santaṃ etaṃpaṇītan'ti* [*santa*[MS]][*santaṃ*[VRI]] *santanti appetvā nisinnassa* [*divasaṃpi*[MS]][*divasampi*[VRI]] *cittuppādo "santaṃ* [*santaṃ"teva*[MS]][*santan"teva*[VRI]] *pavattati, paṇītaṃ paṇītanti appetvā nisinnassa* [*divasaṃpi*[MS]][*divasampi*[VRI]] *cittuppādo "paṇītaṃ* [*paṇītaṃ"teva*[MS]][*paṇītan"teva*[VRI]] *pavattati* . . .(*Sabbasaṅkhārasamathoti-ādīnipi tasseva vevacanāni. Sabbasaṅkhārasamathoti appetvā nisinnassa hi* [*divasaṃpi*[MS]][*divasabhāgaṃpi*[VRI]] *cittuppādo sabbasaṅkhārasamathoteva pavattati . . . pe . . .*) . . . *nibbānaṃ nibbānanti appetvā nibbānassa divasaṃpi cittuppādo "nibbānaṃ nibbānaṃ"teva pavattatīti.* [*Sabbaṃ petaṃ*[MS]][*Sabbampetaṃ*[VRI]] *phalasamāpattisamādhiṃ sandhāya vuttaṃ.* (Mp)

706. *The Middle Length Discourses*, 393–94.

Dve kho, āvuso paccayā animittā cetovimuttiyā vuṭṭhānāyāsabbanimittānañca manasikāro, animittāya ca dhātuyā amanasikāra. (MN43.29)

707. Material phenomena, feeling, perception, formations, and consciousness.

708. See *The Path of Purification*, 729, fn. 7: "It is because he is called 'emerged from attainment' as soon as the life-continuum consciousness has arisen that 'he brings to mind that which is the object of the life-continuum' is said. Kamma, etc., are called the object of the life-continuum."

709. See also Ibid., 729.

Sabbanimittānanti rūpanimittavedanāsaññāsaṅkhāraviññāṇanimittanaṃ. Kāmañca na sabbānevetāni ekato manasikaroti, sabbasaṅgāhikavasena panetiṃ vuttaṃ. Tasmā yaṃ bhavaṅgassa ārammaṇaṃ hoti, taṃ manasikaroto phalasamāpattivuṭṭhnaṃ hoti. (Vism 23.13)

710. See "Appendix 3: Stream of Consciousness," lines H18, 20.

711. *Attheso, bhikkhave, samādhi so ca kho aparisuddho.* (Vin and Vin commentary)

712. The five aspects of absorption are: investigating the *jhānic* factors of the absorption through adverting-consciousness, entering the absorpion, determining the duration of the absorption, emerging the absorption, and reviewing its *jhānic* factors through the knowledge of reviewing. – Tr.

713. *Dve hi khīṇāsavā satatavihārī* [*ca*[VRI]] *nosatatavihārī ca. Tattha satatavihārī yaṃ kiñci kammaṃ katvāpi phalasamāpattiṃ samāpajjituṃ sakkoti, no satatavihārī pana appamattakepi kicce kiccappasuto hutvā phalasamāpattiṃ appetuṃ na sakoti.* (Ps)

714. See also *The Path of Discrimination*, 17.

Uppādo [saṅkhāra[MS]*][saṅkhārāti*[VRI]*]. . . anuppādo [nibbānaṃ*[MS]*] [nibbānanti*[VRI]*]. . . Pavattaṃ [saṅkhāra*[MS]*] [saṅkhārāti*[VRI]*]. . . apavattaṃ [nibbānaṃ*[MS]*] [nibbānanti*[VRI]*]. . . Nimittaṃ [saṅkhāra*[MS]*] [saṅkhārāti*[VRI]*] . . . animittaṃ [nibbānaṃ*[MS]*] [nibbānanti*[VRI]*]. . . Āyūhanā [saṅkhāra*[MS]*] [saṅkhārāti*[VRI]*]. . . anāyūhanā [nibbānaṃ*[MS]*] [nibbānanti*[VRI]*]. . . Paṭisanki [saṅkhāra*[MS]*] [saṅkhārāti*[VRI]*]. . . apaṭisanki [nibbānaṃ*[MS]*] [nibbānanti*[VRI]*]. (Paṭis 1.22)

715. The word *nibbāna* can be possibly regarded as a verbal noun because its verb forms and verbal noun forms (*dhātusiddhapada*) are often found in the Pāḷi Texts and commentaries (such as *nibbantidhīrā, nibbāpenti rāgaggiṃ, parinibbāyati, parinibbātu sugato, parinibbāyeyya, parinibbāyī, parinibbāyissati, antarā parinibbāyī, parinibbuto, khandhaparinibbānaṃ,* and so on).

716. *Nibbāti vaṭṭadukkhaṃ etthāti nibbānaṃ, nibbāti vaṭṭadukkhaṃ etasmiṃ adhigate'ti vā nibbānaṃ, nibbāyate vā nibbānaṃ.* (Sv)

717. *Vānato* [*nikkhantaṃ*[MS]][*nikkhantanti*[VRI]] *nibbānaṃ . . . natthivānaṃ etthāti* [*vā*[MS]] *nibbānaṃ . . . natthi vā na etasmiṃ adhigateti vā nibbānaṃ.* (Sv)

718. *Appaṭṭhibhāgaṃ, Mahārāja, nibbānaṃ. Na sakkā nibbānassa rūpaṃ vā saṇṭānaṃ vā vayaṃ vā pāmaṇaṃ vā, opammena vā kāraṇena vā hetunā vā nayena vā* [*upadissayituṃ*[MS]][*upadissayitun'ti*[VRI]]. (Mil)

719. *The Udana and the Itivuttaka: Two Classics from the Pali Canon*, John Ireland, trans. (Kandy: Buddhist Publication Society, 1998), 103 and 148.

Atthi, bhikkhave, ajātaṃ abhūtaṃ akataṃ asaṅkhataṃ. No cetaṃ, bhikkhave, [*abhavia*[MS]][*abhavissa*[VRI]] *ajātaṃ abhūtaṃ akataṃ asaṅkhataṃ, nayidha jāa bhūa kaa saṅkhaa nissaraṇaṃ paññāyetha. Yasmā ca kho, bhikkhave, atthi ajātaṃ abhūtaṃ akataṃ asaṅkhataṃ tasmā jāa bhūa kaa saṅkhaa nissaraṇaṃ* [*paññāyati*[MS]][*paññāyatī'ti*[VRI]]. (Ud; It)

720. Ibid., 102.

Atthi, bhikkhave, tadāyatanaṃ, yattha neva pathavī na āpo na tejo na vāyo na ākāsānañcāyatanaṃ na viññāṇañcayatanaṃ na ākiñcāññāyatanaṃ na nevasaññānāsaññāyatanaṃ tanaṃ nāyaṃ loko na paro loko na ca ubho candimasūriyā . . . Tatrāpāhaṃ, bhikkhave, neva āgatiṃ vadāmi na gatiṃ na ṭhitiṃ na cutiṃ na upapattiṃ, appatiṭṭhaṃ appavattaṃ anārammanaṇamevetaṃ, esevanto dhukkhassā. (Ud)

721. *Yasmā nibbānaṃ sabbasaṅkhāravidhurasabhāvaṃ* [*tasmā*[MS]] *yathā saṅkhatadhammesu katthaci natthi, tathā tatthapi sabbe saṅkhatadhammā. Na hi saṅkhatāsaṅkhatadhammānaṃ samodhānaṃ sambhavati.* (Ud-a)

722. *The Connected Discourses*, 1848.

Katamañca, bhikkhave, [*dukkhanirodho*[MS]][*dukkhanirodhaṃ*[VRI]] *ariyasaccaṃ? Yo tassayeva taṇhāya asesavirāganirodho cāgo paṭinissaggo mutti anālayo.* [. . .[DN, MN]]*Idaṃ vuccati, bhikkhave, dukkhanirodho ariyasaccaṃ.* (SN 5.13)

723. *The Middle Length Discourses*, 260.

Idampi kho . . . duddasaṃ, yadidaṃ sabbasaṅkhārasamato sabbūpadhipaṭinissaggo taṇhākkhayo virago nirodho nibbanaṃ. (MN 26.19)

724. *The Udana and the Itivuttaka*, 149.

Katamā ca, bhikkhave, sa-upādisesā nibbānadhātu? Idha bhikkhave, bhikkhu, arahaṃ hoti khīṇāsavo vusitavā kitakaraṇīyo ohitabhāro anuppattasadattho [*parikkhīṇābhavasaññojano*[MS]] [*parikkhīṇābhavasaṃyojano*[VRI]] *sammadaññā vimutto. Tassa tiṭṭhanteva pañcindriyāni yesaṃ avighātattā manāpāmanāpaṃ paccanubhoti, sukhadukkhaṃ paṭisaṃvedeti. Tissa yo rāgakkhayo, dosakkhayo, mohakkhayo: ayaṃ vuccati, bhikkhave, sa-upādisesa nibbānadhātu.*

Katamā ca bhikkhave anupādisesa nibbānadhātu? Idha bhikkhave, bhikkhu, arahaṃ hoti . . . pe . . . [*khīṇāsavo vusitavo kitakaraṇīyo ohitabhāro anuppattasadattho parikkhīṇābhavo saññājano*[VRI]] *sammadaññā vimutto. Tassa idheva, bhikkhave, sabbavedayitāni anabhinanditānī* [*sīti*[MS]][*sīti*[VRI]] *bhavissanti. Ayaṃ vuccati, bhikkhave, anupādisesa nibbānadhātu . . .* (Ud)

725. The Buddha is called the Seeing One because he possesses five special powers that are referred to as his "five eyes." These are: the divine eye (*dibbacakkhu*), the eye of path knowledge of arahantship (*paññācakkhu*), the eye of the three lower path knowledges (*dhammacakkhu*), the eye of insight into a person's inclination (*Buddhacakkhu*), and the all-seeing eye (*samantacakkhu*).

726. *The Udana and the Itivuttaka*, 150, fn. 28: "*Tādi*: 'stable,' is a term for an emancipated one, the arahant, and refers to his equanimity towards agreeable and disagreeable sense objects."

727. Ibid., fn. 29: "The 'cord of being' (*bhavanetti*) is craving for being (*bhavataṇhā*), so called because it keeps living beings attached to the round of existence."

728. Ibid., 150.

Duve imaṃ cakkhumatā pakāsitā, nibbānadhātū anissitena tādinā;
ekāhi dhātu idha diṭṭhdhammikā, sa-upādisesā bhavanetti saṅkhayā;
anupādisesa pana samparāyikā, yamhi nirujjhanti bhavāni sabbaso.
Ye etadaññāya padaṃ asaṅkhataṃ, vimuttacittā bhavanettisaṅkhayā;
te dhammasārādhigamā khaye ratā, pahaṃsu te sabbabhavāni tādino. (It)

729. *A Comprehensive Manual of Abhidhamma*, 222.

[*Tadethaṃ*[MS]][*Tadetaṃ*[VRI]] *sabhāvato ekavidhampi sa-upādisesanibbānadhātu, anupādisesanibbānadhātu ceti* [*duvimaṃ*[MS]][*duvidhaṃ*[VRI]] *hoti kāraṇapariyāyena.* (Abhidh-s 6.31)

730. *The Connected Discourses*, 1191.

Tasmātiha, bhikkhave, se āyatane veditabbe yattha cakkhu ca nirujjhati, rūpasaññā ca nurujjhati, se āyatane veditabbe [*yattha sotañca nirujjhati, saddasaññā ca nurujjhati, se āyatane veditabbe yattha ghānañca nirujjhati, gandhasaññā ca nirujjhati, se āyatane veditabbe*[MS]][*. . . pe . . .*[VRI]] *yattha jivahā ca nirujjhati, rasasaññā ca nurujjhati, se āyatane veditabbe yattha kāyo ca nirujjhati, photthabbusaññā ca nirujjhati, se āyatane veditabbe yattha mano ca nirujjhati, dhammasaññā ca nirujjhati, se āyatane veditabbe.* (SN 35.117)

731. Ibid.

Saḷayatananirodhaṃ no etaṃ āvuso, Bhagavatā sandhāya bhāsitaṃ . . . (SN 35.117)

732. *The Udana and the Itivuttaka*, 21.

Tato tvaṃ Bahiya, nevidha, na huraṃ ba ubhayamantarena. Esevanto dukkhassa'ti. (Ud)

733. *Aññe idhāti ajjhattikāyatanāni, huranti bāhirāyatināni, ubhayamantarenāti cittacetasikāti . . .* (Ud-a)

734. *The Connected Discourses*, 103 (Mahāsi Sayadaw's glosses in brackets).

Yattha āpo ca pathavī, tejo vāyo na gādhati;
ato sarā nivattanti, ettha vaṭṭaṃ na vattati;
ettha nāmañca rūpañca, asesaṃ uparujjhati. (SN 1.27)

735. *The Long Discourses of the Buddha*, 179–80.

Viññānaṃ anidassanaṃ, anantaṃ sabbatopabhaṃ;
ettha āpo ca pathavī, tejo vāyo na gādhati.
Ettha dīghañca rassañca, aṇuṃ thūlaṃ subhāsubhaṃ;
ettha nāmañca rūpañca, asesaṃ uparujjhati.
viññānassa nirodhena, etthetaṃ uparujjhati. (DN 11.85)

736. Ibid.

737. See also *The Path of Purification*, 651, and Venerable Mātara Sri Ñāṇārāma Mahāthera, *The Seven Stages of Purification and the Insight Knowledges* (Kandy: Buddhist Publication Society, 2010).

Aṭṭhārasa mahāvipassanā nāma aniccānupassanādikā paññā. Yāsu aniccānupassanaṃ bhāvento niccasaññaṃ pajahati, dukkhānupassanaṃ bhāvento sukhasaññaṃ pajahati, anattānupassanaṃ bhāvento attasaññaṃ pajahati, nibbidānupassanaṃ bhāvento nandiṃ pajahati, virāgānupassanaṃ bhāvento rāgaṃ pajahati, nirodhānupassanaṃ bhāvento samudayaṃ pajahati, paṭinissaggānupassanaṃ bhāvento ādānaṃ pajahati, khayānupassanaṃ bhāvento ghanasaññaṃ pajahati, vayānupassanaṃ bhāvento āyūhanaṃ pajahati, vipariṇāmānupassanaṃ bhāvento dhuvasaññaṃ pajahati, animittānupassana bhāvento nimittaṃ pajahati, appaṇihitānupassana bhāvento paṇidhiṃ pajahati, suññatānupassanaṃ bhāvento abhinivesaṃ pajahati, adhipaññādhammavipassanaṃ bhāvento sārādānābhinibesaṃ pajahati, yathābhūtañāṇadassanaṃ bhāvento sammohābhinivesaṃ pajahati, ādīnavānupassanaṃ bhāvento ālayābhinivesaṃ pajahati, paṭisaṅkhānupassanaṃ bhāvento appaṭisaṅkhaṃ pajahati, vivaṭṭānupassanaṃ bhāvento saṃyogābhinivesaṃ pajahati. (Vism 20.90)

738. See also *The Path of Purification*, 663.

Aniccanti khandhapañcakaṃ. Kasmā? Uppādavayaññathattabhāva hutvā abhāvato vā. [Aññathattaṃ nāma jarā.[khu.ni.aṭṭha.]] *Uppādavayaññathattaṃ aniccalakkhaṇaṃ hutvā abhāvasaṅkhāto vā ākāravikāro.* (Vism 21.6)

739. Ibid., 283.

Aniccatāti tesaṃyeva uppādavayaññatathattaṃ, hutvā abhāvo vā, nibbattānaṃ tenevakārena aṭṭhatvā khaṇabhaṅgena bhedotiattho. Aniccānupassanāti ā aniccatāya vasena rūpādīsu aniccanti anupassanā. (Vism 8.234)

740. *Hutvā abhāvaṭṭhenāti idaṃ itaresaṃ catunnaṃ ākārānaṃ sangahakattā visuṃ vuttaṃ.* (Vibh mulatika)

741. *Aparehipi catūhi kāraṇehi aniccaṃ—uppādavayavantato, vipariṇāmato, tāvakālikato, niccapaṭikepatoti.* (Sammohavinodanī Aṭṭhakathā)

742. *Kiñcāpi uppādāditividhampi saṅkhatalakkhaṇatāya aniccalakkhaṇaṃ, tathāpi jātijarāsu [na diṭṭhāsu*[MS]]*[nadiṭṭhāsu na*[VRI]] *tathā aniccalakkhaṇaṃ pākaṭaṃ hutvā paṭṭhāti yathā [vayalakkhaṇeti*[MS]]*[vayakkhaṇeti*[VRI]] *āha "bhaṅgo nāma aniccātaya paramākoṭī"ti.* (Vism-mhṭ)

743. *Vuṭṭhānagāminī pana vipassanā kimārammaṇāti? Lakkhaṇārammaṇāti. Lakkhaṇaṃ nāma paññattigatikaṃ na vattabbadhammabhūtaṃ. Yo pana aniccaṃ dukkhamanattāti tīni lakkhaṇāni sallakkhenti, a pañcakkhandhā kaṇṭhe baddhakuṇapaṃ viya honti. Saṅkhārāmmaṇameva ñāṇaṃ saṅkhārato vuṭṭhāti. Yathā hi eko bhikkhu pattaṃ kiṇitukāmo pattavāṇijena pattaṃ ābhataṃ disvā haṭṭhapahaṭṭho gaṇhissāmīti cintetvā vimamsamāno tīni chiddāni passeyya, so na chiddesu nirālayo hoti, patte pana nirālayo hoti; evameva tīni lakkhaṇāni sallakkhetvā saṅkhāresu nirālayo hoti.*

Saṅkhārārammaṇeneva ñāṇena saṅkhārato vuṭṭhātiti veditabaṃ Dussopamāyapi eseva nayo. (Dhs-a)

744. *"Aniccan"ti-ādinā saṇkharesu pavittamānena ñaṇena lakkhaṇānipi paṭividdhāni honti tadākārasaṅkhāra*[*gg*[MS]][g[VRI]] *ahaṇatoti āha "lakkhaṅārammaṇā"ti.* [*Sankhāralakkhaṇarammaṇā*[MS]][*Saṅkhārārammaṇā*[VRI]]*evayathāvuttādhippāyena "lakkhaṇārammaṇā"ti vuttāti dassento "lakkhaṇaṃ nāmā"ti ādimāha. Aniccatā dukkhatā anattatāti hi visuṃ gayhamānaṃ lakkhaṇaṃ paññatigatikaṃ paramatthato avijjamānaṃ, avijjamānattā eva parittādivasena navattabbadhammmabhūtaṃ.*

Tasmā visuṃ gahetabbassa lakkhaṇassa paramatthato abhāvā, "aniccaṃ dukkhaṃ anattā"ti saṅkhare sabhāvato sallakkhentova lakkhaṇāni sallakkheti nāmāti āha "yo pana aniccaṃ dukkhaṃ anattāti tīṇi lakkhaṇāni sallakkheti"ti. Yasmā ca aniccanti-ādinā saṅkhārāva dissamānā, tasmā te kaṇṭhe baddhakuṇapaṃ viya paṭinissajjanīyā honti. (Abhidhamma subcommentary)

745. *Aniccādīhi aniccalakkhaṇādinaṃ aññattha vacanaṃ ruppanādivasena pavattarūpādiggahaṇato visiṭṭhassa aniccadiggahaṇassa sabbhāvā. Na hi nāmarūpaparicchedamattena kiccasiddhi hoti, aniccādayo ca rūpādinaṃ ākārā aṭṭhabbā . . . Aniccanti ca gaṇhanto "dukkhaṃ anattā"ti na gaṇhāti, tathā dukkhādiggahaṇe itarassāgahaṇaṃ.* (Abhidhamma subcommentary)

746. See also *The Path of Purification*, 662–63.

Aniccalakkhanaṅaṃ tāva udayabbayānaṃ amansikārā santatiyā paṭicchannattā na upaṭṭhāti. . . . Udayabbayampana pariggahetvā santatiyā vikopitāya aniccalakkhaṇaṃ yāthāvasarasato upaṭṭhāti. (Vism 21.3–4)

747. *Santatiyā hissa paṭicchannattā aniccalakkhaṇaṃ na upaṭṭhāti, sā ca santati udayabbayāmanassikārenajātā* [*paṭicchādikā*[VRI]]. *Udayabbayaṃ passato na udayāvatthā vayāvatthaṃ pāpuṇāti vayāvatthā vā udayāvatthaṃ. Aññova udayakkhaṇo, aññova vayakkhaṇoti ekopi dhammmo khaṇavasena bhedato upaṭṭhāti, pageva atītādikoti āha "udayabbayam pana. . . (pe) . . . upaṭṭhāti"ti. Tattha santatiyā vikopitāyāti pubbāpariyena pavattamānānaṃ dhammānaṃ* [*aññoññabhāva*[MS]][*aññoññabhāvasa*[VRI]] *lakkhaṇena santatiyā ugghāṭitāya. Na hi sammadevi udabbayam sallakkhentassa dhamma sambhandabhāvena upatihanti, atha kho ayosalākā viya asambhandhabhāvenāti upaṭṭhahanti, atha kho ayosalākā viya asambhandabhāvenāti suṭṭhutaraṃ aniccalakkhaṇaṃ pākaṭaṃ hoti.* (Vism-mhṭ)

748. See also *The Path of Discrimination*, 178.

Aniccato anupassanto niccasaññaṃ pajahati. (Paṭis 3.197)

749. *Niccasaññanti niccagāhaṃ, saññāsīsena niddeso. Sukhasaññaṃ attasaññanti etthāpi eseva nayo.* (Vism-mhṭ)

750. *Niccasaññāyāti "saṅkhatadhammā niccā sassatā"ti evaṃ pavattāya micchāsaññāya, saññāggahaṇeneva diṭṭhicittānampi gahaṇaṃ daṭṭhabbaṃ. Esa nayo ito* [*parāsu*[MS]] [*parāsupi*[VRI]]. (Vibh)

751. *Ettha sattānaṃ rāgānusayo anuseti'ti etasmiṃ iṭṭharammaṇe sattānaṃ appahīnaṭṭhena rāgānusayo anuseti.* (Vibh-a)

752. *Ārammaṇasantānānusayanesu iṭṭhārammaṇe ārammaṇānusayanena anuseti.* (Vibh mūla-anuṭika)

753. *Ārammaṇasantānānusayanesuti ārammaṇānusayanaṃ santānānanusayananti dvīsu anusayanesu. Yathā hi maggena asamucchinno rāgo kāraṇalābhe uppajjanāraho thāmagataṭṭhena santāne anusetīti vuccati, evaṃ iṭṭhārammaṇepīti a ārammaṇānusayanaṃ daṭṭhabbaṃ.* (Vibh mūla-anuṭika)

754. *The Connected Discourses*, 1261.

Sukhāya, bhikkhave, vedanāya rāgānusayo pahātabbo, dukkhāya vedanāya paṭighānusayo pahātabbo, adukkhamasukhāya vedanāya avijjānussayo pahātabbo. (SN 36.3)

755. See also *The Path of Purification*, 715.
Chakkhādīnaṃ pana āpāthagate ārammaṇe pubbabhāge anuppajjamānampi kilesajātaṃ, ārammaṇassā adhiggahitattā eva aparabhāge ekantena uppattito, ārammaṇādhigahituppannanti vucchati. (Vism 22.89)

756. *Aniccānupassanā tāva tadaṅgappahānavasena niccasaññaṃ pariccajati, pariccajantī ca tathā appavattiyaṃ ye "niccan"ti gahaṇavasena kilesā, tammūlakā abhisaṅkhārā tadubhayamūlakā ca [vipākākhandhā*[MS]*] [vipākakkhandā*[VRI]*] anāgate uppajjeyyuṃ, te sabbepi appavattikaraṇavasena pariccajati, tathā [dukkhanupassanadayo*[MS]*] [dukkhasaññādayo*[VRI]*]. Tenāha—"vipassanā [hi*[VRI]*] tadaṅgavasena saddhiṃ khandābhisaṅkhārehi kilese pariccajatī"ti.* (Vism-mhṭ)

757. *Anāgāmissa avijjānusayo ca mānānusayo ca bhavarāgānusayo ca anuseti . . . pe. Dvinnaṃ puggalānaṃ avijjānusayo ca kāmarāgānusayo ca paṭighānusayo ca mānānusayo ca bhavarāgānusayo ca anusenti, no ca tesaṃ diṭṭhānusayo ca vicikicchānusayo ca anusenti. Puthujjanassa avijjanusayo ca anuseti kāmarāgānusayo ca paṭighānusayo ca mānānusayo ca diṭṭhānusayo ca vicikicchānusayo ca bhavarāgānusayo ca anusenti.* (Yam)

758. *Yassa kāmarāgānusayo anuseti tassa paṭighānusayo anusetīti? Āmantā . . .* (Yam)

759. . . . *Yamhi santāne anusayā appahīnā, yamhi vā pana nesaṃ santāne uppattipaccaye sati uppatti anivāritā, tattha anuppajjanakkhaṇepi uppannapubbañceva kālantare uppajjamanakañca upādāya yassa kāmarāgānusayo upajjati, a paṭighānusayo upajjatiyeva nāmā.* (Abhidh-mlṭ)

760. See also *The Path of Purification*, 716.
Samathavipassanā vasena pana vikkhambhitampi . . . (Vism 22.89)

761. *The Numerical Discourses*, 1247.
Aniccasaññā bhāvetabbā asmimānasamugghātāya. Aniccasaññino, bhikkhave, anattasaññā saṇṭhāti, anattāsaññi asmimānasamugghātaṃ pāpuṇāti diṭṭheva dhamme nibbānaṃ. (AN 9.1)

762. *Anattasaññā saṇṭhātīti aniccalakkhaṇe diṭṭhe anattalakkhaṇaṃ diṭṭhameva hoti. Etesu hi tīsu lakkhaṇesu [ekekasmiṃ*[MS]*][ekasmiṃ*[VRI]*] diṭṭhe itaradvayaṃ[diṭṭhamo*[MS]*] [diṭṭhameva*[VRI]*] hoti. Tena vuttam—"aniccasaññino, bhikkhave, anattasaññā saṇṭhātī"ti.* (Mp)

763. Sammohavinodanī Aṭṭhakathā, PTS 50. Mahāsi Sayadaw does not include the Pāḷi in his discussion of this passage.

764. *Anattalakkaṇapaññāpanañhi aññassa kassaci avisayo, sabbaññubuddhānameva visayo. Evametaṃ anattalakkhañaṃ apākaṭaṃ. Tasmā satthā anattalakkhanaṃ dassento aniccena vā dassesi dukkhena vā, aniccdukkhena vā, aniccadukkhehi vā.* (Vibh-a)

765. *Anattalakkhaṇapaññāpanassa aññesaṃ avisayattā anattalakkhaṇadīpakānaṃ aniccadukkhalakkhaṇānañca paññāpanassa avisayatā dassitā hoti. Evaṃ pana duppaññāpanatā etesaṃ durūpaṭṭhānatāya hoti.* (Vibh mūla anuṭikā)

766. *Na hi ghaṭabhedakaṇṭakavedhādivasena labbhamānā aniccadukkhatā sattānaṃ ekantato anattadhigamahetū honti. Paccayappaṭibaddhatā-abhiṇhasampaṭipīḷanādivasena pana labhamānā honti, tatthā hi cakkhādīni kammādimahābhutadipaccayapaṭibaddhavuttīni, tato eva ahutvā sambhavanti hutvā paṭiventīti aniccāni, abhiṇhasampaṭipīḷitatthā dukkhāni, evaṃbhūtāni ca avasavattanato anattakānīti pariggahe ṭhitehi samupacitañāṇāsambhārehi passituṃ sakkā.* (Vibh mūla anuṭīkā)

767. See also *The Path of Discrimination*, 178.
Aniccato anupassanto niccasaññaṃ pajahati. (Paṭis 3.197)

768. See also *The Path of Purification*, 663.
. . . *Yadaniccaṃ taṃ dukkhan"ti vacanato pana tadeva khandapañcakaṃ dukkhaṃ. Kasma?* [*Abhiṇhappaṭipīḷanā.*MS] [*Abhiṇhapaṭipīḷanā.*VRI] [*abhiṇhappaṭipīḷanākāro* MS] [*abhiṇhapaṭipīḷanākāro* VRI] *dukkhalakkhaṇaṃ.* (Vism 21.7)

769. *Tīsu dukkhatāsu saṅkhāradukkhatāva byāpinī* . . . (Vism-mhṭ)

770. See also *The Path of Purification*, 662–63.
Dukkhalakkhaṇaṃabhiṇhasampaṭipīḷanassa amanasikārā iriyāpathehi paṭicchaṇṇattā na upaṭṭhāti . . . *Abhiṇhasampaṭipīlanaṃ manasikatvā iriyāpathe ugghāṭite dukkhalakkhanaṃ yāthāvasarasato upaṭṭhāti.* (Vism 21.3–4)

771. Ibid., 651.
Dukkhānupassanaṃ bhāvento sukhasaññaṃ pajahati . . . (Vism 20.90)

772. See also *The Path of Discrimination*, 178.
Dukkhato anupassanto sukhasaññaṃ pajahati. (Paṭis 3.197)

773. See also *The Path of Purification*, 663.
"*Yaṃ dukkhaṃ tadanattā"ti pana vacanato tadeva khandhapañcakaṃ anattā. Kasmā? Avasavattanato. Avasavattanākāro anattalakkhaṇaṃ.* (Vism 21.8)

774. Ibid., 662–63.
Anattalakkhaṇaṃ nānādhātuvinibbhogassa amanasikārā ghanena paṭiccannattā na upaṭṭhāti . . . *Nānādhātuyo vinibbhujitvā ghanavinibbhoge kate anattalakkhaṇaṃ yāthāvasarasato upaṭṭhāti.* (Vism 21.3–4)

775. See also *The Path of Purification*, 663, fn. 3.
Yā hesā aññamaññūpatthaddesu samuditesu rūpārūpadhammesu ekattābhinivesavasena aparimadditasaṅkhārehi . . . *dhammānaṃ kiccabhedassa satipi paṭiniyatabhāve ekato gayhamānā kiccaghanatā, tathā sārammanadhammānaṃ satipi ārammaṇakaraṇabhede ekato gayhamānā ārammaṇaghanatā. ca, tā dātūsū ñāṇena vinibbhujitvā dissamānāsu, hatthena parimajjiyamāno pheṇapiṇḍo viya vilayaṃ gacchanti, "yathāpaccayaṃ pavattamānā suññā ete dhammā dhammattā"tī* . . . *anattalakkhaṇaṃ pākaṭataraṃ hoti.* (Vism-mhṭ)

776. Ibid., 651.
Anattato anupassanto attasaññāṃ[. . .Vism.] *pajahati.* (Vism 20.90)

777. *Visesato dhammānaṃ khaṇikanirodhe aniccatāvohāroti dassento "hutvā abhāvo vā"-ti-ādimāha.* (Vism-mhṭ)

778. *Aniccato tāva anupassanā bhaṅgānupassakassa yuttā "bhaṅgā nāma aniccatāya paramā koṭī'ti.* (Vism-mhṭ)

779. Ibid., 665.
Yasmā bhaṅgo nāma aniccatāya paramā koṭī, tasmā so bhaṅgānupassako yogāvicaro sabbaṃ saṅkāragataṃ aniccato anupassati, no niccato. Tato aniccassa dukkhattā, dukkhassa [*ca*VRI] *anattattā tadeva dukkhato anuppassati no sukhato. Anattato anupassati no attato.* (Vism 21.15)

780. See also *The Path of Purification*, 651.
Nibbidānupassanāṃ bhāveno nandiṃ pahajati. (Vism 20.90)

781. *Nibbidānuppassanāyāti saṅkhāresu nibbindanākārena pavattāya anuppassanāya. Nanditoti sappītikataṇhāto.* (Vism-mhṭ)

782. *Virāgānupassanāyāti tathā virajjanākārena pavattāya anuppassanāya.* (Vism commentary)

783. These terms are taken from Matara Sri Ñānarama Mahāthera, *The Seven Contemplations of Insight* (Kandy: Buddhist Publication Society, 1995).

784. See also *The Path of Purification*, 283.

Khayavirago'ti saṅkhārānaṃ khaṇabhaṅgo. Accantavirāgoti nibbānaṃ. Virāgānupassanāti tadubhayadassanavasena pavattā vippasanā ca maggā ca. (Vism 8.235)

785. See also *The Path of Discrimination*, 178.

Nibbindati no nandati, virajjati no rajjati. (Paṭis 3.197)

786. See also *The Path of Purification*, 665.

Yasmā pana yaṃ aniccaṃ dukkhamanattā, na taṃ abhinanditabbaṃ. Yañca anabhinanditabbaṃ, na tattha rajjitabbaṃ. Tasmā[etasmiṃ[Vism]*][esa tasmiṃ*[Psm Com'y]*] bhaṅgānupassanānusārena "aniccaṃ dukkhamanattā"ti diṭṭhe saṅkhāragate nibbindati, no nandati. Virajjati, no rajjati.* (Vism 21.16)

787. *Nirodhānupassanāyāti saṅkhārānaṃ nirodassa anupassanāya. Yathā saṅkhārā nirujjhantiyeva āyatiṃ punabbhavavasena na uppajjhanti, evaṃ vā anupassanā nirodhānupassanā.[Tenevāha "nirodhānupassanāya nirodheti, no samudetī"ti*[Mula. Ti)]*] Muñcitukamyatā [hi*[VRI]*] ayaṃ balappattā.* (Vism-mhṭ)

788. See also *The Path of Discrimination*, 178.

Nirodheti, no samudeti . . . Nirodhento samudayaṃ pajahati. (Paṭis 3.197)

789. The word *nirodheti*, used in the line from the Paṭisambhidāmagga above, can be analyzed in two different ways to arrive at these two different definitions. In the first, it is broken down into the root *rudha*, the prefix *ni*, and the two suffixes *e* and *ti*. In the second, it is broken down into the noun *nirodha* and the two suffixes *e* and *ti*.

790. *Yathā diṭṭhaṃ sampati upaṭṭhitaṃ saṅkhāragataṃ nirodheti nirodhaṃ mansi karoti, [evaṃ*[MS]*] adiṭṭhampi atītānāgataṃ anvayañāṇavasena 'yathā idaṃ etarahi, evaṃ itarepī'ti anuminanto nirodheti, manasikatassāpi nirodhaṃ [manasi*[MS]*]karoti.* (Vism-mhṭ)

791. *Rāgaṃ nirodhetī'ti rāgaṃ vikkhambhananirodhaṃ pāpeti, vikkhambhetīti attho.* (Vism-mhṭ)

792. The Pāḷi word *paṭisaṅkhāsantiṭṭhānā* in this passage refers to the *vipassanā* knowledge of equanimity toward formations.

793. *Saṅkhārānaṃ paṭinissajjanākārena pavattā anupassanā paṭinissaggānupassanā. Paṭissaṅkha santiṭṭhanā hi ayaṃ.* (Vism-mhṭ)

794. *The Middle Length Discourses*, 234.

Rūpaṃ bhikkhave na tumhākaṃ, taṃ pajahatha. (MN 22.40)

795. See also *The Path of Purification*, 665–66.

Ayampi aniccādi-anupassanā tadaṅgavasena saddhiṃ khandhābhisaṅkharehi kilesanaṃ pariccajanato, saṅkhatadosadassanena ca tabbiparīte nibbāne tanninnatāya pakkhandanato 'pariccāgapaṭinissaggo ceva pakkhandanapaṭinissaggo cā'ti vuccati. Tasmā tāya samannāgato bhikkhu yathāvuttena nayena kilese [ca[MS]*] pariccajati, nibbāne ca pakkhandati. Nāpi nibbattanavasena kilese ādiyati, na adosadassitāvasena saṅkhatārammaṇaṃ. Tena vuccati 'paṭinissajjati no ādiyatī'ti.* (Vism 21.18)

796. *'Sattadhā aṭṭhārasadhā'ti-ādinā vibhattāpi hi anupassanāpakārā aniccānupassanādīvasena tīsu antogadhāti matthakappattā vipassanā tāsaṃ eva vasena tiṭṭhati.* (Vism-mhṭ)

797. See also *the Path of Purification*, 652.

[Yā ca aniccānupassanā yā ca animittānupassanā ime dhammā ekatthā byañjanameva nānaṃ. Tathā "yā ca dukkhānupassanā yā ca appaṇihitānupassanā, ime dhamma ekatthā, byañjanameva nānaṃ.[Vism only]] *[Yā ca anattānupassanā yā ca suññatānupassanā, ime dhamma ekatthā byañjanameva.*[Psm, Vism]] (Vism 20.91)

798. Ibid.

Adhipaññādhammavipassanā pana sabbāpi vipassanā. Yathābhūtañāṇadassanaṃ kaṅkhāvitaraṇavisuddhiyā eva saṅgahitaṃ. (Vism 20.91)

799. *Aniccānupassanāya hi siddhāya nirodhānupassanā, khayānupassanā, vayānupassanā, vipariṇāmānupassanā ca ekadesena siddhā nāma honti; dukkhānupassanāya siddhāya nibbidānupassanā, ādīnavānupassanā ca; anattānupassanāya siddhāya itarāti.* (Vism-mhṭ)

800. *Keci panettha 'aniccato anupassati, no niccatoti-adinā visuṃ dassanakiccaṃ natthi, bhaṅghadassaneneva sabbaṃ diṭṭhaṃ hotī'ti vadaṇti, taṃ bhaṅghanupassanāya matthakappattiyaṃ yuttaṃ, tato pana pubbabhage anekākāravokārā anupassanā icchitabbāva.* (Vism-mhṭ)

801. See also *The Path of Discrimination*, 169.

Vayalakkhaṇupaṭṭhānekattañca vipassakānaṃ. (Paṭis 3.17)

802. *Khayānupassanāti paccuppannānaṃ rūpakkhandhādīnaṃ bhaṅgadassanañāṇañca taṃtaṃkhandhabhaṅgadassanānantaraṃ tadārammaṇacittacetasikabhaṅgadassanañāṇañca.* (Paṭis-a)

803. See also *The Path of Purification*, 722.

Khayānupassanāti pana ghanavinibbhogaṃ katvā aniccaṃ khayaṭṭhenāti evaṃ khayaṃ passato ñāṇaṃ. (Vism 22.114)

804. *Bhaṅgānupassanato paṭṭhāya ā pāripūrīti ghanasaññāya pahānaṃ hoti, tato pubbe aparipuṇṇatāya taṃna hoti. Evamaññatthāpīti paripuṇṇāparipuṇṇatā pahānatīraṇapariññāsu vipassanāpaññāya daṭṭhabbā.* (Vism-mhṭ)

805. See also *The Path of Purification*, 722.

Vayānupassanāti—

Arammaṇnvayena, ubho ekavavatthānā;
nirodhe adhimuttatā, vayalakkhaṇavipassanāti.—

Evaṃ vuttā paccakkhato ceva anvayato ca saṅkhārānaṃ bhaṅgaṃ disvā tasmiññeva bhaṅgasaṅkhāte nirodhe adhimuttatā, tāya āyūhanassa pahānaṃ hoti. Yesaṃ hi atthāya āyūheyya, 'te evaṃ vayadhammā'ti vipassato āyūhane cittaṃ na namati. (Vism 22.115)

806. Ibid.

Vipariṇāmānupassanāti rūpasattakādivasena taṃ taṃ paricchedaṃ atikkamma aññathāpavattidassanaṃ. [*Athavā*[MS]] *Uppannassa vā jarāya ceva maraṇena ca dvīhākārehi* [*vi*[VRI]] *pariṇāmadassanaṃ* . . . (Vism 22.116)

807. *Vayānupassanāti paccuppannānaṃ khandhānaṃ bhaṅgadassanānataraṃ tadanvayeneva atītānagatakhandhānaṃ bhaṅgadassanañāṇaṃ. Vipariṇāmānupassanāti tasmiṃ bhaṅgasaṅkāte nirodhe adhimuttattā, atha sabbepi atītānāgatapaccuppannā khandhā vipariṇāmavantoti sabbesaṃ vipariṇāmadassanañāṇaṃ.* (Paṭis-a)

808. See also *The Path of Purification*, 669.

Nimittanti saṅkhāranimittaṃ. (Vism 21.34)

809. *Saṅkhāranimittanti 'saṅkhārānaṃ samūhādighanavasena, sakiccaparicchedtāya ca saviggahānaṃ viya upaṭṭhānan'ti.* (Vism-mhṭ)

810. See also *The Path of Purification*, 691–92.

Yasmā panesa aniccanupassanāya saṅkhāranaṃ ghanavinibbhogaṃ katvā niccanimittadhuvanimittasassatanimittāni pajahanto āgato, tasmā animitto. (Vism 21.122)

811. See also *The Path of Discrimination*, 250.
Aniccato manasikaroto khayato saṅkhārā upaṭṭhanti . . . (Paṭis 5.55)

812. Ibid., 262.
Aniccato manasikaronto nimittaṃ yathābhūtaṃ [pa[MS]*] jānāti passati.* (Paṭis 5.78)

813. See also *The Path of Purification*, 723.
Adhipaññādhammavipassanāti—
"Ārammaṇañca paṭisaṅkhā bhaṅgañca anupassati;
suññato ca upaṭṭānaṃ, adhipaññā vipassanā"ti.
Evaṃ vuttā rūpādi-ārammaṇaṃ jānitvā tassa ca ārammaṇassa tadārammaṇassa ca cittassa bhaṅganaṃ disvā "saṅkhārāva bhijjanti, saṅkhārānaṃ maraṇaṃ, na añño koci attahī"ti bhaṅgavasena suññataṃ gahetvā pavattā vipassanā. Sā adhipaññā ca dhammesu ca vipassanāti katvā adhipaññādhammavipassanāti vuccati, tāya niccasārābhāvassa ca attasārābhāvassa ca suṭṭhu diṭṭhattā sārādānābhinivesassa pahānaṃ hoti. (Vism 22.118)

814. Ibid.
Yathābhūtañāṇadassananti sappaccayanāmarūpapariggaho, tena "ahosiṃ nu kho ahaṃ atītamaddhānan"ti-ādivasena ceva, "issarato loko sambhotī"ti-ādivasena ca pavattassa sammohābhinivesassa pahānaṃ hoti. (Vism 22.119)

815. *Saṃsayamicchāñāṇānaṃ vasena sammuyhanaṃ sammoho* . . . (Vism-mhṭ)

816. See also *The Path of Purification*, 723.
Ādīnavānupassanāti bhayatupaṭṭhānavasena uppannaṃ sabbabhavādīsu ādinavadassanañāṇaṃ, tena 'kiñci alliyitabbaṃ na dissatī'ti ālayābhinivesassa pahānaṃ hoti. (Vism 22.120)

817. *Saṅkhāresu leṇatāṇabhāvaggahaṇaṃ ālayābhiniveso atthato bhavanikanti.* (Vism-mhṭ)

818. See also *The Path of Purification*, 723.
Paṭisaṅkhānupassanāti muñcanassa upāyakaraṇaṃ paṭisaṅkhāñāṇaṃ, tena appaṭisaṅkhāya pahānaṃ hoti. (Vism 22.120)

819. *Saṅkhārānaṃ muñcanassa upāyabhūtaṃ paṭisaṅkhāñāṇaṃ paṭisaṅkhānupassanā, tāya aniccādīsu [appaṭisaṅkhānaṃ tattha*[MS]*] [appaṭisaṅkhātatthā*[VRI]*] paṭisaṅkhānassa paṭipakkhabhūtaṃ [avijjā*[MS]*] [avijjaṃ*[VRI]*] pajahati.* (Vism-mhṭ)

820. See also *The Path of Purification*, 723.
Vivaṭṭānupassanāti saṅkhrupekkhā ceva anulomañca. Tadā hissa cittaṃ īsakapoṇe padumapalāse udukabindu viya sabbasmā saṅkhāragatā patilīyati, patikuṭati, pativattatīti vuttaṃ. Tasmā tāyasaṃyogābhinivesassa pahānaṃ hoti. (Vism 22.121)

821. *Yathā cittaṃ saṅkhāre muñcitvā vivaṭṭaṃ nibbanaṃ pakkhandati, tathā pavattanato [saṅkhāre*[MS]*][saṅkhārupekkhā ca*[VRI]*] anulomanañca 'vivaṭṭānupassanā'ti [vuttaṃ*[VRI]*]. Niviṭṭhabhāvena ogāḷhabhāvena pavattasaṃyojanādikilesā eva kilesābhiniveso.* (Vism-mhṭ)

Pāḷi-English Glossary

ābādhato	as afflictions
abhāvapaññatti	concept of nonexistence
abhidhamma	higher teaching
abhijjāvisamalobha	covetousness and unrighteous greed
abhijjhā	covetousness
abhiṇhasampaṭipīlana	seeing things as constant torment
abhinīhārapaccupaṭṭhāna	manifestation of conveying
abhiññāpaññā	wisdom of full understanding
abhiññātā	full understanding
abhisamaya	realization
abhisaṅkhāra	store accumulation of kamma, merit or demerit
abhisaṅkhāraviññāṇa	consciousness and volitional mind
abhūta	not-brought-to-being
abhūtattha	not genuinely existing
abyākata	kammically indeterminate, neutral; insensate
abyākata-paccupaṭṭhānā	manifestation as being subject to alteration and insensate
abyāpāda	nonaversion
accantanirodha	complete cessation
accantavirāga	complete dispassion
accutirasa	function of deathlessness
ādāna	taking up

ādānanikkhepana	taking up and putting down
addhā	present time
addhāpaccuppanna	conventional present; referring to the period of time that spans from birth to death
addhātīta	past lives
ādhato	as afflictions
adhicittasikkhā	training in the higher mind
adhimokkha	faith, confidence, determination
adhipaññādhammavipassanā	insight into phenomena that is higher wisdom
adhiṭṭhāna	resolve
adhiṭṭhāyaka	superintendent (an erroneous experience of the self)
adhuva	unstable
adhuvato, addhuvato	seeing that conditioned phenomena are not everlasting
ādīnavañāṇa	insight knowledge of danger
ādīnavānupassanā	contemplation of danger
ādīnavato	as disadvantageous
adosa	nonhatred
adukkhamasukhavedanā	neither-unpleasant-nor-pleasant feeling
agati	wrong ways of behaving
aghamūla	root of unwholesomeness
aghamūlato	seeing conditioned phenomena as the root of unwholesomeness
aghato	as unprofitable
āhāra	nutriment, nutrition
āhāramaya rūpa	materiality arising from nutriment
āhārasammasana	comprehension of nutrition
ahetuka	severe inborn deficiency in spiritual intellect
ahetukadiṭṭhi	wrong view that volitional action does not produce good or evil results
āhuṇeyyo	worthy of gifts

ajāta	not-born
ajīvapārisuddhi	pursuing a pure livelihood
ājīvapārisuddhisīla	morality of right livelihood
ājīvaṭṭhamakasīla	five precepts or the eight precepts topped with right livelihood
ajjhāsaya	aspiration
ajjhattacitta	internally oriented mind
akāliko	immediate; immediately effective
akāmakāriya	not subject to creation by will
ākārapaññatti	concept about the manner; conventional reality defined by manner
ākāraparivitakka	ideas that are accepted based on reason
ākāsadhātu	space element
ākāsānañcāyatanasaññī	beings of the realm of infinite space
akata	not-made
ākiñcaññāyatana	base of nothingness
ākiñcaññāyatanasaññī	beings of the realm of nothingness
akiriyadiṭṭhi	wrong view that there is no good or evil
akkhanti-asaṃvara	lack of restraint due to impatience
akusala	nonvirtuous, unskillful, or unwholesome actions
akusalā dhammā	unwholesome things or actions
alabbhanīya	not subject to control [by desire]
alabbhanīyato	as not subject to control
alābha (-o)	lack of gain
ālayābhinivesa	adherence to conditioned phenomena as something reliable
aleṇato	as without shelter, not a shelter
alobha	nongreed
ālokasaññā	observing light; vivid contemplation
amahaggatacitta	undeveloped state of mind
amata	deathlessness

amoghaparibhoga	consumption of almsfood that is beneficial both to oneself and to one's supporters
anadhigatattā	not yet realized
anāgāmi	nonreturner
ānantariyakamma	kamma that has immediate result
āṇaṇyaparibhoga	consumption of almsfood that is debt-free
ānāpāna	in- and out-breath
ānāpānasati	mindfulness of in- and out-breath
anattā	not-self, impersonal
anattālakkhaṇā	characteristic of not-self
anattānupassanā	contemplation of not-self
anattato	as devoid of self
āṇāvītikkamantarāya	threat to prospects for path knowledge and fruition knowledge; obstacle of knowingly violating the monastic code
aṇḍaja	birth from an egg
andhaputthujjana	spiritually blind people
āneñja jhāna	imperturbable absorption
āneñja samādhi	imperturbable concentration
anicca	impermanent; impermanence
aniccalakkhaṇā	characteristic of impermanence
aniccantikā	as limited by disappearance
aniccānupassanā	contemplation of impermanence
aniccatā	impermanence
aniccato	as impermanent
animitta	signless
animittā-cetovimutti	signless deliverance of mind
animittānupassanā	contemplation of the signless
animittapaccupaṭṭhāna	manifestation of the signless
animittovimokkho	liberation through signlessness
anindriyabaddha	lifeless

anipphannarūpa	nonconcretely produced matter
anissarato	as not under anyone's control
anissariya	not having control
añjali	both hands folded together in respect
añjalikamma	making the gesture of lifting up the hands folded together as a token of respect
añjalikaraṇīyo	worthy of reverential salutation
aññāṇupekkhā	equanimity associated with delusion
antarāparinibbāyī	attainer of nibbāna in the interval
anuloma	adaptation
anulomañāṇa	insight knowledge of adaptation
anulomikakhantī	forbearance in conformity; referring to the composure of the insight knowledge of equanimity
anumāna	inference
anumāna-anattānupassanā	inferential contemplation of not-self
anumāna-aniccānupassanā	inferential contemplation of impermanence
anumāna-dukkhānupassanā	inferential contemplation of unsatisfactoriness
anumānañāṇa	inferential knowledge
anupada	repeated, repetition
anupadadhamma-vipassanā	insight into states one by one as they occur
anupādisesa	without residue remaining
anupādisesanibbāna	nibbāna without residue
anupādisesanibbānadhātu	element of nibbāna without the residue remaining
anupassati	see or observe; contemplate in turn
anuppādanirodha	cessation of arising
anuppādo	nonarising
anusaya	latent [defilements]
anusaya-kilesā	defilements that are latent or domant
anussatī	recollection
anussava	understanding gained from tradition

anuttaracitta	superior state of mind
anvayavipassanā	inferential insight into dissolution
apākaṭadukkha	obscure pain or distress or obscure suffering
aparappaccaya	lacking in causes
apāyadukkhaṃ	suffering of the lower realms
āpo	water
āpodhātu	water element
appākaṭadukkha	indistinct pain or distress
appanā	absorption
appanāsamādhi	absorption concentration
appanidhāyabhāvanā	observing the usual meditation object without letting the mind incline elsewhere
appaṇihita	desireless
appaṇihitānupassanā	contemplation of the desireless
appaṇihitovimokkho	liberation through desirelessness
appaṭicchannadukkha	manifest pain, manifest suffering
appaṭipatti-avijjā	ignorance of suffering and its cause
appaṭisaṅkhāna	nonreobservation
appiyarūpa, asātarūpa	unpleasant objects
āraddhavipassaka	insight beginner; energetic meditator
arahaṃ	accomplished
arahant	fully liberated being
arahattamagga	arahant path
arahattaphala	fruition of full liberation
ārammaṇādhiggahita-kilesā	defilements that lie dormant in sense objects
ārammaṇādhiggahituppanna	defilements that arise when sense objects are not observed
ārammaṇaghana	solidity of object
ārammaṇānusaya	lying dormant in sense objects
ārammaṇānusaya-kilesā	defilements that lie dormant in sense objects

arati	discontent
ariya	noble one, noble person
ariyakantasīla	moral conduct agreeable to the noble ones
ariyamagga	noble path, path of the noble ones
ariyamaggabhāvanā	method of practice to the noble path
ariyamaggañāṇa	one of the noble path knowledges
ariyasaccā	noble truths, truths for the noble ones
ariyūpavādantarāya	obstacle of insulting a noble one
arūpa	immaterial, immateriality
arūpā vutthāti	emerging from mental phenomena
arūpabhava	immaterial existence
arūpabhūmi	immaterial realms
arūpajjhānā	immaterial absorptions
arūparāga	desire for immaterial existence
asaccikaṭṭha	not personally experienced
asamāhitacitta	unconcentrated mind
asaṃhīra	not yielding to temptations of attachment and wrong view
asaṃkuppa	not ruined by attachment and wrong view
asammohasampajañña	clear comprehension without delusion
asaṃvara dhammā	behaviors involving lack of restraint
asaṅkhāraparinibbāyī	attainer of nibbāna without exertion
asaṅkhata	unconditioned phenomena
asaṅkhataparamattha	unconditioned absolute reality
asaññasatta	nonpercipient beings
asāraka	without core or essence
asārakato	as having no solid core or substance
asaraṇato	as without refuge, not a refuge
asātarūpa	unpleasant object
āsava	taints

āsevana	repetition
āsevanajavana	repetition impulsion consciousness
asmimāna	conceit "I am"
assāmikato	as without an owner
assāsapassāsa	in- and out-breathing
asubha	impurities of the body
asubhabhāvanā	contemplation of the impurity of the body
asubhasaññā	perception of impurity
atakkāvacaro	beyond logic
atāṇato	as without a hideout, not a hideout
atiharaṇa	pulling a lifted foot even with the other foot
atimāna	arrogance
atta	self
attadiṭṭhi	view that a self really exists
attasaññā	perception of self
attasāra	substantial self
attavādupādāna	clinging to personality views that are based on the view of self
attha	truth
atthāpannanaya	the deductive method
atthapaññatti	concepts of things
aṭṭhapurisapuggalā	eight types of individuals
aṭṭhārasa-mahāvipassanā	eighteen great insight knowledges
aṭṭhi	skeleton
aṭṭhisaṅghāto	mass of bones
āvajjana	to advert to an object, to attend
āvajjanupekkhā	equanimity of adverting
āvakālika	momentariness
āvāsa	lodgings
āvāsamacchariya	stinginess regarding lodgings

avasavattana	uncontrollable; not subject to anyone's wishes
avasavattīto	not able to exercise mastery
avijjā	ignorance
avijjāniyyānāvaraṇa	ignorance as a hindrance to liberation
avijjānusaya	latent ignorance
avijjāpadaṭṭhānā	ignorance as a proximate cause
avikkhepa	nondistraction
avimuttacitta	unliberated mind
aviparinaṇāta	unchanging
aviparīta	not false
avitatha	not untrue
avuttasiddhinaya	the method established without being said
avyākatakamma	neutral or indeterminate kamma
ayaso	disrepute
āyatana	sense base
ayoniso manasikāra	unwise attention
āyūhanā	accumulation of wholesome actions
bādhanalakkhaṇā	characteristics of torment
bahiddha-citta	externally oriented mind
balava	powerful
bhagavā	Blessed One
bhaṅga	dissolution
bhaṅgañāṇa	insight knowledge of dissolution
bhaṅgānupassanā	contemplation of dissolution
bhava	existence, becoming
bhāvanā	meditation
bhāvanābhisamaya	realization of the path through development
bhāvanākamma	practice of meditation
bhāvanākicca	function of developing the path
bhāvanāmayañāṇa	meditative knowledge

bhāvanāpaṭivedha	penetration of the path through development
bhāvanārati	bliss of meditation
bhavaṅga	life-continuum
bhavaṅgacalana	vibration of the life-continuum
bhavarāga	desire for existence
bhavarāgānusaya	latent desire for existence
bhavāsava	taint of existence
bhavataṇhā	craving for being
bhāvetabbāmaggasacca	truth of the path that one must develop
bhayāgati	act wrongly due to fear
bhayañāṇa	insight knowledge of fear
bhayato	seeing conditioned phenomena as fearful or frightening
bhikkhu	monk
bhikkhunidūsanekamma	raping a virtuous nun
bhojanemattaññū	moderation in eating
bhūmi	plane or realm of existence
bhūta	existence
bhūtārocana	the monastic rule allowing a monk to reveal his genuine attainment
bhūtattha	genuinely existing
bodhipakkhiyādhammā	requisites of enlightenment
bojjhaṅgā	factors of enlightenment
brahmavihārā	divine abodes
brūhanarasa	"function of expansion"; i.e., dampening
buddhacakkhu	eye of insight into a person's inclination
buddhānussati	recollection of the qualities of the Buddha
buddhindriya	sensory faculties
buddho	enlightened
byādhi	sickness

byādhidhammato	seeing conditioned phenomena as subject to sickness
byāpāda	aversion, ill-will
byāpādanīvarana	hindrance of aversion
cāga	generosity
cāgānussati	recollection of one's generosity
cakkhāyatana	eye base
cakkhudhātu	eye element
cakkhupasāda	eye-sensitivity
cakkhusaṃvara	restraint of the eye
cakkhuviññāṇa	eye-consciousness
cakkhuviññāṇadhātu	eye-consciousness element
cakkhuviññānaviññātabbā	mental phenomena that can be perceived along with eye-consciousness
calānupassanā	contemplation of instability
calato	seeing that conditioned phenomena are unstable
cariya	conduct
catudhātuvavatthāna	analysis of the four elements
catusaccakammaṭṭhāna	contemplation of the Four Noble Truths
catuttañāṇavajjho	abandoned by the fourth path
catuttha paccavekkhanāñāṇa	fourth [reviewing] knowledge
cetanā	volition, intention, urge
cetasika	mental factor or constituent
cetasikadukkha	mental pain
cetopariya abhiññāṇa	supernormal ability to read others' thoughts
chaḷaṅgupekkhā	sixfold equanimity
chanda	will, desire to act
chandāgati	to act wrongly due to desire
chandarāga	lust, greed, attachment
chaṭṭhama paccavekkhaṇañāṇa	sixth reviewing knowledge

cintāmaya	analytical knowledge; knowledge gained through study
cintāmayañāṇa	intellectual knowledge, analytical knowledge
citta	mind, cognition, mentality
cittānupassanā	contemplation of mind
cittasamuṭṭhāna rūpa	physical phenomena that are generated by consciousness
cittavisuddhi	mental purification
cittekaggatā	one-pointedness of mind or concentration
citttavīthi	cognitive process; stream of consciousness
cūlasotāpanna	lesser stream enterer
cuṇṇamanasikāra	"deconstructing attention"
cuticitta	death consciousness
dakkhiṇāvisuddhi	perfect offering or donation
dakkhiṇeyyo	worthy of offerings
dāna	generosity
dānavosaggupatṭṭhānekatta	one-pointedness based on contemplation of generosity
dandhābhiññā	weak insight
dāyajjaparibhoga	consumption of almsfood that is passed by inheritance
desanākkama	preaching order
devā	celestial or heavenly being
devātānussati	recollection of the qualities of celestial beings
dhamma	state, phenomena, nature, law, or doctrine
dhammacakkhu	eye of the three lower path knowledges
dhammadhātu	mental object element
dhammamacchariya	stinginess regarding knowledge
dhammānupassanā	awareness of mental objects
dhammārammaṇā	mental object
dhammatārūpa	inanimate objects

dhammaṭṭhitiñāṇa	knowledge that discerns conditionality
dhammavavatthānañāṇa	knowledge that discriminates phenomena
dhammavicayasaṃbojjhaṅga	enlightenment factor of investigation
dhammāyatana	mental object base
dhammuddhacca	practice-related agitation
dhammuddhacca pahānanaya	eliminating practice-related agitation
dhātu	elements
dhātumanasikāra	attention to the elements
dhātuvavatthāna	tranquility meditation of determining the four primary elements
dhutaṅga	asceticism; ascetic exercises
dhuva	stable; durable
dhuvanimitta	sign of stability
dhuvasāra	durable and substantial
dibbacakkhu	divine eye
diṭṭhānusaya	latent wrong view
diṭṭhi	wrong view
diṭṭhi-ugghāṭana	removing wrong view
diṭṭhi-upādāna	clinging wrong view
diṭṭhimāna	conceit of view
diṭṭhinijjhānakhanti	ideas accepted based on personal opinion
diṭṭhivisuddhi	purification of view
domanassa	distress; mental suffering
domanassavedanā	feeling of distress
dosa	aversion, hatred
dosāgati	act wrongly due to hatred
dosamūla-samohacitta	mind rooted in hate and affected by delusion
dubbhāsita	improper conversation
duddaso	difficult to understand
dukkata	improper conduct

dukkha	unsatisfactoriness; suffering; pain
dukkha-ariyasacca	noble truth of suffering
dukkhadukkha	suffering of pain; mental or physical pain
dukkhalakkhaṇā	characteristic of unsatisfactoriness
dukkhama	as painful
dukkhanirodha-ariyasacca	noble truth of the cessation of suffering
dukkhanirodhagāminīpaṭipadā	path that leads to the cessation of suffering
dukkhanirodhagāminīpaṭipadā-ariyasacca	noble truth of the path leading to the cessation of suffering
dukkhānupassanā	contemplation of unsatisfactoriness
dukkhasacca	truth of suffering
dukkhato	as painful, suffering, unsatisfactory
dukkhavatthu	base of suffering
dukkhavatthutāya	source of pain
dukkhavedanā	unpleasant physical feeling; painful feeling
dussīlya-asaṃvara	self-indulgence through immoral conduct
dutiyabhaṅgañāṇa	second insight knowledge of dissolution
dutiyapaccavekkhanāñāṇa	second reviewing knowledge
dvatti	two or three
dvattiṃsa	thirty-two
dvihetuka	inborn deficiency in spiritual intellect
dvikoṭika	two aspects
ehipassiko	inviting inspection
ekabījīsotāpanna	one seed attainer
ekaggatā	one-pointedness
ekatta	unification of mind
ekattagata	one-pointed
ekattakāya	beings alike in body and different in perception
ekattasaññī	beings different in body and alike in perception
etadagga	foremost

gāha	obsession
gambhīro	profound
gaṇḍato	as an ulcer, abcess
gandhabbas	celestial musicians
gandhādhātu	odor element
gandhāyatana	odor base, smellable smell base
garuda (Skt; Pāḷi, 'garuḷa')	mythical bird, a harpy
gati	destination
gatinimitta	image of the new life we will go to; sign of destiny
gehassita-domanassa	home distress
gehassita-somanassa	home happiness
gehassita-upekkhā	home equanimity
ghānadhātu	nose element
ghanapaññatti	concept of compactness
ghānapasāda	nose-sensitivity
ghānaviññāṇa	nose-consciousness
ghānaviññāṇadhātu	nose-consciousness element
ghānāyatana	nose base
gocarajjhatta	lit. "internal domain," referring to mental and physical objects that fall within the scope of vipassanā
gocarasampajañña	clear comprehension of the domain
gotrabhū	change-of-lineage
gotrabhū javana	change-of-lineage impulsion
gotrabhūñāṇa	knowledge of change-of-lineage
hadaya	heart
hadayarūpa	material phenomenon of the heart
hadayavatthu	heart-base
hiri-ottappa	moral shame and fear of consequences
hutvā abhāva	nonexistence of something that has arisen

iṇaparibhoga	use of requisites "on loan"
indriya-asaṃvara, indriyāsaṃvara	lack of sense restraint
indriyasaṃvara	carefully restraining the senses
iriyāpatha	bodily postures
issā	envy, jealousy
issāmacchariya	jealousy
itikirā	hearsay
ītito	subject to calamities
iṭṭhārammaṇa	lovable and pleasant sense object
itthibhāvā	femininity
itthindriya	feminine faculty
jalābuja	birth from a womb
jarā	aging, old age
jarādhammato	subject to aging and decay
jaratā	decay
jāti	birth
jātidhammato	subject to birth
javana	impulsion, mind-moment that is a kammic impulsion that fully perceives or moves toward an object
jhāna	jhāna, absorption
jīva	being or soul; life
jivhādhātu	tongue element
jivhāpasāda	tongue-sensitivity
jivhāviññāṇa	tongue-consciousness
jivhāviññāṇadhātu	tongue-consciousness element
jivhāyatana	tongue base
jīvita	vitality
jīvitindriya	life-controlling faculty
kakkhaḷalakkhaṇā	characteristics of hardness, softness, or smoothness

kakkhalatta	roughness and hardness
kalāpa	whole
kalāpasammasana	contemplation as a whole
kalāpasammasanañāṇa	knowledge that comprehends all phenomena as a whole
kalāpavipassanā	insight that observes all states as a whole
kālavimutta	independent of time
kāma	sense sphere
kāmabhava	sensuous existence
kāmacchanda	sensual desire
kāmacchandanīvaraṇa	hindrance of sensual desire
kāmarāga	lust, sensual desire
kāmarāgānusaya	latent desire for sensual objects
kāmāsava	taint of sensual desire
kāmasugatibhūmi	realms of sensual pleasures
kāmāvacara	domain of the senses, sensual phenomena
kāmāvacaracitta	sense-sphere consciousness
kamma	kamma, volitional or intentional actions
kammabhava	existence based on intentional actions
kammaja rūpa	kamma-generated materiality
kammanimitta	image impressed in the memory when an action is performed
kammaññatā	wieldiness
kammantarāya	kammic obstacle
kammaṭṭhānā	basis or foundation for practice
kammavaṭṭa	cycle of volitional actions
kammindriya	functional faculties
kaṅkhāvitaraṇavisuddhi	purification by overcoming doubt
kāraka-atta	individual or personality who performs wholesome and unwholesome actions
karunā	compassion

kasiṇa	colored disk
kāyadhātu	body element
kāyagatāsati	mindfulness of the body
kāyānupassanā	contemplation of the body
kāyapasāda	body-sensitivity
kāyaviññāṇa	body-consciousness
kāyaviññāṇadhātu	body-consciousness element
kāyaviññattirūpa	bodily intimation manifested as bodily movement
kāyāyatana	body base
kāyikadukkha	physical pain
kāyikasukha	physical pleasure
khaṇapaccuppanna	momentary present, a period of time limited to a single mind moment
khaṇapaccuppannarūpa	momentarily present physical phenomena
khandhā	aggregates
khandhānupassanā	contemplation of the five aggregates
khandhaparinibbāna	cessation of the aggregates
khaṇika	momentary [nature]
khaṇikacittekaggatā	momentary single-pointedness of mind
khaṇikāpīti	momentary rapture
khaṇikasamādhi	momentary concentration
khaṇikasammasana	contemplation of momentary nature
khanti	forbearance
khantisaṃvara	restraint by means of patience
khayanirodha	destruction and cessation
khayānupassanā	contemplation of destruction
khayavirāga	destructional dispassion
khippābhiññā	strong insight leading quickly to path
khuddikāpīti	minor rapture
kiccaghana	solidity of function

kilesā	defilements
kilesābhinivesa	adherence due to defilements
kilesantarāya	defilement obstacle
kilesaparinibbāna	cessation of the defilements
kiriyāparihāni	insufficient practice or instruction
kodha	anger
kolaṃkolasotāpanna	family-to-family attainer
kosajja-asaṃvara	self-indulgence through idleness or laziness
kriyacitta	functional consciousness
kukkucca	regret
kula	relatives
kusala	virtuous, skillful, wholesome
lābha	gain
lābhamacchariya	stinginess regarding gain
lahutā	lightness
lakkhaṇā	characteristic
lakkhaṇarūpa	characteristics of material phenomena
lobha	desire, greed, or attachment
lobhamūla	rooted in desire
lobhamūla-samohacitta	mind rooted in desire and affected by delusion
lokadhamma	vicissitudes of life
lokavidū	knower of worlds
lokuttarā	supramundane
lokuttaramagga	supramundane path
macchariya	avarice or stinginess
mada	vanity
magga	path
magga-appāna	absorption of the path
maggacittuppāda	path consciousness

maggajavana	impulsion consciousness associated with [the attainment of the supramundane] path
maggāmaggañāṇa-dassanavisuddhi	purification by knowledge and vision of what is path and not path
maggañāṇa	path knowledge
maggapahānapariññā	path full understanding by abandoning
maggapariñña	full understanding by means of the path
maggaphala	path [knowledge] and fruition [knowledge]
maggasacca	truth of the path
maggavirati	path knowledge that brings about abstinence from all evil behavior
mahaggatacitta	developed state of mind; sublime types of consciousness
mahaggatacittāni	sublime types of consciousness
mahāpaccavekkhaṇāñāṇa	great reviewing knowledges
majjhimapaññāneyya	person of middling intelligence, wisdom, or understanding
makkha	contempt
māna	pride, arrogance, or conceit
māna-samugghātana	removing conceit
mānānusaya	latent conceit
manasikāra	attention
manasikārapadaṭṭhānā	attention or attitude as proximate cause
mānatta	penance
manāyatana	mind base
mandabhabba-puggala	person of dull intelligence but fit for liberation
manodhātu	mind element
manodvāra	mind door
manodvārāvajjana	mind-door-adverting consciousness, a mind-moment that adverts to a mental object
manoviññāṇa	mind-consciousness

manoviññāṇadhātu	element of mind-consciousness
mārāmisato	as subject to death and mental defilements
maraṇa	death
maraṇadhammato	as subject to death
maraṇānussati	recollection of death
māyā	deceit
mettā	loving-kindness
miccadiṭṭhi	wrong view or belief
micchā-ājīva	wrong livelihood
micchākammanta	wrong action
micchāñāṇa	wrong knowledge
micchāpaṭipatti-avijjā	ignorance of pleasure and its cause
micchāsamādhi	wrong concentration
micchāsaṅkappa	wrong thought
micchāsati	wrong mindfulness
micchāvāyāma	wrong effort
micchāvimutti	wrong deliverance
migapadavalañjananaya	inferring a deer's footprint
moha	delusion
mohāgati	act wrongly due to delusion
muditā	sympathetic joy
mudutā	malleability
muñcitukamyatāñāṇa	insight knowledge of desire for deliverance, insight knowledge that desires deliverance
musāvāda	false speech
muṭṭhasacca-asaṃvara	self-indulgence through forgetting to be mindful
nāga	serpent or Nāga demon, gifted with miraculous powers and great strength
nāma	mental
namanalakkhaṇā	characteristic of inclining toward its objects

nāmapaññatti	conventional reality defined by name, concepts of name
nāmarūpanupassanā	contemplation of mental and physical phenomena
nāmarūpapadaṭṭhāna	physical and mental sense objects that are proximate causes
nāmarūpaparicchedañāṇa	insight knowledge that discerns mental and physical phenomena
nāmasattaka	contemplating mental phenomena
nāmayāthāvadassana	seeing mental phenomena as they really are
ñāṇa	knowledge, insight knowledge
ñāṇadassanavisuddhi	purification of knowledge and vision
ñāṇaniyyāna	liberation through knowledge
ñāṇasaṃvara	restraint arising from wisdom
nānattakāya	beings that differ in body
nānattasaññī	beings that differ in perception
ñāṇavippayutta	without consciously knowing
nandi	delight
ñātapariññā	full understanding of the known
ñātivyasana	loss of relatives
natthikadiṭṭhi	wrong view that everything is cut off or comes to an end when we die
ñāya	right conduct
nayadassana	inferential observation
nayahetu	ideas that are arrived at methodically
nayamanasikāra	inferential attention
ñāyapaṭipanno	practices the true way
nayavipassanā	inferential insight
nekkhamma	renunciation; wholesomeness that arises from insight
nekkhammassita-upekkhā	neutral feeling associated with renunciation
nekkhammassitadomanassa	distress associated with renunciation
nekkhammassitasomanassa	happiness associated with renunciation

nevasaññānāsaññāyatana	neither perception nor nonperception
nevasaññānāsaññāyatanasaññī	beings of the realm of neither perception nor nonperception
neyya	person to be guided
neyyatthanaya	implicit method
nibbāna	liberation; extinction of greed, hatred, and delusion
nibbatthitaparamattha	genuine ultimate realities
nibbatti	arising of present physical phenomena, first arising or generating
nibbattilakkhaṇā	characteristic of arising
nibbidāñāṇa	insight knowledge of disenchantment
nibbidānupassanā	contemplation of disenchantment
nicca	permanent
niccapaṭikkhepa	denying permanence
niccasaññā	perception of permanence
niccasāra	permanent and substantial
nikanti	delight, attachment
nikantipariyādāna	removing attachment
nikkhepana	putting down
nimitta	sign
nindā	blame
nippariyāyadukkha	explicit suffering
nipphannarūpa	concretely produced matter
nirāmisa-adukkhamasukha	unworldly neither displeasure nor pleasure
nirāmisadukkha	unworldly displeasure
nirāmisasukha	unworldly pleasure, genuine happiness
nirodha	cessation, truth of cessation
nirodhanissita	cessation-based
nirodhānupassanā	contemplation of cessation
nirodhasacca	truth of cessation, truth of the cessation of all suffering

nirodheti	causes cessation
nirodhupaṭṭhānekatta	one-pointedness based on knowledge of cessation
nissaraṇa	liberation-related, escape
nissaraṇanirodha	escape by means of cessation
nissaraṇavirāga	escape by means of dispassion
nissaraṇaviveka	liberation-related seclusion, escape by means of seclusion
nissaya	present cause
nīvaraṇa	hindrance, hindrances
nivāsi	permanent resident
niyatamicchādiṭṭhi	to have steadfast wrong views
niyyāna	liberation
niyyānāvaraṇa	hindrances to liberation
nosatatavihārī	not constantly engaged in tranquility and insight meditation
obhāsa	light
obhāsānupassana	contemplation of light
ojā	nutritive essence
okkantikāpīti	showering rapture
opanayyiko	onward leading
opapātika	spontaneous birth
pabhaṅguto	easily destroyed
paccakkha	empirical
paccakkha anattānupassanā	empirical contemplation of not-self
paccakkha aniccānupassanā	empirical contemplation of impermanence
paccakkha dukkhānupassanā	empirical contemplation of unsatisfactoriness
paccakkhañāṇa	personal knowledge
paccakkhanirodhānupassanā	empirical contemplation of cessation
paccakkhattha	empirical reality
paccakkhavipassanā	personal insight

paccattaṃ veditabbo viññūhī	to be experienced by the wise for themselves
paccavekkhaṇa	wise reflection or reviewing
paccavekkhaṇañāṇa	reviewing knowledge
paccayapariggahañāṇa	insight knowledge that discerns conditionality
paccayasanissitasīla	ethical conduct of reflecting on the purpose of the four requisites
paccayasannissita	wisely using requisites
paccekabuddha	silent buddha
pacchimabhavikā	being's final life
paccupaṭṭhānā	manifestation
paccuppanna	present
paccuppannarūpa	present arising of physical phenomena
paccuppannasaṅkhāra	present mental formations
paccuppannasaññā	present perception
paccuppannavedanā	present feeling
paccuppannaviññāṇa	present consciousness
paccuppanne vaṭṭamūlakaṃ dukkhaṃ	future suffering of being rooted in the round of rebirths
pada	state
padaṭṭhānā	proximate cause
padhānanaya	figurative usage
padhāniyanga	element of exertion
paggaha	balanced energy
paggharaṇalakkhaṇā	characteristics of flowing or melting
pahaccaparinibbāyī	attainer of nibbāna upon landing
pahānābhisamayā	realization by abandoning
pahānakicca	function of abandoning
pahānapariññā	full understanding by abandoning
pahānappaṭivedha	penetration by abandoning
pahānekaṭṭha	simultaneous elimination

pahātabba akusula dhamma	unwholesome states to be abandoned
pāhuṇeyyo	worthy of hospitality
pākaṭadukkha	plain pain or plain suffering
pakatūpanissāya	remote condition or prior cause
pakkhandanapaṭinissagga	launching out into
pakkhandanavosagga	release that rushes to nibbāna
paḷāsa	domineering attitude
palokānupassanā	contemplation of deterioration
palokato	deteriorate
pamāda	heedlessness, negligence
pāmojja	delight, spiritual delight
pañcadvārāvajjana	mind-moment that adverts one of the five sense doors to an object, five-sense-door-adverting consciousnesses, adverting to the five sense doors
pañcamapaccavekkhaṇāñāṇa	fifth reviewing knowledge
pañcaviññāṇa	five physical sense consciousnesses
paṇḍitavedanīyo	experienced only by the wise
panidhāyabhāvanā	observing alternative objects of meditation
paṇidhi	desire
paṇihita	craving
paññā	wisdom
paññā-āloka	light of wisdom
paññā-obhāsa	lustre of wisdom
paññācakkhu	eye of path knowledge of arahantship
paññāpajjota	torch of wisdom
paññāsikkhā	training in wisdom
paññatti	conventional reality
paññāvisuddhi	purification of wisdom
pāpamittatā	bad companionship
papañca	proliferation
papātika	spontaneous birth

para	strangers or outsiders
pārājika	offense meriting expulsion
parama	ultimate
paramāna kamma	deeds of noble people
paramasuñña	ultimate emptiness
paramattha	absolute reality
pāramī	noble deeds; perfection; also "deeds of a noble person" (paramānaṃ uttamapurisanaṃ bhāvo kammaṃ)
paramparā	teachers and forefathers
parato	as strangers or outsiders
pariccāgapaṭinissagga	giving up
pariccāgavosagga	release that abandons defilements
parideva	lamentation
paridevadhammato	subject to and a source of lamentation
parikamma	preparation
parikappa aniṭṭhārammaṇa	those that deceptively appear to be unpleasant
parikappa iṭṭhārammaṇa	those that deceptively appear to be pleasing
parinibbāna	complete cessation
parinibbānacuti	mental and physical phenomena
pariññākicca	function of fully understanding
pariññeyya-ariyadukkhasacca	full understanding of the noble truth of suffering
parivatta	probation
pariyāyadukkha	implicit suffering
pariyuṭṭhāna kilesā	defilements that arise as obsessive thought
passaddhi	calm, tranquility
passaddhisaṃbojjhaṅga	enlightenment factor of tranquility
paṭhama paccavekkhaṇañāṇa	first [reviewing] knowledge
paṭhamabhaṅgañāṇa	first knowledge of dissolution
pathavī	earth
pathavīdhatu	earth element

pathavīkasiṇa	earth kasiṇa
paṭibhāganimitta	conceptual object of meditation
paticcasamuppāda	dependent origination
paṭicchannadukkha	hidden pain or distress or hidden suffering
paṭigha	anger, latent aversion
paṭighānusaya	aversion
pāṭikūlamanasikāra	attention to repulsiveness
pāṭikūlasaññā	perception of impurity
pāṭikūlyatā	repulsion
pāṭimokkhasaṃvara	observing the monastic precepts
pāṭimokkhasaṃvarasīla	ethical conduct of observing the monastic precepts
paṭinissaggānupassanā	contemplation of relinquishment
paṭipadāñāṇadassanavisuddhi	purification of knowledge and vision of the path, purification by knowledge and vision of the way
paṭipassaddhi	repeated
paṭipāṭi	successive
paṭipattikkama	practice order
paṭisambhidāñāṇa	discriminating knowledge
paṭisaṅkhā santiṭṭhānā	referring to the vipassanā knowledge of equanimity toward formations, lit. "to be established in re-observation"
paṭisaṅkhāna	thoughtful reconsideration
paṭisaṅkhāñāṇa	insight knowledge of reobserving
paṭisaṅkhānañāṇa	thoughtful reconsideration
paṭisaṅkhānupassanā	contemplation of reflection
paṭisevanāpahātabbāsavā	abandoning taints by proper use
paṭivedha	penetration
paṭivipassanā	counter-insight
paṭivipassanābhāvanā	counter-insight meditation
pavāraṇā	ceremony at the end of the annual rains retreat
pavatta	occurring

pavattaṃ	occurrence
phala	fruition, fruition consciousness
phalacittuppāda	fruition consciousness
phalañāṇa	fruition knowledge
phalasamāpatti	absorbed in fruition
pharaṇāpīti	pervasive rapture
pharusavācā	insulting words
phassa	contact, mental contact
phassapañcamaka	contact-led phenomena
phoṭṭhabba	tangible object
phoṭṭhabbadhātu	tangible object element
phoṭṭhabbāyatana	tangible object base
pipphalī	long pepper
pisuṇavācā	backbiting or slander
piṭakasampadā	in accord with scripture
pīti	joy, rapture, zest
pītisaṃbojjhaṅga	enlightenment factor of rapture, enlightenment factor of delight
piyarūpa	pleasing objects
pubbabhāgamagga	momentum of the preliminary path
pubbabhāgasīla	morality that has been purified before meditation
pubbaṅgamarasa	leading its mental factors
puggalapaññatti	concept of person
pumbhāva	masculinity
purisindriya	masculine faculty
puthujjana	ordinary people
rāga	lust
rāgakkhayo	destruction of lust
rasā	function
rasadhātu	flavor element

rasāyatana	flavor base, tasteable flavor base
ritta	permanence, pleasure, beauty, and the ability to control
rittato	as devoid of
rogato	as disease, as chronic disease
rūpa	matter, physical, fine-material sphere
rūpa upādānakkhandha	materiality aggregate subject to clinging
rūpā vutthāti . . . arūpe vutthāti	emerging from physical phenomena, emerging from immaterial phenomena
rūpabhava	fine-material existence
rūpabhūmi	fine-material realms
rūpādhātu	form element
rūpajjhānā	material absorptions
rūpakkhandhā	physical aggregate
rūparāga	desire for fine-material existence
rūpārammaṇā	[visible] form object
rūpārūpa	physical matter
rūpasaṅghāto	mass of physical phenomena
rūpasattaka	contemplating physical phenomena, material septad
rūpāyatana	form base, visible form base
rūpayāthāvadassana	seeing physical phenomena as they really are
sa-upādisesa	with residue remaining, referring to nibbāna of a living fully enlightened being
sa-upādisesanibbāna = kilesaparinibbāna	nibbāna with residue
sa-uttaracitta	inferior state of mind
sabbasaṅkhārasamatho	peaceful ending of all conditioned phenomena
sabhāva aniṭṭhārammaṇa	those that are inherently unpleasant
sabhāva iṭṭhārammaṇa	those that are inherently pleasing
sabhāvalakkhaṇā	specific characteristics, intrinsic characteristics, unique characteristic

sacchikiriyābhisamaya	realization through direct experience
sacchikiriyākicca	function of directly experiencing
sacchikiriyāpaṭivedha	penetration through direct experience
saccikaṭṭha	empirically experienced
saddādhātu	sound element
saddārammaṇa	sound object
saddāyatana	sound base, audible sound base
saddhā	faith
sadosacitta	mind affected by hate
sahajātanissaya	immediate condition or present cause
sahajātasīla	morality that is purified during meditation
sahuppannattā	come along with
sajjana	dropping the foot
sakadāgāmī	once returner
sakadāgāmiphalasamāpatti	attainment of the fruition of once returning
sakkāyadiṭṭhi	view of personality
salakkhaṇarūpa	matter possessing real characteristics
sallakkhento	bearing in mind; making a mental note
sallato	as thorn, as thorns or arrows
samādhāna	firm and steadfast
samādhi	concentration
samādhisaṃbojjhaṅga	enlightenment factor of concentration
samādhisikkhā	training in concentration
samāhitacitta	concentrated state of mind
samānavāda	universally accepted, generally accepted view
sāmaṇera	novice monk
sāmaññalakkhaṇā	universal characteristic
sāmaññanibbāna	general nibbāna
samantacakkhu	all-seeing eye
samāpatti	attainment

samatha	tranquility
samathabhāvanāmaya	knowledge derived from tranquility meditation
samathanimittupaṭṭhānekatta	one-pointedness based on tranquility meditation
samathapubbaṅgama	developing tranquility prior to insight
samathapubbaṅgamā bhāvanā	method of one who takes the tranquility vehicle to nibbāna
samathayānika	practitioner who uses both vipassanā and tranquility meditation; one who takes the tranquility vehicle to nibbāna
saṃhīra	yields to temptations of attachment and wrong view
sāmīcipaṭipanno	practicing the proper way
sāmiparibhoga	consumption of almsfood that is one's own
sāmisa	worldly
sāmisa-adukkhamasukha	worldly neither displeasure nor pleasure
sāmisadukkha	worldly displeasure
sāmisasukha	worldly pleasure
saṃkhittacitta	indolent state of mind
saṃkilesadhammato	seeing conditioned phenomena as afflictions or impurities
saṃkuppa	ruined by attachment and wrong view
sammāājīva	right livelihood
sammādassana	right seeing
sammādiṭṭhi	right view
sammākammanta	right action
sammapaddhanavīriya	effort that is the right kind of striving
sammāsamādhi	right concentration
sammāsambuddho	fully enlightened
sammasana	comprehension
sammasanañāṇa	insight knowledge by comprehension
sammasanarūpa	matter to be comprehended by insight

sammāsaṅkappa	right intention
sammāsati	right mindfulness
sammāvācā	right speech
sammāvāyāma	right effort
sammoha	delusion
sammutipaññatti	conventional reality
samohacitta	mind affected by delusion
saṃojanāni	fetters
sampajañña	clear comprehension
sampaṭicchana	to receive, mind-moment that receives a sense impression of an object, mind that receives the sense object
sampayuttadhammā	associated dhammas
samphappalāpavācā	frivolous speech
saṃsāra	cycle of suffering
saṃsedaja	birth from moisture
samuccheda	perpetual
samucchedanirodha	perpetual cessation
samucchedapahāna	completely removing evil behavior and wrong livelihood
samucchedavirāga	perpetual dispassion
samucchedaviveka	perpetual seclusion
samudaya	arising
samudayāriyasacca	noble truth of the origin of suffering
samudayasacca	truth of origin, truth of the origin of suffering
samudīraṇarasa	function of movement, pushing, or pulling
samūhaghana	solidity of mass
samūhapaññatti	concept of solidity
saṃvega	spiritual urgency
saṃyojana	fetter

saṃyojanāni	removal of the fetters
sandahanapaccupaṭṭhāna	manifests continuously
sandiṭṭhiko	visible here and now
saṅgahapaccupaṭṭhāna	cohesion or holding together
saṅgha	assemblage, a community; here referring to the community of enlightened beings
saṅghādisesa	offense requiring a convening of the saṅgha
saṅghānussati	recollection of the qualities of the saṅgha
sañjāyana	perceiving
saṅkhāra	volition, conditioned
saṅkhāradukkha	suffering of conditioned phenomena, the condition of being subject to arising and passing away
saṅkhāraghananimitta	concept of a solid form or shape
saṅkhārakkhandhā	aggregate of mental formations
saṅkhāranimitta	signs of phenomena, sign of conditioned phenomena
saṅkhārāva saṅkhāre vipassanti	as if phenomena are observing themselves
saṅkhārupekkhāñāṇa	insight knowledge of equanimity toward phenomena, insight knowledge of equanimity toward formations
saṅkhata	conditioned phenomena
saṅkhatalakkhaṇā	conditioned characteristics
saṅkhataparamattha	conditioned reality
saṅkhatato	depending on causes
saññā	perception
saññākkhandhā	aggregate of perception
saññāvipallāsā	perversion of perception
sannikkhepana	touching the ground
sannirumbhana	pressing
santānānusaya	those that dwell in a continuum

santati	solidity
santatighana	solidity and continuity of phenomena, solidity of continuity
santatipaccuppanna	serial present, apparent continuity or duration of present phenomena, continuity of mental and physical processes happening in the present, a period of time that covers a single mental process
santatipaccuppannarūpa	seeing present physical phenomena as solid
santatipaccuppannavedanā	solidity of present feeling
santatipaññatti	concept of solidity
saṇṭhānapaññatti	conventional reality defined by appearance, concepts of form or shape
santi	peace
santilakkhaṇā	characteristic of peace, characteristic of peacefulness
santīrana	mind that investigates the sense object, to investigate, mind-moment that investigates an object, investigation
sappītikataṇhā	attachment accompanied by joy
sarāgacitta	mind affected by lust
sārambha	disdain
sāsana	Buddha's teachings
sasaṅkhāraparinibbāyī	attainer of nibbāna with exertion
sāsava	associated with mental defilements
sāsavato	as intoxicating
sassata	eternal
sassatadiṭṭhi	eternity view
sassatanimitta	sign of eternity
sātarūpa	pleasing objects
satatavihārī	constantly engaged in tranquility and insight meditation
sāṭheyya	hypocrisy, fraud
sati	mindfulness

satipaṭṭhāna	foundation of mindfulness
satipaṭṭhānabhāvanā	meditation on the foundations of mindfulness
satisaṃbojjhaṅga	enlightenment factor of mindfulness
satisaṃvara	restraint arising from mindfulness
sattāhakālika	food allowed for a week
sattakkhattusotāpanna	seven-times-at-most attainer
sattaloka	world
sattamapaccavekkhaṇāñāṇa	seventh reviewing knowledge
sattāvāsā	spheres of beings
satthā devamanussānaṃ	teacher of gods and humans
sāvaka	disciple
savicāra	sustained application
savitakka	intial application
sayamvasi	commander
sekkha	trainee
sikhāpattasaṅkhārupekkhā	peak-reaching equanimity
sikkhā	training
sīla	morality
sīlabbatāparāmāsa	adherence to rites and ceremonies, wrong belief in rites and rituals as a path to liberation
sīlabbatupādāna	liberation from the cycle of suffering
sīlānussati	recollection of one's morality or ethical conduct
sīlasaṃvara	restraint by means of morality
sīlasikkhā	training in morality
sīlavisuddhi	purification of conduct
sivathika	charnel ground contemplation
soka	sorrow, grief, or lamentation
sokadhammato	subject to and a source of grief
somanassa	happiness; joy
somanassavedanā	feeling of joy

sotādhātu	ear element
sotāpannā	stream enterer
sotapasāda	ear-sensitivity
sotāpattimagga	path of a stream enterer
sotāpattiphalasamāpatti	attainment of the fruition of stream entry
sotaviññāṇa	ear-consciousness
sotāviññāṇadhātu	ear-consciousness element
sotāyatana	ear base
suddhavipassanāyānika	one who takes the pure vehicle of insight to enlightenment
sugati	blissful destination
sugato	sublime
sukha	pleasure, happiness
sukhasaññā	perception of pleasure
sukhasāra	pleasurable and substantial
sukhavedanā	pleasant bodily or mental feelings, pleasant feeling
sukhumarūpa	subtle matter
suñña	empty of a substantial self
suññata	empty
suññatānupassanā	contemplation of emptiness
suññato	seeing conditioned phenomena as devoid of self
suññatovimokkho	liberation through emptiness
sutamaya	theoretical knowledge
sutamayañāṇa	theoretical knowledge
sutta	discourse
svākkhāta	well-preached
taccha	real
tadaṅga	temporary
tadaṅganibbūta	temporary liberation from defilements
tadaṅganirodha	temporary cessation

tadaṅganirodhasacca	truth of temporary cessation
tadaṅgappahāna	temporarily eliminated, temporary or partial removal [of mental defilements]
tadaṅgavirāga	temporary dispassion
tadaṅgaviveka	temporary seclusion
tadārammaṇa	registration, mind that registers the sense object
tādi	stable
tajjāpaññatti	concepts that refer to ultimate reality, concepts that refer to ultimately real phenomena
takkahetu	ideas that are arrived at through logic
taṇhā	craving, attachment
taruṇavipassanā	fledgling insight
tatha	true
tathāgata	Thus Gone One (Buddha)
tatiyañāṇa	third path; attainment of ānāgamimagga
tatiyañāṇavajjho	abandoned by the third path
tatramajjhattatā	balanced state of mind
tatramajjhattupekkhā	balanced equanimity or balanced observation
tattha tattha	then and there
tāvakālika	momentary
tejodhātu	fire element
thambha	obstinacy
ṭhānyupacāra	figuratively
thera	one who has been an ordained bhikkhu for at least ten years
theyyaparibhoga	food obtained by theft
thinamiddha	fatigue or sleepiness
thinamiddhanīvaraṇa	hindrance of sloth and torpor
thullaccaya	serious infraction
tihetuka	rebirth consciousness that is capable of enlightenment

tikkhabhabba-puggala	person of sharp intelligence
tikkhapaññāneyya	person of sharp intelligence, wisdom, or understanding
tīraṇapariññā	full understanding by investigation
tuccha	insubstantial
tucchato	as insubstantial, useless, empty
ubbegāpīti	uplifting rapture
ubhayindriya	faculty that is both sensory and functional consciousness
udaya	appearance, arising
udayabbayañāṇa	insight knowledge of arising and passing
udayabbayappīḷanato dukkhā	suffering of being oppressed by arising and passing away
udayabbhayappaṭipīḷana	mode of being constantly oppressed by appearance and disappearance
uddhacca	restlessness, fidgety
uddhaṃsotakaniṭṭhagāmī	one bound upstream, heading toward the Akaniṭṭha realm
uddharaṇa	lifting the foot
ugghaṭitaññū	person of quick understanding
ujupaṭipanno	practices the straight way
uṇhattalakkhaṇā	characteristics of heat, warmth, or cold
upacāra	access concentration, access
upacārasamādhi	access or neighborhood concentration
upacaya	production
upādāna	clinging or grasping
upādānakhandhā	aggregates subject to clinging
upādārūpa	derived material phenomena
upaddavato	as an accident
upadhāraṇa	foundation or basis

upahaccaparinibbāyī	perfect in moral conduct, perfect in concentration, but only having medium-developed wisdom; attains final path after mid-life
upanāha	revenge
upanissayapaccaya	decisive supporting condition
upanissayapaccayuppanna	resulting conditionally arisen state
upapatti	reappearance
upasaggato	as dangerous
upasamānussati	recollection of peace (of nibbana)
upaṭṭhāna	effortless mindfulness
upāyāsa	tribulation, anxiety
upāyāsadhammato	subject to and a source of trouble
upekkhā	feeling that is neither unpleasant nor pleasant, equanimity
upekkhāsaṃbojjhaṅga	enlightenment factor of equanimity
upekkhavedanā	neutral feelings, feelings of neither displeasure nor pleasure
uppādavayaparicchinna	limited by arising and passing away
uppādavayavantata	arising and passing away
uppādo	arising
uttama	highest
uttamattha	higher reality
utumaya rūpa	materiality arising from temperature
vācā	speech
vacīviññattirūpa	verbal intimation manifested as verbal expression
vadhaka	as a murderer
vadhakato	as murderous
vāna	beyond entanglement
vaṇṇa	beauty
vaṇṇamacchariya	stinginess regarding beauty
vassa	annual rains retreat

vaṭṭa	round of existence
vaṭṭabhedakadukkatā	breach of the rules concerning one's duty
vaṭṭasacca	truths of the round of existence
vatthārammaṇapadaṭṭhāna	sense bases and sense objects that are proximate causes
vaya	disappearance, passing away
vayalakkhaṇupaṭṭhānekatta	one-pointedness based on knowledge of dissolution
vayānupassanā	contemplation of fall
vāyodhātu	air element
vayovuḍḍhatthaṅgama	aging and decay in stages
vedaka-atta	individual or personality who experiences their results
vedanā	feeling
vedanānupassanā	contemplation of feelings
veneyyajjhāsaya	Dhamma audience
vibhāva	nonenduring
vibhavato	not endure
vicāra	sustained application of mind, sustained application
vicikicchā	skeptical doubt, doubt
vicikicchānusaya	doubt
vijānana	knowing
vijānanalakkhaṇā	characteristic of knowing an object
vijjā	true knowledge
vijjācaraṇasampanno	perfect in true knowledge and conduct
vijjamānapaññatti	concepts that refer to what ultimately exists
vikappanā	assignment
vikārarūpa	mutable material phenomena
vikkhambhana	stopping
vikkhepa	restless
vikkhittacitta	distracted state of mind

vimokkhamukha	gateway to liberation
vimuttacitta	liberated state of mind
vinaya	rules for bhikkhus, monastic rules and regulations
viññāṇa	cognition, consciousness
viññāṇapadaṭṭhānā	consciousness basis
viññāṇaṭṭhiti	stations of consciousness
viññānāyatanasaññī	beings of the realm of infinite consciousness
vipaka	resultant
vipākantarāya	obstacle of inborn deficiency
vipākavaṭṭa	cycle of results
vipallāsā	perversions
vipañcitaññū	person who understands through elaboration
vipariṇām	change
vipariṇāmadhammato	seeing conditioned phenomena as constantly changing
vipariṇāmadukkha	suffering of change, the impermanence of mental or physical pleasure
vipariṇāmalakkhaṇā	characteristic of disappearance
vipariṇāmānupassanā	contemplation of change
vipariṇāmato	as change
viparīta	false
vipassanā	insight; insight meditation
vipassanā pāramī	vipassanā perfections
vipassanācittuppāda	mind that arises during insight meditation
vipassanākamma	practice of insight meditation
vipassanāmagga	path of insight
vipassanāñāṇa	insight knowledge
vipassanāpahānapariññā	insight full understanding by abandoning
vipassanāpubbaṅgama bhāvanā	development of vipassanā before/preceeding concentration

vipassanāyānikā	one who practices pure vipassanā meditation. (See also suddhavipassanāyānika.)
vipassanupakkilesā	corruptions of insight, obstacles to insight
vipassanupekkhā	insight equanimity
virāga	nonattachment, dispassion
virāganissita	dispassion-based
virāgānupassanā	contemplation of dispassion
virati	abstinence from evil
vīriya	effort, exertion
vīriyabojjhaṅga	enlightenment factor of effort
vīriyasaṃbojjhaṅga	enlightenment factor of energy
vīriyasaṃvara	restraint through effort
visaṅkhāra	nonexistence of conditioned phenomena
visesanibbāna	specific nibbāna
visuddhi	purification
vītadosacitta	mind unaffected by hate
vitakka	initial application of mind, initial application
vītamohacitta	mind unaffected by delusion
vītarāgacitta	mind unaffected by lust
vīthi	mental process, cognitive processes
vīthicitta	mental processes
vītiharaṇa	pushing it forward in front of the other foot
vītikkama-kilesā	transgressive defilements
vitthambhanalakkhaṇā	characteristic of distension; characteristics of firmness, stiffness, or looseness
vivaṭṭa	beyond the round of existence
vivaṭṭanissita	nibbāna-based wholesome action or a wholesome action based beyond the round of rebirth
vivattānupassanā	contemplation of turning away
vivattasacca	truths beyond the round of existence
viveka	seclusion

vivekanissita	seclusion-based
vivitta	secluded
vivittato	to seclude oneself; to be distinct from cause and effect
vosagga	penetration, release
vosaggapariṇāmī	maturing in release
vosaggārammaṇato	penetration of the objects [of insight]
vosajjana	dropping the foot
votthapana	to determine, mind-moment that determines an object, mind that determines the sense object
votthapanavāravīthi	mental process that ends with determining
vutthānagāminīvipassanā	very clear knowledge that leads to emergence, insight leading to emergence
yamaka	pairs
yāmakālika	food allowed after noon
yamakasammasana	contemplation of pairs of phenomena
yathābhūta	things as they are, real existence
yathābhūtañāṇa	knowledge of things as they really are
yathābhūtañāṇadassana	knowledge and vision of things as they really are
yāthāvamāna	pride in what is worthy
yāvajīvika	food allowed for life
yoni	birth
yoniso manasikāra	right attitude, wise attention
yuganaddhanaya	pairing method

English-Pāḷi Glossary

abandoned by the fourth path	catuttañāṇavajjho
abandoned by the third path	tatiyañāṇavajjho
abandoning taints by using	paṭisevanāpahātabbāsavā
absolute reality	paramattha
absorbed in fruition	phalasamāpatti
absorption	appanā
absorption concentration	appanāsamādhi
absorption of the path	magga-appāna
abstinence from evil	virati
access concentration, access	upacāra
access or neighborhood concentration	upacārasamādhi
accomplished	arahaṃ
accumulation of wholesome actions	āyūhanā
act wrongly due to delusion	mohāgati
act wrongly due to fear	bhayāgati
act wrongly due to hatred	dosāgati
adaptation	anuloma
adherence due to defilements	kilesābhinivesa
adherence to conditioned phenomena as something reliable	ālayābhinivesa
adherence to rites and ceremonies, wrong belief in rites and rituals as a path to liberation	sīlabbatāparāmāsa

aging, old age	jarā
aggregate of mental formations	saṅkhārakkhandhā
aggregate of perception	saññākkhandhā
aggregates	khandhā
aggregates subject to clinging	upādānakhandhā
aging and decay in stages	vayovuḍḍhatthaṅgama
air element	vāyodhātu
all-seeing eye	samantacakkhu
analysis of the four elements	catudhātuvavatthāna
analytical knowledge; knowledge gained through study	cintāmaya
anger	kodha
anger, latent aversion	paṭigha
annual rains retreat	vassa
appearance, arising	udaya
arahant path	arahattamagga
arising	samudaya, uppādo
arising and passing away	uppādavayavantata
arising of present physical phenomena, first arising or generating	nibbatti
arrogance	atimāna
as devoid of	rittato
as devoid of self	anattato
as a murderer	vadhaka
as an accident	upaddavato
as an ulcer, abcess	gaṇḍato
as devoid of	rittato
as devoid of self	anattato
as disadvantageous	ādīnavato
as disease, as chronic disease	rogato
as having no solid core or substance	asārakato

as if phenomena are observing themselves	saṅkhārāva saṅkhāre vipassanti
as impermanent	aniccato
as insubstantial, useless, empty	tucchato
as limited by disappearance	aniccantikā
as murderous	vadhakato
as not subject to control	alabbhanīyato
as not under anyone's control	anissarato
as painful	dukkhama
as painful, suffering, unsatisfactory	dukkhato
as strangers or outsiders	parato
as subject to death	maraṇadhammato
as subject to death and mental defilements	mārāmisato
as thorn, as thorns or arrows in the flesh	sallato
as unprofitable	aghato
as without a hideout, not a hideout	atāṇato
as without an owner	assāmikato
as without refuge, not a refuge	asaraṇato
as without shelter, not a shelter	aleṇato
asceticism; ascetic exercises	dhutaṅga
aspiration	ajjhāsaya
assemblage, a community; here referring to the community of enlightened beings	saṅgha
assignment	vikappanā
associated dhammas	sampayuttadhammā
associated with mental defilements	sāsava
attachment accompanied by joy	sappītikataṇhā
attainer of nibbāna in the interval	antarāparinibbāyī
attainer of nibbāna upon landing	pahaccaparinibbāyī
attainer of nibbāna with exertion	sasaṅkhāraparinibbāyī
attainer of nibbāna without exertion	asaṅkhāraparinibbāyī

attainment	samāpatti
attainment of the fruition of once returning	sakadāgāmiphalasamāpatti
attainment of the fruition of stream entry	sotāpattiphalasamāpatti
attention	manasikāra
attention or attitude as proximate cause	manasikārapadaṭṭhānā
attention to repulsiveness	pāṭikūlamanasikāra
attention to the elements	dhātumanasikāra
avarice or stinginess	macchariya
aversion	paṭighānusaya
aversion, ill will	byāpāda
aversion, hatred	dosa
awareness of mental objects	dhammānupassanā
backbiting or slander	pisuṇavācā
bad companionship	pāpamittatā
balanced energy	paggaha
balanced equanimity or balanced observation	tatramajjhattupekkhā
balanced state of mind	tatramajjhattatā
base of nothingness	ākiñcaññāyatana
base of suffering	dukkhavatthu
basis or foundation for practice	kammaṭṭhānā
bearing in mind; making a mental note	sallakkhento
beauty	vaṇṇa
behaviors involving lack of restraint	asaṃvara dhammā
being or soul; life	jīva
being's final life	pacchimabhavikā
beings alike in body and different in perception	ekattakāya
beings different in body and alike in perception	ekattasaññī
beings of the realm of infinite consciousness	viññāṇāyatanasaññī
beings of the realm of infinite space	ākāsānañcāyatanasaññī

beings of the realm of neither perception nor nonperception	nevasaññānāsaññāyatanasaññī
beings of the realm of nothingness	ākiñcaññāyatanasaññī
beings that differ in body	nānattakāya
beings that differ in perception	nānattasaññī
beyond entanglement	vāna
beyond logic	atakkāvacaro
beyond the round of existence	vivaṭṭa
birth	jāti, yoni
birth from a womb	jalābuja
birth from an egg	aṇḍaja
birth from moisture	saṃsedaja
blame	nindā
Blessed One	bhagavā
bliss of meditation	bhāvanārati
blissful destination	sugati
bodily intimation manifested as bodily movement	kāyaviññattirūpa
bodily postures	iriyāpatha
body base	kāyāyatana
body element	kāyadhātu
body-consciousness	kāyaviññāṇa
body-consciousness element	kāyaviññāṇadhātu
body-sensitivity	kāyapasāda
both hands folded together in respect	añjali
breach of the rules concerning one's duty	vaṭṭabhedakadukkatā
Buddha's teachings	sāsana
calm, tranquility	passaddhi
carefully restraining the senses	indriyasaṃvara
causes cessation	nirodheti
celestial or heavenly being	devā

ceremony at the end of the annual rains retreat	pavāraṇā
cessation of arising	anuppādanirodha
cessation of the aggregates	khandhaparinibbāna
cessation of the defilements	kilesaparinibbāna
cessation-based	nirodhanissita
cessation, truth of cessation	nirodha
change	vipariṇām
change-of-lineage	gotrabhū
change-of-lineage impulsion	gotrabhū javana
characteristic	lakkhaṇā
characteristic of arising	nibbattilakkhaṇā
characteristic of disappearance	vipariṇāmalakkhaṇā
characteristic of distension; characteristics of firmness, stiffness, or looseness	vitthambhanalakkhaṇā
characteristic of impermanence	aniccalakkhaṇā
characteristic of inclining toward its objects	namanalakkhaṇā
characteristic of knowing an object	vijānanalakkhaṇā
characteristic of not-self	anattālakkhaṇā
characteristic of peace, characteristic of peacefulness	santilakkhaṇā
characteristics of torment	bādhanalakkhaṇā
characteristic of unsatisfactoriness	dukkhalakkhaṇā
characteristics of flowing or melting	paggharaṇalakkhaṇā
characteristics of hardness, softness, or smoothness	kakkhaḷalakkhaṇā
characteristics of heat, warmth, or cold	uṇhattalakkhaṇā
characteristics of material phenomena	lakkhaṇarūpa
charnel ground contemplation	sivathika
clear comprehension	sampajañña
clear comprehension of the domain	gocarasampajañña
clear comprehension without delusion	asammohasampajañña
clinging or grasping	upādāna

clinging to personality views that are based on the view of self	attavādupādāna
clinging wrong view	diṭṭhi-upādāna
cognition	viññāṇa
cognitive process; stream of consciousness	citttavīthi
cohesion or holding together	saṅgahapaccupaṭṭhāna
colored disk	kasiṇa
come along with	sahuppannattā
commander	sayamvasi
compassion	karunā
complete cessation	accantanirodha, parinibbāna
complete dispassion	accantavirāga
completely removing evil behavior and wrong livelihood	samucchedapahāna
comprehension	sammasana
comprehension of nutrition	āhārasammasana
conceit "I am"	asmimāna
conceit of view	diṭṭhimāna
concentrated state of mind	samāhitacitta
concentration	samādhi
concept about the manner; conventional reality defined by manner	ākārapaññatti
concept of a solid form or shape	saṅkhāraghananimitta
concept of compactness	ghanapaññatti
concept of nonexistence	abhāvapaññatti
concept of person	puggalapaññatti
concept of solidity	samūhapaññatti, santatipaññatti
concepts of things	atthapaññatti
concepts that refer to ultimate reality, concepts that refer to ultimately real phenomena	tajjāpaññatti

concepts that refer to what ultimately exists	vijjamānapaññatti
conceptual object of meditation	paṭibhāganimitta
concretely produced matter	nipphannarūpa
conditioned characteristics	saṅkhatalakkhaṇā
conditioned phenomena	saṅkhata
conditioned reality	saṅkhataparamattha
conduct	cariya
consciousness and volitional mind	abhisaṅkhāraviññāṇa
consciousness basis	viññāṇapadaṭṭhānā
constantly engaged in tranquility and insight meditation	satatavihārī
consumption of almsfood that is beneficial both to oneself and to one's supporters	amoghaparibhoga
consumption of almsfood that is debt-free	āṇaṇyaparibhoga
consumption of almsfood that is one's own	sāmiparibhoga
consumption of almsfood that is passed by inheritance	dāyajjaparibhoga
contact-led phenomena	phassapañcamaka
contact, mental contact	phassa
contemplating mental phenomena	nāmasattaka
contemplating physical phenomena, material septad	rūpasattaka
contemplation as a whole	kalāpasammasana
contemplation of cessation	nirodhānupassanā
contemplation of change	vipariṇāmānupassanā
contemplation of danger	ādīnavānupassanā
contemplation of destruction	khayānupassanā
contemplation of deterioration	palokānupassanā
contemplation of disenchantment	nibbidānupassanā
contemplation of dispassion	virāgānupassanā
contemplation of dissolution	bhaṅgānupassanā
contemplation of emptiness	suññatānupassanā

contemplation of fall	vayānupassanā
contemplation of feelings	vedanānupassanā
contemplation of impermanence	aniccānupassanā
contemplation of instability	calānupassanā
contemplation of light	obhāsānupassana
contemplation of mental and physical phenomena	nāmarūpanupassanā
contemplation of mind	cittānupassanā
contemplation of momentary nature	khaṇikasammasana
contemplation of not-self	anattānupassanā
contemplation of pairs of phenomena	yamakasammasana
contemplation of reflection	paṭisaṅkhānupassanā
contemplation of relinquishment	paṭinissaggānupassanā
contemplation of the body	kāyānupassanā
contemplation of the desireless	appaṇihitānupassanā
contemplation of the five aggregates	khandhānupassanā
contemplation of the four clear comprehensions	sampajañña
contemplation of the Four Noble Truths	catusaccakammaṭṭhāna
contemplation of the impurity of the body	asubhabhāvanā
contemplation of the signless	animittānupassanā
contemplation of turning away	vivattānupassanā
contemplation of unsatisfactoriness	dukkhānupassanā
contempt	makkha
conventional present; referring to the period of time that spans from birth to death	addhāpaccuppanna
conventional reality	paññatti, sammutipaññatti
conventional reality defined by appearance, concepts of form or shape	saṇṭhānapaññatti
conventional reality defined by name, concepts of name	nāmapaññatti
corruptions of insight, obstacles to insight	vipassanupakkilesā
counter-insight	paṭivipassanā

counter-insight meditation	paṭivipassanābhāvanā
covetousness	abhijjhā
covetousness and unrighteous greed	abhijjāvisamalobha
craving	paṇihita
craving for being	bhavataṇhā
craving, attachment	taṇhā
cycle of results	vipākavaṭṭa
cycle of suffering	saṃsāra
cycle of volitional actions	kammavaṭṭa
death	maraṇa
death consciousness	cuticitta
deathlessness	amata
decay	jaratā
deceit	māyā
decisive supporting condition	upanissayapaccaya
"deconstructing attention"	cuṇṇamanasikāra
the deductive method	atthāpannanaya
deeds of noble people	paramāna kamma
defilement obstacle	kilesantarāya
defilements	kilesā
defilements that are latent or dormant	anusaya-kilesā
defilements that arise as obsessive thought	pariyuṭṭhāna kilesā
defilements that arise when sense objects are not observed	ārammaṇādhiggahituppanna
defilements that lie dormant in sense objects	ārammaṇādhiggahita-kilesā, ārammaṇānusaya-kilesā
delight	nandi
delight, attachment	nikanti
delight, spiritual delight	pāmojja
delusion	moha, sammoha

denying permanence	niccapaṭikkhepa
dependent origination	paticcasamuppāda
depending on causes	saṅkhatato
derived material phenomena	upādārūpa
desire	paṇidhi
desire for existence	bhavarāga
desire for fine-material existence	rūparāga
desire for immaterial existence	arūparāga
desire, greed, or attachment	lobha
desireless	appaṇihita
destination	gati
destruction and cessation	khayanirodha
destruction of lust	rāgakkhayo
destructional dispassion	khayavirāga
deteriorate	palokato
developed state of mind; sublime types of consciousness	mahaggatacitta
developing tranquility prior to insight	samathapubbaṅgama
development of vipassanā before/preceeding concentration	vipassanāpubbaṅgama bhāvanā
Dhamma audience	veneyyajjhāsaya
difficult to understand	duddaso
disappearance, passing away	vaya
disciple	sāvaka
discontent	arati
discourse	sutta
discriminating knowledge	paṭisambhidāñāṇa
disdain	sārambha
dispassion-based	virāganissita
disrepute	ayaso

dissolution	bhaṅga
distracted state of mind	vikkhittacitta
distress; mental suffering	domanassa
distress associated with renunciation	nekkhammassitadomanassa
divine abodes	brahmavihārā
divine eye	dibbacakkhu
domain of the senses, sensual phenomena	kāmāvacara
domineering attitude	paḷāsa
doubt	vicikicchānusaya
dropping the foot	sajjana
dropping the foot	vosajjana
durable and substantial	dhuvasāra
ear base	sotāyatana
ear element	sotādhātu
ear-consciousness	sotaviññāṇa
ear-consciousness element	sotāviññāṇadhātu
ear-sensitivity	sotapasāda
earth	pathavī
earth element	pathavīdhatu
earth kasiṇa	pathavīkasiṇa
easily destroyed	pabhaṅguto
effort that is the right kind of striving	sammapaddhanavīriya
effort, exertion	vīriya
effortless mindfulness	upaṭṭhāna
eight types of individuals	aṭṭhapurisapuggalā
eighteen great insight knowledges	aṭṭhārasa-mahāvipassanā
element of exertion	padhāniyanga
element of mind-consciousness	manoviññāṇadhātu
element of nibbāna without the residue remaining	anupādisesanibbānadhātu
elements	dhātu

eliminating practice-related agitation	dhammuddhacca pahānanaya
emerging from mental phenomena	arūpā vutthāti
emerging from physical phenomena, emerging from immaterial phenomena	rūpā vutthāti . . . arūpe vutthāti
empirical	paccakkha
empirical contemplation of cessation	paccakkhanirodhānupassanā
empirical contemplation of impermanence	paccakkha aniccānupassanā
empirical contemplation of not-self	paccakkha anattānupassanā
empirical contemplation of unsatisfactoriness	paccakkha dukkhānupassanā
empirical reality	paccakkhattha
empirically experienced	saccikaṭṭha
empty	suññata
empty of a substantial self	suñña
enlightened	buddho
enlightenment factor of concentration	samādhisaṃbojjhaṅga
enlightenment factor of effort	vīriyabojjhaṅga
enlightenment factor of energy	vīriyasaṃbojjhaṅga
enlightenment factor of equanimity	upekkhāsaṃbojjhaṅga
enlightenment factor of investigation	dhammavicayasaṃbojjhaṅga
enlightenment factor of mindfulness	satisaṃbojjhaṅga
enlightenment factor of rapture, enlightenment factor of delight	pītisaṃbojjhaṅga
enlightenment factor of tranquility	passaddhisaṃbojjhaṅga
envy, jealousy	issā
equanimity associated with delusion	aññāṇupekkhā
equanimity of adverting	āvajjanupekkhā
escape by means of cessation	nissaraṇanirodha
escape by means of dispassion	nissaraṇavirāga
eternal	sassata
eternity view	sassatadiṭṭhi

ethical conduct of observing the monastic precepts	pāṭimokkhasaṃvarasīla
ethical conduct of reflecting on the purpose of the four requisites	paccayasanissitasīla
existence, becoming	bhava
existence	bhūta
existence based on intentional actions	kammabhava
experienced only by the wise	paṇḍitavedanīyo
explicit suffering	nippariyāyadukkha
externally oriented mind	bahiddha-citta
eye base	cakkhāyatana
eye-consciousness	cakkhuviññāṇa
eye-consciousness element	cakkhuviññāṇadhātu
eye element	cakkhudhātu
eye of insight into a person's inclination	buddhacakkhu
eye of path knowledge of arahantship	paññācakkhu
eye of the three lower path knowledges	dhammacakkhu
eye-sensitivity	cakkhupasāda
factors of enlightenment	bojjhaṅgā
faculty that is both sensory and functional consciousness	ubhayindriya
faith	saddhā
faith, confidence, determination	adhimokkha
false	viparīta
false speech	musāvāda
family-to-family attainer	kolaṃkolasotāpanna
fatigue or sleepiness	thinamiddha
seeing conditioned phenomena as fearful or frightening	bhayato
feeling	vedanā
feeling of distress	domanassavedanā

feeling of joy	somanassavedanā
feeling of neither displeasure nor pleasure, neutral feeling	upekkhāvedanā
feeling that is neither unpleasant nor pleasant, equanimity	upekkhā
feminine faculty	itthindriya
femininity	itthibhāvā
fetter	saṃyojana
fetters	saṃojanāni
fifth reviewing knowledge	pañcamapaccavekkhaṇāñāṇa
figurative usage	padhānanaya
figuratively	ṭhānyupacāra
fine-material realms	rūpabhūmi
fine-material existence	rūpabhava
fire element	tejodhātu
firm and steadfast	samādhāna
first [reviewing] knowledge	paṭhama paccavekkhaṇañāṇa
first knowledge of dissolution	paṭhamabhaṅgañāṇa
five physical sense consciousnesses	pañcaviññāṇa
five precepts or the eight precepts topped with right livelihood	ājīvaṭṭhamakasīla
flavor base, tasteable flavor base	rasāyatana
flavor element	rasadhātu
fledgling insight	taruṇavipassanā
food allowed after noon	yāmakālika
food allowed for a week	sattāhakālika
food allowed for life	yāvajīvika
food obtained by theft	theyyaparibhoga
forbearance	khanti
forbearance in conformity; referring to the composure of the insight knowledge of equanimity	anulomikakhantī

foremost	etadagga
form base, visible form base	rūpāyatana
form element	rūpādhātu
foundation of mindfulness	satipaṭṭhāna
foundation or basis	upadhāraṇa
fourth [reviewing] knowledge	catuttha paccavekkhanāñāṇa
frivolous speech	samphappalāpavācā
fruition consciousness	phalacittuppāda
fruition knowledge	phalañāṇa
fruition, fruition consciousness	phala
fruition of full liberation	arahattaphala
full understanding	abhiññātā
full understanding by abandoning	pahānapariññā
full understanding by investigation	tīraṇapariññā
full understanding by means of the path	maggapariñña
full understanding of the known	ñātapariññā
full understanding of the noble truth of suffering	pariññeyya-ariyadukkhasacca
fully enlightened	sammāsambuddho
fully liberated being	arahant
function	rasā
function of abandoning	pahānakicca
function of deathlessness	accutirasa
function of developing the path	bhāvanākicca
function of directly experiencing	sacchikiriyākicca
"function of expansion"; i.e., dampening	brūhanarasa
function of fully understanding	pariññākicca
function of movement, pushing, or pulling	samudīraṇarasa
functional consciousness	kriyacitta
functional faculties	kammindriya

future suffering of being rooted in the round of rebirths	paccuppanne vaṭṭamūlakaṃ dukkhaṃ
gain	lābha
gateway to liberation	vimokkhamukha
general nibbāna	sāmaññanibbāna
generosity	cāga
generosity	dāna
genuine ultimate realities	nibbatthitaparamattha
genuinely existing	bhūtattha
giving up	pariccāgapaṭinissagga
great reviewing knowledges	mahāpaccavekkhaṇāñāṇa
happiness associated with renunciation	nekkhammassitasomanassa
happiness; joy	somanassa
hearsay	itikirā
heart	hadaya
heart-base	hadayavatthu
heedlessness, negligence	pamāda
hidden pain or distress or hidden suffering	paṭicchannadukkha
higher reality	uttamattha
higher teaching	abhidhamma
highest	uttama
hindrance of aversion	byāpādanīvarana
hindrance of sensual desire	kāmacchandanīvaraṇa
hindrance of sloth and torpor	thinamiddhanīvaraṇa
hindrance, hindrances	nīvaraṇa
hindrances to liberation	niyyānāvaraṇa
home distress	gehassita-domanassa
home equanimity	gehassita-upekkhā
home happiness	gehassita-somanassa
hypocrisy, fraud	sāṭheyya

ideas accepted based on personal opinion	diṭṭhinijjhānakhanti
ideas that are accepted based on reason	ākāraparivitakka
ideas that are arrived at methodically	nayahetu
ideas that are arrived at through logic	takkahetu
ignorance	avijjā
ignorance as a hindrance to liberation	avijjāniyyānāvaraṇa
ignorance as a proximate cause	avijjāpadaṭṭhānā
ignorance of pleasure and its cause	micchāpaṭipatti-avijjā
ignorance of suffering and its cause	appaṭipatti-avijjā
image impressed in the memory when an action is performed	kammanimitta
image of the new life we will go to; sign of destiny	gatinimitta
immaterial absorptions	arūpajjhānā
immaterial existence	arūpabhava
immaterial realms	arūpabhūmi
immaterial, immateriality	arūpa
immediate condition or present cause	sahajātanissaya
immediate; immediately effective	akāliko
impermanence	aniccatā
impermanent; impermanence	anicca
imperturbable absorption	āneñja jhāna
imperturbable concentration	āneñja samādhi
implicit method	neyyatthanaya
implicit suffering	pariyāyadukkha
improper conduct	dukkata
improper conversation	dubbhāsita
impulsion consciousness associated with [the attainment of the supramundane] path	maggajavana
impulsion, mind-moment that is a kammic impulsion that fully perceives or moves toward an object	javana
impurities of the body	asubha

in accord with scripture	piṭakasampadā
in- and out-breath	ānāpāna
in- and out-breathing	assāsapassāsa
inanimate objects	dhammatārūpa
inborn deficiency in spiritual intellect	dvihetuka
independent of time	kālavimutta
indistinct pain or distress	appākaṭadukkha
individual or personality who experiences their results	vedaka-atta
individual or personality who performs wholesome and unwholesome actions	kāraka-atta
indolent state of mind	saṃkhittacitta
inference	anumāna
inferential attention	nayamanasikāra
inferential contemplation of impermanence	anumāna-aniccānupassanā
inferential contemplation of not-self	anumāna-anattānupassanā
inferential contemplation of unsatisfactoriness	anumāna-dukkhānupassanā
inferential insight	nayavipassanā
inferential insight into dissolution	anvayavipassanā
inferential knowledge	anumānañāṇa
inferential observation	nayadassana
inferior state of mind	sa-uttaracitta
inferring a deer's footprint	migapadavalañjananaya
initial application of mind, initial application	vitakka
insight beginner; energetic meditator	āraddhavipassaka
insight equanimity	vipassanupekkhā
insight full understanding by abandoning	vipassanāpahānapariññā
insight into phenomena that is higher wisdom	adhipaññādhammavipassanā
insight into states one by one as they occur	anupadadhamma-vipassanā
insight knowledge	vipassanāñāṇa

insight knowledge by comprehension	sammasanañāṇa
insight knowledge of adaptation	anulomañāṇa
insight knowledge of arising and passing	udayabbayañāṇa
insight knowledge of danger	ādīnavañāṇa
insight knowledge of desire for deliverance, insight knowledge that desires deliverance	muñcitukamyatāñāṇa
insight knowledge of disenchantment	nibbidāñāṇa
insight knowledge of dissolution	bhaṅgañāṇa
insight knowledge of equanimity toward phenomena, insight knowledge of equanimity toward formations	saṅkhārupekkhāñāṇa
insight knowledge of fear	bhayañāṇa
insight knowledge of reobserving	paṭisaṅkhāñāṇa
insight knowledge that discerns conditionality	paccayapariggahañāṇa
insight knowledge that discerns mental and physical phenomena	nāmarūpaparicchedañāṇa
insight that observes all states as a whole	kalāpavipassanā
insight; insight meditation	vipassanā
insubstantial	tuccha
insufficient practice or instruction	kiriyāparihāni
insulting words	pharusavācā
intellectual knowledge, analytical knowledge	cintāmayañāṇa
internally oriented mind	ajjhattacitta
intial application	savitakka
as intoxicating	sāsavato
inviting inspection	ehipassiko
jealousy	issāmacchariya
jhāna, absorption	jhāna
joy, rapture, zest	pīti
kamma that has immediate result	ānantariyakamma
kamma-generated materiality	kammaja rūpa
kamma, volitional or intentional actions	kamma

kammic obstacle	kammantarāya
kammically indeterminate, neutral; insensate	abyākata
knower of worlds	lokavidū
knowing	vijānana
knowledge and vision of things as they really are	yathābhūtañāṇadassana
knowledge derived from tranquility meditation	samathabhāvanāmaya
knowledge of change-of-lineage	gotrabhūñāṇa
knowledge of things as they really are	yathābhūtañāṇa
knowledge that comprehends all phenomena as a whole	kalāpasammasanañāṇa
knowledge that discerns conditionality	dhammaṭṭhitiñāṇa
knowledge that discriminates phenomena	dhammavavatthānañāṇa
knowledge, insight knowledge	ñāṇa
lack of gain	alābha (-o)
lack of restraint due to impatience	akkhanti-asaṃvara
lack of sense restraint	indriya-asaṃvara, indriyāsaṃvara
lacking in causes	aparappaccaya
lamentation	parideva
latent conceit	mānānusaya
latent [defilements]	anusaya
latent desire for existence	bhavarāgānusaya
latent desire for sensual objects	kāmarāgānusaya
latent ignorance	avijjānusaya
latent wrong view	diṭṭhānusaya
launching out into	pakkhandanapaṭinissagga
leading its mental factors	pubbaṅgamarasa
lesser stream enterer	cūlasotāpanna
liberated state of mind	vimuttacitta
liberation	niyyāna

liberation from the cycle of suffering	sīlabbatupādāna
liberation through desirelessness	appaṇihitovimokkho
liberation through emptiness	suññatovimokkho
liberation through knowledge	ñāṇaniyyāna
liberation through signlessness	animittovimokkho
liberation-related seclusion, escape by means of seclusion	nissaraṇaviveka
liberation-related, escape	nissaraṇa
liberation; extinction of greed, hatred, and delusion	nibbāna
life-continuum	bhavaṅga
life-controlling faculty	jīvitindriya
lifeless	anindriyabaddha
lifting the foot	uddharaṇa
light	obhāsa
light of wisdom	paññā-āloka
lightness	lahutā
limited by arising and passing away	uppādavayaparicchinna
lit. "internal domain," referring to mental and physical objects that fall within the scope of vipassanā	gocarajjhatta
lodgings	āvāsa
long pepper	pipphalī
loss of relatives	ñātivyasana
lovable and pleasant sense object	iṭṭhārammaṇa
loving-kindness	mettā
lust	rāga
lust, greed, attachment	chandarāga
lust, sensual desire	kāmarāga
lustre of wisdom	paññā-obhāsa
lying dormant in sense objects	ārammaṇānusaya

making the gesture of lifting up the hands folded together as a token of respect	añjalikamma
malleability	mudutā
manifest pain, manifest suffering	appaṭicchannadukkha
manifestation	paccupaṭṭhānā
manifestation as being subject to alteration and insensate	abyākata-paccupaṭṭhānā
manifestation of conveying	abhinīhārapaccupaṭṭhāna
manifestation of the signless	animittapaccupaṭṭhāna
manifests continuously	sandahanapaccupaṭṭhāna
masculine faculty	purisindriya
masculinity	pumbhāva
mass of bones	aṭṭhisaṅghāto
mass of physical phenomena	rūpasaṅghāto
material absorptions	rūpajjhānā
material phenomenon of the heart	hadayarūpa
materiality aggregate subject to clinging	rūpa upādānakkhandha
materiality arising from nutriment	āhāramaya rūpa
materiality arising from temperature	utumaya rūpa
matter possessing real characteristics	salakkhaṇarūpa
matter to be comprehended by insight	sammasanarūpa
matter, physical, fine-material sphere	rūpa
maturing in release	vosaggapariṇāmī
meditation	bhāvanā
meditation on the foundations of mindfulness	satipaṭṭhānabhāvanā
meditative knowledge	bhāvanāmayañāṇa
mental	nāma
mental and physical phenomena	parinibbānacuti
mental factor or constituent	cetasika
mental object	dhammārammaṇā

mental object base	dhammāyatana
mental object element	dhammadhātu
mental pain	cetasikadukkha
mental phenomena that can be perceived along with eye-consciousness	cakkhuviññānaviññātabbā
mental process that ends with determining	votthapanavāravīthi
mental process, cognitive processes	vīthi
mental processes	vīthicitta
mental purification	cittavisuddhi
the method established without being said	avuttasiddhinaya
method of one who takes the tranquility vehicle to nibbāna	samathapubbaṅgamā bhāvanā
method of practice to the noble path	ariyamaggabhāvanā
mind affected by delusion	samohacitta
mind affected by hate	sadosacitta
mind affected by lust	sarāgacitta
mind base	manāyatana
mind-consciousness	manoviññāṇa
mind door	manodvāra
mind-door-adverting consciousness, a mind-moment that adverts to a mental object	manodvārāvajjana
mind element	manodhātu
mind rooted in desire and affected by delusion	lobhamūla-samohacitta
mind rooted in hate and affected by delusion	dosamūla-samohacitta
mind that arises during insight meditation	vipassanācittuppāda
mind that investigates the sense object, to investigate, mind-moment that investigates an object, investigation	santīrana
mind unaffected by delusion	vītamohacitta
mind unaffected by hate	vītadosacitta
mind unaffected by lust	vītarāgacitta

mind-moment that adverts one of the five sense doors to an object, five-sense-door-adverting consciousnesses, adverting to the five sense doors	pañcadvārāvajjana
mind, cognition, mentality	citta
mindfulness	sati
mindfulness of in- and out-breath	ānāpānasati
mindfulness of the body	kāyagatāsati
minor rapture	khuddikāpīti
mode of being constantly oppressed by appearance and disappearance	udayabbhayappaṭipīḷana
moderation in eating	bhojanemattaññū
momentariness	āvakālika
momentarily present physical phenomena	khaṇapaccuppannarūpa
momentary	tāvakālika
momentary concentration	khaṇikasamādhi
momentary [nature]	khaṇika
momentary present, a period of time limited to a single mind moment	khaṇapaccuppanna
momentary rapture	khaṇikāpīti
momentary single-pointedness of mind	khaṇikacittekaggatā
momentum of the preliminary path	pubbabhāgamagga
monk	bhikkhu
moral conduct agreeable to the noble ones	ariyakantasīla
moral shame and fear of consequences	hiri-ottappa
morality	sīla
morality of right livelihood	ājīvapārisuddhisīla
morality that has been purified before meditation	pubbabhāgasīla
morality that is purified during meditation	sahajātasīla
mutable material phenomena	vikārarūpa
mythical bird, a harpy	garuda (Skt; Pāḷi, "garuḷa")
neither perception nor nonperception	nevasaññānāsaññāyatana

neither-unpleasant-nor-pleasant feeling	adukkhamasukhavedanā
neutral feeling associated with renunciation	nekkhammassita-upekkhā
neutral feelings	upekkhavedanā
neutral or indeterminate kamma	avyākatakamma
nibbāna with residue	sa-upādisesanibbāna = kilesaparinibbāna
nibbāna without residue	anupādisesanibbāna
nibbāna-based wholesome action or a wholesome action based beyond the round of rebirth	vivaṭṭanissita
noble deeds; perfection; also "deeds of a noble person" (paramānaṃ uttamapurisanaṃ bhāvo kammaṃ)	pāramī
noble one, noble person	ariya
noble path, path of the noble ones	ariyamagga
noble truth of suffering	dukkha-ariyasacca
noble truth of the cessation of suffering	dukkhanirodha-ariyasacca
noble truth of the origin of suffering	samudayāriyasacca
noble truth of the path leading to the cessation of suffering	dukkhanirodhagāminī-paṭipadā-ariyasacca
noble truths, truths for the noble ones	ariyasaccā
nonenduring	vibhāva
nonexistence of something that has arisen	hutvā abhāva
nongreed	alobha
nonpercipient beings	asaññasatta
nonarising	anuppādo
nonattachment, dispassion	virāga
nonaversion	abyāpāda
nonconcretely produced matter	anipphannarūpa
nondistraction	avikkhepa
nonexistence of conditioned phenomena	visaṅkhāra
nonhatred	adosa
nonreobservation	appaṭisaṅkhāna

nonreturner	anāgāmi
nonvirtuous, unskillful, or unwholesome actions	akusala
nose base	ghānāyatana
nose element	ghānadhātu
nose-consciousness	ghānaviññāṇa
nose-consciousness element	ghānaviññāṇadhātu
nose-sensitivity	ghānapasāda
not able to exercise mastery	avasavattīto
not constantly engaged in tranquility and insight meditation	nosatatavihārī
not endure	vibhavato
not false	aviparīta
not genuinely existing	abhūtattha
not having control	anissariya
not personally experienced	asaccikaṭṭha
not ruined by attachment and wrong view	asaṃkuppa
not subject to control [by desire]	alabbhanīya
not subject to creation by will	akāmakāriya
not untrue	avitatha
not yet realized	anadhigatattā
not yielding to temptations of attachment and wrong view	asaṃhīra
not-born	ajāta
not-brought-to-being	abhūta
not-made	akata
not-self, impersonal	anattā
novice monk	sāmaṇera
nutriment, nutrition	āhāra
nutritive essence	ojā
obscure pain or distress or obscure suffering	apākaṭadukkha

observing alternative objects of meditation	panidhāyabhāvanā
observing light; vivid contemplation	ālokasaññā
observing the monastic precepts	pāṭimokkhasaṃvara
observing the usual meditation object without letting the mind incline elsewhere	appanidhāyabhāvanā
obsession	gāha
obstacle of inborn deficiency	vipākantarāya
obstacle of insulting a noble one	ariyūpavādantarāya
obstinacy	thambha
occurrence	pavattaṃ
occurring	pavatta
odor base, smellable smell base	gandhāyatana
odor element	gandhādhātu
offense meriting expulsion	pārājika
offense requiring a convening of the saṅgha	saṅghādisesa
once returner	sakadāgāmī
one bound upstream, heading toward the Akaniṭṭha realm	uddhaṃsotakaniṭṭhagāmī
one of the noble path knowledges	ariyamaggañāṇa
one seed attainer	ekabījīsotāpanna
one who has been an ordained bhikkhu for at least ten years	thera
one who practices pure vipassanā meditation. (See also suddhavipassanāyānika.)	vipassanāyānikā
one who takes the pure vehicle of insight to enlightenment	suddhavipassanāyānika
one-pointed	ekattagata
one-pointedness	ekaggatā
one-pointedness based on contemplation of generosity	dānavosaggupaṭṭhānekatta
one-pointedness based on knowledge of cessation	nirodhupaṭṭhānekatta

one-pointedness based on knowledge of dissolution	vayalakkhaṇupaṭṭhānekatta
one-pointedness based on tranquility meditation	samathanimittupaṭṭhānekatta
one-pointedness of mind or concentration	cittekaggatā
onward leading	opanayyiko
ordinary people	puthujjana
pairing method	yuganaddhanaya
pairs	yamaka
past lives	addhātīta
path	magga
path [knowledge] and fruition [knowledge]	maggaphala
path consciousness	maggacittuppāda
path full understanding by abandoning	maggapahānapariññā
path knowledge	maggañāṇa
path knowledge that brings about abstinence from all evil behavior	maggavirati
path of a stream enterer	sotāpattimagga
path of insight	vipassanāmagga
path that leads to the cessation of suffering	dukkhanirodhagāminīpaṭipadā
peace	santi
peaceful ending of all conditioned phenomena	sabbasaṅkhārasamatho
peak-reaching equanimity	sikhāpattasaṅkhārupekkhā
penance	mānatta
penetration	paṭivedha
penetration by abandoning	pahānappaṭivedha
penetration of the objects [of insight]	vosaggārammaṇato
penetration of the path through development	bhāvanāpaṭivedha
penetration through direct experience	sacchikiriyāpaṭivedha
penetration, release	vosagga
perceiving	sañjāyana
perception	saññā

perception of impurity	asubhasaññā, pāṭikūlasaññā
perception of permanence	niccasaññā
perception of pleasure	sukhasaññā
perception of self	attasaññā
perfect in moral conduct, perfect in concentration, but only having medium-developed wisdom; attains final path after mid-life	upahaccaparinibbāyī
perfect in true knowledge and conduct	vijjācaraṇasampanno
perfect offering or donation	dakkhiṇāvisuddhi
permanence, pleasure, beauty, and the ability to control	ritta
permanent	nicca
permanent and substantial	niccasāra
permanent resident	nivāsi
perpetual	samuccheda
perpetual cessation	samucchedanirodha
perpetual dispassion	samucchedavirāga
perpetual seclusion	samucchedaviveka
person of dull intelligence but fit for liberation	mandabhabba-puggala
person of middling intelligence, wisdom, or understanding	majjhimapaññāneyya
person of quick understanding	ugghaṭitaññū
person of sharp intelligence	tikkhabhabba-puggala
person of sharp intelligence, wisdom, or understanding	tikkhapaññāneyya
person to be guided	neyya
person who understands through elaboration	vipañcitaññū
personal insight	paccakkhavipassanā
personal knowledge	paccakkhañāṇa
clinging to personality views that are based on the view of self	attavādupādāna
pervasive rapture	pharaṇāpīti

perversion of perception	saññāvipallāsā
perversions	vipallāsā
physical aggregate	rūpakkhandhā
physical and mental sense objects that are proximate causes	nāmarūpapadaṭṭhāna
physical matter	rūpārūpa
physical pain	kāyikadukkha
physical phenomena that are generated by consciousness	cittasamuṭṭhāna rūpa
physical pleasure	kāyikasukha
plain pain or plain suffering	pākaṭadukkha
plane or realm of existence	bhūmi
pleasant bodily or mental feelings, pleasant feeling	sukhavedanā
pleasing objects	piyarūpa, sātarūpa
pleasurable and substantial	sukhasāra
pleasure, happiness	sukha
powerful	balava
practice of insight meditation	vipassanākamma
practice of meditation	bhāvanākamma
practice order	paṭipattikkama
practice-related agitation	dhammuddhacca
practices the straight way	ujupaṭipanno
practices the true way	ñāyapaṭipanno
practicing the proper way	sāmīcipaṭipanno
practitioner who uses both vipassanā and tranquility meditation; one who takes the tranquility vehicle to nibbāna	samathayānika
preaching order	desanākkama
preparation	parikamma
present	paccuppanna

present arising of physical phenomena	paccuppannarūpa
present cause	nissaya
present consciousness	paccuppannaviññāṇa
present feeling	paccuppannavedanā
present mental formations	paccuppannasaṅkhāra
present perception	paccuppannasaññā
present time	addhā
pressing	sannirumbhana
pride in what is worthy	yāthāvamāna
pride, arrogance, or conceit	māna
probation	parivatta
production	upacaya
profound	gambhīro
proliferation	papañca
proximate cause	padaṭṭhānā
pulling a lifted foot even with the other foot	atiharaṇa
purification	visuddhi
purification by knowledge and vision of what is path and not path	maggāmaggañāṇadassa-navisuddhi
purification by overcoming doubt	kaṅkhāvitaraṇavisuddhi
purification of conduct	sīlavisuddhi
purification of knowledge and vision	ñāṇadassanavisuddhi
purification of knowledge and vision of the path, purification by knowledge and vision of the way	paṭipadāñāṇadassanavisuddhi
purification of view	diṭṭhivisuddhi
purification of wisdom	paññāvisuddhi
the monastic rule allowing a monk to reveal his genuine attainment	bhūtārocana
pursuing a pure livelihood	ajīvapārisuddhi
pushing it forward in front of the other foot	vītiharaṇa
putting down	nikkhepana

raping a virtuous nun	bhikkhunidūsanekamma
real	taccha
realization	abhisamaya
realization by abandoning	pahānābhisamaya
realization of the path through development	bhāvanābhisamaya
realization through direct experience	sacchikiriyābhisamaya
realms of sensual pleasures	kāmasugatibhūmi
reappearance	upapatti
rebirth consciousness that is capable of enlightenment	tihetuka
recollection	anussatī
recollection of death	maraṇānussati
recollection of one's generosity	cāgānussati
recollection of the qualities of celestial beings	devātānussati
recollection of the qualities of the Buddha	buddhānussati
recollection of the qualities of the saṅgha	saṅghānussati
recollection of one's morality or ethical conduct	sīlānussati
recollection of peace (of Nibbana)	upasamānussati
referring to the vipassanā knowledge of equanimity toward formations, lit. "to be established in re-observation"	paṭisaṅkhā santiṭṭhānā
registration, mind that registers the sense object	tadārammaṇa
regret	kukkucca
relatives	kula
release that abandons defilements	pariccāgavosagga
release that rushes to nibbāna	pakkhandanavosagga
remote condition or prior cause	pakatūpanissāya
removal of the fetters	saṃyojanāni
removing attachment	nikantipariyādāna
removing conceit	māna-samugghātana
removing wrong view	diṭṭhi-ugghāṭana

renunciation; wholesomeness that arises from insight	nekkhamma
repeated	paṭipassaddhi
repeated, repetition	anupada
repetition	āsevana
repetition impulsion consciousness	āsevanajavana
repulsion	pāṭikūlyatā
requisites of enlightenment	bodhipakkhiyādhammā
resolve	adhiṭṭhāna
restless	vikkhepa
restlessness, fidgety	uddhacca
restraint arising from mindfulness	satisaṃvara
restraint arising from wisdom	ñāṇasaṃvara
restraint by means of morality	sīlasaṃvara
restraint by means of patience	khantisaṃvara
restraint of the eye	cakkhusaṃvara
restraint through effort	vīriyasaṃvara
resultant	vipaka
resulting conditionally arisen state	upanissayapaccayuppanna
revenge	upanāha
reviewing knowledge	paccavekkhaṇañāṇa
right action	sammākammanta
right attitude, wise attention	yoniso manasikāra
right concentration	sammāsamādhi
right conduct	ñāya
right effort	sammāvāyāma
right intention	sammāsaṅkappa
right livelihood	sammāājīva
right mindfulness	sammāsati
right seeing	sammādassana
right speech	sammāvācā

right view	sammādiṭṭhi
root of unwholesomeness	aghamūla
rooted in desire	lobhamūla
roughness and hardness	kakkhalatta
round of existence	vaṭṭa
ruined by attachment and wrong view	saṃkuppa
rules for bhikkhus, monastic rules and regulations	vinaya
secluded	vivitta
seclusion	viveka
seclusion-based	vivekanissita
second insight knowledge of dissolution	dutiyabhaṅgañāṇa
second reviewing knowledge	dutiyapaccavekkhanāñāṇa
see or observe; contemplate in turn	anupassati
seeing conditioned phenomena as afflictions or impurities	saṃkilesadhammato
seeing conditioned phenomena as constantly changing	vipariṇāmadhammato
seeing conditioned phenomena as devoid of self	suññato
seeing conditioned phenomena as subject to sickness	byādhidhammato
seeing conditioned phenomena as the root of unwholesomeness	aghamūlato
seeing mental phenomena as they really are	nāmayāthāvadassana
seeing physical phenomena as they really are	rūpayāthāvadassana
seeing present physical phenomena as solid	santatipaccuppannarūpa
seeing that conditioned phenomena are not everlasting	adhuvato, addhuvato
seeing that conditioned phenomena are unstable	calato
seeing things as constant torment	abhiṇhasampaṭipīlana
self	atta
self-indulgence through forgetting to be mindful	muṭṭhasacca-asaṃvara
self-indulgence through idleness or laziness	kosajja-asaṃvara

self-indulgence through immoral conduct	dussīlya-asaṃvara
sense base	āyatana
sense bases and sense objects that are proximate causes	vatthārammaṇapadaṭṭhāna
sense sphere	kāma
sense-sphere consciousness	kāmāvacaracitta
sensory faculties	buddhindriya
sensual desire	kāmacchanda
sensuous existence	kāmabhava
serial present, apparent continuity or duration of present phenomena, continuity of mental and physical processes happening in the present, a period of time that covers a single mental process	santatipaccuppanna
serious infraction	thullaccaya
serpent or Nāga demon, gifted with miraculous powers and great strength	nāga
seven-times-at-most attainer	sattakkhattusotāpanna
seventh reviewing knowledge	sattamapaccavekkhaṇāñāṇa
severe inborn deficiency in spiritual intellect	ahetuka
showering rapture	okkantikāpīti
sickness	byādhi
sign	nimitta
sign of eternity	sassatanimitta
sign of stability	dhuvanimitta
signless	animitta
signless deliverance of mind	animittā-cetovimutti
signs of phenomena, sign of conditioned phenomena	saṅkhāranimitta
silent buddha	paccekabuddha
simultaneous elimination	pahānekaṭṭha
sixfold equanimity	chaḷaṅgupekkhā

sixth reviewing knowledge	chaṭṭhama paccavekkhaṇañāṇa
skeleton	aṭṭhi
skeptical doubt, doubt	vicikicchā
solidity	santati
solidity and continuity of phenomena, solidity of continuity	santatighana
solidity of function	kiccaghana
solidity of mass	samūhaghana
solidity of object	ārammaṇaghana
solidity of present feeling	santatipaccuppannavedanā
sorrow, grief, or lamentation	soka
sound base, audible sound base	saddāyatana
sound element	saddādhātu
sound object	saddārammaṇa
source of pain	dukkhavatthutāya
space element	ākāsadhātu
specific characteristics, intrinsic characteristics, unique characteristic	sabhāvalakkhaṇā
specific nibbāna	visesanibbāna
speech	vācā
spheres of beings	sattāvāsā
spiritual urgency	saṃvega
spiritually blind people	andhaputthujjana
spontaneous birth	opapātika, papātika
stable	tādi
stable; durable	dhuva
state	pada
state, phenomena, nature, law, or doctrine	dhamma
stations of consciousness	viññāṇaṭṭhiti
stinginess regarding beauty	vaṇṇamacchariya

stinginess regarding gain	lābhamacchariya
stinginess regarding knowledge	dhammamacchariya
stinginess regarding lodgings	āvāsamacchariya
stopping	vikkhambhana
store accumulation of kamma, merit or demerit	abhisaṅkhāra
strangers or outsiders	para
stream enterer	sotāpannā
strong insight leading quickly to path	khippābhiññā
subject to aging and decay	jarādhammato
subject to and a source of grief	sokadhammato
subject to and a source of lamentation	paridevadhammato
subject to and a source of trouble	upāyāsadhammato
subject to birth	jātidhammato
subject to calamities	ītito
sublime	sugato
sublime types of consciousness	mahaggatacittāni
substantial self	attasāra
subtle matter	sukhumarūpa
successive	paṭipāṭi
suffering of being oppressed by arising and passing away	udayabbayappīḷanato dukkhā
suffering of change, the impermanence of mental or physical pleasure	vipariṇāmadukkha
suffering of conditioned phenomena, the condition of being subject to arising and passing away	saṅkhāradukkha
suffering of pain; mental or physical pain	dukkhadukkha
suffering of the lower realms	apāyadukkhaṃ
superintendent (an erroneous experience of the self)	adhiṭṭhāyaka
superior state of mind	anuttaracitta
supernormal ability to read others' thoughts	cetopariya abhiññāṇa

supramundane	lokuttarā
supramundane path	lokuttaramagga
sustained application	savicāra
sustained application of mind, sustained application	vicāra
sympathetic joy	muditā
taint of existence	bhavāsava
taint of sensual desire	kāmāsava
taints	āsava
taking up	ādāna
taking up and putting down	ādānanikkhepana
tangible object base	phoṭṭhabbāyatana
tangible object element	phoṭṭhabbadhātu
tangible object	phoṭṭhabba
teacher of gods and humans	satthā devamanussānaṃ
teachers and forefathers	paramparā
temporarily eliminated, temporary or partial removal [of mental defilements]	tadaṅgappahāna
temporary	tadaṅga
temporary cessation	tadaṅganirodha
temporary dispassion	tadaṅgavirāga
temporary liberation from defilements	tadaṅganibbūta
temporary seclusion	tadaṅgaviveka
then and there	tattha tattha
theoretical knowledge	sutamaya, sutamayañāṇa
things as they are, real existence	yathābhūta
third path; attainment of ānāgamimagga	tatiyañāṇa
thirty-two	dvattiṃsa
those that are inherently pleasing	sabhāva iṭṭhārammaṇa
those that are inherently unpleasant	sabhāva aniṭṭhārammaṇa

those that deceptively appear to be pleasing	parikappa iṭṭhārammaṇa
those that deceptively appear to be unpleasant	parikappa aniṭṭhārammaṇa
those that dwell in a continuum	santānānusaya
thoughtful reconsideration	paṭisaṅkhāna
thoughtful reconsideration	paṭisaṅkhānañāṇa
threat to prospects for path knowledge and fruition knowledge; obstacle of knowingly violating the monastic code	āṇāvītikkamantarāya
Thus Gone One (Buddha)	tathāgata
to act wrongly due to desire	chandāgati
to advert to an object, to attend	āvajjana
to be experienced by the wise for themselves	paccattaṃ veditabbo viññūhī
to determine, mind-moment that determines an object, mind that determines the sense object	votthapana
to have steadfast wrong views	niyatamicchādiṭṭhi
to receive, mind-moment that receives a sense impression of an object, mind that receives the sense object	sampaṭicchana
to seclude oneself; to be distinct from cause and effect	vivittato
tongue base	jivhāyatana
tongue element	jivhādhātu
tongue-consciousness	jivhāviññāṇa
tongue-consciousness element	jivhāviññāṇadhātu
tongue-sensitivity	jivhāpasāda
torch of wisdom	paññāpajjota
touching the ground	sannikkhepana
trainee	sekkha
training	sikkhā
training in concentration	samādhisikkhā
training in morality	sīlasikkhā

training in the higher mind	adhicittasikkhā
training in wisdom	paññāsikkhā
tranquility	samatha
tranquility meditation of determining the four primary elements	dhātuvavatthāna
transgressive defilements	vītikkama-kilesā
tribulation, anxiety	upāyāsa
true	tatha
true knowledge	vijjā
truth	attha
truth of cessation, truth of the cessation of all suffering	nirodhasacca
truth of origin, truth of the origin of suffering	samudayasacca
truth of suffering	dukkhasacca
truth of temporary cessation	tadaṅganirodhasacca
truth of the path	maggasacca
truth of the path that one must develop	bhāvetabbāmaggasacca
truths beyond the round of existence	vivattasacca
truths of the round of existence	vaṭṭasacca
two aspects	dvikoṭika
two or three	dvatti
ultimate	parama
ultimate emptiness	paramasuñña
unchanging	aviparinaṇāta
unconcentrated mind	asamāhitacitta
unconditioned absolute reality	asaṅkhataparamattha
unconditioned phenomena	asaṅkhata
uncontrollable; not subject to anyone's wishes	avasavattana
understanding gained from tradition	anussava
undeveloped state of mind	amahaggatacitta

unification of mind	ekatta
universal characteristic	sāmaññalakkhaṇā
universally accepted, generally accepted view	samānavāda
unliberated mind	avimuttacitta
unpleasant object	asātarūpa
unpleasant objects	appiyarūpa, asātarūpa
unpleasant physical feeling; painful feeling	dukkhavedanā
unsatisfactoriness; suffering; pain	dukkha
unstable	adhuva
unwholesome states to be abandoned	pahātabba akusula dhamma
unwholesome things or actions	akusalā dhammā
unwise attention	ayoniso manasikāra
unworldly displeasure	nirāmisadukkha
unworldly neither displeasure nor pleasure	nirāmisa-adukkhamasukha
unworldly pleasure, genuine happiness	nirāmisasukha
uplifting rapture	ubbegāpīti
use of requisites "on loan"	iṇaparibhoga
vanity	mada
verbal intimation manifested as verbal expression	vacīviññattirūpa
very clear knowledge that leads to emergence, insight leading to emergence	vutthānagāminīvipassanā
vibration of the life-continuum	bhavaṅgacalana
vicissitudes of life	lokadhamma
view of personality	sakkāyadiṭṭhi
view that a self really exists	attadiṭṭhi
vipassanā perfections	vipassanā pāramī
virtuous, skillful, wholesome	kusala
visible here and now	sandiṭṭhiko
[visible] form object	rūpārammaṇā
vitality	jīvita

volition, conditioned	saṅkhāra
volition, intention, urge	cetanā
water	āpo
water element	āpodhātu
weak insight	dandhābhiññā
well-preached	svākkhāta
whole	kalāpa
wieldiness	kammaññatā
will, desire to act	chanda
wisdom	paññā
wisdom of full understanding	abhiññāpaññā
wise reflection or reviewing	paccavekkhaṇa
wisely using requisites	paccayasannissita
with residue remaining	sa-upādisesa
with residue remaining, referring to nibbāna of a living fully enlightened being	sa-upādisesa
without consciously knowing	ñāṇavippayutta
without core or essence	asāraka
without residue remaining	anupādisesa
world	sattaloka
worldly	sāmisa
worldly displeasure	sāmisadukkha
worldly neither displeasure nor pleasure	sāmisa-adukkhamasukha
worldly pleasure	sāmisasukha
worthy of gifts	āhuṇeyyo
worthy of hospitality	pāhuṇeyyo
worthy of offerings	dakkhiṇeyyo
worthy of reverential salutation	añjalikaraṇīyo
wrong action	micchākammanta
wrong concentration	micchāsamādhi

wrong deliverance	micchāvimutti
wrong effort	micchāvāyāma
wrong knowledge	micchāñāṇa
wrong livelihood	micchā-ājīva
wrong mindfulness	micchāsati
wrong thought	micchāsaṅkappa
wrong view	diṭṭhi
wrong view or belief	miccadiṭṭhi
wrong view that everything is cut off or comes to an end when we die	natthikadiṭṭhi
wrong view that there is no good or evil	akiriyadiṭṭhi
wrong view that volitional action does not produce good or evil results	ahetukadiṭṭhi
wrong ways of behaving	agati
yields to temptations of attachment and wrong view	saṃhīra

Bibliography

Bodhi, Bhikkhu, ed. 1999. *A Comprehensive Manual of Abhidhamma: the Abhidhammattha Sangaha of Ācariya Anuruddha*. Onalaska: BPS Pariyatti Editions.

———, ed. 2005. *In the Buddha's Words: An Anthology of Discourses form the Pāḷi Canon*. Boston: Wisdom Publications.

———, trans. 1999. *The Connected Discourses of the Buddha: A New Translation of the Saṃyutta Nikāya*. Boston: Wisdom Publications.

———, trans. 1995. *The Middle Length Discourses of the Buddha: A New Translation of the Majjhima Nikāya*. Boston: Wisdom Publications.

———, trans. 2012. *The Numerical Discourses of the Buddha: A New Translation of the Aṅguttara Nikāya*. Boston: Wisdom Publications.

Fronsdal, Gil, trans. 2005. *The Dhammapada: A New Translation of the Buddhist Classic with Annotations*. Boston: Shambhala Publications.

Ireland, John D., trans. 1997. *The Udāna: Inspired Utterances of the Buddha; & The Itivutakka: The Buddha's Sayings*. Kandy: Buddhist Publication Society.

Mahāsi Sayadaw. 1971. *Practical Insight Meditation*. Kandy: Buddhist Publication Society.

Ñāṇamoli, Bhikkhu, trans. 1991. *The Path of Purification: Visuddhimagga*. Onalaska: BPS Pariyatti Editions.

———, trans. 2009. *The Path of Discrimination: Paṭisambhidāmagga*. Oxford: Pali Text Society.

Ñānarama, Mahāthera Matara Sri. 1993. *The Seven Stages of Purification and the Insight Knowledges: A Guide to the Progressive Stages of Buddhist Meditation*. Kandy: Buddhist Publication Society.

———. 1998. *The Seven Contemplations of Insight: A Treatise on Insight Meditation*. Kandy: Buddhist Publication Society.

Walshe, Maurice, trans. 1995. *The Long Discourses of the Buddha: A New Translation of the Dīgha Nikāya*. Boston: Wisdom Publications.

Index

References that begin with "A" refer to appendixes, which can be found on the removable insert.

A

abandoning:
  attachment to the body, 507–8
  conditioned phenomena connected with the three universal characteristics, 471–73
  craving, 240–41, 244, 252
  defilements, 37–38, 39, 76, 153–55, 428, 429–30, 476, 506–7. *See also under* latent defilements
  the perception of permanence, 475–76, 480
  the sense of self, 332, 333–34, 354–55, 398–400, 484–85, 521
  See also overcoming; removing

Abhidhamma:
  on "I"/the self, 331–32
  on impermanence, 326
  on latent defilements in noble ones, 482
  on mental contact, 165–66
  on phenomena, 100
  on seeing, 95
  on seeing the three universal characteristics, 470–71, 472, 485–86
  on ultimate reality, 93, 98

Abhidhammatthavibhāvinī, 101, 146, 331–32

Abhiññeyya Sutta: on sensing/seeing, 151, 152

absorption, imperturbable, 452

absorption concentration, 46, 47, 49

abstinence (from immoral conduct/evil behavior), 37, 38, 39–40, 250–51

access concentration, 45–46, 47, 49

access impulsion consciousness, 408–9, 413

access to the Dhamma, 3

action:
  intention and, 106–7, 319
  volitional actions, 315–23, 480–81
  wrong action/ways of behaving, 422, 424–25, 426–27
  See also activities; movement; walking

activities:
  clear comprehension of, 185–95
  insightful vs. ordinary understanding of, 105–8, 183–84, 188
  seeing as they really are, 303–4

adaptation, insight knowledge of, 406, 407–8, 409, 415, 416, 448, 471
  contemplation of turning away, 526–28

adaptation impulsion consciousness, 408–10, 413

adherence to conditioned phenomena, 523–24

advanced insight, 53

adverting consciousness, 160, 179, 313, 376, 382, 408, 409, 527

See also under mind-moments
aggregates. *See* five aggregates
aging, 227
"aging and decay in stages" (of the body), 341–42
agitation, practice-related. *See* restlessness
aggregate, 213–14, 216–17
air element:
  touch characteristics, 177
  walking function, 186
alms:
  gratitude for, 85–86
  obtaining of, 8. *See also* right livelihood
alms donors (lay supporters):
  benefits for, 42–43
  generosity, 9
Ānāpānasati Sutta, 130
Anāthapiṇḍika's story, 368–69, 372
anger, 206, 220
  overcoming, 75
Aṅguttara Nikāya/commentary:
  on fruition, 450–51
  on grave offenders, 10–11
  on impermanence vs. "I am," 484–85
  on loving-kindness and alms donors, 42–43
the animal world, 83
anticipating the future, 79
antidotes to hindrances, 75–76
Anupada Sutta:
  on Moggallāna's method and experience of insight meditation on the jhānas, 113
  on Sāriputta's method and experience of insight meditation on the jhānas, 134
appearance: of not-self, 493
appearance and disappearance. *See* arising and passing away...
arahants, 110, 133, 453–54, 459, 525
arising and passing away of phenomena, 280–81, 282, 349–50, 358–62
  characteristics, 362–64
  insight knowledge of, 53, 216–17, 259, 280–81, 282, 295, 356–79; that discerns the correct path, 378–79; vs. insight, 370–71; return to after cessation, 293–94
  mindfulness of, 282
  observing true arising and passing away, 364–67
  physical phenomena, 194–95, 215–16
  reobserving, 390–91
Ariya's enlightenment, 28–29
arrogance, 220
aspiration for enlightenment, 260
  See also desire for deliverance
attachment, 58–60, 220, 357
  abandoning attachment to the body, 507–8
  becoming attached, 118–19
  and consciousness, 216–17
  removing, 357–58; practice as/as not, 356
  See also sensual desire
Attadattha's story, 70–71
attainment:
  of fruition. *See* fruition
  revealing one's own, 432
  stream enterers reviewing their own, 441–45
attention:
  to repulsiveness of the body, 255
  wise/unwise, 210–13
attention-getting objects, 274
aversion, 61, 209, 422
  overcoming, 61, 75, 88–89
avoiding practice, 288
awareness:
  gender awareness, 179
  noting and, 195
  nutrition awareness, 180, 195, 345
  of sense objects, 144
  See also consciousness

B

bad companionship, 36
balanced energy, 375
balancing excesses in mental faculties, 224–26
basic insight, 52–53
"the basis or foundation of practice," 185
beauty: stinginess re, 423–24
bending, 106–7, 188, 190–91, 214
benefits of practice, 84
birth, 227

birth and death, contemplation of, 335–36
Bodhirājakumāra Sutta: on practitioners' potential for enlightenment, 259
bodily postures, 255
bodily sensations: noting, 177
the body, 148–95
abandoning attachment to, 507–8
"aging and decay in stages," 341–42
faculties, 331
as impermanent, unsatisfactory, and not-self, 338–39, 341–42, 345–46, 348
nutrition awareness, 180, 195, 345
as oppressive, 330
posture. *See* posture
as the primary object of meditation, 260, 264–66, 277
repulsiveness, 255
sensitivity, 173
taking up and putting down, 338–39
temperature sensitivity, 345–46
universal characteristics. *See* three universal characteristics...
body-consciousness, 150, 174
See also the senses; touch
body-sensitivity, 173
bowl story, 470, 471
breaking a precept, 8
breathing: mindfulness of, 174–76, 264–66
See also in- and out-breath
bubble metaphors, 359, 366, 384, 401
the Buddha:
and Attadattha, 70–71
on cessation/nibbāna, 458
on contemplation of turning away, 527–28
on contentment without enlightenment, 74–75
on the five characteristics of appearance and disappearance, 363–64
on freedom from lower rebirth, 437–41
heirs in the Dhamma, 73–75
on inferential insight knowledge (by comprehension), 327
and the louse, 9–10
and Mahānāma, 439–41
and Māluṅkyaputta, 153, 154, 156–57
on mindfulness, 257–58
on the mirror the of Dhamma, 430–31
not-self as the domain of only, 486, 487
offerings to, 72–73, 75
and Potthila, 161–62, 163–64
on practitioners' potential for enlightenment, 258–59
on remembering the past, 117
and Saccaka, 332
and Santati, 26–27
and Sāriputta, 437–39
and Uttiya, 28
on vision/purification and realization, 133
the Buddha-to-Be: lower rebirths, 324–25
Buddhaghosa, 12

C
calm (enlightenment factor), 223
canal crossing simile, 413–14
cause and effect, 277–79, 313–14, 314–15, 522
from previous lives to present and future lives, 316–18
proximate causes of ultimately real phenomena, 145–46, 146–47
wrong views of. *See* defilements
See also creator concept; discerning/seeing conditionality; no cause concept
cautionary word on insight knowledge leading to emergence, 418–19
cessation (of craving/suffering), 154, 156, 412–14, 417–18
of consciousness, 465
contemplation of, 504–7
descriptions, 292–93
duration, 293
"Just this is the end of suffering," 457
of lust, 505–6
mental states following, 294–95
nibbāna as, 454–56, 463–64, 465–66; of the five aggregates, 459–62
noting after, 293–94
one-pointedness based on knowledge of, 91
reflections on, 293
return to insight knowledge of arising and passing away after, 293–94

the truth of. *See* truth of cessation
See also fruition; nibbāna
cessation-oriented insight, 446
change:
contemplation of, 515–17
suffering of, 228
change-of-lineage (impulsion consciousness), 411, 447, 448, 460
insight knowledge of, 406, 407, 411, 415–16, 471, 527–28
characteristics of phenomena, 340, 469
re arising and passing away/appearance and disappearance, 362–63
re the four primary material elements, 176–77
See also three universal characteristics of phenomena
chicken and egg metaphor, 320–21
clarity following cessation, 294
clear comprehension, 255
of activities, 185–95
without delusion, 184, 185–86
of the domain, 184, 187, 189, 190–91, 192, 194
of reality, 187, 191, 192, 193, 194
clinging, 266, 426
craving and, 310, 311
clothes: wearing robes, 9, 191
compassion. *See* loving-kindness
comprehension, insight knowledge by. *See* inferential insight knowledge
conceit (pride), 377
removing, 355–56, 484–85
See also self, sense/concept of
concentration:
developing, 445
enlightenment factor, 223–24
excessive concentration, 225
and fruition, 445
in insight meditation, 33, 47, 50, 51. *See also* momentary concentration
morality and, 40
objects of, 45–46, 53
obstacles to and methods for overcoming, 78–89
path concentration, 40, 55–56
strong concentration effects, 279–80
three types, 45–46, 47
training in. *See* training in concentration
See also tranquility
concepts:
of continuity. *See* continuity
as delusions, 37–38
examples, 102–4
as illusions, 94–96
insight meaning, 106–8
names as, 102, 104–5, 107
ordinary meaning, 105–6
processes as, 104, 106–7
of solid form. *See* solidity
vs. ultimate reality, 107–8
See also creator concept; no cause concept; permanence concept/perception; person concept; self, sense/concept of
concretely produced matter, 110, 111
conditionality. *See* discerning/seeing conditionality; *and also* cause and effect
conditioned characteristics of phenomena, 469
conditioned phenomena, 521–22
abandoning phenomena connected with the three universal characteristics, 471–73
adherence to, 523–24, 524
appearance, 519
characteristics. *See* characteristics of phenomena
relinquishment of, 524–26
stages/phases, 314–15, 335–36, 358, 469–70
suffering of, 228–29, 280–81
conduct: purification of. *See* moral purification
See also immoral conduct; moral conduct
confessing one's offense, 20, 75, 443–44
confidence, 114, 375, 406
confirmation of stream entry, 430–32
consciousness:
as an aggregate, 213–14, 216–17
cessation of, 465
death consciousness, 338
fruition consciousness, 412, 412–13, 445
functional. *See* life-continuum
kinds, 156, 168–69
mental factors/states in each, A2

path consciousness, 412–13, 418
the rising of, 216–17
sense-sphere consciousness, 111, A2, A7
stream factors, A3
unwholesome states, 427, 428–30
See also adverting consciousness; awareness; impulsion consciousness; life-continuum; relinking consciousness; *and also* the senses
considering the disadvantages, 76
contact. *See* mental contact
contemplation/contemplations:
of birth and death, 335–36
of cessation, 504–7
of change, 515–17
of danger, 523–24
of the desireless, 520
of destruction, 512–14
of disenchantment, 501–2, 503, 504
of dispassion, 502–4, 511
on dispelling hindrances, 72–75, 75–78; laziness and restlessness, 80–87
of emptiness, 520–21
of fall, 512, 514–15, 517
of feeling/feelings, 195–206, 256, 348–51
of impermanence, 334–35, 335, 355–56, 468–89, 501, 518, 519
inferential insight knowledge and, 326
of the jhānas, 56, 414
of mental objects, 121, 208–32, 278; wise/unwise attention, 210–13. *See also* five aggregates; five hindrances; seven factors of enlightenment; six senses; ten fetters
of mental phenomena, 334–35, 351–56
of the mind, 206–8, 256, 351
of momentary nature, 352
of not-self, 492–501
and noting, 326
of pairs of phenomena, 275–77, 285, 352
of physical phenomena, 338–51
of reflection, 524–26
of relinquishment, 119, 507–9
of sensation/sensations, 346–48
of the signless, 518–20
the three contemplations, 509–12
of turning away, 526–28
of unsatisfactoriness, 489–92
See also meditation; reflection/reflections
contempt, 429
contentment without enlightenment, 74–75
continuity (concept), 103–4
solidity of, 493, 494–95
continuity of phenomena, 144–45, 473–74
continuity of process, 359, 360–61
continuum. *See* life-continuum
counter-insight, 381
counter-insight meditation, 185
craving, 206, 230, 231, 232, 237
abandoning, 240–41, 244, 252
and clinging, 310, 311
desire for nibbāna as not, 59–60
the end of. *See* cessation
noting, 253
See also desire; lust
creator concept, 37–38, 278, 308–9, 312, 320
crow metaphor, 405

D
danger:
contemplation of, 523–24
insight knowledge of, 297, 385–87, 388–89
dangers of the lower realms, 80–84
death, 227
as no death, 103
and relinking, 322–23
death consciousness, 338
deceit. *See* lying
defecating, 192
defilements (mental defilements), 25, 37–38, 66–67, 115–16, 158–59, 159–60
abandoning, 37–38, 39, 76, 153–55, 428, 429–30, 476, 506–7. *See also under* latent defilements
arising of, 152–53
categories (reviewing knowledge), 420–30, A4
insight knowledge vs., 38

keeping from arising, 41. *See also* abandoning, *above*
latent. *See* latent defilements
nibbāna as not connected to, 464–65
unwholesome states, 427, 428–30
See also hindrances; obstacles
delight, 67–68, 422
enlightenment factor, 223
vs. insight, 376, 377
not delighting in any object, 397–98
in visionary experiences, 284
deliverance: wrong deliverance, 422
See also desire for deliverance
delusion/delusions, 206–7, 425, 478, 522
defilements as, 37–38
removing, 75
See also ignorance
dependent origination: discerning/seeing conditionality as, 314–15
depression in practice, 285–87
description vs. experience, 98–100
desire, 206, 478
See also craving; lust; sensual desire
desire for deliverance, 389, 390, 403–5
aspiration for enlightenment, 260
insight knowledge of, 297, 389–90
longing for liberation, 59–60
the desireless (desirelessness):
contemplation of, 520
liberation/emancipation through, 407, 416
destruction, contemplation of, 512–14
determination, 259
See also effort
determining mind-moments, 158, 159, 160
determining the fruition period/duration, 295, 298, 449
Dhamma:
access to, 3
heirs of the Buddha in, 73–75
listening to, followed by enlightenment, 27–28
mirror of, 430–32
vision of, 417–18
Dhamma inheritance, 73–75
Dhammapada:
on evil views, 3
on Santati's enlightenment, 27
Dhanañjānī's stories, 36–37, 434–35
Dīgha Nikāya:
on effort, 80
on insight meditation on the jhānas, 129
on observing true arising and passing away, 365
on walking, 182–83
diligence, 275
See also effort
the disadvantages, considering, 76
disappearance:
of phenomena/objects of insight, 284–86, 469–70
seeing impermanence and the other universal characteristics through, 469–70, 500–1
See also arising and passing away of phenomena
discerning the path, 378–79
discerning/seeing conditionality:
as dependent origination, 314–15
by inference, 311, 313–14, 318–20
insight knowledge of, 37–38, 308–25, 472–73, 522
by observation, 309–13
as volitional actions and their results, 315–23
discerning/seeing phenomena, insight knowledge of, 37, 303–8, 472–73
discriminating knowledge, 63–64
disdain, 429
disenchantment:
contemplation of, 501–2, 503, 504
insight knowledge of, 297, 387–89, 390
disgust:
for the repulsiveness of the body, 255
for the rot of impermanence, 471
disillusion in practice, 285–87
dispassion, contemplation of, 502–4, 511
displeasure (unpleasant feelings), 181, 197, 394–95
while noting, 279
worldly/unworldly, 200–4
dissolution (of phenomena):
insight knowledge of, 53, 151, 297, 379–84, 512, 521–22

one-pointedness based on knowledge of, 90–91
dissolution of the mind, 381
distinguishing between insight and noninsight, 63–64
distracting thoughts, 266–67
distress, 181
doing good, keeping busy, 18, 76–77
domineering attitude, 429
doubt (skeptical doubt), 63, 64–65, 210
overcoming, 75, 313, 314, 315, 318–19, 324
sixteen skeptical doubts, 311–13
"steadfast purification by overcoming doubt," 324
drinking, 191–92
the drunken minister Santati's enlightenment, 26–28

E

ear-consciousness, 170
ear-sensitivity, 169–70
earth element:
touch characteristics, 177
walking function, 186
eating, 9, 191–92, 272–73
effort (energy):
balanced, 375
diligence, 275
enlightenment factor, 223
excessive effort, 225
five factors of striving, 259
in practice, 3–4, 80–87
effortless mindfulness vs. insight, 375
eight hindrances to liberation, 57–72
antidotes to, 75–76
contemplations on dispelling, 72–75, 75–78; laziness and restlessness, 80–87
eight precepts topped with right livelihood, 22–23, 23–24, 43–44
eight vicissitudes of life, 422–23
eighteen great insight knowledges, 467–528
elements:
attention to, 256
materiality, A5
the six elements, 167–68
See also four primary material elements
elimination of practice-related agitation method, 56
emancipation. *See* liberation
emergence (from phenomena), 407, 415, 470, 471
insight knowledge leading to, 51, 396, 406, 406–19, 470–71, 472; cautionary word on, 418–19
See also cessation
empirical insight, 108, 124, 125
empirical insight knowledge (personal/empirical knowledge), 63–64, 98, 99, 506
See also fruition knowledge; insight knowledge; path knowledge
empirical phenomena. *See* ultimately real phenomena
emptiness:
contemplation of, 520–21
of the five aggregates, 334
liberation/emancipation through, 407, 416–17
seeing the world in terms of, 402
the end of suffering. *See* nibbāna
energy. *See* effort
enjoying the status of a monk on false pretenses, 9–11
enlightenment:
aspiration for, 260. *See also* longing for liberation
contentment without, 74–75
of immoral laypeople, 26–30, 31
after listening to a Dhamma talk, 27–28
of Mahāsīva, 201–4
of Moggallāna, 204, 452
moral violations as obstacles to enlightenment for monks but not laypeople, 23–24, 26–28, 32, 35–36
practitioners' potential for, 258–59
of Sāriputta, 204
seven factors of, 222–24, 226–27, 256
stages of, 294, 299–300
vehicles to, 46–49
See also liberation; nibbāna; realization
envy, 220
equanimity:
of adverting, 376

balancing excesses in mental faculties with, 224–26
enlightenment factor, 224, 226
toward formations. *See under* insight knowledge
vs. insight, 376
insight equanimity, 283, 376
and oblivion, 373
peak-reaching equanimity, 405, 407–8, 408–9, 448
toward phenomena. *See under* insight knowledge
in practice, 283, 289–92
sixfold equanimity, 160–64, 291
the three stages of, 402–5

escape from conditioned phenomena. *See* relinquishment
ethical impulsion to insight, 112–13
everyday language as used in this book, 5
evil behavior. *See* immoral conduct
evil views, 3
the executioner Tambadāṭhika's realization, 34–36, 37
exhaustion from practice, 33
overcoming, 33–34, 76
existence:
planes of, A6
taint of, 425
experience vs. description, 98–100
expiating offenses, 8, 20, 26
explicit suffering, 229
eye-consciousness, 95, 96, 105, 107, 144, 149, 166, 217, 498
eye-sensitivity, 96, 105, 144, 146–47, 148, 217, 218

F

faith, 259, 375
excessive faith, 224
stories of, 432–36
fall, contemplation of, 512, 514–15, 517
falling asleep, 193
false pretenses, enjoying the status of a monk on, 9–11
fatal deeds, the five, 24–25
fear, insight knowledge of, 297, 384–85, 385, 386, 388–89
fear of nibbāna, 310
feeling/feelings, 181, 195–206, 332
as an aggregate, 213–14, 216
contemplation of, 195–206, 256, 348–51
noting, 205
re seeing, 144, 149–51
realizing, 205–6
See also anger; attachment; aversion; craving; delight; disgust; displeasure; doubt; fear; hate; joy; loving-kindness; lust; pleasure; *and also* mental states; sensation/sensations
fetters. *See* ten fetters; three fetters
fire element:
touch characteristics, 177
walking function, 186
the fisherman Ariya's enlightenment, 28–29
five aggregates, 213–17, 256, 334
characteristics of arising and passing away, 362–64
impermanence, 468, 470–71
nibbāna as cessation of, 459–62
as not-self, 492–93
seeing, 415, 416
See also consciousness; feeling/feelings; mental formations; perception; physicality
five causal factors, 316, 317–18, 318–19
See also clinging; craving; ignorance; volition
five characteristics of arising/appearance, 362–63
five characteristics of passing away/disappearance, 363
five destinations, 389
five factors of striving, 259
five hindrances, 208–10, 425–26
five mental faculties. *See* mental faculties
five obstacles, 24–26
See also obstacles
five precepts, 22–23, 43–44, 436–37
five resultant factors, 316–17, 318, 318–19
See also feeling/feelings; mental contact; phenomena; relinking consciousness; six sense bases
five ropes metaphor, 165

five stinginess types, 423–24
flavor basis of taste, 171
fluctuations in practice/insight knowledge, 290–91, 291–92, 292, 296, 405
food: eating, 9, 191–92, 272–73
fools: wise vs. true, 29–30
forbearance: restraint by means of, 16, 17, 18–19, 19
formations. *See* mental formations
forty insights/aspects of phenomena, 391–96, 415–17
foundations of mindfulness. *See* four foundations of mindfulness practice
four clinging types, 426
four foundations of mindfulness practice, 28, 184–85, 257–58, 258–59, 260
four modes of birth, 389
Four Noble Truths, 229–30, 256–57
  as in and beyond the round of existence, 232–34
  mindfulness of, 232–57
  realizing, 234–46, 251; in- and out-breath mindfulness example, 251–54. *See also under* truth of...
  See also truth of cessation; truth of origin; truth of suffering; truth of the path
four primary material elements, 147–48, 176–78
  the six elements including, 167–68
  touch characteristics/functions, 177
  walking functions, 185–88
the four realities, 93, 94, 101
four taints, 425
fraud, 429
freedom from lower rebirth, 437–41
friends: stinginess re, 423
fruition (attainment of fruition/fruition absorption), 295–96, 298–300, 445–54
  benefit, 447
  concentration and, 445
  descriptions, 449–50
  emerging from, 451–52
  entering, 295, 447–49
  insight knowledge of equanimity toward phenomena and, 446
  mastery, 453–54
  period/duration, 295, 447; determining, 295, 298, 449
  resolving to attain higher path and, 298
  unstable attainment, 452–53, 453–54
fruition consciousness, 412, 412–13, 445
fruition knowledge, 98, 119, 155–56, 257, 411–18, 471
  contentment without achieving, 74–75
  development/realization/attainment of, 24, 27, 37, 48–49, 156, 158, 260, 294–95, 300, 417–18
  morality and, 37, 40
  obstacles to, 25–26, 36–37
  at successive stages of enlightenment, 294, 299–300
fruition-oriented insight, 446, 448–49
"full understanding...," 167
function, solidity of, 493–94, 496–97
functional consciousness. *See* life-continuum
the future: anticipating, 79
future phenomena, 114–15, 116, 117–18, 123

G
gain: stinginess re, 423
gender awareness, 179
generosity:
  of lay supporters, 9
  one-pointedness based on contemplation of, 90
getting up, waking and, 272
getting up and getting a drink during meditation, 269–71
going to bed, 271–72
gratitude for alms, 85–86

H
happiness. *See* delight; joy
hate (hatred), 206
  overcoming, 75
"He only apprehends what is really there," 14
health, 259
hearing, 169–70, 218, 219, 305–6
hearsay and such, 97–98
heirs of the Buddha in the Dhamma, 73–75

hell: suffering in, 80–84
hidden pain/suffering, 229
higher insight knowledge, 372, 472–73
higher path and fruition: resolving to attain, 298
higher wisdom: insight into phenomena as, 521–22
hindrances, 256
  the five hindrances, 208–10, 425–26
  unwise attention and, 210
  See also defilements; eight hindrances to liberation; obstacles
honesty, 259

I
"I am": impermanence vs., 484–85
  See also self, sense/concept of
ignorance, 66–67, 206–7, 220
  and consciousness, 216–17
  of suffering and of pleasure, 309–10
  See also delusion/delusions
illusions: concepts as, 94–96, 102–5
  See also delusion
immoral conduct (evil behavior), 14–15
  abstinence from, 37, 38, 39–40, 250–51
  See also moral violations; offenses against the monastic code
immoral laypeople: realization/enlightenment of, 26–30, 31, 34–36
impatience in practice, 288–89
impermanence, 3, 104, 280, 286–87, 325–26, 327–29, 339–40
  of the body, 338, 341–42, 345–46, 348
  contemplation of, 334–35, 335, 355–56, 468–89, 501, 518, 519
  definitions, 468–69
  disgust for the rot of, 471
  establishment of unsatisfactoriness and not-self, 484–85
  of the five aggregates, 468, 470–71
  vs. "I am," 484–85
  insight aspects, 391–92
  seeing through disappearance, 469–70, 500–1
  and unsatisfactoriness: insightful vs. ordinary understanding of, 486–87; as taught to teach not-self, 487–88
  See also permanence concept/perception; three universal characteristics...
impermanent characteristics of phenomena, 469
imperturbable absorption, 452
implicit suffering, 229
improper conduct, 8
impulsion consciousness, 408–10, 410–11, 411, 413–14, 418
impulsion process (kammic impulsion), 149
  seeing without/eliminating, 159–60, 161–63
  wholesome/unwholesome impulsions, 158–59
in- and out-breath:
  mindfulness of, 251–54
  observing, 129–31
inanimate phenomena, 236–37, 351
inattentiveness: noting, 77
inborn deficiency, 25
inferential insight, 108, 113, 123, 124–26, 140–41, 142
inferential insight knowledge (by comprehension), 64, 325–56, 383, 506
  of arising and passing away, 53, 216–17, 259, 280–81, 282, 295, 356–79, 366
  the Buddha on, 327
  of conditionality, 311, 313–14, 318–20
  and contemplation, 326
  of impermanence, suffering, and not-self, 327–34
  peak, 343–44
  re past and future, 311
inheritance, Dhamma, 73–75
insight, 51, 58, 60, 70
  beginner level, 366
  counter-insight, 381
  developing (methods), 56–57
  distinguishing between noninsight and, 63–64
  empirical insight, 108, 124, 125
  ethical impulsion to, 112–13
  forty insights/aspects of phenomena, 391–96, 415–17
  inferential insight, 108, 113, 123, 124–26, 140–41, 142

into phenomena, as higher wisdom, 521–22
objects of. *See* objects of insight
obstacles to, 56, 58–60, 79
as renunciation, 58, 60
sensual desire vs., 59–60
ten corruptions of, 367–78
transformation of, 382
types, 446
See also knowledge; realization; understanding; wisdom
insight equanimity, 283, 376
insight knowledge, 43, 51, 63–64, 66, 98, 119
of actions, 106–8
of adaptation, 406, 407–8, 409, 415, 416, 448, 471; contemplation of turning away, 526–28
of arising and passing away, 53, 216–17, 259, 280–81, 282, 295, 356–79; that discerns the correct path, 378–79; vs. insight, 370–71; return to after cessation, 293–94
of change-of-lineage, 406, 407, 411, 415–16, 471, 527–28
by comprehension. *See* inferential insight knowledge
of danger, 297, 385–87, 388–89
vs. defilements, 38
of desire for deliverance, 297, 389–90
development/realization/attainment of, 24, 27, 32–33, 34–35, 37, 40, 47–48, 50, 57
of discerning/seeing conditionality, 37–38, 308–25, 472–73, 522
of discerning/seeing phenomena, 37, 303–8, 472–73
of disenchantment, 297, 387–89, 390
of dissolution, 53, 151, 297, 379–84, 512, 521–22
the eighteen great knowledges, 467–528
empirical (personal), 63–64, 98, 99
of equanimity toward formations, 76–77, 119, 204–5, 525; contemplation of turning away, 526–28
of equanimity toward phenomena, 34–35, 160–61, 295, 297, 298–99, 300, 396–406; and fruition, 446; mental processes, 160–61, 406–7, 408, 410; peak. *See* peak-reaching equanimity
of fear, 297, 384–85, 385, 386, 388–89
fluctuations in, 290–91, 291–92, 292, 296, 405
higher, 372, 472–73
inferential. *See* inferential insight knowledge
and insight meditation, 51, 54–55
leading to emergence, 51, 396, 406, 406–19, 470–71, 472
vs. learning and logical thought, 151–52
and mindfulness, 185
momentary concentration and, 47–48
morality and, 37, 40
obstacles to, 36
one-pointedness based on, 90–91
of reobservation, 390–96; contemplation of reflection, 524–26
restraint by means of, 15–16
stages/levels, 296–97, 303–466, A1; getting/returning to, 297, 298–99
insight meditation, 3, 46–49, 50–52, 123–24
beginning, 144–45, 191, 264–65, 383, 448
concentration in, 33, 47, 50, 51. *See also* momentary concentration
counter-insight meditation, 185
guidance of the teacher, 5, 301–2, 378
insight knowledge and, 51, 54–55
on the jhānas. *See* insight meditation on the jhānas
mental purification for, 57–91
the mind of, 38, 39–40
objects of. *See* objects of insight
prioritizing, 70–71, 78
regret for not practicing, 4
tranquility meditation and. *See* insight meditation on the jhānas
See also meditation; practice
insight meditation on the jhānas, 126–42
Moggallāna's method and experience, 137–38
Moggallāna's method and experience of, 113, 137–38, 452–53

observing the in- and out-breath, 129–31
purification and realization, 131–33
Sāriputta's method and experience, 109, 133–37, 138–42
insightful vs. ordinary understanding:
of activities, 105–8, 183–84, 188
of impermanence and unsatisfactoriness, 486–87
instruction:
guidance of the teacher in insight meditation, 5, 301–2, 378
insufficient, 36–37
insubstantiality of phenomena, 366
insufficient instruction, 36–37
insufficient practice, 36, 37
insult: encountering, 18–19
insulting a noble one, 25–26
intelligence: and liberation, 131
intensive insight practice, 70–72, 75, 78
intention:
and action, 106–7, 319
noting, 182, 183–84, 185, 277
intermediate insight, 53
investigation (enlightenment factor), 222
investigation process (third mental process), 94–95, 96, 107, 149, 159, 160, 161–63
"...it has no support," 457

J
the jhānas:
absorption in and contemplation of, 56, 414
insight meditation on. *See* insight meditation on the jhānas
mental phenomena: of the first jhāna, 134, 135–37, 138–39; of the highest jhāna, 109, 139–40, 140–41; observing, 109, 110–11, 128–29, 133–42
persons suited/not suited for, 32, 32–33, 109
joy (happiness), 181, 374–75
See also delight
"Just this is the end of suffering," 457

K
kamma: and phenomena, 480–81
See also cause and effect
kammic obstacles, 24–25
kammmic impulsion. *See* impulsion process
keeping busy doing good, 18, 76–77
keeping defilements from arising, 41, 154–55
keeping in mind the purpose for using requisites, 8–9, 12–13, 21, 41
failure to do so, 9–11, 11–12
instructional sources, 11, 12–13
meditation and, 13, 21, 41
as for monks vs. laypeople, 24
keeping silent, 193
Khuddaka Nikāya:
on not-born, 456
on "then and there," 119
See also Milindapañha; Paṭisambhidāmagga/commentary; *Udāna*
kindness. *See* loving-kindness
knowledge, 65–66, 67
discriminating knowledge, 63–64
empirical insight knowledge, 63–64, 98, 99
excessive knowledge, 224–25
experience vs. description, 98–100
hearsay and such, 97–98
inferential. *See* inferential insight knowledge
vs. insight, 370–71
liberation through, 65, 67
practice vs., 139
reason-based knowledge, 64, 97–98
reviewing. *See* reviewing knowledge
stinginess re, 424
wrong knowledge, 422
See also fruition knowledge; insight knowledge; path knowledge; *and also* insight; understanding; wisdom

L
labeling, 144, 182
not labeling, 282
latent defilements (dormant), 41, 115, 426
abandoning, 115, 155, 346–47, 426, 476, 478, 483–84
arising of, 152–53, 478, 479–81

in the mind-continuum, 476–77, 481–84
occurrence singly, 482
in practitioners, 481–82
in sense objects, 476, 477, 478–81
types, 476–78, 481–83
as volitional actions, 480–81
laypeople:
different trainings for different types, 31–34
immoral people's realization/enlightenment, 26–30, 31, 34–36
moral purification for, 22–37
moral violations as obstacles to enlightenment for monks but not, 23–24, 26–28, 32, 35–36
morality as for monks vs., 23–24
as supporters. *See* alms donors
laziness, 62, 68–69, 80
overcoming, 61–62, 69; reflections on, 80–87
learning: insight knowledge vs., 151–52
lesser stream enterers, 323–25
"Let seeing be just seeing," 14
liberation:
the eight practices for and hindrances to, 57–72
intelligence and, 131
through knowledge, 65, 67
longing for, 59–60. *See also* desire for deliverance
loving-kindness and, 41–43
temporary liberation from defilements, 155
See also enlightenment
life-continuum (life-continuum consciousness/mind-continuum), 159, 178, 179, 271–72, 313, 320
arising/awareness of, 160, 285–86, 382, 408, 409–10, 412, 451
defilements dormant in, 476–77, 481–84
light/lights: vs. insight, 61, 367–70, 377–78
See also luminosity
line of termites concept, 102–4
lineage nobility, 84
listening to the Dhamma: realization/enlightenment after, 27–28, 35
livelihood. *See* right livelihood
loan, using requisites on, 9–11, 11
lodgings: stinginess re, 423
logical thought: insight knowledge vs., 151–52
longing for liberation, 59–60
See also desire for deliverance
the louse: the Buddha and, 9–10
loving-kindness, 75
and liberation, 41–43
lower realm dangers, 80–84
lower rebirth, 8, 30, 43, 76, 421, 422, 430, 458
by the Buddha-to-Be, 324–25
freedom from, 437–41
luminosity: nibbāna as, 464–65
See also light/lights
lust (sexual desire), 206, 220
cessation of, 505–6
mind affected by, 206
overcoming, 17–18, 75, 76–77, 88–89
lying (deceit), 427, 429
refraining from, 22–23
lying down, 188

M

Mahāhattipadopama Sutta: on equanimity, 161
Mahāmālunkya Sutta: on jhāna contemplation, 414
Mahānāma: and the Buddha, 439–41
Mahāsatipaṭṭhāna Sutta/commentary: on the body as primary object, 265–66
Mahāsīva's story, 201–4
Mahāṭīkā. See Visuddhimagga-mahāṭīkā
Mahātissa story, 21
Majjhima Nikāya, 26
on intelligence and liberation, 131
on observing true arising and passing away, 365
Māluṅkyaputta: the Buddha and, 153, 154, 156–57
Māluṅkyaputta Sutta, 157–58
manifest pain/suffering, 229
Manorathapūraṇi: on equanimity, 161
mass, solidity of, 493, 495–96

mastery of fruition, 453–54
material elements. *See* four primary material elements
materiality of the elements, A5
matter
concretely produced, 110, 111
seeing the causes of, 309–10
medicine, taking, 11–13
meditation:
counter-insight meditation, 185
distracting thoughts during, 266–67
four foundations of mindfulness practice, 28, 184–85, 257–58, 258–59, 260
getting up and getting a drink during, 269–71
insight. *See* insight meditation
and keeping in mind the purpose for using requisites, 13, 21, 41
moral purification before, 16–20, 40
moral purification through, 20–22, 37–44, 40
and morality, 22, 24, 37, 41–43, 43–44
objects of. *See* objects of insight
odd sensations during, 268–69, 283, 296
physical discomfort during, 267–68
reflections during, 276–77, 278–79, 280–81, 286–87, 288, 291
restraint as a prerequisite for, 22
restraint by means of, 15–16, 20–22
tranquility. *See* tranquility meditation
See also contemplation; mindfulness
meditators: types/classes, 159–60
mental contact (between eye and object), 128, 144, 149, 164–66, 178, 180, 360
mental defilements. *See* defilements
mental faculties (five), 281–82
balancing excesses in, 224–26
strengthening, 336–38
See also concentration; effort (energy); faith; mindfulness; wisdom
mental factors, 111, 112, 127, 138, 165, 178, 181–82, 218, 219, 294, 352, 373–74
in each consciousness, A2
See also mental formations; mental objects; mental phenomena
mental formations, 181–82, 360
mental formations (aggregate), 181–82, 213–14, 216, 360
insight knowledge of equanimity toward, 76–77, 119, 204–5, 525; contemplation of turning away, 526–28
mental objects, 160, 178, 179, 353, 498
contemplation of, 121, 208–32, 278; wise/unwise attention, 210–13. *See also* five aggregates; five hindrances; seven factors of enlightenment; six senses; ten fetters
mental phenomena, 110–11, 128
characteristics. *See* characteristics of phenomena
contemplation of, 334–35, 351–56
distinguishing from physical phenomena, 304–6
of the first jhāna, 134, 135–37, 138–39
of the highest jhāna, 109, 139–40, 140–41
observing, 109, 110–11, 128–29, 133–42, 144–45, 145–48, 344–45
as oppressive, 330
pairing with physical phenomena, 275–77, 285, 352
understanding of one as understanding of all accompanying, 133–34, 151–52, 157–58, 164–66, 166–69
See also mental factors; mental formations; mental objects; mental processes; mental states; noting mind; phenomena; restlessness; visionary experiences
mental processes:
of insight knowledge of equanimity toward phenomena, 160–61, 406–7, 408, 410
in noting, 241
sensory: functions, A7. *See also* mental processes of seeing
See also attention; feeling/feelings; fruition; intention; mindfulness; perception; sensation/sensations; volition
mental processes of seeing, 94–96, 143, 144–45, 149, 217
defilements in, 115–16, 158–59, 159–60
sequence, 14, 94–95, 158–59, 159–60, 574n183. *See also* mind-moments

See also impulsion process; investigation process
mental purification (purification of mind), 45–91
for insight meditation, 57–91
momentary concentration as, 46–47, 48–49, 57
three types of concentration for, 45–46, 47
mental states (states of mind), 56–57, 206–8, 256, 274–75
in each consciousness, A2
following cessation, 294–95
unwholesome states, 427, 428–30
See also attachment; aversion; equanimity; faith; feeling/feelings; one-pointedness; restlessness; sensation/sensations; tranquility; *and also* mental processes
mental volition. *See* volition
Milindapañha:
on attaining path and fruition, 417
on nibbāna, 455–56
the mind, 20
aspects/orientations, 334–35
contemplation of, 206–8, 256, 351
dissolution of, 381
impermanence, 334–35
of insight meditation, 38, 39–40
"no longer expands," 397–98
as oppressive, 330
purification of. *See* mental purification
seeing the causes of, 310–11
states. *See* mental states
steering toward wholesomeness, 18–19
units involved in thought, 112
universal characteristics. *See* three universal characteristics...
See also mental phenomena; noting mind
"mind affected by lust/hate/delusion," 206–7
"mind and matter," 94, 306, 307, 495–96
the mind door, 15, 160, 163, 178, 178–79, 212–13
mind-consciousness (thinking consciousness), 156, 168, 169, 178, 180, 217, 218–19, 279, 498
mind-continuum. *See* life-continuum
mind-door-adverting consciousness, 160
See also adverting consciousness
mind-moments, 14, 111–12
that advert to objects, 111, 112, 159, 179, 217, 382
determining mind-moments, 158, 159, 160
that receive sense objects, 217
mind-sensitivity of the heart, 178, 179
mindfulness:
of arising and passing away, 282
benefits, 257–61
of breathing, 174–76, 264–66
effortless, vs. insight, 375
enlightenment factor, 222
four foundations of mindfulness practice, 28, 184–85, 257–58, 258–59, 260
of the Four Noble Truths, 232–57
of the in- and out-breath, 251–54
insight knowledge and, 185
as the only way, 257–58, 300
restraint by means of, 15, 17, 17–18, 19
wrong mindfulness, 422
mirror the of Dhamma, 430–32
mistake in the *Visuddhimagga-mahāṭīkā*, 410–11
Moggallāna:
enlightenment, 204, 452
method and experience of: insight meditation on the jhānas, 113, 137–38, 452–53
moment of path knowledge, 233, 242, 244–45, 247–48, 250, 254–55
momentary concentration, 46, 46–47, 48, 52, 53, 62
and insight knowledge, 47–48
levels, 52–54
as mental purification, 46–47, 48–49, 57
restlessness and, 62–63
strong, 53–54
See also one-pointedness
momentary nature, contemplation of, 352
momentary phenomena, 359, 361–62

monastic code/precepts:
observing, 7–8, 22; morality as, 12, 28
offenses against. *See* offenses
revealing one's own attainment, 432
violating knowingly, 26
and wisely using requisites, 11–13
monks:
enjoying the status of on false pretenses, 9–11
moral purification for, 7–22, 24, 28
moral violations as obstacles to enlightenment for monks but not laypeople, 23–24, 26–28, 32, 35–36
morality as for monks vs. laypeople, 23–24
raping a virtuous nun, 25
moral conduct, 250–51
noble conduct, 436–37
See also morality
moral precepts (the precepts):
breaking a precept, 8
as the eight precepts topped with right livelihood, 22–23, 43–44
as the five precepts, 22–23, 43–44, 436–37
offenses against. *See* offenses
resolving not to break, 8, 37
See also monastic code/precepts
moral purification (purification of conduct):
for laypeople, 22–37
before meditation, 16–20, 40
through meditation, 20–22, 37–44, 40
for monks, 7–22, 24, 28
as necessary, 37
See also observing the monastic code/precepts; pursuing a pure livelihood; restraint; using requisites wisely; *and also* morality
moral violations (of the precepts), 14–15
as obstacles to enlightenment for monks but not laypeople, 23–24, 26–28, 32, 35–36
See also offenses against the monastic code
morality:
and concentration, 40
as essential, 43–44
five kinds, 37–40
four kinds, 7–22
and knowledge, 37, 40
meditation and, 22, 24, 37, 41–43, 43–44
as for monks vs. laypeople, 23–24
as observing the monastic code/precepts, 12, 28
restoring, 37; by confessing one's offense, 20, 75; by expiating one's offense, 8
restraint by means of, 14–15, 16
training in. *See* training in morality
two categories, 7
two kinds, 40
and wisdom, 40
See also moral conduct; moral purification
movement, 106, 194, 342
See also walking

N

names as concepts, 102, 104–5, 107
negligence, 429
neither displeasure nor pleasure, 181, 197–99
worldly/unworldly, 204–5
"neither perception nor nonperception," 109, 127, 140
"neither this world nor another...; neither sun nor moon," 457
Nettipakaraṇa: on different trainings for different types of people, 31–32, 33
nibbāna, 104, 156, 292–301, 454–66
as cessation, 454–56, 463–64, 465–66; of the five aggregates, 459–62
descriptions/definitions, 416, 454–58
fear of, 310
realizing/experiencing, 462–66
rush into, 406, 411, 527
as a state, 461
taking as an object, 59, 299, 300, 411, 412, 414
as twofold (with/without residue), 458–62
See also cessation; enlightenment; fruition
Niddesa: on restraint, 15–16

nine factors for strengthening the five mental faculties, 336–38
nine spheres of beings, 389
no cause concept, 37–38, 308, 320–21
"...no coming, no going...," 457
"no longer expands," the mind, 397–98
no self. *See* not-self
nobility of the lineage, 84
noble conduct, 436–37
Noble Eightfold Path, 232
noble ones. *See* practitioners
noble path, 51, 55–56
the nobleman Sarakāni's enlightenment, 30, 33–34
the noblest offering, 72–73, 75
nonappearance: of not-self, 493
nonaversion, 60–61
noninsight: distinguishing between insight and, 63–64
nonreturners, 10–11, 258
  latent defilements in, 482
  rebirth for, 437
nontransgression, 37, 39–40
nose-consciousness, 171
nose-sensitivity, 170
not being reborn, 309
not delighting in any object, 397–98
not sacrificing one's own welfare, 71–72
not-born, nibbāna as, 456
not-self, 3, 104, 152, 281, 326, 331–34, 339–40
  the body as, 339, 341–42, 345–46, 348
  contemplation of, 492–501
  as the domain of only the Buddha, 486, 487
  as established by impermanence, 484–85
  the five aggregates and all phenomena as, 492–93
  impermanence and unsatisfactoriness as taught to teach, 487–88
  insight aspects, 395–96
  nonappearance and appearance, 493
  See also three universal characteristics...
noting, 39, 46, 79, 119
  and awareness, 195
  bodily sensations, 177
  after cessation, 293–94
  contemplation and, 326
  craving, 253
  diligence in, 275
  feelings, 205
  after fruition, 296
  inattentiveness, 77
  intention, 182, 183–84, 185, 277
  and labeling, 144, 182; not labeling, 282
  and liberation, 67
  mental processes in, 241
  mental states/states of mind, 208, 274–75
  more persistently, 61, 77–78
  noting mind, 185, 275–77; successive occurrences, 352–54
  phenomena, 333; the moment they occur, 473–75
  realizations while, 278
  seeing, 144, 145, 150–51, 151–52, 163–64, 189, 213–14
  sensual desire, 220–21
  unpleasant feelings while, 279
  visionary experiences, 279–80
  walking, 182, 183–84
  See also noting mind; observing phenomena
noting mind, 39, 56, 119, 158, 164, 277, 289–90, 290–91, 291–92, 303, 379, 451–52
  dissolution of, 381
  noting, 185, 275–77; successive occurrences, 352–54
  pairing with physical phenomena, 275–77, 285
nun, virtuous, raping, 25
nutrition awareness, 180, 195, 345

O

objects:
  solidity of object, 494, 498–500
  taking nibbāna as an object, 59, 299, 300, 411, 412, 414
  tangible objects, 173–74
  See also mental objects; objects...; sense objects
objects of concentration, 45–46, 53

objects of insight, 53–54, 108–18, 189–90, 255–57
  adding/increasing, 273
  arising and passing away of, 280–81, 282
  attention-getting objects, 274
  disappearance of, 284–86, 469–70
  internal vs. external, 113–14, 124, 138, 194
  the present object, 79, 126
  the primary object (the body), 260, 264–66, 277
  relinquishment/penetration of, 54–55
oblivion, 372–73
observing light, 61–62
observing phenomena, 44, 58, 79
  from 2/4/6/8/10/12 aspects, 398–403
  internal vs. external, 113–14, 124, 138, 194
  mental phenomena, 109, 110–11, 128–29, 133–42, 144–45, 145–48, 344–45
  the moment they occur, 473–75
  physical phenomena, 110, 111, 129, 143, 144–45, 145–48, 154–55, 344; walking, 185–88, 342–43. *See also* present physical phenomena, *below*
  in the present moment, 114, 116–17, 118–24, 126
  present phenomena, 114–18, 123–24. *See also* present physical phenomena, *below*
  present physical phenomena, 357–58; as continuous, 359, 360–61; as momentary, 359, 361–62
  reobservation, 390–96, 403–5
  supramundane phenomena, 109
  thoughts, 178–82
  ultimately real phenomena, 144–45, 145–46, 151
  walking, 185–88, 342–43
  See also noting
observing the in- and out-breath, 129–31
observing the monastic code/precepts, 7–8, 22
  morality as, 12, 28
observing thoughts, 178–82
observing true arising and passing away, 364–67
obsessions, three, 377
obstacles:
  to concentration and methods for overcoming, 78–89
  the five obstacles, 24–26
  to insight, 56, 58–60, 79
  to insight knowledge, 36
  to liberation. *See* eight hindrances to liberation
  mental. *See* defilements (mental defilements); mental phenomena
  moral violations as obstacles to enlightenment for monks but not laypeople, 23–24, 26–28, 32, 35–36
  to path and fruition knowledge, 25–26, 36–37
  ten corruptions of insight, 367–78
  See also defilements; hindrances
obstinacy, 429
obtaining requisites, 8
  See also right livelihood
odd sensations during meditation, 268–69, 283, 296
odor basis of smell, 170–71
offenses against the monastic code, 8, 10, 14–15
  confessing, 20, 75, 443–44
  expiating, 8, 20, 26
  insulting a noble one, 25–26
  See also moral violations
offerings to the Buddha, 72–73, 75
once returners, 10–11, 299, 438
  latent defilements in, 482
  rebirth for, 437
one-pointedness (single-pointedness), 54
  states of, 89–91
  See also momentary concentration
"the only way," 257–58, 300
ordinary vs. insightful understanding:
  of activities, 105–8, 183–84, 188
  of impermanence and unsatisfactoriness, 486–87
origin, the truth of. *See* truth of origin
overcoming:
  anger, 75

aversion, 61, 75, 88–89
doubt, 75, 313, 314, 315, 318–19, 324
exhaustion from practice, 33–34, 76
hatred, 75
laziness, 61–62, 69; reflections on, 80–87
lust, 17–18, 75, 76–77, 88–89
obstacles to concentration, 78–89
overzealousness, 87–88
restlessness, 56, 63, 79, 225; reflections on, 80–87
sensual desire, 220–21. *See also* lust, *above*
sloth and torpor, 61–62
See also abandoning; removing
overzealousness: overcoming, 87–88

P

pain, 174
physical discomfort during meditation, 267–68
suffering of, 227–28
See also distress; suffering
pairing mental phenomena with physical phenomena (pairs of phenomena), 275–77, 285, 352
pairing method (contemplation of the jhānas), 56
Pāḷi references: as used in this book, 4–5
Pañcama Sutta: on jhāna contemplation, 414
pāramīs, 300–1, 313
Pariññeyya Sutta: on seeing/sensing, 152
particles: tranquility meditation on, 188
passing away. *See* arising and passing away of phenomena; disappearance
the past: remembering, 117
past existence, 522
past memories, 375–76
past phenomena, 114, 116, 117, 123
the path:
discerning, 378–79
the noble path, 51, 55–56
as the only way, 257–58, 300
purification by knowledge and vision of what is/is not, 378
the truth of. *See* truth of the path
path concentration, 40, 55–56
path consciousness, 412–13, 418
path knowledge, 51–52, 98, 119, 155–56, 257, 411–18, 471, 483
development/realization/attainment of, 24, 27, 32–33, 37, 48–49, 57, 156, 158, 294–95, 300, 417–18
emergence from phenomena into, 51, 396, 406, 406–19
the moment of, 233, 242, 244–45, 247–48, 250, 254–55
morality and, 37, 40
obstacles to, 25–26, 36–37
restraint by means of, 16
stages, 221
of stream entry, 418
at successive stages of enlightenment, 294, 299–300
path-oriented insight, 446, 448–49
Paṭisambhidāmagga/commentary:
on basic concentration, 52–53
on birth and death, 335–36
on cessation, 505
on change-of-lineage impulsion consciousness, 406, 407, 411
on concentration in insight meditation, 55
on contemplation of change, 517
on contemplation of dispassion, 511
on contemplation of fall, 517
on contemplation of turning away, 527–28
on dissolution, 503
on impermanence, 489
on insight knowledge of dissolution, 380–83
on insight knowledge of equanimity toward phenomena and fruition, 446
on insight meditation on the jhānas, 135
on morality, 37
on nibbāna, 454–55
on seeing, 150–51, 151
on seeing the five aggregates, 416
three universal characteristics insights, 391–96
on unsatisfactoriness, 491
peace following cessation, 294

peak of insight knowledge by comprehension, 343–44
peak-reaching equanimity, 405, 407–8, 408–9, 448
penetration (of the objects of insight), 54–55
people. *See* laypeople; monks; practitioners
perception (aggregate), 181 , 213–14, 216
  "neither perception nor nonperception," 109
  See also permanence concept/perception
permanence concept/perception, 38, 66–67, 115–16
  abandoning, 475–76, 480
person concept, 66–67, 115–16, 183, 312
  seeing through, 37, 103, 177, 184, 276, 278, 306, 307, 308, 320–21, 332
  See also not-self; the self
personal knowledge. *See* empirical insight knowledge
persons of quick understanding: training suitable for, 31, 32–33
persons to be guided: trainings suitable for, 31, 32, 33–34
persons who understand through elaboration: trainings suitable for, 31, 32
perversions, twelve, 424
Pessa's story, 36
phenomena:
  arising and passing away of. *See* arising and passing away of phenomena
  aspects (four), 145–48
  becoming attached to, 118–19
  characteristics. *See* characteristics of phenomena
  conditioned. *See* conditioned phenomena
  continuity, 144–45, 473–74
  disappearance of, 284–86, 469–70
  discerning/seeing as they really are, 37, 303–8
  dissolution of. *See* dissolution (of phenomena)
  emergence from. *See* emergence
  empirical. *See* ultimately real phenomena
  equanimity toward. *See under* insight knowledge
  as impermanent, unsatisfactory, and not-self, 349–50, 357, 378
  inanimate phenomena, 236–37
  insight into: as higher wisdom, 521–22
  insubstantiality, 366
  kamma and, 480–81
  kinds/factors/elements (five, of seeing), 111, 143–45, 150, 164, 217–18
  momentary phenomena, 359, 361–62
  as not-self, 492–93
  noting, 333; the moment they occur, 473–75
  observing. *See* observing phenomena
  reobservation of. *See under* insight knowledge
  stages/phases, 314–15, 335–36, 358, 469–70
  understanding of one as understanding of all accompanying, 133–34, 151–52, 157–58, 164–66, 166–69
  See also concepts; future phenomena; mental phenomena; past phenomena; physical phenomena; present phenomena; thoughts; ultimately real phenomena
physical discomfort during meditation, 267–68
physical phenomena, 110, 111, 128
  appearance and disappearance, 194–95, 215–16
  characteristics. *See* characteristics of phenomena
  contemplation of, 338–51
  distinguishing mental phenomena from, 304–6
  observing, 110, 111, 129, 143, 144–45, 145–48, 154–55, 344; present phenomena, 357–58; walking, 185–88, 342–43
  as oppressive, 330
  pairing mental phenomena with, 275–77, 285, 352

present. *See* present physical phenomena
seeing as they really are, 286, 303–4, 306–8
understanding of one as understanding of all accompanying, 133–34, 151–52, 157–58, 164–66, 166–69
walking, 185–88, 342–43
See also the body; phenomena
physicality (aggregate), 213–14, 216
planes of existence, A6
pleasant sense objects, 477
pleasure (pleasant feelings), 174, 181, 195–97, 424, 476
ignorance of, 309–10
worldly/unworldly, 199–200
See also joy
posture:
bodily postures, 255
during fruition absorption, 295–96
potential for enlightenment, practitioners', 258–59
Potthila's story, 161–64
practice (of insight/insight meditation), 263–302
advice on, 201–2
avoiding, 288
beginning, 144–45, 191, 264–65, 383, 448
benefits, 15–16, 84, 158–59
disillusion/depression in, 285–87
effort in, 3–4, 80–87
equanimity in, 283, 289–92
exhaustion from, 33; overcoming, 33–34, 76
faith in, 375
fluctuations in, 290–91, 291–92, 292, 296, 405
going to bed, 271–72
impatience in, 288–89
insufficient practice, 36, 37
intensive practice, 70–72, 75, 78
vs. knowledge, 139
laziness in. *See* laziness
as not for ordinary people, 84
the only way, 257–58, 300
preparations for, 263–64
reflections on, 3–4
rejecting, 3
as removing attachment, or not, 356
sensual desire vs., 58–59
See also insight; insight meditation; meditation; moral purification; noting
practice-related agitation. *See* restlessness
practices:
developing insight (methods), 56–57
for liberation, the eight, 57–72
See also overcoming
practitioners (noble ones/people):
different trainings for different types, 31–34
latent defilements in, 481–82
potential for enlightenment, 258–59
types, 10–11, 438–39
See also arahants; laypeople; monks; nonreturners; once returners; persons...; stream enterers
precepts. *See* moral precepts
preparation impulsion consciousness, 408–9, 413
the present life, 120
the present moment, 119–20, 350
observing phenomena in, 114, 116–17, 118–24, 126
the present object, 79, 126
present phenomena, 115, 359–60
observing, 114–18, 123–24
present physical phenomena, 357–58
as continuous, 359, 360–61
as momentary, 359, 361–62
pride. *See* conceit
prioritizing insight meditation, 70–71, 78
processes: as concepts, 104, 106–7
See also mental processes of seeing
proximate causes of ultimately real phenomena, 145–46, 146–47
pure livelihood. *See* right livelihood
purification:
of conduct. *See* moral purification
by knowledge and vision of the way..., 378–79
by knowledge and vision of what is path/not path, 378
of mind. *See* mental purification

and realization, 131–33
"steadfast purification by overcoming doubt," 324
of view, 146, 303–8
pursuing a pure livelihood, 8, 16, 22
"putting the three characteristics on the mind and body," 339–40, 340–41, 342, 347

R
rains retreat story, 453–54
raping a virtuous nun, 25
rapture vs. insight, 371–72
reading slowly example, 95
reality: the four realities, 93, 94, 101
See also ultimate reality/truth
realization:
of immoral laypeople, 26–30, 31, 34–36
after listening to the Dhamma, 27–28, 35
while noting, 278
purification and, 131–33
See also enlightenment; insight
realizing:
feelings, 205–6
the Four Noble Truths, 234–46; in- and out-breath mindfulness example, 251–54. *See also under* truth of...
the three universal characteristics, 379
reason-based knowledge, 64, 97–98
rebirth:
freedom from lower rebirth, 437–41
not being reborn, 309
secure rebirth, 323–25
for stream enterers, once returners, and nonreturners, 437
See also lower rebirth
reflection/reflections:
on cessation, 293
contemplation of, 524–26
during meditation, 276–77, 278–79, 280–81, 286–87, 288, 291
on overcoming laziness and restlessness, 80–87
on practice, 3–4
on the purpose for using requisites. *See* keeping in mind the purpose for using requisites
See also contemplation/contemplations
registration process, 149
regret for breaking a precept: alleviating, 75
regret for not practicing insight meditation, 4
rejecting insight meditation practice, 3
relinking: death and, 322–23
relinking consciousness, 317, 320, 321, 322, 338
relinquishment (of conditioned phenomena/the objects of insight), 54–55, 524–26
contemplation of, 119, 507–9
contemplation of reflection, 524–26
remembering the past, 117
removing:
attachment, 357–58; practice as/as not, 356
conceit, 355–56
delusions, 75
the sense of self, 332, 333–34, 354–55, 398–400, 484–85, 521
See also abandoning; overcoming
renunciation, 58, 60
reobservation (of phenomena), insight knowledge of, 297, 390–96, 403–5
contemplation of reflection, 524–26
repulsiveness: of the body, 255
See also disgust
requisites, the four, 73
gratitude for alms, 85–86
obtaining of, 8. *See also* right livelihood
using. *See* using requisites
residue, nibbāna as with/without, 458–62
resolving not to break the moral precepts, 8, 37
resolving to attain higher path and fruition, 298
resolving to reach particular insight knowledge levels, 297
restlessness (practice-related agitation), 56, 79, 80, 87–88, 113–14
and momentary concentration, 62–63

overcoming, 56, 63, 79, 225; reflections on, 80–87
restoring morality, 37
by confessing one's offense, 20, 75
by expiating one's offense, 8
restraint (restraining the senses), 13–22, 37, 39
forms of, 14
before meditation, 16–20
through meditation, 20–22
as a prerequisite for meditation, 22
revealing one's own attainment, 432
reviewing knowledge, 98, 221, 419–45
aspects/kinds, 419
defilement categories for, 420–30
occurrence/nonoccurrence, 419–20
re stream entry, 430–45
right action, 241
right attitude (wise attention), 19, 210–11
encouraging, 18–19
right concentration, 241
right effort, 241
right intention, 241
right livelihood (pure livelihood), 241
the eight precepts topped with, 22–23, 43–44
pursuing, 8, 16, 22
right mindfulness, 241
right speech, 241
right view, 241
river concept, 103–4
robes: wearing, 9
rope concept, 103
five ropes metaphor, 165
round of existence: the Four Noble Truths as in and beyond, 232–34
rush into nibbāna, 406, 411, 527

S
Saccaka: and the Buddha, 332
sacrifice: not sacrificing one's own welfare, 71–72
Sakkapañha Sutta/commentary:
on mental contact, 165–66
on neither displeasure nor pleasure, 198
Saḷāyatanasaṃyutta: on defilements, 158–59
Saḷāyatanavibhaṅga Sutta:
on longing for liberation, 59–60
on unworldly pleasure, 200
Sammohavinodanī:
on impermanence, 469
on not-self, 487
on the path, 246
Saṃyutta Nikāya:
Anāthapiṇḍika's story, 368–69
on defilements, 158–59
on the guidance of the teacher, 302
on seeing, 150–51
sand bag concept, 103
Santati's enlightenment, 26–28
Sarakāni's enlightenment, 30, 33–34
Sāriputta:
the Buddha and, 437–39
and Dhānañjāni, 36–37
enlightenment, 204
method and experience of insight meditation on the jhānas, 109, 133–37, 138–42
and Tambadāṭhika, 34–35
Satipaṭṭhāna Sutta/commentary:
on attaining fruition knowledge, 260
on the benefits of mindfulness, 257
on concentration, 47
on enlightenment after listening to the Dhamma, 27
on mental contact, 165–66
on neither displeasure nor pleasure, 198
on objects of insight, 55
on observing phenomena in the present moment, 120–23
on the person/individual, 332
secure rebirth, 323–25
seeing, 37, 94–96, 111–12, 143, 155, 217–18, 304–6
factors/elements of (five), 111, 143–45, 150, 164, 217–18
feelings re, 144, 149–52
without impulsion, 159–60, 161–63
"Let seeing be just seeing," 14
noting, 144, 145, 150–51, 151–52, 163–64, 189, 213–14
processes. *See* mental processes of seeing
tranquility meditation for, 189
See also discerning/seeing conditional-

ity; discerning/seeing phenomena; observing phenomena; seeing...
seeing the five aggregates, 415, 416
seeing the three universal characteristics, 144–45, 152, 178, 280–82, 339, 470–71, 472, 473, 485–88
seeing the world in terms of emptiness, 402
seeing things as they really are, 286, 303–4, 306–8
self, sense/concept of ("I am"/the self), 331–33, 476, 492, 497, 498, 520–21
  seeing through/removing/abandoning, 332, 333–34, 354–55, 398–400, 484–85, 521
  See also not-self; person concept
self-control, 17
self-indulgence, 14–15, 16
sensation/sensations:
  contemplation of, 346–48
  odd sensations during meditation, 268–69, 283, 296
  seeing as they really are, 303–4
sense bases, six, 154, 156, 213, 256, 464
sense doors, 346, 347
sense objects:
  awareness of/contact with, 144
  defilements dormant in, 476, 477, 478–81
  pleasant/unpleasant, 477–78
  six sense bases, 154, 156, 213, 256, 464
  thoughts about, 59
  See also visual objects (visible objects)
sense of self. *See* self, sense/concept of
sense-sphere consciousness, 111, A2, A7
the senses:
  hearing, smell, taste, and touch, 169–70, 218–19
  restraining. *See* restraint
  six sense bases, 154, 156, 213, 256, 464
  six senses, 217–20
  See also seeing; thinking
sensitivity to seeing. *See* eye-sensitivity
sensory mental processes: functions, A7
  See also mental processes of seeing
sensual desire, 58, 208–9, 210, 425
  vs. insight, 59–60
  noting and overcoming, 220–21
  vs. practice, 58–59
  See also attachment; craving; lust
seven factors of enlightenment, 222–24, 226–27, 256
seven latent defilements, 426
seven stations of consciousness, 389
seven types of suffering, 227–29
seven ways to contemplate mental phenomena, 351–56
seven ways to contemplate physical phenomena, 338–51
sexual desire. *See* lust
sight. *See* seeing
the signless (signlessness):
  contemplation of, 518–20
  liberation/emancipation through, 407, 416
simultaneous elimination, 428
single-pointedness. *See* one-pointedness
six elements, 167–68
six kinds of consciousness, 156, 168–69, 304
  See also body-consciousness; mind-consciousness; the senses; thinking
six sense bases (internal and external), 154, 156, 213, 256, 464
six senses, 217–20
sixfold equanimity, 160–64, 291
sixteen skeptical doubts, 311–13
skeptical doubt. *See* doubt
"skilled in the elements," 167–68
sleep:
  falling asleep, 193
  going to bed, 271–72
sloth and torpor:
  and oblivion, 373
  overcoming, 61–62
smell, 170–71, 218, 305–6
snake metaphor, 356
solidity (solid form concept), 115–16
  of continuity, 493, 494–95
  of function, 493–94, 496–97
  of mass, 493, 495–96
  of object, 494, 498–500
sound, 170, 305–6
  See also hearing
speaking, 193
speech, right, 241

speech, wrong, 422, 427
standing, 106, 188
states of mind. *See* mental states
"steadfast purification by overcoming doubt," 324
steering one's mind toward wholesomeness, 18–19
stinginess, 220, 221–22, 423–24
stream enterers, 10–11
  latent defilements in, 482
  lesser stream enterers, 323–25
  rebirth for, 437
  reviewing their own attainment, 441–45
stream entry:
  confirmation of, 430–32
  path knowledge of, 418
  reviewing knowledge re, 430–45
stream of consciousness factors, A3
strengthening the five mental faculties, 336–38
stretching, 190–91
striving: five factors of, 259
  See also effort
strong momentary concentration, 53–54
successive occurrences of noting mind: noting, 352–54
suffering (unsatisfactoriness), 3, 104, 280–81, 326, 330, 339–40
  of the body, 338–39, 341–42, 345–46, 348
  of conditioned phenomena, 228–29, 280–81
  contemplation of, 489–92
  the end of. *See* cessation
  as established by impermanence, 484–85
  in hell, 80–84
  ignorance of, 309–10
  impermanence and: insightful vs. ordinary understanding of, 486–87; as taught to teach not-self, 487–88
  insight aspects, 392–95
  the seven types, 227–29
  three aspects, 489–90
  the truth of. *See* truth of suffering
  See also three universal characteristics...
Suppabuddha's story, 432–33
supramundane phenomena: observing, 109
Sūrambaṭṭha's story, 435–36
swaying during meditation, 269
swinging torch example, 95

T

taints, four, 425
taking medicine, 11–13
taking up and putting down the body, 338–39
Tambadāṭhika's realization, 34–36, 37
tangible objects basis of touch, 173–74
taste, 171–72, 218–19, 305–6
teacher's guidance in insight meditation, 5, 301–2, 378
temperature sensitivity, 345–46
ten corruptions of insight, 367–78
ten defilements, 421
ten fetters, 220–22, 420–21
ten unwholesome actions, 426–27
ten wrongs, 421–22
"then and there," 119–20
the thief's enlightenment, 29–30
"things as they really are, seeing," 286, 303–4, 306–8
thinking (thought), 219–20
  mind units involved in, 112
  about sense objects, 59
  See also consciousness; investigation process; perception
thoughts:
  concepts as illusions, 94–96, 102–5
  distracting thoughts, 266–67
  observing, 178–82
  of past and future, 78–80
  transforming, 17–18, 76–77, 77–78, 78–80
three contemplations, 509–12
three existences, 389
three fetters, 438
three obsessions, 377
three stages of equanimity, 402–5
three stages/phases of phenomena, 314–15, 335–36, 358, 469–70
three universal characteristics of phenomena, 3, 280–81, 325–26, 339–41
  abandoning conditioned phenomena connected with, 471–73
  appearance by themselves, 379

equanimity re, 356–57
insight aspects, 391–96
"putting...on the mind and body," 339–40, 340–41, 342, 347
realizing, 379
seeing, 144–45, 152, 178, 280–82, 339, 470–71, 472, 473, 485–88
seeing impermanence and the others through disappearance, 469–70, 500–1
the three contemplations of, 509–12
understanding of one as/as not understanding of the others, 473, 485
See also impermanence; not-self; suffering (unsatisfactoriness)
Tipiṭka Cūḷānāga Thera, 12
Tissa's story, 9–10
tongue-consciousness, 171–72
tongue-sensitivity, 171
torpor. *See* sloth and torpor
touch, 172–74, 219, 305–6
material element characteristics/functions, 177
tradition-based knowledge, 97–98
training in concentration, 20
persons suited/not suited for, 32, 32–33
training in morality, 13, 20
persons suited for, 32, 33–34
training in wisdom, 13, 20
persons suited for, 31–32
trainings:
different trainings for different types of people, 31–34
types. *See* training in..., *above*
tranquility, 37, 51, 52
vs. insight, 373–74
and oblivion, 373
See also momentary concentration
tranquility meditation, 46–49, 49–50
and insight meditation. *See* insight meditation on the jhānas
one-pointedness based on, 90
on particles, 188
for seeing, 189
transformation of insight, 382
transforming thoughts, 17–18, 76–77, 77–78, 78–80
transgressions. *See* moral violations
transience, 102–5
tree and seed metaphor, 320–21
tree concept, 104
truth. *See* truth...; ultimate reality/truth
truth of cessation, 230–31, 309
realizing, 239–40; mundane understanding, 240–41; in the path knowledge moment, 255; supramundane understanding, 244–45
truth of origin/craving, 229–30
realizing, 237–39; mundane understanding, 240–41; in the path knowledge moment, 255; supramundane understanding, 243–44
truth of suffering, 229–30
realizing, 234–37, 238–39; mundane understanding, 240; in the path knowledge moment, 254; supramundane understanding, 242–43
truth of the path, 231
realizing, 240–41; mundane understanding, 241–42; in the path knowledge moment, 255; supramundane understanding, 244–45
turning away, contemplation of, 526–28
twelve perversions, 424
twelve unwholesome states of consciousness, 427
typographical error in the *Visuddhimagga-mahāṭīkā,* 410–11

U

Udāna:
on imperturbable absorption, 452
on nibbāna, 457–58, 463
ultimate reality/truth, 93–94, 98, 101
vs. concepts, 107–8
ultimately real phenomena (empirically experienced), 93–94, 99, 107, 144
aspects, four, 145–48
as indescribable, 99–100
nibbāna, 104
observing/experiencing/understanding, 144–45, 145–47, 151
the unconditioned: nibbāna as, 457–58, 461, 466
understanding:
"full understanding...," 167

insightful vs. ordinary: of activities, 105–8, 183–84, 188; of impermanence and unsatisfactoriness, 486–87
of one phenomenon as of all accompanying phenomena, 133–34, 151–52, 157–58, 164–66, 166–69
of one universal characteristic as/as not understanding of the others, 473, 485
"seeing things as they really are," 286, 303–4, 306–8
See also insight; knowledge; wisdom
universal characteristics. *See* three universal characteristics of phenomena
unpleasant feelings. *See* displeasure
unpleasant sense objects, 477–78
unsatisfactoriness. *See* suffering
unusual experiences. *See* visionary experiences
unwholesome actions. *See* wrong action...
unwholesome impulsions, 158–59
unwholesome states, 427, 428–30
unwholesomeness, 15, 69
wholesomeness as, 70–72
unwise attention, 210, 211–13
unworldly displeasure, 201–4
unworldly neither displeasure nor pleasure, 204–5
unworldly pleasure, 200
Uppalavannā, 222
urinating, 192
using requisites on loan, 9–11, 11
using requisites wisely, 8–9, 11–13
the monastic code and, 11–13
See also keeping in mind the purpose for using requisites
Uttiya: the Buddha and, 28

V

vehicles to enlightenment, 46–49
verbal precepts, 22–23
Vibhaṅga Aṭṭhakathā: on impermanence, 326
vicissitudes of life, eight, 422–23
views:
evil views, 3
purification of view, 146, 303–8
right view, 241
wrong. *See* wrong views
Vīmaṃsā: on the self, 331, 332
violating the precepts knowingly, 26
See also moral violations
vision of the Dhamma, 417–18
visionary experiences, 56, 59, 279–80, 283–84, 294, 298, 375–76
delight in, 284
light/lights, 61, 367–70
rapture, 371–72
visual objects (visible objects), 45, 98, 105, 148, 217, 218
awareness of/contact with, 144
defilements in, 115, 153, 154
observing. *See under* observing phenomena
Visuddhimagga:
on cessation, 505
on death and relinking, 322
on disenchantment, 502
on dispassion, 502–3
on dissolution, 501, 503–4
on impermanence, 335, 468
on insight meditation on the jhānas, 127, 135
on latent defilements, 483–84
Mahātissa story, 21
on mental phenomena as paired with physical phenomena, 276
on mental purification, 46–48
on mind and matter, 306
on moral purification, 7
on not-self, 333–34, 500
on objects of insight, 109, 110
on physical phenomena, 347
on the present life, 120
on relinquishment, 508
on restraint, 15, 16
on seeing, 305–6
on the signless, 519
on the ten corruptions, 367, 377–78
on unsatisfactoriness, 491
on volitional action, 321
Visuddhimagga-mahāṭīkā (Mahāṭīkā):
on contemplation of destruction, 512–13
on delusion, 522

on disenchantment, 502
on impermanence, 469
on inferential knowledge, 506
on knowledge and ignorance, 66
on lesser stream enterers, 323–24
on mind and matter, 307
mistake/typographical error in, 410–11
on objects of insight, 114
on observing true arising and passing away, 364–65, 365
on renunciation, 58
on the rush to nibbāna, 406
on single-pointedness, 54
on solidity, 499
on the ten corruptions, 367
on the three contemplations, 510, 511, 512
on the universal characteristics, 340–41
on unsatisfactoriness, 490
on using something on loan, 9
vitality, 180
volition, 37, 39, 360, 422
volitional actions, 315–23, 480–81

W

waking, 193
waking and getting up, 272
walking:
elemental functions, 185–88, 342–43
insightful vs. ordinary understanding of, 183–84
noting, 182, 183–84
water element:
touch functions, 177
walking function, 186
wearing robes, 9, 191
welfare, one's own: not sacrificing, 71–72
wholesome impulsions, 158–59
wholesomeness, 57–58, 69–70
as Dhamma inheritance, 73–75
keeping busy doing good, 18, 76–77
steering one's mind toward, 18–19
as unwholesomeness, 70–72
wisdom:
excessive wisdom, 224–25
morality and, 40
restraint by means of, 15–16, 16
training in. *See* training in wisdom
See also insight; knowledge; understanding
wise attention, 210–11
See also right attitude
wisely using requisites. *See* using requisites wisely
worldly displeasure, 200–1
worldly neither displeasure nor pleasure, 204
worldly pleasure, 199
wrong action/ways of behaving, 422, 424–25, 426–27
wrong belief, 220
wrong mindfulness/knowledge/deliverance, 422
wrong speech, 422, 427
wrong views, 118, 220, 424, 425
seeing through/removing the sense of self, 332, 333–34, 354–55, 398–400, 484–85, 521
See also defilements (mental defilements)
wrongs, ten, 421–22

About Vipassanā Mettā Foundation

The Vipassanā Mettā Foundation was incorporated in 1995 with the mission of sharing the liberation teachings of the Buddha, rooted in the Theravāda tradition, with those who aspire to free themselves from suffering of heart and mind. We are fulfilling this mission by offering instruction in retreats around the world and by creating a sanctuary—a secluded environment for silence, solitude, and meditation—on the Hawaiian island of Maui. The Foundation teaches the practices of generosity, ethics, meditation/tranquility, love, and insight/wisdom to foster greater compassion and wisdom in the world through the personal lives of individuals. The Vipassanā Mettā Foundation is a federally recognized 501(c)3 Theravāda church in the lineage of Mahāsi Sayadaw.

The Vipassanā Mettā Foundation supports development of the following values in all mental, verbal, and physical actions.

- *Harmony*. We value sincere, honest communication and action carried out with integrity that do not cause harm in personal, organizational, economic, and communal interactions.
- *Generosity*. We value the generosity of heart that offers compassionate service to others for the relief of suffering through sharing material as well as human resources.
- *Simplicity*. We value moderation through responsible stewardship of financial, human, and environmental assets.
- *Awareness*. We value awareness for the benefits that it brings in the form of clarity, flexibility, stamina, stability, inclusivity, and for its role in understanding that liberation of heart is what brings the greatest happiness—peace.
- *Diversity*. We value living with the full diversity of life. We offer the Dhamma to all who wish and "come to see for themselves."

The Vipassanā Mettā Foundation was founded by Kamala Masters (formerly ordained as Ven. Vipulañānī) and Steve Armstrong (formerly ordained as Ven. Buddharakkhita), who are its guiding teachers. Both have practiced Dhamma in the Mahāsi Sayadaw tradition under the guidance of Anagarika Munindra and Sayadaw U Paṇḍita.

The Vipassanā Mettā Foundation has funded the translation, research, editing, and preparation of this book. All proceeds from the sale of this book will be used to freely distribute copies of this book to monastics, libraries, Buddhist retreat centers and organizations, as well as to provide support for practice of the method outlined in this book.

For more information, please visit our website at www.vipassanametta.org.

Also Available from Wisdom Publications

In This Very Life
The Liberation Teachings of the Buddha
Sayadaw U Paṇḍita
Edited by Kate Wheeler
Translated by U Aggacitta
Foreword by Joseph Goldstein

The State of Mind Called Beautiful
Sayadaw U Paṇḍita
Edited by Kate Wheeler

The Four Foundations of Mindfulness
Sayadaw U Sīlānanda
Foreword by Larry Rosenberg

Buddhist Ethics
Hammalawa Saddhatissa
Introduction by Charles Hallissey

Abhidhamma Studies
Buddhist Explorations of Consciousness and Time
Nyanaponika Thera
Edited and Introduced by Bhikkhu Bodhi

A Heart Full of Peace
Joseph Goldstein
Foreword by His Holiness the Dalai Lama

THE TEACHINGS OF THE BUDDHA

In the Buddha's Words
An Anthology of Discourses from the Pali Canon
Edited and Introduced by Bhikkhu Bodhi
Foreword by His Holiness the Dalai Lama

Great Disciples of the Buddha
Their Lives, Their Works, Their Legacy
Nyanaponika Thera and Hellmuth Hecker
Edited by Bhikkhu Bodhi

The Long Discourses of the Buddha
A Translation of the Dīgha Nikāya
Maurice Walshe
Foreword by Venerable Sumedho Thera

The Middle Length Discourses of the Buddha
A Translation of the Majjhima Nikāya
Bhikkhu Ñāṇamoli and Bhikkhu Bodhi

The Connected Discourses of the Buddha
A Translation of the Saṃyutta Nikāya
Bhikkhu Bodhi

The Numerical Discourses of the Buddha
A Translation of the Aṅguttara Nikāya
Bhikkhu Bodhi

About Wisdom Publications

Wisdom Publications is the leading publisher of classic and contemporary Buddhist books and practical works on mindfulness. To learn more about us or to explore our other books, please visit our website at wisdomexperience .org or contact us at the address below.

Wisdom Publications
199 Elm Street
Somerville, MA 02144 USA

We are a 501(c)(3) organization, and donations in support of our mission are tax deductible.

Wisdom Publications is affiliated with the Foundation for the Preservation of the Mahayana Tradition (FPMT).

Thank you for acquiring *Manual of Insight.*

Please visit https://wisdomexperience.org/wp-content/uploads /2020/07/Manual-of-Insight-Charts.pdf to download a free PDF version of the comprehensive collection of seven charts, including "The Progress of Insight," "Mental Factors Present in Each Consciousness," and "Planes of Existence."